MYTHS
OF THE HERO

Illustrated by

Nikolay Nikolenko

NORMA
LORRE
GOODRICH

THE ORION PRESS

NEW YORK

myths

OF THE HERO

First printing
All rights reserved
© 1960, 1962 by Norma Lorre Goodrich
Library of Congress Catalog Card Number: 62-15017
Designed by Wladislaw Finne
Manufactured in the United States of America

THIS BOOK IS
DEDICATED WITH MY LOVE TO
JEAN JOSEPH LORRE

CONTENTS

INTRODUCTION

Myths are literature, a branch of literature. As much as any other reality, they are a fountainhead of literary and artistic creation.

The myth is a branch of literature which for centuries remained the exclusive domain of the artist and the classical scholar. As a matter of fact, it is rather exceptional as one looks down the ages to find a great artist who was not at the same time a classical scholar. The artist has always been a student of art. Both artist and classical scholar have always been primarily concerned with art and its creation. Their prime questions have always been: What is the essence of art? What are the origins of art? What are its themes and its symbols? How is the artist inspired? What are his sources?

For centuries the artist and the classical scholar were one and the same person as we see today in the case of Edith Hamilton or Gilbert Highet or John Hall Wheelock, as we saw only yesterday in Gilbert Murray and Andrew Lang, in Henry Adams and James Joyce. The writers of antiquity were also scholars. They knew their mythology well. So did the Alcuins, the Boccaccios, and the anonymous writers of the Middle Ages. These writer-scholars complemented the sculptors, the painters, and the architects.

In the ancient world the great poets, such as Homer and Vergil, traditionally called upon their Muse for assistance when they launched into the exacting composition of that epic which was, in the latter's case, the very reason for having lived, and the ultimate concern upon the point of death. Milton and Dante continued the tradition. Even as late as the nineteenth century the French writer François René de Chateaubriand summoned forth the nymph Cymodoce from the verses of Vergil so that she could inspire or *breathe into* him.

In the twenty centuries since the death of Vergil, however, most literary artists ceased to refer directly to the Muse as a source of their creative energies. Instead they drew from the vast treasure house of mythology. The greatest of the English poets—Shakespeare, Milton, Chaucer, Spenser—were all deeply steeped in this field. It was their special domain, available to them either in the original classical texts or in translation. The greatest of the French writers—Racine, La Fontaine, Rabelais—were also authorities on the subject. Then in the nineteenth century such influential writers and thinkers as Chateaubriand and Victor Hugo began to clamor for a more thorough investigation into the whole area of the myth, particularly that of the Middle Ages. Subsequently mythology ceased to be the particular province of the classical scholar and of the creative artist. Other academicians began to scrutinize it.

Within the last hundred years the historian has redoubled his efforts to claim the myth for his academic discipline. He was joined by the new scientists, the anthropologist, the sociologist, the linguist, and the psychologist. Last to arrive in the lists was the philosopher, who for centuries had regarded the myth as a sphere beneath his attention, as an area tabooed by Plato, and therefore fruitless.

Shakespeare and Milton would be very much surprised, indeed, to read what discoveries have been made since their lifetimes. That most prolific writer of myths, the elegant Ovid, would undoubtedly be delighted to learn how important he and his *Metamorphoses* have become to so many technical researchers. He would have all the more reason to insist that the Emperor Augustus allow him to return from his exile in Pontus.

For centuries the artist and the classical scholar reveled undisturbed in their own private domain. The teacher was their student and admiring accomplice. He also had known about this secret area of learning which had never failed to elicit a spark from even the most reluctant schoolboy whose thoughts had for years insisted on wandering beyond the classroom window.

After having thought for so many hundreds of years that the myth was their private property, the classical scholar, the artist, and the teacher must have been amazed to discover the myth finally dignified by scientific scrutiny. They had long realized that there was a secret power in the myth, that the myth intensely lived a charmed and magical life of its own. The classicists had loved Homer and worshiped Vergil—primarily for beauty's sake. Rapt in the sure paradise of form, syntax, and affiliation, they had never thought to be challenged by such a perfectly obvious question as: What is a myth?

Then into their peaceful sancta came trampling the modern world armed with its tools of measurement and a firm determination to know all about everything. The great artists—Shakespeare, Vergil, and Ovid—continued to smile enigmatically as they had done down the ages. They were telling no secrets.

Very much that was brought out into the clear light of day by the scientists had long been known intuitively to the artists. They and the classical scholar were at home in the mysteries of their mythological province. "Research into origins is futile," declared the anthropologist as he assembled his instruments and plunged headlong into mystery.

The great difficulty the modern world has encountered as it has analyzed the myth is its definition at any given point in time, such as the present. Those works which we commonly accept as myths are stories—but stories of unknown origin—many of them so old that even the philosopher arrives, as he traces them, at a point far remote in time when they were perhaps not stories at all, but realities!

The myth, then, says the philosopher, was originally a rite which had no author. By the time this rite reaches us, it has had scores of authors. It is a story told of certain personages in a given locality that we can recognize and identify as Greece, for example, with a certain central event such as a flood. Such a myth the philosopher calls "Greek," until an anthropologist finds a similar flood story with similar characters and similar mountains, only under different names, unfolding on an island in the Pacific! The latter myth is not old; it is modern. The original definition is therefore amended to include the word *recurrent*, for certain myths do recur throughout the world.

The hero stories treated in this volume, which we traditionally think are myths—those stories which we can prove belong to Greece, to Persia, to China, to India, to Egypt, and to Rome, in fact, to all of western Europe, as well—are very old. They seem to date from the Neolithic Age all the way down to the period which saw the last of the Crusades. Some of them can fortunately be fairly closely dated, even to a certain decade in the Middle Ages. Others emerge from some impossibly distant period of the Ancient World. Many were already myths when the great writers of antiquity heard them and recognized, if not their origin, at least their power.

What further characterizes the myth, what separates it clearly from any other story, is the powerful thrill of recognition it evokes in generations of readers. The philosophers believe that this power may perhaps stem from the fact that the myth was not, at its point of origin, a story at all. Once it was a reality!

Such a suggestion leads very far afield. If a myth of ancient Greece was once a lived reality in a given culture, and if the same myth occurs in a Pacific culture contemporary with ours, then may one not assume that all primitive peoples experience the same realities and pass them on in the form of myth? The psychologist C. G. Jung examined this phenomenon and formulated a theory of the "collective unconscious." He spoke of a "racial memory" common to all mankind and of the myth as the product of this common unconscious. From the myth itself he borrowed the word *psyche*. His theory explained the otherwise uncanny sense of identification which people feel in reading a myth.

Jung saw the wisdom of countless ages "lying dormant in the human brain" itself.

Modern metaphysicians, such as Schelling, believed that the "myth expresses a real relationship of human consciousness to God." The anthropologist discovered that all primitive people are haunted by the great phenomena of nature, the rhythmic alternation of light and darkness in the rising and setting of the sun each day, and the cyclical movement of the seasons. All peoples throughout the world performed, and still perform, certain ceremonies accompanied by a liturgy, and attended by magic formulas consisting of names and of numbers. The use of magic was primitive man's attempt to control the forces of nature and to bend them to his will. Centuries after such ceremonies were replaced by religions, their liturgies remained, becoming more and more mysterious as the original pageants were forgotten. These liturgies were the ancestors of the myth.

While it seems tenable that many myths originated as ceremonies celebrating the various passage rites—birth, puberty, marriage, and death—it seems equally possible that other myths were concocted to explain customs retained by certain groups of people who had either forgotten their primary purpose or to whom the primary purpose was no longer either meaningful or necessary. One could imagine why certain people in a given area of India, for example, might perform a rain ceremony upon the success of which their very lives depended. By conserving the rite their leaders might have thought to maintain a cultural unity. Therefore people continued to respect the custom long after they had migrated to a rainy area. Subsequently they invented another myth as a secondary explanation of this vestige.

Long before the attention of philosophers was turned to mythology, other scholars had seen that myths could be studied from the standpoint of history. For years the seesaw has wavered back and forth upon this burning question: Is the myth history? To what extent is the myth historical? A case in point would be the myth of Theseus, one of the best known and most complete of the Greek myths. Even in the ancient world Plutarch so much considered Theseus to have been a real man that he wrote his biography. Cyrus the Great of Persia seems to have fared in a contrary fashion. Here is the case of a real man whose life was treated mythically. The same is true of Alexander the Great. Had Julius Caesar not written two books that have survived, he also might have become entirely mythical. Yet the myth of Theseus, as the Greek and Roman authors have transmitted it, seems quite clearly historical. King Minos of Crete could also have been a real person. Certain scholars have felt the same for Osiris of Egypt. Such was the opinion of the celebrated authority Sir James Frazer, who thought that Osiris had really lived in Africa. "Myths grow like weeds round the great historical figures of the past," he said. One also wonders to what extent mythological thinking has knowingly been applied to such persons as Napoleon and Hitler.

Other myths, such as those of Prince Igor of Russia and Roland of France, are laid in an historical setting which scholars can situate. Yet there is no record of any such French knight as Roland. This key figure, in other words, cannot be found in any genealogical table of medieval France. Some scholars have even wanted to explain this strange fact by arguing that Roland is not to be considered the hero of the poem, that the hero is Charlemagne. The same shadowy identity holds for Lancelot, Tristan, Percival, Heracles, Perseus, and Rustam. Yet the myths that surround all these key figures have always admitted to at least *some* historical gleanings. The myth is in another way, however, historical; as the German philosopher Schelling argued, "the process through which the myth arises is itself a true history, an actual occurrence." Then, too, there is the added complication that writers through the ages have made the myth historical by situating it for themselves and therefore for us.

If it may be assumed that the liturgy which gave rise to the myth antedated history as such, then the question follows: What was the influence of the myth upon history? This is a field open to inquiry, to endless speculation, and to substantiation. It hardly seems possible that the English reader can fail to recognize cultural traits or a kind of ideal man in the myth of *Beowulf*, or that the Spanish reader who knows Spain can fail to recognize them in *Mio Cid*. The philosopher Ernst Cassirer asserts daringly, in fact, that "the history of a people is determined by its mythology."

Certain myths, however, may have very little historical cloak. These are the very ones that the philosopher may hail as the most valuable and which he may hope are the most archaic, the closest to the original premise of the lived reality. Special care should be given to their every word and action. Such are the myths of Osiris-Horus-Isis and the myth of Peredur. It is only if these myths are read in terms of some gigantic drama, some primitive ceremony with the hero as the central actor, that they assume a deeper significance. In these two cases subsequent authors have not overly interpolated, have not rewritten, have not situated in a given culture, and have not re-explained. Neither Ovid, nor Vergil, nor Chaucer, nor Shakespeare, nor any other wizard, has given them a second life more splendid than the primitive one.

If one accepts the theory, held also most positively by Lord Raglan in his book, *The Hero*, that the myth derives from a primitive liturgy, then it must be the anthropologist who furnishes the documentation upon the subject of primitive man and his ceremonies. One such rite is that of separation, the rending apart of sky from earth which many myths speak of after a period called Chaos. The ceremony consisted of sexual intercourse and the separation of the male and the female by the intervention of a third participant—man. In certain cultures the sky was male and the earth female; this was reversed in other cultures.

Another primitive rite was the deliverance from death, the submersion in water, and the rebirth. Death and resurrection in a cave or a cavern, after a long struggle involving pain and heroism, is a common concern of many mythological systems. Still another was eucharistic—and as Sigmund Freud observed, a possible survival of the totem animal, which was sacrificed and then eaten. There was also the rain ceremony —the cloud or dragon vanquished by the arrows or thunderbolts of the hero. A common passage rite was that of initiation into manhood. Still another was the replacement of the father or the king by the son or the new king. Regicide and patricide were, of course, attended by much compensation on the part of the murderer. This "superlative acknowledgment," as Freud called it, is to be seen in reverse in Charlemagne's behavior after the loss of Roland, as well as in Aeneas' excessive grief at the sudden death of his father Anchises.

Other rites seem to be common all over the earth. One such is the flood story, from which life is sometimes saved by means of an ark and a sacred mountain. Another such is the rite that ushered in spring, or that which accepted autumn.

Such ceremonies represented primitive man's conception of the creation of the earth, of his own creation, and of the meaning of his life. He did not see his life as ending at the point of death. On the contrary, he looked upon death as another form of existence. These myths were already ancient when the Roman Lucretius said "death is immortal." In the myth life is immortal. King Arthur, even after Lucretius's pronouncement, did not die; he only "passed" and "will come again." Hiawatha was another such dying god who vanished into the west, but who did not die. In mythology there is generally no such pagan *attitude* as that of Lucretius, but rather the *feeling* of a divine consciousness that orders the world in such a way that all happenings are purposeful, meaningful, and intentional. Therefore, as Ernst Cassirer points out, the "content of the myth is transcendental . . . and stretches towards a divine and conscious religious certainty."

It is also to be noted that none of these great rites could or would be celebrated without the active participation of man. Rain would not fall upon a parched earth until the chosen Rustam went out alone to wage his painful combat in the name of all Persia. If the weeping of the bereaved Isis could be heard all the way from Abydos to the Delta, on the other hand, it was because all the women in that valley wailed until the Nile rose resurrected. Spring could not come in Yorkshire until Peredur had finally met the rusty knight of black winter upon that bleak mountain, until the hero had driven famine from the land. Heracles could not bring back the golden apples until he had found the key to all wisdom in the far eastern land of India.

The myths in this volume are centered about the adventures—or

ceremonies—involving a great hero. Such tales are often called "culture myths." Although such a term applies to all myths, the hero myth may be the one that has most influenced culture down the centuries. Myths centered around a hero have him as a unifying feature and should, therefore, contain a number of similarities. The modern French poet Stéphane Mallarmé, whose book on ancient gods was in its fifth edition in 1925, generalized on the hero of mythology. Mallarmé noted that the hero usually led a short but brilliant life, that he labored for the good of others rather than for himself, that he was invulnerable but for one spot or that he was subject to defeat from one special weapon, that his face was particularly beautiful, that his hair was blond like the sun, and that his propensity was to abandon his lady.

Although Mallarmé's specifications fit a great many heroes, indeed, they are not always applicable, even for the few heroes treated in this volume. Rustam, according to Firdausi, lived a long life, and so did Aeneas, according to Vergil. Sigmund Freud pointed to the duplication or multiplication of incidents centered about such compelling figures as Theseus, for this hero has a whole series of myths taking him from birth to death. The story called *Berta of Hungary* will give the reader an example of this process at work.

The vulnerable spot applies to Sifrit's back and to Achilles' heel, but not to Rama or to Gilgamesh. No special weapon caused the death of Osiris, or that of Moses, or that of Roland. Neither Egypt, nor Persia, nor India loved a blond hero; on the contrary, their preference was for dark hair. One sees this attitude towards hair color persisting into Shakespeare: "dark is not counted fair."

However, it would seem that Mallarmé was correct in that each hero was astonishingly beautiful, that he labored for the good of others, and that he almost always deserted or abandoned or was unavoidably obliged to leave the lady he loved.

Lord Raglan, writing in 1939, also generalized upon the hero. After having tabulated the myths of a great many heroes, he found that the hero's life could be divided into three phases: birth, accession to the throne, and death. The births of heroes often are similar in that they are unusual, if not miraculous. Sigmund Freud has amply discussed this phenomenon in his book, *Moses and Monotheism*. While we do not have the details concerning the births of Rama, Roland, and many others, it is true that Rustam, Achilles, Odysseus, Horus, King Arthur, and a preponderance of other heroes are born unusually. The hero also generally spends his childhood in an isolated place, preparing to do some great deed that will announce his coming. His accession to the throne, or his initiation, often follows a long journey fraught with perils and trials. He often has to solve a riddle, or successfully complete a guessing game. Thus we see Osiris quizzing his son Horus, the Shah of Persia examining Zal, Oedipus solving the riddle of the Sphinx, and Peredur wrestling so long with the meaning of the bleeding lance.

The long journey is a prime characteristic of the hero myth. Osiris and Heracles traveled extensively about the known world, both visiting India, as did the gods Dionysus and Bacchus who so closely resemble Osiris. Rama's journey from northern India to Ceylon follows the lines of the Aryan invasion of India. Rustam traveled constantly from one end of Iran to the other, and then into Arabia, although his seven-day journey to Mazinderan is more likely ritualistic. In the eleventh adventure of Heracles there is a fascinating travel story that finally involves Prometheus on his Caucasian peak. Prince Igor, Sifrit, Beowulf, Roland, Cassandra, Berta—all are involved in stories of wandering or travel. The *Odyssey* and the *Aeneid* are perhaps the most beloved travel books in the western world, the latter authenticated, for Vergil believed in on-the-spot verification as Herodotus had believed before him.

Vergil's treatment of the love story, his development of the relationship between Dido and Aeneas, is both mythological and modern, in the sense that it is so perceptive that scholars have counted it among the ancestors of the psychological novel. According to the myth the relationship between man and woman is not a particularly successful one. Denis de Rougemont in his book, *Love in the Western World*, has shown his great concern with the extent to which the European myths of adultery—the triangular loves of Tristan-Isolde-King Mark and Lancelot-Guinevere-King Arthur—have warped attitudes towards love and marriage. The love story of Sifrit-Brunhilde-Chriemhilde as told in this volume is another case in point. Such unfortunate love affairs seem to have some precedence in the hero myths of antiquity.

One of the most flagrant desertions in all mythology is that of Ariadne by Theseus. In that story as completed in this volume, however, the ardent Roman poet Catullus has arranged affairs so that Ariadne is compensated. Rama will abandon Sita in the *Ramayana*, Rustam leaves Tamineh, Gilgamesh spurns the goddess Ishtar, Osiris leaves Isis, Pepin mistakes Margiste for his bride Berta, Sifrit betrays Brunhilde, Prince Igor has left his wife, and Peredur deserts the empress of Christinobyl. Even Vergil's masterly handling of Aeneas at Troy is not quite satisfactory. Aeneas "lost" his first wife Creusa! Then after the burning of Troy and his sea voyage, he abandons Dido who has rescued him and his men. The theme of abandonment even occurs in the epic of *Mio Cid*, a poem in which a real man has received mythological treatment.

The role of women, the difficulties of their position, and their abandonment by the hero—from Odysseus' Penelope to the strange seduction of Alcmene that resulted in the birth of Heracles, to the rape of Brunhilde—all present a problem that the modern world still finds a suitable subject for the sociologist, the psychologist, and the creative artist.

In a most interesting book published in Paris in 1949, Pierre Gordon points out a series of features that recur in myths and which seem to

him to prove their ritualistic and liturgical origin. Prof. Gordon notes that there is a constant reference to the "sacred island," such as the Greek Atlantis, or Iceland, Thule, Ile-de-France, or even Scandinavia. Sometimes the term "Isles of the Blessed" is used, or Hesperides, or the Avalon to which King Arthur departed.

These far-distant, often western abodes are paralleled by the recurrent preoccupation with a "sacred mountain," which sometimes represents the navel of the earth, or which has the fire of eternal life at its summit, or which receives the ark after the deluge. Mt. Meru in India is such a holy mountain, as Chomolungma is to Nepal today. Parnassus, Olympus with its twelve great gods, the magic mountains in Crete and Phrygia that are both named Ida, the Elburz where the phoenix raised the Persian Zal, and Enlil in Sumer—all are examples of this preoccupation. One should perhaps include the artificial mountains, the Hanging Gardens of Babylon, and the pyramids of Egypt and Central America. When modern climbers say that they scale some great peak or the north face of Eigerwand "because it is there," one wonders to what extent their actions have been motivated by the myth. Gilgamesh traveled to a high mountain in order to kill a dragon called Huwawa. The psychologists have wondered about dragons as father images. In connection with the mountain there is often a cave or a tunnel, and sometimes a sacred spring. In many cases the hero is buried on a mountain. Beowulf's barrow on the Headlands of Hronesnesse is somewhat similar to Theseus's burial on a mountain. Then, too, there is the theme of the revelation on the mountain, of which the enlightenment of Zeus is an example. It was Lord Byron who said that to him "high mountains are a feeling."

The late Ernst Cassirer analyzes another recurrent symbol, the cross, and relates it to early man's structural concept of space. As the reader will see in the Egyptian myth of Osiris, the earth is square or quadripartite and associated with the number *four* which Plutarch, as a Pythagorean, equated with the Athenian Theseus. The myth recognizes four directions—north, south, east, and west. When the center of the earth is included, then the magic number becomes five. Cassirer further points out that certain associations concerning the four quarters of the earth become established. The north comes to mean winter, and war, and warriors. To the south is attributed fire, summer, medicine, and agriculture. The east represents light or dawn, spring, magic, and religion. The west comes to signify the abode of death, plus autumn. "O wild, west wind, thou breath of autumn's being," said Shelley. The west is also related to the frightening sound of the galloping hunter, in European folklore the "maisnie hellequin" which the modern novelist Michel Butor uses so effectively in his recent book *Change of Heart*. Washington Irving used it most successfully in his "Headless Horseman of Sleepy Hollow."

Numbers, as commonly accepted motifs in the myth, were not used necessarily to explain the earth, but rather to represent it. The numbers associated with certain heroes were like their names—latent with magical power. The number four was sacred to the North American Indians as well as to the Athenians. There were not only Nine Muses, but also nine major gods—the Great Ennead of Egypt. There were seven planets, seven days of the week, seven liberal arts, and the seven-days journey of Rustam. The number three occurs in the three persons of language, in the Egyptian triad, and in the Trinity. There were the twelve months of the year, twelve episodes of the Gilgamesh myth, twelve signs of the zodiac, and the twelve labors of Heracles. In Greece it is even now commonly believed that the number thirteen became unlucky because of the fall of Constantinople in 1453. Ever since early Egypt, perhaps earlier, certain numbers have been lucky and unlucky. Numbers in mythology have essence.

The notion of time, according to mythological thinking, is cyclical and moving, not stationary in the sense that there is a marked delineation between the past, the present, and the future. According to linguists, the verb—which expresses relationships in time—was the last part of speech to be developed in all its complexity. In the myth time is often symbolized by a wheel, either a chariot wheel or a spinning wheel. During these revolutions the souls of the dead wait in the underworld until their turn has come to be born again. In some myths time plays chess with men, or wields a scythe and is referred to as "father." The hero, gathering his strength, waits until the proper moment *in time* has occurred so that he may enter the drama, cause himself to be recognized, and admitted to the theater of his actions. Above him is fate, or Three Fates, or Wyrd, or destiny. In all these motifs there is a kind of order, perhaps only a biological or physiological one, but still a universal system, despite the "blindness of fate." In such myths as those of Orestes, Antigone, and Oedipus one sees that there is no use struggling against destiny. Shakespeare called it "outrageous fortune." The goddess Cassandra lives until her present becomes the future she had seen in the past.

If the hero's relationship with his father, or if the father's relationship with his son is a peculiar one, and if the hero's relationship with his wife or betrothed is also a peculiar one—and how few heroes have sons!—his relationsip with his people is the area in which he distinguishes himself. As Stéphane Mallarmé pointed out, the hero performs his labors for his people or for his fellows. This altruism is apparent in each of them, to such an extent that as early as in the *Song of Roland* one hears a strong statement of that chauvinism which will define the French national state four hundred years later. In France the Romantic poets of the nineteenth century longed also to become beacons for mankind, just as Beowulf had done. It was they, in fact, who resurrected the medieval myth and focused attention on its nature and its weird power, they who clamored for its definition.

It can be said, however, that even the basic nature of the hero and his altruistic ideal undergoes some divergence. Not all heroes scorn, as Beowulf did, guile or the unfair fight. Odysseus was and is very much admired for his cleverness on several occasions. The Greeks supposedly captured Troy by trickery: the Trojan Horse. Sifrit also used guile not only in defeating Brunhilde, but also in overpowering her. The hero—as—trickster became common in medieval literature; the many tales of Renard the Fox are cases in point. Among certain American Indians the hero was, as Ruth Benedict showed, Old Man Coyote. Theseus also killed the Minotaur by guile, and then abandoned Ariadne. Rama, on the other hand, used his magic weapon only as a last resort. Rustam returned to water for reinvigoration only to avoid ultimate defeat. In the *Niebelungenlied* Chriemhilde is punished for treachery, however; and Hagen was generally more admired than Sifrit.

Many distinguished scholars have studied the myth from the viewpoint of comparative linguistics, proving interesting correspondences between personages in the mythologies of Greece and Egypt, or Greece and India, for example. Thus Vritra-Python-Sphinx-Libya-Fafnir. Varuna-Uranus-Cronus. Agni-igni, etc. Some have concluded that all myths originated in India, particularly because of the *Vedas'* extreme age. Others have argued that all myths are of solar origin, or at least of astral origin. Among the solar heroes, according to Max Müller, would be Heracles, Achilles, Perseus, Bellerephon, and Theseus.

The psychologists have attacked the problem from the point of view of symbols. They have found that symbols also occur in dreams, in everyone's dreams. They speak of a symbolic language which is the common inheritance of the human race. Thus wild animals become passions, going on a journey indicates death, apples are breasts, water is birth, emperors are parents, rocks and mountains are male organs. Sigmund Freud believed also that these symbols represented a "racial heritage." In his *Essay on Man* Cassirer suggested that man himself should be defined as "animal symbolicum." He further agreed with the artist that "man lives in a symbolic universe" made up of language, art, religion, and myth. It was the myth that shaped his culture; his culture is therefore man-made.

According to Freud the myth occupies a middle ground between dreams and a waking state. Cassirer was more or less in agreement. He felt that the myth "hovered" between the dream world and that of "objective reality." The myth is, then, perhaps a reverie. The modern philosopher speaks of the poet's mythical consciousness and of mythological thinking as a philosophical system. The myth is a milestone on the road which leads from barbarism to religion.

Pierre Gordon says that by its theogony the myth leads the way to a cosmogony, into a cosmology, and into physics. Plutarch, on the other hand, writing *De Iside et Osiride* around the year 100, calls the myth "an image of a certain truth other than scientific." Students of religion see the myth as an ancestor and also as a component part of the world's great religions, particularly of Christianity.

Eric Fromm's ideas are most stimulating in this regard. He speaks of man struggling throughout the ages with historical and existential dichotomies that the myth treats superlatively, particularly early man's craving for a oneness with the world even as his growing awareness of self sets him more and more apart from it. One realizes in the hero myth this sense of "aloneness," how alone Roland would have been if Saint Gabriel had not hovered near him, how alone Rustam feels as he contends with the White Demon, how Aeneas alone, in the last analysis, must found Rome, how Gilgamesh must go alone down the black tunnel of death and must alone swim through the dangerous waters of rebirth. The hero must sacrifice himself; the "I" is repeatedly offered up for the good of the whole. The hero does this through a free and voluntary action of his will. Thus the hero myth is a record of man's inner life.

The question of why the hero feels so little concern for himself, why he has no sense of his own conservation, was raised by Pierre Caillois in his book *Le Mythe et L'Homme*, published in Paris in 1938. An answer comes by studying the hero of the myth himself. It also comes from the great religious figures. It comes from Cape Canaveral. It comes from the artist, as Ernest Hemingway in *The Old Man and the Sea*.

The scientists and the philosophers have, indeed, enriched knowledge, oriented thinking, and enlarged points of view concerning mythology, its nature, its possible origin, and the need it serves. The classical scholar was not able to reserve the myth for himself, he who had been its loving custodian over the centuries. The creative artist has found not only his work, but even his processes submitted to the curious analyses of science. The scientist still wonders how the artist knew most of his findings only by intuition. The artist has never particularly cared to reveal the secrets of his craft. He has preferred to appear full-blown. He has tended to deny his apprenticeship and to disguise his sources.

The creative artist still refuses to unveil his mysteries. He has heard the arguments of the scientists even as, so long ago, Omar Khayyam heard them:

"Myself when young did eagerly frequent
Doctor and Saint, and heard great Argument
About it and about: but evermore
Came out by the same Door as in I went."

From his distant point in the sixteenth century the French myth–maker, François Rabelais, speaks for the creative artist as he asks caustically for all time:

"Do you really believe in good faith that as Homer wrote *The Iliad* and *The Odyssey* he thought of those allegories which Plutarch (and others) have caulked him with? If you do think so, you aren't within hands and feet of my opinion which decrees that he thought as little of them as Ovid thought of the sacraments of the Gospel when he wrote his *Metamorphoses*. . . ."

Rabelais, as he introduces his readers to the giant Gargantua, exhorts them to: "Disport yourselves, my dears, and gaily read the rest."

Dr. François Rabelais is an outstanding example of the highly original artist who was one of the most erudite of classical scholars—and, in addition, a Professor of Medicine. Yet, like so many artists, he preferred to let his public think that art was a natural process which was not only effortless and spontaneous but attended with much good cheer.

Whether he admits it or not, the artist burns the midnight oil over his books and his manuscripts. He studies mythology during his apprenticeship in order to be able to say—when the floodgates that dam his creative energy are ready to be thrown open—that he has composed effortlessly, spontaneously and freely. He carefully disavows his early compositions. He prefers the aura of mystery that he finds in the myth; great art is always mysterious. Mythology, down through the centuries, has remained the artist's basic curriculum. He rejoices to find it, in the words of the classical scholar, Charles Mills Gayley, "simple, spontaneous and beautiful." "Beauty," sighed the medieval poet and scholar, Charles d'Orleans, "I am a prisoner to beauty."

The myth is literature. It is a branch of literature which is, like all great art, only a waking dream.

Norma Lorre Goodrich, 1962

1

BOOK
ANCIENT
MYTHS

ONE
SUMER

The epic of Gilgamesh, of which the following story is a composite, was written in Sumerian cuneiform. This language was studied as a classic until Christian times although the Sumerian peoples themselves, conquered by the Semites, had begun to disappear by 2000 B.C. The reader will doubtless recognize in Gilgamesh the prototype of the semilegendary Oriental ruler of antiquity. Many versions of this story have been found, particularly in the library of the Assyrian King Ashurbanipal at Nineveh. Translations of cuneiform tablets are still going on.

European scholars, particularly M. François Thureau-Dangin, were trying to decipher cuneiform in the early 1800's, and great credit must also be given to Sir Henry Rawlinson's translation of the Behistun inscription around 1850. Noted American Sumerologists are Arno Poebel (1881–1958), Thorkild Jacobsen of the Oriental Institute of the University of Chicago, and Samuel Noah Kramer of the University of Pennsylvania.

Descriptions of Gilgamesh, Enkidu, and Huwawa come from archaeological photographs belonging to the Musée du Louvre in Paris.

GILGAMESH THE WRESTLER

In the beginning was our mother Nammu, the great goddess whose waters were all the universe. As time went by this goddess, lonely in her limitless vastness, bore two children in human form, first a son named An who stretched across the arc from pole to pole, and whom we call "heaven." Her second child was a female whose name was Ki, and her we call "earth." After their birth An and Ki were first united in the shape of a mountain towering high above the clouds, in cosmic space. From their union was born the great deity of the air Enlil, who in his fatherly desire to create separated the earth from her brother heaven. Then Enlil the air god carried Ki away into the privacy of the clouds and from her fashioned all the animals of the earth, all the plants on mountain, river valley, and desert, and finally man.

From his splendid temple in Nippur, Enlil ruled the world with lifted eyes that shone far over to the east where rushed the muddy waters of the Tigris flowing southward from the desolate hills of Assur, and far to the west where the lordly Euphrates, broad and slow, brought its life-giving waters through the plains of ancient Sumer to the sea. On a white throne in a pure place sat Enlil, like a great mountain, tracing with his fingers the lands and the seas, sending sunshine over the plains and spring thaws from the hills over barren deserts, looking upon his creation and wishing it plenty and prosperity. In his omnipotent majesty Enlil appointed a god of wisdom whose name was Enki and whose main task was to superintend above all places the great land of Sumer through which gold and silver were to flow in ships to the temple of Enlil at Nippur.

Great were the deeds of Enki and many were his gifts to man. Like a good teacher Enki yoked oxen to the plow and in due season showed man how to make grain sprout like jewels in the sunlit fields. From the hills he drove ewes with their lambs and built pens for them. The great fishes of the river he persuaded to lay eggs among the river reeds to nourish the people of Sumer. When the barley bent double under its weight, Enki built granaries and filled them with the grains of the fields and all the fruits of the gardens, with peaches, mulberries, pomegranates, bananas, and apricots. From the clay of the rivers he molded square bricks, and taught the black-haired craftsmen how to construct walls and even lofty cities, tier on tier and adorned with precious cedarwood and lapis lazuli. Around each of the lovely cities of Sumer, Enki built dikes which could be opened during the dry season so that the tender wheat would not burn in the hot sun of noon. Above the luxuriant gardens the waving fronds of tamarisks and date palms he had planted whispered in the south wind. Far in the distance gleamed the blue tile walls and lofty ziggurats of the wealthy city-ports of Sumer.

Fom Nippur in the center between the two rivers the land of Sumer, or Shinar as it is called in the Bible, extended southward toward the blue waters of the Persian Gulf and the delta region. The powerful city of Lagash, which at its height might have had a population of 36,000, was ruled by a tall, thin king called Ur-Nammu. He was later deified. The city of Ur, where Abraham once lived, covered 150 acres and had a population of 24,000. Its great ziggurat boasted brick columns "overlaid with copper and mother of pearl." At Kish and Eridu were raised massive brick platforms as much as 700 yards square, upon which were built huge temples to the gods. These cities were often at war, striving for supremacy over their tropical valley, the ancient meeting place between Egypt and Asia Minor to the west and India and the Orient to the east. Greatest even among these cities was Uruk, which lay on the east bank of the Euphrates a hundred miles from the sea, between Ur and Eridu on the southeast and Nippur and Lagash on the north. It was such a lovely city that it could have been the Garden of Eden. Its memory was venerated for centuries, well beyond the golden age of the Babylonian Empire, because of the deeds of its great king, Gilgamesh.

Gilgamesh was a king and the decendant of a king. He was born in the royal palace at Uruk to a mother, Ninmah, who "knew all knowledge" and in whom he could confide all secrets. He grew to be strong and powerful, a huge, courageous king, a great hunter of lions and wild bulls, a peerless wrestler, and a dauntless leader in war. His legs were powerful like cedar pillars in the palace courtyard; with his left arm he could hold a struggling lion and in his right a mighty bronze war club. The fierceness of his face could drive terror into his enemies, even into the Agga of Kish, whose siege of Uruk did not last five days.

Dressed on ordinary days in a short-sleeved garment that fell without folds to his knees, his wrists encircled in heavy golden identical bracelets, and with two pet monkeys on his shoulders, the lord Gilgamesh strode daily among his warriors, inciting them to wrestling bouts. His hair was heavy, black, and curly, and dressed in thick rolls of curls from the crown of his head to his forehead, but falling around his nape like a sleek helmet. His black eyes were prominent and thick-lidded under arched brows, his nose large and aquiline, his lips curved and sensuous. He wore his curly beard carefully arranged in twelve long ringlets that ended in a straight row of little curls about the level of his armpits. On days of high ceremony, such as those of the spring corn festival, his long cloak attached to a round headdress made him appear as tall as a god, as high as a mountain, as dazzling as sunlight on the enameled walls of Uruk. Then, indeed, was he called "He who discovers all," and again in worship "Our lord who saw all." Two-thirds of Gilgamesh was god. The remaining third, however, was man.

With those parts of him that were mortal Gilgamesh loved women. In this desire he was unquenchable, for no one woman could long satisfy his lust. As he rode through the streets of Uruk he would snatch maidens from their father's homes and even wives shopping in the market place or carrying water from the canals. In vain the council protested the rape of their daughters. In his majesty Gilgamesh neither heard their protestations nor heeded their supplications. Even young brides he snatched from their bridegrooms' arms and carried screaming away over his shoulder. Not in all the city, nor even in all the plain of Sumer, was there a man who dared challenge the king to battle or defy him in open combat. So he continued to swagger through the streets, hunt lions in the plains, and steal maidens, especially the slender, almond-eyed daughters of the great nobles, whose perfumed ringlets captured his roving eye.

Finally in desperation the council of elders of the city made sacrifices in the temple to Aruru, the great mother goddess, patroness of Uruk, beseeching her, "Make another man to match him. Create another mortal who will lay his proud power in the dust, for lo! we can endure his tyranny no longer." Aruru was pleased with their rich gifts and listened to their story sympathetically.

After they had prostrated themselves before her altar, weeping and moaning, the mother goddess, taking pity on the parents of Uruk, slowly descended from her golden couch, descended the winding stairs of the ziggurat and walked deep in thought across the plain until she came to the riverbank. There, parting the willows and thick reeds, she bent down with the tips of her golden sandals in the dark, wet clay of the river and began to gather it in her hands. Slowly and patiently, reciting a prayer to the god An, who was so holy he had never left his band of stars to walk across the earth, she began to shape a man in his image. As she worked, the south wind blew on the clay image, fanned it for her until the breath of life began to swell its ribs and flutter under its long, silky eyelashes. In this way Enkidu came to Sumer.

Free as the breeze and happy as a young colt in a green pasture, he bounded away from the riverbank and out into the wide desert. Aruru had fashioned him with the hoofs and thighs and long tail of a bull, but from the waist up he was a man, naked and healthy as a wild animal. His hair grew long and luxuriant and his body hardened with the wild grace of his friends the gazelles. His strength was that of An, of his army of bright stars marching upon the paths of heaven. With a sure instinct he protected the wild beasts of the plains, as their patron saving them from the pits of the hunter and directing their flight to desert fastnesses. In time the reputation of his daring and swiftness of foot was the subject of much admiration in Uruk. Even Gilgamesh was piqued in his pride and touched in his sense of his superiority until he finally hit upon a plan to capture the long-haired Enkidu.

Into the royal chamber he called his bravest hunter and sent him out to the desert watering hole where Enkidu at sunset usually led his animal bands. With him the hunter took one of the most accomplished of the palace courtesans, dressed in a sheer gown, with silver anklets on her bare legs and long carnelian earrings in her ears. As they stood in the slanting rays of summer sun, she anointed her breasts and arms with perfume and unloosed the fillets from her hair. When the animals began to come down their usual path toward the water, they scented her and fled wild-eyed. Enkidu scented her also, but he could not turn away. As he approached warily, the courtesan loosened her garments so that he could see how beautiful she was. Enkidu circled closer and finally clasped her in his arms.

As he later withdrew from her arms and tried to rejoin his herds, to

his astonishment and sorrow his "desert cattle shunned him." Even the gazelles whom he had protected so long ran away at his approach. With his innocence gone, he no longer belonged among them, even as their protector. Sadly he turned back and fell exhausted by the side of the beautiful courtesan. With soft words and flattery she wound herself around his heart, enticing him to return to Uruk with her, extolling the beauty of the city, its comforts, and the delights of the company of men. Hand in hand, with the hunter as their guide, they returned to Uruk. Far from loving Enkidu, however, the woman was thinking only of the jewels the king had promised her if she could induce the wild man to submit to the customs and restraints of life in a big city.

Little by little Enkidu at the hands of the palace women allowed his hair to be cut and his beard trained and coaxed into fashionable ringlets. For the first time he wore a linen shirt and a conical hat. As he learned the rites of civilization—how to behave at a banquet, and how to make ceremonious compliments at court—he gradually lost his wildman appearance and something of his brute strength. On the other hand he gained in moral and mental stature.

Soon after Enkidu had been captured and had come to live in the city, Gilgamesh had a terrible nightmare which persisted even after he was awake. In his anxiety he turned to his wise mother and told her of this dream.

Dear Mother Ninmah, who knows all knowledge,
I have had a dream, a black dream in the night,
Of an army, stars of An, flying toward me,
Of a great warrior, a great stranger, who wrestled with me,
Who conquered me and overbore me!

Gently Ninmah comforted her son the king. She told him that the dream meant he would indeed wrestle with a stranger, but that from this bout he could make not evil but good come.

Soon after this Gilgamesh planned an evening party, a riotous affair during which, as he and his friends roamed through the streets of Uruk, they would enter certain houses of debauchery. Enkidu was a member of this band of gay young men. However, as Gilgamesh was about to enter the evil house, he found Enkidu not only standing before him but actually barring the door. Red with anger, he aimed at Enkidu a great blow on the side of the jaw, which was intended to dash him to the ground. He found his blow parried, however, and the two mighty giants grasped each other by the shoulders, with heads close together and muscles straining, trying each one to throw the other. It was the only time in his life that Gilgamesh, the strongest wrestler in all the world, had ever felt—arm for arm, back for back, thigh for thigh—a strength equal to his own. Surrounded by a breathless throng of courtiers, lit by the flaring red light of torches, the heroes wrestled.

Sweat poured from their mighty muscles, but neither one could budge the other. There was no sound in the night but their sharp breathing. Suddenly Gilgamesh released his hold. He threw back his head and laughed. In a twinkling his anger had vanished. As they stood panting and looking each other full in the face, the prediction of Ninmah came true. Something good came out of the struggle, a friendship that was to last all the days of their lives, that no danger could threaten nor no evil diminish.

From that evening Gilgamesh and Enkidu were inseparable. A fine couch of silk and furs was prepared in the palace for Enkidu. When Gilgamesh presided at the council of elders, his friend sat on his left hand. All the kings of the earth paid homage to him also and knelt at his feet and kissed them. As he and the king walked through the streets or floated down the river in their round skin *kelec*, all the people raised their voices loud in praise, for the old evil habits were gone from their king. Yet in spite of the luxury and opulence of Uruk, or perhaps even because of them, Enkidu was unhappy. From time to time an old longing would come over him, even in the midst of gaiety, for the savage wanderings of his youth when he had roamed strong and free over the desert and even up to the mountains where the rivers were born. One night Enkidu also had a terrifying nightmare.

In the morning, when he heard his friend's dream, Gilgamesh summoned the dream interpreters to study it. In his dream Enkidu had seen a horrible black monster swooping down on him. It buried its long fierce talons into him and carried him off, as an eagle a lamb, into the black Underworld realm of Nergal, king of eternal darkness. There he was forced to stumble among the dead, who lay in great heaps about him. They were like grotesque birds because of their black, feathered garments. In the gloom he could see that their only food was mud. Enkidu covered his face with his hands and trembled as he recalled with a chill of horror that dreadful scene. After long deliberation the wise men of the king agreed that this dream was a very serious matter. They advised him and Enkidu to sacrifice immediately to the sun god Shamash, whose justice could be invoked in cases of extreme urgency.

As servants prepared the sacred oil for the offering, Gilgamesh and Enkidu proceeded, naked as the ritual required, to the House of Judgment. From there Shamash, who riding daily across the earth in his chariot saw all that happened in the world and even into the future, dispensed justice. As the holy oil was poured in generous libation into the basin, the temple priests studied its pattern. Finally the god spoke through them, telling the king that he must go away, must leave Uruk. While Gilgamesh and Enkidu listened, they made more offerings, a pot of honey and a lapis lazuli jar of sweet butter. Again the god spoke to Gilgamesh, telling him that he must journey indeed even to the Cedar Mountain, which the loathsome monster Huwawa guarded. Once there, he must kill the monster, fell seven cedar trees, and deliver all the land from evil.

No sooner had Gilgamesh and Enkidu left the temple than the king began to shout orders right and left. He called upon the cleverest craftsmen of the city to forge for them magnificent weapons of bronze. On every side he met tears and lamentations, for his subjects were certain that they would never see him again or bask in the protection of his might. In haste the elders calculated the problem of distance, pointing out that the land of the great cedars lay 20,000 hours of travel away, that it would take the heroes two and half years even to reach it. Secondly they argued the dangers of such a long journey all the way northwestward over the seven mountains to the horizon of the world. Gilgamesh would have to travel to the western rim, where Shamash at sunset disappeared into the bowels of the earth. Undismayed, the king replied that Shamash had ordered this task himself, and that he had therefore a double responsibility toward them, not only as the instigator but also as the personal deity of travelers.

It was Ninmah, the king's mother, however, who grieved the most deeply. Understanding that her son's determination was not to be shaken, she stepped out on the palace terrace just as the rays of the western sun struck full against it. Dressed in her prayer robes and holding in her uplifted hands a bowl of incense, she prayed to Shamash to protect her child, reminding the god that this battle with Huwawa, guardian of the Cedar Mountain, would be an unequal one since Gilgamesh would be pitted against a horrible monster and not against a man. In her anguish she cried to the god, "Why must it be to my son that you have given a heart that will not slumber?"

Armed with new flashing daggers and war clubs, Gilgamesh and Enkidu set out the next morning on their great adventure. Soon they had left the tropical forests, the buffaloes, and pelicans of the Euphrates delta country, and were striding past the last irrigated plots and out into the rolling yellow plains of the desert. For weeks and weeks they walked through a land that looked as vast as the ocean, guiding their routes always toward the northwest. Under the gorgeous hues of an eastern sky the rolling hills stretched yellow and treeless. Only the hawk and the eagle flew overhead. On certain days black storms would march like succeeding armies along the desert behind them and go crashing into the walls of the Amanus Mountains. It was a desolate land, where they were grateful at night to lie warmly wrapped in their robes, snug in a cairn or against a sheltering boulder. Over all the desert lay a yellowish haze through which the flying clouds cast shadows that stood like gigantic black pillars holding up the sky. Striding through upland pastures of red, blue, and yellow flowers the friends were amused to see that the colors had dyed their own ankles as they brushed against them. At sunset they often turned to look back southward toward their homeland, and watched in awe as the yellow desert slowly turned from lavender to purple.

As they traveled, they discussed the precious cedars they must fell and float down the Euphrates to Uruk, for in the land of Sumer there was neither stone nor timber for building. If Gilgamesh had been alone, he would have dreaded to meet the monster Huwawa, but with Enkidu by his side he did not even fear death or the hideous face of the beast. Every day made them stronger and harder, and more firm in their resolve never to turn back, come what might. Finally they saw over the crest of a hill the magnificent Cedar Mountain. Its dark green trees had been placed in the guard of Huwawa by the god Enlil long before. In delight the two heroes greeted the shade of the scented trees. They quickly followed a path to the very summit, not wanting even to stop and catch their breath. Soon they reached a stockade of seven magic trees, which was the domain of the monster.

Enkidu was suddenly terrified. He begged Gilgamesh to wait until morning so as not to encounter the giant with darkness falling. Gilgamesh would not listen. In a loud voice he cried out to Huwawa, ordering him to come out of his shelter and meet them in battle. Only silence answered his challenge. Huwawa had heard them, but he would not answer. With pounding hearts the heroes listened to the wind in the trees. There was no answer at all from the stockade.

Enkidu then advised Gilgamesh to sacrifice to the gods. The two friends dug a trench in the forest earth and planted the sacrificial seeds they had brought with them. After reciting their prayers Gilgamesh asked their patron Shamash to send Enkidu a dream in the night by which they could either be sure of their victory or prepare for death.

Toward morning Enkidu awoke to find Gilgamesh leaning over him. "It is I who have dreamed," he said. "Or did you awaken me from my slumber? I must have dreamed, for lo! the earth shook, and the heavens

rained fire! All around me death fell from the clouds!" Enkidu listened to the dream and reassured Gilgamesh, saying that his dream surely presaged the destruction of Huwawa. Then, as they prepared for battle, Huwawa breathed. Before the tempest of his breath the lofty cedars bowed their heads in obedience all the way down the mountainside. Gilgamesh and Enkidu had hardly time to draw their daggers before the monstrous Huwawa charged toward them, roaring like a tempest, shrieking like all the winds let loose. Gilgamesh caught only one glimpse of that devilish face as it lunged toward him—a horrible, distorted face with yellow, bared teeth and fierce, bloodshot eyes.

Back and forth the battle raged between Gilgamesh and the monster. His dagger was soon red with blood from the gushing wounds he had inflicted. Harder and harder Gilgamesh pressed the monster. His courage and strength welled up in him as he fought. Harder and faster he swung his war club, unmindful of his own danger. Finally the monster fell over backward; and before he could get his footing and rise again, Enkidu rushed over to him and hacked off his head. The bloody head rolled down the mountainside, bouncing against the trees.

Thus Gilgamesh was free to cut the cedars for the temples of Uruk, and by his courage he delivered the land from evil. The gods of Sumer had abandoned Huwawa and had fought with Gilgamesh and Enkidu.

After the battle the heroes cleansed themselves of blood, put on fresh garments, and made offerings to the gods. Gilgamesh was so handsome in his gold helmet and white tunic that the goddess of love, Ishtar, appeared suddenly before him. While she was congratulating him on his victory, she began to caress his face provocatively and to stroke his shoulders, asking him if he did not begin to love her. Gilgamesh answered her sharply, "What do you do to your loves, Ishtar? When the stallion worships you, do you not put him into the harness and condemn him to pull the heavy war cart? When the shepherds of the hills are charmed by you, do you not transform them into leopards that eat the little lambs? Did you not kill the lovely youth Tammuz, who loved you? Did you not send him to the House of the Dead after the harvest so that every year the snows of winter steal down the river valleys and cover our land with ice?" Thus for the first time was Ishtar spurned by the heroes.

By the time Gilgamesh and Enkidu had felled the cedars and returned to Uruk, the sultry Ishtar had planned a terrible revenge. She had persuaded her father An to send the Bull of Heaven into the city to trample the people, destroy the temples, and slaughter the warriors by the thousands. Gilgamesh and Enkidu rushed into combat. As the king was about to stab the bull, Enkidu seized it by the tail, and summoning all his strength, hurled it against a stone altar. A loud gasp of joy and relief rose from the city residents, who had watched the combat from their walls. Among the temple courtesans lurked Ishtar herself with tears of anger on her face. Quickly Enkidu bent over the dead bull, flayed it, and flung the bloody pelt up into the goddess' face, shouting defiance at her. Laughing over their shoulders, the two friends sauntered to the Euphrates to wash their hands, followed by the acclamations of the people of Uruk. For the second time Ishtar was insulted.

Very soon after this Enkidu became ill, which was certainly due to a curse put upon him by Ishtar. His sickness lasted for twelve days, and at daybreak on the thirteenth day he died in the arms of his friend, who had never left his side. Gilgamesh was frantic with grief. First he tried to call Enkidu back to life by reminding him of their adventures, the wonderful lion hunts they had enjoyed on the plains, their trip to the Cedar Mountain, and their dazzling defeat of the Celestial Bull. Then as the full realization of his loss sank into his soul, he could bear his grief no longer. Like a wild man he rushed out of the palace, fleeing madly from the awful sight of death. Everywhere he wandered, his subjects tried to console the king by holding up to him the memories of his heroism. Gilgamesh could not be comforted, for he realized that as Enkidu was even then in the House of Death, with mud as his only food, so would he be also one day. This terrible thought drove him in his revulsion to leave Uruk just as the yellow spatches of the date palms were bursting into flower, and to roam desolate through the desert, wrestling with the horror of death.

One day in his anguish a possibility occurred to him. There was one man who had received the gift of immortality. Perhaps, if Gilgamesh could find his abode, he would be willing to divulge this secret. Perhaps also Gilgamesh would be able to return to Uruk with it and save the whole race of mankind from their certain death!

This man who had received the secret of immortality was Utnapishtim, the famous king of Shuruppak. Long before the days of Uruk, Shuruppak had been one of the five royal cities of Mesopotamia. Once the possibility of such a scheme entered his head, Gilgamesh knew no rest. Instead of returning to his home and to his weeping mother, he continued his road straight to the west, traveling as swiftly as he could. With such an inspired goal, how could he fear the dangers of the burning desert? At length, weary and footsore, he reached Mount Mashu, the dazzling western home of the sun god. Blinded at first, for the sunlight was white-hot, he finally made out to his consternation rows and rows of scorpion-men who stood in ranks guarding the entrance to the mountain. His heart sank as he looked at their size. The lower parts of their bodies seemed to rise from the Underworld, while their blazing heads reached high up to the ramparts of the sun god.

At first Gilgamesh could not force his quaking legs to advance, but saying to himself that unless he did confront them, he would also have to taste like Enkidu the bitter clay of death, he finally took a deep breath, walked courageously up to the central scorpion, and bowed low before him. This guardian, apparently recognizing the godly parts of Gilgamesh, pointed toward a gate that swung open, allowing him passage into the dark heart of the mountain. As his eyes became used to the gloom, Gilgamesh managed to follow a wet, cold tunnel that lay ahead of him. Gathering courage as he groped his way forward, he walked so long that he almost lost track of the time. For twice eleven hours he walked without once stopping for rest, and at last in the twelfth twinhour he saw far ahead of him a shimmering of light.

With a gasp of relief, he stepped out into the sunlight into the garden of the goddess who lived by the shore of the sea. Never even in Uruk had he seen a more beautiful sight. Amid pools and flowers stood the holy tree of the gods, the tree of life, covered with all kinds of delicious, scented fruits. Its branches were not of wood but of lapis lazuli flecked with gold. Under it lay a profusion of precious gems winking and sparkling in emerald light. At the end of the garden was the house of the goddess, and beyond that the blue waters of the sea that no man had crossed, clearer than a mirror, bluer than a sapphire. Dazzled and happy, Gilgamesh stood admiring the peace of the garden, not realizing how he looked after his months of travel. His beard was long and unkempt. His palace garments, which had worn out long before, he had replaced with animal skins. His body was scratched and burned by the sun, his hands bleeding from the jagged walls of the Mashu Mountain tunnel. When the goddess saw him, it is no wonder that she ran screaming into her house and bolted the door.

Gilgamesh had not come this far to be stopped by a frightened woman. Rapping sharply on her door, he ordered her to come out at once and talk with him. The goddess, however, would not open the door. Gilgamesh told her that she must see him or he would burst the locks and break down the door. Apparently she believed him, for she came out and listened. Gilgamesh told her he must find a passage across the sea to the home of Ut-napishtim, but the goddess only laughed. This, she told him, was quite impossible. It was absolutely out of the question, since nobody could find the way except the boatman of Ut-napishtim himself. When Gilgamesh tried to make her understand his sorrow at the death of his beloved comrade, Enkidu, she counseled him in this way: "Go home to Uruk, King, and accept the inevitable with good grace. Think of all the gifts with which the gods have showered you. Be grateful for them. Live in your fine palace. Fight your great wars. Eat and drink merrily. Take a wife and sleep peacefully with her head on your shoulder. This way you will live out your days and accept the bird of death when it flies over you." No matter how she argued, Gilgamesh could not be persuaded. Eventually he had his way and extracted from her directions for reaching Urshanabi, the boatman.

He found him and his boat down by the shore in a little cove. At first Urshanabi shook his head solemnly and affirmed that Gilgamesh would be swallowed by the sea. All around the abode of Ut-napishtim, he said, the sea waters were turbulent and dangerous and full of black crags. This was the precise reason why no mortal had ever succeeded in crossing the ocean. Since Urshanabi with all his tales of danger could not dissuade Gilgamesh either, he finally thought of a way in which the passage might possibly be made. The main thing would be for Gilgamesh not to touch the water, for that meant instant death. He told the king to go back up on the mountain and cut 120 poles, each one 60 cubits (30 yards) in length. In this way Gilgamesh did arrive at the magic abode of King Ut-napishtim, the only mortal thus far who had been given the priceless reward of everlasting life. As the boat of Urshanabi approached each crag rising among the waters of death, Gilgamesh with his superhuman strength pushed the boat away from it. He dropped each contaminated pole into the water as soon as he had used it.

He found King Ut-napishtim sitting in his throne room alongside the queen. When Gilgamesh told him who he was and why he had come, the king only nodded knowingly to the queen and laughed openly at such a foolish mortal. "Shall I tell you how I won immortality?" he asked.

Ut-napishtim then recounted at great length and in great detail the story of a flood that the gods had once sent upon the earth. Weary and travel-worn, Gilgamesh listened to the old tale which he had heard so often at his mother's knee—how the god of wisdom had counseled the building of a great ship, how the king had gathered into it a pair of all the animals and birds of creation, how it had rained for six days and six nights, how Shamash had destroyed all the face of the earth with the flood waters, how on the seventh day the tempest had abated. He went on to tell about sending out a dove, a swallow, and finally a raven that did not return. The boat had finally landed on the mountain of Nizir, where the King Ut-napishtim made sacrifices to the gods. "Thus," he concluded, "have I won eternal life."

"So would I also," replied Gilgamesh, undaunted.

"You would not enjoy it," answered Ut-napishtim wearily. "I wager you would long for sleep. Look here," he said, "I'll wager you could not remain awake for six days and seven nights, as I did!"

Even before he could answer, Gilgamesh had fallen asleep at the very foot of the throne, exhausted by his long travels and the final task of the 120 poles. Ut-napishtim would have been content to let Gilgamesh lie there on the floor until he sank into the sleep of death. In this way would his thoughts have been confirmed. The queen, however, with her woman's heart, was touched. In her pity for the handsome king of Uruk, handsome in a virility and power that shone even through his tattered garments, she urged her husband, as only a wife knows how to do, to grant Gilgamesh his request. They awoke the sleeping king and told him of the flower of youth. It lay at the very bottom of the sea, however, and it would require lungs of iron to swim to such a depth. Gilgamesh was not afraid. He saw that the end of the quest was near, and his sleep had restored his strength.

He ran down to the shore, tied huge boulders to his feet, and dauntlessly plunged down through the clear waters, deeper and deeper past the white ledges of the sea. There in a deep, dark cavern he plucked the thorny plant of eternal youth, wincing as the barbs pricked his fingers. With tortured lungs he struggled with powerful strokes back upward toward the sunlight in the waters of the surface. Strange painted fishes glided past him, curious at the bubbles that arose from his threshing limbs. Once on the surface he loosened the stones from his feet and regained the skiff of Urshanabi. Without a thought of tasting the flower himself, he clutched it in delight. It was the attainment of his life's ambition, a gift to his people such as no king before him had ever had the courage and perseverance to obtain. Refreshed and happy beyond words to tell, he rested in the boat as it made its tortuous passage back to the shores of the goddess.

The long journey home to Uruk was a pleasant one, for Gilgamesh held the flower in his hand and no danger could threaten him. Now and again he smelled its aromatic fragrance. One afternoon, weary and dusty, not many days' journey from home, he reached the shores of a little lake that, unbelievably enough, lay in a desert hollow. The water smelled clean and fresh after his days of travel over a parched land. Having removed his garments, he placed the precious flower securely on a stone right near the water, and plunged in. After his swim he waded ashore just in time to see a snake, which had been attracted by the pungent odor of the plant, disappear with the flower of eternal youth in its mouth. Search as he might, Gilgamesh could never find it again. He sat naked by the little lake and wept.

Brokenhearted, he returned to Uruk, where no welcome could cheer him. "Yes, it is I who have returned," he told his people. "For this have I labored! For this have Enkidu and I toiled! For this have I braved the monster Huwawa! For this have I encountered the Bull of Heaven! For this have I watched my dear friend Enkidu descend to the feathered House of No Return! For this—to have brought eternal life not to my beloved people, but to the race of serpents!"

TWO
EGYPT

The following account of the story of Horus, Isis, and Osiris in Egypt is an attempt to incorporate various references to it among the writers of antiquity with recent translations of hieroglyphic texts from Egypt itself. The story of this Triad of Abydos is apparently much older than even the earliest records and may go back as far as 7500 B.C., when, according to a foremost Egyptologist, Sir Flinders Petrie, it is a memory of Asiatic invasion (Seth), repelled by a native king (Osiris).

These three main gods were skillfully incorporated into the Great Ennead, or state religion of Egypt, by the priests of Heliopolis. Aside from a part of the story as told by Plutarch (C. A.D. 46–A.D. 120) and his very modern philosophical analysis of it, apparently no complete text exists in a chronological sequence, as it is presented here. The story was certainly expanded throughout Egyptian history, particularly during the first five or six dynasties when the worship of this Triad was prominent. Therefore we find in the finished story various anachronistic references—to India and to the horse, for example.

All writers about the ancient history of Egypt must acknowledge their debt to the tireless efforts of those scholars who through the long centuries have studied this great civilization which has left behind it monuments of such massive proportions and of such an enduring beauty. Great honors must be paid to the French scholar Jean François Champollion, who deciphered hieroglyphic writing early in the 1800's. Most of us Americans first knew the history of this wonderful land from the inspired writings of James H. Breasted, the especial admirer of the Pharaoh Akhenaton of the Eighteenth Dynasty.

HORUS THE HAWK, THE AVENGER

Most ancient among the ancient countries of the earth is Egypt. This land was described in antiquity as those portions of the soil of Africa which were flooded once a year for a period of a hundred days by the waters of the River Nile, and all those people who drank the waters of that mighty river from Elephantine to the sea were by definition Egyptians. The Nile flows from the left side of the earth—said they—through the country of the Hawk, which we call Upper Egypt, between narrow walls of rock into the right-hand side of the earth, which is Lower Egypt. There the river meets its prehistoric enemy, the Great Green Sea, which once covered all the land. In preparation the Nile divides itself into several streams which force their way through papyrus reeds and marshes into this northernmost triangle or extreme right edge of the earth called the Delta. Speak softly, because as we paddle through the reeds and come out into an open space we may glimpse the baby Horus sitting brown and naked in the middle of a lotus bloom, sucking his chubby finger.

The ancient priests of Egypt were the most learned men in all the world. According to their hieroglyphic calculations, time could be divided into units of 360 days, with 5 days left over in each cycle for the birthdays of the gods. Only very intelligent and fearless boys were admitted to a temple school such as the great college at Heliopolis, where they could study the sacred carvings that revealed all the mysteries of the creation. It was in this school that the child Moses is said to have learned the wisdom of the Egyptians. The ordinary people of Egypt knew very little of such lore. They were content to follow the precepts of their own leaders, long since recognized by them as having had powers beyond those of ordinary men, and these had become their gods.

Born on the first of the five epagomenal days, and therefore the greatest of all the gods, was Osiris, the merciful judge of the living and the dead. One could glimpse him in the dark waters of the Nile, his silken black hair flowing with the current. His wife and sister was the lady of heaven, Isis, she of the thousand titles, whose name means chamber of the birth of a god. Her one could see in the golden light of sunrise, clothed in the brilliant green robes of the new day, the lady bountiful who fills one's fields with crops and one's cradle with a newborn son. Isis herself was born on the fourth day. On the second day was born the elder Horus, a fair god, but one so old his story has been forgotten or else replaced by the baby who later bore a similar name. The third day one must mark on the calendar with three signs of bad luck, for on this day was born Seth, or Typhon, from whom sprang all disharmony and the destructive forces of the earth. On the fifth and last day was born Nepthys, the barren sister of Isis. To her are the dominions of the far lands, the treeless deserts of Libya, and the sterile confines of the seacoasts.

Long before the priests and even before the Pharaohs, the great dark King Osiris ruled in Africa. He was a tall man and slender as all devout Egyptians longed to be so that their bodies might fit as lightly and easily as possible about their immortal soul, or *ba*. On his head he wore the lofty white crown of Upper Egypt with an ostrich feather on either side of it because these feathers are as light as the truth. A beautiful plaited beard fell from his chin as befitted a great and powerful ruler whose fertility made life swell even in the dry desert. Around his neck and shoulders he wore a white collarlike necklace made of precious gems, ivory, and symbolic beads. Wherever he stepped grew a lily blossom in remembrance of the water lilies in that great lake at the very left edge of the world where Osiris was born and where the righteous who have kept his commandments might hope to find the Isles of the Blessed. His naked body from ankles to wrists was beautifully decorated with crimson painted flowers. Such was Osiris who ruled in Egypt, powerful and black, for black is the color of youth, as white is the color of old heads. To worship him a man must use pure water where the ibis drinks and bring fig leaves so that he may grow potent as the sacred bull, as Osiris.

Osiris had embraced his sister Isis even before they were born, while both were tumbling in their mother's womb. When he had become a man and a king, he married her and took her from among all women as his queen. Together they ruled Egypt, making it a land of music and delight. Gradually Osiris by his teachings and example persuaded the people to put away their former evil habits, especially that of cannibalism to which his subjects were particularly addicted. He showed them how to cultivate the earth that he made black and fertile each summer with the waters of the Nile. As soon as he saw that the Egyptians had become industrious and skilled husbandmen, he gave them a code of laws by which they could regulate their lives. Then Osiris decided that it was not enough to civilize Egypt, but that he should travel throughout the rest of the world and by the gentle arts of persuasion and music enlighten them also. It may have been during this voyage that the waters of the Nile spread beyond their usual limit of inundation and made fertile even the barren wastelands of the lovely sister of Isis, Nepthys. In any case Nepthys did conceive and give birth to a son, Anubis. Her husband Seth suspected her pregnancy was due to Osiris when he found in Nepthys' bed garlands of such melilot, or sweet clover flowers as Osiris often wore.

However that may be, Osiris traveled far and wide over the face of the earth, Isis ruled Egypt wisely and well during his absence, and Seth grew more and more evil and jealous. Several times he tried to violate the laws laid down by Osiris and even to change the government, but the watchful Isis always prevented him. One day the return of Osiris was announced through all the land. Seth hastened to invite him to a festive dinner party, and Osiris accepted.

Using promises of great reward Seth managed to persuade seventy-two of his friends and also an Ethiopian queen named Aso, who happened to be visiting Egypt at that time to help him murder the king. After the banquet Seth announced to the company that he had a present to give to one of them. Drawing back a curtain, he showed them proudly a beautiful cedar chest made in the shape of a man and exquisitely adorned with gold and designs. As the assembled guests gasped at the skill of its construction, Seth opened its lid and swore that it should belong only to the man present who fitted it perfectly. One by one the eager guests tried to fit themselves into the box, but they were all too short or too wide for it. Finally Seth called tauntingly to Osiris, "Do you try the precious chest, O King!"

Proudly the tall, slender-hipped Osiris stepped into the casket, lay down with his arms close to his sides, and, of course, he fitted it perfectly—for Seth and his seventy-two accomplices had ordered the box made to his exact dimensions. As soon as Osiris was lying flat on his back, Seth clapped the cover on the chest and began to nail it down. Then he and his treacherous friends poured molten lead all along the joints, thus sealing it hermetically. Within a few minutes they knew

Osiris had smothered to death. Then, as previously arranged, they carried the chest to the bank of the Nile and heaved it into the water. As they watched the current catch it and carry it swiftly downstream, the exultant Seth realized that he was the ruler of Egypt. Thus did Osiris die in the twenty-eighth year of his life, on the seventeenth day of the month, just as the moon was beginning to wane.

The news of the king's murder swept swiftly through the land, causing panic and terror in the hearts of the people. The lady Isis was at the time in the city of Coptos. As soon as she heard the dreadful news, she cut off a thick lock of her shining, black hair and put on the long white robe of mourning. Then like a faithful wife she started out along the banks of the river to find the casket and the corpse of her beloved husband. Up and down its banks she wandered weeping and disconsolate, for she could not find it. The longer she searched, the deeper grew her love for Osiris. She hunted especially closely all along the papyrus swamps of the delta, thinking that the casket might have been caught among the reeds.

As she wandered weeping and mourning she asked for news about her dead husband from all the people she met. It grieved her deeply to hear his praises, for this made her loss more unbearable. Messengers told how he had traveled throughout the world with his kinsman Heracles, spreading the science of agriculture, how he had planted grapevines, wheat, and barley in Ethiopia where he had founded many cities. They told of his great deeds in Arabia and how he had carried the ivy plant even into India where he had built the great city of Nysa. In this strange country Osiris had delighted in elephant hunts. Messengers reported that after visiting all of Asia he had journeyed westward across the Hellespont and forced those barbarians who lived in southeastern Europe to accept his government.

Isis also learned how her husband had, like the Nile, strayed from his bed and visited Nepthys. Nine months later a son, Anubis, had been born to Nepthys, who in her terror of her husband Seth had exposed the child among the reeds and left him to die. Isis found the baby, so curious with its dog's head and spotted dog's coat. With great love she became a mother to him, and educated him so that Anubis grew up to be the watchdog of the gods of Egypt and, like that wonderful animal, devoted and faithful. For his service Anubis received the gift of human speech and studied medicine and embalming.

One day, weary from her long search and sore from her sobbing, which could be heard all the way from Saïs in Lower Egypt to the holy city of Abydos in the south, Isis sat down on a grassy bank in the delta to watch some little children at play. Now it was common knowledge in Egypt that children will often in their unguarded speech reveal facts of great significance, especially if they are in a holy place or near a goddess. Isis therefore listened intently and questioned them. To her great joy they alone among all the people of Egypt had not only seen the casket float by but were able to assure her that it had passed through the Tanitic mouth of the Nile, a current forever afterward held in horror by all those devoted to Osiris. Thrilled at the thought that her search was near its end, Isis hastened down the river, following its flow through the Great Green Sea until she came to Byblos on the great coast of Syria or Phoenicia. It was here that she found the casket.

The waves had gently washed the casket up on the shores of Syria, where a huge tamarisk tree, thriving and blooming even in the salt spray of the seashore, had lovingly enfolded the box in its trunk. The tough, reddish wood grew tightly around the box, protecting it from moisture and harm. The king of Syria, Melkarth, passing along the beach one day, had marveled at the gigantic tree and ordered it to be cut down and its trunk used as a pillar in his palace.

To this palace Isis went with the sure instinct of a woman searching for the man she loves, and sat down thankfully beside the pillar, stroking its wood lovingly. Before her splashed a lively fountain where the ladies of Queen Ishtar of Syria came every afternoon to bathe. At first Isis would not speak to them but only sat with her cheek against the red wood of the tamarisk pillar. The palace ladies realized that Isis was an Egyptian because of her white linen sheath dress which left her beautiful breasts exposed. They had often seen the ships from Egypt unloading their papyrus in the harbor of Byblos, and they had heard how famed the women of Egypt were for their beauty. Coming closer, they marveled at the way her glossy black hair was braided so that it fell across her bare shoulders in two long plaits. Finally Isis began to talk to them, and as they stepped from the fountain, she showed them how to comb their hair and train its wet curls.

The women had no sooner entered the queen's chamber than Ishtar, so skilled herself in the arts of seduction, smelled the perfume that Isis' hands had stroked upon their bodies and in their hair. When she inquired about it, they told her of the beautiful foreign lady they had seen in the palace courtyard. Ishtar commanded that Isis be brought to her at once. When Isis in her simple white gown was brought before the queen, Ishtar, although not knowing that Isis was a goddess, wanted to keep her near, especially because of the enchanting perfume that surrounded the Egyptian woman like a cloud. She commanded Isis to remain in the palace where she was to become the nurse to Ishtar's oldest son.

Isis kept her anonymity for some time, remaining in the palace at Byblos to nurse the son of its rulers. Whenever the child was hungry, she let it suck on her divine fingers instead of at her breast. Every evening when the palace courtiers had gone to bed, Isis held the little boy over a flame because in this way she knew how to singe away those parts of him which were mortal only and confer upon this future king the precious gift of eternal life. Then in the dead of night, while the palace slept, Isis would transform herself into a black swallow and fly screaming and chirping around and around the tamarisk pillar, longing to hold her husband in her arms and feel his strong body against her straining breasts. One night Ishtar, awakened by the shrill laments of the swallow, stumbled sleepily into the courtyard just as Isis was holding the baby prince over the flame. Not understanding what the goddess way trying to do, Ishtar screamed; and in that instant the magic spell was broken. Thus Ishtar herself robbed her own son of immortality.

Before the blinded eyes of Ishtar, Isis revealed herself in the full light of her glory as the Lady of the Sunrise, the Queen of the South, the Beautiful, and the Beloved Lady of Abundance. Kneeling at the feet of the great goddess, Ishtar listened to the story of her wanderings, and to the dreadful news of the death of the Nile, Osiris. Gladly she gave the tamarisk pillar to Isis, who with trembling fingers split open its trunk and carefully lifted out the cedar casket containing the body of her lord. Then Isis in veneration gratefully wrapped the tree trunk in pure white linen bands, anointed it with perfumed oil, and caused it to be erected in the temple of Byblos, where ever afterward it was worshiped as the tree that had enclosed a god.

By this time it was morning, and Isis prepared to sail back to Egypt with her husband's body. Very tenderly she placed it in the sun on the open deck, and when the little river that flowed into the sea at Byblos blew chill breezes along its estuary, Isis angrily caused its waters to run dry. Shortly afterward she arrived in the delta of Egypt, where she could easily find a safe hiding place in which to perform the operations that she alone knew. With the help of her sister Nepthys she set about reviving Osiris. From this ceremony comes one of the beautiful hymns to Isis:

Let us praise Isis
Who rules at the beginning of the New Year!
Let us praise her who was a protectress to thee.
What has she not performed!
She has ruled Egypt in dignity and in truth.
She has defended thy rule in thy absence.
She has cut a lock of her hair and has mourned thee.
Her cries of grief have been heard in Abydos.
What has she not performed!
She has sought thee even far over the sea.
She has borne thee home to our land in her arms;
Nor did she rest in her flight,
Not once alight, nor ever rest!
Let us praise Isis who made breath to come from her wings,
Who worked on thy lifeless body with knotted cords,
Who warmed thy body with the warmth of her breast,
Who made air to enter with the beating of her wings,
Who made life to flow from thy body up into Isis,
To the chamber of the abode of life.[1]

[1] Paraphrased from a hieroglyphic translation into French by the Egyptologist François Chabas (1817–1882).

The news of the restoration of Osiris brought great joy to the people of Egypt, who saw immediately that if their king could be brought back to life after his death, so might they also expect to be. The evil brother Seth, however, haunted the delta region, his red hair flaming and bristling on his head. And there was malice in his heart. Forever afterward the Egyptians abhorred the color red, considering it a manifestation of all the forces of treachery, murder, and jealousy. For this reason in after times the inhabitants of Coptos would not permit within their city the presence of asses because of their reddish coats, and if they found such an animal would hurl him from a cliff. Neither would they allow the use of a trumpet, for this instrument reminded them of the braying of an ass. In these ways and others did they recall how Seth hunted until he found Isis and, mercilessly dragging the goddess after him, shut her up in a dark prison.

This was no fit place for the Lady of Light, and soon by the help and magical powers of the poor, doglike Anubis, whom she had saved from exposure and death, she escaped and fled in great pain to the reeds of the river. There, sitting unattended on a stool, like a plain peasant woman, she labored to deliver her child, the child of her love for Osiris. Straining and moaning, the goddess suffered, but the baby could not be born. Then in her agony two gods appeared and smeared her temples with blood, symbol of life. They brought her amulets also, one of the little beetle which comes to life as the waters of the Nile begin to pour over its banks onto the thirsty desert, and another of the shiny green frog from that African region where rain falls and awakens it from its long sleep in a dry soil. With the help of their incantations the body of Isis burst open and out sprang her beautiful son, flooding the world with his light just as in the darkness before morning the golden sun suddenly appears dazzling and glorious over the eastern rim of a black world. Thus was finally born the son of Osiris, he who was awaited, Horus the hawk, the avenger. His birthday fell on the vernal equinox, just at the very moment when the tender shoots of grain were piercing the black earth of Egypt with their green feathers. He was born as the fruits of the earth are born, by the action of fertilizing water flowing over mother land, and he was born in Lower Egypt among the shrubs and papyri of the delta.

The peach tree was sacred to Horus because its green leaves were just the shape of his heart and just the size of his little tongue. The baby grew fat at his mother's breast, drinking her milk and gazing up at her adoringly; and so are they represented in statues throughout all of Egypt and even in later millennia in the cultured domains of the Greek and Roman empires.

The climate of the delta was healthful for the little boy who splashed in the water and playfully hid from his mother under lotus plants. When he was older his father appeared to him often and encouraged him to be strong and manly and to endure pain sturdily. One day

Osiris asked him, "What do you think is the most glorious action a man can perform?"

Without hesitation, for like his mother Horus had the gift of fluent speech, the small boy answered, "The most glorious action a man can perform is to avenge the injuries offered to his father and mother." [1]

Much pleased with this first reply, Osiris then asked the child, "What animal do you think is the most useful to a soldier?"

Quickly Horus replied, "I know, a horse!"

At this reply Osiris wondered, because he had expected his son to name that animal in whose constellation the Nile every year begins its inundation. He questioned Horus again, "Why do you prefer a horse to a lion?"

"Because," retorted Horus, "although the lion is really more useful to a warrior in great distress, yet still is the horse more helpful in overtaking and cutting off an escaping enemy host."

As a result of such conversations with his son and their long exercises in the handling and use of the various weapons of war, Osiris felt sure that the boy was ready for the enemy Seth, whom he would one day have to meet in a deadly battle if ever he was to claim his lawful realm in Egypt and rule. However, before this day could arrive, more trials and horrors were reserved for the goddess Isis.

There happened to the gentle goddess the very catastrophe every mother fears and dreads more than anything else in the world. One morning she had left Horus, who was yet a young child, asleep on a mat in the sun and had gone to the city of Buto to buy some provisions for him. Imagine the fear and horror when she hastened home and found the little boy lying where she had left him, stung to death by a scorpion. The child lay rigid, his body swollen and already growing cold, his lips white with foam, and the mat wet with the tears of fright and pain he had shed. Screaming hoarsely, with the terrible grief only a mother can feel who holds in her arms the lifeless body of her only child, Isis called for help.

From all sides the neighboring farmers came running, and from every little creek in the marsh the fishermen hastened to draw up their nets and paddle furiously to the goddess' side; for these simple people all knew her hiding place and never even at the threat of the torture stick would they have revealed it. From her distant haunts on the barren seacoast the goddess Nepthys also heard her sister's hoarse screams of grief. Swiftly she sped to the scene, pushed through the circle of helpless friends, and counseled her sister wisely, "Call upon the sun god, O Isis! He alone can tell us what to do!"

Together the sister goddesses cried loudly up to the heavens, invoking the aid of the great god Ra; and wonder of wonders, he heard their

---

[1] Quoted almost verbatim from Plutarch's treatise *De Iside et Osiride*.

voices, for Isis was beloved even in the heavens for her devotion, for her loneliness, and for the continuous tribulations she had so dauntlessly undergone. As all the peasants and fisher folk stood with their mouths open in wonder, the sun stopped in its daily course over the cloudless Egyptian sky. For the anguish of Isis the boat of a million years stood still, and slowly from it to earth descended the ibis-headed scribe of the gods, whose name was Thoth.

There are many reasons why the black-and-white ibis was sacred to the inhabitants of ancient Egypt. This bird, which has vanished from the land as have the stories of Isis, Horus, and Osiris, was a tall, slender bird with a long downward-curving bill. It waded in the ponds and marshes of the delta. In most ancient times hordes of flying serpents used to swarm into Egypt through a narrow gorge from Arabia just east of the city of Buto. Every spring the ibises would collect and fly up to this gorge, repel the invasion, and devour the serpents. As late as 450 B.C., if one accepts the word of Herodotus, a heap of serpents' bones could still be seen at the entrance to the gorge between two steep mountains. Thoth, who wore the ibis' head, kept the records of the gods. As he listened to Isis's sobbing account, he began to search his memory, for his knowledge was encyclopedic.

Slowly and patiently he repeated to Isis the very secret words that up until then only he had known. Intent on saving her child, the goddess controlled her sobs and memorized the sacred ritual. As she uttered the incantations, the wound on Horus' body opened and the poison oozed out. In a few seconds he caught his breath with a shudder. A gasp of amazement broke from the rapt onlookers. "Horus lives! He lives!" Another name, Mistress of Magic, was added to the many titles of Isis. Slowly and with great dignity the learned Thoth mounted up to heaven and resumed his travels in the Boat of a Million Years. Isis did not forget to transmit these magic words to her temple priests so that from that time onward no little child in Egypt ever had to die from the sting of a scorpion.

By the time Horus approached manhood, Seth had heard of his birth although he either did not believe or did not want to believe that this boy was the son of King Osiris. Certain of his friends, however, did understand that the young boy Isis was raising with such devotion and secrecy somewhere in the delta would one day vanquish the fiery Seth, and rule the Nile so well that the dangers of his flaming red droughts would forever vanish from the land. As Horus continued to grow tall like his father, strong in arm and limb, and skilled in the weapons of war, certain of Seth's accomplices began to desert him and flock to the growing army of Horus. Even a pretty young concubine from the camp of Seth, intrigued no doubt by stories of the shining skin and handsome eyes of the new leader, decided to join him. As she approached his camp, she was pursued by a huge snake. To the increasing renown of Horus and his soldiers, it must be said that far from fearing any such monster, they rushed out and chopped it into pieces. A survival of this encounter remained for centuries in Egypt; a cord was thrown to the ground at the opening of an assembly and then cut up in pieces by the participants.

After her joyful return from Syria, Isis had very carefully hidden the chest containing the body of Osiris so that only she and Nepthys knew where it had been put. The wicked Seth, although he did not believe in the resurrection of the king, was still very anxious to find the chest and the body. During the daylight hours he never ventured in the delta because of Isis's vigilance, but at night he roamed through its trails under the pretense of hunting. When the moon was full, he peered into every cave and hiding place. In this way he finally discovered the chest one night when the goddesses were absent. Drawing his sharp hunting knife, he dragged out the body of Osiris and cut it up into fourteen pieces, throwing each one into the Nile as soon as he had severed it.

Toward morning Isis returned and found the chest empty. In this last and most appalling calamity that befell her on earth the goddess was not alone, for now she had a full-grown son who had been born with the sharp eyes of a hawk and whose role was to be that of the avenger. Although he was not aware of it, the tyrannous rule of the redheaded Seth was soon to draw to a close. Isis swiftly made herself a light boat of papyrus reeds and, leaping into it, started to find the fourteen pieces of the great king's body. As she found each piece, she carried it to her son Horus.

The fierce, man-eating crocodiles of the Nile never touched the goddess or those parts of the king's body she was so tenderly gathering, but allowed her to pass unharmed in her frail craft. Nor did they ever afterward molest any native so long as he remained in a papyrus boat. For this kindness the inhabitants of Egypt even as far south as Thebes venerated the crocodile. In their temples they raised a baby animal and taught him to be tame. They made him earrings of molten stone and sand, put golden bracelets on his forefeet, and when he died embalmed him with the greatest expense and ceremony. This reptile had already earned a reputation for great sagacity even before its charity to Isis, since the female laid her eggs at exactly that place to which the Nile in its flood would rise. The ancients also associated it with their astronomical calculations, for they had observed that the crocodile always laid sixty eggs, which took sixty days to hatch, and that the oldest of their race lived to the age of sixty years.

One by one Isis gathered together the pieces of the body of her lord and carried them to the holy city of Abydos. Horus and Nepthys stood waiting. Because he was a god who had very special and secret knowledge of both black and white magic, Horus assembled together the parts of his father's body. Slowly and tediously he joined bone to bone and flesh to flesh until there appeared before him the very likeness of the great Osiris. After the jawbone had been skillfully placed in the head and the head joined to the trunk of the body, the great king appeared almost ready to receive from his beloved son the breath of life. However, one piece of the body had still not been recovered, the phallus. At the very end of her search Isis learned that it alone of all of the king's body could never be found. It had been eaten by three fishes of the Nile basin, the Lepidotus, the Phagrus, and the Oxyrynchus (*Mormyrus oxyrhynchus*, a species often mummified and used in sculptured decorations). Because of this Isis was obliged to construct models of the genital organs, which were carried by priestesses in all their ensuing ceremonies. In the fourteen days of the waning of the moon the mutilated body was recovered and made whole again. Wherever Isis found a piece of Osiris' body, she caused a magnificent temple to be built to this god, which explains why there were so many of them throughout the land of the Nile. Of these great edifices the principal one was at Abydos itself, where the wealthy and distinguished of Egypt all built their tombs during the earliest dynasties. The inhabitants of Memphis, opposite which the great pyramids were later built, used to assert that their temple contained the body of the king, but they were mistaken.

Having first like a dutiful son cared for the body of his father, Horus then set out in search of Seth. Not only Isis and Nepthys, but Thoth himself was a witness to this monumental struggle. Sharper than the hawk and swifter in his course, the furious Horus pounced down upon the mottled Seth and with his first burst of strength threw him high up in the air, shrieking vengeance on the brother who had twice attacked the person of Osiris, who had usurped the throne, and who had caused the heat and drought to flame far over once fertile valleys and lush crops. As Seth fell to the ground, Horus, black and terrible in his

wrath, swooped down upon him again and sent him spinning and reeling over the cliffs of the western hills. For three days and three nights the battle raged. It was observed by Thoth, who had come down from the heavens on purpose to judge it, and fortunate it was that he did so, for his help was soon most urgently required. At the end of the third night the youthful Horus succeeded in mastering Seth. Holding him firmly about the middle of his body, Horus delivered him to his mother Isis. Hurling Seth's ugly red head to the ground, he stood with his foot on it. Triumphantly he bound tight chains around Seth and committed him to his mother's keeping. Then Horus set out to pursue the remnants of Seth's infernal legions.

As soon as Horus had hastened away on his errand, Seth began to wheedle Isis into liberating him. He used strong arguments, reminding her that his warmth was necessary to Egypt. He painted dark pictures ·for her of the ruin and famine that would befall that fertile land if the Nile waters remained cold. At first Isis turned away from his pleadings. Then he called on her womanly tenderness, showing her the wounds and bruises Horus had inflicted upon him. Finally he appealed to her sisterly love, saying that after all he was her brother and the brother of Osiris, that it was not seemly for one so close in ties of blood to be kept in a dark prison in chains. At last the goddess felt pity in her heart and released him.

So terrible was the anger of Horus, when upon his return he found that Seth had been released, that he cut off with one stroke the crown and queenly head of Isis. It was then that Thoth asserted his presence of mind and vast store of learning. Before the goddess could even become aware of what had happened, he replaced her head and crown with that of Hathor, the more ancient deity of the female principle. Thus Isis wore ever afterward the ears and horns of the cow and appeared in the likenesses of the seven fates, who supervised childbirth personally.

In the second and even more fierce struggle that followed, Isis joined her son in a relentless pursuit of Seth. In spite of her efforts to help Horus, however, Seth managed to catch him off guard and, reaching upward, tore out his eye, that part of the body which contained his soul. Then Isis and Horus renewed their attack, and Horus was able finally to wrest his eye from Seth's hand. With a final burst of fury they vanquished Seth and pursued him all the way down the Red Sea until he disappeared from the land forever. Then Horus, in ceremonial dress, wearing the feathered headdress of the hawk shining and streaming over his shoulders, advanced into the temple of Abydos where he had left the body of his father. Reverently he approached Osiris and embraced him, thus transferring to that god some of the power of his double spirit, or *ka*. In his right hand Horus bore the eye he had snatched from Seth. Osiris sat on a splendid throne, bearing the flail and the scepter of royalty. Gently opening the lips of Osiris, Horus fed him the eye, and Osiris arose from the dead and lived again! The strength of the eye flowed through his limbs, and he was a *ka-in-harmony*.

Then Horus prepared a ladder of many rungs, lacing it well with leather thongs. Slowly Osiris proceeded from the temple of Abydos to the gateway of heaven. Wearing wings and splendid robes, Isis and Nepthys accompanied him on either side, followed by Thoth, who carried the book of the gods. Osiris ascended the ladder with the help of Horus, who pushed him with the tip of one finger. As he arose higher and higher up the ladder, there came into view on the eastern brow of the world the lofty mountain of the sunrise, while on the western side stood the pillared mountain of the sunset. As the god Osiris ascended, the ladder grew in height also. Already Osiris could feel the fresh breezes from the four corners of the earth stir the ostrich feathers in his crown. The light from the Boat of a Million Years shone radiantly around him. Then he stepped upon the gleaming crystal floor of heaven itself, which rested on the two mountain peaks.

Even as Osiris was ascending the ladder, there was a great convention of the gods at Heliopolis where Thoth appeared as an advocate. By the time Osiris had finished mounting into heaven all the evil accusations of Seth were dismissed, Osiris' life was adjudged to have been pure, and Horus was declared his son and heir on earth.

As Osiris advanced over the crystal floor of heaven, the Boat of a Million Years came to a slow halt. Its crew of gods hailed him as the Lord of a Million Years. For ever afterward Osiris ruled the earth, crossing it every day in his solar boat and at night crossing the Milky Way of stars, the Heavenly Nile. His especial realm was that of the dead. Every Egyptian had to pass before him and answer affirmatively to the forty-two commandments in the Book of the Dead. Then his heart was weighed against an ostrich feather, and if it was truly light and free from sin, he could proceed to the Lake of Reeds and the Isles of the Blessed.

Remaining on earth until his time should come to pass before Osiris, the merciful judge of the dead, Horus ruled Egypt and had four sons who lived pure lives in truth and harmony or *Maat*. Every succeeding Pharaoh of Egypt saw Horus in the graceful flight of the hawks in the southern land and longed for his *sed* festival when he too would become a Horus. In this ancient land the man who was so unfortunate as to kill a hawk had to submit to the penalty of death. For out of the land of the hawk came the greatest Pharaohs of Egypt: Menes, who first united the land and wore the red and white crowns of Upper and Lower Egypt; Thutmose, who in the great battles of Armageddon and Carchemish conquered the world; and the gentle Akhenaten, whose concept of a universal god stretching out his hand to all of mankind alike, regardless of color or race, was such a failure in Egypt.

THREE
CRETE AND
GREECE

1214355

In the following three episodes I have attempted to show by the choice of these interconnected legends—chosen from the thousands of stories of the Greeks—how the mainland of Europe was influenced by the older civilization of Crete, which was in turn deeply affected by Egypt and Phoenicia. As the stories tell, Crete finally fell to Achaean conquerors, to the rising cities of Mycenae, Pylos, and Tiryns.

Modern historians, who keep pushing backward into B.C. times the dates for all these ancient civilizations, now say that the Minoan thalassocracy in Crete passed through three periods: (1) 3000–2200 B.C., (2) 2200–1600 B.C., and (3) 1600–1200 B.C. They tell us that Crete was at its peak under a King Minos in this second or middle period, and also that Knossos was burned at this time. By 1450 B.C., they say, Crete had relinquished its supremacy to early Greek tribes.

The interesting point is that these legends about Crete, once assembled in what would appear to be a chronological order, bear out the archaeological findings of the twentieth century in Crete. These stories, which so many Greek and Roman writers never tired of telling, are more or less true, and interesting because they reveal history from two points of view, the Cretan and the Greek. In our own century Sir Arthur Evans excavated Knossos, found the palace of Minos, his throne, his theaters, and part of his moldering treasure. We may turn with renewed admiration to the words of the poets, particularly to the charming Ovid whose pages were thumbed so carefully and remembered so well by Shakespeare. How unfortunate for us all that Shakespeare did not decide to tell us more of the following stories himself!

THE HOUSE OF CRETE

In the beginning was Chaos created, formless and black and vast. Next was fashioned the broad-bosomed Earth, Gaea, upon whose fertile valleys and snowy mountain peaks the deathless gods of Greece have found their dwelling place. Third was created Love, the most beautiful and best-known of all the timeless gods, who alone causes the knees to tremble, the heart to falter, and the wisest plans to be forgotten. Earth bore Uranus, wide and starlit, as a covering mantle for herself, and ever since the sky has veiled her nakedness with floating cloud and wisps of fog. From a union of Earth and Sky were born the twelve Titans; the Cyclops, who had only one eye in the middle of their fore-heads; and three monstrous giants, each with a hundred conquering arms and fifty heads. Uranus, recoiling in horror before his unruly progeny, imprisoned them swiftly in the very depths of the earth. Gaea lamented their fate and mourned them with floods of tears.

Then when Uranus refused to release them, especially the Titans, her six sons and daughters whom she deeply loved, Gaea turned from sulking to a dark scheme of revenge. Beginning with Oceanus because he was the first-born, she asked each one of the Titans to help her tame Uranus, but they were too frightened or too appalled to dare lift up their hands against their sire. Only the last-born of her sons, the crafty Cronus, volunteered.

When it grew dark and still, Uranus returned to the bed of Gaea, stretched out his enormous limbs, and fell fast asleep. Cautiously the ambitious Cronus crept from his hiding place and stole forward stealth-ily, bearing in his outstretched hand the metal sickle that his mother had shaped for him. With a lunge he slashed at the body of Uranus, rendering him incapable of further creation. From the drops of crimson blood sprang the Furies, who throughout all time punish the guilty, pursue them shrieking, and harass them relentlessly. Out of the muti-lated pieces that drifted in foam across the summer sea arose, all bathed in sunlight and silver foam, the goddess Aphrodite at Cyprus.

Having thus disposed of his father, Cronus proceeded to free his brother Titans, from whom he continued the creation of the divinities, assigning to each one his especial domain or province. Cronus knew all this time, however, that the curse of his parent had fallen upon him, for, cautious as he was to veil his face and brandish the sickle, he was doomed forever after. The only way he could escape this punishment would be to remain childless himself. Inevitably, however, he fell into the warm embrace of nature in the person of the great goddess Rhea. Carefully Cronus watched her, and as she was delivered of her children he snatched each one out of her arms and devoured it. Back into the darkness of their father dropped his three daughters, Demeter, Hera, and Hestia, and two sons, Hades and Poseidon. Rhea, the divinity of nature, longed in vain to clasp her children in her arms. In her sorrow and despair, feeling inside her womb the stirring of a new life, she fled to her parents to ask if there were not some way in which she could thwart the evil fears of Cronus and rear a child. After a long reflection Uranus and Gaea hit upon a plan.

As in a dream of beauty Gaea recalled that, set like an emerald gem in a sea of blue that is darker than a sapphire, south of the shores of Greece and north of the Nile delta, lay an island fastness. From its little coves and gleaming sandy beaches the hills rise through terraces of oak and olive to snow-covered mountain peaks. What a perfect spot in which to bear a child! When the time drew near for the birth of her son, Rhea, remembering her parents' advice, fled far over the sea to the island of Crete. There in a mountain cave she gave birth to her sixth child, the god Zeus. Behind the entrance to the grotto extended a long chamber, and behind that another one running deep into the mountain among huge stalagmites that stood beside the silent waters of a sub-terranean lake. Before this hiding place the mountain terraces stretched broad and sloping to the safe interior of the island. Each side of the entrance was guarded by double-edged axes. In such a refuge the new-born child was safe.

Then Rhea returned home to her suspicious husband, and pretend-ing to be delivered of a child, she picked up a huge stone. Wrapping it carefully in the swaddling garments of an infant, she tearfully handed it to Cronus. Unsuspectingly he gulped it down. Thus no search was made for Zeus, and he grew up peacefully in the sunny olive groves of the Cretan mountains.

The king of Crete assigned the care of the baby to two nymphs, Ida and Adrastea. Watchful and gentle, these two maidens bathed the child and fed him milk from a long-haired mountain goat, Amalthea. Placing him in a golden cradle, they dispatched wild pigeons far and wide to bring him honey. Even the lonely eagle from the high crags of Mount Dicte brought him nectar from the lavender mountain crocus. His nurses made him toys of gold and wreaths of laurel for his head. Around his cradle danced the lithe young warriors of Crete, filing up the mountainsides with their huge shields, singing war songs of courage and defiance, leaping and stamping on the ground in martial unison whenever the baby cried, so that the sound would not reach his raven-ous father, Cronus. As the boy Zeus grew older, the young men en-couraged him to train with them, to leap and dance, to shoot and hunt, to run tirelessly across the mountain terraces in pursuit of horned goats, and to swim in the warm waters of the clear sea. After Zeus had learned to drive his thundering chariot over the peaks as fast as the eagle and to catch the thunderbolts in his bare hands and hurl them unerringly into the valleys, he dressed himself in the gray fleece of a mountain goat and went to Greece to settle accounts with Cronus.

Aided by the counsels of his crafty grandmother, Zeus forced Cronus to vomit up the five children he had swallowed and also the stone he had mistaken for his last son. Snatching the stone away, Zeus bore it to the high slopes of Parnassus in Greece, where he placed it at the shrine of an oracle. There at Delphi he appointed a priestess, the Pythoness, who sat thenceforth upon a three-legged stool over a steep chasm. Above this gorge rose the Phaedriades, two enormous rocks, that towered to a height of 300 meters and made its approach from the north impossible. Out of this cleft in the earth rolled magic vapors which caused convulsions in those animals or men who dared approach them. From her intoxication the Pythoness at Delphi, chewing incessantly on bay leaves, pronounced the oracular prophecies that rivaled those of Apis, the sacred bull of Memphis, or even those of Zeus Ammon in the Libyan oasis. Thus Zeus was the instrument through whom the ancient curse on Cronus was accomplished. Plunged into the wide-eyed slumber of eternity, Cronus was banished to the far-distant end of the earth, where even now he nods immortally.

Zeus reigned far and wide over land and sea, gathering clouds about him on lofty Olympus, punishing, judging, and receiving homage from gods and men alike. In one of his prolonged travels he wandered far into the western confines of the earth, where in a garden of delight he met the goddess Hera, she of the gentle brown eyes and golden robes. They were married immediately, for it was a case of love at first sight. In honor of their wedding the tree of life was hung with golden apples in the far garden of the Hesperides where first they met.

In spite of her blooming cheeks, in spite even of the children she bore Zeus, it was not a peaceful marriage. Zeus, so strong he could not be budged by the combined forces of all the gods together, greatly feared the jealous rages of Hera when she flew across the earth in her golden chariot, searching for him when he was too long absent. She could excuse his several previous marriages and such children as the nine Muses and the four Seasons that were born to him. What she could not condone was that in time the faithless Zeus began to woo not only nymphs of purely divine birth but also to have affairs with mortal women such as Danaë, whose son was the great hero Perseus.

One sunny day the roving eye of Zeus was caught and charmed by a beautiful maiden named Io, the granddaughter of Oceanus. As Zeus strolled up to her through the green fields along a little river, something warned him that Hera was spying on him. Quickly he changed the maiden into a silky white heifer and shrouded them both with a thick gray cloud. This stratagem only aroused deeper suspicion in his jealous wife. Regal in a golden robe and dazzling in her beauty, Hera suddenly appeared before her nervous husband. Brushing indignantly through the cloud that he had hung over the riverbanks, she strolled up to him, her dangling earrings swinging provocatively against her rosy cheeks. "What a lovely little heifer you have here," she remarked languidly. "I wonder where she came from. I don't recall seeing her in any of the herds around here. Does she belong to anyone in particular?"

"Why no, dear love of my life," Zeus answered, trying very hard to be casual. "I believe she was just born, . . . ah . . . I think she is a new creation, as a matter of fact."

Maliciously the goddess Hera pursued her advantage. "Will you give her to me as a present then, dear husband?"

"My dear lady," stammered Zeus, "I am sure I could not offer you so meager a gift as this animal. Ask me for a cloak of stars. This would really be more appropriate. Perhaps you would like our son Hephaestus to make you a golden throne down in his workshop under the sea. This would indeed be a present worthy of your golden beauty." With art and cajolement Zeus did his best to turn Hera's thoughts away from the gentle Io, for the god had no intention at all of letting her escape from him. No matter how skillfully he pleaded, Hera, more and more suspicious, would not be diverted.

"Do you mean you refuse to give me this creature?" she finally asked.

Since he could think of no alternative right at that moment, Zeus had to consent. Reluctantly he handed Io over to his wife. As soon as he had departed, she called Argus and instructed him to watch night and day over the heifer. Now Argus was the perfect watchman, for he had a hundred eyes. While any two of them slept, all the others stayed wide open and vigilant. It was therefore no trouble at all for him to keep ninety-eight sharp eyes on Io, who was still in the shape of a silky young cow. As long as it was daylight, Argus allowed her to roam through the pastures, but every evening he tied her to a tree, and even so he sat nearby. From a distance Zeus watched the disconsolate Io wander up and down along the riverbank. Finally Zeus decided to send the clever Hermes down, for surely he of all gods could outwit Argus.

In the meantime Io herself had at least discovered a way to let her family know what had happened to her. Without letting Argus see what she was doing, she managed to slip closer and closer to the river's edge. Then with one hoof, for the poor girl had no voice with which to call for help, nor any arms to wave with, she managed to trace the letters *I* and *O* on the sand beside the water. Very soon indeed her father, the river god, flowing past toward the sea, saw the letters and realized what had happened. Much as he longed to save her, however, there was nothing he could do.

Then to the delight of Argus the god Hermes appeared in the simple dress of a goatherd, a skin thrown over his shoulder and his pipes in his mouth. After he had prudently called Io away from the river's edge, Argus sat down under a gnarled olive tree and prepared to listen to the concert of Hermes. It was lovely music, indeed, that the god played for him, songs of the birth of Zeus in the hidden groves of Crete and a long tune in praise of country life among pretty white sheep that go jumping over a wall, one at a time, two at a time, three at a time, four at a time. . . . Hermes played more and more softly. Argus began to close his

eyes. . . . Hermes played ever so gently, but after a long time he grew sleepy himself. Argus still sat there leaning on the tree and watching with only a few eyes open.

His vigilance presented a real problem, and Hermes was not ready yet to admit defeat. "How would you like me to tell you a story, dear Argus?" he asked.

It is true that by this time the stars were out, and cool breezes were blowing angrily down the river where Io's father rolled and worried in his pebbly bed. Even so, Argus was more than willing to hear a story. Wrapping his goatskin closely around his shoulder, he first assured himself that the heifer was securely tied and then settled back contentedly. It was not every evening that a glib stranger offered to entertain an ugly giant like him. Dropping his pipes and waving in their place a magic wand of sleep, Hermes began his tale.

"Once upon a time . . . Are you comfortable, Argus?"

"Oh, yes, very much, thank you, shepherd."

"Once upon a time there was a pretty little nymph whose name I can't quite recall," began Hermes. "Anyway, she was a pretty little thing very much cherished by certain satyrs and queer folk of the forests and streams. She followed in the train of the chaste Artemis, running through the woods with her spotted fawns, playing in the moonlight, and perfectly pure. Then one day the great god Pan came leaping through a forest glade and saw her. Well, you know how amorous Pan becomes. He just fell head over hoofs in love with her. He followed her around, and insinuated he had even mistaken her for that beam of moonlight, the goddess Artemis herself. When he became a little bolder in his advances, the shy nymph shook her curls and ran away from him.

"Pan followed her down the forest paths, calling her sweet names, and trying in every way to woo her. He didn't catch up with her until she had arrived at the banks of a little stream. There she stood leaning far out over the water and calling tearfully to her sisters, the nymphs of the stream. Just as Pan reached out to catch her by the waist, her sisters answered her pleas for help. In a twinkling they had pulled her down to the safety of the river bed.

"Poor Pan found he was clutching in his hands a clump of reeds. In his surprise, and panting from his hot pursuit, he gasped, 'Oooh!' He was so delighted with the musical sounds that came from the reeds that he forgot all about the wretched nymph and began to cut them properly and blow through them again. 'Well, I shall possess your sweetness in one way or another,' he panted. Then he blew a little tune and began to dance. . . . Are you listening, Argus?" Hermes questioned. There against the oak tree lay the giant, sound asleep, with all of his hundred eyes closed at once.

Quickly Hermes drew his knife and killed the giant. Then he rushed over to Io who stood trembling with fright at the sight of so much blood, and set her free. Next morning, when Hera discovered Argus slain and the heifer gone, she was very angry. Before starting out in pursuit, however, she salvaged the glistening eyes of her faithful Argus and set them all fancifully in the tail of her favorite bird, the peacock, where they may be seen even today.

Even as Io was standing by the water's edge wondering which way to turn, the goddess Hera found her. Immediately she conjured up before the terrified eyes of the maiden a Fury so dreadful, so monstrous to behold that the poor Io, driven mad by the sight, plunged wildly into the sea. Further maddened and tortured by ceaseless bitings and sting-ings that Hera was causing within her breast as if a million hornets were stinging her to death, she sought refuge in the cool waters of the western sea—which ever since has borne her name, Ionian. No matter where she turned or how furiously she swam, however, the terrible bloody image remained before her eyes, appearing and reappearing just ahead of her. Pitiful and alone, she returned eastward, fighting her way at times through heavy waves up into the sea of Thrace. At length she crossed the Bosporus and began her weary, tormented way southward along the coast line of Asia Minor, past the great cities of Troy, of Byblos and Tyre until she reached the reed bank of the Nile delta. It was that great river that received her, a wanderer over the face of the earth.

Feebly the white heifer struggled with her forefeet to find a firm footing along the slippery banks of the Nile. Raising herself finally upon a grassy plot, she threw back her head, fell to her knees, and gazed up mournfully at the face of heaven. With gentle lowing and with hot tears of anguish, she implored the divinities of high heaven to put an end to her torments.

In the meantime Hera had rejoiced in the sufferings and madness of Io, and had kept a close watch on Zeus so that he dared in no way to alleviate them. When he saw that the maiden had managed to cross the seas and find a willing haven in the black earth of Egypt, he persuaded the vindictive Hera to withdraw her spells. It was, of course, not without difficulty that she consented. Zeus was obliged to promise, to swear even by the black waters of the River Styx, that he would never again woo Io in any way whatsoever. Once the goddess was reassured of this, a transformation occurred in her pitiful victim.

At first Io could not believe her eyes. Suddenly the white hairs that were over her body began to disappear miraculously. Quickly she lifted her hand to her head and found that her horns were growing smaller and that they had soon disappeared. Her eyes returned to their former size and shape. Last of all, the hoofs of the cow were metamorphosed into little toes with pretty pink nails. The only semblance to the heifer which remained in her was its milk-white skin and brown eyes. Very gradually Io tried to stand on her two legs instead of four. For a long time she remained so, standing motionless but erect among the fronded papyrus stems. Most of all she longed to hear her own human voice, but she was afraid to try to speak for fear the goddess Hera had reserved the heifer's lowing as a last punishment for the beauty that had attracted Zeus himself. Eventually Io tried to speak. How happy she was to discover that she could say words just as before! As Io made her way into Memphis, the holy city of Lower Egypt, the inhabitants had no trouble in recognizing her as a manifestation of the beloved Isis, who had worn the horns of Hathor on her head. Io still had other sufferings to undergo, but she was comforted for them all by the love of the Egyptians, by her marriage to the Pharaoh himself, and by her own son, who was later venerated in Memphis as Apis, the sacred bull.

It is not to be supposed, however, that compunction for the trouble he had caused could long deter Zeus from other amorous adventures when an apt occasion arose. One day as he observed the coast of Syria from the heights of Parnassus, his roving eye happened to rest on an exceptionally beautiful blonde. Immediately Zeus moved closer for a better view. He was watching a small island about half a mile off the coast of Phoenicia. It was surrounded by massive walls from which jetties and moles projected into the sea. It was the busy harbor and virtually impregnable fortress of Tyre, a great commercial rival of Sidon and Byblos. It was inhabited by black-bearded Phoenicians whose robes of many colors were so distasteful to the ancient Egyptians, who wore simple gowns of white linen. The merchants of Tyre had prospered and become wealthy from the sale of linen and woolen materials, which they knew how to dye a brilliant shade of cerise or crimson called "purple" by the ancients. This precious dye was manufactured from a secretion exuded near the head of a little shellfish native to their waters (*Murex brandaris*). When this liquid was spread over wool or linen in the presence of sunlight, it dyed the fabric permanently and became the "royal purple" of the ancient world, to the wearing of which one had to be born.

Determined this time to lay his plans well in advance so as not to be frustrated again by Hera, Zeus asked Aphrodite to prepare the blonde maiden, whose name was Europa, for the great love affair that was to ensue. To this fair princess of Tyre the goddess of love sent a dream during the night as Europa slept soundly on her couch in the royal palace. Just before the rosy-fingered Dawn was ready to mount the eastern skies, Europa dreamed that her homeland and beloved Asia were engaged in a terrible war. The whole of her land, the East, rose up wrathful in battle with neighing horses and flashing swords against the whole world of the opposite shores, the West. In her dream she seemed to feel that all of mankind was divided into these two raging camps, the East and the West, which glared at each other through the steady eyes of an old hatred, and then rushed forth to slaughter and utterly destroy the other.

Out of the dust and turmoil of the conflict Europa seemed to see two magnificent women, enemies of old, who faced each other in shining armor and panoply of war. One of them was an Asian woman—or it may have been the mother of Europa, since she hovered about the little princess and sheltered her with naked arms and shield. It was the Western woman, however, who beckoned imperiously to the unresisting maiden. This second person called her loudly with words like, "Come! Hasten to me, Europa!" Out of the fantastic vision her voice came down the wings of the winds and shrieked about the young girl's ears, "Euro . . . pa! Come! Eu . . . ro . . . pa!" Silently and with hesitant feet the princess moved across the spaces of land and sea at this imperious command. "By all the powers above, and by those Fates, daughters of black night, who spin and cut the threads of human lives, you are mine, Europa! The aegisbearing Zeus has ordained it!"

The sound of her own sharply intaken breath of wonder and surprise awoke the princess from her dream. Shivering, her scalp prickling with little needles of excitement, Europa gazed about the massive walls of her chamber. Quickly she rushed to the window and looked out. To her surprise the world was just the same. On one side of her sailing ships were moving along the blue waters of the port. Above the castle walls the hills and meadows of Phoenicia were gay with the green of spring. In spite of all these familiar scenes, she still could not drive the thoughts of the dream from her mind, so vivid did they seem and so significant. Recalling before her mind's eye the panorama of war and armies, and then remembering the kind face and imperious manner of that bold woman who called her away from her mother, Europa could not help thinking that this dream was a prophecy of what was surely to come true. With a feeling of inner excitement she spent longer than usual at her toilette, choosing with pleasure a beautiful new gown of

Tyrian purple which only she as a princess of the royal blood could wear. She dressed her long blond hair in ringlets and wound the curls over her ears into a coronet at the top of her head. Then when she had recited her morning prayer to Ishtar, she asked the goddess to be watchful over her that day and especially to see that no harm came from the weird, prophetic dream.

When Europa was finally arrayed in her prettiest gown, she summoned her girl friends about her and proposed an outing. With this group of noble young girls she usually spent her days either in wading along the shores of the sea, in leading dances in the palace rooms or even in the meadows, or in wandering through the hills near her home to gather lilies among the grasses. This morning they set out gaily, walked across the palace lawns and gardens, and climbed the slopes of the hills that slanted gently down toward the sea. Laughing and chatting, they strolled along, each one carrying a May basket on her arm. Every now and then they stopped to catch their breath and listen to the distant sound of the breakers rolling in to the shore and sending little curling fingers of foam to search the black rocks along the beach.

Europa carried a golden basket, an heirloom in her family. It had been made by Hephaestus, the cunning metalworker of the gods. He himself had presented it to Libya on the day of her wedding to Poseidon, whose trident was still revered along the shores of Africa and even among the dwellers of the Nile delta. Libya had bequeathed the beautiful basket to her daughter Telephassa and so to the grandchild Europa. Among the magnificent works of Hephaestus were the dreadful aegis of Zeus, the winged chariot of Helios, the mansions of the gods on Olympus with their massive bronze doors, and the arrows of Hermes and Artemis. It was a basket well worth description, so dazzling was it to the sight, and so artfully fashioned of pure gold.

Against a background of waves Hephaestus had represented the bewildered Io before her transformation into human shape, standing lowing and pawing at the breakers. Two men stood nearby watching to see if the heifer would leap into the water. On the beach stood Zeus himself leaning toward Io and stroking her flanks with his hand, in true loverlike fashion. On the other side of the basket Io was represented in her human loveliness just as she was after her arrival in Egypt. In the background, rolled all in silver, were the seven mouths of the Nile and Zeus represented in gold. On another side stood Hermes piping his sleepy song to the giant Argus, who dozed at his feet. The rest of this wonderful jewel represented the spreading tail of the peacock, bellying out like a sail before the wind and dazzlingly studded with the hundred eyes of Argus. It was in this basket that Europa planned to gather flowers on the May morning after her dream.

The hills of Phoenicia slope gently down toward the island of Tyre. In the spring their pine trees stand dark and fragrant against a pure blue sky. During April and May the hills are a riot of bloom. Europa and her friends had blossoms to choose from of many colors and varieties. There were purple hyacinths and white narcissuses, golden crocuses that thrust their slender cups up from the dark earth, blue violets, and wild lilies. While her friends filled their baskets with flowers of all kinds, Europa chose only the rose, the pride of all the plants of the earth, burying her face in its strange spicy fragrance. Europa was beautiful. Even among her pretty friends she was truly beautiful in her flowing cerise robe with her yellow curls and her golden basket full of roses. It was as if you were to see Aphrodite herself standing in all her radiance among the Graces and outshining them all.

This is the way she looked when Zeus saw her. He was overcome with emotion, for the arrows of the sly imp of Love can pierce the hearts of gods as well as those of men. In a daze he circled around her, numb with joy at the thought of so perfect a beauty. He remembered, however, to divest himself of his immortality so as not to frighten or burn her. He also remembered to disguise himself so well that Hera could never find him. Hastily he transformed himself into a magnificent golden bull that wore in the center of its forehead a star of silver. His horns were slightly curved and thin, like the horned edges of the new moon. His eyes were large and blue, gentle with admiration and sparkling with the thrill and excitement of love.

Although his transformation was swift, he allowed himself to become visible to them gradually so that the virgin maidens of Tyre thought he had been there all the time. With the natural love of the young for animals and their envy of them, the girls ran up to him exclaiming in pleasure and delight. Gently they stroked his satin sides and velvet coat. His breath was like honey or the fragrance of roses, like the smell of summer blowing down green pastures to the sea. With the tips of her fingers Europa touched his lips. It seemed to her that the bull was actually kissing her fingers and nuzzling the palm of her hand. Without any fear whatsoever, she caressed his neck which was so sleek and soft. Only she could hear the soft loving noises he was making low in his throat.

As she stood patting him, the bull knelt at her feet and motioned with his head toward his back. Then he looked up at Europa questioningly. With a laugh she turned to her friends and said, "Look, dear girls, look at this beast. What do you think he wants us to do? Do you see how he has knelt down before us? Come. Let's take a ride on his back. I am sure he is a gentle creature. Just see his soft eyes. Let's have him give us a ride all around the meadows. You know, if he had a human voice, I would think he was a prince!"

Then the princess, light as a feather, lifted herself up until she was seated on the bull's broad back, her two legs dangling down his left side. As she leaned forward to rest her cheek against his neck, the bull suddenly sprang triumphantly to his feet and with no warning dashed off across the meadow terrace and down the slopes. Europa had hardly time to wave to her friends before she was being carried swiftly across the grass. In vain she tried to turn to call for help. The bull was running too swiftly for her to think of leaping to the ground. When she realized that the beast was heading straight for the seashore, she was certain that she would be drowned in the waves.

But when the bull came to the sea, far from drowning Europa, he glided over the crests of the foamy waves like a swallow. There was really nothing at all to fear. Europa began to like the salt wind on her face and the exhilaration of speed. She saw to her delight that they were no longer unaccompanied. On either side of her, leaping porpoises shot up into the air and dived back under the water only to rise again a few feet farther on. On their backs were the fifty Nereids from the caverns of the sea, riding gaily along beside the princess, only less royally mounted than she. Then as the southern shore of Cyprus flew by on her right side, she saw to her amazement Poseidon himself with his trident, speeding merrily along before them and leading the way across the depths. Europa began to feel that this was as gay as a wedding day, that these were her bridal attendants. She even heard music and turned in delight to see that the Tritons, blowing on their pearly conch shells, had joined her escort.

Her pleasure was not unmixed, however, because she was not sure it was her wedding they were celebrating. Then too, no matter how hard she strained her eyes to look back, she could no longer see either the islands of Tyre or Cyprus or the headlands of Phoenicia. A little pang of homesickness ran through her heart. With her right hand she clung tightly to the polished horn of the golden bull, and with her left held up her robe so that its embroidered hem would not trail in the water. Before them as they almost flew forward, Poseidon was leveling out a broad, smooth path right through the sea.

Then it occurred to Europa that the bull might understand her words. Bending down, she began to talk to him. "Dear bull," she said, "where are you taking me? Who are you, wonderful bull?"

The bull answered her in a man's voice.

"Lovely princess of Tyre," he began, "enchanting maiden, do not be afraid. Take heart and be happy, for misfortune shall never touch the hem of your garment! To your eyes I now appear in the guise of a bull, but soon you shall see me as Zeus, the ruler of the heavens. On earth I shall from this day forth come always before you, my beloved, as Zeus Asterius, an earthly king. As a god I may assume any shape I desire."

Europa's heart filled with happiness at the thought that soon she would see her lover drop the guise of a beast and come before her in the royal robes of kingliness.

With a smile she heard him say, "Look far ahead of you, Europa. What do you see there in the distance?"

"I see a cloud," she answered.

"Look again, Europa. Do you not see an emerald island rising around a lacy ruffle of foam? Those are not clouds you see, but the snow-capped mountains of my beloved Crete, a precious gem in a sapphire sea. For there I was born, hidden by my mother in a cavern deep in the sides of Mount Dicte. Across the steep escarpments of Ida I raced as a boy with the Curetes, warriors of Crete. In my palace at Gortyna shall our marriage be solemnized with all the wreaths and pageants of regal splendor. There shall the highborn maidens lead you, Europa, into my loving arms. Take courage, sweet princess of Asia. This *is* your wedding day. From you shall spring my sons who will rule Crete and the islands of the sea forever afterwards. From you shall rise strong men who will be celebrated in song and story until the end of time."

Phoenix, the king of Tyre, was beside himself with anger when he learned that his lovely daughter had been abducted by the king of Crete. Sternly he commanded her brother Cadmus to set sail at once and never to return to Tyre unless he brought Europa safely home with him. The unfortunate Cadmus, so cruelly exiled from his native land, wandered over the whole world without ever daring to attack the king of Crete. Finally he consulted the oracle at Delphi, who instructed him to found a city, the Boeotian city which he named Thebes. While accomplishing this great project he accidently killed a dragon sacred to Ares while it was guarding a spring on the slopes of Parnassus. This unfortunate deed, even though Cadmus did penance for it to Ares, brought down upon his head the curse of the formidable god of war. The baleful vengeance of Ares pursued him and his children down through the years until they had all killed each other in the generation after the ill-fated Oedipus. The men of the Tyrian nation in truth walked over Greece with accursed feet; but as Zeus had promised her, the fate of Europa was a happy one.

Three sons were born to Europa and Zeus Asterius—Minos, the oldest, who became King Minos I of Crete; Rhadamanthus; and Sarpedon. Europa was eternally honored in Crete because of her beauty and great virtue; and her name, the "Fair One," was given to the women of the west and to their descendants also. Even the lofty plane tree that witnessed her wedding in southern Crete was revered and repaid by the privilege of keeping its leaves throughout the seasons from that day onward. The Hellotia festivals were celebrated in her honor every year throughout the Mediterranean world.

The most famous of all the sons of Europa was Minos. Profiting from the advantageous situation of Crete at a mid-point between Egypt and Greece and also between Phoenicia and Sicily, he made it the junction of the world, through which later travelers from Greece to Asia Minor would pass in the war party of the friend of Crete, Menelaus, as well as where an even more famous one named Paul would stop on his way from Syria to Italy. Its snowy mountains were a welcome landmark to sailors from all ports as they tossed in the heavy seas of the Mediterranean in winter.

Minos made Crete a great commercial center whose hundred cities were known far and wide for their wealth and luxury. The islanders raised wheat and barley, made *retsina* wine from their vineyards, and spun their flax into linen which they learned to dye a bright yellow with saffron as well as brilliant hues of red and blue. Their herds of goats and cattle grew sleek and fat on the summer grasses of the mountain slopes and followed like well-bred animals the calls of their piping herders. In every city were thriving industries, for Cretan artisans exported their goods in all directions. They were skilled cabinetmakers, and wood was plentiful. From the lilies and hyacinths that grew wild in the fields specialists distilled perfumes that sold well in every market. The bronzesmiths of Crete made armor and weapons of excellent design, particularly the handy figure-eight shields that covered a man's whole body. They knew how to cut and polish precious gems, and they made signet rings of gold, little charms of silver designed with the image of Rhea, and bars of copper for their business transactions. In every harbor the shipwrights were busy, for Crete under Minos acquired and maintained the mastery of the seas. The greatest of their ports were royal Knossos in the north and on the southern shore Phaestus, which traded principally with Egypt.

Minos attained his celebrated renown, however, for the system of laws he bestowed on his people. These ordinances were later adopted by the Greeks, according to Plato who greatly admired them. They were so logical and so equitable, in fact, that Plato doubted whether an ordinary mortal could have written them unassisted. Popular opinion explained this by remembering that the king really received them all written out in Minoan script on a tablet which his father Zeus revealed to him in the depths of that Dictean cave where he was born. It was common knowledge that every ninth year King Minos was obliged to retire to the slopes of Mount Dicte where, entering the cave, he sacrificed to Rhea and Zeus, communed with them, and at the end of the ceremonies received a renewal of his mandate of royalty valid for nine more years. After each private discussion with Zeus he inserted new amendments into his legal system.

Although the people of Crete were great builders and their king was immensely wealthy, their cities, unlike most of the others in the ancient world, were completely unfortified. Unlike the Tyrians, who had to live within an *enceinte* of massive black walls that compressed their streets and houses into an island area of less than three square miles, Knossos and Phaestus expanded and built new palaces without fear of enemies, for they controlled the seas. In time they piped water from mountain springs right into the coastal cities through a complicated system of conduits lined with cement. The drainage troughs of Knossos and the sewage systems were unknown in any other area of the world until the time of the Romans. Roads made of stone blocks with shoulders of packed stones and pebbles permitted them to race around from city to city in their chariots.

Fashion and dress were very important in Crete, so much so that they have often been called the Parisians of antiquity. The people were not tall, but they were lithe and athletic. The men wore high linen puttees coming almost up to the knees, and a specially draped short garment or kilt. They wore their hair in long ringlets with a twisted knot at the crown of the head. The ladies of Crete were resplendent in wide ruffled skirts, dainty aprons, bolero jackets, high-heeled shoes, wasp waists, puff sleeves, and naked breasts (in honor of Rhea, the Mother Goddess). They too wore their hair in flowing ringlets. Both men and women had pinched waistlines that emphasized the hips and torso. The men wore wide belts to cinch their waists even more, so that in silhouette they closely resembled the figure-eight shield, one of their prehistoric cult symbols. Bracelets and rings were elaborate and ornate, and often decorated with a fleur-de-lis or a Greek cross.

The black pottery of Crete was one of its principal items of export. Besides pictures of the Mother Goddess, or of religious ceremonies, the artisans used many decorative motifs of the sea. Among lotus and ivy tendrils, they were expert at drawing marine creatures from life, orange coral, the murex from which they extracted the crimson dye, the octopus, and the chambered nautilus, among others. In their palace frescoes they skillfully drew dolphins and olive trees, birds, crocuses, and over and over again the lovely butterflies of the island and their chrysalises— such obvious symbols of death and regeneration. Even the divine Pharaohs of Egypt ordered vases and amphorae from Crete, such fragile objects when compared to the massive pyramids they were building as their tombs.

King Minos devised for his people a prudent and rigorous educational system. The young men were divided into troops led by the father of that young man who was the natural leader and instigator of the group. Every day their parent-leader took them on long marches and exercised them at arms, particularly in the use of the bow and arrow. Since Crete was so hilly, the men preferred light armor and depended in battle upon swiftness of foot and muscular agility. From time to time mock battles between the various youth troops were staged in which heavy blows with iron weapons were borne and inflicted. The disobedient were severely punished while the outstanding athletes were rewarded with extra portions of food and a higher percentage of wine in their drinking water at table. Meals were taken at public tables, by groups. The boys were trained from childhood to notice neither cold nor heat, to endure pain without speaking, to run long miles over mountainous country, to stand behind their fathers' chairs until invited to join any discussion, and to consider arms the most cherished of all gifts or rewards. They marched with rhythmic steps, interspersed with unison leaps and beatings on their shields, and sang shrill, military songs to the tunes of lyres and pipes.

The main task of Minos was to establish Crete as the uncontested naval power of the time. In this way his thalassocracy could protect the unfortified cities that extended around the island, all within short distances from the sea. He proceeded to rid the sea of pirates, to subjugate those neighboring lands that were to become his markets for manufactured goods, and to exact a high tribute from them in return for his naval protection. According to plan he conquered the Cyclades and then the southern shore of Greece, forcing the people of Attica to pay him what Plato called a "cruel tribute."

The rewards of this king after death were even greater than the triumphs of his reign and the fame of his celebrated laws. Both he and his solemn brother Rhadamanthus were appointed by the gods to rule over the dead. Upon the stern, impartial seats of justice they presided as supreme arbiters over the past lives of those who stood trial before them. There was no appeal. The wicked were consigned to black Tartarus, to which certain rivers on the surface of the earth so suddenly and so mysteriously descended. The condemned had first to pass through a grove of quaking aspens and dark cypresses down to the gates of the Underworld which were guarded by Cerberus, a huge hound with fifty heads and a bay like the clanging of bronze. Although Cerberus allowed the guilty to enter the portals of hell, he refused their subsequent exit. Then the dead had to be rowed across the black waters of the Acheron by Charon, the ugly old ferryman. The Underworld was nine times encircled by the ink-black waters of the River Styx. If Charon were not paid for their passage, the dead were condemned to wander eternally along the black shores of the rivers. Knowing this, the Greeks always put a coin in the mouth of their dead.

If, on the other hand, the verdict of the great judges Minos and Rhadamanthus was "Innocent," what a marvelous new life was available to the shades who had left the world behind them! Then they were assured an eternity of dreamless bliss, far to the west in the splendid Isles of the Blessed, the perfumed Elysian Fields of enchantment. In this paradise there was no old age, no hot summers, no snowy winters, no withering, and never any decay. There, crowned with the sweetest flowers of meadow and wood, they reclined in luxury under eternally cloudless skies. Soft winds wafted to them the treble songs of birds. Fresh fruits grew just overhead for their delight. There friends and lovers were eternally young, eternally reunited, eternally at peace. On all sides stretched the silver summer sea that languidly lapped the shores of their Atlantis.

KING MINOS II

During the thousand or so years that Minoan Crete maintained its supremacy over the Mediterranean Sea there were many kings named Minos, the most heroic of whom is the one referred to as Minos II. During his reign the palace of this king at Knossos was the object of admiration and wonder throughout the world, so much so that its memory was preserved in the words of the poets. This palace, with its maze of passages, was built for Minos by a noble Athenian architect named Daedalus.

It was quite by a strange twist of fortune that Daedalus happened to be in Crete in the first place. This famous craftsman, mechanical engineer, and sculptor had the sort of past he preferred not to have his acquaintances mention. Of course, it is very hard to conceal one's crimes when one is so skillful as to have become famous. However great an architect he was, this Daedalus apparently was only happy when he received high praise, and he had also so doubtful an opinion of his ability and talent that he could not endure competition. Inevitably this strange, brooding nature of his led him into the crime that caused his resultant exile from Athenian territory into Crete, where he had to rely on the protection of Minos.

The old scandal about Daedalus says that one day back home in Athens his sister had brought him a pupil, her twelve-year-old son named Perdix, or Talos. Daedalus proceeded to train him as his apprentice and to let the youngster accompany him wherever he went. Daedalus did not like the boy, and as he grew to know him better, this dislike turned to hatred. Perdix was too precocious. While Daedalus was loftily just beginning to demonstrate a problem, Perdix was already waving his hand in eagerness. What was worse, Perdix usually knew the correct solution. One day while he was walking on the beach with his uncle, the boy stooped over and picked up the white skeleton of a fish. Curiously he turned it over and over in his hands. As soon as they were back in the workshop, Perdix set about copying the backbone of the fish in iron. He had invented the saw. In silence Daedalus brooded, thinking how soon he would be supplanted by such a nephew. Perdix then had the misfortune to invent a pair of compasses.

Almost beside himself with jealous rage, Daedalus profited by the next opportunity that presented itself. One day he pushed Perdix off a tower. For this reason, the murder of a boy related to him by blood, Daedalus had to leave his native land. The goddess of architects, the wise Athena, catching young Perdix in his headlong fall from the tower, transformed him into a partridge. As he walked through the groves of Ida, how often Daedalus must have started at the sudden flushing of a partridge almost under his feet. He must often have watched its whirring flight with the bitter taste of envy still on his tongue.

Despite constant homesickness Daedalus was fairly happy in Knossos because he was busy. King Minos had grandiose ideas, and even more, he was wealthy enough to put them into execution. This Minos was a headstrong, persistent man; and Daedalus came to know better than to thwart his will. Like everyone else around the palace, he heard most of the good stories about his patron. One in particular made the architect rather pity the king's wife, Pasiphaë, the All-Shining.

It seems that once while on a hunting trip Minos had glimpsed the chaste Britomartis running through the forests. Now this maiden was especially sacred to Artemis, herself also a virgin huntress. Even though Minos knew all this, he still thought he could catch the maiden and take her virginity. He continued to steal through the woods in her pursuit, and once he even crept close enough to surprise her. To her horror he declared his intentions, extolling the pleasures of love and accusing her of being the authoress of his sufferings. Britomartis refused him. Then the ardent Minos tried to seize her in his arms, but she managed to slip through his eager fingers. Not the least bit disturbed by her refusal, Minos thought he could in time wear down her resistance. Night and day he continued to pursue her until the poor maiden could hardly find an hour's resting place. Minos stalked her like a deer for nine long months. Finally Britomartis grew frantic. She saw that he was driving her into a corner of the island, and out on a rocky promontory. As she stood panting and trembling on the very brink of the cliff with the sea beating on the base far below her, she saw Minos confidently approaching, the wild smile of victory on his handsome face and his arms outstretched to clasp her. With a long scream the maiden turned and leaped to her death in the sea. Peering over the edge of the promontory, Minos could see her broken body floating in the nets of the fishermen. In honor of her virginity, Artemis herself made the maiden a star in the sky.

This was the Minos upon whom Daedalus depended. The king wished him to remodel the palace and to construct a row of eighteen parallel rooms or magazines in which he could store his wealth. Then he wanted also a stepped theater built in rectangular shape on the northwest corner of the palace. Thousands of blocks of shining white gypsum were cut and polished in preparation, and huge wooden pillars were prepared for a hall of colonnades. In the meantime workmen were digging sewers, laying pipes and drains for sacrificial basins under the altars. Artists from all over Crete were submitting their sketches to Daedalus, for the rooms would be gay with red and blue frescoes. Great care was taken with the throne room for the king. When completed, the palace would occupy a square of more than 150 meters on each side. The most magnificent hall after the central court, which was well over 50 meters long, was to be that of the sacred labrys, or double-edged ax dear to Zeus. News of this hall, or Labyrinth, soon spread to Egypt, where the Pharaoh himself was so interested that he ordered a similar structure to be built. His edifice was called Labyrinth also, but it was a temple. The Egyptians built permanently only for the dead.

Minos on the contrary built for the living. The grandeur and intricacy of his palace are hard to imagine. Try to picture twelve massive courtyards erected parallel to each other. Six of them faced north and the other six south. All together there were three thousand five hundred separate chambers, each leading into the other through colonnaded halls carved with colorful designs and brilliant with frescoes. The roofs and wall which surrounded the whole structure were of gleaming white stone. In this maze of corridors one was soon lost, passing from one room into an arcade, then into a courtyard, and through a forest of pillars into another almost identical room. Minos had several grand staircases leading into lofty halls and courts from story to story up to the flat roofs. The queen and her children each had separate suites provided with windows overlooking the sea to the north. Even the inner rooms on the ground floor were lighted by wells that plunged several floors toward steps that led down many flights to the secret altars of the gods. Down deep in these hollow vaults the sacred bull of Crete, he who in the past centuries had kidnaped the fair Europa and founded the house of Crete, could sometimes be heard to bellow. The earth trembled at that holy roar. Even King Minos, the high priest, would grow yellow with fear and prepare to sacrifice to Zeus deep in the caverns of Mount Dicte.

One morning after a sleepless night full of the subterranean rumblings of the huge bull, who seemed to bear the gigantic, labyrinthine palace on his back, King Minos prepared a sacrifice to Poseidon. In his anxiety he began to boast, "Send me a bull, great god of the sea. It is I, Minos, who request it. I am Minos, the great son of our father Zeus. My voice can command vast fleets to walk like centipedes over the Great Green Sea, swifter than the flight of gulls. I am the master of this kingdom. I can request any gift from the gods, anything that I like. Send me a bull, Poseidon, a monstrous bull from the sea. Here on your altar will I pour forth his blood, and the earth will be calmed."

No sooner had Minos finished his prayer, even while the clouds of blue incense still curled up from the altar before him, than he heard roaring and the pounding of hoofs. His rash prayer had been answered, for there stood a bull such as mortal eyes had never seen before. It was white and magnificent, with polished horns like the new moon, around which curled shiny locks of satin hair. With nervous, impatient hoofs it pawed the earth and snorted. Minos had no desire to cut its sleek throat and offer its blood to Poseidon. What a waste that would be! An ordinary bull would do well enough for the sacrifice, and anyway the rumblings in the earth had long since ceased. Pleased with his decision, Minos ordered the splendid animal to be put in a chamber deep under the palace until it was festival time and the baiting games could begin. What sport this creature would make.

In this way Minos made the error which was to cause Crete such long and terrible sorrow. Poseidon was not deceived. He had sent the bull to Minos for sacrifice, not for sport. The wrath of the sea god was terrible to behold. Instead of going quietly with his captors, the huge bull seemed suddenly to go mad. Snorting and blowing foam from his nostrils, he burst loose from his captors and galloped furiously down the corridor, goring those servants who tried to slip a rope over his horns and around his legs. Screaming, the palace women rushed for shelter from the raging animal. The bull dashed wildly for the grand staircase just as Queen Pasiphaë, who had been alarmed by the shouts, started to descend the stairs.

This was Pasiphaë, mother of the three children of Minos, the lovely sister of Circe, another enchantress. She stood right in the path of the bull, and nobody was near enough to save her. Her ruffled skirt blew in the breezes and her naked white bosom rose and fell quickly in amazement under its diaphanous gauze scarf. Minos and the courtiers awaited the terrible moment, but the anger of Poseidon was more cunning yet than Minos had imagined. Instead of lifting Pasiphaë on his horns and tossing her lovely body in the air, the bull knelt at her feet.

In an impulse of love and tenderness Pasiphaë enfolded his neck in her arms. Strolling thus enlaced, and guided by the crafty Daedalus, they passed out of view of the astonished onlookers. The story told by Daedalus spread like wildfire through the palace and out into the town.

"The Queen is enamored of a bull!" From time to time in the weeks that followed, herders claimed to have glimpsed the lovers wandering lost in each other far on the slopes of upland pastures.

As if this was not enough, the bull would leave Pasiphaë at night and, blowing fire from his nostrils, lunge wildly through the village, killing the inhabitants and trampling their gardens and cottages. The terror caused by his sudden appearances was so great that people no longer dared sleep. In the palace Minos sat humiliated, listening to his younger daughters crying for their mother. His son Androgeus, who had been reared among the Curetes and who was already a champion athlete, begged to pursue the bull and rid the island of his havoc. Minos dared not allow his son to attempt such a feat. Finally he sent for Heracles, who happened at that time to be in Crete, begging him to include this great service among his twelve labors. The battle that the peerless hero fought with the bull took its place among the annals of the great bouts of the world. In the end Heracles mastered the wild creature and carried him by the sheer strength of his arms all the way across the sea to Greece. Then, with the anger of Poseidon appeased, the pregnant Pasiphaë returned to the palace, where she gave birth to the Minotaur, a creature with the body of a man and the huge horned head of a bull.

Daedalus, steadfast in his admiration of Pasiphaë, was ordered to construct a special room deep in the lowest story of the palace. There the vicious Minotaur was kept, in a place so difficult to find that only its builder and Minos himself had access to it.

Little by little life in Crete returned to normal. The prince, Androgeus, who had not been permitted to pit his strength against the ravaging bull, dreamed of going to Athens. He wanted above all to make a name for himself in some distant land where his father's power would not overshadow him. He was bored with palace life and the chatter of his two young sisters. One summer he finally persuaded his father to let him travel to Athens for the annual festival of Athena, the Panathenaea, at which the greatest athletes competed. There were competitions in discus throwing, track events, jumping, and wrestling. Androgeus had been in training for many years and he looked forward to the opportunity of showing the Greeks how adept he was.

Minos bent every effort to give his son a royal retinue for the trip. Dressed in his finest regalia and accompanied by his friends and trainers, Androgeus departed in the palace yacht. All of Crete awaited in a state of high suspense the outcome of the games. The news brought back to Minos daily was very pleasing. Like any father he was delighted to learn that Androgeus had captivated the Athenian court by the elegance and refinement of his manners. They heard too how Androgeus had made friends with the nephews of King Aegeus of Athens.

Androgeus won first prize in every one of the athletic events. This was the report he sent back to Crete, and his father was overjoyed. Minos had not realized the physical prowess of his son, overwhelming in comparison with the greatest athletes of Greece. The labyrinthine palace at Knossos was hardly large enough to contain King Minos. Proudly he strutted from court to court, followed by the messengers from Athens. Minos wanted to hear their accounts over and over again. It was the proudest day of his life.

The next arrival from Greece brought Minos the news of his son's death. The king could hardly believe his ears. Sitting down heavily on the nearest bench, he asked the messenger to read the letter to him again.

"To King Minos of Crete from Aegeus. Given by my hand in the city of Athens. We regret to inform you of the tragic death of your son Androgeus. The young prince had charmed us all by his regal bearing and skill in our games, where we awarded him the highest honors. . . . He had left Athens to journey to Thebes in the company of our nephews. Having arrived a little distance, as far as the town of Oenoë, he was set upon by the Bull of Marathon, a huge beast that is still ravaging our outlying districts. We regret that we cannot therefore send you his body . . . receive our expressions of grief . . . tragic end . . . such a regal prince. . . . Aegeus of Athens."

For hours Minos sat alone in his throne room, staring vacantly at the figure-eight shields depicted in fresco on the opposite wall. None of his courtiers dared approach him. High in her penthouse apartment Pasiphaë wept, surrounded by her ladies. Women sobbed in the streets where the Curetes met in silent groups with clenched fists and bitter faces. No one believed the story of any Marathonian Bull. People in Crete remembered how fearful Aegeus had always been of his nephews, how much he had resented their nearness to the throne. Observers from Crete had noted how grudgingly the Athenian king had awarded the prizes, and how closely his uneasy eyes had followed Androgeus and measured his popularity with the masses. What would Minos do, now that he had lost his son and heir? All activity came to a standstill. In quiet lines the sailors waited along the wharves where the great ships of Crete rode at anchor. Even the children stopped their play and listened anxiously, quiet and reflective. The hours dragged by in an ominous silence while above the shores of Greece the monstrous black clouds of a father's just vengeance gathered.

Suddenly the people heard the death bellow of a great bull and saw a thin wisp of incense rising in the clear air above the palace. The high-priest king was sacrificing. Awed and frightened, they awaited the appearance of their king in his altar robes. When Minos walked stiff-lipped from the palace, his face stern and white, the people of Crete knew how truly great he was. Without wasting a word or a gesture, Minos ordered that the great ships of Crete be provisioned for an immediate departure. "I shall leave tonight," he commanded. "Let everything be made ready in the fleet. We will show King Aegeus what happens to murderers. We will show Aegeus what the wrath of a father can do to Athens."

At port after port the war fleet of Minos called. Through the islands of the Cyclades and into the Aegean he swept majestically, acquainting every land of the loss of his son. Although the kingdoms he visited wished him well, not all of them dared to furnish warriors for him. One afternoon Minos arrived at the island of Aegina in the Saronic Gulf. A crowd of people rushed down to the harbor at the sight of the large fleet, all eager to learn the reason for its coming, all anxious to see the face of such a famous king. Minos was courteously greeted by the sons of King Aeacus, and finally the aged king himself tottered down to the pier.

"Tell us the reason for this visit, for this great honor," said Aeacus.

Sadly Minos answered, "I have come like any father in his grief. The sheeted shade of my son Androgeus, so cruelly murdered by the Athenian king, whose name I cannot mention—for even so much do I loathe him—cries for vengeance. Will you assist me?"

King Aeacus, shaking his head, answered Minos, "You must ask this of me in vain. My city cannot grant you this request. We have a very strong alliance with the Greeks. Nonaggression is the very core of our agreement."

Minos left the island of Aegina murmuring to himself under his breath. "This pact you have made with Athens will cost you more than

you think, O Aeacus!" No sooner had he put to sea than an Athenian envoy, bearing in his hand the olive branch of friendship, put in to Aegina. There he hastened to give his right hand to the aged king and to his sons, who promised their support to Athens in the forthcoming war. Although Minos knew full well how some of the islands were leaguing with Athens against him, whose family had so many centuries ruled supreme on the sea, he preferred not to dissipate the main thrust of his attack upon such petty powers. Content to measure ahead of time the girth of his enemies, Minos headed straight for Greece, where he began by destroying the coastal cities, one at a time. Minos was not in a hurry.

Then he laid siege to the large city of Megara. The walls of this stronghold were of a very special nature. The god Hermes had aided in their construction. While they were being built, he had laid his lyre upon the stones so that ever afterward they emitted a musical sound when struck. The ruler of this place was an old man named Nisus. Growing from the crown of his head was a long purple lock, which showed plainly among his white hairs. This lock ensured the safety of the city, as everyone knew perfectly well. The inhabitants therefore felt quite secure even before the imposing forces of the vengeful king of Crete. The siege had lasted for several weeks already, and the new moon was rising without any decisive engagement. Every day the attackers advanced up to the walls, where they were met by an equal force. Victory herself seemed undecided. Life inside the fortress went on very much the same.

One person among all the people of Megara was particularly interested in the outcome of the struggle. This person was Scylla, the young daughter of King Nisus. Every afternoon she would walk in the sunshine around the walls and play little tunes by throwing pebbles against their stones, just to hear the golden notes of the god's lyre. Then she would lean over the walls and watch the daily battle. Like a good audience, since after all it was not her personal war, this young lady soon came to know the participants each by name. "Who is that warrior, the one on the black horse?" she would ask some passing soldier.

"Oh, that's so-and-so, the Curetes officer from Cydon," he would answer the princess.

"Who's that wearing the red crest on his helmet, the one who looks so fierce?"

"Those are the arms of Phaestus, the great port of southern Crete," an archer would inform her.

With ooh's and ah's Princess Scylla watched the clashing encounters. During the thick of the battle, when the horses reared and snorted and some warrior dealt a brain-splitting blow, she would applaud him and jump up and down in excitement. Readily she changed sides and cheered for whoever was winning that particular engagement. She had never enjoyed herself so much. In vain her attendants prayed her to return to her spinning. In vain they reminded her of the trousseau she was supposed to be embroidering. Scylla shrugged them away impatiently and rushed away to hang over the ramparts, afraid of missing some deed of heroism.

It was not difficult to find King Minos, even among the brilliant heroes of Crete. He alone rode a pure white horse, a magnificent stallion with a high curved neck and nervous, prancing legs. He alone wore under his armor a flowing gown of royal purple, the hem and sleeves encrusted with golden threads. He alone wore a helmet of pure gold surmounted with streaming feathers. Rising high in his stirrups, he would draw back his right arm and hurl a slender javelin straight into the breast of a Grecian warrior. With his left hand he would curb the reins tightly enough to bend the proud neck of the stallion. When he took bow and arrow in hand and, pulling the bowstring firmly back to his cheek, let fly the stinging arrow, Scylla would gasp with pleasure and swear he was the perfect image of Hermes. In Scylla's opinion Minos did everything perfectly. If he appeared one day with a golden shield embossed and freshly polished, she would say, "Oh, what a perfect contrast it makes with his helmet." If he galloped to one flank to re-form his battle line, she would shout, "Exactly right, O King. Your line was wavering there. I could see it all from here." Day in and day out, Scylla studied Minos' lineaments and every gesture.

One afternoon when in the heat of battle the king of Crete had pressed the Greeks hard up against their walls and forced King Nisus to re-enter the city, Minos stopped his war horse just under the spot where Scylla was leaning. Breathless and hot, he lifted his heavy helmet from his head to let the cool wind blow on his hair and cheeks. Bending far over the wall, Scylla was able to see his naked face for the first time. "Oh, you are beautiful, Minos of Crete. You are beautiful!" the princess kept whispering to herself. "Oh, you are beautiful. I love you. I love you, King Minos of Crete." Lying flat on the warm wall, her face against the stones, Scylla gazed at him enraptured.

"I wish I were an arrow in the quiver that lies by his hip," she said to herself that night after she was in bed. "How beautiful he is pressing the white horse with his knees! I wish I were the reins of his horse that he encloses in his hand!" Tossing in her soft bed, she indulged in all kinds of fantastic dreams. Perhaps she could throw herself from the tower beside the gate just as he galloped under it. She could see her frail body landing across his saddle. Yes, that was it. He would enfold her in his strong arms and carry her far away over the sea to Crete. If only he would look up and see her! Then he would surely take the city in the storm of his desire and claim her as the spoils of conquest. Maybe he would like it better if she just walked bravely through the gates, her thin dress blowing against her, unmindful of the crashing armor or the hoofs of the rearing horses, straight up to him who was mighty in battle.

Then he would be forced to look at her. He would say, "Oh, my beloved. I have waited for you all my life." At this point Scylla would bury her face in her pillow.

Sometimes in more lucid, daylight moments it would occur to her to wonder what sort of welcome Pasiphaë would make to Minos as he staggered over the threshold carrying a new young wife in his arms. Scylla never particularly cared to dwell on the details. Everyone knew how Pasiphaë had disgraced herself with that Grecian captain named Taurus. Of course, some people were charitable enough to have given the queen the benefit of the doubt. They said—but obviously it was only the gossip of Daedalus—that Pasiphaë had got herself involved with a real bull, and not just a Greek named "Bull." Anyway, she was really a harlot, and Scylla was sure Minos would know how to dispose of her once and for all! Then too it seemed to Scylla that she had heard somewhere that Minos had two daughters, one of them quite a big girl by now. Some gossip had even reported that the older one was quite a beauty, giving promise of a stunning loveliness like that of Aphrodite. Her name began with *A* too—Ariadne, or something like that. Anxiously Scylla rushed to the mirror to see if she was beautiful. Well, she wasn't really homely. Anyway, Minos would be sure to become infatuated, and that was all that mattered.

The next morning, as Scylla looked longingly out toward the white tents of the Cretan king, she said to herself, "I don't know whether to be happy or sad because of this war. Without the war I should never have seen the hero. No wonder Zeus Asterius carried away Europa, if her children's children were to be as beautiful as this! I am sure Minos will win the war. Great as our warriors are, they cannot compare with him. Now since he is going to win anyway, why should not my love throw open our city gate to him? If I did that, I would be worthy of a hero. If I am going to do it though, I should rather do it sooner than later. What if I hesitated and some young fool shot his lance at Minos? What if he were wounded?" This was a thought Scylla could not bear. Between her and Minos stood only Scylla's father and the precious lock of purple that grew on his head.

As soon as it grew dark, she tiptoed up the winding stairs to her father's chamber and listened at the door. All was still inside. Silently she crept into the room and up to the bed where King Nisus lay sleeping. As quietly as possible she cut the purple lock from his head and stole down the stairs, holding thus the key to the main gate in her hand. On either side of her the sentries lay sleeping. Scylla unlocked the portals and ran unchallenged toward the lofty white tent where Minos was sitting alone.

Panting and disheveled, she finally stood before him, so overcome with emotion she could hardly speak. Before the king could question her, she managed to blurt out, "King Minos, I am Scylla!"

With raised eyebrows the king of Crete looked at her without speaking. "I have unlocked the gates of the city for you, Minos. While my father slept, I stole the key. Here it is. The city is yours. I am not bringing you only a lock of hair but the very life of King Nisus, my father." With a toss of her hand Scylla threw the purple lock across his knees.

60

To her surprise Minos rose, his eyes blazing. He brushed the lock away from him as if it had been a loathsome scorpion.

Scylla continued breathlessly, "I ask for no reward, King Minos. I did it all for love. I only ask you to take me back to Crete as your royal bride."

Minos towered fiercely above her. "To Crete?" he gasped. "I take you to Crete?" With peremptory gestures he waved Scylla out of the tent, where two officers had leaped to attention: "You are the disgrace of the century! You are a monster! What kind of girl betrays her father and her city?" By this time Minos was roaring. "What makes you think I need a woman to fight my wars? May you be swept from the earth! You have betrayed your native land forever. May you be driven from the lands and the seas! There is no room on the face of the earth for traitors. Their punishment is death!"

The following morning Minos entered the fallen city of Megara where he imposed just laws in accordance with his family tradition and where he accepted tribute. Then he ordered his men to return to their ships, to weigh the anchors, and to break out the oars. Within a few hours the main force of the Cretans was beating eastward down the coast toward Athens.

Scylla stood long on the shores of Megara watching the Cretan fleet disappear and screaming in terror after them, "What shall I do? Where shall I go? Why do you leave me thus? I cannot return to my father, for I have betrayed him. I cannot go back to the city, for the people will kill me. I closed the gates of the world behind me so that Crete alone might be my home.

"Europa was not your ancestor, Minos! Do you hear me? Your mother was a Caucasian tigress. The story of your birth is false! And so is the tale of Pasiphaë. It is all illusion and dream. Pasiphaë was not bewitched. She preferred a bull to you, Minos!" In despair Scylla leaped into the sea; but as she fell, she was transformed into a sea bird. Since Minos had forbidden her both the land and the sea, she was forever afterward condemned to glide without respite down the draughty winds.

Minos and his fleet arrived safely the same day and laid siege to the city of Athens. Here Minos distinguished himself again for great battles and single combats. While his army sat around the city, well supplied with food from Crete, Athens was ravaged by plague and famine.

At first the city was covered with a heavy darkness. Then within a few days all the animals within its walls—sheep and cattle, dogs and fowl—died from a sudden distemper. Even while their carcasses rotted in the streets and mangers, the citizens were attacked. The first symptom was a burning in the bowels and a difficulty in breathing. The fire was already within them also. Then their tongues grew red and swollen, and their mouths gaped open. The diseased no longer could endure coverings on their beds, but tried to cool themselves by lying on the stones of the roadways. Even the walls and stones grew hot from their fever. The physicians, learned as they were, had no cure for this malady.

Abandoning all hopes therefore of cure, the ill lay as close as possible to the fountains, where they died, sometimes with their corpses rotting in the water itself. People ran wildly from their homes, not knowing the source of their sickness. They died suddenly just as they were about to take the next step, falling on the earth like rotten apples from a moldy tree, or like acorns that the rough winds of autumn scatter and roll over the leaves.

In vain the priests sacrificed to the gods while there was one of them left living or a healthy animal whose blood could be offered in propitiation. Then the elders of the city obtained permission from King Minos to go to the oracle at Delphi. When the Pythoness heard their terrible story, she advised them to submit to the Cretans. She reminded them of the death of Androgeus, of the divine parentage of Minos, and of his heroism. Upon their return they dispatched ambassadors to the Cretan king, begging him for honorable terms of peace.

Minos granted their request, but reminding them of his just and bitter grievance against their King Aegeus, he stipulated that beginning that very year, and every ninth year thereafter, there should be sent to Crete seven youths and seven maidens from among the most comely in the city to compete at the funeral games of Androgeus.

THESEUS AND THE MINOTAUR

King Aegeus of Attica lived on after the conquest by Crete, tormented and bewitched by his hideous wife, the witch Medea whom Jason had abandoned after his quest of the Golden Fleece. Medea had been born on the shores of the Black Sea, a hateful land renowned for its magic. Eighteen years before, Aegeus had loved a gentle maiden named Aethra, whom he had left pregnant in the island of Troezen. Unknown to Aegeus a fine boy had been born to Aethra. His name was Theseus, and he was destined to become one of the most beloved heroes of Greece.

Every year from the age of fifteen Theseus, educated in the tales of his cousin Heracles, had accompanied his mother to the temple of Poseidon. As directed by her he had fought his way through the thickets outside the temple wall and had tried to lift a huge rock that lay half buried at the roots of a plane tree. By the time that he was eighteen he had managed to perform this great feat of strength, which no man before him had been able to do. Under the stone he had found the strong sword of bronze and the pair of golden sandals Aegeus had left there. Knowing Theseus was beloved of the gods who had sent him his superhuman strength, Aethra then told him that he was the son of Aegeus.

Theseus set out for Attica, that fair sunny land that faced south, a land of honey and the olive, with sweet plains and meadows and silver-headed mountains all engirdled by the blue Aegean Sea. It lay across the straits from his birthplace, behind the blue shores of Aegina. "What would you do, my Theseus, if you were lord of such a land?" his mother asked him sadly, for she knew she would soon lose her son.

"I should become the shepherd over my flocks," the youth answered, smiling. "I would rid the land of monsters and rule it so well that all my people would mourn my passing."

"Go then to your father," bade Aethra. "You will find him in Athens on the hill of Athena. Give him the sword, and he will welcome you."

The young Theseus set out on foot for his father's palace, taking the long route by the isthmus. In his heart he hoped to do great deeds along the way so that King Aegeus would be proud of him. First he walked into the monstrous spider web of the wicked Periphates, and slew him. Next he encountered Sinis, the robber who waylaid travelers and, tying their bodies to two pine trees, let them rebound and tear the poor victims apart. Him also Theseus slew with his bronze club, at the narrowest part of the isthmus. After this he walked forward to the shores of the Saronic Gulf, where lay the great city of Megara. There he encountered Sciron, who barred the path and forced his prisoners to wash his feet. Theseus killed this giant by kicking him over the cliffs into the sea, where even the carrion-feeding tortoises would not touch his stinking flesh.

After the adventure stories of Theseus and his prowess began to spread through the land, warriors, in imitation of him, cut their hair short so their enemies could not grasp them by it. Theseus continued his long journey, keeping the sea and the strait of Salamis on his right. In the land of Eleusis he met King Cercyon, whose palace court was full of the bones of the men he had killed. Strewing fresh sand on the earth, Cercyon wrestled with Theseus until the stars came out in the heavens. Finally Theseus grasped him by the waist and one wrist and heaved him over his shoulder to the ground. Cercyon died instantly, and Theseus accepted to rule the land. For this feat Theseus purged himself, for he had unwittingly vanquished a member of his own royal family.

As he passed the white peaks of Parnes, Theseus met a pleasant man named Procrustes, who invited him home to dinner. When the hero learned that his sweet-spoken host lured travelers to his palace on the pretense of hospitality only to torture them, Theseus slew him also. Procrustes for years had been trying to fit his guests into a bed. When they were too long for it, he cut off their limbs. When they were too short, as maidens often were, he stretched them until they died. Theseus divided all the wealth of this tyrant among the poor shepherds of the mountain and then started off again on his journey.

In the early morning he swung along happily down through the mist of the slopes of Parnes where the oak trees dripped on his head. Underfoot, pink arbutus bloomed in patches of snow, and the air was perfumed with laurel and wild thyme. As he passed through the valleys of Attica, people greeted him warmly, for they knew a god was in him. Finally he saw in reverence the plain of Athens and in the distance the holy hill where Athena dwelled. Breathing prayers, he climbed the sacred stairs of the Acropolis and arrived at the palace of Aegeus. He wondered how his father was, when the land was so ravaged with robbers and giants.

The palace was in a state of confusion. Drunken courtiers lolled at the tables. Sternly Theseus sent a message to the king, who was sitting in his chamber watching the evil eye and murderous hand of Medea. As soon as Aegeus saw the fair hair and stately bearing of Theseus, he loved him at once. Bidding him welcome, they all sat down to dinner— all except Medea, who retired to her chambers. She knew, although Aegeus did not, who the young stranger was. Dressing herself in royal robes and wearing her jewels, Medea prepared a deadly poison mixed in wine. Then, returning to the dining hall, she offered the wine to Theseus.

"Greetings, hero," she said, advancing toward him in all her midnight splendor. "Drink from this golden cup, and you will taste the heady wine of the East."

Theseus looked at her raven hair and especially at her black eyes, which were as dry as the eyes of a serpent. "Do you drink first, Medea," he answered. "Drink or die, Medea," he threatened, lifting his bronze war club.

With a scream of anger Medea dashed the golden goblet to the floor. Wherever the red liquid flowed over the marble, it steamed and bubbled. In the silence that followed, the courtiers heard Medea escaping in her dragon chariot that left a trail of flame in the sky. Thus Medea, who had at an earlier time betrayed her father, burned alive Princess Creüsa of Corinth, and killed her own little children, fled furiously across the eastern sky. Far beyond the two rivers of the land that had once been Sumer she founded a country of Asia, Media. Through the descendants of this land she would one day seek her revenge against Greece.

Then Theseus showed his father the bronze sword and golden sandals he had unearthed from under the stone. Smiling and weeping, Aegeus embraced his son who had already rid the land of such evil. "This is my son, Theseus, a better man than ever his father was!" he used to say. Relieved in his old age of the heavy responsibility of the throne, Aegeus recounted his troubles to Theseus. He told him of the long siege of Athens and how King Minos had accused him of the murder of Androgeus.

"Who is this King Minos?" cried Theseus. "Let me behold the man who calls my father a liar!" All winter the young hero toiled to put the land in order. First he killed the plotting, drunken courtiers. Next he sought and overcame the Marathonian Bull. When spring came, he noticed how everyone seemed downcast. Although he asked the reason for their sorrow, no person would tell him. To his persistent questions, Aegeus would only reply, "It is hard enough to face sorrow when it comes. Let us not discuss it now."

Later that spring there arrived from King Minos of Crete a splendid herald. In the market place he called, "Hear ye, citizens! Nine years have elapsed. Have you prepared your tribute for His Majesty of Crete, ruler of the Great Green Sea?"

"What is this dog that dares ask tribute of Attica?" cried Theseus, advancing boldly to the ambassador.

When the herald explained, Theseus listened aghast, for he had not heard of the tribute. In consternation he begged his father to deny the slanderous story of his murder of Androgeus.

Aegeus, turning sadly away, would only reply, "An oath is sacred. The tribute must be sent."

On every hand the people of Athens wept bitterly. They knew the seven youths and maidens would never be heard of again. In horror they pictured what Minos must have made them do. He must have fed them alive to the Minotaur! In their fear and sorrow they had for the moment forgotten Theseus, he who was born to royalty. Before King

Aegeus even realized what his son intended, Theseus stepped before the citizens. "Cast lots for the thirteen, if that is your custom. I myself will make the fourteenth!"

At his words King Aegeus groaned in horror. Theseus continued while all the people remained breathless at his courage. "Blood will be answered with blood, fire with fire, and sword with sword. King Minos himself will be broken and the Minotaur also. I swear it. His power began to wane the day that I was born! I, Theseus, have spoken!"

Aegeus opposed strong objections to this sudden vow of his son. In particular he warned him of the Labyrinth from which no stranger could escape, and reminded Theseus that it had been constructed by the devious brain of Daedalus, that accursed renegade. Theseus grew even more determined. After the lots were drawn, he led the unfortunate young people from Athens down to their ship. Its sails were black in token of their country's grief. Theseus encouraged the thirteen youths who were with him by reminding them of his exploits on the way to Attica. When they saw him so confident, they began to believe that he actually would not only kill the Minotaur but that he would rid their homeland of Cretan domination. In parting from his father Theseus promised that upon his return he would hoist a white sail instead of the mournful black one so that King Aegeus, peering out over the sea from the cliffs of Sunium, would know they were all alive and well.

As soon as the Athenians arrived in Crete, at the palace of Minos, the funeral games in honor of Androgeus were begun. Not unwilling to impress the Athenians who were so soon to die in the bull-grappling games, Minos began the festival with a boxing match in the new theater that Daedalus had built on the northwest side of the palace. Raised stone steps for the spectators faced the opposite end of the rectangular arena. The royalty of Crete had all taken their places when the Athenian youths and maidens entered in single file. Calmly Theseus stood before Minos. The young hero's blond hair shone in the afternoon sun as he remained facing the king of Crete, now ten years past his prime. The little smile on the Athenian's face did not escape Minos. It would be a pleasure to cast this one to the Minotaur, he thought.

Languidly Theseus dropped to a seat in the front row before the king. A herald was proclaiming a champion wrestler named Taurus. The spectators gasped as the great athelete entered. His broad back and chest were swollen with huge muscles of bronze. Huge mounds of iron tissues stood out like boulders under the tanned skin of his shoulders. He was naked except for a loincloth, and a lion's skin which he draped over his shoulder. Massive and leering he stood, his huge legs far apart like the trunks of pine trees.

Even as the herald called for an opponent, a volunteer to meet this champion, Theseus yawned and looked away from the scene in an attitude of perfect boredom. No person rose. No man volunteered. Jeers came from the Cretans, and cries of "Throw him a Greek!" At this taunt two red spots appeared on the cheeks of Theseus, and he rose.

"Do you wish me to fight your champion, Minos?" he asked quietly.

After a nod from Minos, Theseus advanced toward the herald. "Is it a boxing match?" he called over his shoulder. Quickly attendants brought heavy oxskin gloves and bound them on the hands of the two opponents, and strong leather thongs around their arms.

"Kicking is allowed," pronounced the herald. "Do your mightiest with your fists. Remember all your skills."

Then just as the two were about to start for each other, Minos called tauntingly to his man, "Do not kill him, Champion. We have other sports devised for him."

With a furious rush the boxer lunged toward Theseus, his fists flying through the empty air. Lightly the Athenian prince danced to the left and drove his right fist straight home to the other's chin. Then Theseus threw back his head and laughed while his opponent recovered his footing. A second time the huge man rushed forward, head down, hoping by sheer weight to hurl Theseus to the sand. This time Theseus feinted with his right and, having caught the other's glance, landed a left full in his mouth. The monstrous wrestler reeled and spat blood and broken teeth. Then Theseus darted swiftly at the champion and with the heavily weighted glove struck him in the forehead so hard that the skin was ripped from it. But urged on by the shrill cheers of the Cretan spectators, the giant once more rushed toward the slender Greek. This time Theseus rained so many quick blows on his head and pursued him so relentlessly as the other retreated that finally the wrestler sank over backward to the ground and held up his two fists in sign of defeat.

The prize brought Theseus was a garland of lilies. He was about to throw it at the feet of King Minos when, looking toward the royal box, he saw the sweetest of flowers, the princess Ariadne. Looking her straight in the eye, the slow smile still on his lips, Theseus gently dropped the wreath of lilies upon her lap and turned away. Blushing to the roots of her auburn hair, the innocent Ariadne watched the Greek hero until he had sauntered out of the theater. For this she was sent immediately to her chamber and ordered to remain there. Minos had had personal experience with very young maidens. His theory was a practical one: lock them up until they get married. That way one won't have any cities betrayed.

That night while the palace slept, little Ariadne sat at her window looking out toward the shores of Greece. She had been gently reared by Pasiphaë and the palace ladies who were infatuated with her radiant beauty and soft eyes. She had never been outside the palace walls and had never met a stranger. All her life until then had been games with her sister Phaedra. They had tossed golden balls in the courtyards and sometimes been allowed to watch Daedalus as he modeled his speaking statues. She was so young yet that she had not even thought of love, at least not very seriously. Its torture and happiness had been revealed to her in that instant when the laughing eyes of Theseus had met hers. For this reason she sat still and motionless in her chamber, where her father had sent her.

How long she would have continued to sit thus, staring with hopeless eyes out over the dark sea, Ariadne did not know. It was several minutes before she could rouse herself enough to go to her door after she heard the tapping. At the sound of her voice the door was unlocked, and Daedalus entered stealthily.

"Shall I help you, Ariadne?" he asked her. "Do you very much want to see him?"

Silently the little princess nodded. Covering her bright festival dress with a black cloak, Daedalus took her by the hand and led her to the dark, underground chamber where Theseus was imprisoned. There Daedalus left her alone with the Argive hero, while he stood guard outside.

At first Ariadne could not find her tongue. She blushed and hung her head as she felt his eyes move down her body, over her naked breasts and golden girdle. He talked to her softly, praising her long curls shot with gold, her sweet face, the dimple in her chin, her tiny feet. Finally she said that she had come to help him find a way to escape death. Theseus smiled at her childish innocence.

"I am not afraid, Ariadne. I shall not die."

"Oh, but you will," she gasped. "Tomorrow begin the bull-grappling games. Our youths will give a demonstration, and then the Athenians will be thrown into the ring!"

"I have killed giants many times the size of your Cretan bulls," Theseus retorted. "I have crushed their skulls with one blow of my bronze club."

"You don't understand it at all," cried Ariadne with tears in her eyes. "You won't have a club. You will be naked against the bull. Our specially trained youths and maidens let the bull run toward them. They grasp his horns with their hands and vault over his head onto his back. Then they leap toward the youth behind the bull, who catches them with his hands. It is a skill that requires long years of training. If the bull goes mad, our toreadors stab him."

"Very well," replied Theseus. "Then I will wring the bull's neck. How will that be?"

"Even if you escape death," whispered Ariadne between her tears, "you still have to meet the Minotaur."

"Where is he?" questioned Theseus. "Why don't I search him out now and kill him before tomorrow's games?"

Ariadne was just going to tell Theseus how impossible it would be to find his way down through the three thousand five hundred rooms of the palace when Daedalus reentered the cell. Together he and Theseus

worked out a plan, for Daedalus had never forgotten that he also came from the royal Athenian family of Erechtheus, just like Theseus. On a sheet of parchment Daedalus showed his compatriot a plan of the palace and gave him a sword and a long spool of thread to unwind as he went so that by following it he could retrace his steps.

"Will you come with me to Athens, Ariadne?" asked Theseus.

"Oh yes," she answered. "Only you must not hurt my father."

Then Theseus fell at her feet and swore undying love. He told her of the palace at Athens, high on the hill of Athena. He spoke of his aged father, King Aegeus, and how he would love her. He told her how brave she was to end by her marriage the old quarrel between Crete and Attica. He said that through her love the two countries would forevermore live in peace and friendship.

Then, weeping and trembling, Ariadne was led away by Daedalus, who never doubted that Theseus would slay the Minotaur with his sturdy bronze sword, to the Greek ship that had borne the youths to Crete. Afterward Daedalus ran home, gathered his possessions, dressed his boy Icarus, and fled to a secret hiding place he had made on a cliff far from Knossos.

Theseus, sword in hand, ran lightly through the palace, unwinding the skein as he went. Down he sped from one flight to another through corridors dimly lighted with pine torches. To the right he turned through lofty colonnaded halls where the only sound was his breathing and the rapid tread of his sandaled feet. Then he bore left through vaults and arcades and down another flight of dark stone steps. The air grew damp and chill. Once he almost lost his way and had to follow the thread back to a pillared hall. Hurriedly he got his bearings and raced forward and down another flight. Finally he stopped short, for there directly before him stood the awful, deformed brother of Ariadne.

The Minotaur's keen ears had heard the descending steps of Theseus, and he was waiting. His heavy head hung forward on his chest. Huge, protuberant brown eyes, like a bull's, glowered at the hero. Saliva dripped from his open mouth from which long, fanglike teeth protruded. His arms and shoulders were covered with coarse, black hair.

There was a moment before Theseus could recover himself. His first inclination had been to turn in flight, but even at that instant the creature advanced with huge clawlike fingers eager for his throat. Taking careful aim, Theseus slashed him across the left shoulder. The dungeon echoed with the Minotaur's scream of pain, for he had never before felt a wound. Howling and shrieking, he lunged again for Theseus' throat only to be slashed once more. It was a filthy business, for the animal stench in the chamber was almost overpowering. Mastering his revulsion with an almost superhuman effort, Theseus killed the monster with his next thrust through the heart.

Even before the hideous body of the Minotaur had stopped twitching and writhing on the slippery stones, Theseus had fled upward out of

that reeking dungeon. It was not too difficult to follow the thread, but he stopped at every landing long enough to place a smoking pine torch at the base of one of the wooden pillars that held up the ceiling. Panting until his lungs almost burst, he retraced his steps toward the surface, realizing that within a matter of minutes the fumes would give the alarm. His Athenian friends were crouched near the door of their cell. As soon as Theseus opened their prison, they leaped out and helped him set fire to the palace, working their way quickly northward toward the dock. The seven whom Theseus had disguised as maidens stripped off their women's gowns and headed directly for the wharves where the Cretan fleet rode at anchor. Without hesitation—for Theseus had picked them for their knowledge of swimming and rehearsed them well—they plunged into the water and within a few minutes had staved in the bottoms of the wooden galleys.

Within half an hour they had all returned to the Athenian galley, and its thirty muffled oars were dipping into the calm waters of the bay. Before they had cleared the harbor, they began to see smoke and flames rising in long streaks into the black air. When the wind veered, they could even hear faintly the distant cries of the Cretans. Theseus and his friends clapped each other on the back, gulping great draughts of wine, laughing, boasting, and congratulating their great leader. None of them came near Ariadne who crouched sobbing and weeping on the afterdeck near the helmsman, straining to see once more the shores of her home that she had betrayed, moaning over and over under her breath the names of her mother and father, and seeing for the first time the coarseness and vulgarity of these primitive Greeks into whose ruthless hands she had placed herself.

Back in Knossos, King Minos had been awakened by frightened servants. His palace was in flames. Quickly he gave orders to salvage as much as possible and to move his family to an outer palace. He stood in the central court regardless of his own safety, giving orders and directing rescue operations. It was there that he learned how his fleet had been scuttled. Immediately he realized that the Athenians must have done it. Then he was told that the lower floors had collapsed, but no one had seen the Greeks. Last of all he heard the bitter news that Ariadne was not to be found. Still the palace burned all around him with the thundering roar of falling masonry. It was not until morning that Minos began to reconstruct what had happened. His suspicions were confirmed when he was told that Icarus, the young son of Daedalus, was missing also.

It was Daedalus whom Minos cursed not only for the destruction of the palace, but more especially for having treacherously misled the child Ariadne. Surrounded on every side by death and destruction, knowing that the fast Grecian galley could hide out for months among the numerous isles of the Cyclades, Minos determined first to track Daedalus to earth. His orders were categorical. Any Cretan who knew of Daedalus' whereabouts or assisted him either on land or on sea would be instantly executed. Munificent rewards, on the other hand, awaited his captor or any informant.

Daedalus meanwhile, assisted by his boy Icarus, was hard at work in his hidden atelier. "Let Minos rule the land and the sea," he muttered as he finished his design. "The skies above are henceforth my dominion. Let Minos impose his orders everywhere else. He cannot command the heavens!"

For years this cleverest of inventors had been haunted by the flight of his nephew Perdix. For years he had longed to emulate this feat, not content to build great palaces or lifelike statues of men and gods. He had pondered the problem of flight for more than a decade and had kept a sheaf of notes made from careful observations and calculations of weight and wind. While his son played in the workshop and sometimes hindered his father, as children will, Daedalus constructed from feathers, thread, and wax, two pairs of wings modeled exactly on the wings of eagles, only much larger. When they were finished, he led the little boy out to the edge of the tall cliff where they were hiding, fitted the wings to his little shoulders, and instructed him carefully.

"Icarus, my boy, follow my example and you will fly. Stay well in the middle course, neither too near the sea, which would weigh down your wings with water, nor too high, where the heat of the sun would melt the wax. Especially do not look toward the Great Bear or the flashing sword of Orion. Set your course on me, to the north." With tears streaming down his face, for the elderly Daedalus loved his little son dearly, he kissed him good-by and took to flight from the top of the cliff. Looking back, he saw that the plucky lad had taken the plunge and was following.

Their wings bore them valiantly to the north and the Cyclades. Below them they saw Samos, Delos, and Paros, set like little gems in a glittering sea. Fishermen left their catches struggling on the lines as they watched the fliers high overhead. Shepherds on the islands leaned on their crooks in amazement, believing that they were beholding gods. In the valleys the plowman stared up in amazement at these creatures who so upset the laws of nature as to cleave a passage through the fields of heaven.

Icarus grew weary of following his father. Like any lively boy, he wanted to sail forth on his own. He began to soar and dip, pleased to try his wings in his own way. Daedalus did not know what the boy was doing until he heard his scream. Turning, he saw the child, frantically waving his bare arms, plummet down to the sea. The boy had flown so near the sun that its heat had melted the wax, just as Daedalus had warned him. In honor of Icarus the waters where he died were called Icarian, and the island where Daedalus buried him, near present-day Samos in the Sporades Islands, was also called Icaria.

Daedalus wandered from country to country in the Mediterranean, with the fleet of King Minos steadily tracking him. In Egypt he designed a temple to Hephaestus at Memphis. In distant Sardinia he mapped out fortifications for King Iolaos, the towers of which were named in his memory Daedaleia. Then he moved to Sicily. From the vapors of Aetna he made a bath to cure rheumatism. For King Cocalus he constructed a reservoir, treasuries, and castles. It was here at last that Minos found him.

As the king of Crete expected, Cocalus shielded his valuable architect and denied any knowledge of him. Minos, however, relying on the enormous vanity of Daedalus, showed Cocalus a puzzle that could not be solved. It was a spiral seashell, and Minos defied any man alive to learn the secret of its turnings and find a passage through it. Cocalus took the shell and when he next showed it to Minos there was a fine thread drawn through it from outer rim to vertex. Laughing at Minos, Cocalus told him that one of his engineers had tied the thread to an ant which, lured by a drop of honey, had carried it through the coils of the shell and discovered the exit. In this way Minos knew Daedalus was in Sicily, for he alone could so ingeniously have solved this problem. The Cretan king would have killed him too, except that Minos met his own death there in the palace of Cocalus. Some say a daughter of the king drowned him in his bath.

By noon on the day following their victorious departure from Knossos, Theseus and his band of warriors anchored on the coast of Naxos in the Cyclades. This island, the largest in that archipelago, was a center for the cult of Dionysus. Wading ashore, the Greek heroes proceeded to bathe and sacrifice to the gods for their easy triumph. Theseus carried Ariadne ashore and tried to comfort her, for she had neither slept nor stopped crying since they left Knossos the evening before. Her whole body was racked with dry sobs. Annoyed with her lack of courage, he grudgingly made her a bed beside the beach, where after a little while, lulled by the rhythmic rush of the waves and warmed by the noonday sun, the little princess fell asleep. Meanwhile the Athenian warriors finished their prayers, took on food and water, and still boasting and laughing, set sail for Athens.

When Ariadne awoke, it was late afternoon. The sun already cast long shadows among the black rocks that lay around her and stretched far out into the foaming sea. At first she could neither remember where she was nor what had happened. Slowly she recalled with a gasp of horror the red tongues of flames as they leaped above her burning homeland. Then she remembered the grinning faces of the Greeks. Looking all around her, she could see no trace of them except for their footprints in the sand. Shading her eyes with her hand, she scanned the horizon. There was no ship in sight. There was not even a black sail silhouetted against the horizon. Frantic, Ariadne began to climb the jagged rocks that projected out into the sea. She cut her hands as she scrambled over them, Ariadne who had never before yesterday even walked outside her carefully tended gardens at Knossos. Stepping in shallow water between two boulders, she cut her feet on the black spines of the sea urchin. Heedless of the blood flowing from the wounds, she clambered on a higher rock and looked again far out over the sea. Great waves came rolling along the deep toward her and tore at her frail garments. Unmindful of them also, Ariadne let them wash her thin robe from her body. She was alone in a world of sea and sky. There was not a person in sight, not a single habitation, only vastness and the surging, white-crested waves of the sea. Then she began to speak to the departed Theseus:

You traitor! So this is the way you have left me, Theseus,
Deserted here on this wretched shore where you brought me, traitor!
While you go sailing away, completely unmindful.
Yes, scorning the gods you flaunt your broken promise to Athens!
Could nothing bend the iron of your cruel decision?

Had you no tenderness in your heart for Ariadne
That its ruthlessness should at last be melted to pity?
Oh! with your once sweet voice you never promised
Me these rocks, nor urged me ever to hope for this fate;
But an honored queen and a lovely wedding you pictured
Which the lofty winds have destroyed and completely abolished.
From this day forth let no maiden trust any man's swearing,
Nor ever believe that the oaths of a hero are honest
While his crafty brain having schemed ahead how to betray her
Will help him swear anything, nor stop him from promising everything;
For as soon as the lust of his greedy ambition is sated
His words he will not remember, nor care for his swearing!

So Ariadne spoke her farewell to Theseus, adding to her words a curse that he should cause as much sorrow to one of his family as he had brought to her, and to Crete through her.

Ariadne stood on the black rock in her naked loveliness with the setting sun behind her, crowning her long curls in an aureole of golden light. It is in this position that she is remembered, for so she stood in her young beauty when the god Dionysus first saw her. At first he thought she was Aphrodite rising as at her birth out of the green sea foam.

Dionysus was just returning from a long voyage to the East, where he had taught the other men of the world the art of agriculture. His moisture had flowed forth over the banks of the Nile and made the black earth of Egypt fertile. He had crossed the Tigris River on a splendid tiger that Zeus had sent him, and the Euphrates on a cable made of ivy tendrils and grapevine. He had just come from India, at the eastern end of the earth, where he had founded the city of Nysa.

Lifting Ariadne tenderly from her dangerous crag, Dionysus enfolded her in his gentle arms and carried her to the shore. Ariadne had never seen a god before, and so she had no idea how much more beautiful they were than mortal men. The god's hair was black and curly, for black is the color of youth as white is the color of old heads. As a boy Dionysus had been enclosed in a chest that had floated over the sea, but now he was a man, tall and handsome, but with the rounded arms and the graceful gestures of a god. His head was crowned with ivy and laurel. In one hand he bore his insignia, the thyrsus or staff crowned with vines. In the other hand he carried a gleaming wine cup from which he made the princess drink until she had forgotten her sorrow. Then she sat across his lap, resting her shoulder on his raised left knee while he stroked her hair with his left hand and wooed her.

The god of the harvest, Dionysus, and the princess Ariadne were married at Naxos, for this was his particular island. Even the great gods and goddesses from Olympus attended the formal wedding. They had three sons and lived happily ever afterward. On her wedding day Dionysus presented Ariadne with a magnificent golden crown, which she always wore as long as she lived. At her death—for her husband could not give her immortality—he threw her crown up into the northern sky where it may still be seen on a cloudless night as the radiant Corona Borealis.

Theseus and his band of Athenian heroes returned directly home after their short stop at Naxos. With hissing beak their swift galley ploughed the waves while they urged on their oarsmen to greater sweeps with the flashing oars. Theseus could already hear the shouts of the admiring citizens, "Lo! another Heracles!" as they acclaimed him the savior of his people. With shouts of joy the triumphant young men sighted the shores of Greece and the high promontory of Sunium. It was not until he stepped ashore and heard the cries of grief around him that Theseus remembered the white sail. It still lay folded in its chest where his father Aegeus had lovingly placed it. Aegeus, straining his eyes over the blue sea for news of his beloved son, had sighted the black sail over the Athenian galley. Preferring by far a sudden death to the news of the loss of his beloved Theseus, Aegeus threw himself from the cliff of Sunium onto the sharp rocks far below. The gods in this way punished Theseus swiftly for his abandonment and betrayal of the Cretan princess.

Because of his father's suicide Theseus became king of Attica. Using the slogan "Come hither, all you peoples," he persuaded the inhabitants of small outlying towns to move to Athens. In this way he created a powerful state which he administered well and defended heroically for many years. At the confines of his territories he caused a massive pillar to be erected and carvings to be made on its eastern and western sides to indicate to travelers that they were leaving the Peloponnesus and entering Ionia. Theseus was so respected by his citizens that whenever a great task was to be undertaken by an Athenian, he always remembered this king and affirmed that it could be done perhaps, but "Not without Theseus!"

One of Theseus' greatest subsequent exploits was his kidnaping of the Amazonian queen Hippolyta and his destruction of the fierce hordes of female warriors that, bent on revenge, invaded the kingdom of Attica. This famous fighting queen became his bride after four days, in ceremonies long remembered for their glamor. A later poet has described these nuptials in immortal lines. Theseus says,

Hippolyta, I woo'd thee with my sword,
And won thy love doing thee injuries;
But I will wed thee in another key,
With pomp, with triumph, and with revelling.

It was indeed a solemn wedding enlivened with a play about the loves of the Babylonian youth Pyramus and his sweetheart Thisbe.

A son, Hippolytus, was born from the union of Theseus and the queen of the Amazons. At the death of Hippolyta, Theseus married Phaedra, the younger sister of Ariadne. This marriage, however, resulted in great tragedy. Phaedra, far from loving King Theseus, fell passionately in love with the boy Hippolytus. Since this youth had taken vows of chastity, Phaedra's consuming passion caused the death of both of them.

When he was fifty, Theseus began to search for a new bride. Once on a voyage to Sparta he became enamored of a young wisp of a girl whom he saw dancing in the temple of the virginal goddess Artemis. Without reckoning the consequences of his blind passion Theseus kidnaped the girl, who was not even of marriageable age at the time, and hid her with his mother Aethra in the island of Troezen. This young girl had twin brothers, the Dioscuri, who followed Theseus to Athens in an attempt to rescue their sister. Theseus had not realized that this abduction would set off a chain of circumstances that would result in long and bloody wars, and in his own death far from home.

It was not until later years that the huge body of Theseus was carried royally home to Athens and duly buried with great honors in the heart of that city. The ship that had borne him and the youths to Crete was preserved in Athens until 300 B.C. Ceremonies in honor of this greatest hero of Attica were instituted on the eighth day of every month, for it was on the eighth day of the month of Cronus that he had first entered Athens and climbed the holy stairs of the Acropolis in search of his father. The number eight, as the first cube of the first even number and the double of the first square number, aptly indicated the reliable and loyal nature of Theseus, the Immortal Hero.

As the mighty Theseus wandered golden-haired among the immortals in the perfumed Elysian Fields, did he know that the ten-year-old Spartan girl whom he had abducted was becoming, through a chain of violations, one of the most celebrated women the world had ever known, the fateful Helen of Troy?

FOUR
TROY

Many writers of the ancient world—lyric poets, dramatists, and historians—have mentioned the story of Cassandra. Artists throughout antiquity had rather generally agreed in their representations as to how she looked. One poet, Lycophron, wrote a work in Greek of 1,712 lines recounting her many prophecies in the words of her guardian, some of which are in the following pages. As in the case of Ariadne, another favorite heroine, there were widely divergent accounts of the Cassandra story. It was one that apparently held a very special appeal for the ancients.

The historian Plutarch speaks of her tomb, as does Pausanias, who adds that a great hero worship had grown up in Greece around her legend. Vergil, writing from the Roman point of view—since his purpose was to glorify Caesar and the Julian family, who were "Trojans" claiming descent from Aphrodite—mentions Cassandra with great sympathy. Euripides gives her beautiful lines to speak in *The Trojan Women*, and Aeschylus in the climax of *Agamemnon* recounts her death most vividly. Even Cicero in *De Oratore* wittily puts an opponent to rout by retorting "Ajax" when the other styled himself "Cassandra."

The reader will find in the following pages her story as told by the above-named authors, not the more familiar version of the Trojan War as Homer tells it. For a scholarly interpretation of all the classical texts and a detailed study of 123 artists' representations of this princess, the reader may wish to consult the learned dissertation of Dr. Juliette Davreux. This treatise was presented at the University of Liége and published in Paris in 1942.

CASSANDRA

King Priam of Troy was rightfully called the sower of many seeds, for he fathered fifty children. Nineteen of them were born to his royal spouse, Queen Hecuba. Together they lived in a prosperous city which was encircled by lofty walls and which commanded a view over a wide plain watered by the River Scamander. The city of Troy, or Ilion, was on the Asian side of the Hellespont, the strait connecting the Aegean with the waters leading into the Black Sea and its fertile wheat-growing areas.

Priam was proud to trace his ancestry back through seven royal generations to one of the Titans—Iapetus, brother of Cronus. In his family tree he also boasted not only the giant Atlas, but even Zeus himself. Among his allies King Priam could number many lands of Asia—Lycia, Mysia, and Cilicia—and among his friends even the Pharaoh of Egypt.

The royal Priam was not blessed with children alone, but also with great wealth. His forefathers had been accustomed to levy tolls on all vessels that passed through the Hellespont, a practice Priam also continued. By gathering under his protection many of the smaller cities of Asia Minor, he was able successfully to oppose the growing populations of the "barbarian" peoples to the west of his domains, and also to prevent their expansion eastward. Of necessity he kept a watchful eye on the allies and descendants of the kings of Crete and upon their Achaean conquerors. Two of the most powerful lords of the west were the brothers Agamemnon of Mycenae and Menelaus of Sparta, both great-grandsons of the famous King Minos II of Crete. Like them King Priam considered Crete one of the cradles of his race.

The pride and hope of the great Trojan city was its Prince Hector. He was their shield of bronze, the pillar of their palace, sturdy enough to bear upon his shoulders the heaviest of monarchies. Hector had married the white-armed Andromache, and to them had been born a strong son, Astyanax. The home of Hector within the city was a place of peace and innocence, because his wife stayed in her own garden, quiet and contented. She only craved the pleasant company of Hector; and when he returned, she greeted him with gentle words and obedience. For her dear sake, although the most valiant of the warriors of Troy, Hector was a kind and honorable lord.

Among the many brothers of Hector were other brave men, Deiphobus, Helenus, and Troilus. With only one of her sons did Queen Hecuba have any difficulty, and this was a great sorrow both to her and to King Priam. During one of her pregnancies Queen Hecuba dreamed that the child within her body was a burning brand of fire. Her dream was so strange that the priests of Zelia were consulted. Their verdict was an ominous one. They believed that this unborn child would bring about the ruin of the whole kingdom. They affirmed most categorically that he must be put to death. Although Hecuba and Priam would have liked to raise the baby boy who was born to the queen, they decided in order to fulfil the orders of the temple to expose the child on the slopes of the Trojan Mount Ida.

Fortunately the loss of this one son was compensated in some measure by the births of other children. One of their daughters was Creüsa, who grew up to marry none other than a son of the goddess Aphrodite. This mischievous goddess had often plagued the ruler of the gods, Zeus, with a desire to possess mortal women, and thus had brought down on his head the baleful glances and swift revenge of his wife Hera. Zeus decided to repay Aphrodite by causing her to be faithless to her husband, Hephaestus, in a similar fashion.

Zeus caused Aphrodite to fall passionately in love with a Trojan shepherd who was guarding his flocks on the slopes of Mount Ida near Troy. In order to satisfy her burning desire, Aphrodite went to infinite trouble. She arrayed herself in silken robes, and selected bright jewels for her throat and perfumes for her hair. Then she descended to earth and pretended to be aimlessly strolling through the wooded groves. When she had allowed the shepherd to see her naked body, she confessed her passion modestly. He wondered, it is true, how she happened to be accompanied by tame panthers and lions that rubbed against her thighs and rolled like kittens at her feet. Aphrodite invented a plausible story about how she was really the daughter of a minor Phrygian king who was subject to the overlord Priam.

The delighted shepherd led her at once to his humble couch, where among the bearskin covers she fulfilled Zeus's wish and conceived a son. After the love-making Aphrodite revealed her true character to the shepherd. Awed and terrified, he fell to his knees. He begged her to forgive the indignity, the humiliation he had caused her. Aphrodite forgave him. She even managed to spare him the punishment usually meted out to mortals who had soiled the body of a goddess. He was allowed by her good graces to keep intact his youth, instead of being changed instantly into a senile, doddering old man.

Aphrodite accompanied her rare charity with an admonition. The shepherd was never to reveal at Troy who the mother of his son was. Relenting even more, the goddess, remembering no doubt how ardently this shepherd had caressed her and how pleasantly he had relieved her of her tormenting desire, condescended to tell him a great secret. This son, whom she would bear him, would resemble a god! The poor fellow listened spellbound to this revelation.

"When he is born," she instructed the shepherd, "you are to call him Aeneas." After a thoughtful pause she added, "I think I shall love him very much in memory of our most enjoyable few hours together." The deity turned back over her shoulder and called to the shepherd, who still remained humbly on his knees, "What did you say your name was, boy?"

"Anchises," he answered.

"Very well," smiled Aphrodite. "I shall remember you too one night in the very midst of hell. Good-by, Anchises."

It was this son of Aphrodite, the godly Aeneas, who married one of the princesses of Troy. Another of Priam's daughters was the Chosen One. This was the pure and holy Cassandra.

From her earliest childhood this daughter had set herself apart as a servant of the gods, and her parents had acquiesced in her wishes. This Cassandra had a rather boyish look. She was not tall. Her hair was blond and very curly, but her eyes were large and black. She had a round face, fair skin, and a slender nose. With quiet, calm steps she went about her duties as a virgin priestess who knew very little about the world and whose thoughts are only on the gods. Both Priam and Hecuba sensed the tranquil strength in this consecrated daughter, and they were very proud of her. Bearing her keys, her forehead bound with the fillets of a priestess, she moved through the shrine of Apollo with gleaming eyes, inspired with the beauty of the world.

The royal baby abandoned by the rulers of Troy upon the slopes of Mount Ida did not die. His hungry cries attracted a she-bear, who nursed him until he grew tall and strong, able to care for himself. He grew up to be a handsome, blond shepherd dressed in leopard skins, and he was happy. Far from the cares of the world, he led an enchanted existence among docile flocks. He was beloved of the nymph Oenone. Then one day an order from Zeus came to interrupt his carefeee life.

The goddess of discord had incited a quarrel between the three great divinities Athena, Hera, and Aphrodite. Zeus had suggested that the handsome shepherd, whose name was Alexander, settle the argument by awarding a golden apple to the most beautiful. Confused by such a difficult choice, and yet preferring quite clearly the gifts of love to those of lands and possessions or wisdom and valor, Alexander chose the goddess Aphrodite. Immediately afterward he set out for Troy, where his parents, forgetting the oracle, welcomed him. Now the goddess of love had so inflamed him with her promise that he should have as his own the most beautiful woman in the world that Alexander did not even cast a backward glance toward his erstwhile love, Oenone. Once established in Troy as a prince of the blood, he set out royally, this perfumed youth, to visit King Menelaus of Sparta.

When ill fortune happens to a family—for, as the oracle of Zelia had predicted, Prince Alexander would bring no good fortune—it never seems to fall singly. As if the very return of this prince had raised an ill storm, evil fortune then blew about the dedicated priestess Cassandra. Her very distinctive charms, her quiet and modest manner, and the singleness of her rapt devotion brought her to the attention of the god

Apollo. One day he appeared, splendid and powerful, before his altar. Blinded by the glory of his presence, Cassandra would have fled or fallen before him in adoration. The god's purpose was very different.

"Cassandra, you must yield to me," he commanded.

"I cannot," answered Cassandra. "I have taken vows of chastity. I have sworn to remain a virgin as long as I live. I cannot break such an oath."

"You are to break it for me," answered Apollo. "A god desires you. I wish to possess you now."

"I cannot. I cannot," Cassandra kept moaning, as she twisted her hands in mortification.

"Cassandra, you must lie here now and allow me to embrace you," commanded Apollo, beginning to be impatient at such a whimsical reluctance. "It is a great honor to offer one's virginity to a god. I release you from your vow."

"Oh, no," pleaded the priestess. Clutching her gown across her body, she backed away from the god, who pressed close after her, swollen with passion.

"Come, Cassandra," he panted. "You will be rewarded. Well rewarded. Look. I have already given you the gift of prophecy."

Even as he spoke, the trembling Cassandra felt the walls of her head split open with a maze of moving pictures. Swiftly she closed her eyes and held her fingers over them. It was no use. With regularity the awful pictures flicked on and off before her sight. In horror she shook her head and turned it blindly from side to side.

"What do you see, Cassandra?" intruded the voice of Apollo, who hoped to embrace her while her vigilance was relaxed.

Her voice rose to a shriek. "Oh, I see . . . I see my father lying on the ground in a pool of blood, his drawn sword dangling from his lifeless, blue-veined hand. His white beard is stained in blood . . . oh . . . oh," screamed Cassandra. "Do not let me see these horrors!"

"Then will you yield to me?" insisted Apollo.

"No! No!" she answered, sobbing now and raising her hands to her eyes in an effort to erase the flood of pictures. The god abruptly released her rigid, protesting body.

"Then," decided Apollo, "let me give you one kiss before I go." Imperiously he approached her again as she cowered kneeling at the foot of the altar. "Open your lips, Cassandra, and receive one kiss from a god."

Cassandra did as he commanded. She finally opened her lips and closed her eyes. Apollo bent his gleaming face down to hers and instead of kissing her, he blew in her open mouth. "Good for you, stupid girl," he sneered. "You may keep your virginity for a while. Now, you must henceforth prophesy as long as the gods of Troy shall stand on their altars, and almost as long as you shall live, for all I care. You are a prophetess, Cassandra. I have given you this gift as a souvenir."

The god was already taking his leave. Cassandra could see through the bloody images that his radiance was fading, but she could still hear his parting words. "Prophesy, Cassandra. Look every day at your future. Dare to live what you see is going to happen to you. I have given you a second gift, however. Would you like to know what it is? It is this: you will never be believed! That was my second gift. No matter how truly you see into the future, you will never be believed!"

Hopeless and tortured, bloody scenes of battle and sword succeeding one after another before her bursting eyeballs, Cassandra rushed from the temple and into the audience room of the palace. A polite reception was in progress there, for Prince Alexander had found his mortal bride, the most beautiful woman in all the world. He was just then presenting her to his royal parents. King Priam had just extended his right hand to the couple. Queen Hecuba was appraising the bride with critical eyes that rejoiced in her loveliness and in the full lines of her body that would surely make her a warm lover and a tender wife to Alexander.

Cassandra burst in upon this tranquil scene with a piercing wail of despair. It froze their hearts like the sudden icy blast of winter that clarions sleet and driving snow. Transfixed with fear they heard that long shriek curl about their ears and go moaning along the draughty

walls of cold stone. The hair stood up on their heads, and their blood turned cold in their bodies. Still Cassandra screamed, another long, vibrating wail of agony. In horror they looked at her torn garments and recoiled. Not even her father could bear the burning, vacant glare of her bright eyes.

"She has gone mad," whispered Priam to himself. "Cassandra, my dear Cassandra, stop!" he moaned.

Her body stiff and rigid, and her face a chalky, distorted mask, Cassandra stole across the marble floor as if she were a tattered wraith treading on air. Her hair fell in damp ringlets over her eyes, but she did not seem to know it. Straight up to the throne she went and, pointing to her brother, Alexander, screamed again in accusation, "Never call him Alexander! This whelp of a she-bear! This soft and perfumed, loathsome lover! He is the breath of murder, the red-hot, scorching breath of destruction and death! He will kill us all! I see our bloody deaths before my eyes! Kill him before it is too late! Kill him! He is a filthy, swollen worm that will send us all into a violent hell! Step on him! Kill him! His name is *Paris*, he-who-is-wed-with-ghastly-death!

"And as for her," she continued, focusing her blazing eyes on the gentle Helen of Sparta, "send her away. Be rid of her! Send home this voluptuous queen, or you will see how the bees will swarm. They will assemble in clouds and swarm leather-shielded over the seas to sting us all to death. Oh, Hector! My beloved Hector!"

Turning to her brother's wife, Andromache, Cassandra knelt at her feet and touched the hem of her garment. The incredulous spectators began to recover their composure and cast pitying glances to the throne where the aged Priam sat flushed and humiliated. "Save Hector, Andromache. You of all women will know how to do it," pleaded Cassandra. Then her head sank to the marble floor, and she appeared to sleep.

At a command from the king two courtiers lifted the limp, fragile body of Cassandra and carried her down to a cell under the palace where her screams would no longer be heard. Everyone in Troy regretted her madness and pitied her, but no one cared to see her again. Within a few weeks she was, in fact, almost forgotten in the press of an emergency. Troy was indeed besieged by an enormous force from Greece and Crete, led by great warriors, Agamemnon, Menelaus, Achilles, Ajax, Idomeneus, Odysseus! Between Troy and the sea they erected a great stockade to protect their fleet; and there on the damp shore, amidst the fogs of summer evenings and the fierce, howling storms of winter, they besieged Ilion for ten long years.

One day the guard whose duty was to sit outside Cassandra's prison requested an audience with King Priam. Although he did not believe her wild dreams, this rough soldier still felt that he must share the responsibility of his knowledge with the king himself, so terrible was it!

"This war drags on, O King," the soldier began, "and still the priestess Cassandra affirms that the Spartan Helen must be returned to her husband, Menelaus. She says Prince Paris has given indeed a just grievance to the kings of the Peloponnesus. She says Prince Paris was a guest in the court of Menelaus. He broke bread with him and ate salt from his table. Then when Menelaus left on a voyage for Crete, Paris persuaded his wife to elope with him to Troy. Thus was a great crime committed. Helen of Sparta brought vast treasure with her. 'She must be returned, and the treasure a hundredfold,' says Cassandra. O King, please hear her prophecies, for I can no longer sleep at night, they so ring in my ears!"

At the words of the guardian, Trojan courtiers had begun to gather around to listen to the prophecies of Cassandra. Somewhat abashed to be speaking before such a large and important assembly, the soldier proceeded, however, to enumerate them.

"Cassandra says that one tragedy above all others shall eat away her heart. She says her brother, our Prince Hector, will die in this war, that he will topple over like a slender pine on the mountainside. Hector will be slain by the swift Achilles, who will hitch the body of our prince to his chariot and drag it through the dust and rocks." Incredulous murmurs came from the palace courtiers.

"When we of Troy ask for its return, Achilles will refuse us; and you, O King, will go a suppliant to the tent of this hero to sue for it. The eagle will make us all pay dear the body of our Hector. He will not render it for pity, but only for gold. With Hector dead from a gaping

wound in his throat, his body soiled and desecrated, we shall have lost the pillar of our house. Cassandra says so shall Troy fall!

"She further says Odysseus and Diomedes will enter the city by night and steal the Palladium itself, our holy image of Pallas Athena upon which our lives and safety depend. They will not fear to touch the sacred stone with their polluted hands, even though it fell to us from the very skies themselves. Odysseus will creep into the city disguised as a Greek deserter. He will dare to profane the image, and will send it over the seas to Greece. Cassandra says we have a traitor in our midst, a false woman who will see these furtive thieves, who will recognize the fabled boar's-tusk helmet of Odysseus, and who will not reveal their presence to us. This woman is the white dove, Helen of Sparta.

"Now the Princess Cassandra tells another story which is very wild indeed. She says the Greeks will pretend to leave Troy because they have angered Athena. She says they will construct a mighty horse of fir and oak planks. She says you are not to touch the horse, not to trust it, not to tear down the walls of Troy in order to pull its mighty mass into the city. She says this horse will bring us all to ruin. She says it will be some trick of Menelaus, some stealth of his to enter the city in search of his long-lost wife whom he covets even now. Cassandra says you are not to negotiate with Menelaus or to trust his word, but only the word of Agamemnon.

"Cassandra says our fair city of Troy will fall in the night while its soldiers are sleeping, while we think the Greeks have left for home. Then will come fire and destruction. Then will walls come crashing down over our heads. Then will friend kill friend, for no one will see in the flames and darkness who is Greek and who Trojan. Then will the bloody Pyrrhus storm our cedar portals with his ax. His father Achilles will be dead by that time. For even the great Achilles will die at Troy.

"It will be good to see Achilles dead, Cassandra says, the valiant Achilles whose mother so feared this war that she concealed him in Scyros dressed up as a virgin. Her love and care will not follow him forever. He will die in the temple of Apollo while bargaining for the hand of Princess Polyxena of Troy. Then will Paris shoot him through the heel with a poisoned arrow; and like a man, not like a hero, will he die while Ajax and Odysseus quarrel over his new armor. Your vengeance will also be swift and cruel, for Troy will haggle over his body with the Greeks.

"Next will die the dainty princess of Troy, Polyxena, not for any sin of hers, not for any quarrel with the Greeks. She will die because she had been promised to Achilles. Cassandra says the Greeks will cluster armor-clad about the altar and pray. Then at a nod from Odysseus will two strong ones lift the maiden high above the altar as you would lift a fawn, hunched forward, its thin neck over the blood basins. Her weak cries of 'Hector! Hector!' will pierce the air in vain,

for Hector will lie rotting in his shroud. Her desperate eyes will roam about the temple searching for one kind face among the throng of bearded veterans, war-black, bloodthirsty, foreign warriors. Then will her immolators bind her mouth, for her pitiful cries of pain and fright will have driven the quiet Agamemnon from the temple. So died in her saffron robes his own little daughter when the seas stormed and the winds prevented the Greeks' thousand galleys from setting sail for Troy.

"Agamemnon, king of Mycenae, would have prevented the sacrifice of Polyxena, had he been able, says Cassandra. He will not be able, and so shall perish in agony the frail maiden, Polyxena, at the command of Achilles' ghost. Into the basins will flow her bright, red blood.

"The Greeks will not let Paris live long either—he who should have been put to death at birth, this wretched cause of all our sufferings. He will die too, just as Achilles died, with the sting of a poisoned arrow, with his flesh bloating and putrefying from the jagged wound. Then will Paris remember old friends in his distress. Then will he turn his head away from the gentle dove of Greece when she tiptoes in to measure his minutes with her beautiful, soft eyes.

"Only one person will know the remedy for the envenomed arrows of Heracles, and she will be far away on the slopes of Mount Ida. She will turn deaf ears to Paris' messengers. Only when she sees her faithless lover stretched in rigid death, will Oenone relent and mourn him. Then the nymph in her sorrow will hurl herself from our battlements and die.

"Cassandra says she will return to serve the temple of Athena. She says you will eventually call her up from her dungeon but keep far away from her wild eyes. There will her own story be re-enacted, says Cassandra. This time the lesser Ajax will force his way into the sanctuary, breathing lust all over his stupid, ox's face. Even though Cassandra clutches the feet of the goddess, he will tear at her garments and seize her by the hair. There, in the temple itself, the bearded Ajax will rape Cassandra.

"The goddess, shocked at man's brutality, will avert her eyes from such a horror. Not yet will a Trojan maiden live to be pure and serve the gods! Not yet will a Trojan hero dare to hope while the Greek conquers and burns the city.

"Even Your Majesty, King Priam, you also—Cassandra says—must die in this war. She says the beastly son of Achilles, snakelike in new armor, will tear down the bronze-bound doors of our palace. Like an executioner Pyrrhus will swing his ax from right to left splitting skulls and mangling bodies. The young prince, Polites, will he send bleeding unto death right in the courtyard shrine where his mother Hecuba is crouching. Then, O King, clad in your armor of youth, you will raise a trembling old hand to save your son. You will hurl your feeble spear against the Greek's breastplates. Pyrrhus will laugh at the light blow. He will advance and plunge his steaming sword into your body, up

to the hilt into your flesh. . . . How can I bear to hear such horrors?"
the soldier cried. "Cassandra says then will our royal ladies be taken
prisoner, our Queen Hecuba, Hector's wife Andromache, and herself."

"What of our grandson, Astyanax?" Priam questioned.

"He is to die in babyhood, Cassandra says. They will not leave a son
of Priam to grow up in whatever corner of Asia he might find a haven,
for fear of his eventual revenge. The sly Odysseus will snatch this child
from his mother's arms and hurl him down from the walls of our burning citadel. 'Not yet do I see a Trojan hero who will live,' cries Cassandra.

"Andromache will fall to the lot of Pyrrhus. She will follow him
gently and without complaint, for she who has known the arms of
Hector encircling her in the night will best bear the insults of captivity.
Andromache alone will one day remarry a prince of Troy, the courteous
Helenus. Together they will make a realm beyond the sea. There, once
more secure, Andromache may pray again to the shade of her beloved
Hector.

"As for our queen, the lady Hecuba, she will become the slave of
Odysseus and be borne by him to Thrace. She will never forgive him
for his baseness, particularly for the murder of the child Astyanax. An
old, nagging, fearless woman, Hecuba will never cease taunting this
Greek, never cease calling him foul names until in desperation and
anger, he will lapidate her as one does a mongrel bitch. 'Bitch' he will
call her, as he hurls the first stone at her white head.

"May I go on, O King?" the guardian asked. All around him the courtiers of Priam listened with smiles of amusement on their faces at the child's tale he was recounting.

"Go on," King Priam commanded. "What of the Greeks? What kind of story does our daughter make up about them?"

"First Cassandra spoke of Ajax the Locrian, he who will violate her in the temple of Athena. This lesser Ajax will die, she says, but not by his own hand and the sword he had as a present from Hector, as will the great Ajax. This Locrian Ajax will die by drowning in the wild waters of the sea. The goddess Athena will not let them all escape, these impious Greeks. Great winds shall drive this Ajax on stormy rocks where he will cling for dear life and boast how beloved he is of those on Olympus. Then will Poseidon split the rock and flood great waves over his head. Then will the sea god choke Ajax with huge throatfuls of sea water.

"Then Athena will send a plague to devastate the Locrians as further retribution for the desecration of Ajax. For the rape of Cassandra, she says, they will be taxed to furnish two maidens per year for the temple of Athena at Troy. The punishment is to last a thousand years. The first maidens will be stoned to death just like Queen Hecuba, their bodies burned, and their ashes strewn over the sea. As for her punishment to the other Greeks, Athena will disperse them with storms that will rage over their guilty heads for years and years.

"Acamus, son of the Athenian Theseus, will be shipwrecked on the shores of Cyprus. The curse of the gods shall rest above his head until the son of this Acamus is killed in Thrace. Idomeneus too shall drag out his unfortunate life in a strange, new land. This handsome king of Crete shall return to find his island desolate, weed-ridden, its inhabitants decimated by a plague. During his absence at Troy his queen and her daughter will be cruelly murdered.

"Helen of Sparta will return to the Peloponnesus with her doting Menelaus, the curse of thousands upon her lovely head. As a parting gift to Troy she will light torches and lead the Greeks into the palace, where they will fall upon Hector's brother, Prince Deiphobus, as he lies sleeping on his nuptial couch. This prince too will she have added to the list of her conquests after the sudden death of Paris. Menelaus will rush upon the sleeping youth, slit his nostrils, rip off his ears, lacerate his upraised palms, and send him headlong to join the throngs of illustrious dead in the dark Underworld. Menelaus will take his Helen, but they will also be punished with long, sea-tossed voyages along the coasts of Asia and Africa before they ever regain their Spartan court.

" 'Our little war shall be forgot,' Cassandra says. 'It is only one of the many wars fought and to be fought by men of the East against those of the West.

" 'Do you remember the great hero Perseus, he who slew the Gorgon?

Far to the east, beyond the double rivers, high on the plateau of Asia, Perseus will father a race of warriors, a band of rulers, whose magnificent King of Kings will laugh before Athens' wooden walls. Their great King Xerxes will burn those walls to the ground before he returns to Persia.

" 'Perseus will then provide a champion for the West, who will grow up dreaming of subduing Persia. The world will not soon forget his name. While still young, he will visit his vengeance upon his Persian brother and roll his tide of battle from Macedon to Egypt and even to the land of India. His name will also be Alexander.' "

King Priam sat pensive as these words of prophecy rolled about his ears. Affected in spite of himself, he mournfully asked the guardian, "Is that all? Sees our daughter no hope at all for Troy? Sees she not one of us to live, not one hero to bear our household gods out of the city's burning? Must we all die and our children's unborn children?"

At these questions the soldier shifted from one foot to another and hesitated to answer. Finally he began reluctantly to speak, "Yes, there is one more prophecy. However, I do not understand it at all.

"Cassandra says there is among us, within the walls of our windswept citadel, a gentler hero than the world has seen up to now. He is," and here the soldier looked about and lowered his voice, "he is . . . not even the son of a king. He is the son . . . I cannot understand this secret. How could a hero be only the son of . . . He is the son of a shepherd! Yes, that is what Cassandra says. He is the son of a Trojan shepherd, but his mother is Love. His mother is the goddess of Love. His name is Aeneas.

"Now this Aeneas is married to Creüsa, a princess of Troy. It is therefore true that their son Iulus, or Ascanius as he is sometimes called, has the blood of Hector in his veins.

"Cassandra says the night Troy burns, a golden light will come to play around the head of Iulus. This will be a sign from heaven. For that night Aphrodite herself will walk through the city beside them, and they will pass through fire and never feel the flames. That night in the very midst of hell the goddess will save Anchises, her son Aeneas, and the grandson Iulus. Not Creüsa. She must stay in Troy to pray for our dead. She will stay to worship the earth goddess Cybele whom our ancestors brought with them from Crete.

"Aeneas will carry our household gods safely from Troy. With twenty ships he will wander through the sea until he comes to the land of Hesperia, a fabled country in the portals of the west. His son Iulus will reign in this place of Italy for thirty years. Then for 300 years the lineage of Hector shall be crowned in this western kingdom. After that will be founded from our race a great eternal city. Its name will be Rome. Mankind by that time shall have reached another Age of Gold.

"This is all Cassandra's dream and all her prophecy."

It was not believed. None of it was believed, for that was the curse of Cassandra. Nonetheless the machines of the gods ground out their irrevocable happenings. Troy fell. The peerless heroes, Achilles and Hector, fought and died. Troy burned and toppled, lofty towers and all. Everything occurred as the prophetess had foretold. Cassandra moved from her temple with the line of prisoners and saw her mother wrapping the tiny broken corpse of Astyanax in bands of linen and laying him to rest on Hector's shield. The sea was red with flames, and the night hideous with wailing. Cassandra moved slowly forward among the women of Troy, down the hill for the last time, across the plain and to the seashore where the loaded galleys from Greece danced, impatient to walk the waves toward home.

Behind her, high on the summit of Mount Ida, flared the bright beacon that would flash its news of victory westward across the Hellespont, to the Lemnian Rock of Hermes, to the heights of Mount Athos, on to a dozen watchful sentinels, and so to the valley that sloped toward the plain of Argos. Here in this valley, surrounded by lofty hills, the wealthy city of Mycenae awaited the return of Agamemnon its king.

When Cassandra reached the bottom of the hill, she was motioned toward the galley of Agamemnon. This king himself stood by the shore waiting for her. As she approached where he stood tall and somber on the beach, she slowly and deliberately tore from her hair the sacred fillets of the priestess. Untying her keys to the temple from her golden girdle, she dropped them on the wet sand. She neither looked directly at Agamemnon nor spoke to him.

"Is it really you, Cassandra?" he whispered. "My sweet Cassandra. My nightingale." Gently he bent over her bowed head, hoping that she would look up at him. "To me," he murmured, "has fallen the chosen flower of all the beauties of Troy. You shall be met with every gentleness. The gods alone have loved you until now."

The signal fires had done their work well. The news of the fall of Troy had arrived at the golden citadel of Mycenae long before the galley of the king. In her opulent court Queen Clytemnestra welcomed the tidings, for she had waited ten long years for the day that her husband Agamemnon would return.

Hers was not the fate of so many women of Hellas who had to endure the news of their loved one's death and the more awful thought that their bodies lay unburied upon a foreign shore where no loving hands could bathe them and prepare them for their long journey after death. Clytemnestra had not shared her sisters' fortunes. She had not spent ten loveless years awaiting the possible return of her lord. During all this time her hatred of Agamemnon had rankled and festered in her violent heart. She loathed him even to the sound of his name.

Ten years before, when the gods had prevented the starving Greeks from setting sail for Troy, the warriors in compliance with the wishes of

Artemis had demanded a human sacrifice. Agamemnon as their king and the leader of the expedition had yielded and reluctantly summoned his own young daughter Iphigenia under the pretense of marrying her to Achilles. There she had been sacrificed as Polyxena was later offered to the gods at Troy. Because of the loss of Iphigenia, Clytemnestra had hated Agamemnon.

All this time she and her lover Aegisthus, who was a cousin of the king, had planned a royal welcome. The sharpened ax that Clytemnestra would swing down upon Agamemnon's skull stood ready just inside the bath. The woven, intricate carpets of Tyrian purple more valuable than gold were ready to be spread between his chariot and the door. Clytemnestra had, folded and ready also, the swathing robe of royal purple she would throw around him so that with its folds enveloping his hands and arms he would never be able to defend himself.

Amidst shouts of welcome the chariot of Agamemnon rolled through the Lion Gate and up to the portal, followed by another splendid one in which stood the princess of Troy, Cassandra. Before her eyes the future was clear and unconfused, only one picture left. Ever since her awakening that morning there had been no more scenes of horror before her eyes except the last one of her death. Her ears were clear from shrieks and groans. There was no sound at all except the false welcoming words of the yellow-faced Clytemnestra. As if from far away Cassandra heard her arguing with her husband. She realized that Agamemnon had finally yielded, that he was allowing his sandals to be removed, that he had agreed to tread upon her crimson carpet royally.

Then Agamemnon, in disregard of protocol, turned to Cassandra's chariot and helped her to descend. Once more she felt the strong, warm touch of his hand. Smiling to his courtiers and friends, Agamemnon entered the portal first, followed by Cassandra.

There was a silent pause while he allowed his wife to shroud him in the crimson gown. Then the cortege advanced majestically into the central courtyard.

The evil distorted face of Clytemnestra did not frighten Cassandra, for she had grown used to it in her dreams. In her last moments she concentrated on Hector. At the thought of him whom she would see so soon, her eyes filled with tears.

With yellow teeth bared in her mighty effort to swing the ax powerfully, Clytemnestra brought it down across the head of Agamemnon who fell heavily to the floor waving his arms to disengage them. As Clytemnestra's ax struck Cassandra and she fell gratefully, she saw one last thing she had never noticed in her dreams. As she fell dying, Cassandra saw the hand of Agamemnon raised to save her.

FIVE
PERSIA AND
AFGHANISTAN

The extensive legends of Persia were collected by one poet and rewritten by him over a period of more than thirty years. Modern scholars have found from their own research that these stories are faithful retellings of much older material taken from Pahlavi or Middle Persian sources. The poet's name was Firdausi, and he lived from 941 to 1019.

The *Shah Namah*, or *Book of Kings*, of Firdausi covers the history of Persia over a total period of 3,874 years, or from 3223 B.C. to the Mohammedan conquest of Persia in A.D. 651. In the *Shah Namah* we are given the names of the rulers of Persia, whose reigns are divided into four dynasties.

There are several obstacles to the reconciliation of these dynastic lists with the Western beliefs concerning Persia. The greatest difficulty is one of names and the people or places to which the names refer. The territories of Persia varied extensively over its long history from a small area west of the Persian Gulf to the empire of Darius with its twenty satrapies, which included parts of northern Greece and Africa, all of Asia Minor and the Middle East through Afghanistan, and extended into India on the east and China on the north. It would be difficult to say at what time separate dynasties were coruling in these wide domains, and only an extensive knowledge of all the dozens of lost and half-forgotten languages of these many and varied peoples could hope to straighten the tangle of references. Another difficulty is one of geography, particularly for the westerner.

The ancient Persians looked about them from the central plain of Iran and concluded that the earth was encircled by mountains, a theory similar to that of the Greeks who had decided that it was surrounded by the waters of a stream they called Oceanus. Persia is, indeed, practically surrounded by mountain ranges. The poet Firdausi followed ancient tradition in calling all of them the "Elburz." Modern scholars of Persia, such as Professor James Darmesteter of the Collège de France, have struggled to be more specific.

As far as Persia is concerned, people there have less of a problem. They are not bound by the writings of Herodotus as we are. We speak of their kings by Western names, which were given by the Greeks— Darius, Cyrus, Cambyses, and Xerxes. Persians recognize their own kings by their Persian names, and they regard the *Shah Namah* of Firdausi as verbatim truth.

Occasionally the Western and Eastern views of Persia's history almost coincide. If in the celebrated account of Cyrus the Great as told by Herodotus, we substitute wherever he says "Media" or "Mede" the Persian word of "Turan" or "Turanian," the two versions are substantially the same. Early Western geographers and Matthew Arnold supposed Turan to have been east of the Caspian Sea, and have talked about battles along the Oxus (Amu Darya) River. Since Firdausi did not commit himself, more recent scholars believe that his Turan referred to the highly contested area in the Caucasus west of the Caspian Sea.

The Persians performed one of their last great deeds in the ancient world by stopping the eastward expansion of the Roman Empire and by taking prisoner the Emperor Valerius himself. By A.D. 651 they were conquered by the Arabs, as the *Shah Namah* predicts, and converted to Mohammedanism. Followers of the Persian religion of Zoroaster fled to India where they live today as the Parsees. Fortunately the old history of Persia did not die entirely, thanks to the lifework of the patriotic Firdausi, who was born in the city of Tus near Meshad in eastern Iran where some of his story takes place.

The following chapter is a condensation of Book I and about half of Book II of the *Shah Namah*. The entire poem is 60,000 couplets long, an unbelievable feat for one poet. Four translations have been used:

1. French	Jules de Mohl	prose	7 vols.	3,500 pp.*
2. Italian	Italo Pizzi	poetry	8 vols.	4,000 pp.*
3. English	George and Edmond Warner	poetry	9 vols.	4,500 pp.*
4. English	Atkinson abridgment	prose	1 vol.	412 pp.

* *Approximate figures.*

The poem has been partially translated into German, and other fragmentary translations have been done.

Western readers know the *Shah Namah* from Matthew Arnold's superb poem "Sohrab and Rustum." Arnold was accused by a contemporary of having plagiarized Jules de Mohl's French translation which was announced to the public by none other than Sainte-Beuve. However, Arnold's poem was printed in 1853, and the de Mohl translation appeared only in 1876. Arnold's source was Sir John Malcolm's *History of Persia*. Arnold said, "For my part, I only regret that I could not meet with a translation from Firdausi's poem. . . . I should certainly have made all the use I could of it."

The modern lover of Persian poetry must give homage where it is due—to the pioneer work of Jules de Mohl, a professor at the Collège of France, whose long labors were interrupted by the Revolution of 1848, so that he died without having finished his translation of the *Livre des rois*. One of the Warner brothers also died before the work was finished, but the other brother continued it alone. All of these scholars were most erudite men; in addition to Persian the Warners knew Hebrew, Syriac, and Arabic. Of all the translators, however, the Italian scholar Italo Pizzi, whose version appeared in 1886, is the most unreserved in his love for this great epic. He says that the poem from its very beginning gives one the impression of vastness like that of a starry sky which unites in its dazzling constellations the infinite plurality of the world. (*"L'epopea persiana, nel suo insieme, produce l'impressione dell' incommensurabile, simile alla vista del cielo stellato, che ruinisce nei suoi fulgidi sistemi di stelle l'infinita pluralità dei mondi."*) He felt that there is no other country in the world that has such a rich poetic treasure as Persia. (*"Non vi ha forse in tutto il mondo paese più ricco della Persia in leggende eroiche."*)

The American admirer of Persian poetry may remember one of our great scholars, Professor A. V. Williams Jackson who wrote four splendid books on Persia, who visited Iran in 1903, 1907, 1910, and 1918, who swung on a goat's-hair rope down the side of Mount Behistun to verify the cuneiform translations which Rawlinson had made of Darius the Great's trilingual inscription. Professor Jackson was a Columbia graduate and a professor at that university from 1883 to his death on August 8, 1937. No westerner ever loved Persia more than did this great scholar. He has also left us in his book *Early Persian Poetry* several translations of the same material the reader will find in the following pages. Professor Jackson's very beautiful poetry is the only one I know that follows the style of Firdausi, rhyming couplets of tetrameter verse with anapaestic feet prevailing.

Firdausi has been compared to Homer, to Chaucer, to Layamon, and to the author of the *Beowulf* epic. While all of these comparisons have some grain of truth, it seems rather that there is no work in the western world of such length and completeness. Our epics are episodes by comparison.

The government of Iran assures us that even children in the streets of Teheran know whole chapters of the *Shah Namah* by heart. The reader may be interested to know that Columbia University possesses two manuscripts of this work. One from the sixteenth century is in book form with a dark red, lacquered cover and a Persian design of roses and lilies. Unbelievably beautiful, it has many full-page illustrations, hand-painted in brilliant colors and with brush strokes so fine that they show every blade of grass and even the hairs in Rustam's eyebrows.

THE COMING OF RUSTAM

By 2400 B.C. the ancient land of Sumer, the oldest in Mesopotamia, began to be invaded by Semitic warriors whose original homeland may have been Arabia. These fierce invaders, known to us as the Akkadians, swept down over the Tigris and Euphrates valleys under their great King Sargon, as the Amorites under the lawgiver Hammurabi, and as the Assyrians. The Assyrian empire furnished the idea and pattern for later conquests and the organization of conquered nations. According to western historians, the Assyrian kings ruled in unparalleled cruelty and savagery a vast realm that extended from western Egypt across Arabia, through Babylon and eastward toward the Indus River and the great mountain ranges of central Asia. Western historians date their hated conquests and their mass deportations of subject peoples—such as that of the Ten Tribes of the Jews in 721 B.C.—from the fall of Babylon in 910 B.C. to the battle of Carchemish in 612 B.C.

Now, the battle of Carchemish was fought in Syria, a little to the west of the headwaters of the Euphrates, near the Amanus Mountains where Gilgamesh had sought his precious cedars. To this westward spot, close to 300 miles away from the Assyrian capital at Nineveh, near the northern reaches of the Tigris, were the Assyrian wolves driven.

They were defeated by the learned Chaldeans of Babylon, who hired and persuaded Asiatic tribesmen—bigger, more savage, and more warlike, mounted on swifter horses—to hunt down and utterly annihilate the Assyrians. These tribesmen were the Medes and Scythians (Persians and Bactrians) from Iran. From that day onward in history the story of these Asiatic tribesmen has of necessity, and by all rights, also to be heard and considered.

The ancient land of Iran, say the Persians, extended from the Zagros Mountains and the Persian Gulf on the west to the Hindu Kush Mountains and the Indus River on the east. It reached northward on the western shores of the Caspian Sea up to the Caucasus Mountains of what is today the Azerbaidzhan Soviet Socialist Republic. On the eastern shores of the Caspian its borders reached into Turan, or well into the modern province of the Turkmen S.S.R.

This vast tableland of Iran was settled by Asiatic tribesmen whose name was "Aryan," or "noble." They had all come originally from the area of Balkh in the northern province of what is today Afghanistan. From Balkh, this "beautiful city of high flags," successive migrations spread southward from the shores of the Amu Darya River into the Land of the Seven Rivers (the Punjab) and into India.

A second and third wave of peoples moved slowly southwestward across the high plateau of Asia, or Iran. There they may be identified as the Medes who settled the south shores of the Caspian and built their capital of Ecbatana halfway between the Tigris River and the Elburz Mountains. A second group called Iranians or Persians settled in the area along the Persian Gulf in the land of the Elamites, and their capital was at Susa. The remaining Aryans continued to occupy eastern Iran or the area around Balkh and Herat, the capital of modern Afghanistan. Leaving aside for the moment those Aryans who invaded India, we find that the three kingdoms of ancient Iran were Media and Persia in the west and Balkh, or Bactria, in the east.

The first king, say the eastern historians, was Yama who ruled at about 3500 B.C. from the city of Balkh. He explained the science of agriculture to his people and the use of metals. With the latter knowledge they forged arms, mounted their horses, and set out to conquer the "eastern and western hemispheres." The horse was one of their great contributions to the western world. This King Yama is also mentioned in the sacred *Avesta* and in the *Vedas* of India. He founded the Peshdadian Dynasty, which was followed by the Kava or "Wise" Dynasty. The third dynasty of Balkh was called Aspa from its founder Lahra-Aspa, or Lord of Swift Horses. During the reign of the third Aspa king, around 1000 B.C., the great prophet Zarathustra appeared in Balkh.

This prophet converted the King Gusht-Aspa to his way of thinking. Zarathustra said that religion should be a practical way of life, that each man should be able to choose light from darkness, right from wrong, good from evil. He said a man should apply his powers of reasoning directly to the problems of his life and distinguish clearly by his own powers of thought the beauty of pure and abstract truth. The thinking of Zarathustra appeared in the five books of the *Avesta* which were carried into Hind, or India, by the Aryans of Balkh. Fire temples of the Zoroastrian religion were constructed throughout Iran from Kabulistan in the east to Mazinderan on the Caspian Sea.

The second group of Iranians were the Medes. One remembers them in western history for their wise priests or magi. Three of the magi are said to have traveled once, much later, bearing gold, frankincense, and myrrh, to Bethlehem in Judaea. Their journey, which had been foretold by the prophet of Iran, Zoroaster, was made possible by the light of a star which showed them the way to Bethlehem and also guided their homeward journey to northern Iran. The descendants of the Medes worshiped fire and lived in modern times in Kurdistan in the southern Caucasus. It was here that Zeus had chained the fire-bearing Prometheus. It was to this same area also that Jason sailed in search of the Golden Fleece and the Dragon Queen, Medea.

According to the Persians, the third group of Aryan people who finally became all-powerful in Iran, their first king was Kauimers. He gave them a code of laws and ruled them for thirty years, or from about 3600 B.C. Then came King Husheng whose reign lasted for forty years. After him ruled a glorious king named Tahumers, who destroyed a great many wicked magi, or evil demons, in Media.

The reign of Jemshid, fourth shah of Iran, lasted for 700 years. In Indian and Afghan tradition he is identified with Yama. This king constructed a *var*, or huge underground palace, in anticipation of the flood that would destroy the earth. Like a bright shepherd he ruled over the seven climatic zones of the earth and divided all his subjects into four castes, thus making the rulers and warriors distinct from the artisans and peasants. Jemshid built a throne at Persepolis, a platform adorned with forty columns each sixty feet high. It was upon this platform that the splendid white palaces of his successors could rise proud and gleaming in the southern plain. To this stronghold King Vishtaspa of Balkh later sent the gold-embossed original copy of the *Avesta;* and here it was burned, along with the palace of Persepolis, in one of Alexander I's drunken orgies.

The rule of Jemshid, so gloriously begun, ended in a darkness that was to last a thousand years. Iran was conquered and Jemshid killed. The conquerors were relatives of the same Semitic warriors from the Tigris-Euphrates valleys to the west of Iran. For a thousand years their awesome king, named Zahhak in eastern tradition, lorded it over the Medes and the Persians. The Assyrians also advanced toward the third kingdom, or Bactria, and besieged the city of Balkh with an army of two million men. Eventually this last stronghold capitulated to them.

The despotic king named Zahhak had come, according to Persian tradition, from Arabia. His capital was in Babylon. From his great palace he ordered tribute from all of Iran, thousands of stallions and tens of thousands of Persian lambs. For a thousand years the heroes of Persia dreamed of unseating this monstrous, three-nosed, triple-skulled, six-eared foreigner. They also thought about liberating and possessing his two wives who were reputed to be beauties of unequaled charms.

Finally, at the end of the thousand years, a dragon king named Feridun was born in Persia. After good advice, aided by the blacksmith Kava, and escorted by a vast army reinforced with elephants, Feridun conquered Zahhak. Winding him in fetters of lion's hide, he carried the tyrant to Mount Damavand. There in a cave on this more than 19,000-foot mountain he bound him eternally for eleven millennia to come. He was wise enough not to kill Zahhak, for from his severed body would have crept toads and frogs, and other loathsome creatures. Feridun then proceeded to rule all of Iran for 500 years.

The next shah of Iran was Minuchir, son of Manu, who reigned for

120 years. This ruler gave the southeastern part of his realm—over toward the Indus River, Seistan and Zabulistan—to the command of a great hero named Sam. The hero blessed the shah, wished him a long and prosperous reign, swore to defeat all the enemies of Iran, and left the coronation ceremonies homeward bound for Seistan. His capital lay near a lake into which the Helmand River, which rises near the Khyber Pass, brings its waters after its 700-mile journey. Sam would have been perfectly happy, for the land was delivered of Assyrian rule, and a good shah was on the ivory throne. One sorrow grieved him deeply. He had no son to follow in his footsteps.

It was with great secret joy that he learned upon his return to Seistan that one of his wives, a lovely beauty with a gentle face like a moon and long, curling ringlets, was expecting a child shortly. Soon after Sam's return a baby was born, but the palace women did not dare to show it to him. It was a very lusty baby with pink cheeks, bright eyes, and strong limbs. But its hair was the color of snow, and so were its eyelashes. For several days the palace women tried to decide what to do.

Finally one of them courageously lifted the beautifully swaddled baby and bore him directly to Sam. "Great warrior, rejoice," she told him. "You have a strong son to follow in your hero's trade. He is a boy fashioned of the whitest silver. Even his hair is silver! Therefore, hero, give thanks to our Maker who willed it thus!"

Sam glanced only once at the child and motioned for him to be taken away. He realized sadly that he would be an object of ridicule throughout Persia with a son whose locks were white with old age. Sternly Sam commanded that the baby Zal be carried to a lonely mountain in India where rise the loftiest peaks on earth. Here the luckless infant was exposed to die, naked. His father never thought of him again because he knew it must have been the Median demons who had played such a trick on him in order to ruin his otherwise terrifying reputation.

Many years later Sam, perhaps because he was beginning to feel in his bones the first signs of old age, dreamed of Zal, his snowy-haired son. In his dream a caravan laboring northward out of India brought him word that the boy was still alive. When Sam recounted his dream to the magi priests of his palace, they berated him sharply. They told him that even the wild animals of the desert care more for their young than Iranian heroes. They said if Zal had been born to a leopard, that animal would have shielded him from the burning sun and let him nestle close to her at night. The priests advised Sam to spend the rest of his days searching for Zal, if need be. They gave him, however, one word of comfort, saying that the Creator would never let perish from either heat or cold one whom he loved. Sam was sorely ashamed, for looking at his own graying head, he no longer had any such reason to despise a white-haired son.

Calling around him a large band of warriors, Sam galloped away across the Punjab and into India. There on a lofty peak he made out a large bird's nest. It belonged to the simurgh, the fabled bird who nursed her young from breasts like a bat's, while she spread her ruby wings around them to keep them warm. She had taken the baby Zal into her eyrie, had raised him among her young, and had loved him dearly. When Sam shaded his eyes and looked again toward the high black crag, he discerned a handsome youth standing on the rim of the gabled nest. Then the warrior Sam prayed as he had never done in battle, for there was no possible way to scale the rock needle, no way at all.

Fortunately the devoted simurgh, looking down from her unassailable crag, saw the richly dressed paladins of Persia. Saying good-by to her beloved Zal, the kind bird carried him to earth and set him at his father's feet. Zal's eyes were full of tears, for though she had taught him the speech of men, he had never seen a man before. Zal reproached the simurgh for returning him to his father. Then because she loved the boy, the radiant bird plucked out one of her brilliant scarlet feathers. Giving it to Zal, she said, "You will also be my child always. If you ever need me, if you are ever betrayed or in great danger, burn this feather. Then I will fly to your aid at once."

With tears in his eyes Sam thanked the simurgh for having nursed his son with her red milk, and he begged the stalwart Zal to forgive him. Before all the noble paladins of Persia he swore solemnly that he would always treat Zal gently, and that he would allow the boy to rule him in every way that would bring about his son's happiness.

Great was Sam's joy and his heart full to bursting as he saw how the bearded warriors of Iran greeted his son. They walked about Zal marveling at his broad shoulders, his well-developed thighs, his sturdy body. They praised his clear eyes and his hand that seemed so apt to grasp the Indian scimitar. Black silken trousers were brought for him, a gold-brocade tunic, a wide belt, and a dagger. His long, white hair flowing over his shoulders, Zal mounted an Arab steed, and then the whole company set out for Zabul and Seistan.

Before them the drummers kept up an exciting rhythm from their perches on the lead elephants. Clarions sounded. Golden gongs and bells from India shrilled the news far and wide. In his palace at Amul the shah Minuchir heard the glad news and sent a courier posthaste to offer Sam his congratulations. This horseman was followed by a caravan laden with gifts from the shah to Zal—slaves bearing silver platters, loaded high with emeralds and turquoises, Arab horses with golden furnishings, rich carpets from Kerman, suits of armor, brocade cloaks with wide golden belts, bows and arrows, and a gleaming signet ring.

Then Sam entrusted all his kingdom to Zal, for the warrior had been commanded by the shah to exterminate a vulture-headed tribe that were robbing and pillaging the shah's domains in Mazinderan, the land of the Medes. Sam left Zal the key to his treasuries and full powers to govern as he pleased during his father's absence. After a sincere exchange of compliments and long farewells, the trumpets sounded, the drums rolled, and Sam set out for war. Zal watched his father's army march out of the city gates until the whole plain beyond was a cloud of dust from their thundering hoofs. Then he sat upon his ivory throne, took counsel with the elders, and ruled Seistan, Hind, and Zabulistan wisely and well. Everyone praised his judgment and respected him so much that they would have sworn his white locks were as black as ebony.

One day Zal decided to travel forth from Seistan and see the vast lands that he was governing. To the north of his capital lay a great city called Kabul. It was a picturesque spot because of the Hindu Kush Mountains that rose to snow-capped peaks behind it. Here reigned a powerful and wealthy potentate named Mihrab who was descended from the hated Assyrian conqueror Zahhak. His domains were not powerful enough to allow him to raise an army against Sam, and so Mihrab contented himself with paying tribute and accepting Sam as his overlord. When news reached Mihrab that the newly found Zal was going to pay him a visit, coming in a lordly procession with minstrels and harpists for the sole purpose of travel and diversion, he ordered his city made festive to receive the youth. Then Mihrab prepared rich gifts—caparisoned thoroughbreds, slave boys, gold coins, spices, and furs—and set out richly dressed to meet Zal's troupe. When Mihrab saw the new prince's cavalcade on the horizon, he and his noble Semitic chiefs dismounted and, leading their horses, advanced on foot toward Zal. Then, kneeling, they kissed the ground and awaited his greeting.

Zal was highly gratified by this proper reception. The youth was in holiday mood. He and Mihrab sat down to a sumptuous feast. Mihrab regaled his guests with dancers and music. The wine cups were kept filled to the brims. Zal discussed his realms learnedly and judiciously, and Mihrab thought to himself, "This is indeed a witty as well as a wise, young ruler. I have apparently nothing to fear from him. Surely his mother was immortal like the phoenix herself."

Flushed with wine and overjoyed to be traveling alone so royally and seeing his rich domains, Zal reflected also upon the grace and manners of his host. "No wonder the Semites ruled Iran so long," he thought. "This Mihrab is a prince. I have never seen a more handsome man. He is tall and as slender as a poplar. His shoulders are broad, his waist narrow, his fingers nervous for the scimitar, and his manners impeccable."

While Zal was inwardly admiring the Semitic Mihrab, one of the noble chieftains at the banquet whispered in Zal's ear, "Noble paladin, this Mihrab has within his palace a beauty such as mortal eyes see once in all a generation of women. This is his daughter Rudabah! She is descended from the fabled beauties of Zahhak's court. Her portrait hangs in every court from Hind all the way to the China Sea. The lords of Turan sigh as they gaze upon such loveliness. The great master of the easternmost world, the Khan of Chin, dreams of possessing her.

"Her skin is fairer than the palest ivory which gleams in a starlit hall at Persepolis. When you smell the pungent musk, that is the very perfume of her hair. Her ringlets fall to her feet in curls so wide that they would make you an ankle bracelet. Her lips are red as cherries and her glowing cheeks as pink as the sun-kissed pomegranate. Her slender nose is like burnished silver. She is tall as a teak tree growing in a Chinese garden, and as slender as the cypress. Her silver breasts have in their centers two ruby buds as rosy as pomegranate seeds. If you were to see her, you would swear you were in paradise where angels sing with nightingales and all is music and delight."

All night long Zal could not sleep but sat in his golden tent gazing upon the moonlit river and imagining the glowing face of Rudabah. When the first rays of the sun had turned the land of Kabul to crystal, Mihrab came again to pay his respects to his guest. Courteously he asked Zal what he could do to satisfy his desires.

Zal answered that he invited Mihrab and his court to visit him in Seistan. The proud Mihrab replied that this alone he could not grant. "Your father Sam would never allow it," he replied. "Nor would he approve our drinking together until late at night, or your sitting here at Kabul among our Semitic idols." Then since Zal's religion and customs were different from his, Mihrab refrained from praising the Persian lord overmuch.

Zal, on the other hand, quite beside himself with love for the fair Rudabah whom he had not even seen, praised Mihrab and his court so much that the lord of Kabul began to relent and treat the young Zal with less suspicion.

In the palace of Kabul, Queen Sindukht and her daughter nervously awaited Mihrab's return. They hoped all had gone well, for the might of Sam could crush their kingdom like a blade of straw in his left hand. "How is this young lord?" Sindukht questioned anxiously. "Does he resemble some nestling of the mountain peaks? Does he walk like a ruler, or like a fledgling bird?"

"Why, silver lady," replied Mihrab, "he treads the earth like a Persian paladin, with steps so large no other lord except his father could fit his slippers into them. In battle he is as fierce as a crocodile, snapping off heads with one blow of his steely blade. Mounted on his galloping charger, you would say he was a horned dragon. His hands are as encompassing as the branches of the River Nile. He has a lion's heart like a true Persian and the son of a hero, and the shrewdness of an elephant. When he surmounts his turquoise throne and scatters gold on every side of him, you would think him as mighty as the shah. His eye is wise and thoughtful, and on his cheeks the handsome bloom of youth. There is only this one defect in him: his hair is as white as snow."

Mihrab was exceedingly unwise to speak such words before his daughter. The great teachers of the East have often said: "Refrain from describing masculine beauty when women are within earshot. In the heart of every female lurks a living devil. If you only suggest, a woman will search out the way. When desire enters a woman's heart, wisdom flies out the window."

The lovely Rudabah hurried to her chambers completely inflamed with love. She clapped her hands for the five serving girls who had come to her as a gift from the northern province of Turkestan. To them she confided her passion. "I shall not sleep," she cried. "Do you hear me? I cannot eat, I am sure. You must help me out of my distress. I am in love with the lord of our lands, the princely Zal!"

Her damsels were aghast at such folly. They implored her to listen to reason. "Your portrait has been sent even to the great Semitic rulers who dwell in far-off Palestine," they reminded her. "You cannot marry a Persian, a man of another religion and customs, and even more, your father's lord! Think too of your beauty. How could a peerless maiden like yourself wish to wed the nursling of a bird? You have not even seen this lord of Seistan! His hair is as white as that of an aged man! And besides, this Zal could never marry you! What would the warrior Sam say? What would the shah of Persia say? Why, he would bury you in sand up to your ears!"

Furious with love and anger, Rudabah screamed at them, "What do I care about his face or his hair? I am in love with *him!* No other man shall ever stir my heart as he has done. Do you understand? What I have just said are not light words but an oath! If I told you that I wanted to eat mud in the dark Underworld, would you offer me roses instead? Perhaps he is neither tall nor dark-haired! He is tall enough for me. He is handsome enough for me. He will give me peace in the burning depths of my passion. Talk not of any other man. The princely Zal alone will bring me peace in my body and peace in my soul!"

Then the maidens of Turkestan took counsel and swore to Rudabah that they would use all their foreign arts of guile and even of magic, and that they would bring Zal to her feet. They urged her to remain hidden in her chambers, to be patient, and to count on them. Above all, they cautioned her not to let her parents guess her secret desire.

Rudabah promised to be discreet. She told them that her love with Zal would be like a lofty tree that dropped precious rubies on the grass instead of petals, as long as she should live.

The slave girls dressed themselves in the five hues of spring and ran toward the rose garden that lay beside the river. On the opposite bank they could see the royal tents of Zal's encampment. Laughing and chattering loud enough so that their shrill voices would carry across the water, they began to gather roses. Slowly they wandered closer and closer to the stream's edge. There on the banks they bent to gather violets. Soon they saw Zal, attracted by their laughing voices, stroll along the opposite bank with his bow and arrows in hand, and attended by a single slave boy. When Zal saw a water bird on their side of the stream, he shot it so that it fell near them. Then he sent his boy across the water to fetch the fowl.

The girls called to the slave boy and began to converse with him. "Tell us," they teased him coyly. "Who is that handsome warrior whose aim is unerring?"

"That is my master, Zal of Persia, a sun for radiance and beauty," he told them.

"Go and tell your master," confided the slave girls, "that if he is the sun in all his radiance, we have within our palace the beauteous moon herself. Surely the sun and the moon should meet on the silken cushions of love."

Zal's heart leaped when he heard their message. Ordering them to await his return, he rushed to his tent and had five lengths of golden brocade prepared as gifts for them, and coins and jewels. When the slave boy carried the presents to the girls, he warned them, "My master says if you are faithful, you are like to find jewels often among the roses of his garden."

The slave girls exchanged knowing looks as if to say that a princely lion of Iran was not so hard to enmesh in their silken coils. Then Zal called the maidens to him and inquired about Rudabah. "Tell me the truth about your mistress," he commanded. "If you lie to me, I shall have you trampled by my elephants!"

The slave girls knelt and kissed the earth at his feet. Then the youngest and prettiest of them spoke to Zal. "Our mistress is the very perfumed breath of spring flowers. She is a rose. She is as beautiful a woman as your father Sam is a matchless man, and almost as tall. She is a whole head taller than yourself. Her face is like a tulip when only one flower is blooming in a garden. She is as sweet as jasmine that blooms in the snow of winter." Then at his further questions they vouched for Rudabah's intelligence and education.

Neither Zal nor Rudabah could wait to see the other. Back and forth all day went the careful messengers who succeeded in not arousing the suspicions of the palace guards. All the arrangements were finally made. The following morning, just at the first hint of dawn, Zal stole silently to Rudabah's pavilion and called up to her balcony.

The night had been spent in feverish preparation in Rudabah's private chambers. Her whole pavilion had been hung with silken curtains and decorated with the portraits of great kings and heroes. A royal feast had been set out on low tables, and the roasts well marinated in rose water. Dancers and musicians stood ready for her summons. The room was gay with precious vases filled with all the perfumed flowers of the gardens of Kabul. Rich pink and blue carpets covered all the floors with their silky softness. Cushions of brilliant hues and rich fabrics were piled high on Rudabah's couch.

As soon as she heard Zal's voice, the princess of Kabul leaned over

her balcony, loosed her scarlet veil, and let her two long ringlets fall down to his feet. Then in soft words she begged him to climb up to her heart.

Zal tossed his lasso up to the parapet where it caught firmly. Then, hand over hand, he mounted and stood before Rudabah. She had not known that his eyes were blue, the color of lake water at sunrise. Hand in hand the lovers walked into her pavilion, blushing and speechless with joy. It was there that Zal whispered his eternal love to Rudabah. He vowed that neither torture nor death could ever make him unfaithful to her. The passionate Rudabah responded to his love in every detail. She also swore to him undying devotion.

While soft music played and the Indian dancers floated behind the gauze curtains, Zal and Rudabah spent their few moments together. As the first rays of sunlight fell upon their couch, the slave girls announced to them the coming day. Tearfully they parted, cheek from cheek, and hand from hand.

"O sun, could you not wait one minute more?" Rudabah called despairingly. "Please do not leave so soon," she whispered to Zal through her tears. Brushing his own tears from his eyes, Zal retied his lasso to the balustrade and descended. He strode toward his camp as if the strength of a hundred elephants were in his body. Masterful and imperious, he called a meeting in his tent, to which all the magi and wise men of Persia hastened to assemble. Briefly and succinctly he disclosed his situation to them and asserted his firm resolve to marry the lovely Rudabah. After some deliberation the counselors declared themselves unequal to such an affair of state, and they suggested that Zal inform his father at once.

Sam saw the messenger from Zabulistan as the rider approached his mountain camp. He had recognized from afar the white horses of Persia. When he had read his son's letter, written in the most ardent and yet respectful terms, Sam puzzled greatly. He was not surprised that his son, raised so far from civilization in the weird nest of the simurgh, should fall so violently in love. Shah Minuchir, who hated the Semites most cordially, would naturally be furious. After Sam had slept on the matter—for considering himself bound by the oath he had made to Zal, he could make no hasty decision—he summoned his astrologers and bade them draw up horoscopes of Zal and Rudabah.

All day Sam waited while they prepared their information. Toward evening they approached him, and to his astonishment they were smiling broadly. "Great hero of the golden belt," they cried, "let us announce to you a most glorious event! The blessings of heaven are above our heads in Persia. Let your son Zal be wedded to Rudabah!"

"What have you found, O wise men?" Sam asked eagerly.

"We have seen the sign of an elephant, mighty Paladin. The land of Iran never saw his like. From your son Zal and the lady Rudabah there will be born a hero who shall carve on his ruby signet ring not only the lands of Iran and Hind! To them he shall add the western land of Greece. What is more, he will defeat our enemies from Turan, and drive them howling like jackals into the Turkestan deserts!"

Sam rose joyously and sent a messenger to Zal to say that he was leaving at once for the palace of the shah. Sam said in his letter that although this longed-for marriage had really nothing exceptional in its favor, yet was he bound by oath and would try to arrange something. Sam had a thousand prisoners bound and fettered to take along with him as a present to the shah.

As soon as Zal had received his father's message, he sent an old woman who had been acting as a liaison between him and Rudabah to tell his sweetheart that Sam had hemmed and hawed and finally given his consent. This time the old woman was not so clever, and she was caught by Sindukht with gifts up her sleeves from Rudabah to Zal. Sindukht made her daughter confess that she had a lover. At first, Sindukht was very angry and accused Rudabah of throwing herself from a palace into a ditch. Then when she heard that it was Zal of Persia whom she loved, Sindukht grew frantic with despair. She saw before her eyes the clouds of dust the shah would raise around her palace. Even when Rudabah assured her mother that Sam consented to the marriage, Sindukht was not reassured.

Her anger was nothing compared to the fury of Mihrab. He wanted to kill Rudabah immediately. "The shah of Iran does not even like me to mount my horse," he screamed. "Do you think he will let my own daughter rise to a throne in Persia? Look at this wretched child," he yelled. "I wish that I had strangled her at birth." Like a snarling leopard he pointed a shaking finger at Rudabah, who had not come to the audience humbly as her mother had suggested, but stood proudly before her father, dressed in gold brocade and wearing a ruby crown that Zal had smuggled to her.

Sam in the meantime had ridden hard to the palace of the shah, preferring to have their sovereign hear the news from himself directly. Minuchir received him well. All during the feasting the shah listened avidly to Sam's victories up north in Mazinderan. The following morning, however, when Sam broached the question of Zal's marriage, the shah's wrath was terrible to hear. He ordered Sam to horse immediately. His mission was to proceed at once to Kabul. There he was to burn the palace to the ground, to kill Mihrab, his Queen Sindukht, and also Rudabah. The news of the sentence traveled fast. All of Kabul was in an uproar of terror.

Zal also heard of the shah's order. Pale and determined, he rode out to meet his father. On every hand his courtiers advised him, "You have embarrassed your father. Your father is angry. He has reason to be displeased with you. Be humble. Forget Rudabah. She is lost. All is lost!"

Zal answered them all quietly, "What should I fear? Man's only end is dust. Without Rudabah why should I care to live at all?" He greeted his father lovingly, and all the time as they rode side by side toward their palace at Seistan, tears rolled down Zal's cheeks.

In the evening he spoke alone to his father. "What are your quarrels with the Assyrian to me? I am the nursling of an Indian bird, no son of yours. You never rocked me gently in a cradle. You never let me feel my mother's tender arms. You sent me naked to a distant mountain. You deprived me of my childhood, and also of love. It was my Maker who caused my hair to be white. It was no sin of mine. Before the simurgh you promised to help me be happy. Here I stand before you. Do whatever your wrath dictates against me. Only know that whatever you say or do against Kabul, you do and say to me."

Sam's heart was touched. He called the scribes and dictated a long letter to the shah in which he carefully inserted a reference, toward the end, to the effect that it might be better for him and Zal to attack Amul, the shah's palace, rather than the Assyrian Kabul. In the morning he sent Zal himself with the letter, for the shah had never seen the boy. After Zal, desperate with love, had spurred out of the palace, Sam sat alone and reflected on how much more difficult it was to be a father than a hero.

In Kabul, Mihrab pondered the harsh exigencies of fate. There was no warrior in his city who would dare to lift a mace to Sam. The only thing that Mihrab could think of to do was to execute Sindukht and Rudabah publicly. Several times he was on the point of putting his daughter to death, and yet he realized that this would be no solution either if what she swore about Zal's love and Sam's consent was actually true. In calmer moments too he savored the sweetness of the revenge if by some chance Rudabah managed to marry this Persian hero. Then would Assyrian blood be close to the throne of Persia, perhaps for a second thousand years.

While Mihrab was debating what course he should best follow, his wife Sindukht, laboring now to save herself and her child from death, proposed another solution. "Why not try buying our lives, my husband?" she inquired.

"Who would dare mention such a solution to Sam?" he retorted impatiently.

"I would dare it," replied Sindukht seriously. As she spoke, she folded her arms gravely across her silver breasts and looked the very picture of courage. "Entrust to me the key to all your hoarded wealth," she demanded.

Mihrab was struck with the daring of her proposition. Without grumbling or even regretting the treasure, he watched her prepare it for Sam. She took 300,000 pieces of gold, 30 horses with silver saddles, 60 slaves bearing golden goblets filled with jewels and rare perfumes, 100 red-haired camels, 100 baggage mules, a jeweled crown suitable for a shah, a gold and inlaid throne as high as a mounted horseman, and 4 Indian elephants loaded with precious carpets and bales of materials. All this she dispatched in haste to the warrior Sam.

Then Sindukht dressed herself in trousers, belted tunic, and helmet like an Iranian warrior. Once she was astride a long-legged stallion you would have thought her a youthful paladin as she spurred her horse as fast as he could gallop along the dusty road to Seistan. She overtook her caravan at the gates of Sam's palace, from which it stretched two miles along the track. Imperiously Sindukht requested an audience with Sam who sat bemused upon his ivory throne. Sindukht took off her helmet so that her gleaming black hair set off her face to best advantage. Advancing with the light tread of a pheasant, she kissed the earth at his feet and begged him to accept the treasure.

Sam couldn't imagine who she was or what he was to do. Should he commit himself by accepting? If he refused, then there would be Zal to deal with. Then Zal would reproach him and flop around weeping like the simurgh herself. "Very well, Messenger," he finally acceded. "We accept the treasure in the name of our son Zal." Sindukht's spirits rose, for the old warrior was now committed.

"Your words have made me young again," smiled Sindukht. "Now may I beg of you why you wish to destroy Kabul? It is Mihrab who was to blame for letting these children meet in his palace, and he has been weeping blood for his fault these many weeks. Please do not punish the innocent, great warrior."

While she was talking, Sam sat watching her narrowly through half-closed lids and stroking his silken beard. "Tell me, lady, if you are not by some chance the wife of Mihrab herself," he asked.

"If you will first swear never to injure me or my family, I will reveal my identity to you, great paladin," she answered swiftly.

With a half smile on his lips and a twinkling eye, for Sam dearly loved quick wits, he extended his hand to her. Solemnly they shook hands, and Sindukht fell and kissed the floor at his feet gratefully.

"O, paladin of Persia," she continued without daring to lift her head, "I am the wife of Mihrab and the mother of Rudabah. If you will spare our lives, I swear that we will praise your name forever."

"Never fear, lady," answered Sam. "I admire your courage. I shall uphold the pledge I just made even if it is to cost me my life. You have my word. Zal shall marry this priceless moon, your daughter Rudabah.

"My son has already gone—not gone, but rather flown like a bird to the shah with a letter. The shah will eventually give his consent, I think, just to be rid of Zal, if for nothing else. My son sighs and weeps so that he is forever standing in a puddle of mud caused by his own tears. The shah will be relieved to be rid of such a dismal companion. As for you, lady, you have the kind of spirit that would make you a good grandmother to my grandson."

Sindukht waited deferentially while the old man mused, "I have seen things in my life," he continued. "I have seen the Assyrians fall and the lowly elevated. It will do my old heart good to see this fabled beauty

of yours. They say she is a very moon. I have heard that her ringlets are so wide they would make anklets. Of course, she has the blood of the Assyrian dragon in her veins. Even so," he mused, "I long to see the mother of my grandchild."

Then Sindukht answered him warmly, for she could see he had no more hate in his heart for the Assyrian. "If I were to bring such a king as you into Kabul, my daughter's head would reach the skies." The next day Sam granted Sindukht leave to return to Kabul with her good news.

In the meantime Zal had hastened to the court of Persia where he was well received as befitted the son of the shah's most renowned warrior. The shah had secret horoscopes drawn up regarding the proposed marriage, and having heard the exciting prognostication, had privately decided to give his consent. However, before doing so he subjected the boy Zal to several tests to determine his fitness for marriage and the responsibilities of such a position.

In solemn audience the wise men of Persia asked Zal the following questions:

1. What are the dozen cypresses decorated with thirty boughs?

2. What are the two horses, one crystal and one pitch, that try in vain to overtake each other?

3. What are the thirty attendants of our king, who seem to be twenty-nine but always count off to be thirty?

4. What is the meadow where a fierce reaper cuts ripe and withered grass alike and hears no cry of despair?

5. What are the two trees, one withered and one green, to which a solitary bird flies? What is the bird that nests on one in the morning and on the other in the evening?

6. What citizens preferred a thornbrake to a highly fortified city, a preference they will regret one day when the earth quakes?

Zal was allowed to think before giving his answers. All the courtiers awaited the results of his examination. Finally he replied:

"The twelve cypresses are the twelve moons, each with thirty days.

"The two horses are day and night, which gallop fast but never overtake each other.

"The thirty attendants of our shah are the phases of the moon, one of which from time to time escapes observation.

"Time is the mower in your field who cuts down the old and the young alike, and respects no plea.

"One tree is the lighter, summer season and the other the darker or wintertime. The bird is the sun which alternates between one and the other.

"The citizens of the swamp are ourselves who live, whether we prefer it or not, in this wayside inn of life. The city we have lost is our life's work, which is more often than not usurped by others. It will do us no good in time of danger to regret our past achievements. All we can hope to keep on earth is our good name. No one of us is born for anything but death. We enter life by one door and leave by another while time counts our every breath."

On the morning following his highly acclaimed examination, Zal presented himself before the shah. He was dressed for the road and requested permission to depart, alleging that he was very anxious to see his father. The shah only congratulated him on his interrogation, smiled, and answered that he had other plans for the day. The shah even expressed his incredulity, suspecting that Zal was not really that impatient to see his father. The whole day was spent in a magnificent tournament where Zal displayed his horsemanship, his skill, his fearlessness, and his respect for the shah. It was only on the following morning that he was allowed to return to his father.

The wedding of Zal and Rudabah took place at her home in Kabul with festivities that lasted four weeks. Mihrab and Sindukht had arrayed Rudabah in all the rest of their golden treasures and placed her on a throne in the pavilion where she had first met Zal. Sam and his son advanced toward the city royally attired. They were met by Mihrab, who dismounted as they approached. When Sam was formally escorted into Rudabah's chamber and saw her at last, he was overcome by her beauty and by his own emotion. Turning to Zal, Sam congratulated him on his choice and said that no princess in Persia had ever been so lovely.

After the long celebration the wedding party returned to Seistan. Rudabah entered her new capital riding in a silk-curtained couch. Almost at once Sam left again for war, and the young couple ruled together from the ivory throne. Very soon the news was carried to Sam that Rudabah was pregnant. The old warrior smiled to himself, for he knew of the wonderful son she would bear. He sent word that he would hasten to Seistan as soon as the child was old enough to be presented.

All was very far from well at Seistan, however. The body of the lovely Rudabah grew larger and larger. The nine months came and went without bringing a child. Sindukht in agony watched her daughter grow thin and weak. Finally Rudabah went into labor, but the child was too large and could not be delivered. Her screams filled the palace. Over her bed Sindukht tore her hair and cut her cheeks. Neither she nor any wise woman had a remedy. Rudabah screamed and pleaded, and grew weaker by the hour.

Then servants were sent to Zal to tell him that his princess was dying. He hastened to her rooms and saw that she was already unconscious. By this time the palace resounded with the wails of her attendants. Zal ordered them to be silent. He cleared the room and asked Sindukht to light a small fire in the censer. When the flames appeared, Zal held the simurgh's feather over them. Within a matter of seconds the great red bird flew into the curtained chamber, dripping pearls about her like droplets of peace. Zal asked the simurgh to save Rudabah, since this mother-bird had promised him one great favor. "Princess Rudabah is worth more than my life to me, dear bird," he explained.

The simurgh gave her counsel. "The birth of your son will be unnatural," she told Zal. "The Creator has not made him like ordinary mortals. He is an elephant for size, and a lion for courage.

"First you must give your lady the strongest wine you have in the palace. Then you must ask an arch-Mage to come to her. He is to carry a blue-steel dagger. While Rudabah sleeps, he must make an incision downward from the side of her waist, turn the child's head toward the cut line, and draw him carefully from her body. Then he must sew up the incision, cover it with the juice of certain herbs I will give you, and bandage her tightly. She will live to hold the child against her breast, after a day and night of sleep.

"Some fruits do not fall into the world naturally but have to be plucked from the golden bough of life's tree." With these cryptic words the simurgh flew back to India.

It was some minutes after the baby had been drawn from the mother's open body before Zal could recover from the marvel of it. Then he was astonished at the size and beauty of the child. Finally he collected his wits enough to send a messenger posthaste to notify the warrior Sam.

The newborn child was the wonder of all Persia. He was from head to toes the very image of his grandfather Sam. Everyone thought so except Mihrab who privately felt the baby looked just like him. The child was born without a mark or defect on him, tall, broad-shouldered, long-armed, with wide-open eyes and fists flailing the air. It took the milk of twenty nurses to allay his hunger. His mother named him Rustam, which means "I have borne fruit."

By the time Sam was able to leave his war and return to see his grandson, Rustam was walking. He had grown so strong that his parents were able to seat him on a golden throne atop a splendid elephant. Mounted thus royally, the child Rustam rode out of the city gates to meet his grandfather's procession.

Flags flew along either side of the road, over the heads of the army that had been drawn up at attention. Drummers kept up a rhythmic tattoo. Children strewed the route with flowers. Zal and Mihrab on foot escorted the elephant upon which Rustam balanced proudly. They were amazed to see Sam, who was galloping toward them on a magnificent bay stallion, rein in his horse and dismount. The valiant warrior paid his grandson the unparalleled honor of advancing to meet him on foot.

When Sam had strode up to the side of the elephant and looked up into his small grandson's face, he halted. The child returned his gaze without lowering his black eyes or blinking.

Sam spoke his first words to Rustam in a voice choked with emotion. Holding his hand on his heart he said, "Greetings, great paladin! May you live long and happily and have the heart of a lion."

To the amazement of the spectators, the child Rustam replied in a clear, treble voice, "Greetings, great paladin! May I draw my courage from my grandfather Sam, a lion among men."

RUSTAM AND KAI-KAUS

(*Note to the reader:* The following episodes from the reign of Kai-Kaus may be of interest for several reasons. First of all, there is the reference to an eclipse of the sun during a battle between the Persian and Median armies. Some modern historians have assumed that this refers to the eclipse of the sun which occurred on May 28, 585 B.C., and which, according to Herodotus, stopped a battle in the sixth year of a war between the Lydians of Asia Minor and the Medes. The famous Greek astronomer and mathematician Thales, who was born in Miletus on the coast of Asia Minor, is supposed to have predicted this eclipse. Other scholars think the *Shah Namah* could refer to another eclipse, such as the one recorded at Nineveh in 736 B.C. The people of Asia were in any case remarkably good observers. Among the astronomers of the ancient world were the Chinese, whose records contain eighty or so eclipses recorded by Confucius, most of which have been verified by modern science.

Most western historians are surprised by the account of the Persian conquest of Arabia. The geography of this part of the *Shah Namah*, however, comes from the research of Professor Darmesteter.

Most people who read Persian agree that Firdausi rose to his greatest poetic achievement in the part of the poem that treats the reign of Kai-Kaus. The climax of the *Shah Namah*, however, comes during the subsequent reign of Kai-Khosrau, who the Persians *know* is the shah we in the West do not believe is Cyrus the Great.)

After a glorious reign of 120 years, Shah Minuchir, calling before the peacock throne his son Nauder, entrusted the empire to him, saying, "My caravan is ready to depart. We may all tarry here, but not abide. Put not your faith in a world like this one." Then Minuchir closed his eyes and departed, and Nauder ruled in Persia for seven years.

During this reign the warrior Sam died of old age in Zabulistan. A marble tomb was erected in his memory, and all Iran mourned this great and noble paladin. His death was a signal for an invasion by Afrasiab, the son of the Turanian king. Afrasiab marched against Shah Nauder with 400,000 soldiers. In the ensuing battle he slew 50,000 Persians, took Nauder prisoner, and finally executed him. Persia was only saved by the combined efforts of Zal and Mihrab. Zal, however, would not then accept the crown of Iran, which it was a tradition in his family to refuse, and he put in the palace an aged prince named Zav, who ruled for five years.

The next shah was Garshasp of Balkh, who only reigned for nine years, and who died at the moment when Afrasiab was preparing a second invasion. Courtiers from the west of Iran reproached Zal bitterly for not having slain Afrasiab in the preceding war, a deed which would have ended the threat of his ambitious schemes. Zal, who was beginning to suffer from his long years as a champion warrior, asked for his son Rustam to be brought to him.

"My boy," said Zal, "even though you are too young for the horrors of war, yet must I send you on a dangerous mission, for our land is without a ruler. You must journey alone to Mount Elburz, and bring back our new shah, Kai-Kobad."

Rustam answered that he was ready to go out into the world as a warrior. He called for the mace of Sam, which had remained in Zabul as a trophy since the death of that great hero. No other man had been able to wield it. The future ruler, however, swung it over his head joyfully. Then he asked what he was to do for a horse, since he had outgrown the fabled stallions of Zabul, whose strong white backs had carried even his grandfather to war. Rustam needed a taller, stronger mount.

Zal ordered all the herds from Seistan and Kabul, where the special white horses were bred, to be driven past Rustam. The young boy singled out several promising two-year-olds, but they were all too weak for him even without his armor. Then he saw a spirited mare with a broad chest and sleek flanks. She was followed by her colt, which was as tall as its dam. However, when Rustam inquired about that particular colt, the herders told him that, unlike ordinary horses, mother and colt were inseparable. Several paladins had tried to lasso him, but the unnatural mare had attacked them with bared teeth and murderous hoofs. This was the kind of spirit Rustam needed in his own horse.

The colt was a three-year-old, a velvety roan with saffron-colored back and hard, black belly. His conformation was flawless—a deep, broad chest and powerful hindquarters. Rustam caught him on the first toss of his lasso and drove the mare away with a loud cry and a cut across her muzzle.

Expertly Rustam slipped a bridle on the colt, mounted him, and gave him his head. By the end of the first lesson the sturdy animal accepted Rustam as his master. He bore his rider easily at any pace, almost effortlessly. The herders were delighted, for man and horse seemed molded together. Rustam called his colt Raksh. From that day onward the two were a team. Everyone in Persia believed that Rustam and Raksh would put the Turanians to rout and defend the country for centuries to come. At night when Rustam slept in his tent on the battle-fields of western Iran, his followers would burn wild rue on either side of Raksh so that no tiger from the Tigris reed beds would steal upon him in the darkness. Even to this day in Afghanistan shepherds will proudly show you Raksh's manger, and about a mile to the west of it, marble slabs to which his hind feet are said to have been tethered at night. Raksh was well-paced, soft-mouthed, and clever. He was so sharp-eyed that he could make out an ant's feet on black cloth at night two miles away!

Their first adventure together was to cross the Great Salt Desert of central Iran and notify Kai-Kobad that, as the only living prince of the blood, he had succeeded to the throne and was requested to found a new dynasty. This they accomplished. The reign of Kai-Kobad lasted a hundred years, and it was a glorious one. The next shah of Persia was his son, Kai-Kaus the Astronomer.

This shah was a personable young man who came to the throne of the richest country on earth in a time of peace. Afrasiab had been driven by Rustam back into Turan, and was happy to have escaped with his life. Rustam would certainly have killed Afrasiab when he pulled him from his horse by grasping the Turanian's wide belt, but fortunately for that dark prince the belt broke, and he escaped. It would take Afrasiab many years to recover from the fright he felt when the mighty hand of Rustam grasped at his waist.

In the unparalleled splendor of his sculptured palace at Persepolis, Kai-Kaus ruled Persia with its plains covered with wild almonds and oaks, its sequestered valleys and lofty mountains, its rich villages surrounded by date groves, its magnificent Alpine terraces, and its wheat fields strewn with scarlet poppies. The country was prosperous and contented. With Afrasiab hiding in Turan, with Zal and Rustam ready to come at any sign of danger, Kai-Kaus could look forward to a long and memorable reign.

What prompted him then to listen to that demon from Mazinderan who, disguised as a harpist, presented himself at Jemshid's throne, and asked to sing to the shah? What caused Kai-Kaus to listen to that devilish lay in praise of Mazinderan? What made him seriously believe that the narrow strip of land between the Elburz Mountains and the Caspian Sea was the richest, the largest, the sweetest in all of Asia?

When Zal was summoned to Persepolis in great urgency by the courtiers and warriors, he could not believe his ears! The shah in person was planning to traverse the Elburz Mountains and conquer Mazinderan! In vain Zal expostulated! To deaf ears he pointed out the hazards of this long journey across the plateau of Iran. Zal spoke of the horrid race of white-skinned people, demons rather, who inhabited the caves of these mountains.

To all of Zal's arguments Kai-Kaus opposed his wealth, his powerful army, his thirst for glory, and his desire to hear the nightingales of

Mazinderan which warbled so much more melodiously on a moonlit night than the plain *bulbuls* of Persia. When Zal saw that the shah was, although young, as pliable as a withered tree, he shook his head sadly, returned to Seistan, and tried to bear with some degree of equanimity the news of the departure northward of the entire Persian host.

Kai-Kaus advanced by slow stages, resting often and admiring the beautiful mountain country. His route lay upward over the three terraces that rise from the Persian Gulf to the 5,000-foot plateau of central Iran. Here the sure-footed white horses mounted single-file steep cliff walls where the rock strata lay upended from some primeval convulsion. Its white and yellow layers showed bright against the treeless plains. At night they camped in some small, green valley bright with glossy orange trees, and Kai-Kaus mused over his wine glass and remembered sometimes to listen for the nightingales.

One morning when his head was clearer, the shah remembered the prime purpose of his expedition. He sent 2,000 warriors ahead of him to plunder Mazinderan. He ordered them to kill every inhabitant without quarter, and to burn every hamlet and town. For one week his champions slaughtered and looted. Then on the eighth day an unheard-of occurrence brought disaster to the Persians. The great White Demon appeared. Zal had warned Kai-Kaus of him, but the shah had not listened. This was a monstrous demon, whose skin was a clammy, white mass; he protected with very special magic the land and the king of Mazinderan. He had been summoned from his huge cave on Mount Damavand.

All of a sudden the sun began to be swallowed up! A great stillness fell over all the earth, and an increasing blackness. As it grew darker and darker, a huge storm gathered, slowly rolled in its icy winds, tucked them methodically under its belly, and began to suck them up into its huge bellows. Terrified, the Persians listened as the sky inhaled. There was a moment of silence. Then the storm burst. In an explosive onslaught it blew across the flat tableland where the Persians huddled unprotected. Great chunks of ice ripped through their brocade tunics. Hailstones beat upon their armor and stung the horses, which plunged wildly across the plain.

Arrows fell among the warriors from the bows of the white demons. The pack animals trampled madly over the fallen warriors. The earth was in total darkness. Kai-Kaus and his paladins became completely blind. They could not even see the face of the White Demon when it appeared leering and ghostly white at the horizon's edge. They surrendered quietly to his 12,000 demons, who ripped off their jeweled collars and rings, and tore their weapons from their hands. Kai-Kaus had just time enough to whisper to one warrior to dash for safety through the elephants, and to try to reach Seistan alive. Zal must be notified of their fate. Then the shah and his nobles were driven, battered and blind, to a cave where the demons guarded them closely. They were allotted just enough food and water to keep them alive. The White Demon sent word to Kai-Kaus that if the shah reflected—now that he had all the time in the world for thought, and no more treasure to bother his head about—he might come to hear how beautifully the nightingales of Mazinderan sang!

The shah's messenger flew like smoke the 300 miles southeast to Seistan, stopping only long enough for a fresh horse as each one foundered. Zal listened wearily to his breathless account. "The shah says to tell you that he set forth from Jemshid's throne, his army scented and bedecked like a rose garden in spring. Then came a great darkness and a wind that scattered their silken petals over Mazinderan. The shah says he sighs deeply for not having followed your advice, although what has happened to him was demonstrably no fault of his. He says you are to come at once to his rescue."

Zal called Rustam and to him alone confided the dreadful news of the shah's humiliation. By no means must such news reach Turan. "You must go alone to Mazinderan, my son," he said. "Persia has lost its monarch and its army. Go find these demons and their chief, and crush them crown to spine. Beware, however, of the White Demon himself, for he can turn day to night.

"There are two routes into Mazinderan, the long one taken by the shah, which passes across the terraces and into the mountain game country. This road takes fourteen days. There is a shorter way that you can make in seven days. Its issue is through the Elburz by two precipitous passes. The first of these is a mere fissure in the rock wall only the width of a horseman and very dangerous because of icy water that trickles down it constantly. The second pass lies through a black chasm in the mountain, but you must brave its murky depths. Only beware of lions and demons that infest this gloomy waste.

"I shall pray for you night and day," Zal told his tall, young son. "I know the sure hoofs of Raksh will bear you bravely enough. I shall not worry because your fate is in the hands of our Maker, and your fame so well established that you could never be forgotten."

On the first day Rustam covered a two days' journey, sparing neither himself nor Raksh. Toward evening, as he began to feel faint from hunger, he rode over a wild plain where game abounded. With his lasso he snared a wild ass, and lighting a fire with his arrow tip, he roasted the animal and lay down to sleep until morning. Raksh grazed nearby. During the night a lion crept through the tall grass and sprang upon Raksh. The valiant stallion attacked the lion with his sharp hoofs and sank his teeth deep into the lion's back. Rustam awoke to see Raksh grazing tranquilly, and the lion dead in the grass. Then Rustam scolded his horse. "You were very foolish, Raksh, to fight a lion all alone. Why didn't you awaken me? If something happens to you, I shall have this terrible journey to finish on foot, carrying my tiger skin, my helmet, my lasso, my bow, and my sword." Then Rustam gathered

dried grass and rubbed Raksh down, saddled him, and continued his journey just as the sun was rising over the eastern horizon.

All day long Rustam and Raksh traveled through the Great Salt Desert, where the heat was intense under a burning sun. Hour after hour they pressed on without a sign of life in a dazzling inferno. Even the birds had been shrivelled into powder. Raksh grew so blinded and stumbled so often that Rustam had to dismount and lead him by the bridle. Slowly they staggered onward with the afternoon sun full in their faces. At last neither man nor horse could advance any further. Rustam's lips were cracked and his tongue swollen and parched. He sank to the hot sand wearily, unable to continue. Then as he lay prostrate and despairing, he saw a fat ram run past them. With his last ounce of strength Rustam rose to his feet, pulling Raksh behind him, and saw that the ram had led them to a desert spring. He let Raksh take a sip or two of water, and then, bone-weary as he was, Rustam washed his suffering horse, and made his coat clean and glossy again. Then he killed another wild ass, roasted it, and lay down to sleep while Raksh grazed and wandered near the water's edge.

During the night a huge dragon, such as those that inhabited the primeval wastes from the beginning of time, dragged its scaly length across the hard sand to see who had passed the salt wastes of the desert unscathed. Raksh saw him come and galloped to Rustam, pawing the earth and neighing in shrill alarm. When Rustam awoke, the dragon had vanished. Rustam scolded Raksh and told him not to disturb his slumber again. No sooner had Rustam fallen asleep, however, than, breathing fire through his nostrils, the monster reappeared. Once more Raksh beat upon the sand and neighed. Again the dragon vanished. This time Rustam was very angry. He threatened to cut off his stallion's head and carry his weapons on foot to Mazinderan.

When the monster appeared for the third time, Raksh tried to lure him away into the desert where he could outrun him easily. The cumbersome beast only lumbered closer to Rustam. Then the frantic Raksh awoke his master. This time Rustam too saw their peril. "Tell me your name, foul creature," he cried. "Then I shall kill you surely."

"No matter my name," roared the dragon. "This is my land. For centuries not even an eagle has dared to fly over it. Tell me your name so I can dispatch you to your death!"

"My name is Rustam. I am the son of Zal and the grandson of Sam Suwar, champion of Persia."

Rustam joined battle with the dragon in a fight so difficult that Raksh had to come to his aid with hoofs and teeth. When Rustam cut off the monster's head, the whole plain was deluged with gushing streams of steaming blood. After this battle Rustam thanked his Creator humbly for having given him such strength and such an intelligent horse. "I am on earth to fight all enemies of man," he mused. "Dragons, demons, raging elephants, burning deserts, and the storm-tossed seas are all alike to me." This was his third adventure.

On the evening of the fourth day Rustam rode down into a fertile, green valley. There to his surprise was a banquet table set with a feast of venison, wine, and crusty loaves of fresh-baked bread. At the sound of a human voice the demons, who had prepared the feast for their mistress, vanished in a twinkling. Rustam lolled on the bench and ate until he could eat no more. Then he picked up a lute from the table and sang a little ballad, just to himself and Raksh, about the rigors and lack of leisure for love in a hero's life. While he sang, the enchanting mistress of the grove joined him. She was dressed in beauty like a starry sky, but Rustam did not trust her. He poured her a glass of wine, and as he handed it to her he mentioned the name of the Creator. Instantly she leaped away, screaming like a hideous hyena. Rustam threw his lasso unerringly and pulled her back to him. Then he saw to his disgust that she had resumed her true shape, that of an ugly, shriveled witch. Drawing his sword, he slew the repulsive hag.

Rustam and Raksh toiled all through the fifth day in the pass of Mount Elburz. Choosing the shortest route, they plunged bravely through underground caverns, guiding themselves by the courses of subterranean rivers. You would have said that the sun itself had been taken prisoner and that even the bright stars had been lassoed! Sometimes overhanging cliffs were so precipitous on either hand that you could not even see the sky. Soaked to the skin, they finally found the exit and looked joyfully across cultivated fields that lay below them like a picture puzzle. As soon as they had picked their way down the mountain, Rustam let Raksh have his fill of tender wheat while the hero laid out his tiger-skin cuirass in the sun to dry. Rustam dropped to the warm earth contentedly and savored the fresh air and spring sunshine.

Then as he dozed Rustam was attacked by Ulad, the young ruler of that land. "Who are you, young man, and why do you let your dappled horse eat my wheat?" cried Ulad.

Rustam was angry. Truly there was not a second's peace in a hero's life. "My name is Cloud," he cried, "if a cloud has the steely claws of a lion and if it rains arrows and war clubs." Swinging to right and left of him, Rustam cut off the heads of Ulad's hunters, two at each stroke. "My name is Cloud," he panted, "for if I were to tell you my real name, your blood would freeze in your bodies." He dispersed Ulad's warriors, pursued Ulad, and pulled him over backward from his horse, the lasso tight about his neck. Then Rustam, riding Raksh, drove the frightened prince along the road ahead of him.

"Be merciful for once and spare my life," pleaded Ulad.

"If you will guide me the hundred leagues to the White Demon's cave where the shah of Iran is imprisoned, I will give you as your reward the whole kingdom of Mazinderan," offered Rustam.

"Between us and the Demon's land," warned Ulad, "are such cliffs that not even a gazelle could scale them, and a river so well guarded that no man can cross it. The White Demon is himself as high as a mountain. You could not, even with your powerful arms, reach up to his waist. These demons command twelve hundred elephants of war. Your shah is closely guarded in their huge cavern. You cannot hope to advance beyond the frontiers of Mazinderan."

Ulad's words only made Rustam laugh. "You come along with me, Ulad," he shouted gaily, "and I will show you how to fight demons. Before I finish with them, they will be so dizzy that they won't know their reins from their stirrups."

Rustam and Ulad galloped all that day and all night. On the morning of the sixth day the Persian hero bound Ulad to a tree for safekeeping, for they had arrived at Mazinderan. After a short nap Rustam awoke refreshed, happy to have come so near to the journey's end. Before him lay the camp of the devil Arzhang, who guarded the entrance to Kai-Kaus' prison. Well protected with his tiger-skin cuirass and bronze helmet, Rustam rode up to the camp at daybreak on his sixth day and shouted for Arzhang.

It was a cry so loud it seemed the mountain trembled. Hoping to catch Rustam by surprise, Arzhang spurred out at full gallop and charged headlong. Raksh sidestepped; and as the devil flew past, Rustam shot out his hand and caught him by the throat. So great was the impact that Arzhang's head was torn from his body. Then with the head still in his hand, Rustam trotted forward a few paces and tossed the bloody trophy full in the enemy camp. Screaming with terror, the demons fled far over the mountain.

Deep in their cave the Persian prisoners heard the demons departing. Early that morning Kai-Kaus had told his companions that he had recognized the shrill whinny of Raksh, but none of his fellow prisoners had believed him. "Our shah is suffering from hallucinations," they said. Imagine their surprise then when Rustam himself strode into their cave! The young hero's eyes were full of tears. He fell at the shah's feet and thanked the Creator that the ruler of Iran was still alive. The shah ordered Rustam, tired as he was, to set out at once for the White Demon's cave that lay overlooking the Caspian.

"Bring back his vitals," commanded Kai-Kaus. "Three drops of its blood will cure our eyes of blindness."

On the seventh day Rustam crossed seven mountains and saw before him the yawning cavern of the White Demon. He waited patiently until the noonday heat became so intense that it forced the demons to hide their corpselike white skins within their grottoes. In complete silence Rustam walked alone into the central cave, carrying in his hand Sam's heavy mace. It was so dark inside that at first he could see nothing. He strode resolutely forward while his eyes became accustomed to the murky gloom. Then looming directly ahead of him like a mountain with a lion's mane, lay the chief Demon, sound asleep. Rustam could have killed him treacherously. Instead, he shouted at him to rise and fight a man.

The Demon lunged at Rustam, hurling a millstone as he came. Rustam thought, "This is surely my last fight. I'm going to die deep under this mountain." At the thought he remembered the shah of Persia, humiliated and blind. After the monster had passed him in the gloom, Rustam saw him silhouetted against the entrance. Quick to seize his opportunity, Rustam hacked off a hand and a foot.

It was the White Demon's turn to despair. "My hope is gone," he thought. "This must be some great hero come to destroy me. What if this is Rustam, that grandson of the champion Sam? Even if I live, I shall be maimed for life." In his despair the Demon lurched about the cave, groping for the hero and pouring slippery blood all over the walls and rock floor. Sam's mace smashed at his knees and thighs with ruthless accuracy. Viciously Rustam and the Demon tore at each other's flesh and sought a hold.

Then Rustam, using his great strength, pushed his attack to the utmost. Time and again the great war club crashed against the head and vitals of the monster, gouging out great masses of hide and flesh. Even the floor of the cavern shook under the impact of the blows. So murderous was the assault that not even this greatest of demons could long withstand it, and soon he sank to the floor battered and helpless. "If I live through this day," thought Rustam, "I surely must be immortal." Then he threw himself once more upon the monster and plunged his dagger deep into the Demon's heart. He tore out the liver, and without sparing Raksh, rode swiftly back to the cave where he had left Kai-Kaus the day before.

"May your mother be praised, my boy," cried the shah. "May Zabulistan that raised you be praised! May I be praised, for truly I am the most brilliant ruler on the earth to have at my command so worthy a young fellow!" Then he directed Rustam to squeeze the blood from the Demon's liver into their eyes, and so the paladins of Persia were cured of their blindness. Ulad was rewarded with the kingdom of Mazinderan, and the shah returned in triumph into Persia. For some months Kai-Kaus busied himself with building observatories in Babylon and the Tigris area. Loaded with gifts, Rustam returned home to Zabulistan.

Very shortly, however, Kai-Kaus wearied of his palaces in Persia. In royal state he toured his realm from Turan into Chin, thence southward to Baluchistan and to Seistan, where he spent a month feasting with Zal. Then he learned that the Arabs of Hamaveran, or Yemen, were inciting trading nations along the Gulf of Aden to rise up against Persia. The leader in this plot was the crafty king of Hamaveran. Kai-Kaus hastened angrily to Baluchistan, and there on the shores of the Gulf of Oman he had a splendid fleet built. Embarking with his armies, he sailed along the southern shores of Arabia to Berberistan, the land called Punt by the ancient Egyptians. From this point in Africa, with Egypt on his left and the Berbers on his right, Kai-Kaus launched a mighty offensive against Hamaveran in Arabia.

The war was a great success. Kai-Kaus controlled once more the sea routes between Africa and Asia. The king of Hamaveran sent him tribute and uncounted riches. What then possessed the Persian Kai-Kaus to covet the daughter of Hamaveran's king? Why could he not have burned for a Persian princess? How did he not realize that this union would involve Persia in a series of wars with the western states?

Ambassadors were sent from Kai-Kaus to the wily king in Hamaveran, asking for the hand of his daughter, Sudaba. Nothing could have been more unwelcome. The Yemenite king had only this one child whom he loved dearly. He could not bear the thought of losing her, of letting her go away across the sea. Nothing but the Persian victory could ever have persuaded him to part with her. Try as he might, there was no way out of the dilemma for the king of Hamaveran, especially as his daughter Sudaba relished the prospect.

"Do not consider this a tragedy," she answered her father. "It will be a joy for me to wed the shah of Persia." When Kai-Kaus saw Sudaba arrive in her golden litter, he was overjoyed at her rosy cheeks and slender waist. He declared himself completely satisfied with the Arabian princess. His courtiers were delighted, for they hoped this marriage would steady the shah.

Shortly after the wedding Sudaba's father invited the shah and a few of his chosen heroes to visit Hamaveran, not in war this time, but in peace. He alleged that he was very lonely for his daughter and longed to see her once more. Sudaba tried to warn her royal husband that the invitation was full of guile, that treachery was intended. She pleaded with Kai-Kaus not to venture into Hamaveran at all, and certainly not with a mere handful of warriors. "Who would dare betray the shah of all Persia, Turan, Baluchistan, Chin, Mazinderan, Hindustan, Balkh, and Seistan?" the shah demanded scornfully. "An attempt on my person is inconceivable!"

Ten days later desperate messengers spurred into Zabul to tell Zal and Rustam what had befallen the Lion of Persia. Kai-Kaus had spent a week feasting and being regaled at the royal city of Shaha in Hamaveran. Then when the Persians least expected it, they had been seized, roughly bound, and transported to a snow-covered fortress where they were guarded by a thousand picked warriors.

"What of Sudaba?" asked Rustam.

"This lady, strangely enough, defied her father's attempts to win her back to his court. She screamed, tore her hair, and with her rosy nails tore deep mourning grooves in her polished cheeks. Then preferring her husband in exile to her father on a throne, she followed Kai-Kaus to tend him in his captivity."

This time the fate of Persia's shah spread to Turan, where Afrasiab began to assemble his warriors for an invasion of Iran. Rustam after careful deliberation decided he should go first to Africa before some worse harm could befall the shah. Then he would return to face Afrasiab in Iran, for sooner or later he and Afrasiab were destined to meet in mortal combat.

Rustam wrote to the king of Hamaveran and ordered him to liberate Kai-Kaus at once. All he received in reply was a taunting letter saying that there were pits dug and waiting for Persian champions in Yemen, and one big enough even for Rustam. Meanwhile the combined armies of Egypt, Punt, and Arabia prepared to meet the Persians led by Rustam. Another letter was sent secretly to Kai-Kaus so that he would not despair when he heard how massive a force was being assembled against his Iranians. "Do not fear, great ruler," Rustam wrote him. "When I have finished with them, these foemen won't know their heads from their feet."

"Whip them soundly," replied the shah. "They deserve it. I command you to level your lances at your horses' ears. Think not of me. The world was not spread out to be my banquet solely."

The morning of the battle the three monarchs—of Hamaveran, Berberistan, and Egypt—mounted on three superbly caparisoned elephants, paraded before their troops. Their battle line stretched for two miles. It looked as if all the enemies of Persia, entirely clad in iron, had come together that day. The very earth was weary from their weight and the trampling hoofs of their animals. And what with the thousands of pennants—red, yellow, and purple—it seemed as though all the birds of Africa had lent them their plumage.

Rustam drew up the small force of warriors he had brought with him from Hindustan and Seistan. He assigned his right and left wings to two heroes who were his friends, while he reserved the center, which would spearhead the attack, for himself. Heavily armed, his coiled lasso hanging ready on his saddlebow, Rustam rode up and down his line of battle so that the sight of the celebrated Raksh would give his army courage. The dappled stallion, fat and rested from the plains of his native Zabul, pranced before the Persian warriors. Then Rustam harangued his troops, "Today we must keep our eyelashes wide apart, men of Iran! Today we must look steadily over our horses' manes and level our eyes at our spear points! What do we care for a hundred thousand foes? Our shah has been seized by trickery, through no fault of his own! Today we shall free him from his lonely prison, and all Persia shall thank us! As for Hamaveran and its allies, their noses shall breathe dust! Forward! After me!"

The enemy line was pierced at the first onslaught, and Rustam took sixty enemy chiefs prisoner before he reached the king of Syria. This proud monarch he lassoed around the waist and pulled him through the throngs of enemy warriors as if he were playing polo with his head.

Spurred on by Rustam's bravery, the Persian lords did great deeds that day. One by one they saw Rustam single out the enemy leaders and cleave a passage toward them with his polo-playing Raksh. When the king of Hamaveran realized that it was his turn to fall, he sent a messenger to Rustam. He offered total surrender, the return of Kai-Kaus and Sudaba, reparations for the trouble the war had caused, a restitution of Persian valuables, and a reinstatement of Persian suzerainty over the ancient trade routes.

The first act of Kai-Kaus when he had resumed command of his Persian subjects after the battle was to dictate a letter to Afrasiab, who had by that time seated himself upon the throne of Persia. "I am surprised at what I hear of you," wrote Kai-Kaus to the Turanian chief. "It cannot be true that you are trying to fill the throne of Iran! You should be satisfied to remain in Turan, a country which is from all reports by far too large for you. Surely you know what happens to the grasping, to the covetous! They stretch out their cat's paws for honey and prick themselves upon the thorns of Persian roses. Before this happens, you should try to save your pelt, dear Afrasiab! Does the puny cat insist upon annoying the Lion of Iran who sits by all rights of excellence and birth upon his ancestor's throne, upon Jemshid's throne?"

Afrasiab's dark face grew black when he read Kai-Kaus' letter. "Tell your monarch without a country not to give me lessons in covetousness," he snarled to the Persian envoy. "If he had not been so covetous himself, he would not have landed in a Yemenite jail. Tell him that I also am descended from Jemshid, and from Feridun the Dragon King. And secondly, I have been protecting Iran during Kai-Kaus' absence. For otherwise the Arabs would have ravaged it themselves. If he is a king, then let him remain in his own country and rule. Let him not go wandering off to the ends of the earth, leaving his realms shah-less. If he is a lion, then let him hasten to meet the Leopard of Turan!"

Afrasiab was as good as his threat. He waited for the Persian forces to re-embark, traverse the sea, and mount to the central plateau of Iran. The Turanian king had heard that Kai-Kaus was planning to meet him in person. Afrasiab gave orders to seize Kai-Kaus. What Afrasiab did not know was that Rustam had remained among the Iranian warriors and that he was to lead the central charge as he had done so effectively in Hamaveran. When Afrasiab saw a great hero spearhead the offensive right through his front lines, with thousands of veteran Iranian warriors pressing close behind him, while the two flanks remained powerful enough to drive around the Turanians in an encircling movement, then Afrasiab called his bravest warriors. "That hero is certainly Rustam," he cried. "Is that not the mace of Sam that he is wielding? If you will take that man dead or alive, I will give you each a kingdom. The parasol of royalty will henceforth be borne above your heads, and you shall marry my daughters!"

Even as he spoke the swarthy Afrasiab saw Rustam bearing steadily toward him! He felt his scalp tingle with the old fear that haunted him still at night. A few minutes later he ordered a retreat. Leaving half his troops wounded or dead on the plain, and his treasure in the silken tents, he collected a bodyguard around him and fled at top speed toward Turan. He did not stop until he was well northward of the Caspian. Men saw his face and cringed, for his lips were dour and drawn. Twice had Rustam made his wine of life turn to vinegar.

After this brilliant victory Kai-Kaus gratefully turned all his thoughts to his realm. Efficient and serious, he collected his tributes from Africa and Arabia, and sent garrisons to the conquered lands. In his proper place, dispensing justice from his ivory throne, he made the people of Persia happy. So great was the wealth of Kai-Kaus that men and demons kissed the earth before him and hastened to do his will. Kai-Kaus said that he had had his fill of adventure. "Our shah has grown tranquil in his maturity," his subjects said. "Now he is going to rule us well. Now he will stay at home. Our land will reach the pinnacle of power and dominion."

In a magnificent ceremony Kai-Kaus honored Rustam by conferring upon him the title of Jahani Pahvlan, Champion of the World. Thus the tireless hero was elevated even above the kings who did service at the court of Persia. Rustam heaved a sigh of relief. He was delighted to see the shah so serious about his kingly duties, and he turned Raksh's head toward Seistan gratefully.

To pass the time away Kai-Kaus gave orders for the building of two palaces in the Elburz Mountains, each one ten lassos wide. One was made of silver and the other of gold. In the bedrock under them he had tremendous stables excavated in imitation of the *var* his great ancestor had built before the flood. Then he erected a pleasure dome entirely out of crystal with a cupola of black onyx imported from Arabia. From Hind he brought rubies and emeralds to decorate its walls. Inside his lofty crystal dome he stationed learned men who were to spend their lives mapping out the stars and planets. Kai-Kaus took a great interest in their complicated calculations. In such pursuits he spent his time and lived in a perpetual spring, moving from one palace to another as the seasons changed.

As wise a ruler as he had become, Kai-Kaus could not be expected, however, to have discovered every demon in all his wide domains. There were still some evil creatures left who met and plotted in the hidden wilds. "One of you must wean this ruler from his kingdom," said an archfiend. "Otherwise the world will become so insufferably pure that demons like ourselves will find no pleasure in it!" One demon volunteered for the difficult task.

Kai-Kaus was returning merrily to his palace from a hunting trip when he was stopped by a pleasant youth who offered him a bouquet of roses and bent to kiss the earth at the feet of the shah's horse. "Great ruler," said the youth, "you have indeed conquered all the civilized lands. You have imposed your sway from sea to sea. I am amazed that you have not thought of leaving the world some lasting memory of your greatness. Why have you not attempted some feat unparalleled in the rolls of history?"

Why did Kai-Kaus listen to that youth? What made him send his learned courtiers away? How was it that he did not recognize a devil in disguise? Eagerly the shah drew the youth into his private chambers and ordered all his attendants to withdraw out of earshot. Then Kai-Kaus, reclining on his silken cushions, let the false words of the demon drive his wisdom out of his brain.

"You have only conquered bits of earth," the demon urged. "Other men have done the like before and will again. Your very grandson will overtop your conquests and build a pontoon bridge from Asia into Europe. Another of your descendants will conquer the whole world. You have yet performed no feat that is unique," insisted the demon.

"Perhaps you are right," nodded Kai-Kaus. "Continue."

"Excuse me for speaking so frankly," apologized the youth. "Has it not occurred to your royalty that earth is not the proper place for one so glorious? You are a gracious shepherd, that is true, a loving shepherd to these nobles, your blatting sheep."

"You are right," sighed Kai-Kaus. "I am engirdled with stupidity."

"What have you learned as you have peered through your crystal dome?" pursued the devilish boy. "What is the secret of the sunset? Have you discovered that? Do you not also long to ferret out the eastern sun's abode? Do you not wish to see the Elburz Mountains as they lie encircling the earth?"

"Why, yes," Kai-Kaus replied. "These are studies worthy of my greatness. Certainly I desire to pierce the secrets of the universe."

"Do you not wish also, great Lion of Persia, to unravel the mysteries of day and night? Your proper place is in the skies. Why do you not turn your piercing brain to its elucidation? How can so glorious a monarch as yourself be satisfied with dust? Unless, of course, you really believe the sky is ladderless!"

The demon talked on and on, but the shah was deep in reverie. All night long he thought and thought, more and more wretched when he considered his transitory fame, less and less interested in his palaces and usual delights. Toward morning he sent a servant to the observatory to ask the wise men, "How far is it from Persia to the moon?" They sent their answer back to him, and still he pondered. He no longer gave audience or attended to his royal duties. Day after day he wrestled with his problem. No person dared disturb his meditation.

One morning he reappeared wreathed in smiles. His orders were secret and urgent. Brave men were dispatched to the mountain eyries and ordered to capture eaglets while the mothers were sleeping. The young birds were carefully nurtured on chicken and breast of lamb. Then when they were full-grown, Kai-Kaus had each one tested. The four strongest, so powerful that each one could lift a mountain sheep in its sharp talons, were selected. The shah inspected them, praised their keepers, and kept his own counsels.

In the greatest secrecy the shah had a frame built of special aloe wood imported from Cape Comorin, the southernmost tip of India. On each of its four corners he had affixed one upright spear. Then from each of the spear's points he let a juicy leg of lamb dangle. In the center of the frame his cabinetmakers lashed a golden throne. Without confiding in any of his ministers, the shah dressed himself in a golden tunic and a jeweled crown. Then he settled back comfortably on the gleaming throne, his feet on a silken cushion, and ordered that the four strongest eagles, which had not been fed for twenty-four hours, be tied by their feet to the four corners.

At once the hungry eagles saw the pieces of meat which hung above them, just out of their reach. Flapping their wings powerfully, they flew toward the meat, and in their attempts to reach it bore the shah of Persia lustily through the air. Kai-Kaus looked smugly from his great altitude. He saw with interest the palace fade from view below him. With a wide smile of achievement on his face, he sipped wine from a golden goblet he had thoughtfully requested just before take-off.

Not many hours passed before the palace had forced the secret of the shah's whereabouts from his confidants. Consternation reigned. Horsemen were sent across the land to Rustam, who donned his battle dress, called Raksh from the meadow, and galloped toward the court. A disorder, indeed, had fallen over the land. On every side fierce wolves devoured the lambs! How sad a country is when no shah rules from his ivory throne! Rustam gathered a band of horsemen and scoured the countryside, sure that the eagles could not have flown too far, dinnerless as they were. Drums rolled as the searchers fanned out over the plateau.

The older warriors of Persia were very disgruntled. By twos and threes they cantered up to Rustam and complained. Old Gudarz was particularly angry with the shah for having drawn him out of his retreat on such a wild-goose chase. "You know I have been a confidant of kings," he grumbled to Rustam. "I have been devoted to our shahs of unsleeping renown. But, never in all my long years, have I met any man whatsoever, of either high or low estate, who was so perverse as this present shah, Kai-Kaus. There seems to be no particle of ordinary sense in him. Do you think his heart is as rotten as his brain?" When Rustam did not answer, Gudarz continued, "Now, take this last prank of his! What man in his right mind would do such a thing? Do you suppose his head was put together upside down?"

Other warriors, friends of Zal, bent close to Rustam's ear to say, "Our shah is insane. See how he is carried off his feet by every wanton wind!"

Rustam thought his own thoughts and made no comment. He

pressed the searchers hard and urged them to scan every hill and valley carefully, for Kai-Kaus if still alive would be extremely hungry by that time. Toward evening on the second day, as the riders came up on the crest of a mountain spur, they saw sparkling in the rays of the setting sun what looked like a golden object. It was the throne of the shah. They galloped closer, and there was the King of Kings seated calmly on his chair. He had just finished roasting and eating a wild duck. All in all he looked very well and extremely pleased with himself.

Kai-Kaus was about to greet his heroes graciously when they burst out at him like angry hornets, "You, sir, belong in a madhouse and not in Persepolis," shouted Gudarz as he dismounted stiffly.

"You have vacated your throne without consulting us," cried another. "What do you mean by dragging us all over the country in search of you?"

"We sent our warriors with you to Mazinderan. You made merry with wine cup and song all along the way. Then what happened to you? Rustam alone could have saved you from the White Demon! Do you realize that?"

"What will we answer," cried another wealthy Persian paladin, "when visitors to our land ask us, 'Where is your shah?' Think occasionally of our embarrassment. 'Oh,' we have to answer. 'Ahem! Our shah has just gone on a little junket, just up to count the stars and see the sun and moon.'"

"Why don't you try to serve the Creator?" cried another. "Haven't you ills enough in your land of Persia? Are there not wrongs enough all around you? First put your house in order before you go meddling with the world of sky!"

All this time Kai-Kaus sat on his golden throne with his head in his hands. Although he gave no sign, they knew he was listening to their tirade. When every paladin had aired his grievance—all except Rustam, who had remained apart without speaking, as befitted a young man— the shah lifted his weary head and answered them, "Your judgment of me is just. You have convinced me." Then the shah called on the Maker, burst into tears, and crept into the litter that had been brought for him. All the way back to Persepolis he only wept and prayed. He spoke to no one otherwise.

Royally accompanied by surly, red-faced warriors, Kai-Kaus was driven back to his palace. He refused obstinately, however, to mount upon his throne. There were no more banquetings and no more audiences. For forty days the shah did penance for his latest indiscretion. He would see no one, but sat alone, his head in the dust. At last he reappeared, smiling and forgiven. "The sun is shining on its favorite land," went out the glad news as Kai-Kaus emerged from his retreat and reigned again.

This is the story of Rustam and Kai-Kaus that every man, woman, and child knows very well—in Persia.

RUSTAM AND SUHRAB

Rustam awoke one morning with a strange feeling of expectancy. He was restless and tense as if something important were about to happen. All day long he wandered about the palace with this sense of inner excitement. He was bored and exhilarated at the same time. His brother Zuara passed him with the words, "Have you seen the foals? Spring is early this year!" Then Rustam realized the cause of his unrest. It was spring. The New Year had indeed come early.

Tender blades of grass had grown up overnight all over the meadows around Zabul, and overhead the birds flew noisily in pairs. Rustam called for Raksh, prepared his weapons, and set out from the palace on a hunting trip. He felt like leaving the comforts of Zabul behind him and just wandering northward across the plains with no place special to go and no other purpose than to renew himself by living close to the earth. It felt good not even to hear voices. He loved the warm spring sun on his bare head and the clean smell of mold and soil. It was wonderful to be young and free. Raksh liked it too after a winter in the stables. He kept tossing his head mischievously and bursting into a mad gallop every now and then.

Day after day they meandered toward the open country of the north until they were almost on the Turanian border. At night Rustam would kill a wild ass with his arrows. Then he would collect dried grass and thorns and get a small fire going. After it had caught, he would pile large branches on it, make a spit, and roast his supper. Throughout the evening hours he would sit by the embers, peacefully wrapped in his blanket, and think of his past adventures. He slept soundly at night beneath the stars.

One night a band of Turkman horsemen riding home across the plains came upon Raksh, who had wandered far from his master. Spurring their horses, they skillfully surrounded the stallion and tried to capture him. Raksh defended himself well. He managed to unseat two of them and wound their horses. The Turkman nomads finally managed to lasso the roan stallion, however, and drive him into their city of Samangan. They planned to share the prize money the king would be sure to give them.

When Rustam awoke in the morning and realized that Raksh was gone, he was white with fury. He saw the deep marks in the meadow and Raksh's hoof tracks blended with those of the nomads' ponies. Shouldering his weapons, he set out in pursuit. His heart ached at the thought of Raksh, who would be hours away by that time. He was discouraged at the possibility that he might have to fight a band of mounted Turkman warriors on foot. He blushed at what the gossips at Afrasiab's court would soon be telling about him. "Here is Raksh. Bold Rustam lost him in the chase. Brave Rustam slept his horse away!"

Rustam had only passed the outskirts of the provincial Samangan when mounted horsemen galloped past him to warn their king that a Persian youth, extremely tall and broad-shouldered, and very kingly in his appearance, was approaching. The opinion was general that it might be none other than the famous Rustam. The king of Samangan and his courtiers hastened to put on their crowns. Then they nervously set out on foot to meet the stranger.

"Can it be the rising sun or the heroic Rustam?" the king inquired anxiously. "Who in my country has dared to meet you in a quarrel? We are all your friends here and your devoted servants. We have no love for Afrasiab! Our lands, our possessions, and our heads, most dear to us, are all at your disposal."

"While I was hunting in your meadows, my Raksh, without halter or rein, strayed away from me," replied Rustam. "I have tracked him to your city. If he is found at once, you will have my thanks and the reward due the honest. If by some chance he is not brought to me forthwith, I shall separate several heads from your chieftains' bodies."

"Do not be angry, noble paladin," answered the king of Samangan. "A horse so well known as your priceless Raksh could not remain hidden. Let me proceed with all gentleness to recover him. Meanwhile, honor us with your company at dinner. Fortune has favored us generously since we have this opportunity of receiving you in our midst. Set your mind at rest. Raksh shall be found."

Rustam accepted the invitation. At once messengers were dispatched to convoke the army chiefs and city dignitaries, who hastened to meet the most famous man in Persia, the champion whose very existence kept Afrasiab north of their own borders. The notables of Samangan outdid themselves in an effort to make their small town palace look as festive as possible. Dancers and musicians were hastily assembled. The cooks bustled and shouted in the kitchens. The wine stewards rushed busily about. Until late at night the guests lolled on cushions and begged Rustam to tell them again of his adventures. Old warriors thrilled and shivered as he talked. Young nobles hung on his every word and studied his face and gestures so that one day they could tell their grandchildren, "The night I had dinner with Rustam, *he* said to *me* . . ."

The guests were still celebrating when Rustam asked to be shown to his chamber. There the king had laid out perfumes and rose water for his bath. Rustam fell on the bed dizzy from the quantities of wine he had drunk. As he drifted into sleep he saw the door open and slave girls approach his couch with lighted tapers. The room was suddenly full of the heavy scent of roses. Rustam looked dazedly up from his pillow to see bending over him the most beautiful girl he had ever seen in his life.

"Are you real? I cannot believe it," he murmured. Then he lifted himself on his elbow and looked at her face as she bent over him. It was like looking into the heart of a rose. Her cheeks were like petals of dark red velvet. Her eyes gleamed in the soft light of the candles. Her dark hair fell like a cloud over her shoulders and ripe breasts, and her lips were as firm and full as a lover's heart!

"Who are you?" Rustam asked her. "Am I awake? Are you real?"

"I love you, Rustam," she murmured, and ran the soft tips of her fingers reverently across his forehead, down his cheeks, and onto his lips.

Rustam tried to shake the clouds of wine from his head. He stared in amazement at her beauty. "Who are you?" he insisted. "What are you doing in my chamber at night?"

"I am Tamineh, daughter of the king," she whispered. "Until tonight no man but my father has ever seen my face. No man in Samangan has ever heard my name. I vowed that no man should ever possess

me because I intended to wait all my life for you. Inside my own chambers and high-walled gardens the tales of your renown were brought to me."

"What do you know of me, Tamineh?" Rustam whispered. Gently he pulled her down beside him on the bed, so that as she talked he could linger over the beauty of her eyes and lips, and run his fingers through her soft hair.

"What do I know of you, my beloved?" she whispered, smiling. "I know you are the bravest man who ever walked the earth. You went alone into the White Demon's cave to rescue the glorious shah. I know that in Arabia you defeated three kings and made them bow their insolent heads in the dust before your feet. The stories of your deeds are more wonderful than a romance. I know you wander lonely through the world, living only to defend mankind from danger, able to bear wounds without a cry and cold and hunger without blanching. You are the only man whom I could love. The wary eagle wheels high overhead when you are near. The fiercest lion fears the sting of your lasso. Whole armies fly in terror at the mention of your name.

"I have so longed to touch your beloved face. I have so longed to feel with my fingers, as now, how broad your shoulders are. I have so dreamed of just the sound of your voice. . . . And more than that, I have a present to give you, Rustam."

"What is it that you have to give me, Tamineh?" he murmured.

"Everyone else in all the lands of Iran seeks you, Rustam," she replied. "They all run after you for one great service after another. 'Rid us of demons. Rescue the shah. Brave dangers we could not face. Do not think of yourself. Come at our bidding,' they say."

"Yes, that is true," he encouraged her.

"I know how lonely you must be," said Tamineh. "I want to give you this gift so that you will never be alone again. I want to give you the most valuable gift a woman can offer the man she loves. Hold me in your arms, closely. I want to bear you a son."

Without letting her move from his side, Rustam dispatched the slaves to notify the wise men of the palace and have Tamineh's father brought immediately. When he arrived, sleepy and slightly drunk from the festivities, Rustam made him understand somehow that he wished to marry Tamineh, and never any other. The king of Samangan could hardly believe his ears. There was no request for dowry, no demand for authentication of lineage, no complication, and very little ceremony. In a daze he regained his quarters, leaving the newlyweds alone, and tried to make himself believe by saying it out loud as if he were really convinced, "My daughter is the wife of Rustam. Naturally, *the* Rustam. My Tamineh is wedded to the grandson of Sam Suwar of Zabulistan, Seistan, and Hindustan." The oftener he said it, the less he believed it. How could such an honor fall upon a desert chieftain?

The next few days sped swiftly by, and Rustam's nights were not lonely. He could not caress his bride enough. He delighted in her silken skin, her slender body, and in her wit and intelligence. When news was brought him that Raksh had been recovered, he hardly listened. He answered yes to all questions that were asked him without taking his eyes from the eyes of Tamineh. He realized, however, and so did she, that he could not stay much longer in enemy territory. His rich kingdoms in the south and his aging parents required his presence. Tamineh only watched him with her soft eyes, and never asked him either when he would go or if he could not remain longer. She was content that her life's desire was being fulfilled.

All through his last night in Samangan, Rustam held his bride closely in his arms and comforted her. No one will ever know what words he said. Then in the early morning, when he had saddled Raksh, he bade farewell to her father and praised him highly. Turning to Tamineh, who stood pale and dry-eyed stroking Raksh's muzzle, Rustam gave her his last directions: "Take my amulet, my beloved Tamineh. It is a famous one. If a daughter is born to you, choose a time when the stars are auspicious, and plait it in her hair. If a son is born, let him wear it. Then he will grow powerful and brave. No fear will ever make my son tremble, and no desert sun will ever scorch him."

Rustam drew Tamineh tenderly against him and held her willowy body once more in his arms. Then he mounted Raksh and rode away among the cheering people of Samangan. Tamineh did not weep until he was out of sight.

Although from that day onward caravans bearing gifts of the value of a king's ransom were dispatched regularly by Rustam from Zabulistan into some unknown area of Turan, Zal never asked his son for whom they were intended. No one in Persia ever heard Rustam mention what befell him on his hunting trip in spring.

When nine months had come and gone, Tamineh gave birth to a beautiful son, whom she named Suhrab because of his smiling, sunny nature. In a month the baby was as large as a year-old child. When he was three his chest was so broad and his arms so strong that he played at warrior with much older boys. By the time he was five, no other lad dared pick a quarrel with him. At ten years of age Suhrab seemed fully grown. Then Suhrab went to his mother and asked her why he had no father. "What can I say when people ask me? Was he some shameful person, or some enemy of Turan? Who was my father? My heart breaks to know!"

Tamineh looked at her handsome son, so much taller and stronger than any of the Turkman warriors in her palace. "Your father is alive, Suhrab," she said. "Here are three priceless rubies from Hind and three purses of gold he sent you at your birth."

"What is his name then?" persisted the boy. "Is he the king of Hind?"

"Yes, he is the ruler of all the southern lands, of Hind, Seistan, and

Zabulistan. He is the Jahani Pahvlan, Rustam."

At her words Suhrab's eyes filled with tears. He had never dreamed in the long years of wondering and imagining that his own father could be the greatest of all men alive, the kingly Rustam.

"Afrasiab must not know of this," warned Tamineh. "If he knew you were Rustam's son, he would have you killed. I do not want Rustam to know either," she continued, "how tall you are or how gallant. If he knew, he would order you to his side. I cannot lose you, dear Suhrab. You are the child of my love. If I lost you, I would have nothing left."

Suhrab did not agree with his mother at all. "You cannot hide such a thing as this," he cried. "Men have only to look at me to know I am not a Turkman. See how tall I am. Men as tall as I am come only from the blood of Rustam and Sam."

Tamineh pleaded as a mother will. Her caution and prudence were lost on Suhrab whose will had never been curbed by a father's voice. Dazzled with the knowledge of his glorious ancestry, the boy made plans and built his dream castles high into the clouds. By the time he was fourteen, Suhrab had found a suitable horse—a swift roan from the breed of Raksh—had persuaded his grandfather of Samangan to outfit him, and was ready to seek adventure far from home. Tamineh wept in vain. She could not stop him.

Suhrab's plan was this: he would advance with an army into Iran and with Rustam's help defeat the ridiculous puppet, Kai-Kaus, who was so obviously no proper shah in any sense of the word. Rustam alone should be shah of Iran. Then with his father at his side Suhrab would return northward and depose Afrasiab. At this happy event Suhrab would rule Turan, where his mother Tamineh would be the queen and most honored lady. She would emerge from her desert hiding place and become the envy and admiration of all Asia. All Suhrab would need to put his plan into execution would be to fight his way bravely into Iran so that he could at last meet his father.

Afrasiab, well informed of all that took place in his own kingdom, was delighted with such news. He shook his head with glee, seeing at once that with care he could ruin Rustam. "Of course, this is the son of Rustam, who tarried so long at Samangan." Summoning two of his most valiant warriors, men of proven character and weighty experience, Afrasiab discussed the situation with them. "Go with this youth," he instructed Barman and Human. "By no means let him recognize his father. It will all work out admirably. Either Rustam will be slain by this rash youngster and Kai-Kaus defeated, or Rustam will kill Suhrab. Then when Rustam realizes that he has killed his own son, the heart will go out of him—so much so that we will be able to finish him, or Kai-Kaus without his interference. It will be child's play to dispose of Suhrab, should he be the victor. You can dispatch him any night while he is asleep."

Along with Barman and Human, Afrasiab sent a flattering letter to

Suhrab that enjoined him to invade Iran with all confidence. He gave the boy 12,000 picked troops, horses, pack animals, gold, and many rich presents. The two Turanian chiefs were overwhelmed with the stature and prowess of Suhrab. They wrote to Afrasiab that this lad on his roan stallion, so similar to Raksh, loomed more formidable to them than Mount Behistun itself. Thus bravely accompanied, Suhrab invaded Iran, burning everything in his path, wheat fields and villages alike.

Then Suhrab with his Tartar army encamped around the White Castle, a famous fortress commanded by a seasoned warrior named Hajir. Shouting insults back and forth, Suhrab and Hajir fought in single combat. Without much difficulty Suhrab struck the Iranian warrior from his horse. Before Hajir could rise from his heavy fall, Suhrab had dismounted, thrown the warrior on his back, and sat heavily on his chest. Hajir managed to twist himself to one side. He begged Suhrab for mercy so piteously that the youth complied. Binding Hajir's hands behind his back, Suhrab sent him to Human as a prisoner and returned to the castle gates just in time to meet a second champion who spurred out of the fortress and charged him.

Suhrab set his Chinese helmet well over his head and leveled his spear. As this new champion charged, he pulled back his bow and sent a stinging arrow toward Suhrab. Then this warrior, displaying superb horsemanship, wheeled and careened so intricately that Suhrab was unable to catch him. When Suhrab finally managed to send his dart against the enemy's waist with an accuracy and force that would have unseated a less expert cavalier, this champion managed to rise again in the saddle and keep his seat. Then instead of returning to combat, the champion galloped furiously across the plain and out of sight of the castle and the Tartar forces. Suhrab followed hot on his heels and jostled the other's horse so as to break its stride. The two rode side by side until Suhrab, leaning over, managed to yank off the enemy's helmet.

To his amazement he saw that his enemy was a young girl whose long curls blew in the wind behind her head. "If their girls can fight like this one," thought Suhrab to himself, "what must their young men be like in Persia?" Then he expertly coiled his lasso and, standing tall in his stirrups, caught the maiden round her waist. Then he reeled her in, her arms pinioned tightly by the rope.

"What are you doing in all this battle gear?" he asked her. "Who are you?"

"I am Gurdafrid," she answered. "My father is an aged warrior in the White Castle. Are you going to kill me, Champion, or shall we make a truce?" As she spoke, the handsome maiden tossed her hair and showed her pearly teeth.

Suhrab blushed before her saucy charm and could not answer. Pertly Gurdafrid spoke for him, "Oh, come, untie your lasso! You're hurting me." Then as the young giant started to obey her, she enmeshed him well with her flirtatious looks. "You'd better let me go, you know," she told him. "Your soldiers would die laughing if they knew you dueled with girls. We surrender, great warrior," she told him. "Our city and all its wealth is yours."

"Do you surrender also?" Suhrab questioned.

"Oh!" laughed Gurdafrid. "You make hard terms, young Lion. I see that!"

"Shall we make a bargain?" Suhrab asked her, looking straight into her eyes. He still made no move to loosen the ropes that cut her arms.

"I have spoken," she answered, smiling. "The castle and all its treasure is yours. Only let's not stand here all afternoon. You have my word."

Together they rode up to the fortress where her father hastened to unbar the gates. Then quickly Gurdafrid spurred her horse and dashed inside. Before Suhrab's nose the heavy gates swung shut. Soon he saw the maiden's saucy face over the battlements.

"Warrior! You there!" she called down to him. "Why give yourself such trouble? Go home to Turan. You will never catch me!"

"What of your promise?" Suhrab called up to her. His only answer was her mocking laughter. Then Suhrab swore that he would storm her castle and raze its walls to the ground. "The next time it will be my turn to laugh," he warned her. "Wait till I get you helpless and writhing again in my lasso. Then you will see."

"Suhrab, you won't find a person in Iran to help you win your war," she called. "You may live, but not long. Soon the shah will march his armies out against you. Why don't you go home while you still can? You are no Turanian, anyway! What are you doing in their army? We never saw a champion like you among Turkman chiefs. If you wait here, you are sure to be destroyed. We of Persia have a warrior of our own. Against Rustam you cannot hope to stand, even with arms and shoulders as powerful as you have. Rustam is no youngster either, to be fooled by a girl!"

Suhrab wheeled away from the walls and rejoined the troops. First he gave orders that all the fields and hamlets around the White Castle should be mercilessly laid waste. "We will storm the fortress at dawn tomorrow," he announced, and then retired to his tent, for darkness was falling.

Inside the fortress Gurdafrid and her aged father, left alone to command since the capture of Hajir, dictated a letter to Shah Kai-Kaus and selected their swiftest messenger to stand ready to bear it at top speed. After having extolled the shah, his wisdom, courage, and valor, they told him frankly of their plight. "If you so much as stop to breathe, Persia is lost," they dictated to the scribe. "There is no man in Iran who will stand before the Turanian champion who breathes fire at our gates. Hajir, arrayed in his strongest armor, folded like kindling before his burning lance. This champion's name is Suhrab. He is young, surely not more than an adolescent, but he is as tall and as powerful as Mount Damavand. We cannot believe him to be of Turanian stock. Picture rather Sam at the first flush of his career, rather than Rustam.

"It would be foolish to cast any more of our warriors to this living mountain, and so we will steal out of the castle tonight and leave the place to him. The greatness of this Suhrab surpasses our poor powers of expression. Therefore arm yourself in might and hope all is not lost."

At daybreak Suhrab and his warriors battered down the gates and stormed into the White Castle only to find it undefended. The few people left within its walls knelt weeping and implored the Turanians' mercy. From them Suhrab learned how the garrison had crept out under cover of darkness through a secret passage cut in the rock foundation. An extensive search was made for Gurdafrid, but she was not to be found. This Suhrab regretted more than the escape of the forces. He would have liked to have held this impertinent girl in his arms and heard her cry for mercy.

Kai-Kaus read the letter he received from the White Castle aloud to his courtiers. The shah was very pained, particularly at the fact that Gurdafrid and her father gave him no consolation. "What do you advise?" he asked his champions.

"We must certainly send for Rustam," they replied.

The shah then dictated a long letter to Rustam and ordered the great warrior Giv to prepare his horses and stand by to carry it to Zabul. The shah praised Rustam in the highest terms, reminded him of his past services to the crown of Persia, and explained the present emergency. Kai-Kaus made the point very clear that he personally was very pained, that in fact his heart ached that Turan should have at present inconvenienced his realm. "At whatever moment this letter falls into your hand," he wrote, "whether by day or in the darkest hours of night, if you should tarry long enough to speak, Iran is doomed. If you should be holding a fresh-plucked rose in your fingers, stop not to smell it! Unless you march forth instantly with your well-known green battle standard, Persia is lost, and your shah is lost! Clothe yourself in valor. The situation, from what I hear, is critical."

The shah ordered Giv to leave immediately and to return without stopping. Giv ran from the palace and leaped on his horse. Away he went like smoke and never halted except for a fresh mount all the way to Zabul. Over 300 miles he sped with neither sleep, nor food, nor rest, nor water. It was Zal who heard the cry from the watchtower, "A rider from Iran as swift as the wind!"

Rustam and his attendants met the weary Giv and drew him into their palace. Here Rustam read the shah's letter while servants bathed and fed Giv. At the end of the first line Rustam began to laugh. "This is just like Kai-Kaus," he said between gales of laughter. When he came to the passage about Suhrab, he could not contain his merriment. He slapped his thighs and stomped around the room, pointing out the words to his friends. "This is really too much," he cried. "A warrior like my grandfather Sam Suwar has appeared. But that's not all! Where has this noble lion come from, if you please? He has sprung from the wilds of Turan, from Afrasiab's soil! This is really too much to ask me to swallow!

"Come! Let us go to my father's palace for feasting," shouted Rustam to Giv and his warriors. "Let us tell this story to the honorable Zal and ask his advice in this matter." While a feast was being served, Rustam continued to joke about Kai-Kaus and his false alarms. Once he fell silent as the thought occurred to him to search his mind well about Tamineh and her son.

"It could not be this champion," Rustam decided. "In the first place, my son is still only a child. Not long ago I sent Tamineh rich gifts for him, and she answered that he was not growing very fast, that in fact he still preferred milk to wine. No, it could not be. Secondly, this Turanian champion is a seasoned warrior. In one onslaught he unseated the valiant Hajir and trussed him hands and feet like a fowl for the oven. That was not the work of a boy, not even my own son."

While Rustam reflected, Giv grew more and more anxious. "We must leave," he told Rustam. "The shah expressly told me not to stop."

"Oh, let us not worry," answered Rustam. "The more we hurry in this world, the quicker we get to the end of our lives, which are only dust anyway. Let us relax a day and lift the wine cups to our thirsty lips. Then we will gird ourselves for war. Battles must wait upon heroes, once in a while." Nothing could move Rustam when he had made up his mind. Giv settled back on the cushions and, listening to the music, dozed off. Every now and then the voices of Rustam and his friends reveling and singing would intrude on his slumber.

"This Turanian champion will have to wait for me," Giv heard Rustam say. "He won't run away, at least not until he sees my face and might. At the sound of Raksh's hoofbeats the heroes of Iran will rouse from their fear. They will rush on this Tartar themselves, without needing me at all. This matter is nothing to worry about anyway. Who ever heard of comparing a Turkman to my grandfather Sam? It's almost insulting."

Rustam had intended to start the following morning, but his head was so foggy with wine that he ordered another banquet instead of his horse and armor. For three days he and his warriors feasted and made merry from dawn until the middle of the night. It was only on the morning of the fourth day that Giv could persuade Rustam to depart. "Don't even give this Suhrab a thought," Rustam reasserted. "The shah won't be angry. By this time their Turanian champion will probably have tripped on a pebble and broken his spine!"

Two Persian champions, Tus and Gudarz, met Rustam and Giv a day's journey from the shah's court. They were reassured by the sight of Rustam and began to agree with him that the whole story was a farce. Laughing and joking, as old comrades in arms will do after a long separation, they strode into Kai-Kaus' presence and saluted him. The shah glared at them in silence without acknowledging their obeisance. They saw his face become purple with rage. He burst forth at them like a caged lion, berating Giv for his delay. Then the shah turned to Rustam, "Who does he think he is that he can disobey my express commands? If I had a sword, I'd lop off his head like a rotten orange. Seize him," the shah ordered Tus. "Seize both of them, him and Giv. Hang them alive, at once!"

Tus in wonderment moved to Rustam and took his hand, intending to lead him out of the palace until both he and Kai-Kaus had time to become calmer. Rustam never moved, but stood looking defiantly at Kai-Kaus. "You are not powerful enough to indulge yourself with such a display of temper," Rustam told the shah. "You rule us worse and worse every day. Very soon, indeed, I see you will not be sane enough to govern at all. Since you no longer need my services, you can go and hang your own enemies yourself! Mazinderan, Hamaveran, Zabulistan, and Hindustan obey my sword, not yours! Why take out your wrath on me?"

Rustam struck Tus's hand with such violence that the warrior dropped to the floor. Then he strode from the audience chamber, down the marble steps of the palace, whistled to Raksh, and was gone. His thoughts were very bitter. How could Kai-Kaus presume to punish him? When just a lad Rustam had placed his line upon the throne. Every man in Rustam's family, for generations back, had deferred to tradition, law, and order in refusing for themselves the crown of Iran. Here was an example of the basest, most thoughtless ingratitude. "Let Suhrab invade Iran, for all I care," mused Rustam. "Kai-Kaus can henceforth fight his own wars!"

After Rustam had left, so angry you would have said his skin was cracking, the warriors of Iran conferred anxiously. Then they sent the oldest and most respected among them to the shah. This was Gudarz. Patiently the old man reasoned with the shah, asked him where Rustam's fault was, and how the shah could be so unmindful of past services. "A great ruler like yourself dare not be hasty or rash in his judgments," he told the shah. Then Gudarz reminded Kai-Kaus of the letter from the White Castle, which expressly stated there was no horseman at all in Iran who would avail against Suhrab. "If you do not persuade Rustam to return," added Gudarz, "then we must fly your palace for our lives instead of rallying to you as we ought to do."

Kai-Kaus admitted the logic of his arguments and ordered Gudarz to persuade Rustam to relent. Gudarz with Tus and Giv overtook Rustam on the road. In vain they apologized for Kai-Kaus. In vain they called the shah stupid, rash, impulsive, thoughtless. In vain they described him as sitting in the palace menaced by Turan, so troubled he was chewing on the backs of his hands. Rustam was not moved by their words.

Deferentially the warriors listened with bowed heads while Rustam raged. "What is your shah to me that I should fear him? He is less than the grains of sand that sift through my fingers. What can he offer me, since he has shown his ingratitude? Do I care for his riches? I have crowns and lands of my own. I have eaten his insolence up to my ears! My only master is the Creator. My only end is dust!"

The only way the three warriors could persuade Rustam to return was to insinuate that his quarrel with the shah would be interpreted—not by his friends, but by others who only knew him by reputation—as cowardice, as fear of this Turanian champion. Because of this Rustam became reconciled with Kai-Kaus and accepted his profuse apologies. "I am like a tree that planted crooked is unable to grow straight. Any sudden emotion, such as this emergency, puts me out of my normal good humor," said the shah in his own excuse. They spent the evening in revelry, and the following morning Kai-Kaus, accompanied by Rustam and an army of a hundred thousand soldiers, set out to meet Suhrab.

The shah's army encamped upon a plain before the castle seized by Suhrab. When Human the Turanian looked out over the battlements and saw the Iranian host which stretched to right and left as far as eye could see, he was frightened. Suhrab on the contrary marked only the brilliant pavilions of the Persian nobles. "This war will be fought by me in single combat," he assured Human. "You have nothing to fear whatsoever." With a shrug of his shoulders the youth rejoined the merrymaking.

After darkness had fallen, Rustam requested leave of Kai-Kaus to enter the Turkman camp. He left his helmet and royal belt and set out covered with a dark cloak to have a look at the Turanian champion. Unobtrusively Rustam stole outside the circle of the feasters and looked upon Suhrab for the first time. Standing in the unlighted area he marveled at the boy. Suhrab was seated on the turquoise throne Afrasiab had sent him. On its ivory steps knelt fifty slaves with golden armbands who chanted verses in his praise. Suhrab's shoulders and back were so massive they filled the throne from edge to edge. His naked biceps were as large as a camel's thighs. His merry face gleamed in the firelight, and he was handsome, glowing with health and animal spirits.

Then as Rustam watched fascinated, a Turanian warrior who had stepped outside for a moment saw the strange cloaked man, noticed his extraordinary height, and making a passage through the throng, accosted Rustam roughly. Without seeing the man's face, Rustam reacted like lightning, with the instinctive speed of thought and action that is developed over a period of warring years. Rustam chopped the Turanian across the neck with the outside edge of his hand. The blow was so swift and so accurate that the Turkman fell dead on the ground. Rustam had already made his way quietly out of the camp before Suhrab missed his warrior. When he found Zanda Razm dead on the ground, Suhrab was deeply grieved. This was his uncle, Tamineh's brother, who had accompanied his nephew at the mother's request. Zanda Razm was the only person in Samangan who had seen Rustam years before during his wedding week. Suhrab had counted on his uncle to point out Rustam to him and to introduce the son to his father. Suhrab ordered his uncle's body to be honorably borne to Samangan, and then the boy returned to his guests. "The treacherous fiend who has stolen into my camp to kill in the darkness shall not spoil our festivities. Tomorrow early I will wield my lasso in revenge."

Rustam returned through the darkness to his own lines. He was accosted by Giv who was standing sentry. Overjoyed to see Rustam safe and sound, Giv accompanied him to the shah. Kai-Kaus heard from Rustam himself corroboration of the information sent him by Gurdafrid and her father. "This Suhrab is a champion indeed," admitted Rustam. "To begin with, he is as tall as a cypress tree, like my brother and myself, children of our mother Rudabah." Then Rustam told how he had almost been captured by a Turkman warrior.

"What happened?" asked the shah.

"He never returned to the feast," replied Rustam laconically. Then the champion retired to his tent after having instructed the officers that the troops should stand in readiness all through the night.

The following morning, just as the sun flashed full upon the Iranian camp, Suhrab rode out with Hajir, the Iranian whose life he had spared in their battle before the White Castle. Suhrab was stern-faced and intent. He wore his battle gear solemnly—Chinese helmet, Indian sword, and his sixty-coiled lasso upon his saddle horn. From a hill he could survey the brilliantly colored tents of the Iranian nobles. "Hajir," he said, "I spared your life in battle. If you want to be free, not only free but well rewarded, answer my questions truthfully. I want you to identify for me the tents of the Persian paladins which we see spread out below us." Hajir swore that he hated lies more than a crooked arrow. "Do you see over there," asked Suhrab, "a magnificent tent of gold brocade? It is enclosed with many flags and awnings of leopard skin. Beside it are tethered a hundred or so elephants. Before it is a turquoise throne above which beats a purple flag with yellow sun and moon. Whose tent is that?"

"That is the tent of Kai-Kaus, shah of Persia," answered Hajir.

"To the right of the golden tent is a black one. Do you see it? Beside it are chained lions and many troops with golden boots. The banner is black with elephants upon it. Whose enclosure is that?"

"It belongs to Tus, son of a shah named Nauder," replied Hajir. "His standard bears an elephant. I know it well."

"Now," continued Suhrab, "do you see the large red tent? Before it floats another purple pennant with lions rampant. Beside it are many paladins in armor. Whose tent is that?"

"It belongs to Gudarz, a great general. The paladins are his forty sons who came along to war with him," said Hajir promptly.

"Look sharply now," said Suhrab, "for you shall die if you lie to me. There is a massive tent of bright green silk. Before it on a throne sits a paladin so tall that even seated he towers above his throngs of warriors. Behind him are lined Indian elephants all in chain mail. His banner is green with a dragon on it. A golden lion stands upright on the flagpole. Who is that warrior?"

"I do not recognize him," lied Hajir, who knew Rustam's colors very well. He thought it better to lie for fear Suhrab would go charging impetuously down the hill and slay Rustam as he sat on his throne.

"Why do you not know this one?" persisted Suhrab. "Look how wealthy he is. He must be some very famous paladin."

"I think he must be some lord of Chin who joined Iran since I was your prisoner," was all Hajir could think of to say.

Fate had arisen early that morning. Her web was woven tight about them all. Patiently Suhrab went over the Iranian host one by one until Hajir had identified them all. Then he questioned Hajir again about the green tent.

"See the stallion who tosses his mane so restlessly. Is it not Raksh? Is it not Rustam's horse? The coiled lasso reaches almost to the ground. Is it not Rustam?" cried Suhrab.

"No," lied Hajir again. "Rustam remained home in Zabulistan. It is the annual feast of roses there. He would not come to war."

"What kind of tale is that!" Suhrab replied scornfully. "Rustam not go to war? He is the first in every battle line! Kai-Kaus for all his might would never face an enemy without Rustam! The shah, foolish as he is, still remembers what befell him alone in Mazinderan!"

"Rustam did not come," reaffirmed Hajir. "You would recognize him easily enough. He is so much mightier and handsomer than any paladin you have ever seen. Whole empires topple when he lifts his hand." Hajir would say no more. In his heart he despaired, for he gave Rustam no chance at all to vanquish Suhrab. Hajir would not have minded dying then and there, for he considered the war as good as lost. Angry and frustrated, Suhrab dealt Hajir a blow that sent him headfirst from his horse. His heart ached that after all these toils he had not found his father.

It was the Creator who laid out the world. Would you be the one to criticize its workings? He it was who sent their fates to all the warriors of that battlefield. If you will loiter about in this Wayside Inn of Life, you also will see similar tragedies, pain, sorrow, and all kinds of poison!

Suhrab left Hajir on the gound where he had thrown him. Gathering his reins, he spurred his horse down the hill and across the plain to Kai-Kaus' enclosure. Warriors and slaves fled panic-stricken at his approach, and the shah remained hidden in his tent. "Where is this shah of Persia?" Suhrab called sarcastically. "Why does he not ride forth and fight me? One of his brave men stole into my camp last night and slew my faithful uncle, Zanda Razm! Because of this treachery I have sworn a solemn oath: I shall not leave one single Iranian noble alive upon this field! As for the Shah of Shahs, Kai-Kaus, I shall have him strung up alive upon my scaffold!"

The loud cries of Suhrab echoed across the plain while the Iranian army listened in silence. Huddled inside his tent, the shah sent off a messenger for Rustam. Again Suhrab shouted, "Will no one come to fight me?" When there was no answer, Suhrab, laughing and mocking them, circled the shah's encampment and with his spear uprooted seventy tent pegs so that the whole tent collapsed upon its shivering royalty inside.

Rustam was dressing when he received the shah's frantic message. Calmly and methodically he continued to adjust his leopard-skin doublet, buckle his wide girdle, and loosen his sword in its scabbard. Stepping out of the tent, he smiled to see Giv himself tightening Raksh's cinches. Clapping his old friend on the back, Rustam mounted and gathered up the reins. Before leaving he turned kindly to Giv, who looked up at him with tears flowing down his wrinkled cheeks. "Did you ever see such a shah as this one?" Rustam asked. "He never invites me to banquets, only to war!" Then, laughing and slapping the reins across his stallion's neck, Rustam rode off with the words, "Do not advance unless you hear from me. Obey no other's orders!"

A hundred thousand Iranians watched their champion and his color-bearer canter across the plain up to Suhrab. Even Kai-Kaus mustered enough courage to step out to his throne while all around him the older warriors of Persia shook their heads sadly to see their champion ride so nonchalantly to what must be his death.

"Oh! A champion at last!" called Suhrab scornfully. "And an old one at that!"

"Let us withdraw to some quieter spot where we can meet," replied Rustam calmly.

"Hurry up then, old man," called Suhrab, wheeling his mighty roan stallion. "In truth, the field of battle is no place for you. I shall receive no added glory by killing you in plain sight of your troops. You may have been a fine man once, but your powerful limbs are long stiff with age. One cuff, and I will send you to the dust!"

Rustam looked at him and smiled to see so much ardor and impetuosity. "Young man," he answered pleasantly, "I wonder if you have any idea at all of how cold and hard this earth is upon which we stand. Do you perceive the mildness of the summer air and yet desire to leave it? Have you any notion at all of death?

"I may be old by your standards," Rustam continued, "but I have never been beaten. I hope you are paying attention to what I say," he added, for Suhrab was obviously impatient to begin. "I have fought elephants, fierce crocodiles, demons, and armies, but I have never been overpowered. You will know fear if you insist on fighting me. If you survive, then never fear again. The stars above be witness to my words: my heart aches for you, young man, young Suhrab. I do not want to take your life. There is no other champion like you in Turan. I know, because I have fought them all."

Despite his arrogance Suhrab was moved by the words. "Tell me one thing, great warrior of Iran. What is your name and lineage? Are you not Rustam, son of Zal?"

Shaking his head, Rustam answered slowly, "No, I am not Rustam. He is a mightier paladin with crowns and empires. I am only a lowly warrior. You will have many more like me to vanquish before you meet Rustam and the shah. You have a false opinion of your importance. We would not send Rustam to meet a youngster like you."

For Suhrab all the day was spoiled. It was as if a cloud had overcast the sun. He and Rustam withdrew to a small area far from the troops, and there they met in battle. First they fought with javelins until their weapons' points were broken. Then, wheeling their mounts, they closed with Indian scimitars until the sparks flew red above their heads. The struggle was a draw. Then they wielded maces so strong their armor cracked and the mail dropped from their staggering horses. After these onslaughts each one drew aside to rest a moment, Suhrab exhausted, and Rustam in anguish.

How mysterious are the workings of the world! Wild lions, horses, fishes know their young. A newborn foal totters to its dam. Only the race of men feel no strong stirrings of love for their brothers. Only the father does not recognize his child!

Rustam laid his hand across the mane of Raksh and sighed to hear the stallion's labored breathing. Thoughts of old feuds and wounds ran through his mind. "The White Demon in all his insensate fury was nothing compared to this boy," he mused. "Here before armies an unskilled youth has made me long for death!"

Looking up, the champion saw Suhrab on horseback again and stringing his bow. Heavily Rustam mounted, and the battle began afresh.

Arrow after arrow they shot, stinging and clanging on each other's armor, but neither was seriously wounded. Then Rustam grabbed Suhrab by the belt, an old trick of his that had succeeded with Afrasiab once. Suhrab gripped his mount with knees of iron, and Rustam could not unseat him. Then Suhrab brought his heavy iron mace down across Rustam's shoulder so hard that the champion winced in spite of himself and let go Suhrab's girdle. The youth yelled in triumph and taunted Rustam, "Champion of Iran, I saw you flinch beneath my mace. Go home, old man. You cannot fight with me! That nag of yours ambles rather like a donkey."

Rustam spurred away, the youth's exultant cries following him. All along the Turanian front line Rustam galloped, lopping off heads in his anger and driving the troops and horses in panic back upon each other. Then there came to his ears the moans and cries from the Iranians. Rustam, realizing he should not have left Kai-Kaus' side, tore off across the plain to his own lines where Suhrab was plunging like a maddened elephant. "Stop it!" he ordered. "Save your blows for me." Since darkness was falling, they agreed to meet again at dawn.

Suhrab returned to his camp where Human hastened to help him dismount and anoint his cuts. "How was their champion?" questioned the Turanian chiefs.

"I hold him peerless," answered Suhrab. "He has the heart of a lion truly, but I have won the day, for I killed many Iranian chiefs while all he did was to ravage our front lines. We fight again tomorrow. Come. Let us feast. You may be sure I shall kill him tomorrow."

Rustam was met by his old friend Giv. "How did you fare?" asked Rustam, for he was worried about the shah.

"This Suhrab is a raging lion," answered Giv. "I kept your rule and made him fight our champions one by one. Perhaps in that way will we wear him out."

The shah greeted Rustam warmly and anxiously scanned his weary face. He courteously made Rustam lean back on the throne itself and rest while he reported what had happened. "We fought all day," said Rustam. "We strove with javelins, arrows, and maces. This Suhrab never felt my blows. I tried to lift him from the saddle, but I could not even rock him from his horse. We fight again tomorrow, but for once I can promise you nothing. I will do what I can for shah and country, but only the Creator can say which of us will prevail." Then Rustam strode stiffly to his own tent where his brother was waiting. Rustam would let no one else help him. Zuara bit his lips as he cut away the mail and saw how cruelly Rustam had been wounded.

Half through the night Rustam conversed alone with his brother. "I want you to have our troops in readiness by sunrise," Rustam told him. "Bring Raksh around to me and set out my golden boots. If I manage in some way to vanquish Suhrab tomorrow, we will set out for home as soon as you see me return. Therefore have all the baggage ready to depart. If I am vanquished, as seems will be the case, you will command our forces. Do not tarry one second, not even to mourn me or lament, but push on without stopping to Zabulistan.

"Think of our mother first, and bear her first the news. You will know what to say. Tell her my life was good. Say that I remained undefeated until the day of my death. Especially tell her I forbid her to weep or mourn for me. I have been knocking at the door of death each day, ever since I mounted Raksh and sought for battle. No man can live forever. Tell her to think of Jemshid on his Golden Throne, and of Zahhak. Even they left this world as all must do. Comfort her, for a woman does not understand what a man's life is.

"Tell our father Zal I bid him to fight for the shah. Prepare for siege as soon as you reach Zabul." Then Rustam and his brother searched their minds for precedents and discussed old battles in an effort to decide how best to defeat Suhrab the following day.

At sunrise the two champions rode across the shimmering plain toward each other, and Suhrab was smiling. He greeted Rustam cordially as if the two of them had spent the night banqueting together. Rustam listened sternly to the boy's words, "Let us not fight today, you and I," Suhrab suggested. "Let us sit in the warm sun and clear our brows with some ruby wine. I blush to admit it, old man, but I have a strange affection for you. One could almost say there is some link between us. If we were to stretch out here on the grass, I'll wager you would see we are identical in length and breadth. Surely you will tell me you are Rustam. Indeed, you ought, for enemies should always announce their names to each other."

Rustam dryly replied, "As I recall, our appointment today was for the purpose of wrestling. I am too old for tricks, young hero. Do not attempt to beguile me. You cannot disarm me with words."

"You will regret it if I cannot," answered Suhrab shortly.

The warriors tied their chargers to a rock and, huge in their mail, advanced to grapple with each other. Like two fierce lions they wrestled until the sweat and blood poured from their skins and mingled with the dust. All day long they struggled, almost without stopping to breathe. Then, as long shadows fell across the ground, Suhrab gained the advantage. He somehow seized the belt of Rustam with both hands and, yelling with rage and triumph, threw him to the dust. Then Suhrab pounced upon him and drew his dagger to cut off his head. Rustam caught his breath in time, however, and told him, "You cannot kill me yet. We are in Persia and therefore must abide by Persian custom. It is only the second time that you throw a man that you become a Lion. It is only then that you may cut off his head."

His words stopped Suhrab. Wiping the sweat and blood from his mouth, the youth arose, confident now that he could kill Rustam whenever he chose. Fate had not willed that Rustam should die yet. Who knows whether Suhrab also complied through magnanimity? In any case he returned toward his forces and was roundly scolded by Human and his fellow warriors.

"When will you learn not to despise an enemy, no matter how puny he appears to you?" growled Human. "This is the third time you have underestimated a foe. You never should have let the Iranian chieftain go. You say you had him in your power. Why didn't you kill him?"

Suhrab stood crushed before his fury. "Well, never fear," he answered them. "He will return tomorrow, and then will I kill him for you!"

What happened to Rustam when he raised himself from the ground where Suhrab had hurled him is shrouded in mystery. In after years people used to wonder what occurred, and old men who had known Rustam personally told it this way. It seems that when Rustam was a very young man he had suffered greatly because he was different from his friends and fellow warriors. His tremendous height and strength embarrassed him and made him feel ashamed, since he could so effortlessly vanquish any foe. It seemed to him that he was taking undue credit for his victories. In his sorrow he had prayed to have his force diminished. He had wept and prayed to be like ordinary men so that he could walk into a hall without bumping his head, and stride over sand without sinking deep into it. His prayer had been answered, for Rustam's request was honorable.

In after years old men believed that the day Rustam almost met his death at the hand of Suhrab, he arose from the dust and walked alone to the banks of a nearby river. There he unbuckled his armor and plunged into the icy water. As he bathed, he prayed to have his former strength restored. The cool water flowed over his bruised body, and his prayer was granted a second time.

The warrior who met Suhrab on the following morning was a different man. As soon as the two had tied their horses to the same rocks, Suhrab advanced confidently. The moment he felt the hands of Rustam bending his body backward, however, Suhrab became like a helpless toy. Rustam grasped him firmly by the belt and, lifting him high in the air, hurled him to the ground. Then as Suhrab struggled violently beneath him, Rustam without a word drew his dagger and gave his son a mortal wound.

"Ah," groaned Suhrab as the sharp blade pierced his chest. "Ah," he cried again. "It is all my fault and the fault of my fate that bore me up so soon to cast me down so fast. My mother warned me not to go to Persia." Then looking up at Rustam through anguished eyes, Suhrab lashed out at him. "Run and hide yourself, paladin. Transform yourself into some crawling worm and hide beneath the surface of the earth. For were you some slimy fish that lurks among the weeds of a bottomless pool, or an eagle that soars a mile above us, my father would seek you out. When Rustam hears you have slain his only son, he will choke you with his bare hands. You shall die for this day's work!"

Rustam stood above the writhing youth, his dripping dagger in his heavy hand, when those words struck him. Before his eyes the world spun in a huge maelstrom with him at its center, upside down. Blinded and numb, he fell to his knees, and his tears gushed over his face.

"Suhrab," he moaned. "I am Rustam."

"Cut open my mail, and you will see the amulet my mother bade me take you," sobbed the boy. Rustam did as he bade and saw the brilliant gem.

Then he covered his head with dust as the words of his son pierced his very heart. "Why did you not tell me?" wept Suhrab. "I came to you yesterday in love. Why did you not know me for your son?"

Rustam then held the dagger to his throat, but the hand of Suhrab stopped him. "It must have been my fate to die so young," he cried. "What good will it do to kill yourself? Swift as the lightning came I to this world and on the wind's breath shall I glide away. Perchance you will be my father in heaven. It was the wish of fate for me to die. You could do nothing. Therefore live."

With his head in the dust beside his dying son Rustam crouched, and here the Iranian warriors found him. Their joy turned to consternation when they saw that he had rent his garments and covered his head with dust. "I have killed my son," he whispered to the aged Gudarz who

knelt beside him. Fast as a prairie fire spread the word through the Persian army.

In honor of Rustam men everywhere rent their garments also and bent their heads to the dust. Even the Turanian chiefs sat in rows along the ground and wept. Then Gudarz remembered the famous elixir of Shah Kai-Kaus, a marvelous medicine that would stanch the blood of any wound. He told Rustam to take courage and hastened to the shah.

Kai-Kaus refused. All he could remember was Suhrab's threat to hang him, and so Suhrab died. All hostilities ceased between the two hosts, and the Turanians began quietly to withdraw. Zuara fashioned a superb litter of gold cloth and on this Suhrab was transported to Zabul. As the cortege entered the home city, all the warriors removed their belts and fastened them to the bier. Their horses' manes and tails were docked, and their hair covered with dust.

Rustam lifted the cloth from his son's face so that Zal and Rudabah could see him. "He is like a tawny lion," all people said, "who has fallen asleep while playing with war." Rustam sent word to Tamineh and to her also Suhrab's stallion. This sorrowing mother did not long survive her son.

Rustam had an intricate tomb constructed in the shape of a horseshoe for his son's body. For months he mourned Suhrab, but eventually he was able to lift his head and bear his suffering with understanding.

I have written *The Book of Kings*, which will remain as a memory of my life in this world. The palaces men build fall into ruin under the rain and the heat of the sun; I have built with these verses a magnificent palace which the storm and rain will not injure; the years will roll over this book, but men everywhere will recite it. . . . I learned how to weave this golden cloth because I discovered long ago the secret of words.

Oh, you who look into the past, how often are you also joyous like me, and how often like me are you full of sorrow. How astonishing is the swift motion of this vaulted sky above all our heads! How often is the soul burdened with still more recent troubles!

One man's lot is all honey and sugar, good health, sheltered life, and high fortunes; the years of another are so filled with grief and toil that his heart breaks in this fleeting world; a third man's life is spent in disappointment—sometimes he wins, but oftener he loses. That is the way fate lifts us up, and the pain caused by the thorns is greater than the pleasure we felt at the color of the rose. . . . If only the sixty nets of the years were like fishnets, then a clever man could find his way out; but we can none of us escape from this sky that revolves at the will of Him who made sun and earth.

Even the great conquerors of Persia struggled painfully in vain, loved combat in vain, and ceased to take pleasure in their wealth; they too departed for another world and left here all the fruits of their labors.

Consider the fate of the greatest Shah of Shahs, Cyrus the Great; examine once more the old, old stories of the world. Learn how even Cyrus did not remain upon the earth, how men by the millions ceased to obey his commands.

That is the law of every man's life; therefore rid your hearts of all anxiety.

Abu'l-Kasim Hasan
(Called "Firdausi," which means "of Paradise.")
Tus, Iran
c. 1000

SIX
INDIA

Historians agree that the history of India is very long. According to *Ancient India*, published in 1911 by S. Krishnaswami Aiyanger, the original home of the Aryans who conquered India was in the Arctic Circle. He believes the Aryans were living there in 7000 B.C., and that changes of climate forced them to move south. Geologists confirm that the strongest climatic change the world has known in 100,000 years occurred in this area between 10,000 B.C. and 5000 B.C. A rapid rise in temperature and flash floods would have driven the inhabitants to seek in central Asia conditions similar to those with which they were familiar. Indian scholars think that the *Vedas*, or hymns of the Aryans, had already been composed by 3800 B.C. They base their belief in part on interior astronomical evidence, which is also confirmed by modern science.

In the third millennium B.C. the Aryan tribes were moving through the Khyber Pass into the Punjab. By 1500 B.C. they had settled along the Doab, Ganges, and Jumna River valleys of northern India. Their language, Sanskrit, which is the parent of the major languages of India, corresponds to Latin, the parent of the romance tongues. Sanskrit is believed to be much older than Latin.

The two epics of India were composed in Sanskrit. Many Western historians, such as Pierre Meile (*Histoire de l'Inde*, Paris, 1951), feel that these poems cannot be dated. Indian students, on the contrary, would assign the *Mahabharata* to the years 1500 B.C.–1000 B.C. This long and very spirited epic tells the story of wars fought when the Aryans were contacting the older residents of India, the civilized Dravidians. Prior to the Aryan invasion there existed two extensive kingdoms along the Indus River, one in the area called Sind (Mohenjo-Daro) and a second in the Punjab (Harappa). Some scientists believe they see similarities between these Dravidians and the early Egyptians, and also with the Australoids. The Dravidians are usually referred to as a short, dark-skinned people.

Most Indian students fix the *Ramayana*, the second long epic of India, at around the year 1000 B.C. Romesh Dutt, its best-known translator, concurs. The following chapter will retell the story of Rama, a story that describes those virtues that for millennia have characterized all that is best in Indian men and women. Mr. Dutt points out the striking contrast between the *Ramayana* which extols faithfulness, piety, and steadfastness, with the Greeks' reverence of beauty and their emphasis upon gaiety and joy. Like the epic of Persia, the *Ramayana* is the work of one man, the poet Valmiki, whom you will meet in the following pages.

Persia was always the link between India and the West in ancient times. According to a Persian historian named Mohammed Kazim Farishta (translated by Lieutenant Colonel Alexander Dow, Dublin, 1792), Shah Feridun ruled Hindustan before 1429 B.C. Then in 1072 a Persian noble named Rustam deposed an Indian prince named Feros-ra, who later died in Bengal, thus ending a dynasty that had reigned for 137 years. Rustam then placed upon the throne a ruler named Suraja because Rustam felt this area was too distant for him to govern it efficiently. It seems quite certain that Cyrus the Great ruled a part of India around 550 B.C.; and according to the Mount Behistun inscriptions so did Darius, from 521–485 B.C. Through Persia the western or Byblos alphabet made its way into India. Persian annals also tell how that great shah of Persia whom we usually refer to as Alexander the Great also crossed the Hindu Kush Mountains into the Punjab in 327 B.C.

Ancient India apparently never returned the compliment by wishing to conquer or possess any part of the Western world.

One of their ideas was that their Himalayan peak, which they called Mount Meru, was at the center of the earth. Paradise was at its summit, and similar beliefs exist about Mount Everest today. They pictured the land of India as lying around this mountain, encircled by a sea of salt water. Other lands lay in concentric circles around India, surrounded by other seas—of wine, milk, sugar-cane syrup, and juices.

The Indians knew of a western land they called Rómaka, where it was midnight when it was sunrise at Lanka in Ceylon. To their immediate west were the Párasica (Persians), then the Yávana (Greeks), and the Raúmaca (Romans). Anyone else was a Barbara, an unidentified foreigner. While the Indians for religious reasons were poor geographers, they were great mathematicians, grammarians, philosophers, and poets. They claim Pythagoras learned his mathematics in India.

Mr. William Robertson, historian to His Majesty of Scotland, writes in Edinburgh in 1791 that India was "the original station of man." He adds that in the mild and fertile regions of the east the most useful of the domestic animals, the horse and the camel, were first bred.

Early historians noted how envious the West always was of the riches of the East. India itself is a country that, judging from the vast numbers of histories and the hundreds of travel books written about it, particularly in the nineteenth century, has always attracted the West. The library shelves on Persia are bare by comparison. The following chapter incorporates descriptions from one of the most novel travel books, *L'Inde* by Pierre Loti. This book was written in India at the turn of the century and tells also of Loti's conversion. Unlike the *Shah Namah*, the *Ramayana* does include descriptions of scenery.

One other Indian work is included because it is representative of the most ancient writing of India and also because it contains the thought of our hero's religion, or an answer to a problem that had been plaguing heroes all the way from Gilgamesh. The philosophy or scriptures of Rama come from the *Katha Upanishad*. The sacred *Vedas* of the Aryans were divided into four types of writing: (1) poetic, (2) Brahmanical, (3) philosophical, and (4) ritualistic. The *Upanishads* are the best philosophical thinking of Brahmanism. They are the commentaries of great thinkers whose pupils sat down beside them (*upa*—near; *ni*—down; *sad*—sit).

The Lieutenant Colonel Dow of Dublin, mentioned above, in addition to being a translator from the Persian and an historian, was an early student of Sanskrit. In the middle 1700's he persuaded a learned pandit from the University of Benares to give him lessons in this mysterious language. The colonel's personal conclusion was that Sanskrit had been artificially created by the Brahmans, just as hieroglyphics had been devised in Egypt and restricted to an educated elect. In his preface Colonel Dow has this to say about India: "Though, in an advanced stage of society, the human mind is, in some respects, enlarged, a ruinous kind of self-conceit frequently circumscribes its researches after knowledge. In love with our own times, country and government, we are apt to consider distant ages and nations, as objects unworthy of the page of the Historian."

RAMA AND THE MONKEYS

Once upon a time there lived in the fair kingdom of Ayodhya a prince named Rama who was without an equal for comeliness, courage, and learning. His father was a wise old rajah named Dasa-ratha. Prince Rama was beloved of his father and of his father's wives, who had borne Dasa-ratha three other sons, both handsome and brave—but not so outstanding as Rama.

One day the rajah of the neighboring kingdom to the east sent a challenge out to the civilized lands of northern India to say that he would bestow his oldest daughter on whatever prince could bend a mighty war bow in his palace. Rama traveled to this land of Videha as soon as he heard the pronouncement. Everyone had spoken of the extraordinary beauty and gentleness of this Princess Sita, and people wondered who would win a maiden so lovely. Suitors hastened to the court of her father Janaka, but they soon left it in great humiliation. No matter how strong they were, they could not even lift the bow of the Rajah Janaka, to say nothing of bend it.

Rama and his three brothers were ceremoniously received at the eastern court. Rama asked to be shown the marvelous engine that no prince could move. Before the whole court of Videha the monstrous bow was hauled into the audience chamber. It lay on an eight-wheeled chariot pulled by eight hundred men. Everyone gasped as Prince Rama lifted the bow quite easily. He strung it also, and then asking King Janaka's aid and blessing, Rama bent it until it split asunder with a crack like a clap of thunder. In this way did the Sun Prince Rama, descendant of mankind's father Manu, win his sweet-faced bride.

Messengers rode back to Rama's kingdom of Ayodhya to notify the prince's father, Dasa-ratha. Seven days later the elderly rajah himself arrived in Videha for the wedding. He was most courteously welcomed as an enlightened ruler and a devoted student of the holy *Vedas*. After the early morning rites had been scrupulously performed, a high altar was raised, richly adorned, and encircled by Igni, the holy fire. Then slender Prince Rama advanced to the altar, where he took the hands of Princess Sita who was arrayed in flame-and-golden draperies. Then Rama's three brothers—Lakshman, Bharat, and Satrughna—all sons of Dasa-ratha by two different mothers, advanced and were wedded to Sita's sisters—Urmila, Mandavi, and Sruta-kriti. After each couple had humbly stepped around the altar, the princes led away their resplendent brides through a shower of drifting petals, and all Videha rang with music and acclamation.

A few days later Dasa-ratha's train, returning homeward to Ayodhya, saw their own fair city of Kosala bright and shining like the Himalayan mountain Meru. The people had sprinkled the ways with rose water and swept them clean. Then they had strewn yellow, perfumed jasmine all along the route. The kindly Dasa-ratha smiled down at his subjects as his chariot bore him among them. All in Kosala were healthy and plump, and no one so poor he could not wear gold earrings and bracelets. Men of all occupations were free from the disgraceful passions—servility, egotism, and the lust for gold. All had leisure to study the *Vedas* and mind enough not to question the will of heaven. In Videha hard labor was not done by men, but by ponderous elephants brought down from the Himalayas or captured in the Vindhya Mountains.

Dasa-ratha and his sons were met by the royal wives—first Kausalya, the mother of the oldest prince and heir, Rama; then Kaikeyi, whose brother ruled in a fierce and warlike western land and whose son was the tall and very handsome Bharat; and thirdly by Sumitra, mother of the twin sons, Lakshman and Satrughna. Each one of the royal mothers was greeted affectionately by the princes, who approached and humbly touched their feet. Then the gentle brides were admired and made welcome. Dasa-ratha looked on his royally married sons and decided it would be safe for him to relax somewhat from the exigencies of kingship. Within the next few days he dispatched his second son, Bharat, to see the world and pay a visit of state to his mother's kingdom, that fierce land in the west.

Then the aged rajah of Ayodhya called a formal assembly of all the Brahmans and chieftains of his lands. Addressing them respectfully, he told them of a suggestion. He asked them if they agreed that he had ruled so long he might be allowed to spend his last few months of life prolonged and served by his three young wives. Dasa-ratha appealed to the wise Brahmans for their thoughts in this matter. He said that he desired their sanction for the coronation of his oldest son, Rama. At once the priests and warriors gave him their consent. Even when Dasa-ratha begged them to speak freely, to reveal any misgivings they might have thought it polite to conceal, his council continued to approve his decision.

Rama was notified that he was to be crowned the following morning. This prince had won the trust and affection of the whole kingdom. From childhood he had been unfailing in his religious observances, humble before the Brahmans, eager to memorize the *Vedas*, and in war the world had never seen his equal. Even the lowliest workingman could obtain audience with this tall prince at any time whatsoever. Rama saw to it that there was no unemployment and no beggars in his land. To his father and the queens he had always been unfailing in his devotion, touching the feet of each of his mothers with equal respect and affection. Rama placed virtue and truth above all else, so that people called him the prince of righteousness. As soon as Rama received his father's directions, he retired to fast and pray so that he would be ready for the coronation in the cool hour of sunrise the following day.

The three queens rejoiced also in the news, as much as the city dwellers. From their private apartments and secluded gardens they could hear preparations for the ceremonies. Poles were being driven into the ground along the roads so that lanterns could glow all through the next evening. Golden bells were strung from the elephants' howdahs. A new white umbrella was being sewn for Rama, wide enough to protect his broad shoulders from the sun.

Kaikeyi, the mother of Bharat, she who had come from the western land, was selecting jewelry to wear on the morrow when her maid Manthara stalked into the room. The choice of jewelry was very important to Kaikeyi, for she was Dasa-ratha's favorite wife. No matter how much the old rajah respected and admired Rama's mother, Kausalya, he could not take his eyes from the bewitching charms of this Kaikeyi.

The old servant Manthara glared at her mistress and sulked. To Kaikeyi's questions she replied sullenly, "What matter?" or "What is there to be festive about?"

"Stop moping this way, Manthara. There is every reason to celebrate. Our dear son Rama will be crowned at sunrise. He is so beloved of us all, and surely he will make an excellent rajah. He will rule well, and Dasa-ratha will have more time for me!"

"I do not rejoice," Manthara replied angrily. "While Bharat is far away, Rama rises to supreme power. Why Rama? Why not Bharat? Why not your son?"

"That is a mere technicality," Kaikeyi assured the old servant. "Rama and Bharat love each other and will share the rule."

"Do not believe it," retorted Manthara. "If you let Rama gain the throne, that will be the end of your son Bharat." Manthara spoke so convincingly that she succeeded in arousing Kaikeyi's fears. Although this queen had never been jealous of Rama before, now she was thoroughly so. Tearing off her jewels and precious gown, she hurried sobbing and angry to the mourning house. Stormily she threw herself on its unswept earthen floor.

In the cool hours of evening Dasa-ratha, perfumed and freshly bathed, strolled to the apartments of his favorite wife only to find them desolate and empty. Her weeping attendants told the bewildered old ruler that Kaikeyi had been seen weeping wildly and running toward the house of anger. He hurried there, thoroughly alarmed, and found his most treasured wife lying disheveled on the floor. Dasa-ratha lifted her to his lap and petted her.

"Now why is my pretty bird weeping?" he cajoled. "Who has ruffled her silken feathers? Tell me at once, and they shall be punished. My darling shall have anything her heart desires!"

"Do you remember how once years ago I nursed you during a long and dangerous illness?" Kaikeyi asked him. "Do you remember how I healed you of two dangerous wounds?"

"Yes, I remember," answered the king. "You are my charming little bird."

"Do you remember that you promised to grant me two requests, anything that I should ask? Do you remember giving me your sacred word?" persisted Kaikeyi.

"Yes, I remember," answered the rajah. "Only you never made your two requests."

"I am ready to make them now," answered Kaikeyi. "That is why I have come to the house of tears. For if you do not grant them, I shall die of grief this night."

"You shall have your requests," smiled the king. "Do you wish more more cities? Do you desire gems, or pearls from Ceylon?"

"My first request is that my son Bharat be recalled from his visit, and that he be crowned in the place of Rama. My second request is that Rama be exiled to the most savage jungles for a period of fourteen years!"

The old king's eyes opened wide in horror. He stared at his wife in amazement and could say nothing. He lifted a trembling hand to his head as if to clear it of this terrible thought.

"Will you dare to refuse me?" asked Kaikeyi. "If you do, people everywhere will call you a liar forevermore."

After a long silence Dasa-ratha spoke. "How shall I tell Rama? How shall I admit this shameful disinheritance of my first-born? How can I expose my son to this cruel banishment?" Looking at Kaikeyi as if he saw her for the first time, he asked, "What are you? Are you some serpent I have pampered and nourished in my heart?"

The following morning at dawn Prince Rama approached his father's throne and, joining his hands in greeting, bowed to Dasa-ratha and Kaikeyi who sat beside him. Rama was astonished to see his father's worn face and to notice that he had been weeping. He was grieved to note that the rajah did not even acknowledge his son's reverence. Turning to Kaikeyi, whom Rama had always held as his mother also, the prince begged her to tell him what he could have done to offend, what injury he could have unwittingly performed. Kaikeyi then coldly told Rama that Dasa-ratha was bound by the oath he had made her. Rama replied that he too was bound by any oath of his father, and he asked Kaikeyi to reveal the oath. "Whatever my father desires, I desire it also," swore Rama. "You have my word."

As Kaikeyi revealed her will, Rama bowed his head. Then without speaking he bowed out of the palace and returned directly to his quarters to prepare for his departure. His instructions to Sita were detailed, "I must leave Kosala to wander through the jungles for fourteen years. I know you will uphold my name and honor during this long separation. Respect my father and serve him like a dutiful daughter. Pay every homage to my mother, and equal duty to Kaikeyi. Let no one say that the wife of Rama showed bitterness or revenge. Take your place among the palace ladies with a serene and open face. Serve also my brother Bharat, for he will be especially aggrieved at his mother's baseless fears. Be careful not to speak my praises or let anyone see you grieve for me. Remember that we are not the victims of my father's vow, but his children happy to accomplish his will. Now we must part, my dear Sita."

Rama would have left his wife then and departed from the palace, but Sita held him back. "My father is a rajah also," she reminded him. "He and my mother taught me, Rama, that a woman's place is beside her husband. They did not tell me that my lot was yours only so long as your fate was an easy, perfumed path. They instructed me to follow you all the days of my life, through luxury and through poverty, through carpeted halls and jungle paths. In Videha also we have wise Brahmans whose teachings could not mislead a princess."

Rama described for Sita the horrors of the jungle. "I must spend fourteen years among tall coconut palms which spring up so fast all around me in the warm rains that I shall go for days among them without seeing the sky. My road shall be through hot green tunnels of vine that are so tightly interlaced no ray of sunlight ever pierces them. I shall have to climb up and down over the roots of banyans that writhe and turn like the gnarled trunks of primordial elephants. For company I shall have only the wild creatures of the jungle, snakes, monkeys, and hordes of crying birds. My only lodging will be a hut of palm fronds, my only food the wild fruits and roots, my only clothing a hermit's coat of bark. Parrots and crows and the white-feathered eagle will roost above me at night. You cannot leave our palace, Sita, to wander fourteen years under giant trees where the tiger crouches to drop on your shoulders!"

"How could I fear tigers when Rama is near to protect me? What sun shall I lack when I am warmed by his love? I shall serve you like a true wife. While you are busy, I will collect food. I will carry your tools. At night we will nestle snugly in our palm hut, and the years of banishment will fly. Let me go with you," pleaded Sita.

Rama consented. Then his brother Lakshman fell at Rama's feet and made a similar request. He begged to be allowed to accompany them both to the forest. Rama refused, primarily because he could not think of leaving his mother alone and unserved since Dasa-ratha was so obviously a prisoner to his craving for Kaikeyi. However, Lakshman reminded Rama that first of all his mother, Kausalya, was a wealthy and powerful queen in her own right, that she owned a thousand villages and had many soldiers at her command. Lakshman also spoke to Rama of Bharat. "When our brother returns, you know he will be horrified at what has occurred. You know he will blame his mother Kaikeyi, and all the more revere and honor your mother Kausalya." Lakshman also argued that Rama should not take the gentle Sita into the jungle all alone. "While you are away for any reason," Lakshman urged, "I will be needed to remain beside Sita. It will take the two of us to protect her from rain and dangers!"

Finally Rama consented to both their requests. Then they all three made their preparations for departure. Sita took with her only her best bracelets and bangles, and only her most perfect gold hoops for her ears. She could fold several saris into a very small square. She took no perfume, for the jungle was full of scented flowers. She took no mascara, for Rama would be there to drive away all demons. Rama and Lakshman, however, made lists and sent the palace smiths and armorers scurrying busily to and fro. They required a supply of swords, daggers, scimitars, shields, suits of mail, bows, cords, and bronze-tipped arrows. All this was loaded into the royal car, where the charioteer Sumantra stood flicking his whip proudly.

The three exiles bade farewell to Rama's mother first. This gentle lady wept so bitterly that Rama took her aside and consoled her with scripture. "Reflect upon the spirit of man; it has no body though it dwells in bodies; it is not corruptible though it dwells in the midst of corruption. Meditate upon the permanence of the spirit. Think how vast it is. See how penetrating. It alone is changeless. It alone never dies. Therefore it is not wise to grieve." Queen Kausalya was calmed. She kissed Sita's long braids that were still wet from her morning's devotions and blessed her for knowing her wifely duties. She praised Lakshman for fulfilling his proper service to his elder brother. Then the three passed out of the queen's palace with Sita between them looking like an amber butterfly.

In the chariot where Sumantra waited were piled high gifts from Dasa-ratha for the three of them, more precious fabrics and jewels than Sita could ever wear. Once they were seated, Sumantra cracked his whip, and the horses started forward. The populace was silent at first, for they could see Rama was praying. To his wife and brother he was saying, "Know that you are the lord of your chariot, the master of your body. Know that your Buddhi (Reason) is the driver who holds in check your impulses, which are the reins." Their progress was slow, for on every side people crowded to praise the three of them, and to catch a last glimpse of their prince. As the chariot passed the palace, Rama was heartbroken to see Dasa-ratha, supported by his courtiers, try to totter toward them. Overnight his father had become an aged, almost a helpless man. Rama ordered Sumantra to whip up the horses so that the parting would be swift.

All day they traveled in the heat and dust through masses of people who knelt all along the route. In the evening they arrived at the banks of the Tamasa River, where they bathed. Rama would neither eat nor drink. Finally he and Sita slept a few hours while Sumantra mounted guard. Then during the night they quietly crossed the river so that the citizens of Kosala upon awakening would find them gone and would return to their families and occupations. On the following day they continued their journey southward, crossing the parallel rivers, until they came to the north shore of the holy river of India, the Ganges, Bride of the Sea. Reverently they watched its russet waters flow majestically before them. Before traversing this river, Rama sent their driver Sumantra home to Kosala, for they had reached the southern boundary of Dasa-ratha's land.

After having prayed, they crossed the sacred Ganges. Rama then led the way through open meadows, traveling single-file with Sita and Lakshman after him. When they grew hungry, they roasted a deer; when they were thirsty, they knelt on the ground and drank spring water from their cupped hands. Sita followed Rama bravely and let no word of complaint escape her lips. At night the brothers made her a bed of sweet grasses under the clusters of bloom of the asoka tree, and she slept peacefully while the courteous tree waved its feathery pink blossoms and kept the starlight from her eyes.

On the fourth day of their travels they arrived at the junction of the Ganges and Jumna Rivers, where the dark blue waters of the Jumna embrace the ruddy ones of its older sister. In this triangle between the two streams lived a celebrated scholar and hermit to whom students flocked from all of civilized India so that they could sit at his feet and hear him lecture on the holy writings of their land. Rama asked this anchorite for hospitality, and it was granted. The scholar invited Rama and his friends to spend their fourteen years of exile with him. He had already learned of their causeless banishment. Rama was overjoyed because he knew that in studying and learning the years would pass most delightfully, but he was afraid to stay too near the hermit for fear that throngs of curious pilgrims would come to visit the royal exiles and so disturb the holy man's meditations. It was arranged that Rama should cross the Jumna and build a small hut for the three of them only twenty or so miles away. During the fourth night the wanderers slept in the peace and holiness of the hermit's hut.

The next morning Rama and Lakshman felled trees on the north bank of the Jumna River and bound them together with creepers to make a strong raft large enough for themselves and for their possessions. Lakshman wove a seat for Sita, and folded beside her all the precious stuffs Dasa-ratha had sent his oldest daughter-in-law. Sita made their craft gay with wreaths of flowers; and as the princes shoved out into the current and plied their bamboo oars, she prayed to the River Jumna for their safe return and decked its dark blue waters with yellow carnations. Pelicans and herons waded along the sand bars of the southern shore. Beyond that lay the pathless wilderness to which they were condemned.

Shouldering their bundles, they turned bravely away from the sunny riverbank and plunged into the dark tangle of jungle. Lakshman walked first, wielding his ax to cut away the matted vines that barred their route, and Rama lifted his fragile wife over the slippery roots of trees that towered high above their heads. They stopped often with Sita to admire strange berries and flowers that gleamed in the dark tunnel of this forest. Toward afternoon their path began to climb steadily toward the slopes of the mountain Chitra-kuta. In its foothills they paid a courtesy visit at the hermitage of the greatest poet of India, the saintly Valmiki.

Coming out of his simple shelter, this poet greeted them and blessed them. He told the three wanderers that in after ages countless generations of Indians would retrace their travels every year and would hold in high esteem the peak of Chitra-kuta, their refuge. Smiling at the beauty of the lotus-eyed Sita, the poet Valmiki pointed to the garlands she was wearing and told her that in future millennia the women of India would weave wreaths of flowers from this very mountain. They would call them "Sita's Blossoms" in praise of the princess who had braved these wilds for the love of Rama. "I shall write a poem about love, and I shall call it the *Ramayana*," he said.

Farther up the mountain, Lakshman and Rama built of forest timbers and palm leaves a shelter where they slept on the sixth night of their banishment.

On this very night in the kingdom of Ayodhya, Dasa-ratha dreamed of his youth, a dream that presaged his death. Calling his two good wives, Kausalya and Sumitra, the rajah told them of his vision. More than a half century before, when Dasa-ratha was the prince of the realm, the sin of pride ate deeply into his heart. Wherever the young prince went, or whatever he did, adulatory courtiers praised him to the skies so that Dasa-ratha forgot the lessons of humility the Brahmans had taught him and became overconfident and boastful. The one achievement of the youthful Dasa-ratha that was considered most extraordinary by the other warriors of his caste was his ability to shoot at a target by sound, even when the animal was not in sight.

One evening as Dasa-ratha hunted among the reeds of a riverbank he heard the gurgling sounds an elephant makes with his trunk when he plays in the water. Silently Dasa-ratha sent his arrow in that direction, as swift and as venomous as the fangs of a cobra. He heard his arrow strike flesh, and then, instead of the trumpeting of an elephant, a long, human wail that sent shivers down his back rose in the still night. Dasa-ratha plunged through the underbrush to see a young man lying pierced by his arrow. It was the young son of two holy hermits who lived nearby. The boy had been filling his pitcher with water for their frugal evening meal.

Piteously the boy begged Dasa-ratha to pull out the burning arrow, and pitifully he asked the prince why he had murdered him. After the boy had died, Dasa-ratha filled the pitcher with water and bore it to the aged parents. At first they mistook the young prince for their own son, but when they understood what a tragedy the young heir to the throne had caused, they cursed him. The aged couple sought death on their son's funeral pyre. Their curse was that years hence—when he also was old and feeble—he should be deprived of his son and die of grief. "Now I feel the agony of their curse," whispered the aged king. Even as Kausalya and Sumitra stroked his blue-veined fingers, Dasa-ratha died, soon after midnight on the sixth day.

When Bharat arrived home, he was distraught with grief, first at the exile of Rama, which had been ordained while he was absent, and secondly at the death of his father. Accompanied by the two widowed queens and throngs of courtiers, Bharat left Kaikeyi weeping in her palace and set out to bring the wanderers home. Joyfully the charioteer

Sumantra led the way to the banks of the Ganges. From there on local residents thronged to show Bharat the wanderers' route. The progress of the royal party was slow, for they had long since left the highways. Engineers were obliged to cut roads through brush and jungle so that the heavy chariots would bear Kausalya and Sumitra comfortably. Their grief was acute when they saw Prince Rama clothed in the bark robe of a hermit, his hair in an unkempt tangle on his head. Queen Kausalya sighed to see Sita's soft skin torn by brambles and her face burned by the wind.

Bharat embraced his brother and begged him to return. He described the sad state of Kosala with its old rajah dead and Queen Kaikeyi sunk in self-reproachment. Rama was not swayed in his purpose. Then Bharat asked Rama to listen to the words of a wise philosopher, a Sophist. While the wanderers attended courteously, the Sophist began to speak.

"Your mind is twisted, Rama, with idle words and false teachings. Why must you care now for the oaths of a dead man? Dasa-ratha has gone, and you should now assume the rule in his place. You must be more sensible, dear Prince. Think not of immortality or of a future life after death. There is no such thing. Learn to live for the present, for this day only. Return to Kosala and joy in your wealth and power. Today is what counts, and there are not enough tomorrows. You also will soon be swallowed by the ravenous jaws of death."

After the philosopher had spoken, Rama and Sita replied, both of them, that they would not consent to return. Rama reasoned in this way, "I know the arguments of the learned Sophist are well-intentioned, but I think they are none the less false. If I were to break my father's oath and return to Kosala, I should become only the shadow of a real man, disguised under the cloak of truth. As far as death is concerned, we can all of us free ourselves of that fear. Your counsels, learned philosopher, may indeed help me to own a fair palace here on earth, but what of the mansions of heaven that I should rather be preparing for myself and for my subjects? Therefore let me follow my own studies in my own way. Let me learn to know that which has neither color, taste, touch, sound, nor smell. Let me meditate upon the infinite, that which is ever constant, so that when I have mastered all base passions I may tread upon the other path that leads not to transient pleasures but to permanent wisdom."

Neither the tears of Bharat nor his pleading could move Rama. Instead he counseled his younger brother to return to Kosala and with the aid of the wise Brahmans to rule the country for the fourteen-year period as his father and mother had ordained. Then Bharat, before bidding farewell, asked Rama for the sandals he was wearing. When Rama had unfastened them and handed them to his brother, Bharat said, "These sandals of our Rajah Rama shall I set upon the throne of Ayodhya. They shall rule our land. As for me, I shall wear also a cloak of bark like my brother Rama. Like him shall I dwell in a hermitage outside our city gates until this prince returns. I too shall seek immortality as he does. I too shall strive to know Purusa, that which is not of this world and which shall set me free also."

To the north returned Bharat with the sorrowing queen mothers and their court. To the south went Rama with Sita and Lakshman following. This time Rama wanted to make sure there would be no pursuit. Week after week they traveled steadily through the Vindhya Mountains and into the Deccan. There they visited a very famous hermit named Agastya, who first had journeyed into southern India to study and to teach the doctrines of Brahma. This holy man gave Rama the magnificent bow of the god Vishnu, which could pierce any enemy as straight as the rays of the sun, and it was Rama as an incarnation of the sun's force, Vishnu, that was revered in later ages in the holiest city of India, Benares on the Ganges. Agastya also gave him the quiver of the thunder god Indra, and the shining dart of Brahma, saying that soon Rama would have need of all these weapons. Agastya pitied Sita for her months of footsore travel. He advised Rama to descend along the steep gorges of the Godavari River until he found an especially beautiful forest. There he and Lakshman were to build a permanent home for the tender princess, who although she had never complained was weary and thin from her long weeks of walking. Agastya warned Rama that they were leaving civilization far behind them and were penetrating into an area where savage tribes lived more like monkeys and bears than like men.

It was late autumn before the wanderers arrived on the cliffs of the Godavari River and found, as Agastya had described, a perfect earthly paradise haunted only by the timid deer. Just as the hermit had instructed, the princes located an open meadow where the grasses were pale and dried, for the sun's chariot was far away in the land of snow, Himalaya. Here on this peaceful meadow the princes built a spacious home with earth walls and floor. Tall bamboo trunks held up a lofty thatched roof scented with the drying herbs of summer. The entrance faced the river where the three bathed every morning. Then the brothers made a couch for Sita, woven from the softest grasses of meadow and field, and perfumed with the petals of the last blooms of the summer. As the winds of winter swept down over them, the little princess lay warm and dry inside her shelter. Even the wild ducks flew far overhead. Along the frozen river the last lotus buds dropped and died. Winter blew over the earth, and the three sat about their fire and tried not to think of home.

The forest where they spent the winter so peacefully was sparsely inhabited by fierce bands of uncultured peoples called Rakshas, who could change themselves into any form that they chose. One day an uncouth Raksha maiden of royal blood discovered the travelers' hut. Her burning eyes fell on Rama. She had never seen a prince with such a lotus-pale skin before, so straight and so handsome. Now this Raksha maiden, called Surpa-Nakha, was overcome by love. In her passion she felt herself to be beautiful and able to inspire his love. Surpa-Nakha could not see herself as uncultured and unattractive, nor did she realize that the brothers would mock her.

"Who are you, handsome warrior?" she called to Rama.

The princes looked up from their hut to see this ugly, misshapen woman peering in at their door. Rama answered her calmly by recounting all the story of their adventures. Then he asked her if she were not one of the southern races, a member of the Raksha tribe that possessed special powers of magic.

"I am Surpa-Nakha. I am the princess of Lanka in Ceylon. I hunt in these woods. I am free. I am very powerful. I have magic. My brother is the dread Ravan before whose face all these forests bend. He lives in Lanka in a great palace. I roam wherever I please with only two warriors." Then without invitation the savage woman entered the cabin and, pointing her dirty fingers at Sita, asked, "Who is the aging, white-faced woman you have on the couch?"

"Please show more respect," Rama cautioned her. "This lady is Princess Sita, my honored wife."

"I am much younger and much more passionate," declared Surpa-Nakha. "Get rid of your woman and marry me. I am very pleased with your appearance, Rama, and will consent to have you as my husband. Don't bother killing your Sita. I will enjoy doing it myself. And I will do the same to your brother. Then you and I will be free to roam like ardent newlyweds all through my forests."

"That is a novel proposition," Rama drawled with a quick smile toward Lakshman. "I doubt if you would care to be my second wife, however, and watch me daily pour out my love to Sita. Why don't you propose to my brother here? He's very handsome and quite alone these days. Why don't you ask him to marry you? He would probably jump at such a chance!"

Lakshman was quick to enter the spirit of the game. Bowing humbly to Rama, Lakshman looked at the Raksha girl over carefully and told her, "Surpa-Nakha, you are as pale as a parrot in all your croaking charm and as neat of line as a pregnant elephant. Could such beauty wish to be the bride of a slave? For I am Rama's slave and the Lady Sita's slave."

Surpa-Nakha's ruddy face grew mottled with anger. "You dare to mock me?" she screamed. "Prefer your withered Sita, only prefer a corpse!" Furiously she leaped across the hut toward Sita, who huddled pale and trembling on the couch. In that instant Rama leaped between them and stood with open arms to protect his wife. At the same moment Lakshman picked up a dagger and, grasping the Raksha by her matted hair, pulled back her head and sliced off her nose. Then before Surpa-Nakha could defend herself he sliced open each of her ears. While Rama strove to revive Sita, the Raksha fled screaming from the cabin, calling for her warrior escort.

The battle Rama and Lakshman fought with the two demon warriors was long and dreadful. Sita huddled on her couch of grass, hearing their loud cries reverberate through the trees. Once Lakshman hurried back for a fresh sword. The Rakshas kept transforming themselves into rocks and blunting his weapons. Finally Rama and his brother cut them into pieces and sent Surpa-Nakha howling southward to the palace of Ravan in Ceylon. Once there she emphasized the beauty of Sita and made her brother promise to avenge her.

Ravan, the warrior ruler of Ceylon, was not only vengeful by nature, but devious as well. He dispatched a Raksha disguised as a deer to wander through the forests and lure Sita away. Lakshman and Sita saw the deer standing at the river's edge at sunset. His antlers were all of gleaming sapphires and his manners timid and gentle. Instead of following it, Sita pleaded with Lakshman to capture the deer for her. She told him how lonely she often was in the cabin and how she would love to have this creature as her pet. Lakshman was unwilling to attack the deer.

"You have never seen a real deer with so soft a coat or with jewels on its head," said Lakshman in refusal. "It cannot be an ordinary creature. It must be some trick of the Rakshas, for they will never allow their princess to go unrevenged. Rama and I were very wrong to have angered her. Primitive peoples do not react as civilized ones would do. She did not enter into the spirit of our jesting, and we have made powerful enemies. Do not attempt to approach this deer."

All that evening, however, Sita could not forget the beautiful animal. She described it over and over again to her husband, insisting that its possession would make her so happy. She told Rama how she would care for it, and how fast the long days would pass if she only had this dazzling creature by her side. "When our years of exile come to an end," Sita pleaded, "we could take this jeweled deer home to Kosala with us. Think how thrilled all the palace ladies would be to let it feed from their hands. No other princess in India has so lovely and so rare a treasure." Then when Rama did not appear convinced, Sita told him that if it were really so difficult for him to capture the deer alive, he could kill it and dress the hide so that she would have a carpet to take home with her. "Think what a lovely keepsake that would make!" she sighed. "I want to have some token of our wanderings so I will remember this distant forest."

In the morning Rama strung his bow, and before setting out to chase the deer warned Lakshman to remain with Sita during his absence. All through the daylight hours Rama stalked the magical animal, but although he set his snares carefully, the creature evaded capture. The only way Rama could seize him was to pierce him with an arrow. Cautiously he crept up on the deer and drove him toward the clearing at the river's edge. Then as the animal stepped out of the brush, Rama sent his arrow true to the mark. As the deer lay bleeding, it called out in a piercing wail, in perfect imitation of Rama's voice, "Lakshman! Come to me! I have been wounded! Here in this wood I die!"

Sita and Lakshman heard the throbbing call. "Go to him, Lakshman," Sita screamed. "My beloved Rama is hurt!"

"No, I do not believe it," Lakshman replied calmly. "It is some trick of the Raksha to lure me away from your side. Did you notice how the call came magically, from no particular direction? Rama has never been defeated by an enemy. And even if he were, he would not call like a coward upon his younger brother for help!"

"You have dared to call my husband a coward!" accused Sita, turning upon Lakshman in a sudden fury. "You are a wicked man. I never should have thought it of you!"

"Calm yourself, gentle Princess," said Lakshman soothingly. "I have never heard your voice in anger before. Rama bade me remain here with you."

"You want to betray Rama," screamed Sita. "I see it now. You hope he will be killed so you can usurp the throne. That's why you won't go to his aid. Perhaps you think after he is gone that I will be your bride!"

"Your words cut me like whips," replied Lakshman sadly. "I do not see how I can have merited such an evil opinion. I will go. Despite Rama's orders I will do what you request. Nothing but sorrow can come from the words you have just spoken." Then Lakshman shouldered his weapons and went from the hut, sad and troubled.

After he had left, a twilight silence fell upon the forest. The leaves hung motionless from the trees. Over the Godavari's wide expanse not a wavelet rippled. All the forest creatures, sensing the approach of evil, crept into their burrows like witnesses reluctant to behold its stealthy approach. Only Sita sat unaware in the cool evening air, arrayed in beauty like the new moon. Her jet-black hair fell over her shoulders on the flame-colored sari she had draped about her. As she sat and listened, she saw a poor old hermit approach her hut. His hair was matted and tangled. His feet were naked in coarse sandals. His robe was ragged and the color of russet bark. Over his shoulder he carried a staff with a gourd hanging from it.

Sita was glad of his company. She offered him water and a place to sit beside her. Then the hermit expressed his astonishment at finding such loveliness and refinement in a wilderness. "Are you a nymph? My eyes have never glimpsed your equal. Your slender waist was surely meant for some royal arm to clasp. Your delicate ears were surely intended for the jewels of a king. How can you dwell here and alone in such wretchedness?"

Pleased at the hermit's interest, Sita told him how she was worried about her husband. Then the stranger continued in a soft, insinuating voice, "Why remain here, gentle lady, with a prince who can only provide a thatched roof for your lovely head?"

"I am very proud to be Rama's beloved wife," Sita confided. "Why are you dressed in an anchorite's poverty? Surely you have known palaces and thrones also," she said.

"Indeed I have," said the hermit, throwing off his disguise. "I am Ravan, king of Ceylon!"

Sita screamed in vain. Ravan caught her by her long plaits as she tried to run down the forest path, lifting her easily in one arm. Then, smiling down into her face, he told her, "I have just seized the woman of the peerless Rama. She will make a nice addition to my wives. Do not struggle. Ravan will not let you go."

"My husband *will* return. He will kill you for this," panted Sita. "You don't know how brave he is. He is much stronger than you, much taller than you. I love my husband. I will never be your wife. I am the faithful Sita. Men everywhere praise my virtue."

Ravan carried Sita as an eagle carries a writhing snake. With her in his arms he mounted his golden car that was drawn by winged asses, and they rose high in the air and over the treetops. Sita screamed for Rama without ceasing. Then she invoked the forest creatures and even the mountaintops, calling upon them to tell Rama what had happened to her. She remembered to ask Lakshman's pardon even though he could not hear her, for she knew her own distrust and suspicion had caused her fate. The only creature she saw was the vulture king, who flew along beside them. Sita appealed to him to save her, but the courageous vulture was helpless before the lance of Ravan, and he fell wounded to the ground far below. Sita could only hope some woodland creature had witnessed her abduction.

Her hopes were answered when Rama and Lakshman, searching furiously over hill and stream, came upon the dying vulture. He had been king of his kind for 60,000 years, and Rama was very sad to see his huge body racked with pain. Before he died, the vulture told how Sita had been carried through the air by the dread Ravan. The dying bird could not say, however, in what direction they were heading. To this day the vulture's bones, long since hardened into rock, lie bleaching in the sun and rain of southern India.

The next day Rama and his brother met the monkey king Sugriva and his counselor Hanuman. Rama had heard of these dark-skinned races in southern India, but he had never met them before. The monkeys were amazed to hear of the loss of Sita, and Hanuman sent messengers leaping and chattering through the trees in all directions. Within a few hours he was proudly showing the grief-torn Rama various signs of Sita that his envoys had collected. On one mountain peak they found her sari, and among the tall grasses their sharp eyes spied bangles that she had thrown away to mark her route. Rama was very grateful. He asked Sugriva what he could do to return the favor. He suggested that they swear an alliance, the four of them.

Sugriva told Rama how he also happened to be a wanderer in the forest. Some time before, Sugriva's wicked brother, a gigantic beast named Bali, had stolen Sugriva's wife and driven him from the kingdom. Ever since that day Sugriva and Hanuman had been unable to force Bali's city and depose him. Sugriva shivered when he heard Bali's name and confided to Rama that he would never dare face his beastly brother in single combat. Since they were now sworn allies, Rama encouraged Sugriva and assured him that together they would reconquer his land. Sugriva promised that once he disposed of vast wealth and subjects he would send his forces swinging through the trees so that they could discover the whereabouts of Sita. To seal the bargain and give Sugriva confidence, Rama shot one of his magic arrows. Before the monkey king could recover from the fierce twang of the bow, the arrow had pierced seven palm trees, passed through a hill, and returned to drop at Rama's feet. At the sight of such prowess Sugriva declared himself convinced.

The following morning Sugriva charged Bali's fortress, striking his chest and shrieking defiance. Bali answered him from inside the palace as he armed himself; and then the two, screaming in high-pitched voices, wrestled mightily in sight of Rama and Lakshman. For a long time Sugriva was inspired by Rama's example, but after several hours he began to tire. Bali was much heavier than his brother, his nails were longer, and his teeth sharper. When Rama saw that he was about to kill Sugriva, he went to his friend's rescue. With one arrow Rama slew Bali. When Sugriva invited Rama into his city, the two princes turned sadly away. "My penance is to live in a forest," Rama reminded his ally. "I may not accept your invitation."

Rama and Lakshman retraced their weary steps toward the jungle. No search for Sita could be made then because the rainy season had begun. Gray clouds as huge as mountains came rolling in from the sea, so thick they looked like solid masses instead of air and water. Within hours the hard earth had become a mass of mud through which no travel was possible. Rama and his brother would have welcomed the rain that fell not in drops but in long lines of water from the heavens if their hearts had not been sad for this delay. In silence they plodded through the dripping forests, made themselves a shelter, and waited until the rains had stopped and Sugriva could fulfill his promise.

Eventually the skies cleared. Eventually the sun shone forth once more, flooding the forest with radiance. Rama and Lakshman smiled again and hurried through the burgeoning jungle to Sugriva's city. There were the monkey bands assembled, 10,000 strong, whom the king divided into four groups. To the first he assigned the regions of the east, exhorting his warriors to scan carefully the seacoast and even the mountains of the sea all the way to where the sacred Ganges and the Brahmaputra transform themselves into ocean. To his greatest and wisest warrior, Hanuman, he assigned the southern lands from the Vindhya Mountains along the dark ravines of the Godavari. "Look carefully," warned Sugriva, "for the forests touch the sea. Look all along the mountains of Mysore and question our people who dwell by the southern sea. Ask our relatives who live by Cape Comorin."

The third group were to depart for the western sea, where coconut palms wave their fronds over a heavy jungle that stretches along deep lagoons. "Look carefully through each busy seaport on this endless western sea. Ravan may be hiding in some leafy bower. Swing from tree to tree, and you will find him. Look most closely along the delta of the Indus. He could be lurking there."

To the mountains of the north Sugriva sent the last search party. "Leap over raging torrents," he urged them. "Fear not the wooded slopes of Himalaya. Look around the fringes of the goddess Nanda Devi. Move to the higher peaks of Dhaulagiri. Fear not Mount Meru itself, though the plateau of paradise be at its summit! We shall not fail the noble Rama. Search northward until you come to the vast, treeless regions of Scythia where dwell the horse-faced women!"

It was the crafty Hanuman who ended all their labors. He it was who had the agility to leap across the sea. Hanuman knew no fear. Gathering his strength in his haunches, he stretched out his slender arms and leaped, borne by the ocean breezes, all the way across the Mannar Straits until he touched the green island of Ceylon, the private domains of Ravan, king of the Rakshas. Swinging noiselessly through the trees, Hanuman glimpsed the disfigured Surpa-Nakha surrounded by her slaves. Around her lay the white-pillared palace of Ravan. Its walks were paved with gold, and its staircases made of ocean coral. Then Hanuman noticed in a far corner of the gleaming court a secluded area hidden under the dense foliage of asoka trees whose masses of crimson blossoms dropped in a thick screen. The entire courtyard was guarded by fierce-looking females, dark and threatening. Silently and nimbly Hanuman swung through the lower branches.

Then he saw a silent woman sitting sorrowful and alone. Her hair fell in a heavy braid down her back. She wore the ugly bark cloak of a hermit. As the monkey warrior studied her appearance, he saw that she was wearing a jewel that Rama had described. Around her neck lay the polished tiger's tooth Rama had given her. This lady must be Sita. Hanuman could see by her attitude of mourning and by her ornaments that she must have resisted Ravan's offers of wealth, that she must, indeed, have remained faithful even in her prison to her lord and master. Softly Hanuman called her name, but she did not lift her head. Then he began in his high voice to sing and chatter the story of Rama. He related it from the very beginning and continued through Sugriva's war with Bali, and he told of the armies of monkey warriors and bears who were massing all the thousands of miles from Mount Meru to rescue the faithful Sita.

"It is a dream that I hear," sighed the princess. "It cannot be true that Rama is so near."

Then Hanuman leaped to the ground and, peering up at her with his wrinkled, kindly face and round, brown eyes, urged Sita to hope again. Into her hand he dropped a ruby ring that Rama always wore, as a token to Sita that her husband was alive, that he loved her still, and that he would rest neither night nor day until he had saved her from her ravisher's sight and palace. "Prince Rama tastes neither food nor drink, takes no pleasure in perfumed champac, neither rests nor ceases. Day and evening he longs for Sita. He will overstride this ocean like a rivulet. No Raksha warrior will stand long before Rama in his wrath. There will be such a war when Rama espies the treacherous Ravan that its echo will ring among the Himalaya until the very end of time."

Then Sita took from her forehead that holy jewel which the god of thunder Indra had given her father on the day of her birth. This jewel had been fastened to Sita's hair on her wedding day, and Rama had never seen her without it. "Give this to my husband," she requested Hanuman. "Tell him how I weep."

Hanuman had remained too long talking to the prisoner. Even as he sensed the danger and leaped into the asoka tree, he was attacked by

Ravan's guard. Although the monkey warrior defended himself hero-ically, he was finally captured and brought before Lanka's King Ravan. His execution was ordered, but the king's younger brother, Vibishan, who had always opposed keeping Sita a prisoner, persuaded Ravan not to kill the courageous monkey. "He was an envoy sent by Prince Rama, and his passage should be assured," urged Vibishan. Ravan then ordered a rag soaked in oil to be tied to the monkey's tail and set on fire. Owing to the prayers of Sita, however, the monkey felt no pain. Instead he leaped wildly through Lanka, spreading fire as he went. When he was sure that even the palace had caught on fire, Hanuman jumped back across the strait to the mainland of India and hastened to Rama.

Rama held Sita's jewel in his hand and thought of all the sorrows that had befallen his gentle wife since her wedding day. He also wept. Even so, he questioned Hanuman closely, "Did Sita weep for love of me, or did she weep for loneliness? Has she remained faithful even in a prison?"

In the spacious white-walled city of Lanka, Ravan called a council of war. Sternly he put the problem of Rama's invading army and asked what he should do. His warriors belittled Sugriva with his army of wild and uncivilized legions that crowded together to fight for Sita and her prince. One after another they boasted of their courage, fine weapons, high battlements, and glory in war. Every warrior approved war except for the younger brother Vibishan. "Ravan had no right to capture the lady of Kosala," said Vibishan. "She will one day be a powerful and noble queen. Her reputation is so spotless that I am not surprised even the beasts of the forest pay her homage and offer to avenge her with their untutored skills.

"This Rama from the north is no ordinary man. He is the mortal aspect of the great god Vishnu. Year after year pilgrims travel to the mountain of Chitra-kuta to worship where he and Sita prayed at the beginning of their exile. He is the idol and star to every boy in India. Would you dare oppose the righteous anger of so just a man?"

Then Ravan's other brother, Khumba-Karna, who had nodded through the long meeting, gave his opinion. "I agree," he said ponder-ously, "that our brother Ravan should not have kidnaped this high-born lady. This is not the first time that he has succumbed to his crav-ing for women. However, the deed is done, and I consider brother must stand by brother, and subject by king." Then Khumba-Karna yawned and stretched his massive legs that projected five feet beyond his chair. "Just send me the northern sapling, the pale lotus-faced hero. He won't get a second shot. Maybe not even a first. Oh, and one more thing: since you have the woman, Ravan, then possess her." Without waiting for their reactions, this giant fell asleep again.

After Khumba-Karna's well-received discourse, the warriors and Ravan condemned Vibishan by word and contemptuous looks, calling him false and cowardly. Ravan scorned his brother in scathing words— "Relatives are all alike! They smile and lull you with honeyed sounds, but in their hearts they hate you. No one takes so much secret pleasure at the misfortunes that befall a man as do his cherished relatives. Like hungry vultures they hover over his death couch, feeding him healing draughts with one hand, and hastening him out of this world with the other. So is my brother, Vibishan. No doubt he thinks to seize the throne. No doubt he hopes to wed my wife. . . . I will not taint my hands with his murder. Therefore, Vibishan-the-Evil, depart from my lands. Join the other cobras that lie in wait to destroy us."

Bravely Vibishan stood his ground, alone in the circle of hostile faces. "You are wrong, Ravan. You are not only wrong but sinful to say such words and harbor such thoughts. I only want to avoid death and bloodshed. Will you not listen reasonably? Will you not redress your wrong? . . . You will not? . . . Then defend yourself without me." Vibishan then left Ceylon's capital and joined the forces of Rama whose army had arrived at the Strait of Mannar.

How to pass this channel with a host of bear and monkey warriors presented a problem. Rama solved it by shooting his powerful arrows into the ocean's bed and, when he still received no answer, by threatening to dry up the very seas themselves with bolts of lightning. Then the ocean god appeared upon the horizon, completely amenable and open to suggestion. It was agreed that the architect of the gods could be consulted. At his direction Rama's host began to roll boulders into the channel until they had made a splendid causeway, the vestiges of which can still be seen today. Upon this highway the army of Rama passed and surrounded the capital city of Ravan.

The battles commenced as the Rakshas opened their gates and tried to force a passage through the ranks of Rama's army. Wave after wave poured from the city only to fall in heaps before the onslaughts of the monkey warriors, who threw boulders and uprooted trees at them. Then the fierce Ravan mounted his heaven-made chariot and cut a path through the helpless foot soldiers. Chieftains rushed bravely to meet him, but they could do nothing against the thundering of his terrible war engine. Sugriva fell wounded to the ground, and after him the clever Hanuman. Ravan then heard the call of Lakshman inviting him to battle. Furiously the two shot volleys of arrows at each other, and for a long time the Prince Lakshman managed to cleave Ravan's darts in midair before they pierced his body. But the human skill of the Kosala prince was puny compared to the demoniac force of the savage Ravan. Lakshman fell wounded, but Ravan too had felt the sting of arrows. He quit the field and returned to his walls.

On the second day of battle Ravan succeeded in awakening Khumba-Karna, who had once even worsted Indra, the thunder god. Brahma had intervened and decreed that this terrible giant should slumber for six months and then remain awake for only one day. Ravan, however, overcame his brother's sleeping sickness and urged the giant to fight. He cautioned him to swallow the monkey warriors by the thousands as he had done in the past, and this time to chew them well so that they could not crawl out by working their way hand over hand along the hairs inside his ears and nose. Armed in bronze, Khumba lurched through the opened gate. As Rama's army hurled trees at him, he caught these missiles in open flight and threw them shudderingly back into the ranks of the warriors, mangling them. First the giant sent Hanuman reeling over backward, and one after another all the native chieftains. There was sore need that day for the magic healing medicines from the slopes of Himalaya! Even Sugriva was dashed unconscious to the ground.

It was not these leaders Khumba was seeking. "I have worsted the god Indra!" he shouted. "Send me not these puny mortals! Where is this Rama we have heard so much about?" There Khumba-Karna made his fatal error. Who was he? Who was a giant to think of conquering Rama?

Pushing Lakshman out of his path like a crumb from the table, Khumba strode toward the tall and deadly Rama. He was met by a flaming arrow that singed off his hair. Another followed and another. Rama fitted at last into his bow an arrow of fire, which pierced the giant's armor and severed his head from his body. Disgusted at the jets of steaming blood that discolored the earth, Rama lifted the body and threw it into the sea. The tidal wave that ensued did not exhaust itself but swept over the entire western sea, which is endless.

A more dreadful war lord even than the giant Khumba was the son of Ravan, Indrajit. This fierce prince was not slain by Rama because he could surround himself in a magic cloud and remain invisible in the midst of the host while he shot swift arrows at his enemies. Once he terrified Rama by conjuring up on the field of combat the likeness of Sita, and then pretending to kill her before her husband's very eyes. It was Vibishan who saw through this trick. Although he had been converted to Brahmanism and had joined the forces of India, he still remembered all the Rakshas' black arts. He and Lakshman penetrated into the heart of Lanka and, catching up with Indrajit in his visible form, dared him to fight openly. It was Lakshman who killed this black prince.

Ravan in his grief and fury at the loss of his son decided to kill Sita, as Indrajit had done in semblance on the battlefield. Her attendants barely managed to avert the blows and save the sad queen. "It would bring you too much misfortune, O Ravan, to slay this woman," they cried. "Do battle rather, for it is the fourteenth day of the waning moon. You will have great strength today. After your victories return and claim this Sita. We will array her in splendor for you."

Ravan mounted his golden chariot. From every house in the city his warriors hastened. The sky was darkened. Red flashes of Indra pierced the heavy air. Angrily the earth shook at so much destruction, at so much hatred, at so many deaths.

Ravan first encountered his brother Vibishan and sought to kill him. The lance he threw was caught in mid-flight by Lakshman who cleft it in two. Meanwhile Indra himself dispatched his own chariot drawn by swans, so that Rama could meet Ravan. Using this and the weapons the hermit Agastya had given him, Rama killed Ravan and ended the war.

A mighty funeral pyre was built for Ravan at Rama's orders. On it were placed the body and arms of Ceylon's king. Vibishan, who inherited the kingdom, lighted the funeral fire. Rama and Lakshman then laid aside their weapons and, standing among the warriors and King Sugriva, awaited the arrival of the princess.

Arrayed in a golden robe, her hair parted in the center and brushed smoothly back from her forehead, the gentle Sita was carried in a golden litter through the city and up to the Kosala princes. At Rama's command she had unveiled her face so that all men could see the princess for whom they had fought. Sita stepped down from the litter in a stilled hush. The assembled warriors had never seen such grace and beauty before. Slowly she walked toward her husband. Lakshman knelt to touch her feet.

Rama neither acknowledged her presence nor spoke. In silence also Sita stood before her lord. Rama seemed to be looking over her head. Little by little Sita's cheeks grew red. Her head fell. Then, turning to Lakshman, she asked him to build a funeral pyre for her also. "Since my husband does not receive me, I must die," she said in a broken voice. "The beginning of the world was in fire and the end of each miserable body."

The throng of warriors moved back so that wood could be placed high in the center of the square. With tears running down his face Lakshman placed the last branches, and at a nod from Sita lighted the fire. Then the princess spoke again, "I swear that I have remained faithful to my husband even in the palace of Lanka." Slowly and with great calm of manner Sita stepped through the ring of flames and was swallowed from view in clouds of gray smoke.

A gasp went up from the assembled crowd. "All desire has fallen from Sita, and she has become immortal," the warriors murmured. "Her heart has one hundred and one nerves, and she has chosen the one leading to the head and immortality! So may we all gain immortality if we seek to know our higher self!" All this time Rama remained motionless with folded arms. The sounds of crackling flames and gusts of smoke blew in his face. People moaned and wept, for they knew the world would never again see such beauty, such devotion, such courage in a woman.

Then before their astonished eyes the great god Brahma appeared above the fire. Parting the flames, he lifted the princess in his arms. Not a strand of her hair had been singed. Not a wisp of her gown had been scorched. "She is pure!" cried the warriors. "The ordeal by fire has shown us her virtue." It was Brahma who placed the princess in her husband's grateful arms.

SEVEN
ROME

The following chapter is in part a summary and in part a translation of the *Aeneid* of Publius Vergilius Maro. (The chapter sections, indicated by Roman numerals, correspond to the twelve books of the original.) Vergil created for Rome not only a thrilling hero story. The *Aeneid* is also a travel book in which the poet has incorporated those events of great historical significance that he witnessed during his lifetime (70–19 B.C.) with his own ideas as a poet, scholar, and historian. He is dealing with the world of around 1000 B.C. It was a world in turmoil, marked by the decline of the ancient continental civilizations, the fall of the wealthy maritime powers such as Crete, Phoenicia, Ugarit, and Troy, and the rising threat of the Assyrians from the east.

Vergil, from his point of view—Rome at its height under the Augustan principate—can look back 300 years or so to the Punic Wars. He tells us of the founding of Carthage and Rome. He thinks of Aeneas as the father of his country and explains by legend the old hostility between these two nations.

Modern historians such as Gilbert Picard (*Le Monde de Carthage*, Paris, 1956) inform us that by the year 876 B.C. Tyre was forced to pay tribute to the Assyrian King Ashurnasirpal, and that by 814 B.C. they had sent colonists under Dido to found a permanent colony in Africa from which they could protect their shipping routes from their tin port in Spain. Vergil's description of navigation and his geography seem also to be corroborated. M. Picard calculates that the round-trip voyage from Tyre to Tarsis in Spain would have taken three years, at an average distance traveled per day of twenty-five miles. Mariners usually sailed only at night and only between the spring and fall equinoxes. Every winter they beached their ships and raised crops, as Vergil describes. Even the story of Dido, as told by our poet, seems substantially correct, except that Dido may have been sacrificed.

When we come to Vergil's vivid description of the war in Italy, there seems to be less agreement. Our poet accepted, as the reader will see, the classical theory advanced by Herodotus that the Etruscans had gone to Italy from Lydia. In this many modern scholars disagree; Professor Pallottino of the University of Rome supports the theory that the Etruscans were part of the general Indo-European invasion. Vergil departed from classical beliefs in having these famous people fight with Aeneas. Some scholars have suggested that Vergil did this because he wanted them to appear in a sympathetic light, that Vergil believed himself to be of Etruscan origin. In any case, Vergil described the scenes in Italy from actual observation, as Professor Carcopino of the University of Paris has demonstrated.

Vergil through the ages has been and remains a controversial writer. Many people think that in his Fourth Eclogue he announced the birth of Christ. St. Paul is supposed to have visited Vergil's tomb in the Bay of Naples and to have said, "*Quid te fecissem, si te vivum invenissem, maxime poetarum!*" ("How much I would have made of you, had I found you alive, O Greatest of poets!") A practice called *Sors Vergiliana*, consisting of selecting oracular passages from his writings, has been practiced even in our century. Professor Toynbee has quoted Vergil's Fourth Eclogue to demonstrate his idea of history. Professor Carcopino has written a book (1930) to refute the Messianic predictions attributed to him.

Another controversy concerns Vergil's use of the word "Caesar," for the *Aeneid* is not always clear as to which Caesar he had in mind. In any case, as Professor Whitehead says, they were both "men of genius." "That we are seated here, in the clothes we wear, and uttering some of the thoughts we do, is in part thanks, I believe, to Augustus," he says.

Almost countless volumes have been written about this poet through the ages, and he has been widely imitated and admired. He was a man whose love for his country breathes through his poem, a poet who was tolerant of other cultures, and a fine human being who was inspired by country life and the deeds of noble people. Tennyson said of him:

> I salute thee, Mantovano,
> I that loved thee since my day began,
> Wielder of the stateliest measure
> Ever moulded by the lips of man.

ANCIENT MYTHS

THE WANDERINGS OF AENEAS

I

Arma virumque cano, Troiae qui primus ab oris
Italiam fato profugus Laviniaque venit
litora, multum ille et terris iactatus et alto
vi superum saevae memorem Iunonis ob iram,
multa quoque et bello passus, dum conderet urbem
inferretque deos Latio, genus unde Latinum
Albanique patres atque altae moenia Romae.
    Musa, mihi causas memora, quo numine laeso
quidve dolens regina deum tot volvere casus
insignem pietate virum, tot adire labores
impulerit. Tantaene animis caelestibus irae?

I sing of arms and of the man who first from the shores of Troy, driven by fate and the ire of the rancorous Juno, came to the Lavinian shores of Italy. He suffered greatly, this hero, buffeted by winds and stormy seas, uncertain of his route and knowing only that his task was to bear the gods of Troy in his arms, and to found a nation on seven hills in Latium, from which would come the Alban Fathers and the lofty walls of Rome.

Let the Muse tell this story, let her remind us of why Juno bore this grudge against Troy. Let her say why this great hero, so outstanding in his goodness and unselfish devotion, had to endure so many hardships, had to bow under the vengeance of this goddess, until he could fulfill his destiny.

There was once an ancient city called Carthage, which had been founded by Phoenicians from the trading nation of Tyre. These colonists had built their "new capital" (Qart Hadasht) upon the northern coast of Africa, directly opposite Italy and the mouth of the Tiber River. Juno protected their settlement, hoping that it would develop into a maritime power that would in time control the western Mediterranean, as Troy and Tyre had, between the fall of Knossos and the rise of Assyria, dominated the eastern. Juno kept her chariot and her armor in Carthage, so dear was it to her.

The goddess knew that the Trojan Aeneas had escaped from Troy and was even then wandering over the seas to find a home in a new land called Latium. It irked Juno to think that Pallas Athena had destroyed some of her beloved Greeks. It angered her to know that a son of Venus should think of founding a city intended to become a rival of Carthage. Therefore Juno sought Aeolus, the king of the winds, on his floating island, and asked for his help. Aeolus kept the hurricanes and cyclones imprisoned deep in a cave. He had heaped rocks and even mountains over their prison. There he sat on his throne, scepter in hand, holding them down with his weight.

"Help me, Aeolus," pleaded Juno. "These hated Trojans are even now on the sea, driving the bronze beaks of their biremes through the waves. Help me to destroy them, for I wish to keep them out of Italy. If you will annihilate them for me, Aeolus, I will give you fourteen nymphs. One of them is so lovely that you will want her for your wife. I guarantee she will bear you fine sons. Will you help me?"

"Whatever service you ask of me, I will perform for you, fair Queen," answered Aeolus. "You and great Jove have entrusted me with the mastery of these violent winds. I will just let some of them loose. You will see how they will make your Trojans disappear!"

Then Aeolus struck against the hollow mountainside with his spear. At his signal east, south, and sou'wester winds rushed from their dark cavern and swooped like eagles of death huge-winged over the Mediterranean. Gray squalls collected into granite formation, marching over the waves, and rolling darkness and rain under their tread. The winds picked up mountains of water and aimed them at the Trojan ships which quivered like sparrows poised on a thrashing treetop. The waves grew so gigantic they laid bare between each swell the white rock depths of the Mediterranean.

Aeneas clung to the rail of his plunging ship. The vessel clawed frantically with its oars to climb the steep water walls and then dropped sickeningly into the abyss. Tons of water broke over its prow and crashed along the decks, light-green water flecked with foam. "They were thrice blessed who found their death on the plains of Troy," he thought, wiping the stinging salt spray from his face. "Oh, Hector, why did I not fall beside you?" Even as he called to the helmsman to hold her firm, a blast from the north caught their square sail and blew them broadside to the waves. Down they dropped into the trough of the sea. The waters were strewn with men fighting to stay afloat, clinging to the salvaged wealth of Troy that floated on the waters. Other ships were lifted high by their sterns and scattered on rocks and beaches. Whole shoals of sand were washed up alongside them.

From his home in the depths of the sea Neptune was stirred by this upheaval. Majestically he rose to the horizon's edge and peered over this tumult of waves driven wild by the violent winds of Africa and the frozen north. Neptune sternly called the Zephyr to him and sent him to say to Aeolus that his province was that of wind, but not of water.

Neptune ordered Aeolus to recall the winds at once. Then he drove over the green water in his chariot, drawn by prancing, golden-maned horses; and the waters were calmed once more. It was just as when through a crowd of angry, surly people a great hero of famous deed strides confidently. At once the unruly mob grows still and obedient. Then the sea nymphs and Triton hurried to the rescue of the shipwrecked crews, boosted them on board their vessels again, and helped to collect their floating gear. With his trident Neptune himself pried vessels loose from the sandbars and set them bobbing on calm waters again.

As soon as the hurricane had subsided, Aeneas collected the seven remaining ships and led them toward the nearest land, which was the coast of Libya. There they found a sheltered cove with a small island to seaward and two tall cliffs to landward. Its sandy beach was protected on either side by curving rocks. As soon as the battered ships had dropped anchor in shallow water, the sailors leaped ashore through the surf and threw themselves exhausted upon the warm earth. Their clothing was wet and stiff with salt. Achates struck spark from tinder and lighted a small fire in dry leaves. Soon the weary men had gathered resinous kindling and logs so that they were able to dry themselves. Others searched through the stores for dry grain which they began to pound with stones into meal for their frugal supper.

Aeneas left his men on the beach and climbed the cliffs to the forest. From this high point he looked out over the island and sea hoping to sight some of his Trojan biremes, but the waves to east and west were empty. There was not even a fishing craft in sight. Turning toward the woods, he then had the good fortune to see a herd of deer feeding peacefully under the trees, all in line like a battle formation. It was a perfect target. Aeneas shot seven of the deer, one for each ship, and had them carried down to the beach. Then he broke out jars of wine, for his comrades were discouraged and beaten.

While the stags were roasting, Aeneas tried to encourage his crews. Choking back his own tears and trying to smile, he told his friends, "Now we have indeed seen trouble and dangers! Fresh from the fires of Troy we have been plunged into the stormy depths of the sea. We have passed shoals and dangerous crags. We have lived through a hurricane, at least some of us. Take courage, Trojans, for there are certainly more perils ahead. Someday, I have no doubt, we shall sit about our own hearths again, in new homes that we must strive to build in the land of Latium. We may look back even upon this dreadful day with a kind of fondness." After his words the men ate warm food and sat about their campfires talking of the missing ships and wondering what the land of Italy would be like.

Jupiter, reigning on Olympus at the very vertex of the sky, looked down over the world and the Libyan coast. As he surveyed it, Venus approached and spoke tearfully to him, "Why have you changed your mind? Why did you promise me that my son Aeneas would survive the fall of Troy only to allow him to be battered and driven almost beyond a man's endurance? What crime can my son have committed against you, O ruler of the lands and skies, that all the earth is barred to him, even the distant shores of Italy? Did you not promise me that from the Trojan stock would come a great empire—that men called 'Romans,' born to rule the world, would build an Eternal City? I stood by and watched Troy fall to appease the anger of Juno. All I could do was to lead my son and his boy out of the holocaust. Why are they still being punished?"

Jupiter smiled and softly kissed her pretty lips. "Lady of Cythera, delicate as the sea foam, I have not decreed otherwise. I shall keep my promise. You shall see with your own eyes this city called Rome, and the high-flung walls of Lavinium. When his task is accomplished, you shall bear your great-souled Aeneas, your sublime hero, to the heavens of stars themselves. Your son must live to wage a decisive war in Italy. Shall I show you the hidden scroll of fate?

"Aeneas will vanquish proud warriors and set forth laws and government. His little boy Iulus shall build powerful bastions at Alba Longa. The race of Hector will rule for 300 years until the priestess Ilia gives birth to twins, sons of Mars, Romulus and Remus. Nursed by a she-wolf, Romulus will found the toga'd empire whose great senators shall be called by his name, Romans. I put neither hour nor limit to their dominion; I have given them sway over the earth throughout all time.

"Even Juno, when she sees their reasonable government and their magnanimity, will change her opinion for the better. She too will come to admire the rulers of Rome, draped in their togas of peace or clad in the iron armor of war. She will also love their Caesar named Julius, who will ride in fourfold triumph through Rome, laden with the spoils of the Orient. Greece will fall to Rome, and Egypt. Europe will fall to Rome and bear the imprint of her language and laws. Augustus Caesar will force shut the iron gates of War for the first time in 200 years. Within the Temple of Janus he will bind the clenched fists of Rage with a hundred chains and let him sit there trembling at his bloody jaws."

Jupiter spoke. Then he sent Mercury flying down through the air to Carthage in order to inspire the Tyrian queen who ruled that city with hospitable feelings toward the Trojan wanderers who had just landed on her coast. Thanks to his winged cap and sandals, the messenger of the gods performed his pleasant errand easily. Dido, queen of Carthage, heard from Mercury that by decree of Jove she was to entertain distinguished visitors.

During the night Aeneas worried and made plans. The next morning he had his ships drawn up into a little river and moored along its banks, with branches pulled down over them so that their hiding place could not easily be discovered. Then he and Achates took spears, climbed again up the cliffs, and set out to explore the country. It appeared uninhabited. There were still no signs of the lost ships. As they walked along in the sunshine, they met Aeneas' mother, the goddess Venus, who had disguised herself as a Spartan huntress. The goddess strolled through the trees, her quiver slung over her shoulder, her hair unbound and blowing in the fresh sea air. When she had come up to them, Venus inquired if they had seen her sister.

"We have met no one on the path this morning," Aeneas answered her courteously. "Are you not Apollo's sister, the huntress Diana? Perhaps you would help us. We are lost. If you would tell us what land this is, and who lives here, we will be sure to make many offerings at your temple."

"Oh," replied Venus, "I am not worthy of such honors. I am not Diana. Tyrian maidens often dress in purple, knot their garments above their knees, and go hunting through the woods. However, I can tell you where you are. You are on the coast of Libya not far from the new seaport city of Carthage, which was built by the Phoenician Dido. Have you heard of her?

"Dido, queen of Carthage, was born in the maritime city of Tyre. Her brother Pygmalion is its king. As a young girl Dido was married to a wealthy Tyrian named Sychaeus. She was a virgin of great beauty. Sychaeus was happy to possess her. Dido returned his love, and they lived in peace. Then one day Sychaeus did not return home. Dido asked her brother, but Pygmalion knew nothing of her husband's whereabouts. The young bride grew sad and longingly searched many days for her husband with no success. Then one night Sychaeus appeared to Dido in a dream. He said he had been murdered by Pygmalion who coveted his riches. Since the body had received no funeral, Sychaeus was condemned to wander eternally through the world. He showed his wife the dagger wounds in his breast and told her that he had been stabbed while at the altar, before the penates (Household gods.) themselves.

"Fortunately Sychaeus was able to advise his young wife as to a course of action that would save her life and give her full revenge. He told Dido to inform her friends secretly and to collect about her other Phoenicians who were smarting under Pygmalion's tyranny. Dido was a clever woman. She followed her husband's directions, sought friends and found ships that would carry them all safely from the island harbor of Tyre. She dug where Sychaeus had directed and found not only his but also Pygmalion's treasure. All of it was stealthily loaded on biremes, and late one spring night they stole out of the harbor and headed due west. After months of travel they found a perfect site for a harbor and city here on this very coast.

"Then Dido bargained for land upon which to build a city. The native Libyans, fierce and unconquerable tribes, thought to cheat her by giving in exchange for her silver only as much land as could be

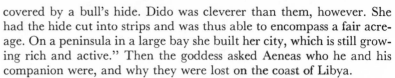

covered by a bull's hide. Dido was cleverer than them, however. She had the hide cut into strips and was thus able to encompass a fair acreage. On a peninsula in a large bay she built her city, which is still growing rich and active." Then the goddess asked Aeneas who he and his companion were, and why they were lost on the coast of Libya.

"I am Aeneas, whom men call 'good,'" he answered. He told her how he had wandered so long and why, and how he had lost fourteen of his ships. "I am an obscure Trojan driven from both Europe and Asia," he said.

"Whoever you are," replied Venus, "I am sure you are not forgotten by heaven. Do you see those swans that fly over the bay of Carthage? Some will alight in the safe haven of the harbor, and others will follow. So is it with your lost ships; some have already arrived at Dido's city. Others are even now folding their great white wings and gliding insid the breakwater. . . . Follow this path into the city, Aeneas!"

As the goddess walked away from them, her short robe lengthened and fell to her feet. The characteristic perfume of Venus was wafted to their nostrils. She had resumed her divinity. Aeneas started to follow her, but she was already fading from view. "Why do you always trick me with these curious disguises, cruel one?" he murmured. "Why may we never join our right hands together, or speak openly to each other as do mother and son?" His mother had already vanished, happy to know that Aeneas would be well received at Carthage. Through the sunlit air she headed for her birthplace in Cyprus where a hundred flower-decked altars burned incense from Saba to her and where blood sacrifices were never accepted.

Following the path the goddess had indicated, Aeneas and his faithful friend strode to the top of the hill. Below them spread the city of Carthage. As they walked toward it, Aeneas marveled at what a beehive of activity it was. Venus had surrounded her son and Achates in a gray mist so that they could enter the city unseen. They saw work squads paving roads. Other men were hewing stone from the hill for a large theater and carving columns for its stage. All along the way newly arrived Phoenician immigrants were digging trenches around the lots where their homes would be built. Beside the waterfront other groups were dredging the harbor and building piers and docks. It was like watching a hive of bees on a summer morning, whose labors also are divided. The pleasant perfume of thyme and honey was blown by the sirocco through the streets. Aeneas was envious at the sight of so much happy toil. How he wished it were the high walls of Rome he was seeing grow stone by stone before his eyes!

In the middle of the city was a grove of trees where Dido was having constructed a temple to their patroness, Juno. Here it was that the Tyrians during the first few days of their arrival on the African shore had dug up a horse's skull. Dido had said this was a good omen, for the men of her city would be as fierce and energetic as a fine-blooded horse.

Aeneas and Achates walked toward the temple and mounted its broad flight of steps. They felt sure the queen of Carthage would come there for her morning devotions and to dispense justice. Meanwhile they admired the temple, its rows of pillars, and its bronze doors with heavy hinges. Suddenly Aeneas stopped short and grasped his friend by the arm. There upon the temple wall were depicted scenes of the Trojan War; its fame had preceded its heroes!

Holding their breaths in wonder, the Trojans examined the murals. There is the crested Achilles dragging Hector's dead body three times around the walls of Ilium! There is old Priam come with the gold of Troy's treasure to buy back his son's body! There towers Memnon with his Ethiopian armies hastening to the aid of Troy! There is Rhesus, king of Thrace, another friend of the Trojans, with the white horses he lost to the Greeks! There is the Amazon queen Penthesilea lying dead from the lance of Achilles who afterward regretted having slain one so young and so beautiful. There lies poor young Prince Troilus, no match for Achilles—his spear trailing in the dust. Even in death the youngster still holds the reins of his horses which are dragging him along beside his empty chariot!

A sound of voices woke them from their memories. A throng of courtiers were approaching the temple, and at their center, moving with smiles and the dignified mien of a queen, came the golden Dido of Carthage. This royal personage took a seat in the temple where she began to dispense justice, offer sacrifices, and settle the business of the day. Aeneas was about to speak to her when he saw to his amazement three of his Trojan captains, men from the lost ships. While their commander listened, these captains asked Dido for the use of her port and supplies. "We have come not in war but in peace," they said. "Your harbor patrol has refused our men permission to go ashore." Then they explained how they needed to beach their ships and repair them with new timbers. They asked her for materials and explained their plight. "If our leader, the princely Aeneas, were here, he could surely persuade you of our good intentions and establish credit with you.

"We are bound for a land in the west which the Greeks called Hesperia. Once we arrive there, we plan to construct a city also, great Queen," they said. "Only do not receive us as enemies. We are pious people, not sea robbers, not lawless pirates!"

Dido, looking down at them from her lofty throne, answered graciously, "You must excuse the vigilance of my harbor guards. We are always on the alert for any ships that might even now set out from my brother's kingdom of Tyre. As far as Troy is concerned, we learned long ago her terrible fate. We may live here in the far fringes of the western world, but Apollo's chariot passes over us also, bringing us news from the east. You may certainly have the full use of my port. Repair your ships at leisure and in entire security. Commandeer whatever supplies you need. Or, if you will, settle here in Carthage. Join forces with me, and I will swear to govern Tyrian and Trojan with equal consideration. I too long to see your famous leader Aeneas. Scouts in fast ships shall be sent out at once all along the Libyan coast. Perhaps he is not so far away."

At that moment the mist that had shrouded Aeneas and Achates was dispelled. Dido and her courtiers looked at the Trojan chief to whom Venus had given at birth some of her radiant health and physical beauty. He stood before the Carthaginian queen in an aura as if of sunlight, his fair hair like gold that the artist has inlaid on his ivory statue. Stretching out his hands in welcome to his captains, Aeneas thanked Dido for her hospitality. "How shall I ever repay such generosity?" he asked. "What a wonderful century we live in that has given birth to so magnanimous a queen! How fortunate the parents who reared you! As long as the rivers seek the sea, or the clouds cast shadows over mountain slopes, or stars graze in the pastures of heaven, so long shall men revere you name and honor your reign!"

"Well do I know your Trojan stock, Aeneas. Often have I heard my father tell of the fortunes of Troy. You are the Aeneas whom the goddess Venus bore to the Trojan shepherd Anchises, are you not? I beg of you to be my guest. I who am not unacquainted with grief know how to succor the unfortunate." Dido proclaimed ceremonies of rejoicing to be performed in her temples. Before preceding Aeneas into the palace, she ordered twenty bulls, with swine and sheep, to be sent down to the Trojan ships so that the sailors could feast also.

Aeneas sent Achates back to their vessels to fetch his son Iulus. Since the child's mother had been separated from them during that worse-than-nightmare, the burning of Troy, Aeneas had assumed the double responsibility for his son. He liked to have Iulus near him as much as possible. Aeneas also asked Achates to bring back gifts for Dido. Fortunately not all their treasure had been ruined by sea water. They still had with them a wool mantle that was stiff with embroidery and gold thread, and a saffron-colored veil bordered with a design of golden acanthus leaves, both of which the Spartan Helen had brought with her to Troy for her licentious marriage. Achates was also to bring the scepter of Priam's eldest daughter, a necklace set with pearls, and a double circlet or crown of gold and gems.

Meanwhile the banquet hall of Dido was being prepared for a dinner. Tables with silver platters and bowls were covered with embroidered cloths and set in the middle of a great hall. The heavy silver was chased and embossed in gold to illustrate famous episodes in the history of Tyre. Counterpanes of royal Tyrian purple were draped over the couches.

Venus was aware of all these preparations. Instead of rejoicing at the honors Dido was heaping upon Aeneas, the goddess was uneasy. She knew the Tyrians by reputation. They traded throughout the seas and were proverbially bilingual in more ways than one. To give a man one's

"Tyrian word" or "Punic word" meant as often as not no promise at all. Venus finally called her son, the mischievous Cupid, and explained to him what she wanted him to do. "I will lift Iulus out of the ship and keep him slumbering on a bed of sweet marjoram somewhere in the pine groves of Cyprus, just for tonight. You take his place, and when you draw near the Phoenician woman, pierce her with your subtle arrow. Set her on fire with such a burning flame that she will swoon over Aeneas, and never dream of betraying him."

Cupid gleefully took off his wings as Venus had commanded, and with mischief in his heart solemnly imitated the person and voice of Aeneas' son. He played the part to perfection, making his father very proud of his son's precocity. Dido received the gifts from "Iulus" and could not praise him highly enough. All through the banquet she reclined on her golden couch under a luxurious canopy and drank in the faces of Aeneas and the boy she thought was Iulus. Starved for love

after her years of widowhood, Dido feasted as much on their masculine appeal as on the dinner. For the first time in years this young queen forgot her dead husband Sychaeus, and how much she had loved him.

As members of the court joined the banquet, they were invited to lie on sumptuous couches. Fifty maidservants brought bowls of perfumed water for their fingers and held out soft napkins to the guests. Another hundred girls served the meats and breads fresh from the ovens. A hundred youths bore goblets and poured into them fragrant ruby wines from the palace cellars. The hum of voices reached the rafters. Everyone admired the boy Iulus, and not even Aeneas suspected there was Cupid in their midst. The saffron veil of the Spartan Helen was lauded as well as the other rare and storied presents Aeneas had made to Dido. Fresh torches were lighted so that the hall at Carthage burned with a cheerful, welcoming light. Even the gilded panels in the ceiling glowed high up in the raftered roof.

After the tables had been cleared, Dido called for the sacred patera of her ancestors. Into this shallow dish she poured a libation of pure wine. Then she sacrificed to the gods, saying, "O Jupiter, may this day when the Trojan and Tyrian are united together in fellowship be an auspicious one! May it be remembered throughout the generations to come." Then after having invoked Bacchus and the patroness of Carthage, the good Juno, she touched her lips to the bowl and passed it to her guests.

The rest of the evening was spent in conversation and song. A celebrated minstrel named Iopas, who was a Numidian taught by Atlas himself, recited a poem to the accompaniment of his lyre. He told of the stars, the sun's labors, the origins of beast and man, the nature of rain and fire—all songs that Atlas, that first master of astronomy, had composed. All marveled at the skill of the singer and were enthralled by this flowing-haired poet. Dido sighed with longing. She could not bear to dismiss her guests. Again and again she drank deep draughts of love.

"How tall was Achilles?" she kept asking Aeneas. "How were the horses of Diomedes? Tell me again in your words," she begged him. "Speak about Hector again! How I wish I might have seen him! What about Priam? Would you describe again the arms of the Ethiopian Memnon, son of the dawn Aurora? What a shame you were separated from your wife Creüsa during the burning of the city! Tell me again about Hector. Speak of the Greeks and of their tricks. Tell me yourself of your travels, for it has been seven summers now since Troy fell. All this time you have been wandering over lands and through seas. Talk to me of yourself, Aeneas," pleaded the unhappy queen, Dido of Carthage.

II

Silence fell upon the assembled guests. All turned toward the godlike Aeneas, who spoke from his couch, "Unspeakable is the grief you ask me to recall for you, how the Greeks swept over our lofty walls and laid in dust the proudest city of Asia. I was there. I saw it all happen." Aeneas covered his eyes with his hand and bowed his head. After a pause he began again, "Yet, if you wish to hear the death agony of our civilization, if your love for the Trojans urges you to inquire into such an appalling disaster, although my very soul shudders to recall it, I will begin."

Then Aeneas told the whole story of Troy's capture, how through the wiles of Sinon the wooden horse was drawn inside the city's walls despite Cassandra's warning, how Laocoön and his sons were strangled by snakes that rose from the sea, how Priam died at the courtyard shrine, how the victors drew lots for the Trojan women. "It was Hector who saved those of us who are here in your palace tonight, Queen Dido," he continued. "You are wise to ask again for Hector. He was the greatest of us all. I doubt if the world will ever see his like again, a man devoted to his city, unsparing in his toils to the extent that even after death he would not rest for thinking of us.

"There was that time when the first sleep of night, gift of the gods, stole over my aching body—when, behold, in my sleep there seemed to come up to my bed, before my very eyes, Hector himself! But oh, how sad he was! . . ." Aeneas could not go on.

In a rapt silence Dido hung on his words. Murmurs of sympathy rose from the Tyrian nobles. What a terrible story to hear! What could be worse than to see the city your forefathers had built stone upon stone with their bare hands burn and fall in a single night! Dido brushed tears from her eyes at the thought of Andromache's baby, the smiling little Astyanax, torn from his mother's breast and hurled to his death at the foot of the very walls he had been born to rule one day, had the gods willed it.

"Hector!" spoke Aeneas again. "How changed he was from that Hector we knew! His hair was matted with dust and his beard with blood! In his poor body were the gaping wounds of Achilles. His feet were swollen and still bore the marks where the thongs that had attached him to the chariot had cut into his flesh. I spoke to him. . . . He only groaned in reply, at first. At last Hector spoke to me, almost in his old voice, the voice we all in Troy had listened to with such respect and love. 'Go, Aeneas,' he said. 'Go, you who were born of a goddess. Take your household gods, and leave this falling ruin. There is no more hope here, none at all. Believe me, Aeneas, if human hands could have saved these walls, mine would have done so. Take from the temple of Vesta the sacred fire of Troy. Carry it with you into the western world. There you will place it in another temple to Vesta and find other virgins to guard it. I pass on the torch to you. Take your son and run. My son and I are . . . dead.' The word 'dead' broke from his lips and rang around the hollow rafters long after he had gone. . . ."

Aeneas then told of his combats in the city, how he saw his sister-in-law, Cassandra, with streaming hair and chains upon her wrists, and how he could not deliver her. He also spoke of Helen, whom he had passed crouching at the altar, and how he had longed to slaughter her but was stopped by the goddess Venus from doing so. After having escaped from the city he met his friends on the mountains southeast of Troy. At least he had managed to save his father, Anchises, and his son, Iulus.

III

"There on the slopes of Mount Ida we built ships," Aeneas continued. "All through that spring we toiled. Hard work is the best cure for heart-sickness, hard work, and the passage of time. We built ourselves twenty strong biremes with square sails, and at my father's command we shoved off from the shores of Asia forever. Our first thought was to make for the sparsely settled shores of Thrace. We thought of this land because in the olden days, when its King Lycurgus was still alive, Thrace and Troy had known close ties. This was the Lycurgus who was killed by the gods because he resisted the worship of the Thracian Bacchus. There on the indented coast we marked out our walls and built a city which we named Aeneadae.

"One day we prepared to offer a thanksgiving sacrifice to my mother Venus and to the gods who had also favored our enterprise. We had slaughtered a white bullock to Jupiter, as you know is the custom. Then, looking around for some green branches to lay on the altar, I saw not far away a little mound or hill where myrtle and cornel bushes were growing. I strode over the sand and, grasping a small myrtle tree the trunk of which was large enough for arrow shafts, I ripped it from the ground. To my horror its roots dripped huge clots of blackish blood. Shaking with fear now, I pulled at a cornel or dagger-wood bush. The same black omen met my eyes. Clotted blood dripped from its bark and seeped into the sand at my feet. Praying to the local gods of Thrace—for I knew I had to discover the meaning of this omen—I tugged at a third branch.

"Even as I braced my feet and pulled, I heard a voice coming from the mound beneath me, that made my hair stand up on end. 'Why are you tugging at my grave? Why do you pull out the spears that rise from my mangled body?' cried a hollow voice. 'You are a good man, Aeneas. Why do you desecrate a Trojan grave?'

"Great drops of sweat broke out on my forehead and dripped on my hands. Imagine my horror. I recognized that sound! It was the voice of Polydorus, an old friend and confidant of Priam!

"'Leave this accursed land of Thrace, Aeneas!' he told me. 'Here I lie struck by the sword of treachery.' At once I understood what had happened to him. Priam, seeing Troy beleaguered, had prepared part of Troy's vast treasure and shipped it secretly in care of Polydorus to his friend, the king of Thrace. Then when the war went badly for us, the Thracians had changed sides. They had rallied to the winning Agamemnon, murdered Polydorus, and confiscated Priam's gold for themselves. What crimes will men not commit when the lust for riches taints their hearts?

"I returned to the beach, where our men surrounded the altar, and told what I had seen and heard. My father, as the oldest of our chiefs, gave his opinion. We all concurred that we must leave that land at once. First we made a funeral for Polydorus. Our women loosed their hair and bore him offerings of warm milk and foaming blood. We made him a high tomb and planted dark cypresses about it so that his shade might finally find repose. Then we packed our goods, hauled our ships down the beach to the sea, and as soon as a fresh south wind sprang up broke out our sails and took to the waves again.

"The wind held strong and steady. Our vessels cut the waves merrily and bore us down the Aegean until we sighted the island of Delos in the center of the Cyclades, birthplace of Apollo. Long ago he had prudently moored this floating island between two others so that mariners in our modern times have no more trouble making toward it. Here we dropped anchor. We were met at this port by the king-priest Anius, an old friend of my father. He and Anchises discussed our troubles and then led me to the rock shrine of Apollo that stands beside its sacred laurel tree. I prayed to the oracle, asking Apollo to breathe upon us, to fill us with some of his wisdom, to tell us where to go, whom to follow, and how to rebuild another Troy that would withstand the storms of time and the malevolent hands of the land-hungry Greeks.

"Then as my prayer echoed through the sunny air before the shrine, the god answered. While the caldron bubbled, the earth shook, and the sacred laurel whipped in the wind, the voice of Apollo rolled clearly about our ears. 'Return, O Trojans, to the home of your ancestors!' No more was said. Silence followed the oracle's pronouncement.

"My father gathered around him our chiefs and together we deliberated. The words of Apollo were clear, except . . . where was the birthplace of the Trojan race? My father Anchises searched his memory. Fortunate for us it was that he had obeyed the gods at Troy and consented to join with us! For, you understand, all the learning and records of our city had been burned. We had no wise priests with us to interpret our history. After some thought Anchises said, as he recited over to himself old poems he had heard as a child in Priam's palace, that we must have come from Creta Minoan. 'Surely Crete was the cradle of our civilization. We know its hundred cities ruled the Mediterranean and brought under their sway the blue Aegean. If we wish to go back to the beginnings of time, we must return to Crete. There is also other evidence that should be conclusive. Our great Mother Goddess Cybele, she who is driven in her car by lions, came from Crete.

Then too our Trojan mountain was surely named Ida for that high peak of Crete where Jupiter was reared. Our citadel in Troy was also named Pergamum from a town in Crete,' said Anchises.

"Joyously we sacrificed to Apollo, without forgetting white bullocks for the sea god Neptune and a white lamb for the westerly Zephyr. Thanking Anius, we set out for Crete. Three days would see us there, for the journey was not long, only 150 miles. We sailed past Naxos, sacred to Bacchus and his heavenly Queen Ariadne. On the third day our lookout spotted the white mountains of Crete, and soon we were leaping ashore through the clear, warm waters. We found the island deserted.

"Rumor told us that Idomeneus, the descendant of the famous kings Minos of Crete, had returned there after the fall of Troy. He had sworn, for a victorious warrior makes loud boasts, that he would sacrifice the first living thing he met upon the shores of his native land. That creature was his own son, who had been watching for his father's fleet to come bounding over the horizon. Idomeneus slew the boy too, and fled those shores like one pursued. . . ."

More wine was poured in the glasses. Fresh torches were lighted in the banquet hall of Carthage. Queen Dido hung on Aeneas' words while in her childless arms she cuddled the sly imp of Love, thinking that she held the boy Iulus. Everyone listened intently, for it could happen to them. Someday in the future they too like Anchises might have to interpret the dictum of an oracle by recalling the adventures that befell their fellow wanderers from Troy.

"There on the silent, deserted shores of Crete, from which our ancestor Teucer had drifted to the headlands of Phrygia, we traced out other walls and built another city, which we called Pergamea after Troy's fortress. The young planned weddings and new houses for themselves. I laid down laws and ordinances by which we could be governed. We pressed oil from ancient olive trees, gathered grapes, and planted crops. . . . Our toil was all in vain. The dog days of July were upon us in all their malevolent heat. In the evening sky Sirius, the Dog Star, directed pestilential winds across Pergamea that withered all our fields and cast a sweatless sickness over our people. The silent hills of Crete, which once had rung to the cymbals of Cybele and the stamping rites of the Curetes, burned in the cloudless heat. My father counseled us to return at once to Delos and beg the priests of Apollo to enlighten us. Perhaps we had not heard correctly what the oracle had commanded.

"Then in my despair, as I lay on my couch that night, I seemed to see our penates—those that I was bearing at the words of Hector—rise before me in a stream of light. Their faces shone illumined. From their kindly images wise words fell upon my troubled ears. 'Troy had more ancestors than one, Aeneas,' they told me. 'Dardanus also was a founder of Troy, he whose brother married Teucer's daughter!' My heart leaped, for in truth I had not remembered before this detail of our storied

196

ANCIENT MYTHS

lore. 'Dardanus came from the portals of the west, from a sunny land the Greeks have always called Hesperia. Teucer, it is true, came from the Dictean shores, but Dardanus came from Italy. Therefore you need not return to Apollo's shrine, for the answer will always be the same. Trust now in your own gods and their inspiration. Do not shirk from new hardships. Your wanderings have only begun!'

"My father Anchises laughed when I told him of our mistake. 'Of course,' he told me. 'We were naturally confused and leaped too suddenly to an obvious conclusion. Now that I reconsider the question,' he continued, 'I remember our priestess, Cassandra. Wasn't she always talking about the west? Wasn't she forever babbling about Hesperia? Not that anyone ever paid any mind to Cassandra's wild words!'

"Once more we set out rollers. Once more we slid our vessels into the surf. Once more we embarked with sacrifices and prayers, for this new voyage was into the unknown. Very soon deep water flowed under our keels. Looking down over the sides, we no longer saw the white reefs of the coast line. The sea became a blue so dark and deep that as one looked down one became dizzy at those bottoms as soundless as the depths of the sky. Our pilot Palinurus, a most skilled mariner, frowned anxiously as he set our course due west into waters none of us had ever dreamed of daring to sail. The lead vessel plowed bravely forward. Our stomachs tightened as we looked to stern and saw the Cretan Ida drop from view below the eastern wave.

"Our fears were not baseless, as you shall hear. Along about noon Palinurus called me to him and pointed upward. There I saw what he meant. We were riding into a storm. A dark blue cloud enveloped the sea before us. There was no escape. Within a matter of minutes it fell about us. Oily waves rose in huge billows and tossed us eagerly from one crest to another. For three days we rolled, battened down, into the storm, struggling only to keep her prow toward the shifting winds. Palinurus swore he could not tell night from day, and so we drifted over the evil waters of the Ionian Sea. On the morning of the fourth day, however, we sighted land, two islands rising out of the sea. Quickly we broke out the oars, and the men rowed toward them for dear life. Palinurus said we had reached the Strophades, the point of no return. To westward lay the uncharted depths. We had drifted far northward of our course. Not many miles to the east lay the shores of Greece!

"We thanked the gods that had led us to dry land safely. In the meadows by the shore of these islands we saw herds grazing untended. We killed enough steers for our supper, and setting up couches and tables there in the grass, roasted the animals. We had no sooner begun to eat, however, than the Harpies swooped down upon us. These were huge birds that the sons of the north wind Boreas had driven out of Thrace as far as these wretched islands, the turning place. They had the scaly bodies of lizards, the wings and claws of birds, but the white, famine-pinched faces of girls. Darting down over us, they snatched the

meats from our tables and filled the air with their foulness. Their stomachs and tails were smeared with their own filth. Their cries were hideous.

"At my orders we fled to a cave, where we relighted our fires, set up our altars again, and cooked fresh food. All that the Harpies had touched reeked from their droppings. Just as we lifted the meat to our hungry mouths, there they came upon us again. Their fierce claws brushed our shoulders as they trod over the tables and perched squawking on the platters. This time I told our men to prepare their weapons. We lay in wait. As they wheeled down another time, we swung our swords at them. It was no use. Aside from a few filthy feathers that drifted down on our heads, we could not kill them.

"Then their leader, a croaking maiden named Celaeno, perched on a crag over the cave entrance and called to me, 'You Trojan liars, do you want to wage a war on the Harpies? You shall be punished for it as your ancestor was punished when he refused Apollo payment for helping to build the walls of Troy, as he was punished by Hercules, who labored to rescue his daughter. You are not supposed to be here in our islands. Apollo told you where to go, and he told me also. Your are bound for Italy. So go there! You have the god's permission and will arrive. Why do you have to come to the Strophades and kill our cattle? Then why try to kill us when we protect our food? My curse is on you! You shall found your great Rome because Apollo is willing, but before you do you shall be as hungry as we are, so hungry you will devour your own tables. Now get out!'

"Anchises bade us loosen the hawsers, unfurl canvas, and fly those ill-omened islands. We begged the Harpies to forgive our intrusion. Fortunately the waves were leveled by this time. The south wind freshened, blowing us easily northward. We were in dangerous waters now. We all prayed that the wind would not drop and leave us drifting upon Greek shores!

"We passed the wooded shores of Zacynthos to port and before long the coasts of Ithaca. You may be sure we thronged to the rails and cursed that land of Ulysses! Then we beached near the promontory of Actium, for winter was upon us. There our young men oiled their bodies and wrestled in honor of Apollo whose shrine in this place will witness, so I hear, a great battle in future ages. We hauled up our ships and spent the winter overhauling them so that they would be ready for sea at the first breath of the spring equinox. Before leaving Actium I nailed to the gate the bronze shield of that Argive King Abas, a shield sacred to Juno, that we had captured from the Greeks at Troy. I carved these words above it: 'Aeneas dedicates these weapons taken from the victorious descendants of Danaus. "*Aeneas haec de Danais victoribus arma.*" '

"Then we embarked and drove along the coast of Epirus until we came to the town of Buthrotum. There we heard an incredible bit of news that gladdened our hearts and quickened our steps as any news from home will do to strangers who wander weary and heartless over stormy seas and along hostile shores. Who do you think was ruling Buthrotum? None other than our old comrade in arms, Prince Helenus of Troy. And who was his wife? The gentle Andromache, she of the white arms, who had fallen to the bloody Pyrrhus. Fate plays strange tricks in this life. Pyrrhus had died, and Andromache had married once more a son of Ilium. Happy at this glad news, I walked along the shores until I came to an altar in a grove of trees. There I saw Andromache herself who was making her yearly offering to the spirit of Hector. I came upon her unaware. When she looked up from her rites and saw me standing there, a Trojan, from home, in Trojan armor, her body stiffened. She fell almost fainting to the ground.

" 'Can it be you, O goddess-born, whom I see before my eyes?' Then her tragic eyes lighted up. She grasped my arm and cried desperately, 'If you live, Aeneas, then where is Hector?' Realizing her foolishness, she burst into tears.

"My heart broke so at her grief I could hardly stammer out, 'Yes, I live, Andromache. How is it with you, dear sister?'

"I put my arms about her shaking shoulders as she told me of her sorrows, of how cruel fate had been to force her into the bed of a Greek, she who was so in love with Hector; to force her to become pregnant and bear other children, she who could never forget Hector's baby under her heart. As I tried to comfort her, she questioned me about Iulus. 'Does he remember Troy? Does he speak of his own mother who remained in the burning city? Does he grow up to be honorable and prudent like his Uncle Hector?' We stood there talking by the altar until Helenus came with open arms to greet me. Together the three of us returned to Buthrotum where they showed me proudly the little Troy that they had built. I rested my hands upon their gate, so like the Scaean gates of home, that Hector had wanted to close against the dogs of war.

"Two days went swiftly by with feasting and talk of home. At last I approached the shrine of Apollo with reverence, asking what omens the winged flight of birds, what auspices were in the stars for us, what counsels he could give us; for I was haunted by the dire prophecy of the Harpy Celaeno. Helenus unbound the fillets from his priest's brow and, leading me bewildered to the temple gates, answered as a seer my request for guidance. 'There would appear no doubt at all but that you will arrive in Italy. However, the omens foretell a long and very perilous crossing. While it is true that the eastern shores of this land lie only across a narrow neck of sea from us, the oracles still predict a long voyage. They tell quite clearly that you cannot settle on the eastern or southern coasts. These are already claimed by colonists from Greece and veterans from the Trojan War who, returning home to Greece, were shipwrecked in Italy. They call their land Magna Graecia.'

"Helenus went on to tell me how I should not try to pass the straits between Italy and Sicily because on the Italian side was the fierce monster Scylla, that barked like a dog and dwelled in a rocky promontory. On the Sicilian side was a whirlpool named Charybdis which would suck my ships down into the sea's depths. Many more counsels Helenus imparted, particularly about the Cumaean Sibyl and how to profit from her knowledge and vision. Helenus told me that when we sighted, beside a western river, a white sow stretched on the ground and thirty newborn pigs lying at her udders, this would indicate the site of our future city.

"We bade farewell to Helenus and Andromache sadly. They loaded us with gifts, especially fine ones for my honored father, Anchises, he who had been deemed worthy of the goddess Venus' love, and for Iulus presents made by the loom of his aunt. Andromache's tears fell as she clasped my son, for he and Astyanax would be about the same age. Then, after inviting them to come in future years to visit us at 'Rome,' we set off to sea again, our minds stored with their advice and admonitions. When dusk fell, we put in to shore for a rest. At midnight Palinurus awoke us all and announced that he could tell by Orion what course we should make westward. Aurora, the pink-fingered dawn, had hardly started to bathe the eastern sky when we saw clearly before us a low-lying coast.

"It was the faithful Achates with whom the glory rests. 'Italy!' he called. We all rushed forward, and almost with one voice echoed his glad cry, 'Italy! Italy!' My father Anchises wreathed a bowl with flowers, filled it with wine, and prayed to the gods of land and sea to favor us, to let us touch this promised land. We found a harbor sure enough, although it was almost hidden in a curve of shore. Set back from the sea, across a bright, green pasture, was a white marble temple to Pallas Athena (Minerva.). There we intended to pray.

"On stepping ashore I saw grazing by the temple four beautiful white horses. 'That is a sign of war all right,' said my father. 'However, it could also be an omen of peace, for horses can be yoked to a plow as well as to a war chariot.' We prayed in the temple for the first time on Italian earth and remembered to placate Juno, as Helenus had advised us to try to do. Then as quickly as we could, we regained our ships, fortunate to have met no Greek inhabitants of that coast.

"We set sail at once, traveling southward that day across the Gulf of Tarentum known in the old days to Hercules. From time to time we sighted towns and passed the area settled by the Locrians. Then on our port side we viewed the dread, smoking peak of Aetna. Even as we stared in horror at huge columns of belching fire and smoke that rose from its thundering crater, we were met by a closer danger.

"At once our ships were caught by some powerful current and drawn forward at a dizzy speed. 'We have come too close to Charybdis!' cried my father. Palinurus urged all hands to the oars. We swung the rudder hard to port. All of our other ships maneuvered likewise as the sea currents tugged at our frail planking. Out of the growing darkness came the ferocious baying of Scylla somewhere to starboard. We fought for our lives during those twilight minutes as desperate men must fight the sea, black rocks, and darkness. Three times we almost despaired. The elements sought savagely to drag us forward while we struggled to swing to port away from this swirling chasm.

"By the time we had cleared these dangers, night had descended. The sea was calm. The wind had fallen. Thankful and exhausted, we drifted southward under the fiery shadow of the volcano. On the Cyclops' coast we found a gravel beach where we spent a restless night under the smoke of the burning mountain. Every now and then the earth heaved as the giant Enceladus who lies buried under Aetna stirred to ease the pain of his burns or turned over in his sleep. Boulders were cast up to the sky from the lurid crater. The woods where we lay without sleeping were lighted every few minutes by explosions of red and orange fire. The vault of sky above our heads was black. Not a star shone. The night seemed endless.

"We were up and astir long before dawn, anxious to be on our way as soon as there was light enough to guide our course. Suddenly we were aware of eyes watching us. You know how one feels such a presence. Finally we saw a wild man at the edge of the trees. There he hung with hunched shoulders, watching us. He was a Greek. We saw that at once, just as he must have recognized us as Trojans. His garments were tattered, his clothing held together by thorns. His feet were naked; his hair and beard were tangled and matted. With a rush he came across the clearing toward us and fell on his knees.

" 'Take me with you, Trojans. I beg of you to take me with you.' Sobbing, the strange Greek clung to my knees. 'I was your enemy, it is true. I helped to storm your walls. Only do not leave me here on this horrible shore. Cast me into the waves, if you must. Let me at least die by human hands!'

"While we urged him to explain himself, my father Anchises extended his hand to the youth as a token that he was safely received. Then the fellow mastered his terror enough to tell us his queer story. It seems that he was an Ithacan, a member of Ulysses' crew who had been left behind when the Greeks had escaped from the Cyclops' cave. For three months he had been managing somehow to hide in the woods and escape detection. He told us the horrid story of Polyphemus. This Greek had crouched in the cave and seen the giant, lying on his back, take two Greeks in his huge hands. Beating their bodies on the rock walls to soften them, he had eaten them, gulping them down and biting into their twitching limbs. Then as he lay belching bones and clots of blood, Ulysses' men had thrust a sharpened stake into his eye. They had escaped, all except this one man.

"Even as the Greek finished his sickening tale, we heard a thumping behind us on the mountainside. Turning around in horror, we saw the giant Polyphemus coming down the slopes with his flock of woolly lambs. He leaned upon a pine-tree trunk and felt his way down the mountain by pounding it along the ground before him. Petrified with fear, we watched him wade into the sea up to his middle. Bending down, he scooped sea water in his cupped hands and washed out the bleeding eye socket. From where we crouched, we could see him grimace and whine with pain. Then in a wild rush of activity we leaped on our ships and bent to the oars.

"Polyphemus heard us. At once he lurched through the surf in our direction, stretching out his huge hands in the hopes that he could catch one of our vessels in his fingers. His roars of anger echoed against the cracked sides of Aetna and brought from their caverns all the race of the Cyclops. As we leaned frantically to the oars, we saw them standing in groups together like clusters of oak trees far away on a hill. We rowed furiously, forgetting even in our panic our close escape of the preceding night, the menace of Charybdis. Fortunately the gods were more mindful than we were. They sent us a brisk north wind that drove us spanking down the coast of Sicily. The Greek we had rescued gave us valuable information. We passed Syracuse, rounded the southern promontory, bore past vast harbors and cities, and arrived finally at Drepanum.

"It was there that I lost my father. It happened suddenly, with no warning. Neither the Harpy nor Helenus had prepared us for the blow. He was the best father a man could ever have. He lightened all my weariness. . . . I hardly know how we got from Drepanum to Carthage, great Queen."

Prince Aeneas finished his story and sat silent.

IV

After the banquet and the story of Aeneas, Dido could not sleep. She
knew intuitively that she had heard the words of a man of destiny. She
lay all night tossing on her couch, envying him. All at once, in one
evening, her own life had lost its significance. Her city now meant little
to her, her former pleasures were empty, her life meaningless unless it
could be somehow attached to his. She could only dream of Aeneas,
of his manly beauty, of his vitality that transcended that of ordinary
men, of the glamor that surrounded him. She had not thought of
love since the murder of her husband Sychaeus, nor ever thought to
feel its burning desire again. Now all she could see before her eyes,
whether she opened or closed them, was the face of Aeneas. All she
could hear in her ears was the ring of his prophetic words. She believed
him, that he *would* lead his people into a promised land that she, Dido,
could never share.

At the first light of dawn she summoned her sister Anna, to whom she
confided her turmoil. "I know this Aeneas is a god," she confided to
Anna. "What magnificent stories he has told me! How has he drained
the cup of heroism to its last drops!" Dido went on to explain her pre-
dicament. "I love him, Anna." She went on to say that rather than
bring shame upon herself, however, she would infinitely prefer to die.
"I gave my heart to Sychaeus, and he is dead. Since that tragic day
I have thought I was free. I never desired to follow the marriage torches
to another wedding bed!"

Anna felt very differently about her sister and Aeneas. "Why must
you think, dear sister, of wasting your years in widowhood? Why for
the death of Sychaeus must you spend your whole life alone and childless? Surely you have paid enough honors to your husband's shade.
Surely you have earned this opportunity for love by having spurned
Iarbas, the African king!" Then Anna went on to paint a bleak picture
for the queen. She reminded her of how small Carthage was and how
vulnerable. She told Dido of the great sandbanks, the Syrtes, that
menaced them from the ocean. She reminded her of the fierce Numid-
ians, the Barcaeans, and the Libyan tribes that rode their desert
horses through the unknown depths behind Carthage. She spoke also
of the danger, how their brother Pygmalion could still at any moment
appear with a vast armada at the narrow harbor entrance and force a
passage before even the chains could be lowered into place.

"Now on the other hand," Anna reassured, "if this Trojan prince
were to fall in love with you, he would want to stay and become our
king. You must learn to depend on your allure. Perhaps he has come to
us through the powerful graces of Juno. She will help you seduce him.
The goddess and you can surely make this son of Venus forget his

mother's plans for him. What a glory for Carthage with such a king and queen! This Prince Aeneas has come to us at just the right moment. Look out your chamber window; the storms of winter hold the seas in their icy clutch. He could not leave Carthage in such heavy weather. By the time summer comes, he will never think of leaving you for Italy!"

Comforted and hopeful now, Dido studied her face in the mirror. Carefully dressed, she left the palace and moved in stately procession into the temple. There she sacrificed to Juno, the supervisor of marriage and the personal helper of women, and then to Ceres and Apollo. Royally dressed in Tyrian purple, and more beautiful than any other woman in the city, Dido herself poured a libation on the forehead of a white heifer. Such ceremonies, however, have no power to soothe a woman in love. She roamed in torture through the city's streets just as a deer whose side some shepherd has pierced with his barbed arrow runs to exhaustion over hills and through streams without easing its pain. When she met Aeneas with his Trojan friends and tried to show them her wealth from Sidon and Tyre, her cheeks flushed and her words failed. So day after day she took less interest in her construction projects, failed to order her soldiers out for maneuvers, and neglected to give her captains permits for port clearance. Night after night, perfumed and jeweled, she dined with Aeneas. All she could do was to ask him to tell her again of his adventures. After the guests had left, she sat alone in the deserted banquet hall, miserable and lonely for him who had just left her side.

Juno saw Dido's embarrassment. This goddess sought Venus to complain that Dido, her protégée, should be entrapped by the goddess of love and her bewitching son. Juno proposed an alliance, offering to give Carthage and its peoples to Aeneas as a wedding dowry. Venus saw through this proposition. To her it looked as if Juno were trying to divert Rome's future greatness to African shores. Aeneas' mother astutely objected that it was probably not Jupiter's will that Trojans and Tyrians unite. She added that Juno ought to know her own husband's thoughts better than Venus could ever do. Juno replied that she would sound out Jupiter on the subject. In the meantime she proposed a plan for uniting Dido and Aeneas. Venus approved, but secretly she laughed.

The following morning, just as Aurora was rising from the eastern sea, a select band of nobles set out from Carthage on a hunting trip. Dido waited at the gate on a slender horse caparisoned with purple and gold. The boy Iulus made his steed prance and cavort; he had received a desert stallion as a present from the queen. Then Aeneas cantered through the gate with the sun about his shoulders and head, just as Apollo looks in spring when he leaves his winter home in Asia and crowned with a golden wreath strides forth to join the dancers at the springtime rites in Delos. The royal party prepared their hunting gear, woven nets and iron-tipped spears. Loosing the hounds, they galloped over the dunes, up steep sand slopes, and into the thick coverts of the Libyan wilderness. Before their compact charge the game fled, wild goats from the rocky ridges of the hills and deer that leaped frantically and bounded through the thickets. Iulus led the way, hoping in his boy's heart that he would come across a fierce boar. He imagined himself struggling alone against the most dangerous creature of the woods and killing it all by himself. He would have tackled a lion singlehanded. This boy, who could hardly wait for destiny to give him great deeds to perform, spurred far ahead of the others.

A storm burst upon them without warning. Amid claps of thunder, the rain poured down as if all the heavens had opened wide. Aeneas galloped to Dido's side and, guiding her horse by its bridle, found a shelter for the two of them in a nearby cave. He did not know that Juno had contrived the whole affair with the tacit acquiescence of Venus.

It was a makeshift wedding, but an impressive one. The lightning acted as marriage torches, the wind as wedding congratulants, and Juno as the matron of honor who led the bride to her marriage bed. Dido wished for no more. She called that her "wedding." In her joy she never heard the wailing of the mountain nymphs who deplored her yielding to such light love, and she a queen!

Rumor saw Dido's surrender. Before the next day she had spread the story with many additions and tasty embellishments through every town in Libya. "Dido has wedded the Trojan Aeneas! Together in sweet love they dally away the winter while their subjects go to rack and ruin. They are both of them heedless of empire and careless of responsibility." This foul-mouthed Rumor, sister of the giant Enceladus, flew like a monstrous bird between heaven and earth every night, spreading gossip, causing friend to fear friend and whole cities to grow alarmed and destroy themselves through hatred engendered by fear and misinformation. Rumor had an eye at the tip of each of her feathers and as many ears. When she swooped over nations, she hissed her lies or half-truths indiscriminately. By day you could see her perched on some city tower, sleepless and avid for careless words which she hastened to distort into scandal.

Rumor liked this story. She licked her lips as she flew to Dido's rejected suitor. He was Iarbas, not only a ruler of Libya but a son of Jupiter Ammon from the oasis. His father long had ruled and been worshiped in the hundred-gated Thebes in Egypt. Rumor poured out her tale to him, how Dido was sleeping nights in the arms of the perfumed Trojan, how Troy was infamous for the rape of innocent women, how this was another Paris with a Carthaginian Helen. The fierce Libyan king went wild at the thought of Dido in the embrace of another. How dare this Phoenician woman refuse him on the pretext of widowhood, only to fall into the arms of any wandering outcast? Iarbas rushed to an altar—for he had a hundred burning in his desert realm— and cried out in rage to Jupiter Ammon. "Have I not sacrificed faithfully? Have I not fed the gods my choicest rams? Have I not poured libations from my damask couch? See how I am insulted! This woman, to whom for silver I tendered lands so she could build her coastwise station, so she could feed her few miserable followers, has forfeited my tolerance! Will you not punish her?"

Jupiter heard the protests of Iarbas. At once he sent Mercury to ask Aeneas what he was doing in Carthage, whether or not he intended to seek Italian shores, and if he was not concerned over his son's future. Mercury hooked on his ankles his golden wings and flew through the winds to the sandy shores of Libya. On his way the messenger passed close to the giant Atlas, who stood bowed by the weight of heaven, which he balanced on his cloud-covered head. From the pines on the summit heavy snows dropped on his sloping shoulders. From his icy chin glaciers cracked and streams formed. Mercury drifted down through frigid currents until he was poised above the walls of Carthage. To his surprise he saw Aeneas wearing a jasper-studded sword and a Tyrian purple mantle and superintending the construction of ramparts. "Jove wants to know why you are idling away your time, Aeneas! He wonders if you have become so smitten that you neglect your mission! Why do you think you were saved from Troy when Hector was allowed to die? Was it to build the walls of Carthage?" The god only poised above Aeneas' head long enough to speak.

Aeneas was overcome with confusion and guilt. What was he in fact doing so long in Africa? Horrified at what the gods must be thinking about him, he summoned his captains and bade them prepare the fleet at once, but secretly. Aeneas planned to choose the right moment for breaking the news of his departure to Dido. Rumor, of course, forestalled him. She saw the skids being greased. She saw the Trojan sailors stream toward the beach where the ships were being readied. By the time Aeneas re-entered the palace, Dido knew all about his decision.

"What! Did you plan to leave my shores without even telling me?" Dido asked Aeneas. "Did you really think my love would not have warned me of this cruel departure? Have you not loved me at all, or respected the vows we exchanged? Have you not thought once of what will happen to me? Look! It is winter over sea and land. Where Troy still standing, no vessel would reach her coast through such seas! Are you running away from me?

"I beg of you, Aeneas. Do not desert me so cruelly. Do not leave me here to die alone, just because I have loved you. For your sake I foreswore myself. For you I made enemies of the Libyan chiefs who surround me. For you I have lost both honor and reputation among them. You were my guest. I have treated you well, and loved you deeply. If you leave me now, I shall die. Aeneas, if you could only wait until I bore a child, a child of yours to comfort me and give me a reason for struggling against the pain that you cause me. . . ."

"I never intended to leave secretly and without explaining my purpose," replied Aeneas. "Furthermore, nothing I do comes from my own wishes. I was chosen by the gods for the life I lead. The weight of my responsibility, my own and my son's, hangs heavily about my every waking thought. My father's image rises constantly before my eyes. And even now in broad sunlight have the gods sent a messenger to me to command my obedience."

Dido pierced him through and through with steady eyes. "Now he wants me to believe the gods have no more urgent business at hand than to send him orders," she said. "You are no son of a goddess. You are as hard as a rock in the Caucasus; your nurse was an Hyrcanian tigress. Did this man ever show pity to me? Did he ever console me? Does he care if I am torn apart by desert chieftains? Let Juno be the judge of what has happened between us! There is no such thing as honor any more. He was starving, shipwrecked, lost, and forlorn—and I welcomed him to my palace! I sought out his lost ships and rescued them! How can I argue with such a man? Go, Aeneas. Seek Italy and your Lavinian shores. I shall not prevent you. Only I hope someday you have to suffer as much as I do. Of one thing I am sure, you will never be free of my curse. From bleak Tartarus where you are consigning me, I shall follow your fortunes. News of you will seep down to me in hell where I am headed." Then Dido called her servants who helped her to her chambers. There she threw herself on the bed and wept.

Aeneas would have liked to remain. He would have liked to comfort her, but Mercury's command had been too grim. Instead he returned to the shore to help in the launching of the fleet.

The Trojans hurried about like ants that have come across a heap of grain which they are efficiently transferring to their tunneled quarters. They form two columns across the plain, and those that are going push huge kernels ahead of them or carry them in their mandibles. Others follow behind as if to urge on the stragglers. So the beach seethed with hurrying black figures, loading stores, unfurling the sails, running to their stations. From her high window Dido watched the piers black with men until she thought her heart would break. Finally in desperation she sent for her sister Anna to plead once more with Aeneas, to ask for just a short delay, a few more days, a last few hours even before he sailed away forever. "Tell him, dear sister, he has no reason to leave so suddenly in this winter weather. I will not injure him. I never sent a fleet to help the Greeks burn Troy. I never plotted to march my soldiers through his Scaean gates. I never violated the grave of his father Anchises. Why does he treat me with such suspicion? Beg him to stay a little longer. It is all I ask—no marriage, no contract, no promise— only that."

Aeneas listened to Anna's pleading. He was moved and sorrowful, but he did not yield. Her entreaties swept over his bowed head like the gusts of wind that beat against an aged oak grown on the very crest of an Alpine slope. Though gales may strew its yellow leaves far into the valley, whip its limbs, and bend its trunk almost to the ground, the tree will cling to the depths of the earth, and it will resist their violence. So Aeneas remained rooted to his purpose.

Dido mourned in her palace. People spoke to her, but she did not hear them. In the temple her sacrifices turned to black blood. The gods were angry. Dido prepared another sacrifice. The auspices were so dreadful that she hid them from sight. It seemed to her that her husband Sychaeus was calling her from some midnight land with wails like those of an owl under a thick, black sky. Wherever she walked, she was followed by the mocking image of Aeneas. It tracked her, stalked just behind her shoulder as Orestes was pursued by the Furies for having slain his mother Clytemnestra and avenged the death of his father Agamemnon. In anguish of body and mind the Phoenician queen came to a decision.

Dido called Anna again to tell her that she was going to attempt a desperate remedy. She cautioned Anna to follow her directions meticulously, for she had found a way to cure herself of her love for Aeneas. "This is a ritual I learned from an Ethiopian priestess," Dido confided. "I would not use such magic if I could think of any other solution." She requested Anna to have a funeral pyre built in the courtyard outside her window. "Take the weapons of Aeneas and all his clothing that he has left in my room, and place it all at the very top of the mound. Take this bed we slept in too. Put it all on the pyre, everything you can find that has belonged to this Trojan." The pyre was erected and sanctified with special herbs cut in the dark of the moon with bronze sickles. To these were added black milk and a lock from a newborn foal. Three hundred gods were invoked. Altars flamed around. Priests chanted litanies. The charm would be potent indeed, thought the Tyrians. What could their queen not do when she set her mind to magic?

That night as Dido paced her chamber, Aeneas and his men slept on the decks of their ships. The water casks were filled. All was in readiness for their departure. Silence and black night mantled the earth. Not a sound came from the slumbering city. The gentle waves of the inner port slapped against the wooden hulls of the vessels as they lay moored to the wharves. Suddenly Aeneas sprang to his feet. In sleep he had heard again the voice of Mercury and seen his intent stare. "Man your stations! Unfurl the sails! Leap to the oars!" he shouted. "There is not a second to lose! We are still in grave danger!" Without waiting for the sleepy men to tumble out, Aeneas jumped to starboard and slashed the twisted ropes that held his fleet to the piers of Carthage. A west wind caught their sails so that when dawn broke and Dido looked out of her window, the Trojan fleet stood well out to sea.

Wildly Dido watched them rise and fall on the ocean swells. Her hatred rose in her throat, and she cursed them and herself. "Why didn't I send out torches last night and burn their ships to bits of charred and blackened refuse? I could have done it. Why didn't I take his beloved Iulus and serve him up to his father in the meats of a banquet? Why didn't I have every last one of their evil, treacherous, lying race put to the sword? I could have done it!

"Today they shall have my answer! I shall make a blood offering to the Tyrian nation, for a nation shall rise beside my bones. May you men of Carthage yet unborn listen well to my story. Trust not the men of 'Rome'! Live to avenge me! May great men of my race in our god Baal rise in their strength and chase the Roman from his Italian shore. From the family of Barca let a conqueror come who can endure all toils, all campaigns, mountain cold, and blindness—but track the Roman down! Let a Hannibal avenge me! From this day forth my people shall hate and loathe the treacherous men of Trojan stock!"

Then Dido and her priests performed holy rites. With one sandal unfastened, garments rent, and blonde hair streaming in disorder over her pale face, Dido officiated as high priestess. She mounted the pyre herself, murmuring strange holy chants. When she had reached the summit, she paused and contemplated the garments of Aeneas that lay at her feet, his shield, and the bed.

"I avenged my husband," Dido thought. "Even an animal could have remained faithful. Why could I, a human being, not have done as much? I built a city, watched it grow beneath my feet, led my people into a new world. The future is theirs . . . I could have been happy if the Trojans had never contaminated my palace and myself." Dido lifted Aeneas' sword and looked at it lovingly. Without another word she thrust it into her heart.

As soon as the priests grasped what she had done, they shrieked aloud in protest. Frantically Anna mounted the pyre and tried in vain to rivive her sister. The sword was well stuck. Three times Dido tried to rise. She opened her eyes and tried to find the sunlight. Moans rose from the courtyard. People despaired to see their queen leaving them. They ran madly about, tearing their garments and their hair. Sunk on the bed of Aeneas, Dido writhed and moaned.

Proserpina was about to mount from the Underworld to liberate the dying queen when Juno took pity on Dido. She quickly dispatched Iris to help her. The goddess of the rainbow arched from the top of heaven to Carthage, in multiple waves of iridescent color. Down this bridge Iris floated in her pink-and-yellow gown. She stooped over the suffering queen and severed the tenuous thread of her life. With a sigh of relief the spirit of Dido darted out into the eastern wind.

THE WAR IN ITALY

V

Aeneas and his Trojans saw from the sea the flames of Dido's funeral pyre rise into the air above Carthage. "I have committed a crime against love," thought Aeneas. Although he mourned for Dido, he was still relieved to have escaped with his ships and to feel once more the roll of the deck beneath his feet. They crossed the strait between Africa and Sicily safely and then put in at Drepanum again to celebrate funeral games for Anchises. Prizes were given to the winners, to men who would shortly found many of the greatest families of Rome. The first contest was a race between four galleys, the second a foot race, the third a boxing match, and the fourth event an archery contest. These games were followed by the Troianus, a demonstration of equestrian skill led by Iulus. Before the Trojans left Sicily, they sorted out those people who were tired of travel, or who were too ill to continue such a life of hardship. King Acestes of Sicily offered these Trojans a home at Drepanum, and Aeneas set out once more, taking with him into Italy only the most hardy and adventuresome from among his followers.

VI

Italy! Almost before the anchors had splashed into the surf, eager Trojans leaped ashore like youngsters. After so many years of travel and danger they had reached the western shores of Italy at Cumae, the oldest colony in that unknown west. Here was the abode of the Cumaean Sibyl, a most renowned prophetess of Apollo. While the men explored this new coast eagerly, and then settled down to bringing water and building fires, Aeneas walked to the temple of Apollo.

He paused to look up in wonder at its golden roof. This edifice had been built and its doors carved many years before by Daedalus. On the portals of his last masterpiece this artist had worked two scenes from his homeland—one showing the death of the Cretan Prince Androgeus and a second the drawing of lots in Athens for the Minotaur's victims. Daedalus had also represented King Minos' wife Pasiphaë, and on the last panel Theseus and Ariadne in the Labyrinth. The sculptor-architect had never finished his work; he had never been able to master his grief enough to carve an image of his boy Icarus whose wings had melted into the Aegean.

Beside Apollo's temple was the cave of the Cumaean Sibyl with its hundred doors that blew open suddenly and echoed from within its hollow caverns the purposes of the gods. Aeneas prayed and asked the

Sibyl to direct him. He remembered not to let her write her prophecies on leaves as she usually did so that the winds within the cave could blow them about and garble or obscure their meaning. By means of the golden bough of Proserpina, to which his mother's doves had directed him in the forest, Aeneas persuaded the Sibyl to accompany him to the Underworld so that he could once more consult with his father. He reminded the oracle that four heroes had dared the journey before him —Orpheus, Pollux, Hercules, and Theseus—and that they had returned safely. The ancient Sibyl finally consented to show Aeneas the way.

The entrance to the Underworld lay through a black, sulphurous cave on the shores of Lake Avernus, an area so poisonous that not even a bird could fly over it and live. Wielding his sword, Aeneas strode resolutely into the yawning tunnels of the earth. What horrors met his eyes as he descended into the blackness! The dead sat about him, those

diseased, those senile, those dead in babyhood wailing endlessly for their mothers' breasts. In the shadows he glimpsed King Minos of Crete judging cases before a voiceless jury. A little further on he saw those dead of spurned or unrequited love. Pale and golden in a dark corner, like a slender crescent moon in a midnight sky, he saw, but not at all clearly, the wan silhouette of the Carthaginian Queen Dido.

"Oh, my lost lady, can it be you?" cried Aeneas. "Is it true what I heard about your death? I swear to you, Dido, by all I love above and below the earth, I could stay no longer in Carthage. I really did not know you would take my departure so tragically." Although he begged her to listen further to his explanation, Aeneas could neither make her stay nor heed his words. Like a new moon she looked over him with light about her but no warmth. Despite his pleas her eyes were hard and full of hatred.

Aeneas and the Sibyl also passed the entrance of black Tartarus where the guilty souls were plunged to be scourged, tortured, starved, and judged by the inflexible Rhadamanthus of Crete. Beyond this, in the green pastures of the Elysian Fields, Anchises had been counting the days until he could see his son once more. Here the blessed dwelled throughout a thousand years until their spirits were cleansed with forgetfulness and they again consented to inhabit mortal bodies. While father and son talked together, Anchises let Aeneas glimpse crowds of young men waiting to be born, all the future great men of the empire Aeneas would found. Anchises spoke carefully, advising his son, and encouraging him to be brave, for the perils he had passed were trifles compared to the gigantic trials ahead.

When it was time to say farewell, Aeneas and the Sibyl climbed carefully up to the world, entering it through the gate of false dreams. In the harbor of Cumae his ships still dipped peacefully at anchor where he had left them. The men slept soundly on the decks. No one even heard Aeneas return.

VII

On the following day the Trojans moved northward along a pleasant coast. At dawn on the second day they spied yellow sand beaches where a swirling river flowed into the sea. Swinging to starboard, they entered the Tiber. They had come to the land of Latium. This was the journey's end.

A hush came over the crews. Silently each ship glided to an anchorage. In the high prow of the lead vessel Aeneas stood with his hand on Iulus' shoulder. "This is Hesperia. This is Italy, my son. This is the land to which the gods instructed me to bring you."

Still under the spell of the momentous day, the crews disembarked upon the soft bright grass of the riverbank. Great chunks of ship's bread were laid on the grass, and the last of their dwindled stores divided on them for the company. Still silent and thoughtful, the weary men ate apples and the crumbs of food. Then they munched on the dried biscuits. Iulus laughed, "Look! We are eating our tables!" Aeneas realized that the words of the Harpy Celaeno had come true. Truly the gods were with them!

He thought otherwise a few days later when fierce Juno herself rushed savagely to the city of Latium to swing open the savage gates of Mars. From her act all Italy burst forth, armed to push Aeneas back into the Tyrrhenian Sea. As far as anyone could remember, there had been twin gates in that place dedicated to the god of war, and overlooked by the two-headed Janus. It was the custom to leave them closed in times of peace and open in days of war. This tradition continued down through the ages even after great Rome had reared her walls beside the Tiber's banks. When the elders voted war, the consul himself, dressed in the striped toga of Romulus, strode to the gates, unbolted their hundred bronze bars, and shouted "War!" as trumpets blared.

This was the land of Latium. Its king was the aged ruler Latinus, who had one daughter, a lovely girl named Lavinia. Latinus had heard from oracles and even more understood from unusual portents that he should save Lavinia so that she could marry a tall, blond warrior who would one day arrive from over the sea to claim her. Therefore Latinus would not betroth his daughter to a neighboring prince named Turnus. This warlike prince ruled a people called the Rutulians from his capital of Ardea. He was not only eligible, but in love with the girl. Latinus had refused Turnus, however, and welcomed Aeneas' ambassadors eagerly, thinking that this must indeed be the ruler from over the sea to whom the oracles referred. Latinus sent gifts to the Trojans and asked to meet their leader.

Two people in Latium did not agree with King Latinus' policy. One was Lavinia's mother, Queen Amata, and the other was Turnus himself. Encouraged and even enraged by Juno who saw that it was a question of stopping Aeneas then or never, Queen Amata spread hatred of the Trojans among the women of Latium. They poured from their houses, shrieking and tearing their hair; on the mountain they indulged in bacchanalian orgies, plotted violence, and advocated war. A Fury sent by Juno drove Turnus mad with jealousy of Aeneas. Turnus rushed for his armor, leaped into his chariot, and thundered about the countryside urging neighboring princes to drive Aeneas from his slender foothold at the Tiber's mouth. In order that the farmers and shepherds of the vicinity might clearly see the necessity for war, Juno's Fury contrived to have Iulus and his playfellows kill a deer, not knowing that it was an especial pet of King Latinus' household. When the aged King Latinus hid in his chambers rather than declare war, Juno herself swooped down and opened the bloody gates.

Let the Muse of History remember their names, those long-dead men of Italy who turned their ploughshares into swords, or unclipped their spears from their hearth walls, who fitted old heads to new arrows and answered the call of Turnus. Let Clio not forget either the simple tillers of fields who dropped the goad beside the ox and, picking up two smooth stones from the furrow, loped down the hillsides with no other weapon than those, at the brazen call of war. From mountain pasture, from fertile valley, and from the cold banks of northern rivers an army of men descended to fight Aeneas.

First came the renegade King Mezentius and his more worthy son, down from the shores of Etruria. Close after, crowned in the palm leaves of victory, strode Aventinus, the Italian son of Great Hercules. After him rushed the twins from Tibur. Next came Caeculus, who had founded the town of Praeneste. Along with his simple, barefooted subjects rode the great horseman Messapus, whose father was the sea god Neptune. Also came Clausus from the olive groves of the Sabine Hills, he whose descendants were the Claudian *gens* of Rome. After Clausus arrived that great loather of Trojans, Halaesus, himself a son of Agamemnon. Next came warriors from Capri, whose shields were of cork, and men from the rich apple orchards of Abella. Virbius came to war also, a descendant of the Athenian Theseus.

Most dauntless of all the enemies of Aeneas was the mighty king of the Rutulians, the suitor of Lavinia, Turnus. He was the chief of all this host, a tall man with a chimera on his helmet that breathed flame in the heat of the battle. Turnus was followed by a band of warriors who despite their valor and arms were dwarfed by their leader. On the bronze shield of Turnus was embossed in gold the story of the Greek maiden Io who had been turned into a heifer. Warriors marveled at the skill of the artist who had depicted in gold the hundred eyes of her guardian Argus and the despair of her father, the river god Inachus.

Up from the southern lands below the Tiber, Camilla rode proudly to war. This virgin maiden, dear to the huntress Diana, trotted gallantly at the head of her Volscian cavalry. Her hair was bound with golden clips, as was her robe of purple. In fingers unused to spinning and weaving, she bore a quiver such as fierce Lycian warriors had used against the Greeks at Troy. This maiden had been brought up from infancy to be a soldier. Camilla was so fleet of foot that she could run over a field of wheat without ever bending the bearded heads, so swift she could skim over waves without ever denting their undulations. All along her route people ran out of their houses to see Camilla, who would fight with Turnus against the Trojan Aeneas.

Throughout Latium even children lisped the name of Camilla. She was the daughter of an old-time king named Metabus who had ruled in Privernum until he had become so despotic that his subjects drove him from the land. Metabus had just time to grasp in his arms his baby girl Camilla. Through woods and fields he fled with his pursuers close at his heels. Somehow Metabus managed to elude them. The arrows they shot after him somehow overshot and missed the mark. Hour after hour the despotic Metabus stumbled desperately through ploughed fields and willow thickets until he came to the banks of the Amasenus

River. Here he stopped short. The river, swollen with melting snows, swirled wildly before him. There was no way to cross it without wetting the baby, and in any case how could he swim well enough with her in his arms? Then, as he reflected, he heard behind him the cries of his enemies in pursuit.

Praying to Diana, promising her that if she would help him he would devote the baby Camilla to her service, Metabus resolved to attempt a daring feat. He wrapped the baby in layers of cork and bound her to his heavy oak spear, enfolding her with many rows of rope. When he thought that the weight was fixed at the proper place on the spear, he poised it carefully and hurled it, baby and all, across the river. To his great joy he saw them land in the wet turf of the opposite bank. Then Metabus swam to the other shore and pulled the spear from the grass. Eluding all pursuit as well as subsequent offers of hospitality, he raised Camilla to be a warrior and a virgin huntress particularly beloved of Diana. No wonder the residents of Latin towns rushed to their garden gates to see this fabled maiden pass. Many a mother would have liked to have chosen Camilla as a bride for her son, but the maiden was bound by her father's oath and would never consent to marry. Warriors and farmers rushed by the hundreds to fight beside Camilla and Turnus.

VIII

Aeneas heard that his offers of peace had not been accepted. He knew that an army was collecting around the standards of Turnus and Camilla. He ordered his men to build a strong camp, but even with that Aeneas wondered how he could ever withstand such an attack as was massing.

One evening while the land and its creatures slept, Aeneas lay thinking. Before his eyes a fog appeared over the Tiber, and the current seemed to cease. The cloud collected in one nucleus, became gray-blue, darker, until there rose through its shifting veils the kindly, white-haired head of the river god. "I am Tiber come to comfort you, Aeneas," he said. "You are not wrong. This *is* the place where the gods of earth and river welcome you. We will proudly bear the weight of your city and of its traffic. Row upstream until you come to the tiny hamlet of Pallanteum. There you will find friends and the site." The god sank back to his sandy bed, but he had stopped the current's flow. Aeneas chose two ships and set out upstream, a passage swiftly cut as through a placid lake.

Shortly he saw on the riverbank a white sow with thirty white piglets, just as the oracle had predicted. Beside it was the small village of Pallanteum. Aeneas was welcomed by its chief Evander and his tall son Pallas. Evander and a few friends had migrated from the mountain-engirdled land of Arcadia in the Peloponnesus all the way to these hills on the Tiber. Here they lived in poverty and fear, never free from Latin incursions. Evander was delighted to give Aeneas 200 men, first because he would be striking an old enemy, secondly because as a child he had once met Anchises, and thirdly because he wanted his son Pallas to learn warfare from a great master like the Trojan hero.

Evander told Aeneas that there might be in Italy a people who would join with him. They would be a formidable ally. To the north of the Tiber lived a proud Asiatic race called Etruscans. They had come from Lydia in Asia Minor and had always been a warlike people, wealthy and very artistic. These people had been ruled by a cruel king named Mezentius, whom they had driven out of Etruria when he began to chain living men face to face and wrist to wrist with the dead. Mezentius had fled to Turnus' land, where he flaunted his wickedness. The Etruscans in their chariots would have fought Mezentius and Turnus gladly except that one of their venerable seers had told them not to rally to the leadership of any man born in Italy. "Otherwise," said Evander, "I would have offered them my son Pallas. Now you, Prince Aeneas," he continued, "could lead them into battle. Your lineage is fine enough, even for so proud a people as the Etruscans!" As they talked, Evander showed Aeneas his poverty-stricken farms, walked with him through the hedgerows and fields where one day Aeneas would erect a magnificent temple to Venus and a Forum Julium for the citizens of Rome, a place where they could congregate to transact business in the open like the Persians.

It was while Aeneas strolled meditatively along the banks of the Tiber at Pallanteum that his mother was able to bring him gifts as she had promised to do. Appearing before her son, Venus laid against an oak tree the new armor that Vulcan had just completed for him. On the shield the clever smith had stamped the story of Rome. Tears came to the eyes of Aeneas as he saw the fame and exploits of his descendants, whose hopeful young faces he had glimpsed in passing through the Underworld. Reverently he ran his fingers over the shield. Here were Remus and Romulus twisting their heads up to grasp the she-wolf's teats. Here were the Roman seizing Sabine maidens, for they had no women of their own. There were the sacred geese warning Marcus Manlius of the Gauls' approach, the sacred geese that saved the Capitol. Beyond the blond Gauls with their dog collars of gold and Alpine spears you could see two Romans, the wicked conspirator Catiline and the lawgiver Cato insisting that Carthage be destroyed.

On the shield was the fierce battle of Actium, where Augustus Caesar and Agrippa stood for Rome, with Antony backed by the riches of Egypt and the Orient against them. To think that there could be a Roman who would rally the forces of the Red Ocean, the lands of the sunrise, against the might of Rome! A Roman with an Egyptian wife! Beside this horror the monstrous zoomorphic gods of Egypt—a dog-headed Anubis, for example—dared to brandish outlandish weapons in the faces of our great Venus, Minerva, Neptune, and Mars.

On the other hand you could see great Caesar borne in triumph through Rome, followed by the kings he had conquered, chieftains who came from Africa, Spain, Cisalpine and Transalpine Gaul, and even those of the Morini who lived the farthest away, opposite an island Caesar had also subdued, a bleak, windswept place called Britannia. Behind Caesar the Rhine grumbled to feel its first bridge, which he had forced upon it.

Proudly Aeneas lifted the shield, felt it well balanced on his arm, and smiled in pity for Turnus and the warrior maiden Camilla.

IX

While Aeneas was absent in the Etruscan cities north of the Tiber, Turnus and his allies from Latium and the land of the Volscians led their army across the plain to the Trojan camp. Aeneas had left orders that in the event that his men were attacked, they should remain behind the walls of their *castra*, defend their gates from the towers they had built beside them, and on no account venture outside these ramparts. He, Aeneas, would engage in single combat upon his return. His men were obedient. From their walls they watched the enemy host spread out across the plain under a cloud of dust. While the attackers were still a good mile away, twenty or so horsemen broke away from the main body and galloped toward the Trojan camp.

Turnus in all his glory was at their head. The Rutulian king rode a Thracian stallion, a tall black horse with white markings. Turnus was resplendent in shining armor. His gold helmet flashed and sparkled in the sun, and over it rose a stiff red crest, curved and proud like the mane of a war horse. Turnus, holding the reins in his left hand, yanked the stallion's head and forefeet high in the air, and then hurled his spear against the Trojan gate. Then this fierce king called for a champion to come out and fight him. There was no answer from the Trojans inside the camp. Infuriated by this unexpected turn of events, Turnus shouted insults, twitted those inside with the loss of Troy, and galloped his horse around and around the walls, hunting for a way to get inside.

In such a way on a cold winter's night a lean and ravenous wolf circles about a sheepfold. Inside the pens the lambs scent his presence and lie bleating against the warm ewes. So Turnus, starved for blood, panting for murder and the pleasure of the kill, looked for a crack, a hole, an opening in the Trojan wall. With clenched jaws and poised sword Turnus circled, wishing he could reach up to the wall's summit and grab by the throat one of those silent strangers that stood looking down on his fury with level eyes. Meanwhile the allied Latin and Rutulian forces had arrived and were drawn up in silent lines watching Turnus threaten and circle in vain. There was apparently no weak spot in the defenses. Aeneas had designed them well. Racking his brain for some impressive deed to do, Turnus' eyes fell upon the Trojan fleet that lay tied up along the Tiber's bank, protected only by a semicircular earthen wall. Here was at least something to do, thought Turnus. "Make pine torches," he called to his men. "Burn their hated ships! Then we shall be sure to drown them in the sea, those who manage to escape our swords!" Turnus rushed toward the river with the first torch flaming in his hand.

This was the fleet Aeneas had built under the supervision of his father Anchises at Antandros, south of Troy. These were the very planks that had carried him and the Trojans through so many adventures. They were more than ordinary fibers, more than just pieces of wood. The kind Mother Goddess, Cybele, she in whose service the wife of Aeneas had remained at Troy, had given her favorite grove to Aeneas. It was a grove of pine and hardwood trees, oaks and maples, that had long stood drinking the rain and the sunshine on the southern slopes of Ida. These trees the mother of mankind, out of pity, had granted Aeneas. When the goddess had asked Jupiter to protect the ships built from her sacred trees, to save them from storm and disaster, the ruler of Olympus had not agreed to do so. "Aeneas is a man. Like every man he must know all danger, all trials, storm and shipwreck, heartache and disaster. No man can do less!" However, Jupiter did promise Cybele that once the fir and hardwood planks, the beams and masts, had done their task, he would release their spirits from their material form.

Jupiter was just about to take care of this engagement when he saw Turnus and his bloodthirsty followers swarming over the breastworks toward the little fleet. This was the promised day: the Fates were watching the last few minutes fill up when the curses of Turnus warned Cybele to keep the pine flares away from her sacred vessels.

Suddenly a strange cloud of light flushed the faces of the spectators, where crowded on the walls they gasped to see it travel across the sky from east to west. At the same time they heard the music of the choruses from Mount Ida near Troy. Then a voice to make you shudder cut through the heavens, filling the ears of the Trojans and the Rutulian hosts. "Do not tremble to defend my ships, you Trojans! Arm not yourselves for me! Turnus shall succeed in burning the sea before he lights one of my sacred pines!" With tears in their eyes the strong warriors recognized the accents of the generative force of the earth speaking again. "Go free, you swimmers! Go free as goddesses of the deep! The Great Mother orders it!"

As her words blew away like smoke and the bright cloud faded, each brass-beaked ship snapped its cable, lifted its pointed prow, skimmed a few feet over the water, and plunged headfirst under the waves. One

after another they glided forward, rose, and plunged like blue porpoises under an ink-blue sea. The Trojans moaned to see them vanish. Turnus stood alone, silhouetted against the blue water, his red crest blowing in the ocean breeze and his lighted torch flaming in his hand. All his followers had crept back and stamped on their torches, guilty and fearful of the wrath of a goddess. Then before their amazed eyes burst rosy and sparkling from the crests of the waves twenty nymphs of the sea. They breasted the swell together, their pink arms flashing as the ships' oars once had done. The fierce soldiers watched them as they bore out to sea.

Only Turnus was unimpressed. All other men were speechless and awed. Even their horses pawed the earth and rolled their eyes uneasily. Even the river god of Tiber lifted an admonishing hand and waved his currents backward upstream lest their force intrude upon the sacraments of Cybele. Only Turnus shouted contemptuously, "Oh, come on, men! These portents are strictly for Trojans. You have seen Jupiter deprive them of their fleet. That saves us the trouble. Isn't that a fact? Follow me, and we'll shove them all into the Tiber as well! We are no Greeks to sit ten years outside a beleaguered Troy! No Vulcan, husband of Venus, had to be cajoled into making armor for me! We don't need a Trojan horse to cover our intent! Here we stand talking while the day is spent. Let food be prepared. Then we'll ring their camp with our campfires and tomorrow let them taste the metal of Italy."

During the night two Trojan youths named Nisus and Euryalus persuaded the chiefs to let them make a dash for it through the Latin troops that sprawled in drunken sleep beside their chariot wheels and dying fires. Iulus urged that the boys be permitted to go, gave them many messages for Aeneas, and promised them rich rewards. The two youngsters, eager for glory, made a wide path of death through the Rutulian soldiers, killing Turnus' favorite augur and many prominent chieftains. They had reached the path that leads up through the trees to Alba when Euryalus stopped to try on a suit of Italian armor and to fit a burnished helmet over his curly head. The glint of metal against a sky brightening with dawn caught the attention of a cavalry column riding down to join Turnus.

Both boys ran through the scrub oak as the horsemen dismounted and fanned out through the bushes after them. Nisus made it! Noiselessly he hoisted himself up over the rocks of Alba where the path to Pallanteum was broad and flat. Euryalus had been caught in the branches because of the plunder he would not or did not let go. Nisus crouched with thumping heart and heard his best friend struggle with his captors. Then Nisus rose and shot two spears that killed two of the Italian cavalrymen. Finally he revealed his whereabouts in the hope that Euryalus would be saved. It was too late, however, and so both were killed in their youth and beauty. Both bent and toppled as does a summer flower uprooted by the cunning, underground plow blade, or as do slender crimson poppies crushed by the overwhelming weight of one summer raindrop.

Their names and their courage are not forgotten. So long as mighty Rome wields her dominion over the lands of the Mediterranean world, so long as the great Capitol rests upon its rock foundation, the names of these brave boys will be remembered!

When morning came, the Trojans grieved to see the Italians parade before their walls bearing—with spear shafts for bodies—the bloody heads of Nisus and Euryalus. The black blood had not stopped dripping down before Rumor had swooped with the news into the Trojan camp and set all the women to screaming. Staggering and moaning like an animal in labor, the mother of Euryalus clutched at the walls and stared at her son's vacant white face. Her shrieks and reproaches took all the fight out of the Trojan men, who abandoned the walls and squatted hopelessly in groups of three and four.

They roused themselves, however, when the boy Iulus walked among them. The Italians had begun their attack. Under heavy, cylindrical shields they moved up to the walls like huge tortoises and began to batter. Others raked the defenders with clouds of arrows as, leaning over the ramparts, they pried at the tortoises with spears and rolled boulders down on the besiegers' heads. Iulus was particularly incensed at the obscenities and boasts of an Italian youngster named Numanus of the Remulus family. "Ha! you Trojans, dressed up in purple and saffron with girlish ribbons on your helmets and sleeves in your tunics. Come out and fight! Come and see what real men are like! We Latins are tough! We bathe our infants in ice-cold mountain streams and train them to hunt, ride, and raze cities for a pastime. You dancing Trojans, either fight or give up!"

Iulus, a golden circlet of royalty on his blond curls, drew back his bow and split the youngster's forehead with his arrow. The archer Apollo saw this feat, and replacing the absent Aeneas, stepped down and told Iulus to stay out of battles until he was a man. Of course, Apollo also praised the boy for his feat. Iulus obeyed, withdrawing to the center of his forces. He remained where the men could still see him, however, and where he could still hear the thud of boulders as they were hurled into the walls by the enemies' catapults.

At one point after a tower had burned and crashed to the ground, the Trojans in the heat of battle forgot and opened one of their gates, pressing hard against the besiegers. By the time one of their chieftains had swung it shut again, Turnus was inside! Like a wolf among lambs he leered at the cowering Trojans and began to lop off their heads. Then a hero, Pandarus, stood up to Turnus. "You are insane, Turnus!" he told him. "We have you now! You are as good as dead!"

Turnus raised his sword and brought it down with such force that he separated Pandarus' head from his shoulders. He smiled sarcastically at his adversaries and said, "Begin, all of you, if you have the courage to oppose me. You can tell old Priam that an Achilles came here too!"

After the swift death of Pandarus, the two Trojans whom Aeneas had appointed as leaders during his absence rallied their forces behind them. Both mature men and brave warriors, they led the Trojans in an encircling movement against Turnus. Well protected by their shields, they pointed a hundred swords eager for his throat. The Trojan Capys was there too, he who would live to found Capua south of Rome!

Step by step they forced the Rutulian backward, nor cringed before his feints, until they had driven him to the riverbank. Sweat dripped over his whole body. Turnus could not even breathe. He had retreated right to the night-black water. Before they could come close enough to stab him, however, Turnus leaped into the river, fully clad in armor. Buoyant in the dark water, he floated across to his own men, washed clean of slaughter and ready to begin again.

X

Late that same night Aeneas came sailing down the river with Evander's son Pallas at his side, asking him questions about war and navigation. Aeneas did his best to educate the lad. Behind them came the formidable war fleet of the Etruscan peoples. Even the Muse could not have memory enough to name them all. King Tarchon had sent them from the cities of Clusium and Cosae. The island of Elba, rich in mines, had dispatched 300 warriors, Populonia 600, Pisa 1,000. Men poured from Caere, Minio, Pyrgi, Graviscae swept with malaria, from Liguria, and from proud Mantua on the Tuscan River. In thirty ships the Etruscans swept to the aid of Aeneas, rallied to the standard of this chief from Asia.

Aeneas was holding the rudder of his flagship when he saw the river nymphs encircle him. One of them called Cymodocea told him how she had been changed by Cybele from a ship into a maiden. The nymph held onto the ship's side with her right hand and splashed along with her left. She warned Aeneas how the Rutulians and Turnus lay in wait for him at the beach, and she spoke of the beleaguered camp. "Prepare for battle!" shouted Aeneas. Ship after ship echoed with the order. As they sailed around the bend of the river, the prince lifted high his new war shield so that it blazed in the sun and flooded his own camp with light. The Trojans, recognizing their leader's sign, sent a fresh shower of arrows toward Turnus.

While the Etruscan King Tarchon maneuvered to drive his ships through the waves and onto the beach—not caring whether or not he split their hulls so long as he gained a beachhead—Aeneas and Achates leaped ashore through the waves. No man could stand before the Trojan

Aeneas, no man at all! Aeneas killed them so fast he once had to send Achates back to the ship for fresh weapons. With the prince cutting a passage for them, the Trojans came ashore.

A unit of the Etruscan cavalry led by Pallas met stiff opposition. They would have fled before the attack of young Lausus except that the boy Pallas fired them with his courage the way a spark will catch in an autumn field and before you know it send out flames in all directions. Pallas fought like a young lion and so did Lausus on the other side. These two equally matched youths were about to meet when Turnus went to the aid of Lausus. Pallas watched the Rutulian king clear a way through the host in his battle chariot and speed to duel with him. Although Pallas faced him bravely, he was no match for a full-grown man like Turnus. After the second exchange of spears, the boy fell pierced, spurting blood from his mouth. Then Turnus put his heavy left foot on the boy's body and yanked off his wide belt, tugging and pulling at the body as if it were nothing to respect. How foolish those men are who do not curb themselves when they ride on Fortune's crest!

Word of the death of Pallas was brought Aeneas by a runner before foul Rumor could invent more revolting details than those that had actually occurred. The prince grew almost blind with anger. Before his eyes he saw the welcome Evander and Pallas had given him and the Trojans, how they had been the first to offer advice and assistance. In a fury of revenge Aeneas left his own troops and cut a path across the battlefield toward Turnus. The Trojan founding father listened to no pleas for mercy, but killed right and left, and also captured four young men to use as a sacrifice for the offended spirit of Pallas. Aeneas cut his swath straight across the meadow until he had reached his own camp, where Iulus opened the gate and ran out to meet him. Aeneas did not find Turnus because Juno had spirited him away from the field.

Turnus' place was well supplied by the tyrannical King Mezentius, who, expelled by the Etruscans, had sought refuge at the Rutulian court. Mezentius was a giant of a man, and his son Lausus was proud of him. Word was brought to Aeneas of the Etruscans Mezentius was slaying. The prince cut his way toward the center. Mezentius, who saw him coming, sneered and hurled his spear. It missed Aeneas but struck one of his comrades. Then the prince hurled his spear. It pierced Mezentius' groin, but his youngster Lausus rushed to cover his father's escape. Again and again Aeneas tried to persuade Lausus to withdraw, for the prince pitied his youth and the boy's foolish temerity. Lausus would not flee, however; Aeneas had to kill him, had to pierce his pitiful, thin shield and the woven, gold tunic his mother had made him.

"Poor youngster," said Aeneas to him, bending down to lift Lausus' head from the trampled earth. Then the Trojan prince, oblivious of the weapons Lausus' escort were leveling at him, curtly ordered the enemy to lay the boy upon his shield.

"What reward can Aeneas offer such a brave fellow?" he asked while Lausus stared at him with eyes that still understood his words. "I shall not take your armor, son," spoke Aeneas to him softly. "One so brave has every right to keep it. I consign you to the spirits of your fathers. Console yourself that you were not vanquished by a mortal. You fell only before Aeneas."

Meanwhile Mezentius, who lay concealed beside a stream, heard of his son's death. He called for his horse and rushed out at Aeneas. Three times he circled the Trojan prince, who had just finished caring for Lausus' body. Aeneas aimed for his horse and then slew Mezentius, who welcomed death but only begged Aeneas to give him funeral rites. "You know how hated I am by both Trojans and Etruscans," were his last words.

XI

After this day the Latins asked Aeneas for a twelve-day truce, which he granted. During this time each army erected funeral pyres upon which they burned their dead. Aeneas sent the body of Pallas home on a bier woven of osier and willow, accompanied by all the trophies the youngster had won by his own right, to which were added many other rich presents from Aeneas. While the Trojans mourned and prayed for their dead, great confusion reigned in Latium.

King Latinus still wanted to welcome Aeneas as a son-in-law and thereby put an end to the war. Turnus and Queen Amata still hoped to win, however, and redoubled their efforts. Courtiers were of various opinions. Many believed the war should be decided by Turnus and Aeneas in single combat. Others wanted to follow King Latinus in his desire to exile Turnus and welcome Aeneas. Still others suggested offering the Trojans a piece of worthless land along the coast to which they could be safely relegated.

Before any line of policy was reached, Aeneas and his forces were well on the way to Latium. The Latin women, with the girl Lavinia in their midst, rode to the temple of Minerva in their chariots. As they passed through the streets where preparations for combat were being made, Queen Amata and her friends admired Turnus and urged him to bring Aeneas to his knees. Turnus rushed about the palace in a blaze of golden armor. As he finished buckling on his sword and setting his red-plumed helmet on his head, Camilla arrived with her Volscian cavalry. She leaped from her horse at the sight of Turnus. "Remain here to guard the castle," she told him. "I have no fear of Trojans either. I will ride out to meet them." She and Turnus arranged that he would set an ambush for the main body of Trojans led by Aeneas, who had to pass through a mountain defile. Camilla would ride out on the plain and engage the Etruscan cavalry.

Camilla organized her horsemen in a long line facing the Etruscans. At her uplifted arm each warrior drew back his spear, and at her dropped hand spurred forward toward the foe. Darts rained among them like driving snow propelled from all directions by the swirling winds of winter. The riders bore down upon each other in rows like the crests of waves that sweep in from the deep. After the first impact the troops of Camilla reversed their shields behind their backs and fled. Then when the Etruscans were in full gallop behind them, the Volscians turned and let the foe impale themselves upon their long spears. Again it was their turn to wheel and charge down from the castle walls with a roar of fury and neighing of horses like an undertow that dangerously gathers sliding sand and pebbles and attacks the oncoming wave insidiously, from beneath.

Then the two lines closed in single combat, each man marking out his opponent. None could stand long before Camilla, who wielded sword and battle-ax fiercely about her. She rode superbly, with knees alone, guiding her horse to right or left at a touch or change of weight. Her purple gown blew about her shield and left her left breast exposed. Tarchon, the Etruscan king, worked hard among his men to keep them from fleeing headlong before her. Camilla killed one after another of the Etruscan and Phrygian nobles, usually marking those whose raiment would make the richest gifts at the shrine of Diana. No one noticed that she was being stalked by a wily warrior named Arruns, who kept a certain distance from her during the engagement, looking for a chance to pierce her escort. Finally he sent a dart straight to her breast. As Camilla lurched forward, her maiden warriors caught her in their arms. Camilla had just breath enough to send her black news to Turnus before she died.

Turnus recalled his men from their ambush. Ordering them to fall in, he started down the hill and across the plain just a few minutes before Aeneas and the main body of Trojans loped through the pass. As darkness fell, the two columns of Turnus and Aeneas galloped almost neck to neck across the plain toward the city.

XII

Turnus arrived first and closed the gates behind him. King Latinus, joined this time by Queen Amata, begged Turnus to end the war and forfeit the hand of Lavinia. Instead Turnus sent Aeneas his challenge, saying that he would meet the prince in single combat between the lines of the two armies at dawn. During the night Turnus inspected his favorite white horses, which would draw his chariot on the morrow. Meanwhile Juno sent Turnus' sister, a maiden who had lost her virginity to Jupiter, down to earth to help Turnus win the combat.

Soon after dawn King Latinus rode out across the plain in a chariot drawn by four horses. He was followed by Turnus behind his white pair. They were met by Aeneas and Iulus, dressed in pure white robes. Before an altar Aeneas sacrificed, prayed, and established the conditions of the combat. "If I lose, I swear that my son Iulus will leave Italy forever and make no claim whatsoever to rule in this western world. If I win, then we Trojans shall build a city called Lavinium in honor of my bride, the princess Lavinia. I swear that I shall not deprive King Latinus of his crown, nor try to impose my power over any peoples who do not wish to live under my sway and protection."

A murmur of admiration rose from the Latin chiefs who saw that Aeneas was other than the perfumed, curly-haired monster Turnus had described. Juturna, Turnus' sister, was quick to spread riot among them, however. If only one dart could be shot at this Trojan, there would be a general rush to arms. Only the presence of Aeneas standing high by the altar restrained the men. Somewhere from the crowd of Rutulians beside Turnus came an arrow that wounded Aeneas. As he was helped from the field, the battle began in earnest. Turnus' spirits rose to the skies. Laughing and eager, he leaped into his chariot and, using his sword like a scythe, drove frightened Trojans before him.

It did not take Aeneas and his physicians long to draw the barb from his leg. Immediately he started to buckle on his shin guards. As he settled his helmet and cheek straps he bent over to kiss Iulus. "Learn courage today, my son, and true work. Let others teach you the accidents of fate. Today my right hand will protect you. When you are a man in your turn, repeat over to yourself the tales of the others who have gone before you. Think of your father and your Uncle Hector."

Aeneas mounted and drove into the battle. From a distance Turnus heard him come. He grew pale and trembled as a farmer shudders before the violence he knows is at the center of a black cloud bearing toward his wheat field. Juturna too heard the ominous thunder of the Trojan cyclone. Using her special powers, she hurled her brother's charioteer from his place and, assuming his guise, whipped up the horses so adroitly and guided them so well that Turnus was borne up and down through his cheering men without ever approaching Aeneas. Disdaining to strike a man who flew from him, Aeneas pursued the elusive Turnus in widening circles through the confusion of battle.

Hour after hour Aeneas stalked the Rutulian hero without ever being able to meet him face to face. Then in anger he summoned his Trojan leaders and told them the time had come to attack the city. "It is no use waiting for Turnus' pleasure," decided Aeneas. "We shall force the city, by arms and by fire, and obtain our treaty from Latinus." At his direction ladders were brought and torches. Battering rams pounded at the gates. The city guard was killed. Queen Amata, seeing that the Trojans had arrived at the palace and supposing that Turnus was dead, hanged herself.

Out on the plain where he wheeled magnificently, Turnus also heard the outcry and saw wisps of black smoke rise from the city's rooftops. Sadly he spoke, "Juturna, I have known for some time that you were my charioteer. You must leave me now. Is it so difficult to die?"

Even as Turnus struggled with himself to make a decision, one of his friends rode up to him. "Turnus," he moaned, for his face had been cut open by an arrow, "how can you desert us now? We are all there in the city trying to stop the Trojan Aeneas who looms above us like the peaks of the Apennines! How can you still drive about this deserted plain when your friends are dying?"

Still Turnus could not decide. As he looked toward the city he saw one of its towers, a structure he himself had helped to hew and bolt, fall in a crash of burning beams. This decided him finally. He drove toward the walls of the castle.

Aeneas heard the word "Turnus" breathed by the crowds, who stopped in their tracks wide-eyed, arms raised, mouths falling open. King Latinus stepped to the wall and watched Turnus approaching the gates and Aeneas striding from the inside through an opening in the ranks.

All were hushed to see those two brave men, born in opposite ends of the earth, come up against each other in a battle to the death. The mobs of soldiers drew back. Latins moved over to make room for the Trojans they had been trying to kill the minute before. Women crept from their houses on tiptoe,—like heifers that wait to see which young bull will be master of the herd.

And like two bulls they met, Aeneas and Turnus, horn to horn and shield to shield, struggling for footing, swords flashing and then locked to the hilt, forehead to forehead. You would have said Jove held scales where each man balanced evenly the other. Which one is heavier by the added weight of death?

Blow after blow they land until the blood flows from a hundred cuts. Then Turnus lifts his sword in what he hopes will be the final stroke, but Aeneas catches the blow glancing on his shield, and the weapon breaks. For an instant Turnus stares unbelieving at his broken weapon. Then he turns in flight. Aeneas, limping from his wounded knee, follows him close after. As Turnus calls to his men for a sword, Aeneas forbids them to throw him one. Five times they circle the plain inside the ranks of soldiers.

Juno on Olympus saw that her cause was lost. "Let me ask only one favor," she said to Jupiter. "Since the Trojans must win, let the new men of Rome keep the antique courage of the Latin peoples. And let them discard the Trojan tongue and keep the Latin language for their own."

In passing a gnarled olive tree Aeneas was able to pull out his spear, which he had lodged there before. Turnus countered this weapon by lifting a boundary stone and trying to heave it at Aeneas. Turnus hardly knew what was happening any more. He was like a man who even as he starts to speak feels the paralysis of sleep creep down his tongue. He saw his soldiers in a blurred background, at their center the clear-cut image of Aeneas, stern-faced, deadly. As Turnus shook his head to clear his vision, Aeneas raised the spear and hurled it; for it was the only blow he would have the chance to make. The sharp point pierced the seven layers of Turnus' shield and penetrated his thigh.

A groan came from the Rutulian warriors who pressed forward as if to come to the aid of Turnus. Their king, however, had already raised his hand to Aeneas. "Spare me," he cried, "for the sake of your father Anchises. Yours is the kingdom. Yours is Lavinia as bride. Only spare me."

Aeneas lowered his sword and gazed at Turnus. Not a sound came from the ranks. Aeneas hesitated. As he thought, he saw displayed across Turnus' shoulder the gilded belt of Pallas. The youngster had been so proud to wear his father's trophy! Turnus had stepped on a dead boy's body to wrench off that belt. "Do you ask me for mercy and wear my young friend's trophy? Turnus, this blow is for Pallas."

Thus Aeneas defeated Turnus, killed him, and built Lavinium not far from the white walls of high Rome.

While I have been singing these deeds, our great Caesar has thundered his war chariots across Europe and up to the deep Euphrates where, a victorious conqueror, he administers justice to willing subject peoples, and has set his feet firmly upon the path to Olympus.

But you and I have finished our journey over the boundless sea;
Now it is time to loose the yokes from the necks of our steaming
    horses. *Vergil.*

2

BOOK

MEDIEVAL

MYTHS

EIGHT
SCANDINAVIA
BEOWULF

The early history of Britain from 55 B.C. to A.D. 1016 may be divided into four periods corresponding to four groups of Indo-European peoples, each of whom left their mark upon English culture, and each of whom contributed to that composite language which is our own.

The first group were the Celts, whom Julius Caesar described in his *Gallic War*. This book is a most valuable historical document, giving us our first direct account of the peoples living (55 B.C.) in northern Europe. According to Caesar the Celts were a warlike people whose priests were called Druids. The Arch-Druid lived in Britain and from there controlled and incited the Celtic tribes on the continent. These priests were well educated, Caesar assures us, and they kept their archives in Greek. Caesar himself wrote Greek fluently and had studied as a young man in Rhodes. Celtic languages are still spoken today—in Wales, Ireland, and Brittany (France), for example. Subsequent Roman legions remained in Britain until about 410, when they began to be recalled. A "barbarian" emperor replaced a Roman one in the city of Rome in 476.

Both Celtic and Latin, however, failed to prevail linguistically in Britain. Soon after the recall of the Roman legions, tribes from Scandinavia and Germany—the Angles, Saxons, and Jutes—settled in Britain. Unlike the tribes who were at the same time invading Gaul and Italy, the Anglo-Saxons did not adopt the language of their subjects. They continued to speak their own Germanic tongues which became in time the basis of the English language.

Their chieftains, such as Hengist and Horsa (*c.* 449), acquired land by circling it with oxhide strips much in the same manner that Vergil describes the Tyrian Queen Dido as doing in Carthage. At approximately the same time (*c.* 445–453) Attila the Hun was ravaging Gaul and Italy. The Anglo-Saxon poem *Widsith*, from which you will read material in the following pages, dates presumably from this period. Scholars have said it could be the oldest poem in any modern language!

There were no major invasions in England from 445 to about 800, except for the Anglo-Saxons. During these years the Merovingian Dynasty was ruling in France (486–751). One Germanic people, the Angles in Northumbria, were creating a literature. St. Augustine had begun their conversion in 597, one result of which was the introduction of the Latin alphabet. By adding to it their own runic characters to represent the sounds (such as "th") that did not exist in Latin, the Angles had a convenient tool.

Poetry and learning flourished in monasteries, such as the one of the Abbess Hilda (658–680) where the poets Caedmon and Cynewulf may have lived. Around the year 500 lived in Wales the great Celtic hero King Arthur, whose life became later an inexhaustible inspiration for poets and chroniclers.

Before 750 the greatest literary work of the Anglo-Saxon culture was composed, probably also in Northumbria. The following pages will retell its story. It is the epic *Beowulf*, a work so beautiful that students continue to learn Anglo-Saxon in order to read it.

Beowulf has 6,359 verses or half-lines. Each verse may have two accented syllables, a pause, and then the second hemistich of two accented syllables. Instead of rhyme there is an interesting alliterative device, often consisting of a repeated consonant in the first verse that is echoed again in the second half.

God mid Geatum	*[God amidst the Geats*
Grendles daeda	*Grendel's deeds]*
wlanc Wedera leod	*[The proud Weder lord*
word aefter spraec	*Words after spoke]*

It is a type of trochaic meter, a rhythm that has survived in one form or another in English poetry. Alliteration is also a prime asset to English poets.

Another feature of the poem that has attracted the reader is the great number of kennings, or compound words that evoke vivid pictures. A woman is called a *freodwebbe* or "peace-weaver." The poet says his hero went *ofer swanrade*—"over the swan-road" in his "foamy-throated" ship. This Germanic propensity to form compounds has also persisted. The reader will note that in the following adaptation some attempt has been made to exclude words of French-Latin origin except the few words such as "name," "gem," "dragon," "north," "south," "female," etc., which are in the original text, either because they represent a common Indo-European origin or because they were words (such as "candle") learned from the Romans. A few Celtic words were used because

MEDIEVAL MYTHS

they are historically justifiable. The principal anachronism is the use of many Danish words ("sky," "anger"), which only came into English after 800. They were too evocative of the mood of the poem to be banned.

The vocabulary of Anglo-Saxon was not extensive. English, which takes its name from the literary Angles, therefore set out upon a long career of appropriating words from scores of other languages, a process that still continues. Because of this propensity to explore other literatures and other lands, English has one of the largest vocabularies of any modern language.

During the ninth century England underwent its next invasion, this time that of the Danes, who finally had their King Canute crowned there in 1016. There had been a great interest in learning and culture during the reign of Alfred the Great, who was born about 843 and who became king in 871. He was a learned scholar himself. He had lived and studied in Rome. King Alfred attracted scholars to his court, founded schools, and himself translated from the Latin into Anglo-Saxon Boethius' *Consolation of Philosophy*.

Alfred's predecessor and example was Charlemagne, during whose reign in France scholars from many lands were persuaded to come and produce works of history and literature that have, in very fact, made this king immortal. One of the prelates and poets whom Charlemagne attracted was an Anglian named Alcuin. In 782 this distinguished scholar left the city of York in Northumbria to become the Bishop of Tours.

There were two results of the Danish invasion: (1) the fusion of Danish and Anglo-Saxon which resulted in the simplification of the resultant language, and (2) the destruction of the monasteries in Anglia, the previous center of literary life. There are other reasons for interest in the *Beowulf* epic aside from its age and linguistic value. One is its story. Another is the unique insight it gives us into the heroic age of the earliest literate Germanic people. Tacitus, who completed his *Germania* in A.D. 97–98, has given us after Caesar almost the only document of value concerning the barbarians, who even in his time were already on the move, in vast migrations that at the end of a few centuries produced not only the modern languages of western Europe, but also its modern cultures and states. Between Tacitus and *Beowulf* there is a long silence of more than 600 years while these peoples and cultures were becoming stable. It would be a mistake to call them "Dark Ages," as the great poet who wrote *Beowulf* has little difficulty proving.

Our poet confirms much of what Tacitus has said. He tells how these people lived, and where. He describes their lives and customs. He makes us understand their thoughts, their aspirations, and their notion of life. More than that, he shows us in *Beowulf* their idea of what a man should be. Many of their ideas survive in the modern world.

Without this poem the modern world would be at a loss to explain the institution of feudalism that suddenly confronted classical tradition and Roman law with a way of life often in complete variance with such Roman ideas as the divine right of kings. The historical period that ended about 1500, and which is known as the Middle Ages, was in a way one long struggle between two very different cultures. *Beowulf* shows us in formation many of the feudal ideas that were to flow so gloriously in knighthood and the code of chivalry. It also demonstrates how the old Scandinavian gods were supplanted, with extreme difficulty, by Christian theology.

The reader will find a strange mixture of paganism, nature worship, the conflict between good and evil so reminiscent of Zoroastrianism, Hebrew traditions, Christian teachings, Oriental dragons, and funeral pyres like those of India, Greece, and other Teutonic myths. Scholars believe that the Asiatic traits go back to the common Indo-European heritage.

Some inconsistencies in the text may be due to interpolations made in the original poem by the two scribes who copied the manuscript. They must, indeed, have been shocked by it! If, on the other hand, they were Anglians, they must have been thrilled. The love of the sea and ships runs all through Anglian literature, and it would seem that the strain of sadness in this great poem also runs through English literature.

Only one copy of *Beowulf* in its original form has ever been found. It was discovered by Sir Robert Cotton in the seventeenth century. Two copies were made of it in 1786 by the Danish scholar G. J. Thorkelin. It has been published and translated frequently since 1833, when Mr. John M. Kemble of Trinity College, Cambridge, prepared the text a retelling of which follows.

Beowulf is prefaced by a part of the *Widsith*, or *Wanderer*, which may be of interest because of its antiquity and secondly because it should refute any preconception about the Anglo-Saxons as having lived in anything resembling a "Dark Age."

BEOWULF AND THE FIEND GRENDEL

"I shall unlock my hoard of words at your will. I shall unfold before you, O King, the story of my wanderings, for truly I have roamed long years over this wonderful world."

The fire burned brightly in the castle hearth. On his high seat the king of Anglia, well wrapped in furs, lounged carelessly while his earls took places below him preparing to hear a renowned bard who was raising his harp and clearing his throat. Gusts of wind blew fragrant wood smoke out the open doors or curled it about the heavy oak rafters. The night had fallen early, but the hall door stood wide open at either end of the rectangular room. . . . No enemies would enter, for the land was at peace. The Angles had long before stopped their restless wanderings over the North Sea. They had cut Northumbria into marches, and the marches into shires. The once fierce Vikings had long since become peaceful farmers; their leaders were called earls. Over them all ruled a fair king, noteworthy because he upheld the freedom of his people, earls and carls alike.

These Angles, lovers of poetry, had ages before skimmed over the North Sea, westward from Sweden and Denmark, until they founded their new kingdoms in Britain: Mercia, Northumberland, and East Anglia. In the south of their new homeland their brothers, the Saxon kings, ruled Sussex, Wessex, and Essex. The Roman legions who for four hundred years had kept order in Britain were only a distant memory. Their missionaries had returned, however, to convince these settlers from over the seas to put away their worship of their pagan gods— Freya, Woden, Thor, Eostre, and the awesome Wyrd, goddess of death.

"O King," sang the bard, "I have tramped the whole world over in the course of a lifetime. Every mighty king have I seen with these eyes. Every land have I understood, each with its own customs and habits, each with its own law. One truth have I learned above all others! A king who seeks to rule his people and his lands without warfare must take this as his plan: he must work first and foremost for his people's good!

"Therefore since the world began, this wandering star upon whose breast we live, one king has shone more brightly than all others. He was Alexander of Macedon.

"In the far-flung realms of Rome have I wandered as a guest made welcome for his songs. In imperial Rome have I seen great Caesar ruling in all pomp and majesty. Through the lands of Greece have I also roamed, and farther eastward even than that. I have seen the splendor of Persian kings. I have glimpsed the sands of Africa and watched the foreign folk who dwell in Egypt's land. I have looked eagerly upon the wealthy men of the East and gaped at their trading vessels proudly riding the waves of Italy's harbors. Men have I seen who dwell by the Ganges' waters, whose flood waves ride down into an unknown sea near Eostre's far home. Lombardy have I seen also, and Franconia.

"In the halls of great kings the mead has always flowed freely; there gold armlets were the reward of my songs. . . . I have sung before the chiefs of the Angles here in Britain, and before the Jutes on the Island of Wight, and in the cold lands of the northernmost Picts and Scots. I have sung before the Saxons and the Swedes and the Danes, and wayworn fared to where the Elbe River joins our northern sea. I have willingly sought the hordes of fierce Huns over whom Attila holds sway, and stopped on my way home at the mead halls of the Franks across the sea. Pirates of the northern coasts have I recalled in my songs, and fought my way into the eastern land of the Finns. Six hundred shillings of pure gold has been my fee, and acres of land as a gift from the Queen of Mercia. Born was I in the Anglian land of Britain, and there shall I die, a faithful son of song.

"One truth would I set high above all others," repeated the glee-man. "Only the king who loves his people is beloved in turn of them. That king alone shall never be forgotten. Bards even now unborn shall sing of his feats, his strength, his faithfulness, and his openhandedness. Let the bards be ever entrusted to write the songs of a hero, and his people will have them to sing always."

The last sound of the harp drifted across the hall. Slowly the king roused himself. Pulling one of the massive gold armlets from his own arm, he sent it to the bard. The world was, indeed, very wide; and he for one had too much to do at home in Anglia ever to fare so far. What was the life of a man? What, indeed, was the life of a king unless he worked hard for his people who had raised him to the throne? What more than the flight of a gull through the mead hall, a sudden bright sweep of white wings against the smoke-blackened rafters? Only the unselfish, only the great in heart were worthy of being sung by the bards.

"Sing us the song of the Angles," ordered the king. "Tell us again our own story that we may steep ourselves in kingship. Sing of *The Hero.*"

Like a distant foreword to the swelling song the heavy rumble of the waves driven by the evening tide moaned and tore at the shore. They were the same waters that washed the headlands of Denmark, the olden home of the Angles. . . . The great hall was still. The song they would hear was such an old one, sung down the ages, recalling a time so long ago that only the great in heart had been remembered from it. . . . Gently the gleeman stroked his harp, in long, lonesome chords like the mournful sound of a wild wind shrieking through darkness. Shivers pierced the bones of the listeners as the old, homely words rang again in their ears:

Sing of the Danes in the days gone by, deeds of our kings who were scatheless in war! Tell about Scyld, the son of Scef, how he stole the mead from the foemen's halls, how he ripped their thrones from under their feet, how he drove his prow through the ways of the whale, how he gulped down tribute from all of the tribes that clung to their cliffs by the chilly sea.

Shout about Scyld with his strength and his might, building wide mead halls ribbed with gold. That was an earl—that Scyld, son of Scef! Ah, what a king we had! In the distant days of the Danes!

The great king called Scyld ruled for many years over the seafaring peoples of the north, and God gave him a fair, strong son to rule after him. According to the old king's will, his body was borne down the sea cliffs and placed on the earlmen's ship. Bronze shields bright with gold flashed along her gunwales, and from her masthead flew the shining flag of Scyld. The dead king, dressed in full mail and wearing his gem-studded crown, was laid on the open deck. On his chest lay heaped the wealth he had gathered during his long rule over the sea realms. Battle-axes and swords lay flashing in the winter sunlight about his body. Sadly the earls pushed the shining ship away from the jetty and watched the first deep swells of the sea catch her and sweep her along over the deep. To this day no man can say what became of King Scyld or his seaworthy ship! The waves hold him in trust—the wild, western sea.

The Scylding kings, descended from Scyld, reigned in Denmark for countless ages until the people became a whole, one in heart and mind. Then ruled an unselfish king named Hrothgar, who dreamed of a deed that would awe the bards so deeply that his name would be recalled among the Vikings forever more. Hrothgar unfolded his plan. He would have built in Denmark a great hall, so lofty, so heavy with gold, so braced with iron bands, that its like the northern folks had never thought to witness! There on a lofty seat Hrothgar would sit in state, night after night, giving rings to his earls, granting wealth to young and old alike, sharing even before his death all the gold of Denmark.

In this way and to this end was built Heorot Hall, the house of the deer, a wonder so famous that gleemen from all over the sea-swept lands came to gasp at its rows of stag's antlers, its bronze-bound doors, its lofty ceiling, and the lavishness of King Hrothgar. There every evening sat the Danish earl with his Queen Wealhtheow beside him, the handsome two, givers of gifts. From the lands around earls came to swear fealty to Hrothgar.

Night after night, however, the fiends of evil, those who live in the underworld, writhed and curled with hatred as the sweet sound of the harp rose from the hearthside. Jealous and full of anger, they leered as the soft song of the scop praised the All-Powerful,—He who had fashioned the earth, with its level fields and shimmering pools, with its girdle of sparkling green sea. He it was who had thrust the sun and moon up into the blue skies where they could stand as torches, as beacons for all homecomers over the seas. He it was who had bespangled the soils with russet leaves and reeds and who had breathed the breath of life into beings.

Hrothgar and his eldermen lived happily in Heorot Hall until the day that Grendel, a living fiend out of hell, a Satan who ruled over the swamps and marshes, came stalking toward them. Grendel and his folk had been banished to the fens eras before because of their slaying of Cain. To Grendel's accursed folk belonged the ghouls, the dragons, the lemurs, the elves, and all evil curs. The giants also had been out-lawed along with Satan because they had fought against God. Therefore God was giving them a fitting reward through everlasting ages.

So in the dark night, gliding among the shadows, Grendel crept stealthily toward Heorot. Drooling with spit, stinking and hairy, he leaped the outside walls, and stopped to listen. . . . No one had heard him. Only the leaves rustled overhead . . . Then with a blood-curdling scream he rushed headlong into the hall where the Danish warriors were sleeping. Careless and carefree they slumbered on the benches, heedless of woe, until Grendel's scream tore them from their sleep. Before they could think, he had crashed through their midst, his claws sunk deep in two warriors. Hurriedly he snatched up others, one or two at a time, until he had slaughtered thirty of Hrothgar's doughtiest earls. After the whole company had awakened, he lurched from the hall and took flight, leaving the partially eaten bodies strewn and mangled among the rushes of the floor.

The deaths were not discovered until dawn. King Hrothgar was appalled. He gathered at once that his strength or that of his earls together could do nothing against the evildoer. The struggle was too uneven. Within a few days Grendel crept back, and again the king awoke to find his fair hall in a shambles, the boards all overturned, and his warriors, torn by the monster's claws, spread about the floor.

Whoever had escaped the ogre's greediness fled for his life across the land of Denmark. In time the great hall was empty. No suppers were held. No scops or gleemen came to Heorot any more. Nor was there any more giving of rings. For twelve long years Grendel haunted the realm of Hrothgar.

No treaty, no peace, no ransom, no fee—nothing could allay the wrath of Grendel against the kingdom of Denmark! Night after night the accursed Shadow of Death crept through the woods, prowled about chieftains' dwellings, snatched his prey at random without thought for rank, youth, or years. Stealthily he lay in wait, caught men in his traps, and flung them headlong into an endless darkness.

Men looked for him, straining their eyes fearfully to peer through the rolling fogs of the moors, dreaded the thump of his heavy paw on their shoulders as they hauled in their nets. They scanned the beaches for him at twilight. They saw him behind every bush and stone of the path, or stood stock-still listening for the crunch of his bare pads on the pebbles. So many bloody deaths! So many screeching loved ones! How could a man know where the fiend would turn up next? What does a man know anyway of the fiends that crawl through the black night?

In the dark of evening Grendel lumbered into the empty hall hunting for food. One thing alone he could not touch—the throne of Denmark! Only that had God forbidden him to soil.

There was wretchedness in the land, sorrow, wretchedness, and cold fear! Hrothgar and his few trusty earls held meetings and tried to find an answer. They prayed to their idols. They cooked up new magic broths. They called upon their pagan gods to thwart all dragons, all fiends, all evil, all nightmares. . . . In their hearts they thought only of hell, not knowing, not having yet heard of the Lord God. . . . Cursed is he who slips from the true path and hands his soul back to the hell-fires! Blessed is he who on the day of his death finds peace in the breast of his Maker!

Hrothgar lived on, his days flowing from a cup of sorrow, powerless in the grip of the ogre, beaten and heartsick.

Those were black days shadowed by the awesome blackness of night . . .

Meanwhile in the land of the Geats across the sea the bitter news had come. The sorrows of Denmark reached in time the ears of the Geats. King Hygelac heard it and mourned! His earls heard it and shuddered!

Beowulf heard the news.

Of the race of men he was the strongest. Boldest among the bold was this vassal of Hygelac! Greatest in heart among all great hearts was this chief of the Geats, this Beowulf!

"Come! Let us haul down the ship!" cried Beowulf. "Over the path of the sea bird, through the wake of the swan, let us fly to Denmark," he said. "This king of the Danes needs men!"

At first the wise eldermen nearest King Hygelac's throne worried and fretted, for the sea was wide, and Beowulf dear to them all. Finally they yielded, however, and helped him choose fifteen strong warriors. Then they studied their hidden lore and found that their gods were willing. One of their number was called who knew the paths of the sea and who spoke to Beowulf of the tides and the landmarks. He warned him of black rocks and swirling shoals.

Under the sea-girt cliffs the shining ship was readied, laden with coats of mail, swords, and gleaming war harness. Bidding farewell to their king, the sturdy warriors embarked. Last of them all strode their mighty leader, his feet strong and steady on the bobbing craft. Turning their backs on Sweden, the fearless warriors cast off and leaned to the oars.

Like a bird, like a swallow, like a slender gull the glistening ship sped forward. She cut a path through the clear, green sea, her prow wreathed in bubbles and foam. The winds caught her like a bird and blew her swiftly southward. Across unknown waters the light floater lunged and ploughed into the swells. The salt spray blew strong on the warriors' foreheads.

By the first hour of the second day the dark fjords of Denmark rose on the skyline, reaching up toward the clouds from their tide-beaten sands. Sounding cautiously and tacking, the pilot brought the swift craft unharmed to the shore. The sea lanes had been followed aright. The coast had been won.

From his lighthouse on the cliff, the coast guard of Hrothgar saw the

Geats disembarking. Spurring his horse, he galloped down to the shore and bespoke them.

"Who are you, warriors in war dress who clamber from your sea-going ship? I am an earl of Hrothgar, king of the Danes. Never have shield-bearers so grim of face ever landed before on our shores! Do you at least know the password?"

Then as he spoke, the Danish earl suddenly saw the leader Beowulf. In fright and amazement he stepped backward. His hand shook on his horse's reins. "Never in my life," stammered the Dane, "have I seen a man like this one! Who in the world is this warrior?" he asked, still staring at Beowulf. "Surely this is a hero, one we must know for his deeds of strength. Please, may I know your kindred and the aim of your trip to this coast."

Beowulf unlocked his word hoard. "We come, indeed, from across the sea. We are folk and vassals of Hygelac, king of the Geats. Perhaps you have heard of my father. His name was Ecgtheow." The Dane gasped. His guess had been right. This was, in truth, a hero and the son of a hero.

"My warriors and I have come to your lands as friends," Beowulf went on. "Have no fear of us! We have heard of some fiend of darkness who is foully mistreating your king. Perhaps we can help him."

"Then hasten back to your ships," bade the coast guard. "Dress yourselves in your coats of mail. Grasp your shields and your axes. Hurry! I will lead you to Heorot Hall. Take no thought for your ship. I shall see that she is well guarded and circled about with hawsers. Her mighty heart shall find rest in our waters."

Setting their boar helmets well over their ears, the fierce warriors from Geatland strode up the sea cliffs after their leader. Shortly the lofty gables and gleaming roof of Heorot Hall came into sight. They stopped and wondered at its cunning workmanship, for truly there was not a building like it in all the world. The coast guard left them. Still gazing up at the high turrets, the warriors drew near the hall over a street of stones. Their swords clanged against mail. On an outer gate to the castle they rested their shields and then climbed the stairs to the door.

They were met by the herald Wulfgar. He curtly craved to know their names and their will in striding so roughly over the roadway. In one glance he noted their arms and their bearing.

"We are vassals of King Hygelac," answered Beowulf. "We will speak of our errand to your king, that most worthy of men."

Leaving them standing at the door, Wulfgar stepped into the hall and drew near his king. This herald was himself an earl from the high-born kindred of Wendel. He knew how to speak to a king, how to stand behind his chief's shoulder.

"We have here, newly sprung from the sea, a band of Geatish warriors. Their leader is a man named Beowulf. They beg leave to tell you their errand, O king. Do not forbid them entry. They have the mien of earls, and their chieftain is a mighty warrior. Greet them as earls, O Hrothgar!"

King Hrothgar answered his herald at once. "Surely I know this leader, or knew him when he was a child. He is the son of Ecgtheow. Hrethel the Geat gave that leader his only daughter in wedlock. This is their child Beowulf! Now, indeed, has he come over the sea to me in my sorrow. I heard that this youngster had the strength of thirty men in his handgrip! Call for gifts to be brought at once! Round up our warriors! All you can hail are to come here at once! Go quickly first to the door and make them welcome."

Wulfgar escorted Beowulf and his men into the hall, allowing them to keep on their coats of mail and their helmets, only begging them to leave their swords, axes, and javelins outside the building. With fitting words he led Beowulf to a dais.

In this way Beowulf and King Hrothgar faced each other, each one from his dais on the opposite side of the hall. The younger man spoke first. "Hail to thee, Hrothgar, king of the Danes. You know my kindred, my name, and my rank. In my youth, it is true, I have done some deeds that have been held worthy of my father. We of the Geats have sorrowed to learn how you are beset in Denmark by a bloody fiend named Grendel. My own king and earl has sent us to offer whatever strength we have against fiends. My own kinfolk have watched me, drenched to the skin with foul-smelling blood, struggle to the death with a lemur. I am the one who crushed the wicked Elves. Swimming far under the waves I have oftentimes wrestled with whales in the deep. In war I overcame the Westerners, who were riding ahead of their own downfall anyway! I crushed those bold warriors out of their lives!

"Today I am ready for Grendel. Grant me this trial, O King! You see that I have come from far over the sea to try it. I would do battle with your Grendel! I would seize your monster barehanded. Without sword or shield I would grapple this fiend as a token of my fealty to King Hygelac. Here in your hall shall sleep whichever one of us our Lord may will. If this beast of yours worsts me, then only send to my uncle and king the gems that are set on my shield. It is the work of Weland the smith; it is thus a priceless heirloom that should be shipped home to my kinfolk."

"This I thought was your errand, dear Beowulf," answered King Hrothgar. "This I thought was the aim of your wandering over the deep. I knew your father back in the days when I was a young man, newly throned. Now I am old and heartsick. My head bows. My eyes weep with shame to have to acknowledge my weakness. My throne, as you see, is almost a barren spot. My lands are becoming a wilderness. What has Grendel wrought in this kingdom! Often at night, swollen with beer, have my warriors sworn to topple this fiend. Then when the bleak, white light of dawn has crept over the misty fields, we have strode through this very hall strewn with their bloodstained bodies!

"Let me speak no more of my woes, great hero. Take your seat at my board, and let me drink to your health. Eat and be merry, my friend, who have sailed over deep water so boldly to save us all."

Straightforth a bench was drawn out from the wall and a meal set before the warriors from Geatland. Highborn vassals waited on them at the board, poured the sparkling mead into their cups from carved beakers with scrollwork handles. As they ate and drank, Hrothgar's gleemen sang them songs of the bygone works of the Danes.

Then one of Hrothgar's earls, a warrior named Unferth, who sat legs-sprawled at his king's feet, began to bait the guests. He was a spiteful man who could not stand hearing about the wonderful trip over the sea from Sweden. He could not let anyone best him in war-work!

"Say! Are you that Beowulf who swam a race with Breca when both of you, swollen with pride, wanted to fathom the depths of the fiords and risk your lives in deep water? Why, there isn't any man, friend or foe, who wouldn't blame such a shameful feat! Under the wintry waves you swam for a week, sliding the slopes of the sea, learning its hidden kingdoms while the waters boiled and hissed in the storm above you? Breca beat you, though. He was stronger by far than you, Beowulf! So the morning tide swept him to his home shore, where he lived to carve out a realm all by himself. He was a good man, that Breca! He kept his word at least.

"What, you Beowulf," Unferth continued. "I look for a far worse fate for you if you think you dare spend a night in this hall with Grendel!"

"Now listen, friend Unferth," snapped Beowulf. "I have kept still while you, drunk as an earl, have poured forth your flood of words about Breca. Now I'll tell you the truth. So hearken! I happen to have more strength in the sea, more breath for the dive, than any other man.

"If you truly care to hear that tale, I'll be glad to tell you myself how it was. I speak the truth. When Breca and I were boys, in the first hot glow of our manhood, we swore an oath that we would pit our strength against the sea. And so we did. We bore our naked swords in our hands, thinking to use them against whales as we struggled up through the tideraces of the coves. In deep water Breca could neither outswim me nor lose me among the peaks of the swells. Nor did I try to outstrip him. Thus we were together for five days and nights upon the sea until a huge flood swept us asunder. That happened during the height of a storm, through a night so black we couldn't see where we were heading. A wind so fierce, as wild as a battle, shrieked down from the north. It drove tons of gray water into the fiords. The waves were unleashed.

"Then all the daring of the big fishes was awakened. The winds had stirred up their cold blood. Well, against such foes my hand-knotted mail stood me in good stead. My gold-heavy harness buffered my chest just as in battle. A thousand-hued beast pulled and dragged at my limbs, striving to suck me down to the depths with him. He held me close in a death grip. However, I was happy enough to stab him in the belly with the point of my blade. I gave him the taste of death with this hand of mine that you see.

"Those aren't the only foemen, Unferth, who have threatened me. with their snarls. I have known for some years how to wield a weapon. No loathsome fishes, not even all of them together, have yet been able to drag me down against my will.

"Well, dawn broke. The eastern light flooded the sea, and I finally caught glimpses of land. I finally saw bleak crags and the headlands buffeted by the gale. There in shallow beach water rolled my foes of the night, put to sleep as it were, by my sword. True it is, indeed, that they ceased henceforth to prey upon war ships on the shores of my native land.

"Wyrd often saves the earl who is not yet marked for death—when he still helps himself in the fighting. I also had the good luck to kill nine sea prowlers, or nicors. Under heaven I have never heard tell of a mighty battle so hardly waged. Have you, Unferth? . . . Still I kept up my even stroke. The waves bore me ashore amidst the jagged crags of Finland. It was there on a sandy strip that I waded ashore.

"Neither Breca," said Beowulf, "nor any one of you in the flashing of swords has ever done deeds of worth so dearly won. I do not boast before you—even though I know that you, Unferth, have murdered your own brethren. You shall be doomed for it too, to hell, in spite of your cleverness. Let me tell you one more thing. Grendel would never have dared such outrage here in this hall if your might in war were as great as you say it is! Grendel found out long ago that he had nothing to dread. So has he lusted after this hall and wanted to suck your blood. He knows he can kill more of the Spear-Danes! He knows he can tumble you all down to death!

"But I, a Geat, have brought a gift for your Grendel. Without his foreknowledge I have here to give him three things: a fighting heart, my dauntless will, and my great strength. After this night whoever may wish to sing in your mead hall may do so. After tomorrow's sun rises in the east upon the sons of men, each one of you may enter this house in freedom. I, Beowulf, swear it."

King Hrothgar heard Beowulf and believed him. He, the aged, baldheaded king of the Danes, felt a hush steal into his heart. So among his heroes there were songs of happiness, and jokes, and toasts drunk to the Geats.

Then through the great hall Queen Wealhtheow walked. She, from whose garments gold dropped, greeted the men in the hall. First she bore a cup of mead to her beloved husband, the king. She begged him to take it from her own hand, and to drink. Hrothgar thanked her and took the goblet. Then the queen passed from earl to earl, young and old alike, bearing to each one a golden gift. She was a queen and the daughter of a queen. Then the highborn lady held out her hand, heavy with rings, to Beowulf. Wise in her words, she thanked him first and then thanked God that her prayers had been answered. She said that she had faith in Beowulf, that she trusted his earlship, and that she was deeply beholden. The freeborn queen held out a cup to the hero.

Beowulf answered the queen, "I wished when I let float my sea-wood on the whale's way, when I set sail with my war-band, to answer with my life the challenge of Grendel. I shall live out my years, as befits an earl, or I shall end my days right here in your lofty hall."

Queen Wealhtheow was gladdened by his words. Then she took a seat beside the king. After that there were boastings in Heorot! Then did the warriors brag before their stainless queen. Then were they light of heart! Their oaths grew bigger and bigger!

At last King Hrothgar arose. He knew what a fray was shaping up for the small hours of the night. He felt the cold of the evening shrinking his limbs. He felt in his bones that the fiend was even then prowling outside in the misty half-light, searching for men's blood. All the warriors stood as the king bade farewell to Beowulf.

"Never before in my years as a king have I given my realm to another, as I give it now to you, Beowulf, son of Ecgtheow. This night, stand in my stead. Uphold my name with all your might. I give you my hall, this proudest of buildings. Be wakeful, Beowulf, against our foe. He is coming tonight. I feel it. . . . If you fulfill this deed, know that no wish of yours during all your lifetime shall go unfulfilled by me."

Then King Hrothgar left the hall with his earls. He wanted to go to bed with his queen.

Carls stood ready to take from Beowulf his coat of mail, his helmet, and his heavy sword. Then the Geat lay down on the pile of furs that had been set for him, laid his cheek against the bolster, and waited. His men also lay down to sleep, tired from their long sail and the frightening tales of the day and evening. They could not know whether they would ever see another sunrise, or if they would live through the night to follow the sea tracks home to Sweden. The night was cold and very still. The fire in the central hearth had burned low. Soon all but Beowulf slept. . . .

Then through the black moors wreathed in fog, Grendel came creeping, God's ire upon him. Out of the swirling mists he stalked with outstretched claws, hunting toward the dimly lighted hall. To his wonderment the door was barred. Grendel had not foreseen that! With a snarl the fiend stepped backward, stiffened his muscles, and lunged at it. Iron bars sprung loose. Wood splintered. The door burst from its hinges.

Grendel was inside the great hall. All about him the Geatish warriors lay stretched out on their fur beds, sunk in sleep, heedless, unhearing. For a second Grendel stopped to scan them. Darts of red fire shot from his deep-set eyes. Rolling his huge head from side to side, Grendel glared about him. Then he laughed.

From his end of the hall Beowulf watched the ogre, weighed his endowment, and waited to see how Grendel would strike. Quick as a wink the fiend pulled at the warrior nearest him, cracked his bones with one twist, ripped at the body with his talons, split open the jugular and drank the hot blood as it gushed from the torn throat. Then he ravenously broke apart the hands and the feet, and swallowed them.

Without warning, Grendel suddenly dropped the mangled body and sprang straight across the hall at Beowulf. The hero had raised himself on his left elbow. Beowulf had just time to stretch forth his right arm as the ogre rushed upon him. He caught Grendel's right hand, and still without rising from his bed, stopped the monster's onrush. For an instant the two stood stock-still. The shepherd of evil then looked down into the icy-cold eyes of the hero. Grendel was chilled. The cold shiver of death ran through his spine as the fingers of Beowulf tightened like steel over his bones.

Wild waves of fear rang over the ogre. His only thought was flight! Without even gathering his strength, he lurched backward, away from the vise, away from the eyes that were working foreign magic on him. As Grendel began to pull, Beowulf sprang to his feet. He did not let go Grendel's hand. On the contrary, he began slowly but surely to push it backward—despite all the strength of Grendel. Of the two Beowulf was the stronger. Grendel felt his hand, his arm, being slowly pushed backward. Great shudders rolled over him. Then Beowulf began to twist the ogre's arm.

With a howl of pain Grendel leaped wildly backward, Beowulf still gripping his hand, into the benches and boards. Back and forth across the hall the two fought, the hunted and the grim hunter. Boards crashed to the floor. The beakers of mead spilled in huge puddles. Against the walls the Geatish warriors huddled in knots or scrambled to safety as the two threw each other against the oak timbers. The wood cracked from the blows as if the iron bands about the outside of Heorot would be burst, as if the roof would cave in at any moment over the din of the struggle. Grendel lurched madly toward the door, hoping to pull Beowulf outside into the black night. Back and forth the two giants wrestled.

Then Grendel began to scream. Mouth open, eyes shooting red fire, he howled in mournful, quivering bursts of pain. Again and again he howled his death shriek until all the ruffians in hell stopped to listen. Beowulf would not let go the hand. His heart was bent on the ogre's death.

As the twain stood locked together, Beowulf's squire roused himself from his fear and strode forth behind the fiend. Lifting his sharp-biting sword, he tried to rescue his master. Then did the Geatish earls see before them another wonder. Blow after blow of the sword fell upon Grendel's shoulders without even leaving a scratch. Then did the earls know the matchless wisdom of their leader! Beowulf had somehow known to doff his coat of mail and to lay down his weapons. No tool

made by man had any strength against Grendel. Daunted and shivering, the squire stole back to his corner. Breathless, blanched with fear, the warriors awaited the outcome.

Beowulf to their amazement had not yet squeezed out the last of his strength. Before their wondering eyes they saw him suddenly wrench the ogre's arm backward and snap the armbone from the shoulder. A gaping wound spurted blood from Grendel's armpit. Beowulf's face, white with anger, flashed back cold fire into the red eyes of the fiend. Eye to eye they glared in unspeakable hatred for one last moment. . . . Then the arm gave way utterly. The bones parted, the muscles burst, the flesh tore, and the fiend—at last free from the grip of Beowulf—fled full-tongued into the darkness.

Grendel knew that his days upon earth were numbered.

In the hall Beowulf the Geat stood alone. He had done what he swore to do. He had rid the house of evil. He had saved the kingdom of Denmark. Gladly Beowulf fastened the token of battle, the bloody arm of Grendel, in the rafters of Heorot.

The next morning the Danish warriors began to creep back to their king. As soon as they heard the bright tidings, even the earls from their far-off homes and byres set out bearing gifts for the hero. All day long they crowded into the hall and stood speechless. Awkwardly and gladly they nudged each other and gawked at the hero. There in the roof above their heads hung the arm of Grendel!

No one spoke of where he had gone, or of how he had ended his days. Wyrd had doomed him to die. No one stopped to think that he must have fled to the boiling pool of the nicors. There Grendel was watching his blood flow out into the seething tarn. Warriors and eldermen never went near that poisoned pool. As they rode through the woods, they always swerved their horse's heads away from those paths.

In the hall of the kind King Hrothgar the scops were already at work shaping with beat and flashing words the story of the black night's struggle between Beowulf the Geat and Grendel. In their song they did not forget about Sigmund and how his name was still renowned long after the day of his death.

They said again how Sigmund had dealt with a dragon, a fierce, writhing, wealth-hoarder hid in white rocks. They told how the many-hued worm had burnt up in his own fire, and how Sigmund had out-fitted a ship all loaded down with his heirlooms. Sigmund was the greatest of wanderers since ever the world began, they said. The tales of his might were a refreshment and a challenge to warriors. They also sang of Sigmund and his many fights with the Jutes. His very name was a beacon, for men throughout the earth had faith in that hero. They thought of him as always behind their shoulders. They said he was a faithful friend in evil days.

Now here was Beowulf a like hero, he too standing alone and beloved in full daylight, before the eyes of men!

Hrothgar, the keeper of golden rings, walked forth from his wedding bed, his queen beside him. Together they climbed the steps to their hall and gazed in wonder and speechlessness at the arm of Grendel.

"May God be thanked," sighed the king. "I have withstood so long the wrath and wolfishness of this ogre. This Beowulf has the strength of a god. Whatever woman bore the body of this child in her womb, whether or not she still lives I cannot say, may well enough know that she was blessed in her childbirth. My dear Beowulf," cried the king, "now shall I love you like a son." With tears running down his cheeks the king clasped the hero. "Inasmuch as I can reward your work, ask me for any boon. Ask only, and it shall be awarded. Beowulf, you have won already by this deed a deathless tomorrow. May God uphold you!"

"It was the deed of gladness," answered the hero. "Still I could wish that you had seen the bloodshedding yourself. I am sorry that I could not keep more of Grendel to show you than just his hand, his arm, and his shoulder. I guess by now, however, that his life's blood has flowed out of his body."

Of all the warriors in Heorot only Unferth was closemouthed that day. Hour after hour crowds gathered, and people talked about the arm of Grendel—how its claws were stronger than metal which no metal could cut. Then carls were bade to bedeck the House of the Hart. The wine house and the guest house were hung with curtains shining bright against the wooden walls. Gold cups and dishes were set on the boards. Despite their best efforts, however, the women could not hide all the cracks in the walls.

The iron bands had been sprung during the struggle of Beowulf. The wood was weakened and splintered. Only the rafters were unharmed. Lucky it was for the hall that Grendel fled when he did! He could not escape Wyrd. He could not fly his tomorrow! That's very hard to do. Let him who wishes only try it! Every man in this life will go lay him down on the bed where Wyrd has decided to nail him after life's meal.

I have never heard tell of so many tribes as came to the winehall that night! I never saw so many great chieftains surrounded by so many brave warriors!

Then Hrothgar gave to Beowulf a golden flag, a chest for heirlooms with handles of wrought iron, a helmet, a coat of chain mail, and a sword of great worth which had been borne once before by an older hero. Hrothgar held the cup to Beowulf's lips. Before so many great warriors Beowulf blushed.

That was not all either. Then Hrothgar called for eight war horses to be driven to the steps of the hall. Each one bore a saddle as finely wrought as a throne. Nor was that all. The king gave a fine, worthy gift to each of the warriors from Geatland and handed out a sum in gold for the one that Grendel had eaten.

After the giving of gifts the gleemen brought forth their joywoods, tightened the strings, and began to sing the *Finnsburgh Lay*. During the evening Queen Wealhtheow also thanked Beowulf, gave him an heirloom ring, and asked him to watch over her children in the case that her husband died before they had reached manhood.

It was with a hush in their hearts and smiles on their lips that the weary Danes dropped on their beds of furs. Henchmen had placed, as was their habit, each warrior's gear and trappings above his pile of skins. Thus you could see the burnished helmet of each warrior set in readiness above his head. It was the Viking habit. Even as a man plowed his fields or chopped trees in the woods, his byrnie and his sword were always at hand.

The northmen were a dauntless people.

They were to pay dearly those few winks of sleep in the hall, the Danish warriors! Down in her lair the mother of Grendel seethed with ire at the death of her only son. This ogress too was begotten of the blood of Cain, whose brood had been doomed forever to the icy floods and freezing waters of the earth.

When night had fallen, the she-demon stole forth toward the hall, which she entered unheard and unseen. In her unholy hatred she grasped the first warrior she found and killed him as he lay slumbering. Then there was an uproar in the hall. Midnight terror seized the Danes, the same cold ache of fear that chills a virgin so that she stands helpless in her tracks, or the pangs that make women wince when they stand beside the battle and watch their men.

Among the furs and the cots the Danes, without stopping for helmets or byrnies, wielded their swords at the ogress. Some had time to grasp their shields. The ogress, however, did not linger. She had made her kill and wanted no more of a fight. The frightened warriors watched her dart out the door and head for the moor. As soon as King Hrothgar heard what had happened—learned also that the slain warrior was his boon companion and dearest friend—he sent for Beowulf. That hero had been lodged in a neighboring guest house.

"Did you spend a dreamless night?" asked the hero.

"Do not ask after me," cried King Hrothgar. "My beloved friend has been slain right in my own hall, he who stood nearest me year after year in my wars, he who was my trusted friend and elderman. Look! Grendel's arm, which you so proudly hung up in my rafters, is gone. His fond mother came in the dark of night and carried it back to her den! Ah, woe is me! Alas, for my kingdom and my kinfolk!

"It is true," added the king, "that the husbandmen for years have glimpsed these twain, the he- and the she-fiend, tramping the moors at night. Folks believed that one was the dam of the other. Who the father could have been, they never knew. These ogres dwelled in the forsaken and untilled meadows, in the secret haunts of the wolves, on barren headlands storm-beaten and wild, in the doubtful paths of the swamps, or under the swift-rushing waterfalls as they thunder into a glen and sink to an underground stream.

"A mile from here is a tarn with rocky caverns and gulches. Around its edge the tree roots are entwined so high and so thick that they cast black shadows out over the water. It is a dreadful sight after dark. There are shooting fires on these waters. Not one of the sons of Denmark knows the hidden lore of this spot.

"If you hunt a stag through the woods and drive him across the heather right to this tarn, he will halt and let the hounds tear at his hide and his throat rather than jump into its blackness. Whenever the thunder grumbles, huge billows will rise from the depths and slap at the sky.

"I leave it to you, Beowulf. You should make up your own mind even though you cannot foresee the traps that will entangle you. If you will do this for us, and if you live, you know what wealth will be yours, for you and your men."

Then Beowulf, son of Ecgtheow, pondered a while and spoke. "Do not let yourself fall into glum grief, O King. Is it not better for a man or a king to avenge his friend rather than to let an old misgiving rankle in his heart? We all of us know the end of our days; therefore let him who can make the reckoning with wrongdoers. After his death men will say that was his greatest deed.

"Lift up your head and your heart, O King. We must follow after this dreadnought, hard on her tracks. I swear to you she shall not slip away from us. She shall not dodge me though she hide in unfathomed waters, or in the earth's bosom, or in lonely woods, or on crags! Let her try it and see!"

Shaking with happiness, the king called for horses, and the band of warriors set out from the hall behind footmen who bore their shields and carefully followed the tracks of the ogress. Their path led them past sharp cliffs, along narrow trails unknown and untrodden, past headlong boulders strewn across barren, treeless, wind-haunted heights. Underneath a black cliff where the incoming tide smashed on the shingle, they stumbled upon the mail hood of Hrothgar's murdered vassal.

Looking down, they saw that the water bubbled with blood or burning venom. From time to time the warriors blew their war horns. They sat on the beach and watched the hissing wavelets. Strange things swam just under the surface. Ever and anon a huge, scaly back of some sea snake would ripple darkly on the oily waves. From the crags over their heads, cumbersome dragons leaned over the water. They stretched out full length to catch in their claws any ship that heedless of jeopardy might round the point. When they heard the sharp sound of the horn, they withdrew, bitten with anger. Beowulf cut one of the sea snakes off from its life. His lance stuck quivering in its still living flesh. Other warriors harpooned it and hauled it on the shingle for all to see.

Meanwhile Beowulf made himself ready for war. He donned a garment of hand-linked mail of many hues. It was strong enough to safeguard the trunk of his body from neck to groin. On his head he fitted his white helmet, heavy enough to protect his skull from the weight of deep water, sharp enough to cleave a path as he swam, and shaped like the lovely body of a white swan. Beowulf bore in his hand a sword lent by Unferth, who now that he was sober had forgotten the bitter jealousy he had shown when drunk. This weapon, named Hrunting, was made of brass, dyed with drops of poison, and dipped in blood. Hrunting had never failed its wielder, yet Unferth did not have the courage to wield it himself, but gave it to Beowulf.

When he was ready to dive, Beowulf spoke a few last words to the king. "First, O King of the Danes, remember that whatever happens, I hold you as my father. It was you who so swore. Then I ask you to send my wealth to my king, Hygelac of the Geats. My sword I bequeath to Unferth. I hold you to your word as regards the safety of my followers. With Hrunting I shall live or shall die." Without waiting for an answer, Beowulf leaped into the oily tarn.

Down and down he swam for the better part of a day before he came to the bottom. Soon the ogress, fierce and bloodthirsty, she who for more than a hundred years had queened it in the depths, saw that a man—a queer being of the upperworld—had sunk to her realm. Quick as a wink she grabbed the hero and hugged him tight around his middle. Her long claws fumbled to tear his flesh from his bones. His byrnie, however, was so skillfully woven that she could not pierce it.

Seeing this, the ogress began to swim, still holding the hero tight in her grip, farther and farther, deeper and deeper into the holes of the sea floor. No matter how fiercely he squirmed, Beowulf could not get his sword arm free. Goggling fishes swam up against him, cutting his thighs with their sharp horns, jostling and bunting the unlucky Geat.

Then Beowulf saw that they had at length reached the entrance to a cave, the upper part of which was above water. He was able to suck huge mouthfuls of air into his lungs. He shook his head and began to peer about him. Huge, overhanging vaults rose high above his head. From somewhere shone a queer, pale fire, a blinding light that hurt his eyes.

Despite the glare he made out the ogress all right. There she loomed, the huge giantess of the sea. At once he lunged for her with his sword. It was no use. At the first blow the fabled sword Hrunting bent and chipped on her hide. This was the first time that the wonderful weapon had ever betrayed a hero! Since the sword was useless, Beowulf would have to rely on his strength. So must every man, in the last face-to-face.

Therefore the peerless warrior grasped the ogress by her shoulder, with no thought for the blows she was raining on him. Before she slipped from his grip, he had bent her back to the ground. However, she wormed out of his hands, backed away for a bit, and then rushed him. Wearied and short of breath, Beowulf lost his footing, rolled over on the ground, and sprawled there helpless at her feet. Then it was that she thought to pierce his chest. Her blow was well-aimed and thrust with a mighty will, but the breastplate of Beowulf stopped the blade. Before she knew what had happened, he was up on his feet again.

Now there has existed in the world, time out of mind, a truly unbeatable weapon. It is an old-time sword, crudely fashioned, and so clumsy that humans cannot wield it. This sword had been smithied long ago by the giants. It was their own personal blade. Beowulf could hardly believe his eyes! There it hung, on the wall of the cavern, just above his hand. He knew it at once from the songs of the bards that he had heard in his childhood. Without thinking twice he reached up his hand and pulled it toward him. Without it he was lost and beaten. Swinging it high above his head, he brought it down on the ogress. It was not too heavy for him. It was indeed a wonderful weapon; it did its work well. The sword severed the little ring-bones in the ogress's throat, and sundered her body.

Before his amazed eyes the ogress staggered and sank to the rocks.

Great drops of black blood dropped from the sword blade. In his turn Beowulf slumped against the stones. He could hardly believe it! The blade had obeyed him! The awesome deed was done!

As Beowulf leaned thankfully against the rocks of the cavern wall, panting and shaken to the marrow of his bones, a golden light fell about him in the den, as if some heavenly candle had been lit. By its friendly glow the hero made out the lifeless body of Grendel sprawled on the slippery shale. With one blow he cut off the head, in earnest of the ogre's murdering trips to Heorot, in full reward for his foul deeds.

Above, in the world of men, the warriors who had sat all these hours, their eyes fixed on the hissing caldron, saw streaks of blood on the waves. "The she-wolf of the deep has killed Beowulf," they whispered. By that time it was high noon. Sad and disheartened, King Hrothgar and his Danes left the shore and tramped back to the hall. Only the Geatish men stayed by the tarn, hoping against hope that their leader would return, or that they could recover his body.

Although Beowulf looked long at the wealth amassed in this underworld realm, he took nothing but the sword hilt which he still held in his hand. Even the blade of the often-sung sword had melted in the seething blood of the ogress. It had thawed just as ice does in spring at the word of the Lord, and sets free the tumbling waves from their jail.

Trailing the head of Grendel, Beowulf swam upward through the cloudy water until he at last set foot gratefully on the shore. There his thanes awaited him, overjoyed to see their earl safe and sound. They helped him off with his war gear, and then setting the ogre's head on a pikestaff, they set out on their homeward trip. Four of his Geats staggered under the weight of the fiend's dripping head! How the Danes gasped when they saw Beowulf and the Geats bring that ugly sight into the hall! The women were close to swooning!

"Now your warriors and thanes may sleep without dreams in your hall," Beowulf told the king.

Hrothgar answered, "Let every king and earl acknowledge henceforth that you are a well-born hero! Your rewards shall be great. I foretell that you will long be the delight of your people, for your strength is as great as your coolness and you are a beacon for all our offspring. Is it not wonderful how Almighty God in the breadth of his thought has spread out wisdom, lands, daring, and might among menfolk over the earth, all under His kingly sway?

"Ponder this," continued King Hrothgar. "Think how sometimes God grants to one man, to some gifted son of one tribe, lands, towns, hamlets, and wealth! This man begins to live without weighing the warnings of illness, or old age, or the whispered curses of his foes. Then one day when his guardian angel is asleep, death strikes him down with a well-shot arrow. Such a man had scorned Death because of the gifts God had bestowed on him. His mind had become mean and selfish. He had not thought to lavish gold rings upon his trusted friends. The reckoning comes, and another—perhaps even a foreigner—reaps all his lands and wealth!

"Therefore, good Beowulf, trust not the promptings of pride! The bloom of your youth is upon you. Someday you too shall fall, to the biting dart, or to the sea's unleashed fury, or to the cold bite of iron. I too ruled as a proud king here in Denmark, until the coming of Grendel."

With such words and more Hrothgar thanked Beowulf and stood as a father to him. Because of the deeds of the hero, the land of Denmark slept soundly. The hero's work was done.

As soon as the morning fowl had announced the sunrise, Beowulf and his men bade farewell. Loading their fees and newly won wealth on their ship, they pushed out into the sea. King Hrothgar wept to see their ship grow small in the distance. He feared that he would never clasp Beowulf in his arms again.

BEOWULF'S BARROW ON THE HEADLANDS OF HRONESNESSE

Upon his return to Geatland, Beowulf gave over to his own King Hygelac all the gifts, the horses, and all the wealth he had won by his hardihood. Every good vassal should do likewise. It is shameful to keep wealth for oneself, or to stir up one clan against another.

Hygelac was also the uncle of Beowulf, the brother of Beowulf's mother. By this tie the hero belonged to the kingly house of the Waegmundings, rulers of old in Sweden. Beowulf the Geat behaved fittingly, bestowing his heirlooms on his friends at home. Men spoke well of him from golden tongues—that he was plucky, that he was law-abiding, that he was a lion in battle—and the strongest warrior alive. They also added that he was manly, that he had never struck a carl or a woman in his own house, even when he was roaring drunk. It was a shocking thing that the Geats did not choose him for their chief earl and king, a man of such golden mettle.

Some evil fellows said behind his back that Beowulf was white-livered and a slacker. This kind of talk was a great sorrow for the hero to bear. Hygelac, however, rewarded Beowulf. He gave his nephew lands, a throne, and a hall of his own. After Hygelac's death there was a war in Geatland until finally Beowulf came to the throne and ruled the whole land for fifty years. He was a wise king, careful and safe. Then after fifty years a foul worm, a dragon, took it upon itself to hold sway through the heavens at night.

I don't know how all this wrack came about.[1] It seems there was a worm that slept upon a pile of treasure, which it had zealously heaped up under a stone bluff. Leading to this hoard was an underground way cut through the rock. Anyway, a man, a culprit, some craven fellow, some outcast from the tribes of men, either stumbled upon or wandered into the dragon's lair. However it came about, some fellow spied the treasure.

In the olden days earls often amassed great wealth which they added to their tribe's heirlooms. Some bygone race of men had all died leaving their hoard under the sea cliffs at the very edge of the waves. They had carried it there, this heavy gold hardened in fire, saying, "O Earth, take back your wealth. Now there are no more heroes to gloat over it from their hollow eyesockets. Those who earned this wealth were undoubtedly men of backbone. In their youth they wrestled and wrested it from you, O Earth. After their years of feasts and mead halls, bold death has borne them away out yonder. No Jute is left to wield a sword to save this hoard. No one is left to swing the battle-ax skyward. No man will ever again drink from this golden goblet! Even those who burnished it have stolen away, beyond the beaches. All, all are dead.

"Let it sleep in the earth. Let the helmet molder along with the coats of mail, along with the shields that stood up well in war against the bite of the foeman's blade. Since he who wore them so pluckily is dead, let his wealth and trappings rust also. In our halls the joywood is silent, no longer stroked by the gleeman's swift fingers. The hawk no longer darts forth from the gauntlet to soar through the air for his prey. No prancing steed champs at the bit and neighs before our hamlets. Such a plague has wasted our tribesmen!" Then the one last singer faded away, too. His flesh wasted from his bones. He too died. Death rotted the skin from his body.

Then the old scourge of dusk swooped down upon the warderless hoard. It is he who burns up the sky at night in long trails of yellow flame, who flies above houses in a whirlwind of shrieking wings and gagging smoke. He it was who wanted the hoard for himself, and who crouched over it in the heart of the headland, gloating and rubbing his scaly loops round it and over it. For three hundred years it had been his, not that it brought him any true warmth or gladness.

At last a man robbed the worm of a goblet, took the golden gift to an earl and tried to win his freedom with it so that forgiven he could belong to some tribe of the Geats again. The earl granted his plea and stared in amazement at the well-wrought gold.

The worm awoke. At once he sniffed the smell of a man. At once he feared his hidden lair had been looted while he slept. How had a man dared to come so close? He must have trod next to the dragon's head so as not to be spellbound. Quickly the worm sniffed around the rocks,

[1] The manuscript is incomplete around verses 4426–4455.

and coiled his bulk through the boulders. If only he was not too late! If only he could catch the thief, he would blow fire over every inch of his body. He would singe off his hair and melt the fat from his bones! When he had made sure that the man was no longer lurking about, the worm hunted through his hoard. Yes, one goblet was missing, indeed! Then in his baleful heart he waited for night to fall so that he could make his reckoning. His throat burned, for the stolen goblet was the one from which he used to drink.

Then as soon as the cloak of darkness had shrouded the lands and the restless sea, the worm took to the air, burning the houses of men, belching red fire in his anger and sorrow. Neither chick nor child was left living the length of the seacoast. The roar of the fires and the thunder rolled inland to warn the Geats. It was already too late. Before daylight, when the dragon flew home to sleep, he had burned up the hall and even the throne of the Geatish king.

The black news was brought to Beowulf. The white-haired king took the tidings with calm, believing that he must have in some fashion broken a law without knowing. Then was Beowulf heavy of heart as he saw the woe of the Geats. Then did his kingship weigh mightily on his shoulders. His will, however, did not falter. He never once thought to ask of another that which he feared in his bones to undertake himself.

Beowulf called for his blacksmiths and said what he would be needing—a buckler of steel—for wood or hides would be burned by the dragon. It was in his mind to fight to the death with the worm. Beowulf never once thought to summon his warriors from their far-flung houses and byres. He alone would wrestle since he alone was king. Nor would he listen to tales of the dragon's havoc. It was better to rehearse the thoughts of his past deeds.

It was Beowulf who had cleansed the mead hall of Hrothgar! He it was who alone and unweaponed had struggled with Grendel, and he who heedless had swam to the depths of the tarn to kill the she-ogre. He was also there at that fight when Hygelac folded under his death-blow.

King Hygelac of the Geats had been struck down by one mighty swipe of the foemen, the Frisians. From that dreadful fight Beowulf had survived, only because of the undaunted will in his body. He had leaped into the sea, bearing the weight of thirty war harnesses, and swam for his life. Only a handful of Frisians lived after to tell the tale. Alone and wretched, Beowulf fought the cold and the tons of sea water. He followed the sea tracks all the way from Friesland across the North Sea to the shores of his homeland.[1] There Beowulf swore fealty to the son of Hygelac and kept his word until that earl's death.

No man could shake a finger at Beowulf. All the days of his life he

[1] The story is corroborated by Gregory, Bishop of Tours (538–594), in his *History of the Franks*. He was the "historian of the barbarians."

had sought the path of right, escaped traps, killed foes, and ruled fairly. Now it was time for him to stand up to the fire-breathing worm. Taking thirteen earls with him, he set out from his mead hall, angered in heart and mind, against the peace-breaker. He had already found out the cliff where the dragon slumbered during the daylight. Beowulf had also seen the goblet; it had been given into his hand by the thirteenth man, the one who had started the broil. Sorry and frightened, this man was their pathfinder across the fields. Half against his will, the thirteenth man led them to the dark cliff and showed them the cavern, its mouth toward the sea. Cold waves broke against it.

From their high place on the cliff Beowulf and his band could look down and see the yawning opening of the cavern, where the worm hid watching his wealth. Threads of gold hung in long festoons from the rock walls. Thousands of costly stones flashed brightly upon their pile of gold. They threw beams of light far over the foamy waves.

After he had planned for the struggle, Beowulf sat down on the rocks and bade farewell to his warriors:

"How well it all comes back to me now, the length of my days! I was seven years old when King Hrethel took me away from my father to bring me up by his throne. He fed me, taught me, and gave me gifts in token of our kinship. I was as dear to King Hrethel as any one of his own stalwart sons—as Herebeald, or Haethcyn, or my beloved Hygelac.

"Those were bleak days when Haethcyn drew his bow taut, standing afar off, let fly the straight-aimed arrow, and so killed the heir to the throne. What a bloody deed it is for a boy to kill his own brother because he stands in line first for the throne! Hrethel was brought low by his grief. How sad it would have been for a king to see his second son dangle from the hangman's gibbet! What sleepless nights for King Hrethel! His flesh crawled and tingled with sweat, for he could not bring himself to avenge the murder of one son by that of another. He could not stand the thought of black, raucous crows picking at Haethcyn's flesh as his body dangled from a gibbet. The breaking of each new day only made more bitter his sorrow.

"Wild-eyed and disheveled, King Hrethel roamed every night through his throne room, which was empty and still. Only the face of his dead son peered at the king from the dark corners. How much death must an old king have seen on the field of war, in the play of swords, without its grinning jaw coming over his own hearthside.

"To drown the soughing of the wind through the treetops old King Hrethel tried to sing to himself. Old sad songs came out of his throat one after the other. Grief for his oldest boy, lying streaked with his own red blood, rose in sobs to his throat. There was no way to cast off this sorrow, since no deed of his could wipe out the misdeed. Therefore Hrethel turned from the gladness of earth to the gladness of God. He kept on walking until he had passed out of the world, leaving his lands and his wealth to others.

"After the leave-taking of the king, war broke out between us and the Swedes. It was in this fight that the second son, Haethcyn, tasted red death in his mouth. I earned my fees that day. In that loud battle I strode forward alone, cutting a swath with my sword, as I swore I should do as long as breath stayed in my lungs. That was the day I killed the dreaded crow, the warrior Hugh. I marked him out in the fray, for he carried the banner of Sweden. My sword, it is true, could not break a hole in his harness, so I grabbed him in my arms. I gripped Hugh so hard that I squeezed his heart out of his bone-box."

The warriors heard him carefully. Then Beowulf stood up and looked down at them threateningly. "You know I have wagered my life time and again in my youth. Now that I am old, I still will not shirk the hardships of kingship. If I can in some way lure this snake from his hole or cut my path even into his very den, you know that I am ready to do it."

"You are my witness," he added, "that I take neither sword nor ax nor any weapon at all to this struggle. I am hoping to hug this worm, as I did years ago with Grendel. I am planning to crush his shiny body in my grip and grapple this vermin against me. But since I foresee that the heat from his fiery breath would kindle and burn me, I shall hold this iron shield as a curtain.

"I swear to you now, as I've sworn before, that I never shall yield one foot's length before him. May God hear my words and see that I keep my oath! I here swear it before you and Him. The winged worm and I are about to do battle. Keep yourselves here on the cliffside. You will be out of harm's way and far enough from the fire's tongues. From here you will see which one of us two stands up . . . when the fiery vomit is quenched."

Then Beowulf fixed tightly his helmet and coat of mail. Holding his new shield before him, he picked his way down the turf of the cliff and strode proud and alone up to the cavern's mouth. Such a fight is not for cowards! Let only the bold fight dragons! . . . He had come to a cleft in the rocks through which poured a red-hot torrent. There was no way at all to go further.

Beowulf stood and taunted the dragon. His words were rough and his curses resounding. "Come out of your hole, filthy, murdering fiend," shouted the hero. The hollow echo bounced on the rocky cliffs and awoke the dragon. He knew it was the hated words of a man. His answer was a roar and a belching of fire that swept around Beowulf, licking his legs and his feet, which the shield did not cover. Beowulf crouched low so as not to fall, for the very ground shook underneath him.

Then the huge worm uncoiled his length and rolled forward to do battle. For an instant he and the hero stood ready. Fear gripped them both. The snake wavered back and forth, and then darted forward. He breathed out long curls of reddish fire. Beowulf, behind his shield, thrust forth only his right arm. In it he had picked up the sword of Ing, well known in olden lore. To his grief the blade bent and burnt up as it flashed on the hide of the worm.

This showed that Wyrd had already written—and none could change it—that this was the day of death. In this battle would Beowulf die. None could gainsay it.

The sword of Ing betrayed its earl. This should not have happened, for it was old and tried, well-smithied and strong, the sword of Ing. Beowulf could only hammer away at the dragon, who burned him up with his breath. That day Beowulf would yield. He would step back, give ground to the snake. That very day would Beowulf step backward, out of his life. His body was charred in the fire. His breath was halting and sore.

From the top of the cliff the warriors never uplifted their shields. Their swords lay ungrasped and idle. Instead, they looked down on their dying earl; their mouths fell open with fear, and they fled away into the bushes. Only one of them stayed. He was a real earl whom even the sight of death could not turn from the bonds of friendship.

This one earl who did not flee was named Wiglaf. When he saw his king bent low in fire but still fighting, Wiglaf recalled the pledges of a vassal. He thought of the oaths he had made as an earl. Frightened though he was, the young Wiglaf could not run away. With tear-stained eyes, he watched his king still struggling like an earl with the worm. In the boy's ears sounded the old high deeds of the Waegmunding line, his kinfolk and Beowulf's also. Wiglaf recalled the high seat of the king before which he had stood to be dressed in the tokens of manhood, the heirloom sword, the shield, and the mail of his father. Up till this day he had done no feat of arms. This would be his first battle.

Turning in wrath to the earls who cowered behind trees, Wiglaff called, "I remember our oaths. Have you all forgotten? Don't you recall in the house of our king we swore great words? When the king bestowed rings, we bragged very loudly how in the day of death we would pay him back—and many times over—with the weight of our deeds! Why do you think he picked us from among all the warriors? He only a few minutes ago reminded us all of our duty and said that he held us faithful. He only just warned us to be worthy of sword and helmet.

"Well, the day when he needs us is almost spent! Are you going to fail him now, when he has never failed you? Let's go! Let's hurry to him in his sorrow! Pick up your swords! Follow me! God knows I would rather die licked in the fire by the side of my king than to live out my days twitted and scorned as a craven. How could I carry my sword across fields to the mead hall of Beowulf if everyone knew it was only a pretty toy in my hands?"

Without waiting for their answer, Wiglaf brandished his sword, scrambled headlong down the steep path until he stood shoulder to shoulder with Beowulf. Amidst the heat and the choking smoke he tried to shout to his earl, "Dear Beowulf, carry on the deeds as you did in your youth. You said you would never stand evil. You swore you would fight all the foes of mankind!"

Beowulf did not hear him. "Now I bid you, dear Earl," Wiglaf continued to shout through the clouds of black smoke, "to save your own life in this struggle. You are not alone any more. Take new heart. I am here beside you. Can you hear me?"

Now the dragon became all the more swollen with anger, red with hate, to see his two foemen still standing. With evil guile he swirled his tail around their limbs and blew billows of flame at their bucklers.

In a twinkling the wooden shield of Wiglaf was in ashes. Nor did his coat of mail save his skin or his flesh. Wiglaf did not turn tail, however. Instead, he hid behind the left arm and strong shield of his earl.

Then Beowulf felt his young kinsman's shoulder against his. Beowulf's heart rose. He gained new strength for another last rush at the worm. With a mighty blow he thrust his own beloved sword Naegling into the head of the dragon. What had Wyrd fore-ordained? Naegling blunted and this time broke into kindling. Naegling, spotted with rust of the years, lacked in strength. The fine sword betrayed its wielder. Beowulf's arm was too strong. It was not given to him to win his fights with man-smithed weapons. The sword bent in his hand, splintered, twisted, and broke.

Then the scourge of the earth, the fire-belcher, rushed for the third bout with the heroes. This blow cost Beowulf dear. The burning jaw and red-hot fangs of the dragon came within inches of his face. Then the worm sank his claws deep into Beowulf's neck, buried them deep below each ear.

The bards through the ages have said how the young Earl Wiglaf stood daring and strong by the side of his king. In this he only fulfilled his sworn oaths. He took no thought then of saving his skin. He did not flinch or cower, even when his hand was burned by the foe. Without a yellow streak in his body, Wiglaf kept hitting the worm from under the shield, aiming low at his guts. Again and again he thrust at the soft white belly of the snake until little by little the fire began to lessen. Then Beowulf too rallied. With his whetted dagger he slit a gash in the serpent's middle. Thus did Beowulf bring him low! Thus did he shorten his days of harm and evil. Thus the two earls brought the snake down from his lofty sway over the world.

Beowulf lived still, long enough to have his heart gladdened once more. Once more was his life made worthy of praise, even as his eyes grew dim. The gaping tears in his throat burned and stung, for the poison from the worm was slowly seeping through his body. Shortly he felt that it had reached his chest. Still clear-headed, however, Beowulf sank down on a rock near the wall of the dragon's cave. From there he could look inside. He sat and wondered at the hoard of gold and winking stones. They reached almost to the roof. Beowulf marveled to see how the walls were upheld by huge trunks of rock that the waves had cut from the headland.

As the king fought Death, his earl brought him water in his cupped hands. Wiglaf washed out the gaping tears in his earl's throat. He smoothed the torn flesh and cooled it with more water. Then he carefully slid off Beowulf's helmet. Both knew that the king's days were running out quickly. They both saw how Death waited at his elbow.

"Now would I send my battle gear to my son, if only I had one," whispered Beowulf more to himself than to Wiglaf. "For fifty winters no neighboring king has dared to set foot on my soil. I have bent my head to the will of Wyrd. I have kept what was entrusted to me. I have never sought an unrighteous broil. I have never broken my word. Therefore I leave this life with a light heart.

"Would you go into the dragon's lair, my peerless Wiglaf? Fetch me out some of his hoard. It will brighten my eyes as I take leave of my lands and my kinfolk. The world grows dim already."

Wiglaf had never thought to see on earth such wonders as the hoard of the dragon. Weapons of bygone ages, their hilts encrusted with sparkling gems, tall goblets, chain mail, gold armlets lay in a heap. In the half-darkness they winked and glowed. Scooping some up in his hands, and shouldering a golden battle flag, Wiglaf hurried back to his earl. He hoped to find him still alive.

The king had slumped. With eyes closed he struggled to catch each breath. The poison welled out of his throat. Wiglaf brought more water and finally roused his earl.

"I have not much longer among you," sighed Beowulf. Then his eyes fell on the wealth that Wiglaf had brought from the cave. "I am glad. This gold shall be for my tribe. Will you ask our oldest warriors to build me a barrow? Ask them to climb this headland and build me a death pile high on its top. Let my deathbed rise high above Hronesnesse. So in other years will incoming ships take their bearings by its shape against the sky, and follow its beacon into harbor. This will be my last deed for the Geats."

Then slipping his golden collar from his shoulders and his ring of kingship from his finger, he handed them to Wiglaf. He said:

(V. 5621)   "Du eart endelaf
Usses cynnes
Waegmundinga
Ealle wyrd forspeof
Mine mazas
To metod-sceafte
Eorlas on elne
Ic him æfter sceal."

"You are the very last of my kin, the only son left of the House of Waegmunding. Wyrd has swept them all before her. They were all warriors mighty and true. I shall go after them . . . now."

Those were the last words of the dying Beowulf, king of the Geats. Wiglaf's heart broke to see his earl slacken and drop to the wet sand. Not far from Beowulf lay the charred remains of the worm, eaten by the fire that had fed it. He would never again streak fiery-tongued across a midnight sky spreading death and shuddering fear. There he sprawled on the ground, brought low by the hand of a hero. What man do you know who has fought such a fight for his people?

Beowulf had scarcely died before the faint-hearts came crawling out of their burrows. Still and ashamed, they crept up beside Wiglaf. That earl had not budged from the body of Beowulf. Bent with grief, he stood staring down at the mighty king whose soul had fled to its Maker. Finally Wiglaf noticed that the warriors stood round him.

"Look here," spat Wiglaf, looking them scornfully in the eyes, "you can tell the truth to the others. You were here at least. You saw our king stride forth alone to the battle. You saw him stand up to the fiery worm that burned the flesh from his body. With all the true men of the Geatish tribes ready and eager to help him, why did he have to pick you?

"Did you stand shoulder to shoulder with Beowulf at the hour of his death? No . . . You let him drain the cup alone. You hid and watched Beowulf die. You saw that I tried to fight, but my puny arms could do nothing. Do your greedy eyes catch the glints of the gold he won? Yes, Beowulf won this for you, but I say it shall never be yours!

"You are hereby stripped of your ranks and your lands, from this day henceforward. Your sons will be penniless! Your children shall wander from here to there and never find a dwelling to shelter their nakedness! Your craven hearts shall be loudly sung through all of our mead halls! For a warrior death is much better!"

The shrill sound of the war horn blared the news of Beowulf's death inland to his people. Men shuddered throughout the land. Women wailed and bemoaned their loss. Folks knew there would be wars now that no dauntless leader breasted the foemen for them. They recalled with fear how the Franks and the Frisians had fought them of old. They knew the Merovingian lords would be only too happy to sail proudly up to their towns with fire and with sword. The Swedes too would come hungrily over to harass them, to steal their crops. The Swedish kings would darken the land with their scaffolds and run them through with their swords, as a pastime.

"Let us bear our king to his barrow. Let us lift the body of Beowulf and raise it high on the wood we have piled. Our warrior will hear no more the sweet sound of the harp. Let not the raven brag to the eagle how he plucked out his eyes, or how he grew fat and sleek on his flesh. I say to you now, 'Let us lift up our earl. Let us take him in our arms for the last time. He was a ring-giver, mighty and true!' "

The Geatish warriors gathered beside the cave. In sorrow and hot tears they gazed for the last time on Beowulf. They saw by his ashes the length and breadth of the dragon. He had been fifty feet long at least. Long had he flown through the air. He never would quiver again. For one thousand years he had lorded it over the hoard. Beowulf had laid him low.

How amazing it is to wonder on what day, on what shore, a warrior will find his death. Even an earl of world-wide song cannot sit in his mead hall forever. Even he cannot know when the time will draw near. So was it with Beowulf. He had not forseen it either.

The chiefs of the Geats, wise and white-haired, passed beside the barrow. They muttered queer oaths through their beards. "May the man who treads on this hoard be swallowed. May he who soils this holy spot be tied to the stone slabs of the olden gods. May he be hurled into hell. May he be eaten by bloodsuckers. For our earl-king was not greedy for gold. If he gathered wealth, it was not for himself. Our king was not a hoarder, but a giver of golden rings."

Then Wiglaf spoke to them. "You see where our earl lies dead through the sin of one man. We could not stop Beowulf from grappling hard with this worm. Let us search out this hoard, load it in wagons, and carry it all to the headland."

A crowd of carls had been gathering timber for the barrow at the very edge of Hronesnesse Cliff. Around its sides were stacked the helmets and shields that Beowulf would never wear again. The body of the dead earl was sorrowfully placed at the peak. Then the fire was lighted. Sobs came from the warriors who watched their earl vanish. The wind was hushed. Huge clouds of smoke rose straight up into the heavens. Men moaned as they heard the heart of Beowulf burst.

An old woman with disheveled hair began weeping and singing a doleful song of the sorrows that would soon befall them all. She sobbed and sang of the bloody wars that would burst upon them, of the Viking raids from the stormy sea, of the yoke of serfdom they would all likely wear. The smoke from the burning barrow faded into the blue sky.

During the following weeks the Geats built a stone lighthouse on the spot where the barrow had stood. For ten days they worked, piling it high and making it strong so that sailors in after years could sight it from the sea even when they were still afar off. They surrounded the whole with a wall. Under this lighthouse they dug a hole and buried the hoard of the worm, the rings and the sparkling stones, all the wealth that their earl had ever won. They gave back to the earth what had been stolen from her in the bygone days. They wanted the gold to become sand again, and the gems to return to stone. There it still lies today, as worthless to us as it was to them.

As night fell, when the sun was only a thin, red streak on the western rim of the world, twelve of the worthiest earls moved in a line around the tomb, singing the Song of the Hero.

They boasted of his might as a warrior should who holds his king as peerless. They sang the song of Beowulf as kinfolk will do to cheer their dead king as he leaves this world, as his soul rushes out to fly through the sea wind.

They said that he had been among all the kings of the earth the kindest and sweetest. They said he had been the most beloved of them all, of his people. They said he had been watchful to save his good name and theirs. They said he had never broken an oath nor ever recoiled from a needful deed. They said he was not a taker, but a giver.

They said their King Beowulf had walked upright down the paths of his life like a true man and a hero, that the light of his life should rightfully shine far out over the northern sea and be a beacon to others.

NINE
WALES
PEREDUR
SON OF YORK

The story of the hero Peredur belongs to the Cymry or Welsh, one branch of the Celtic-speaking peoples. The Celtic languages may be divided into three groups: Gaulish, Brythonic (Welsh, Cornish, Breton), and Goidelic (Gaelic, Irish, Manx).

A hero named Peredur, who died fighting the Angles in 580 according to a Welsh chronicle, was buried near Pickering, Yorkshire. Celtic tradition has always associated Peredur with King Arthur and his knights; but, although Peredur may have been a contemporary of Arthur, his story is much older. It was told by Welsh bards, or *storiawr*, long before the Arthurian legends of the Round Table developed.

There are, in fact, elements of the Peredur hero myth that are common to other Indo-European heroes such as Perseus, Cyrus, Theseus, and Romulus and Remus. However, there are elements in it that also recall the revenge motif of the Isis-Osiris religion in Egypt as well as the death-and-birth of the seasons in the Ishtar or Venus-Adonis stories. Still another interesting feature of the Peredur myth links it to European folklore, particularly to that of another Celtic people—the Irish.

Wales has a poetic tradition that is well documented. Poems in Welsh, or Cymraeg, date from the sixth century when four of their great poets lived: Aneurin, Taliesin, Llywarch Hen, and Myrddin (the Merlin of Arthurian legend). As early as the ninth century the bards of the Cymry held song festivals or eisteddfods. There was a great flowering of Welsh literature during the reigns of Rhys ap Tewdwr and Gruffyd ap Cynan, who came to Wales from Brittany and Ireland respectively in 1077 and 1080. Geoffrey of Monmouth had written, or translated into Latin, his *History of the Britons* by 1135. Into this work later writers would delve for material on Arthur, who kept growing in importance with the passage of time, particularly among the Celtic refugees in the French province of Brittany.

The four ancient books of Wales are the *Black Book of Caermarthen*, the *Book of Aneurin*, the *Book of Taliesin*, and the *Red Book of Hergest*. This last book contains eleven tales or *Mabinogion*, among them the Peredur story, long known and told in the area around the Irish Sea. By the twelfth century the story had found a great number of skillful adapters in France, in Holland, and in Germany. Thanks to their efforts we have from the primitive Celtic Peredur the most famous of medieval knights, Sir Percival of the Holy Grail, and the German Parzifal.

Then in the thirteenth century authors had moved on to subjects other than those that glorified chivalry. Scholars have speculated as to why such a popular hero as Percival should so suddenly have been abandoned. Miss Jessie L. Weston in her book *The Quest of the Holy Grail* (London, 1913) wondered if this sudden loss of interest could have had anything to do with the dissolution of the powerful order of the Knights Templars, and whether any of their mysterious rites had some direct relation to Percival. Sir Walter Scott observes in *Ivanhoe*, Chap. 35, that the phrase *Ut Leo semper feriatur* (Let the Lion always be struck—or killed) seems to be a signal word of the Order of the Knights Templars.

Miss Weston has suggested two theories of this Peredur myth that seem to stand close examination very well. She believed that the original story was Druidic and not Christian, and that it concerned a secret initiation ceremony. All the adventures of Peredur were examinations which the hero either passed or failed.

The association of Peredur with the Grail was a French addition to the original story, as were later ideas about his chastity. Such subsequent heroes as Galahad, Lohengrin, and Sir Launfal seem to have been patterned after Peredur.

This story is very similar to the rites of primitive cultures celebrating the death and rebirth of vegetation. The reader will note how often Peredur rides through a wasteland and through snow, how the women wail as in the ancient festivals of Adonis or Tammuz, and how we assume that Peredur can heal and restore life to the earth. These ancient cults were called mysteries. As the reader will see, Peredur's is a very mysterious story. It is moreover a traditional one, the real meaning of which may even have been forgotten by the time the *Red Book of Hergest* was actually written.

The following is a fairly close but somewhat abridged translation from the Welsh version. Miss Mary Williams of the Universities of Wales and Paris has commented upon the Peredur story at great length in her dissertation of 1909. Her suggestion that it falls into three parts has been adopted. Her study reveals that Parts I and III do resemble accounts of Percival as told on the Continent. Part II, however, which occurs neither in the French nor in the German account, probably represents the original Welsh myth. In Part II references to Irish folklore are numerous, and Arthur's role less apparent. Here Peredur is the real hero who keeps the vassals he conquers for himself.

Not only was Peredur-Percival-Parzifal the most distinctively human and also the best beloved hero of the Middle Ages. His myth has had a strange fortune and a strong influence upon European letters, apparently even having traveled into Spain where Cervantes seems to have taken material from it. The idea of this myth has been regenerated very recently in twentieth-century fiction, particularly among such French novelists as Samuel Beckett and Robbe-Grillet. For this reason his story may be of very special interest to us now.

Owing to the very unusual nature of the hero Peredur, one has more than an inkling about a medieval ideal that could have been patterned after the teachings of Jesus Himself. Peredur is the pure in heart. He is simple, honest, modest, guileless, a child in the hands of his motivator. There is a pathetic quality about his story that strikes a responsive chord. He makes one wonder if there did not live once during the Middle Ages a person who was the living example and spiritual descendant of this traditional hero whose story was so widespread that it became almost a way of life. There is a strange, haunting quality in Peredur that reminds one of Joan of Arc.

PART ONE

The Childhood of Peredur

The Count of York owned estates in the north. He did not maintain himself principally by his revenues, however, but rather by tournaments, combats, and wars. As usually happens to him who seeks, the count was killed as were six of his sons. His last son was named Peredur. He was the youngest. Since he was too young for combats and wars, he survived. Otherwise he would have been killed along with his father and brothers.

Peredur's mother was an intelligent and resourceful woman. She thought a great deal about her son's future and about his domains. She finally decided to flee to an uninhabited, out-of-the-way spot. Besides her only surviving son she took with her only women, other children, and peaceable, industrious men who were either unable to fight or indisposed to do so. None of these people ever dared mention either horses or weapons in Peredur's presence for fear he would acquire a taste for them.

The little count used to go out into the forest every day to play games with lances he had cut out of holly wood. One day he saw his mother's herd of goats with two does near them. Peredur was surprised to see hornless animals. He decided they were goats that had strayed alone so long that they had lost their horns. He rounded them up with the herd and shut them all up in a forest enclosure. Then he went home.

"Mother," said Peredur, "I just saw an astonishing thing! Two of your goats went wild and strayed so long in the forest that they lost their horns. You can't imagine what a trouble I had to drive them into the pen with the others!"

Immediately everyone went to look. Their amazement was great to see that any child could have had the courage and agility to drive wild deer into a pen!

Another time three knights rode along a forest path. It was Gwalchmei, Gweir, and Owein. They were following the trail of a knight who had shared apples at Arthur's court.

"Mother," asked Peredur. "Who are they?"

"Angels, my boy," she answered.

"Then I am going with them as an angel," said Peredur, and followed them into the woods.

"Tell me, my soul," said Owein to Peredur, "did you see a knight go by here today or yesterday?"

"I don't know what a knight is."

"What I am," said Owein.

"If you would tell me what I ask, I would tell you what you ask," replied Peredur.

"Willingly."

"What is this?" asked Peredur, pointing to the saddle.

"A saddle," answered Owein.

Then Peredur questioned him about all his equipment and harness until he had learned their names and their functions. Owein explained them completely. "Ride forward!" Peredur told them. "I saw the sort of man you are seeking. As for me, I shall follow you as a knight. Right now. Today!"

When Peredur returned to his mother he said, "Those were not angels. Those were *knights*, Mother!" Peredur's mother fainted away.

Then Peredur ran out to the yard where the pack horses were kept, those that carried firewood on their backs and brought back food and drink into the deep woods. He picked out a sway-backed gray nag which was bony and thin, but in his opinion the strongest of the lot. He threw a pack saddle over it and then returned to his mother.

"Well," said she. "You want to leave us?"

"Yes," said Peredur.

"Wait first to hear my counsels."

"I'll wait. Talk fast."

"Go straight," said she, "to the court of Arthur, where live the best, the most generous, and the most valiant of men. Whenever you see a church, say a *Pater* near it. If you see food and drink that you need and if no one is courteous enough or good enough to offer it, then help

yourself. If you hear screams, go in their direction; there is no yelp more distinctive than that of a young woman. If you see a beautiful jewel, take that also and give it to somebody else. That way you will acquire a reputation. If you see a beautiful girl, make love to her. Even if she doesn't want you, she will consider you more courteous and more powerful than as if you hadn't seduced her."

With sticks and branches Peredur managed to imitate the various accouterments of a knight as he had seen them on Owein's saddle. Then he left home, holding in his hand a bunch of pointed spears just in case.

For two days and two nights he rode through various wild and uninhabited forests without either food or drink. Then as he passed through a dark and solitary wood, he saw a little glade. Since there was a lodge in its center, Peredur dutifully recited a *Pater* as if it had been a church. Then he rode toward the lodge. The door was open. Near the door was a dark-haired girl seated on a golden chair. She wore on her head a diadem of gold set with precious stones and on her finger a heavy gold ring.

Peredur dismounted and entered. The virgin greeted him kindly and made him welcome. Inside the lodge was a table set with two flagons of red wine, two loaves of white bread, and some slices of milkfed pork.

"My mother told me," said Peredur, "that in whatever place I saw food and drink, I was to take it."

"Go to the table, Prince," she said, "and may God bless you."

Peredur went to the table, ate half of the bread, drank half of the wine, and left the rest for the girl. When he had eaten, he stood up and walked over to her. "My mother," said he, "instructed me that whenever I saw a beautiful jewel, I was to take it."

"Take my soul, if you like," said she. "Don't think I'd hinder you!"

Peredur took her *ring*. Then he bent his knee before her, gave her a kiss, jumped on his horse, and rode away. No sooner had he left than the knight who owned the glade arrived. He saw the hoofprints of Peredur's nag.

"Tell me," said the Knight of the Glade to the maiden, "who was here after me?"

"A strange man, sir," she answered. Then she told him in detail about Peredur's lamentable equipment and the aim of his travels.

"Tell," he replied, "whether he had you."

"On my word," she said, "he did not!"

"On *my* word, I don't believe you! And until I meet him and avenge my anger and shame, you won't sleep two nights in the same spot." Then the knight arose and set out after Peredur.

Peredur at Arthur's Court

Now Peredur was still riding toward Arthur's court. Upon his arrival there, he saw a strange knight ride up and give a gold ring to a groom for holding his horse. The knight clanked into the hall where Arthur and his attendants, and Gwenhwyvar and her ladies, sat in state. A bedchamber page was just holding a goblet out to Gwenhwyvar.

The strange knight seized the goblet from the queen's hand. Without saying a word, he dashed its contents over the queen's face and her bosom. Then he slapped her cheeks and said, "If there is anyone who wishes to dispute with me over this goblet and avenge the insult to Gwenhwyvar, let him follow me into the meadow. I'll wait for him there." Amid a dead silence the knight strode from the hall.

Then the courtiers bowed low their heads for fear they would be asked to avenge Gwenhwyvar's injury. It seemed to them that no knight would have dared such an outrage if he did not possess such strength and valor—or else have such power in sorcery and enchantments—that he was proof against their lances.

Just then Peredur made his way into the hall, still mounted upon his bony gray nag with his makeshift, clumsy trappings. Kay was standing in the middle of the hall.

"Hey! you long fellow over there," called Peredur. "Where's Arthur?"

"What does the likes of you want with Arthur?" said Kay.

"My mother told me to go to him and have myself dubbed a knight."

"My word," said Kay, "you are too ill mounted and too ill armed!" Even as he spoke the courtiers began to laugh and to mock Peredur. They threw sticks at him, happy that such a fellow should have turned up in time to change the subject from Gwenhwyvar.

Then came into the hall a dwarf, who had sought refuge there the year before for himself and his female. During the whole year neither one nor the other had ever spoken a word. As soon as the dwarf spied Peredur, however, he cried, "Ha! Ha! May God bless you, fair Peredur, son of York, leader of warriors and flower of chivalry!"

"Truly, valet," said Kay to the dwarf, "one would have to be ill advised to have spent a whole year dumb and mute at Arthur's court, free to choose one's companion for chatting and drinking, and then to go call, in the presence of Arthur and his train, a man of this sort 'leader of warriors and flower of chivalry.'" Kay gave the dwarf such a blow on the head that he sent him reeling and unconscious the entire length of the hall. Then the female dwarf arrived.

"Ha! Ha! May God bless you, Peredur, fair son of York, flower of knighthood and light of chivalry!"

"Truly, woman," said Kay, "that's what I call stupid, to have remained mute for an entire year at Arthur's court, without saying a single word to anyone at all, and then today, in the presence of Arthur and his warriors, to call such a sight the 'flower of knighthood and the light of chivalry.' " Then he kicked her so hard that she fell in a faint.

"You long fellow, over there," insisted Peredur. "Point out Arthur to me, I said."

"Hush your song," replied Kay. "Look, why don't you go after that knight who waits in the meadow! Take the goblet away from him. Unseat him. Then, you see, you can keep his horse and his armor. After that we shall talk about your becoming a knight."

"Long fellow, I'll do it," said Peredur. He turned his nag about and outside to the meadow. There he found the knight riding up and down, very proud of his strength and his effrontery.

"Tell me, boy," said the knight, "did you see anyone from Arthur's court following me?"

"That tall fellow there ordered me to unseat you, to capture the goblet, and to take your horse and your armor for myself."

"Hush up, silly. Go back to the court and command Arthur from me to come out and fight. And if he doesn't come right away, I won't wait either."

"Upon my word," said Peredur. "You can choose. Whether by your leave or by force, I have been told to take your goblet and your armor." At this, the knight charged Peredur so furiously that with the butt of his lance he hurt the youth between the neck and the shoulder.

"Ah, man," said Peredur. "My mother's people didn't play like that with me. Let's take turns playing that game!" So he hurled one of his holly spears. It pierced the knight's eye so deeply that it came out the nape of his neck. The knight fell over backward dead on the grass.

"In truth," said Owein to Kay, "you were badly inspired to send that young fool after the knight. Either one or the other: he got tumbled off his horse or killed. If the knight threw him, he will count him among the gentry of the court. The result will be eternal shame for Arthur and us. If he killed the boy, the dishonor will be the same, with one more sin for you. May I lose my own honor if I don't go see what happened."

Owein went to the meadow. When he arrived, he was amazed to see Peredur dragging the strange knight the length of the field. "Ah, sir!" said Owein. "Wait! I'll help you off with his armor."

"Never," answered Peredur. "This iron dress is a part of him. It will never come off."

Owein showed Peredur how to take off the armor and the rich robes of the knight. "These are for you, my soul," he said. "Wear them in joy to Arthur's court with me." ·

"May I be disgraced if I go," said Peredur. "You carry the goblet for me to Gwenhwyvar. Say to Arthur that in whatever place I may go, I am his man. Whatever service or advantage I can achieve for him, I shall do it willingly. Add that I shall never go to his court before I have met that long fellow who was there, so that I may avenge the injury to the dwarf and his she-dwarf."

Owein returned to the court and narrated this adventure to Arthur, to Gwenhwyvar, and to the courtiers, without forgetting the threat against Kay. From time to time a vanquished knight rode up to the court from Peredur, and told the same story.

The Fisher King, or the Next Examination

Peredur rode forth until he came to a vast wasteland. There on the edge of the wilderness he found a pond on the other bank of which was a tall castle surrounded by massive ramparts. By the edge of the water sat a white-haired man on a cushion of gold brocade. His valets were fishing from a rowboat.

When the man saw Peredur, he stood up and returned to the castle. He limped badly. Peredur followed him into the courtyard. The door was open. They entered the hall. There the old man sat on a cushion of gold brocade. The great fire in the hearth had been lighted.

The attendants in the castle all rose courteously to greet Peredur. They assisted him from his horse and lifted off his armor. The old man patted the cushion with his hand, thus inviting the youth to sit by him. They sat beside each other, and they talked. When the time came, the tables were set, and they ate. Peredur sat beside the master. After dinner he asked Peredur if he knew how to use a sword.

"I believe," answered Peredur, "that if I were taught, I should know. He who can use a staff and buckler should know how to fight with a sword."

The old man had two sons, one blond and the other dark. "Stand up, young men," said the man, "and fight with the staff and buckler." They skirmished.

"Tell me, my soul," said the man to Peredur, "which one is better."

"In my opinion, the blond could draw blood whenever he wanted."

"Then take the dark one's weapons and draw blood from the blond, if you can."

Peredur struck the blond youth such a blow that one eyelid fell over his eye and his blood flowed in torrents.

"Good, my soul," said the old man. "Now come and sit by me. You are the most skillful in all this island. I am your uncle, your mother's brother. You will stay with me a while to learn courtesy and manners. Give up your mother tongue. I shall dub you a knight. This is what you are to do from now on: should you ever see something extraordinary, do not inquire about it so long as no one has the courtesy to explain it. The blame will never fall on you, but upon your teacher."

The Second King and His Examination

The next morning Peredur arose early, saddled his horse, and with his uncle's permission set out on his quest. First he came to a lonely wood and a flat meadow beyond which he saw a huge fortress and a magnificent palace. The door was open, so he entered. On one side of a large hall sat a majestic man with white hair. Pages surrounded him. They arose to greet Peredur ceremoniously. They seated the youth beside the old man. After dinner the man asked Peredur if he knew how to wield a sword.

"If I were taught, I should know," Peredur answered.

There was in the hall a great iron bar, so large that a man's hand could not grasp it. "Take the sword," said the old man to Peredur, "and strike this iron ring." When Peredur struck the iron bar, he broke it and the sword into two pieces. Then, following instructions, he fitted the pieces together and joined them. Again he struck the bar, and broke it and the sword, and fitted them together. The third time, however, although he broke both the ring and the sword, he could not make them stick together.

"Very good, young man," said the lord. "You may come and sit down, and may God bless you. I see, however, that you have only two-thirds of your strength; you still have to acquire the remaining third! When you have your strength entire, no one will dare to oppose you. I am your uncle, and the brother of the lord who received you last night."

On the heels of these events, there came into the hall two men bearing an enormous lance. Three streams of blood flowed down its head to the floor. At this dreadful sight all the company began to lament and to moan so bitterly that it was unbearable to hear them. Despite all this, the nobleman did not interrupt his conversation with Peredur. He gave no explanation of this occurrence, nor did Peredur ask for one.

After a moment of silence two maidens entered holding between them a huge platter upon which was a man's head resting in a pool of blood. Again all present began to weep and to scream so pitifully that it was embarrassing to be in the same hall with them. Finally they grew still and began to drink as much as they could hold.

Peredur in Disgrace

The next morning with his uncle's consent Peredur set forth again. He came to a wood from the depths of which he heard screams. Riding in that direction, he came upon a dark-haired gentlewoman standing beside a caparisoned horse. In her arms she held a man's corpse. Every time she pushed the body into the saddle, it fell stiffly to the ground. Then she screamed.

"Tell me, Sister," said Peredur, "why you are screaming."

"Oh, it's Peredur, the excommunicated!" she cried angrily. "Little help we have ever had from you in our sorrow!"

"Why do you say I am excommunicated?"

"For one thing, you caused your mother's death by leaving home against her wishes! Then the two dwarfs you saw at Arthur's court you failed to recognize. They used to belong to your own father! You and I had the same wet nurse; I am therefore your sister. This is my husband, who was killed by the knight of these woods. Don't go near that knight, for he would like to kill you too."

"You are wrong to blame me," protested Peredur. "Now I *shall* have trouble killing him because I have lingered so long with you! If I had stayed longer, I never should have been able to kill him. As for you, stop that screaming. It does no good! I'll bury your dead. Then I'll follow your knight. If I can get revenge for you, I'll do so."

Peredur followed the knight, met him in a clearing, charged and unseated him. When the knight asked for mercy, Peredur said, "I grant it on condition that you take this woman as your wife, and that you leave in her hands all the wealth you owe her as an indemnity for having murdered her husband without reason. Then you will go to Arthur's court. You will tell him that I vanquished you in Arthur's name. You will add that I shall never go to his court before I have met the long fellow and avenged the wrongs to the dwarfs."

The knight lifted the lady into his saddle and rode to Arthur's court. There he told his story without forgetting the threat to Kay. The latter bore the reproaches of Arthur for having caused such a courageous man as Peredur to shun the court.

"This youth will never come to court, nor will Kay ever leave it," said Owein.

"By my faith then," cried Arthur, "I shall search him out in all the islands of Britain until I find him. Then let the one do his worst to the other!"

Damsel in Distress

Peredur rode forward until he came to a lonely wood where he saw no traces of man or beast, only wild grasses and bushes. At the end of the wood was a tall castle of rich exterior surrounded on all sides by massive, high towers. Before its entrance the grass grew thickest.

A scrawny, red-haired boy stuck his head over the battlements and called down, "Choose, lord. Either I open the door myself or I'll go notify our master that you are at the gate."

"Tell him I am here. If he wants me to enter, I will."

The boy returned at once, unbarred the gate, and preceded Peredur into the hall. There Peredur saw eighteen skinny valets all in red, all about the same age and size, all dressed alike. He praised their skill and courtesy in disarming him. Then they all sat down and talked.

Later five maidens entered. There was one more noble in bearing than the others. Peredur was sure he had never seen such a beauty. She wore an old dress of precious brocade which had once been elegant but which was now so tattered that you could see her bare skin through it. Her skin was whiter than a flower of white glass. Her hair and brows were blacker than jet. On her cheeks were two red spots, redder than the reddest red you ever saw. The maiden greeted Peredur. Then she threw both her arms about his neck and drew him down on the cushions beside her. Soon afterward Peredur saw two sisters enter, one bearing a crock of wine, and the other six loaves of white bread.

"Lady," they said, "God knows there was nothing but this to eat at the convent tonight." Everyone sat down to supper. Peredur noticed that the maiden wanted to give him a larger share of food than to the others.

"Sister," said he, "it is I who will apportion the bread and the wine."

"Not at all, my soul. It is I."

"Then shame on my beard," he answered, "if I don't!" Peredur took the bread, cut equal shares for all, and gave each one his phial of wine. After the meal he called for a room and went to bed.

"Listen, Sister," said the valets to the damsel, "here is what we advise."

"What?" she said.

"Go find the youth in his chamber and offer yourself to him, as a wife or as mistress, whichever he wills."

"That's very improper," she answered, "that I who have never had anything to do with a man, should give myself to Peredur before he has even courted me. I wouldn't hear of such conduct for anything in the world!"

"Then let God be our witness," said they, "that if you don't do it, we'll abandon you here to your enemies."

The maiden, weeping floods of tears, rose and went into Peredur's chamber. The squeak of the door awoke him. He saw her standing there with tears rolling down her cheeks.

"Tell me, Sister, why you weep."

"I will tell you, sir. My father owned this castle and the richest fiefs all around. The son of another count asked my father for my hand. I would not go to him willingly, nor would my father force me. Since I am an only child, I inherited all these lands at my father's death. Then I wanted this suitor even less. Therefore he declared war on me, took all my lands, leaving me with only this castle. Thanks to my valiant servants I have been able to resist. Now our food is gone. For the last few days we have lived on what the sisters have been able to forage in the country around us. Now even they have nothing more to eat. Not

later than tomorrow the count will renew his attack. If he captures me, he will throw me to his stableboys. Therefore I come to offer myself to you, if you want me, so that you will rescue us all or help us defend this castle."

"Go, Sister," said Peredur, "to bed. And nothing of that sort." The maiden went out of the room and to bed.

Peredur remained with the damsel until he had vanquished her enemies and re-established her authority. On his way from her castle he also met and overcame the Knight of the Glade. After that he met the witches of Kaer Loyw (Gloucester), who took him to their castle for three weeks in order to perfect him in the art of chivalry.

The Red, The Black, and The White

Toward dusk one day Peredur came to a valley where dwelled a servant of God. This hermit welcomed Peredur to his cell. The next morning the youth set out through the fresh snow that had been falling all night. He saw before him a hawk that had just killed a wild duck. At the sound of the horse's hoofs, the hawk flew away. Then a crow settled down on the duck. Peredur reined in his horse. In silence he meditated on the sight of the dead bird. He gazed upon the blackness of the crow, the whiteness of the snow, and the redness of blood. He recalled that he had seen these three colors upon the lady he loved the best. Her hair was blacker than the crow's feathers, blacker even than jet. Her skin was as white as snow. Her two cheeks were as red as red blood.

Just at that moment Arthur and his courtiers came into sight.

"Do you recognize that knight of the long lance, he who is stopped in the woods?" asked Arthur.

"Sir King," said a page, "I will go see."

Peredur was so deep in his trance that he neither heard the page ride up nor his question. When the page pricked him with his lance, Peredur turned and absently toppled the page over his horse's ears into a snowbank. He did the same to the twenty-four knights who came up, one by one, to ask who he was.

Then Kay trotted up to Peredur. His questions were sharp and rude. Peredur caught Kay under the chin with his lance and threw him to earth so hard that Kay's arm and shoulder blade were broken. Kay lay there, unconscious in the snow. His horse, snorting and rearing, galloped back to Arthur. At first the king and his courtiers thought that Kay was dead. Then they decided that if a good doctor could be found, the bones could be made to knit and heal. They carried Kay to Arthur's own pavilion, for the king loved him dearly.

Peredur still did not awaken from his deep meditation. Gwalchmei remarked that no one should trouble a knight so inopportunely when he was sunk in reverie. He observed that the strange knight had perhaps suffered a loss, or that he was thinking of the lady he loved. "The knights who importuned him probably did it rudely. If you wish, Sir King, I will ask if he is ready to leave off his meditation, and if so, whether he would not like to come along nicely to see you."

Gwalchmei found Peredur still leaning upon the shaft of his lance, still lost in thought. Gwalchmei said quietly, "If I thought it would be as welcome to you as it is to me, I would ask you to speak with me. Two of Arthur's men have already come to invite you to his pavilion."

"I know," said Peredur, "but they introduced themselves in a very displeasing fashion. They quarreled with me because I was upset. They disturbed me during my meditation. I was reflecting on the lady I love the best.

"This is how the memory came upon me. I was gazing at the snow, the crow, and the drops of blood from the duck that the hawk had killed on the snow. I recalled that her complexion had the whiteness of snow, that her hair and brows were as black as these black feathers of the crow, and that her cheeks were as crimson as these drops of blood."

"Such a meditation," said Gwalchmei, "has, indeed, a certain character of nobility. It is not at all astonishing that you did not wish to be withdrawn from such a lofty subject."

"Will you tell me if Kay is at Arthur's court?"

"He is. You fought with him last. He has no cause for self-congratulation. You broke his arm and his shoulder."

"Good. I am glad thus to have begun my revenge for the dwarfs."

Gwalchmei recognized Peredur. He threw both arms around the youth's neck and swore his friendship. Then Gwalchmei and Peredur rode side by side to Arthur, joyful and merry. Arthur welcomed Peredur and bade him remain at his side. Peredur returned with Arthur to Caerleon.

PART TWO

The Valley Round

During his first evening, as Peredur was exploring Arthur's castle, he met Angharat of the Golden Hand. (Law Euraw.) "On my honor," Peredur told this damsel, "you are a charming and quite delicious young girl. I could bind myself to love you more than anybody, if you so desired."

"I give you my word," Angharat answered, "that I do not love you and that I shall never desire any part of you."

Peredur replied, "As for me then, I swear that I shall never speak another word until you realize that you love me and long for me more than any man alive!"

Next morning Peredur set out. He followed the high road as it wound along the crest of a mountain. When he had crossed its heights, he saw below him a circular valley with a rocky, wooded rim and a flat, green bottom. Fields and plowed lands alternated. In the center of the forested area was a group of houses crudely built of black stone. As he wound past a rocky spur, he saw a lion hitched to a chain. The sleeping beast barred the path. Behind it was an abyss filled with the white bones of men and animals. Peredur unsheathed his sword and *dealt the lion such a blow* that it dropped into the chasm. Then he cut the chain from which it dangled and watched the huge beast fall on the pile of bones. After that Peredur led his horse down the winding path into the valley.

There he came to a beautiful castle. In its courtyard sat a gray-haired man, the tallest man Peredur had ever seen. A dark-haired youth and a blond one were flipping knives. Their knife handles were made of whalebone. When the old man saw Peredur, he growled, "Shame on the beard of my porter!" Peredur knew he referred to the lion.

At supper they were joined by a lady and her daughter, both taller than any ladies Peredur had ever seen. During the meal Peredur and the girl chatted until her face became clouded and she fell silent. She whispered to Peredur that she had fallen in love with him and therefore feared his death in the morning. When Peredur asked for her help, the girl managed to have his horse and armor left beside his lodging that night. The next morning he arose early, armed himself, and vanquished in succession the giants who dwelled in the crude stone buildings, the two youths, and then the lord of the castle. He sent the white-haired man to Arthur's court to swear homage and be baptized.

"I thank God," Peredur said to himself, "that I did not break my oath not to speak a word to a Christian!"

Peredur's Wound

As Peredur rode forth again, he saw only a forlorn and barren country The only house he found was a poor cottage. There he heard of a huge snake that crouched over a golden ring. This snake would allow no one to live within a radius of seven miles. Peredur sought out the snake. He fought him furiously, tirelessly, and with glorious success. He killed the snake and took its golden ring. Then for a long time Peredur lived a wanderer's life without ever exchanging a word with any kind of Christian. This was why the color faded from his cheeks, and he lost his great beauty. His pallor was the result of the extreme sorrow he felt not to be at Arthur's court, near the lady he loved the best, and near Gwalchmei. Finally he rode toward Caerleon.

Along the road he met the people of Arthur, riding with Kay at their

head to deliver a message. Although Peredur recognized them all, he was so thin and so pale that not one of them recognized him.

"Where are you coming from, sir?" said Kay. He asked Peredur the question again and a third time. Peredur said not a word. Kay then struck the youth with his lance and pierced his *thigh*. Since he would not break his vow, Peredur passed on without avenging the injury.

Then Gwalchmei protested, "By me and by God, Kay, you behaved badly in mistreating that youth as you did, only because he could not speak!" Gwalchmei escorted Peredur to Arthur's court and said to Gwenhwyvar, "Princess, do you see with what cruelty Kay has treated this boy who could not speak? For God's sake and for mine, have him attended by doctors until I return. I shall repay this service!"

While Peredur was living, still unrecognized, at Arthur's court, a knight rode up to the meadow at Caerleon. He wanted to fight. And he found what he sought. However, this knight overcame every opponent for a week. There he strutted in the meadow, vanquishing his one knight per day!

One morning as Arthur and his knights were coming from church, they passed this saucy knight in his meadow, his battle standard raised to invite combat. "Ah! my courageous ones," sighed Arthur, "by your valor I shall not leave this spot until I have had my arms and my horse brought to me so that I can fight this oaf!" As pages were leading Arthur's horse to him, they passed by Peredur. Still without speaking, Peredur put on Arthur's armor, mounted Arthur's horse, and rode across the meadow.

Then everyone, seeing the mute knight mount and ride to combat, climbed on the roofs of the houses or on the hills to look. Peredur gave a sign with his hand that the challenger could begin the combat. Even when the knight charged him full tilt, Peredur never budged from his place. Then it was Peredur's turn. He spurred his horse across the meadow, furious and valiant, terrible and mighty. He gave the knight such a sharp, poisoned, hard, and searing blow under the chin—a blow worthy of a knight that has three-thirds of his strength—that Peredur lifted his challenger clear out of his saddle and hurled him a good distance away. Then Peredur trotted back, returned the horse and armor to the squires, and trudged on foot along the dusty road to the court. People lined the way and called him "the mute youth."

As Peredur entered Arthur's hall, he met Angharat of the Golden Hand. "By me and by God," said she, "it is a great pity that you cannot speak. If you could, I should love you more than any other man, and upon my word, even though you cannot speak, I will love you even so, the best in all the world!"

By his faithful love for Angharat was Peredur recognized. He remained in the company of Gwalchmei, Owein son of Urien, and all those of Arthur's court, and he lived at Arthur's court, at Caerleon on the Wyse.

MEDIEVAL MYTHS

The Empress of Cristinobyl

During this time Peredur accomplished successfully the quest of the one-eyed Black Knight. On his way to kill the Serpent of the Cairn he met the most beautiful damsel in the world. She gave him a magic stone and told Peredur that if he wished to find her, he could ride in the direction of India.

Holding the stone in his hand, Peredur rode toward a valley which was traversed by a stream.

Ac ynteu a doeth racda6 parth a dyffryn avon. A gororeu y dyffryn oed yn goet. Ac o pop parth yr avon yn weirglodeu g6astat. Ac or neill parth arall y g6elei kad6 o defeit duon. Ac val y brefei vn or defeit g6ynyon y deuei vn or defeit duon dr6od. Ac y bydei yn wen. Ac val y brefei vn or defeit duon y deuei vn or defeit g6ynnyon dr6od ac y bydei du.

Its slopes were wooded, but from the two banks of the stream stretched even meadows. On one bank was a flock of white sheep; on the other a flock of black ones. Every time a white sheep bleated, a black one would cross the stream and become white; whenever a black sheep bleated, a white one crossed and became black.

At this river's edge stood a tree which was on fire from roots to tip on one side, but green and leafy on the other side.

Through the amazing virtues of the stone Peredur overcame the reptile. He won vassals for himself, including a Red Knight who loved the Countess of Prowess. Then he rode forth in search of the beautiful maiden who had given him the magic stone.

Peredur rode eastward until he came to the prettiest river valley he had ever seen. There were pitched many brilliantly colored pavilions; but more strange, the valley was dotted with watermills and windmills. The first man Peredur met was tall and swarthy. Although Peredur took him for a carpenter, the man said he was the chief miller of all the windmills.

"May I find lodging with you?" asked Peredur.

"Willingly."

Once Peredur was lodged in the miller's house, he borrowed money from his host to provide food and drink for the household, saying that he would earn the sum in the tournament before he left. He asked the miller why there were so many pavilions of knights and such crowds of people.

"Either one or the other," answered the miller. "Either you come from far away, or you are not in your right mind. There resides here the most beautiful lady in the world. She is the empress of Cristinobyl the Great, the lady who will only have as her husband the most courageous man in the world, for she has no need of riches. That is why you see so many mills; we have to provide food for all her suitors."

The next morning Peredur, clad in full armor, set out for the daily tournament. On his way he spied his beautiful girl, she who had given him the magic stone. She was looking out of a silk pavilion. Peredur had never gazed on one so lovely. The longer he stood and gazed, the deeper in love he fell. He stood without moving or speaking from early morning until noon, and from noon until evening. When that day's tournament ended, he returned to his lodging, obliged to borrow more money from the miller. The miller's wife was displeased, particularly when Peredur spent the second day as entranced as he had been the first.

On the third day as Peredur still stood enthralled, gazing upon the exquisite beauty of the lady, the miller came up behind him and cracked him on the shoulder with a hatchet handle. "Do one or the other," the miller told Peredur. "Either clear out of here, or go enter the lists."

Peredur grinned at the miller and went forth to joust. When he had overcome all his opponents, he sent them as presents to the empress. With the horses and their trappings he was able to repay the miller's wife. Peredur returned each day to the tournament until he was the sole remaining knight on the field. Then the empress sent for him. Peredur paid no attention to her summons the first time. She sent again. Still he ignored her. The third time she dispatched one hundred knights with orders to bring Peredur to her feet, by force if necessary.

Peredur played straight with the one hundred knights. He trussed them up as one would a kid and tossed them all into the moat. Then the empress in despair sent a wise old man, who politely requested Peredur to call upon the empress. He told Peredur that the empress loved him passionately. That time Peredur went to her hall, but he took the miller with him. Peredur sat down on the first seat he came to, so the empress was obliged to walk across the hall to him. After he had exchanged the time of day with her, Peredur returned to his lodgings.

The next day he waited upon the empress again. No seat of honor had been prepared for him, for no courtier could guess where he would choose to sit. As the lovers were chatting, a black man entered. He carried a golden goblet filled with wine. Falling upon his knees, he entreated the empress to bestow the cup only upon that man who consented to fight him for her hand. Peredur took the goblet, drank the wine, and tossed the goblet to the miller's wife.

Then an even taller man entered, bearing a horn goblet filled with wine. Peredur took that one also. The third man was even bigger than the first two. His hair was curly and red. His goblet was made of crystal. The next morning Peredur left his lodgings, killed the three warriors, and sat down in the empress' hall.

"Beautiful Peredur," said the empress, "do you remember that you promised to love me more than any other lady if I gave you the stone that helped you to slay the crocodile?"

"Princess," he answered, "it's the truth. I remember." Then Peredur stayed in Cristinobyl and governed with the empress for fourteen years.

PART THREE

The Black Girl at Caerleon

Four knights—Owein, Gwalchmei, Howel, and Peredur of the Long Lance (Baladyr Hir) were seated on a brocade carpet in the main hall of Arthur's castle when the Black Girl entered. Her hair was black and curly. She rode a yellow mule which she slapped with thick leather thongs. Her appearance was uncouth and ugly. Her face and hands were blacker than the blackest iron dipped in pitch. Even that was not the most striking aspect of her.

The most striking aspect of the Black Girl was her body. Her cheekbones were too high, and her chin was too long. Her nose was too short, and her nostrils were too wide. One of her eyes was a shiny greenish-blue. The other eye was jet black and sunken in her skull. Her teeth were long and yellow, yellower than the flowers of the furze bush. Her belly was pointed and so high it met her chin. Her spine was as crooked as a scythe handle. Her thighs were wide and bony over legs like sticks. Her knees and feet were huge.

The Black Girl greeted everyone at the court politely, except Peredur. "Peredur," she said accusingly, "I won't greet you because you don't deserve it! Destiny was certainly blind when she allowed you to become favored and famous! When you went to the Court of the Lame King, when you saw the bleeding lance brought in before you, when you saw with your own eyes the three streams of blood and other prodigies too, you neither asked the reason nor the cause of them. If you *had* asked, the Lame King would have recovered his health for himself and prosperity for the land. Because of you there will always be wars and famines, women left widowed, and damsels without wealth or food! All these winter calamities just because of you!"

Then the Black Girl shamed Arthur with her sad stories of beleaguered castles, damsels in distress, and five hundred and sixty-six fierce knights still to be overcome. Gwalchmei and the other knights hastened to right these wrongs. There was a bustle of departure and a clanking of armor in the hall. Horses were saddled posthaste. Only this time Peredur was not duped. He remained thinking. "Upon my word," he said finally, "I see that I must not sleep until I have solved the mystery of the bleeding lance!"

Peredur set out on this quest through all the islands, hunting night and day for news of the Black Girl. Finally in the valley of a strange river he met a priest of whom he requested a blessing.

"No, unhappy Peredur," said the priest, "you don't deserve my blessing. Nor will it ever bring happiness to wear armor on a day like this!"

"Why, what day is it?"

"It is Good Friday."

"Please don't reproach me," cried Peredur. "I didn't know it was spring. I have then been wandering a year to the day!"

Peredur walked along the forest paths until he came to Bald Castle. There in the hall he met the priest again. This time he received the Father's blessing. For three days the priest instructed Peredur, and taught him how to find the end of his quest. He directed Peredur to a nearby castle where he could inquire about what he had always sought, Castle Marvelous!

Castle Marvelous

Peredur found Castle Marvelous, which he had sought so long, in the middle of a lake. Its gate stood open. When he entered the hall, he saw a chessboard where the pieces were playing all by themselves. He sat down and helped one side, but his side lost. Then the winners all began to boast and to shout so loudly that Peredur lost his temper. He grabbed the chessmen and tossed the board into the lake.

He had no sooner done this than the Black Girl appeared. She was very angry. "May God never forgive you!" she screamed. "You're always doing everything wrong!"

"*Now* what do you expect of me, Black Girl?" asked Peredur.

"Look what you just did! You threw the princess' game away. She wouldn't have had that happen for all her vast empire!"

"Is there any way that I can recover it then?"

"Well, yes, if you went to Kaer Ysbidinongyl. There's a black man there who is laying waste the domains of our princess. If you killed him, you could win back her chessboard. However, if you go to Kaer Ysbidinongyl, you will be killed."

"Will you serve as my guide to that place?"

"No," said the Black Girl, "but I *will* show you the road." Peredur traveled all the way to Kaer Ysbidinongyl where he overcame the black man, who in exchange for his life promised to return the chessboard. Peredur rode back to Castle Marvelous only to find the Black Girl angrier than ever.

"Now may the curse of God fall upon your head for your trouble, for having let live such an accursed ravager. Now he will continue to ruin our lands and our crops! I told you to kill him!"

"I left him his life," replied Peredur, "so that he would put back the chessboard."

"Well, it's not in the same place as it was before," she retorted. "Retrace your steps, and this time, kill him!" Peredur went all the way back and killed the black man.

Then when he had returned to Castle Marvelous, he insisted upon seeing the Princess. "By me and by God," said the Black Girl, "you won't see her this time either unless you kill the demon that haunts our forest."

"What sort of demon is it?"

"It's a deer as fleet as the swiftest bird that flies. It has in its forehead one horn as long as the staff of a lance, and as pointed as the most pointed lance there is. He nibbles up all the branches of all the trees and eats all the grass in all the forest glades. He kills every living animal he can find, which doesn't matter so much because those he doesn't hunt out die of starvation anyway. Worse even than that, he comes down every evening to the fish pond. He drinks all the water in it so that we have no fish to eat either. Even the minnows die before fresh water can seep into the pool."

"Maiden," said Peredur, "will you show me where this creature is?"

"Certainly not," she retorted. "I have helped you enough. Not a soul has dared go into the forest for over a year. You may take the princess' little spaniel with you, however. He will drive the wild beast toward you, and then you can kill it."

The little dog scented the animal and drove it toward Peredur. The beast with lowered horn attacked furiously. Peredur side-stepped, let it rush past him, and as it did so, cut its head clean off with his sword. Before Peredur could lift up the head, a lady on horseback galloped up to him, crying, "Ah, Sir Knight, you have conducted yourself in a most unchivalrous fashion in so destroying the most rare jewel in all my domains." Then she settled the dog in the folds of her cloak and the deer's head, with its brilliant red collar, next to her body.

"I was asked to do it," replied Peredur. "Is there no way at all for me to win your friendship?"

"Yes. Go up to the summit of that mountain you see over there. Then hunt for a bush under which lies a flat stone. Call aloud three times for a champion to fight you. Thus you will deliver us all."

This time Peredur did exactly as he was told. Out of the ground beneath his feet rose a black knight with antique, rusted armor. He rode a bony, emaciated horse. Every time Peredur struck him from his mount, the aged knight vaulted to the saddle again. Finally Peredur dismounted and drew his sword. Then before he even saw what happened, the rusty knight disappeared before his eyes. He took Peredur's horse with him, and also his own.

Peredur set out on foot down the steep mountainside. As he walked, he saw across the valley a castle with massive towers. When he arrived there, the door was unbarred, so he entered. In the hall sat of all people the gray-haired king who limped. Seated by his side was Peredur's friend, the knight Gwalchmei. Then Peredur noticed that his own horse was stabled beside that of Gwalchmei. Both the Fisher King and Gwalchmei greeted Peredur with great joy. The king made room for Peredur on his other side.

Soon afterward the blond youth entered and knelt before Peredur, begging his friendship. "Sir," he said, "it was I who traveled to Arthur's court disguised as the Black Girl, and I so disguised also when you threw away the chessboard of the princess, and when you killed the dark man of Ysbidinongyl, when you rid us of the devouring deer, and when you combated the wintry knight at flat rock. It was I also who carried the bleeding head on the grail, and I who showed you the lance with its stream of blood the length of the blade.

"The head was that of your first cousin, he who was slain by the witches of Kaer Loyw. It was they who also crippled your uncle. I am also your cousin. It was written that you, Peredur, would avenge all these wrongs."

Peredur and Gwalchmei decided to send for aid to Arthur's court. Then all the knights of Britain campaigned against the witches. One witch tried to kill a knight, but Peredur prevented her. A second time she also wanted to kill a knight before Peredur, but he prevented her. The third time a witch did kill a knight before Peredur. Then Peredur unsheathed his sword. He struck her such a blow upon the point of her helmet that he bent it inward, cut through the metal, and slit it in two.

With a piercing scream the witch ordered the others to retreat. "It is our pupil Peredur, he whom we instructed in chivalry. It was written ages ago that he would kill us!"

Then Arthur and his knights began to wield their swords through the air, right and left, as the witches whirred past them. They fought until they had killed every last one.

That is the story they tell of Peredur in Castle Marvelous.

TEN
FRANCE
THE SONG OF
ROLAND

The Song of Roland is probably the most famous piece of medieval French literature. Its renown is due in great part to the enthusiasm it created among the French Romantic poets of the nineteenth century. It is a curious fact that, although the enormous and largely unknown body of literature produced in France from 1000 to 1500 is vastly more extensive than that of any other European nation, by the French it is still held in a disrepute that dates from the sixteenth and seventeenth centuries. Where England has the one great epic, *Beowulf*, France has eighty of them. The *Roland* poem belongs to one cycle of epics centered about the life of Charlemagne.

Because of the great popularity of the *Roland*, the epic became one of the chief literary forms for those writers who wished to compose in French. Latin was the language of education in all the western European countries. Latin literature continued to develop side by side with works in the vernaculars, and popular pieces such as the *Roland* were translated into Latin so that everyone could read them. Although the *Roland* is not the oldest extant literary document in the French language, it is the oldest masterpiece.

France dominated the European literary scene during the Middle Ages. The reader will see how the themes from *Beowulf* as well as those from the story of Peredur appear in French literature, vastly polished and developed during those centuries when Old French was also the language of England. Into France, the center of learning and culture, hundreds of stories converged, were treated, and then radiated throughout Europe.

The author of *The Song of Roland* is unknown; its date (*c.* 1100?), its origin, and its purpose are still highly disputed. It seems obvious from the tone and language of this poem, however, that it was composed by one man, and that he was not only a great poet, but also well educated. He knew not only certain classics but also a great deal about history and geography. He was patriotic, religious, and chauvinistic. He certainly did not attempt to write about Charlemagne with any degee of exactness, for that emperor's engagement at Saragossa was not the brilliant victory the poet pretends. Like all artists he has transformed his initial situation. Régine Pernoud, one of the most distinguished of modern medievalists, points out that using the subject as a pretext is a characteristic of medieval art.

As the reader will see, our poet is partial to certain localities in northern France, and also to those churches and monasteries along the pilgrims' route to Saint James of Compostella. This was noted by the greatest scholar of this epic, Professor Joseph Bédier (1864–1938).

Upon the barest framework of historical fact—his Charlemagne was a real king—our author has given us a picture of a cultural and national ideal, the imaginary Roland. He was writing at a time when the great nobles of Europe were embarking upon that fantastic series of foreign wars they called the Crusades. The First Crusade lasted from 1096 to 1099. It is also true that Charles Martel had stopped the spread of Islam into France at Poitiers in 732. He is supposed to have fought an army of 90,000 Mussulmans.

In *The Song of Roland* we have a kind of meshing of the earlier themes —the horn, the sword, and the lance—which will be further expanded, by such great writers as Chrétien de Troyes, into the final Grail stories and Arthurian legends. There is no longer any trace, in the *Roland*, of either resistance to Christianity, of survivals of Scandinavian gods, or of Druidism. France was devoutly Christian; her Vikings or Normans outdid the rest of France in religous fervor. France was, indeed, the right arm of the church. The scene is already set for Saint Louis and the subsequent Crusades.

The religious aspects of this poem, its prayers in particular, have been exhaustively studied by Sister Marie Pierre Koch in her dissertation published in 1940 by the Catholic University of America Press. No definitive explanation has been given, to my knowledge, of the letters *AOI* that occur in the text. Scholars have suggested that they have a religious significance, such as has the word "Alleluia."

As *Beowulf* testified to the earliest known origins of feudalism, so the *Roland* explains the operation of a feudal court where the king is only a vassal among his vassals, where appointments are made by nomination, and where the majority vote prevails over the king. Here is Act I of the great drama between the Roman concept of divine right of kings and the equally well entrenched Germanic system that will succumb under Louis XIV. His absolute monarchy entailed the swift destruction of that institution in France.

The *Roland* is written in Old French, a beautiful language with a vocabulary much larger and far more expressive than that of modern

French. Many of its most picturesque words and expressions were systematically reduced by the French writers and scholars of the seventeenth century. A great many of these words remained, however, in English, and it is much easier for the American student to read Old French than would be imagined. Some of its themes and attitudes were also saved for us by our foremost medievalist, Shakespeare, who could very well have agreed with the author of the *Roland* that lyric poetry and epic poetry harmonize, and that historical events make the finest setting for the development of a poet's political and personal convictions.

Although the fifteenth-century French poet, who is known to English lovers of poetry as Charles of Orleans, said "Roland and Saint Louis" when he thought of the heroes of France, the "Roland" poem was "discovered" at Oxford University by a French scholar, Francisque Michel, in 1837. Another copy dating from the fourteenth century was later found in Venice, for Roland—renamed Orlando—was wholeheartedly adopted in Italy.

Among the legions of great authorities on this poem, aside from M. Bédier, are Gaston Paris, Maurice Wilmotte, Gustave Cohen, Ferdinand Lot, Ernest Curtius, Camille Jullian, and Dean Arthur Sideleau of the University of Montreal.

The *Chanson de Roland* is contemporary with the *Shah Nameh* of Persia. Proper names have often been left in Old French because of their musical effect: Rollanz, Carles, Carlemagne, etc.

ROLLANZ

Carles li reis, nostre emperere magnes,
Set anz tuz pleins ad estet en Espaigne:
Tresqu'en la mer cunquist la tere altaigne.
N'i ad castel ki devant lui remaigne;
Mur ne citet n'i est remes a fraindre,
Fors Sarraguce, ki est en une muntaigne.
Li reis Marsilie la tient, ki Deu nen aimet.
Mahumet sert e Apollin recleimet:
Nes poet guarder que mals ne l'i ateignet. [Verses 1–9]

Carles the King, our great Charlemagne,
Seven full years has campaigned in Spain,
Up to the sea has conquered proud domains.
There is not a castle that before him remains,
Not a rampart nor city has he to gain
Save Saragossa, which is on a mountain.

King Marsilie holds it whom God disdains;
He serves Mohammed and Apollo acclaims
Marsilie found *they* were not sovereign!

[V. 815] High are the peaks and the valleys dark! The Pyrenees tower
into the clouds above their dizzy passes. All day long Carlemagne and
the Franks ride northward through the mountains in such great numbers that the very earth shakes. Straining their eyes, the knights gaze
across the foothills, hoping to catch their first sight of France. Thoughts
of their home and families whom they left seven years before bring
tears to their eyes. More than his knights is King Carles full of grief,
for behind him at the gates of Spain he has stationed his nephew Rollanz. The twelve peers of France and twenty thousand knights are still
back in Spain to assure the rear guard!

Now Carlemagne weeps; he cannot hide his tears. "I feel danger
behind me!" says the king. "I fear Rollanz is in danger, for Guenes
named him to command the rear guard. . . . If I lose Rollanz, I
shall never have exchange!"

[V. 999] Clear is the day in Spain, and radiant the sun! Four hundred
thousand Sarrazins under King Marsilie of Saragossa spur their horses
northward! Crimson, blue, and white flash their banners in the sun. A
thousand trumpets shrill as they ride in serried ranks. Their clarions
call through the thin mountain air, and alert the rear guard of the
Franks who are almost at the pass.

"Sir Companion," asked Oliviers of his friend Rollanz, "can it be
that the Sarrazins have followed?"

"If they have," Rollanz answered Oliviers, "then it is the will of
God. We shall make our stand here. Every vassal knows what he must
suffer for his king—distress, and heat and cold. Let every baron strike
great blows for Carlemagne!"

Oliviers climbed a hill to look toward the south. There he saw such a
host of Sarrazins coming that he could not even count them. Their
helmets glittered in the sun and their shields; their satin banners
floated over a sea of rhythmic, mounted knights. "Rollanz, sound the
horn!" cried Oliviers. "Carlemagne will hear it and come back!"

"I shall not call for aid! I shall not sound the horn!" Rollanz answered his friend. "In doing so I would lose my good name in my
beloved France. Durendal will run in blood today up to its golden hilt!
Let the pagans spur northward to the portals! I swear to you here; they
are bent unto death. May neither God nor the angels suffer shame
because of us! Halt! Let us wheel about and fight them!"

Among the twelve peers was the Archbishop Turpins. Standing on a

hillock, he called the Franks to him. "Dismount and pray, for the battle draws near." Then he blessed the valiant knights and gave them absolution. "As penance I command you to strike a blow for God!"

The sunny-faced, the smiling Rollanz reviewed the peers. He rode his swift war charger and brandished high his lance. Its pennants were pure white with long, streaming tassels. "Sir Barons, before evening we shall have won a wealthy prize. These pagans that spur after us are seeking martyrdom." As Rollanz, sheathed in armor, cantered Veillantif down the line of the Franks, their battle cry "Mountjoy" rose from twenty thousand throats. They knew Guenes had sold them to King Marsilie of Saragossa. Then Guenes had appointed Rollanz to the rear guard. They knew they were betrayed.

Opposite the Franks lined up the hosts from Spain, vassals and allies of Marsilie of Saragossa. "Cowardly French, ride forth and tilt with us! Today your Carlemagne will lose his *right hand*. Foolish was your king to leave his nephew Rollanz at the pass! Do you know you were sold and betrayed into our ambush by your own Baron Guenes?"

Rollanz struck the first blow that day at Roncevals. With his sword Durendal he split the taunter's body. "No, son of a slave, our King Carles knew whom to trust! No shame shall fall on him, on us, or on our gentle France!" Second to Rollanz, Oliviers marked out his man, dug his golden spurs into his horse's flanks and charged the pagan foe. Third into their ranks lumbered the Archbishop Turpins, marked out a prince of Barbary, and slew him with his boar spear. Then the good Sir Gerin sent a heathen's soul to Satan. Gerin's friend, the Knight Gerier, next pierced a pagan peer. Duke Sansun attacked next, and after him Anseïs. "That was a worthy arm," cheered Rollanz. Then Engelers of Gascony, Oton, and Berengier accounted for three more. Of the twelve Spanish peers, only Margariz and Chernubles still lived a few minutes more.

The twelve peers of France fought like lions on that field. With each blow Rollanz split a Sarrazin's skull, sectioned his body, and severed the horse's spine. He swung about him in scythe strokes. At one moment he passed Oliviers who was braining enemies with his shivered lance. "Where's Halteclere, your sword?" Oliviers had been too busy to unsheathe it! . . . By hundreds, then by thousands, they strewed the field with pagan dead. Many a gallant French knight also gave up his young life at Roncevals.

Across the Pyrenees all France waited. All France knew that it was a tragic day. From the Mont-Saint-Michel to Saints, and from Besançon to Ouessant, walls crumbled in every house! At noon there grew a darkness in the sky and a great hush broken only by streaks of chain fire and thunder. A hollow wind swept from mountain to seacoast. Huge chunks of hail rattled on the thatch. People crowded together for comfort. They spoke only in whispers. "Here has come the day of judgment and the end of the world!'' They did not know and therefore could not say the truth: it was grief sweeping across fair France for the coming death of Rollanz!

Even as the Frankish peers stood masters of the field, they heard a distant rumbling like the waves of the seacoast. Then hove into sight the main body of the Spanish army, twenty battalions on the double, and seven thousand trumpets sounding the charge. At their head galloped, his dragon pennant streaming in the hot summer sun, Abisme, the daring leader of the infidels. The Archbishop Turpins marked him well. ''That Sarrazin is a heretic. Much better I should kill him, for I have always hated cowards!'' Turpins spurred his yellow-maned Danish charger and smashed his lance into the amethysts and topazes that gleamed on Abisme's shield. Turpins ran him through. Then he wheeled back and encouraged the Franks, ''Sir Barons, go not with somber thoughts! Beyond this last day we shall live no more on earth. Therefore strike your blows today for God and for France! I am here to guarantee you all a seat in Paradise.''

Then a count of Saragossa, Climborins by name—he who had kissed Guenes on the mouth for his treason—unhorsed and killed Engelers of Gascony. What a loss was that for the Franks! Oliviers saw it and took revenge. Then the heathen Valdabrun—he who had taken Jerusalem by treachery, violated the temple of Solomon, and killed the Patriarch before his fonts—slaughtered the distinguished Duke Sansun. ''God! What a baron was he!'' moaned the Franks. Rollanz struck down Valdabrun, split his skull, his byrnie, his jeweled saddle, and his horse's spine. Then charged from the Spanish ranks an African son of a king who cut the vermilion-and-azure shield of Anseïs, killed that noble baron. ''Baron Anseïs, what a pity is your death!'' moaned the Franks. Then from the middle rode out the Archbishop Turpins. Never tonsured priest ever did such deeds of prowess. ''You have just killed a baron whom my heart regrets,'' said Turpins as he struck the African dead.

Grandonie, the heathen son of Cappadocia's king, crushed the crimson shield of Gerin, then killed Gerier his companion, and after them Berengier. ''See how our numbers dwindle!'' moaned the Franks. Rollanz saw those heathen blows. Grandonie had never seen Rollanz in his life, and yet he recognized him. Despite the noise and confusion of battle, Grandonie knew Rollanz at once.

Rollanz was the open-faced, proud-eyed, the graceful, handsome knight. All at once Grandonie was afraid. Rollanz did not let him escape. With one stroke of Durendal he slit the helmet of Toledo steel as far as the nose, then cut through the teeth and lips, unthreaded the chain mail, ripped through the silver pommel, and crushed the horse's spine. Then cried the Franks, ''Carles's *right hand* guarantees us!'' Drops of bright blood trickled through the green field of Roncevals.

In the Book of Deeds it is well written that the Franks had killed up to this moment four thousand of their foes. They stemmed the first four attacks, but the fifth one cost them dear. All the Franks were dead except for sixty knights whom God had thus far spared. They saw what there was to do: they must fetch a high price!

"Sir Knight and dear companions," shouted Rollanz to Oliviers, "with all these knights dead, France will remain a desert! I shall now wind the horn!"

"To sound it now would be unworthy of us all! . . . How bloody are your arms, dear Rollanz!"

"I have been dealing bloody blows. . . . Why are you angry with me now?"

"All this carnage is your fault! You outstretched yourself today. If you had listened when I spoke, King Carles would be here now. You have lost us by your *pride*, Rollanz! Before evening you and I will say farewell."

As Rollanz and Oliviers stood quarreling, the Archbishop Turpins came between them. "Sir Rollanz! Sir Oliviers! By God, I beg you to stop! The horn can no longer save us. Yet, on the other hand, it would still be better for Rollanz to sound it. Why? Because the Franks will return with our army. They will gather up our bodies and carry them over the mountains. They will not leave us as carrion for wild dogs and wolves. They will inter us in the crypts of our cathedrals."

"Sir, well spoken," answered Rollanz. He lifted the horn to his lips and blew with all his might, until his temples burst and the salt blood burst through his throat.

High are the peaks and loud the voice of the horn! For thirty leagues around its shrill tongue blared. Far up on the passes of the Pyrenees, Carlemagne heard it and halted. "Our men do battle!" cried King Carles.

"No," answered the traitor Guenes. "You know how playful Rollanz is. He'd blow his horn all day on the track of a hare. Who'd dare to attack our rear guard? Let's ride forward into France."

"Listen," commanded Carles. "That horn was winded long!"

Duke Naimes agreed with Carles. "Rollanz does battle. I am sure of it. And that man, Guenes beside you, Sir King, has betrayed him! God, Sire, do you hear that desperate horn?"

"Answer Rollanz," cried Carles. "Sound the horns and arm yourselves all!" In haste the Franks dismounted from their palfreys, slipped on their mail shirts, grasped their spears, and mounted their war horses. Under their breaths they prayed Rollanz would live to see their avenging arms.

What is the use of words? They were too late.

Already the vesper shadows crept down the mountain slopes. At the head of his army Carlemagne galloped hard, his face intent and angry as he leaned forward on his horse's neck. Before turning southward, Carles had ordered Guenes seized and put in the guard of the cooks and kitchen knaves. "Watch him closely," commanded the king, "for he is a base felon! He has handed one of mine over to the enemy today!" The kitchen boys pulled out Guenes's hair and his whiskers. They fastened a peg and chain about his neck, the sort a bear wears. Then they hoisted him on a pack animal and beat him with switches and sticks.

[V. 1830] High are the hills and shadowy and dark, the valleys deep and the torrents swift! Rollanz looked over his shoulder toward the mountain peaks and then at the dead lords of France who lay at his feet. "I saw you lay your sweet lives down for me, and yet I could not save you. May God bear you all to Paradise. May he rest your gallant souls in sainted flowers! Greater barons than you have I never seen." Then Rollanz returned to battle, so terrible and so swift that the archbishop gasped to see him drive the heathen like packs of yelping dogs before him.

"That's what a true knight should be," thought Turpins, "either strong and proud like Rollanz, or else I wouldn't give four cents for him. Either let him be like Rollanz, or let him go to a monastery and pray for our sins." Rollanz gave no quarter that day and took no prisoners. Through the thick of battle he spied the King of Saragossa. "May God damn you!" cried Rollanz as he struck off King Marsilie's right hand. Then he cut off his prince's head. At that one hundred thousand pagans, screaming to Mohammed for aid, fled from the field of battle . . .

Call them, as you will! They will not return!

Then Marsilie's uncle, a king who held lands all the way from Carthage to Ethiopia, led his troops against the Franks. His warriors were black and fierce; only their teeth showed white under their helms. When Rollanz saw them coming, he knew that he was lost. They were gallant, those men! Rallying the few remaining Franks, however, Rollanz plunged dauntlessly into their midst. As the African king rode past on his sorrel, he struck Oliviers a deathblow in the back. Before he fell, however, Oliviers turned and killed that king. "You shall never go brag to some lady how you killed Oliviers," he cried. Then he summoned Rollanz, for he knew he soon would die.

Hurrying to Oliviers' side, Rollanz scanned his friend's face sadly. Oliviers' cheeks were already pale and bloodless. Great clots of blood dripped from his body to the ground. Rollanz' eyes blurred, and his head swam at the sight. Oliviers did not even recognize Rollanz. Thinking he was an enemy knight, Oliviers swung his sword at him and dented his helmet. When Rollanz spoke, then Oliviers came to his senses, knew the voice, and asked forgiveness. "I have no injury, Oliviers," said Rollanz gently. "I pardon you here and before God." Then each knight bowed to the other. So did Rollanz and Oliviers part in their lifetimes.

"Sir Companion," murmured Rollanz in farewell, "what a pity for one so brave! Together have we two been both in years and in days. When you are dead, it is pain for me to live!" In his grief Rollanz would have fallen from the saddle if his golden spurs had not held him upright.

There were only three French barons left alive. One was Gualter of Hum, who had fought all day on the mountains. Now, a sole survivor, he rode down to the plain toward Rollanz. "Where are you, gentle Count? Where are you, Rollanz? I was never afraid when I could fight beside you!" Side by side, Rollanz, Gualter, and the Archbishop Turpins of Rheims faced the Sarrazin host. None of them would abandon the others. Forty thousand mounted Sarrazins face them, and one thousand on foot. No pagan stirs a foot to meet them. Instead, they shower volleys of spears, lances, arrows, and darts; Gualter falls. The archbishop's horse falls. The archbishop's body is pierced through with four spears!

Yet the gallant archbishop still struggled to his feet. His eyes sought Rollanz. He gasped, "I am not defeated! I do not surrender!" Then the huge Turpins advanced boldly toward the enemy, swinging his sword about his head in a frenzy of anger and will to defy them. The Book says he injured four hundred more, and so says the eyewitness, the Baron Gilie who built the monastery at Laon. Anyone who doesn't know this, understands nothing about History!

Count Rollanz stood alone. He trembled from fatigue, from the heat of battle, and from his bursting temples. He still did not know whether or not Carlemagne had heard his call. He tried once more to sound the horn, but his strength was almost gone. Even so, the emperor heard the feeble notes. "Sirs!" called King Carles. "That was my nephew's last breath! I can tell by the sound that he is near death! Ride on, whoever wishes to see him yet alive! Sound all our horns at once!" Then sixty thousand trumpets blared full-tongued through the hills and echoing vales.

On the plain of Roncevals the pagans stopped to hear that blast. "Carles will soon be upon us! Then there will be havoc. If Rollanz lives one hour more, we are lost and so is Spain." Then four hundred banded together and advanced toward Turpins and Rollanz.

Count Rollanz of France, nephew of the king, drew himself up cold and haughty. He clenched his teeth and waited. He would never retreat an inch while breath stayed in his lungs. "I am on horseback while you have lost your mount," said Rollanz to the archbishop. "Therefore let Durendal bear the brunt. Know only that I am beside you, whatever happens."

Turpins laughed and answered stanchly, "He is a felon who will still not strike them hard! Carles is coming. He will avenge us."

The four hundred Sarrazins stood face to face with Rollanz. Not a man of them dared attack, and yet there was not a moment to lose. Even then they could hear the advance body of the Franks thundering down the mountain. The blaring war cry "Mountjoy" floated to their ears. Instead of rushing the two French barons, the Sarrazins let fly another volley of spears, arrows, lances, and beribboned darts. Then they turned tail and fled for their lives across the field.

Rollanz stood alone on the field of battle. His armor, his helmet, his mail were pierced and shattered. His valiant war horse Veillantif was dead of thirty wounds. Rollanz turned to the archbishop. As gently as he could, he lifted off his armor and stanched his wounds. Then raising the prelate in his arms, Rollanz laid him on thick grass. "Take leave of me, gentle sir," pleaded Rollanz. "All our friends and companions, all are dead. I shall go and carry their bodies here before you. I shall lay them in a row here on the sod."

Still the archbishop lived and so did his great heart. "Go and return, Rollanz. This field is ours, thank God—yours and mine!"

Rollanz walked across the battlefield. He searched through the vales and he searched through the hills. First he found Sir Gerin and Sir Gerier, then Sir Berengier, Sir Anseïs, and Sir Sansun. Then he found the body of that great hero Sir Gerard of Rusillun. These he laid at the archbishop's feet so that they could be blessed. Then Rollanz sought and found his dear friend, Sir Oliviers the Wise. As he carried Oliviers in his arms, Rollanz spoke soft words to his friend, and wept. After he had laid Oliviers on the earth, Rollanz could endure no more. His face became drained and white. He sank to the ground.

"How I pity you, Baron," said the Archbishop Turpins. The compassion he felt for Rollanz was the sharpest pain he had felt all that day. Unsteadily the worthy prelate rose to his feet. He wanted to bring water for Rollanz from the little stream that flows at Roncevals, but he had lost too much blood. Before he had traversed the length of an acre, his heart faltered and stopped beating. The throes of death gripped him. He fell forward on the grass.

As Rollanz struggled to regain consciousness, he saw the archbishop join his hands and raise them to the heavens imploring God to give him Paradise. Then his head fell, and he died. Through many great battles, and many fine sermons, he had campaigned all his life against the pagans. May God grant him his sainted benediction! AOI

Rollanz was alone. Sensing that his own death was near, he prayed for the archbishop. He saw how he lay, his beautiful white hands crossed on his breast. "Ah, gentle man, knight of illustrious ancestry, I recommend thee today to the celestial Glory. Never will any man do more willingly Your service. Nor has any prophet equaled thee since the Apostles in keeping the faith and attracting men to it. May your soul suffer no hardship. May the gate of Paradise be open when you come."

Rollanz feels death very close. His brains bubble out through his ears. His every thought is a prayer to God to summon to Him the dead peers of France. He prays to the Angel Gabriel, who is near. Then

taking his ivory war horn in one hand, and his sword Durendal in the other, Rollanz walks in the direction of Spain toward a hill where there are four marble steps. There he falls over backward on the green turf.

High are the peaks and very tall the trees. Four marble steps there were shimmering and white. On the bright green grass Count Rollanz falls fainting. Now a Sarrazin, who had smeared his face and body with blood, pretending to be dead among the dead, had all this time been watching Rollanz. As soon as he sees the count lying alone, the heathen in his pride and folly rushes over to him. He tugs at Durendal. Rollanz feels his hands and recovers his strength long enough to strike one last blow with his war horn, so true that the pagan's brains come oozing out his eye sockets.

Rollanz' one thought is for his sword. He cannot risk its falling into enemy hands. Ten times he brings the steel blade down upon a rock, but in vain. It neither blunts nor breaks. "Holy Mother, help me! Ah, Durendal! How sad I am for you. With you in my hand how many lands, how many kingdoms have I subdued that Carles of the curly white beard now holds in sway! You must never fall into the grasp of a man who would flee before the foe!" Even though he strikes the blade full against brown chalcedony, it neither shivers nor cracks!

Rollanz gazes at the twinkling sword, murmuring to himself, "Ah, Durendal, how beautiful you are, how you shine, how white you shine! How against the sun you gleam and return fire for fire! How well I remember that day God commanded Carlemagne to bestow you upon a count and captain. Then gave he you to me, King Carles the Great. Together we have conquered Anjou and Brittany. Together we have won Poitou and Maine, and fair Normandie, Provence and Aquitaine, Lombardy and Romagna, Bavaria and Flanders, and even Burgundy! Together we have won Constantinople and Poland. Saxony. Scotland. England. All these lands does Carles hold, who has the whitest beard. For you, Durendal, I feel such heavy grief. May France never have to say that you are in pagan hands!"

Desperately Rollanz strikes the brown rock with all his power and might. The sword neither splinters nor breaks, only bounces away from the rock. Rollanz speaks to it again, "Ah! Durendal, how lovely and how holy art thou! Thy hilt holds the most holy relics: Saint Peter's tooth, Saint Basil's blood, Saint Denis's hair, and a precious remnant from Saint Mary's own robe. No pagan must ever lord it with you! I pray that a coward's hand may never defile you! By your aid I have conquered so many fair lands!"

Now Rollanz feels that death, stealing its way from head to heart, creeps over his whole body. He runs toward a tall pine tree, where he falls face downward on the ground, his sword and horn safely under his body, his face pointing toward the enemy. He confesses his sins. In atonement he holds out his gauntlet toward God. "*Mea culpa. Mea culpa.* Forgive me my sins, the great and the small, throughout my

299

FRANCE: THE SONG OF ROLAND

life from birth to death." Again he offers his right gauntlet to God. . . . The angels from heaven hover softly over him. AOI

Count Rollanz of France lies under a pine tree. Toward Spain he has turned his sweet face. All his memories surge through his mind—how many lands he has won, his beloved France, the strong men of his lineage, his liege lord, and King Carles who raised him and fed him from childhood at his own table.

"True Father, Thou who never lied, Thou who called back Lazarun from the dead, Thou who saved Daniel from the lions, guard my soul from perdition despite the sins of my life." Rollanz holds forth his right glove to God. . . . It is Saint Gabriel himself who stoops and takes the glove from the hand of Rollanz. Then, and only then, Rollanz drops his weary head to his arm. Hands joined, he goes to his end. God sends his angel cherubim. He also sends Saint Michael-of-the-Peril. With them comes Saint Gabriel. Together they bear the soul of Rollanz to Paradise.

[V. 2397]   Rollanz is dead. God has his soul in Heaven. . . . Now the emperor reaches Roncevals. There is not a road or a path, not an ell or an inch of ground where does not lie a Frenchman or a pagan. Carles cried aloud, "Where are you, my fine nephew? Where is the Archbishop? Where is the Count Oliviers? Where is Gerin, and Gerier, and Berengier, the Gascon Engelers, Duke Sansun, the worthy Anseïs, and that great hero, Gerard de Rusillun the Old? Where are my Twelve Peers of France whom I left at the pass? No matter how I call, will no voice answer mine? Answer me! . . . How greatly am I dismayed that I was not here when this battle commenced!" King Carles tears at his beard, so appalled is he. His twenty thousand Franks kneel upon the sod and weep.

Upon the field of Roncevals the Frankish army weeps. They mourn aloud their sons, their brothers, and their nephews. They weep for dear friends and honored liege lords. Then Duke Naimes first of all speaks to Carlemagne. "Sire, lift your head. Do you see that cloud of dust not two leagues away? That's the pagan host retreating! Let us first avenge our grief."

"That far away already?" mused King Carles of France. "Grant us this grace, O God. These men have stripped from me the gentlest flowers of France." Then Carles summons four knights, "Guard this field of combat, with its hills and its vales. Let these dead be, exactly as they lie. Let neither beast nor lion come near them. Let neither squire nor servant lay a finger on these dead! Let no man touch a one of them until God lets me return." A thousand knights patrolled and mounted guard.

Bugles sounded. Ranks formed. Carles rode to the head of the columns and signaled them to ride. He set a hard pace against the

Sarrazins' backs. Not until vespers did the army slacken speed. Then the king dismounted in a meadow to pray. He knelt and touched his forehead to the earth. There he asked *his* Sovereign Lord to hold back the night, to stretch out the day. Then came to Carles that angel who communed with him and directed his prayers. The angel's words were rapid and clear: "Carles, mount. The daylight shall not lack. God knows you have just lost the finest flower of France. Vengeance is yours today upon these criminals." The emperor set out at once. AOI

For Carles the king, God made a mighty show. He held back the sun, as it was. Less than two leagues ahead the pagan host rode hard. Carlemagne followed harder. Mile after mile the Franks closed the gap. In the Valley of the Shadow (*Val Tenebrus*) the Franks caught up with the Sarrazins. With bursting hearts they wielded swords and axes upon their backs. Detachments forged a circular path ahead on either side and barred the main road and the paths to the south. The pagans were trapped with the dark waters of the Ebro River behind them. The stream was deep and marvelously swift; there was neither barge nor ferry nor warship standing by with ready oar. The pagans called upon their god Tervagant to help them. Then they plunged into the Ebro.

No god helped them. Those who wore rich armor and mail sank first, swifter than rocks to the bottom. Others floated downstream, gulping great draughts of river water before they drowned in agony. The Franks lined the riverbank and cried aloud, "Ah, Rollanz, what grief we feel for you!"

As soon as Carles was certain that not a pagan lived, that all had perished either by sword or by water, he dismounted and like a noble king lay on the ground to thank God. His men looked about them. They were astonished at the amount of riches that strewed the field. By the time Carles had finished his devotions, the sun had set! He spoke then to his knights, "Let us find shelter here for the night. It is too late to return today to Roncevals. Our horses are weary and worn. Unloose their girths, lift off the saddles, and unfasten their golden bridles. Let them graze in these fields."

"Sire, you speak well," answered the knights.

The emperor took lodging there by the Ebro waters. His Franks dismounted in that wasteland, lifted off the ornate saddles, and slipped the bridles from their horses' heads. Then they turned the animals loose to pasture. They could give them no more attention than that. The knights were so tired that they slept there on the ground. Not even a guard was set on their camp.

The emperor also slept in that meadow, his boar spear close to his head. He would not even disarm. He slept in his white hauberk, his jeweled helmet still tightly laced and his massive sword Joyous cinched to his belt. The great sword of Carlemagne lay in beauty, it that changed colors thirty times a day. In its pommel lay encased the point of the lance which had pierced Our Lord on the Cross. Because of the treasure it enclosed, the sword of Carles was called Joyous. It was this joy that the Franks were remembering when they called their battle cry, "Mountjoy!" This is the reason that no people can stand against them.

Clear is the night and the moon glimmering. Carles lies on the ground grieving for his nephew Rollanz. His heart is heavy too for Oliviers, for the Twelve Peers of France, and for the French knights whom he has left dead and blood-smeared on the field of Roncevals. He cannot change his nature; therefore he weeps for them and laments. He begs God to guarantee their salvation. The weight of his affliction wears him so sorely that he finally falls asleep. Even the horses have lain down. Those that have the strength to eat, champ the grass where they lie. *Mult ad apris ki bien conuist ahan*—that man has learned much who has known agony deeply.

Carles sleeps like a man in travail. Then God sends Saint Gabriel to watch over the emperor. All night long the angel stands close by his head. He sends Carles a dream of a great battle he will fight, and of the deaths he will still see. Then in his dream Carlemagne sees mighty cold winds and frosts, storms and marvelous huge tempests, and a monstrous wall of fire and flame that engulfs his whole army. As the ash and apple-wood spears catch fire in the hands of the men, Carles groans. Then the bucklers catch fire up to their golden hasps. The boar-spear shafts explode! The steel and mail and helmets curl and buckle in the flames. Carles sees his knights in torment.

Then the scene changes. Bears and ravenous leopards leap out of the woods and devour the Franks. Serpents and fabled vipers, dragons and demons come to feed on the bodies! More than thirty thousand winged griffins swoop down upon the host! Carles's Franks cry out to him frantically, "Carlemagne! Help us! Help!" The king, though wracked with grief and anxious to go to their aid, is hindered. Finally from a wood lumbers a huge lion, enraged, lordly, treacherous, dauntless. It leaps upon the emperor himself! They fall to the ground, struggle, tumble, fight. Carles cannot tell which one is uppermost. . . . Even through this dream Carles does not awaken.

Then the scene changes. In his next dream Carles is in his castle at Aix. There he sees before him a bear held by two chains. All of a sudden, from the forest of Ardennes he sees thirty bears burst! They seem to speak in the language of men, for Carles hears them say to him, "Sire! Give him back to us! It is not just to keep him any longer! He is our relative. He deserves our succor!" Even as the bears grow angry and threaten, a greyhound runs down the palace steps toward them, darts between the chained bear and his relatives. It leaps for the chained bear's throat. The two fight furiously, but Carles cannot tell which one is vanquished. . . . All these presages the angel of God shows the noble king. Then Carles sleeps dreamlessly until the broad daylight.

[V. 2845] The next morning at the very break of day Carlemagne awakens. Saint Gabriel, who has watched him all the night, makes his sign over the king's head. Carles stands up. His first act is to lay down his weapons and to divest himself of his armor. All the Franks watch him and do likewise. Then they mount their horses and return by high road and byroad to Roncevals. They are going to see by morning light the terrible damage there where the battle was. AOI

When Carles finally comes to Roncevals itself, he can no longer refrain from tears. Holding up his gauntlet, he stops the troops behind him. Then he turns in the saddle and tells them, "Sirs, advance at a walk, for I myself must go ahead of you, especially now. I should like to find my nephew's body first. I remember one day at Aix there was a splendid feast day. My knights were boasting of their chivalry, of their great battles, and of the escarpments they had stormed. Then I overheard my young nephew Rollanz talking. Rollanz said, 'If ever I trespass, if ever I die in a strange land you will know where to find me. You will find me lying farther into enemy territory than any other man in our ranks. You will find me lying in death with my face turned not away, but full toward our foes. Thus in the very act of conquering, I swear I shall die like a baron.' "

The emperor of the Franks walked his horse forward, not much farther than one could throw a stick. He climbed a mound. The flowers of the field between his horse's feet were every one stained with scarlet blood. Tears ran down the old king's cheeks. He rode slowly along until he came to two trees. There he saw on the brown stone the cuts from Rollanz' sword. There he saw stretched in death upon the greensward his nephew Rollanz.

A shudder ran over the king. He dismounted and ran toward his nephew. In his two hands he held the knight's body and rocked back and forth in bitter convulsions of grief. When his sobs had begun to subside, Duke Naimes, Count Acelin, Geoffrey of Anjou, and his brother Tierri lifted the king from the body and bore him under a pine tree. From there Carles looked down upon his boy and said to him softly, "My friend, my Rollanz, God have mercy on thee! For no man ever saw a knight like thee joust and tilt so nobly in such awful wars. *La meie honor est turnet en declin*—my honor is turned to its decline."

The four knights clasped the old king's hands. Again he spoke to Rollanz, "My friend, my Rollanz, may God put thy soul in flowers, in Paradise, among the glorious! Not a day shall henceforth dawn but I shall suffer because of thee. No one now will uphold my honor. I have not a friend left on this earth. Relatives perhaps, but none noble like thee.

"My friend, my Rollanz, I shall go from here to France. When I am in my own estates at Laon, foreign vassals will inquire, 'Where is your count, the Captain?' I shall have to answer that he died in Spain.

"My friend, my Rollanz, valorous and beautiful knight, when I am at Aix in my Chapel (Aix-la-Chapelle), men will come to me asking for news of thee. Then I shall have to say to them, 'Dead is that youth who conquered so many domains for me.' Then will rise up the Saxons, the Hungarians, the Rumanians, the Bulgars, the Poles, the Italians, the Africans, and those of Californe . . . I wish that I were dead."

Geoffrey of Anjou said to the king, "Do you not, Sire, abandon yourself entirely to your grief. Let us seek our knights, our priests, our abbots, and our bishops, and let us inter them honorably according to our rites."

Carles stood by as the bodies of Rollanz, Oliviers, and the Archbishop Turpins were opened, their hearts wrapped in silk, and their bodies enfolded in deerhides. He ordered them placed on three carts and draped in silk gauze.

He had hardly taken these dispositions when messengers from Saragossa announced the approach of the Sarrazin reinforcements from Arabia. Carles turned toward them and pursued the war.

[V. 2980]

THE VENGEANCE OF CHARLEMAGNE

(v. 3633)   White is the heat and high the clouds of dust. The pagans are in flight, and the Franks press them hard. The chase lasts right to the gates of Saragossa.

To the highest tower of the palace Brandimonie, wife of King Marsilie of Saragossa, has climbed. With her are her scholars and her canons of the false faith, those who are neither tonsured nor ordained. When Brandimonie sees the Arabian forces so confounded, she screams aloud, "Mohammed, help us! Ah, gentle Marsilie, they are vanquished, our men! Our emir has been killed, to our great sorrow. And you have been wounded by Rollanz, to our great shame!" Upon hearing her wild words Marsilie turned his face to the wall. He shed tears, his face clouded over, and he died of sorrow. Loaded as he was with sin, he gave up his soul to living devils.

The pagans are finally dead, and King Carles has won the war. First he orders the portals of Saragossa to be burst wide open. He knows perfectly well that it will not be defended. He takes possession of the city. His troops file through its streets and find lodging for the night. Proud is King Carles of the flowerlike white beard. From Queen Brandimonie herself Carlemagne receives the towers and the dungeons, the ten large and fifty small ones. He whom God aids can carry out his plans.

That day passes, and the night is full of stars. The emperor of the Franks has captured Saragossa! By orders of the king, the pagan idols are destroyed so that neither evil nor sorcery can work any more harm. The bishops bless the waters and convert the heathen. If any man protests, he is burned or put to the sword. More than one hundred thousand listen to exhortations and accept the faith. Carles makes exception for the Queen Brandimonie. She will be carried captive back to France. Carles wishes her to be converted also, but through love.

Swiftly sped the night, and dawned a cloudless day. Carles left one thousand trusty, proven knights to rule the city in his name. He garrisoned its towers. Then mounting at the head of his troops, taking beside him Brandimonie—to whom he only wished well—Carles set out happy and joyous. On the way home he seized Narbonne and passed by. Then he came to Bordeaux where he left in the Church of Saint Seurin the ivory war horn which pilgrims go to see even today. He crossed the Gironde on great ships. He bore his nephew's body, that of his highborn friend and companion Sir Oliviers, and that of the Archbishop Turpins to the Church of Saint Romain at Blaye. In white sarcophagi he laid them to rest, the valorous barons. Then over mountain and down dale he journeyed without stopping to his own city of Aix.

As soon as Carles arrives in his capital, he orders the presence of ponderous and learned judges from all parts of his empire. He requests the instant attendance of ambassadors, both authoritative and wise, from Bavaria, from Saxony, from Lorraine, from Friesland, from Germany, from Burgundy, from Poitou, from Normandy, from Brittany, and from France (they are the wisest). Then he declares in session (October 16) the court that will sit in judgment upon Guenes.

[V. 3705] The Emperor Carles has returned home from Spain; he has made his way to Aix, the chief seat of his empire. He climbs the degrees to his throne, where he sits in regal state. Then hastens to his presence the lovely damsel Alde. "Where," Alde asks the king, "where is Rollanz, our noble captain? Where is he who swore to take me as his wife?"

Tears came to Carles's eyes. Averting his eyes, he pulls at his long, white beard. "Sister, dear young friend, after whom do you inquire?"

"Rollanz."

"Do you seek from me a dead man? My nephew Rollanz died in Spain. I will grant your suit, however, in the person of my son Louis. I can do no more than that for you, dear lady. Accept my son and heir Louis, a count of the marches."

Alde replied to Carles in swift, breathless words, "Your answer rings strangely in my ears, O King. May it please God. May it please the Saints. May it please the angels in heaven that after Rollanz, I do not remain in this world at all. . . ." Color drained from Alde's cheeks, and she slipped to the marble floor at the king's feet. She was already dead, this promised wife of Rollanz. God have mercy on her soul.

Carles the king did not know that the damsel had died. He thinks she only swooned. He is so sorry for the pretty maiden that he weeps. He rises from the throne and chafes her hands. Then he lifts her in his arms. Only when her head droops on his shoulder does he realize that she is dead. Carles summons four countesses. He orders the maiden's slender body borne to a minister, laid in state by an altar, and waked by nuns. He has Alde buried there. He can do no more to honor this maiden.

The emperor Carles has returned to Aix from his seven-year campaign in Spain. The felon Guenes, attached to a stake, has been brought before the palace. Serfs have tied his hands with deerhide thongs; they beat him with sticks and switches. Guenes has not merited better treatment. There the traitor awaits the commencement of his trial. As the Book of Deeds records, Carles has summoned his leading vassals who have convened in the Chapel at Aix. It is the high feast day of that great baron of France, Saint Silvestre. On that day begins the judgment to which the traitor Guenes has been carted.

"Sir Barons," says Carlemagne the king, "judge me the case of Guenes. He was in my host all the way to Spain. He stripped from me twenty thousand of my Frankish warriors and my own nephew whom your eyes shall never more behold. He caused the death of Sir Oliviers, the chivalrous, the courageous. He betrayed my Twelve Peers for goods and for gold."

"Felon indeed," shouted Guenes defiantly, "if I hide that fact! Rollanz did me wrong both in goods and in gold. It was for that I sought his death and his distress. But treason, no! That did I never do!"

Answer the Franks, "We will take it under advisement."

Before Carles the king stands Guenes on his feet. He is a strapping fellow with a high-colored face. If he were only loyal, you would call him a noble man. He holds the gaze of all Franks and of his judges. Thirty of his family have come to be with him. Then Guenes shouts loudly, in a very deep voice, "Sirs, I was in the host when the emperor whom I serve still with fidelity and love received hostages from Marsilie of Saragossa. We all suspected the Sarrazin was lying. Carles asked for a messenger from among us to send into Spain, into almost certain death, since our previous heralds had been slain. His nephew Rollanz proposed me for the post. I went, since I was so named and commanded; and I managed to survive. Before all the host I openly swore vengeance upon Rollanz. I got my revenge, but there was no treason in that!"

Answer the Franks, "We shall see."

Guenes understands that upon their decision hangs his life. Thirty of his relatives are there, but one among them is most reliable and influential. This is the knight Pinabel who knows not only how to plead well but also how to compose an excellent brief. Pinabel, in addition, is courageous. He handles weapons extremely well. Guenes tells him, "Friend, get me off. Get me out of here, out of death and calumny!"

Pinabel reassures Guenes, "You will certainly be saved. If any French baron here present casts his vote for your death, rather than see you hanged, I shall meet him sword to sword, my body for yours. In such a trial I shall demonstrate your innocence. Never fear." Guenes bows low to Pinabel.

Judges from all the territories of the Carolingian Empire debate what they are to do, and lower their voices when Pinabel is present. They are finally unanimous in their verdict, all except the young Count Tierri. This count and his brother Geoffrey of Anjou had lifted the body of Rollanz on the field of Roncevals. Tierri voted for the death of Guenes.

The judges advance to Carles, saying, "Sire, we beg you to call it quits with Count Guenes who will henceforward serve you in all good faith and honor. Leave him his life, for he is a very gentle man. You cannot have back Rollanz, not for lands or for gold."

The king replies, "You are felons!" When Carles sees that they have all failed him, his heart and brow grow sad.

Then steps before the king the younger brother of Geoffrey of Anjou, the youngster Tierri. He is a slender youth and not very tall. His skin is dark and his hair very black. He says courteously to Carlemagne, "Sire, great King, do not lose your spirits so. You know how long and how willingly I have served you. According to the tradition of my ancestors I am bound personally to uphold your accusation before this court. No matter what the forfeits of Rollanz to Guenes may have been, Count Rollanz acted in your service, which should therefore have guaranteed his safety. Guenes, in so betraying Rollanz to his death, broke both his feudal oath and our laws. Let him therefore be viewed and treated as a perjurer. If he has a champion from among his family, let that man advance with his sword against mine, let us put the innocence of Guenes here to trial again before this court and our king. Accordingly, I also claim my right. I ask to challenge Guenes."

Answer the Franks, "You have spoken well."

Then strides before the king the tall, strong Pinabel. He is a valorous baron. He says, "Sir King, this court has convened at your insistence to judge your accusation. Let this affair make less stir. I see before me Tierri, and I hear his request. I cancel his vote, and herewith ask to fight him." Pinabel strips off his right gauntlet of deer hide and hands it to the king.

Carles says, "I require now a guarantee. Who will give his word and bond for this man?" The thirty relatives of Guenes step forward.

"I shall set you at liberty on your oaths," announces Carles. Then he assigns guards to watch them. When Tierri sees that there will be a trial by conflict, he also presents his right gauntlet to Carles and gives bondsmen who are placed under like surveillance.

The king orders four benches to be set up before the palace, and there the challengers and their bondsmen to sit. In due procedure and plain sight of all, the quarrel is provoked. The great hero, Ogier of Denmark, bears the challenges from each to the other. The knights ask for horses and arms. When they are dressed, they each confess and are absolved. Each one makes generous bequests to the ministers of his preference. Both bow before the king. They wear spurs, white hauberks, gleaming helmets, and shields with coat of arms. Their swords are sheathed. Their boar spears are ready. Then each is raised to the saddle of his war horse. One hundred thousand knights weep for love of Rollanz and pity for young Tierri. What the outcome will be, only God knows.

Before the palace at Aix, the meadow is very wide. There the two knights meet to render justice. They are both great vassals and both of them valorous. Each one mounts a horse that is savage and aggressive. Both knights spur forward, slackening the reins. Each one strikes the other with all his strength and might. At the first well-aimed blow the shields are shivered, the hauberks split open, the girths broken, the cantles turned, and the saddles thrown to the ground. The spectators weep to behold this awful sight.

Both knights fall heavily to the ground. Quickly both rise to their feet, however. Pinabel is much swifter, lighter-footed, and more agile. Each one looks about for the other. Their horses are gone. They unsheathe their swords with golden hilts and strike great ringing blows at each other's heads. Both helmets are crushed and pierced. The Franks who watch moan aloud. "Oh, God," says Carlemagne, "may the right triumph!"

Pinabel speaks first. "Tierri, call off the fight. I will be your vassal in all love and faith. At your pleasure I will give you my wealth. Only let Guenes be reconciled with the king."

Tierri answers, "I take no thought of what you propose. May I be dishonored if I consent to such a thing! Between us two today must God *show* who is right. You, Pinabel, are chivalrous, strong, and brave. This I know. Your body is well molded. The peers hold you as a peer among them. Therefore do you break off this combat. Such Justice will be done to Guenes as men will remember every day of their lives from now forward."

"May God not so please," replies Pinabel. "It is my duty to uphold my family. I will never unsay myself for any man alive. I prefer death to dishonor."

Then they renew their struggle so violently that sparks fly from their swords. No man can come between them. They are fighting to the death. Pinabel of Sorence is of very great valor. On his helmet from Provence he strikes Tierri so hard that sparks land in the grass and set fire to it. He thrusts the point of his sword in Tierri's face so fiercely that he cuts a gash the length of the young knight's cheek. He slits open Tierri's hauberk down to the belly.

Tierri feels the hot blood running down his face. He sees it dripping into the grass. Then he strikes Pinabel a blow that severs the nosepiece from his helmet and lets the sword pierce his skull. Tierri stirs the blade about in the brain and so kills the valiant Pinabel. The Franks cry loudly, "It is a sign from God! Let Guenes be hanged and also his relatives who answered for his good faith!"

Carles, accompanied by four of his greatest knights—Duke Naimes, Ogier of Denmark, Geoffrey of Anjou, and Guillaume of Blaye—strides to Tierri and enfolds him in his arms. With his own sable tippet Carles wipes the blood from Tierri's face. Squires hasten to disarm Tierri gently. Then they place him upon an Arabian mule and lead him among great shouting to the palace.

Again Carles sits in session with his judges, of whom he enquires, "What is your will for those I hold in bond? They came to swear for Guenes."

Answer the Franks, "Not one of them has the right to live."

Carles orders all of Guenes's relatives strung up on the hangman's tree. One hundred sergeants carry out this sentence promptly. The man who betrays, kills others along with himself.

The court then turns its attention to Guenes. Their verdict is that he should die in the most excruciating agony. Four horses are brought. Guenes is tied to each one by his hands and feet. Then four sergeants whip up the horses, driving them toward a stream. Guenes dies, indeed, in great pain. When a man betrays another, it is not right that he live to brag of it.

Then Carles asks the court its pleasure concerning the captive Queen Brandimonie. "I have in my palace a noble lady prisoner. She has heard so many sermons that she desires to be baptized."

Answer the Franks, "Let godmothers be found. Receive her into the church." They rechristened her Juliane. Then the judges were dismissed.

Carlemagne retires to sleep in his high-vaulted chamber. As he rests, Saint Gabriel descends to him, saying, "Carles, arise! Call up your army! Christianity needs you and cries aloud for you!"

Carles did not want to rise. "O God," prayed the king, "you see how painful is my life!" Then he pulled at his long, white beard and wept.

CI FALT LA GESTE QUE TURDOLDUS DECLINET.[1]

[V. 4002]

---

[1] This is the last line of the Oxford manuscript. It is highly controversial. It seems to say, "Here ends the Deeds [poem] that Turold recites [or composes, or writes]."

ELEVEN
FRANCE
BERTA OF
HUNGARY

The word "minstrel" and the special function of that medieval person who was so closely allied to three art spheres—poetry, music, and drama—are well known. It is unusual, however, to read and to know a composition actually written by a minstrel; very few such compositions have come down the centuries to us. The following story was written by a Belgian minstrel who has also left us three other poems. His name was Adenes li Rois—Little Adam, King of Minstrels. Although his tale—it is neither a true epic nor a true romance, but halfway between the two—is usually classified with the Charlemagne cycle, it is not particularly historical so far as one can say. The Queen Berta about whom the story revolves died in 783. Our poem of 3,482 verses dates from about 1270.

In the *Roland* epic we have had a view of medieval life from an aristocratic level. That author, learned, pious, conversant with the attitudes and manners of the great nobles, looks *down* into only one level of medieval culture and seems to know well only one area of northern France, such as that near the Mont-Saint-Michel, a new church in his day,—only about 350 years old. Adenes li Rois, on the other hand, looks *up* toward the nobility from his humble station and birth. He therefore brings constantly into what he writes a social awareness of the people around him—the peasant, the citizen of Paris, even the coal miner—which is new in literature. Medieval romances and their descendants, our novels, will continue to present and later to plead for social reform and for justice.

Just as scholars compute that the *Roland* must have been composed between the conquest of England (1066) and the capture of Jerusalem by the Crusaders (1099), so one can say also from internal evidence that Adenes wrote during the Crusades and at a time not too distant from the discovery of the New World. The reader will note that our celebrated minstrel was a man of the world, that he knew women and understood well their intimate fears, that he traveled, and that he took real joy and pride in his artist's eye for the evocative image.

His technical skill is wonderful! He chooses a rhyme and then ends every verse on it, sometimes for pages at a time without exhausting his store of words. One can easily see how such a talented man must have been as loved by medieval lords and ladies as our own actors are cherished by millions of us today. One thinks of Adenes li Rois adding a new poem to his repertoire and then delighting audiences in Brabant and France with it. A good word for such an artist is "virtuoso."

Not only is his poem different from the *Roland* in tone and viewpoint; it also differs in subject matter. Great forests, already noticed and described by Julius Caesar, stretched across northern and central Europe. Small groups of people lived in scattered towns where they were not safe from plagues and wars. One feels the dread of the forest in the *Berta* poem, similar to the dread the early settlers in America felt after they had crossed the Ohio River and plunged into "the trees," to use the term of the novelist Conrad Richter.

The sort of story Adenes tells will give encouragement to thousands of fairy tales throughout Europe. In France it will be followed by "Sleeping Beauty" and "Rose Red and Snow White," which seem so close to our story. Similarly, its themes—known to both high and low—will be repeated in other languages than French. There is a medieval students' song that comes to mind in connection with the Princess Berta:

> *Rosa rubicundior*
> *Lilio candidior*
> *Omnibus formosior;*
> *Semper in te glorior!*

(Redder than a rose, whiter than a lily, shapelier than all others; I'm always delighting in [or boasting about] you!)

The reader will see many of our previous symbols as well as new ones understandable and familiar to us because of Freudian studies. One which will gain in importance is the *rose*. Certain scholars of ancient history and architecture—and a comparison of myths seems to corroborate this opinion—believe that the rose was imported by the Crusaders from Persia. One realizes the significance of this symbol in the cult of the Virgin, which is coming into prominence as Adenes writes. Along with this emphasis upon the Virgin we shall see in France an emphasis upon women and the code of chivalry which they in large part designed. The rose windows at Chartres and Notre Dame de Paris are ample evidence of the importance of this symbol. Our poem further testifies to this trend by the emphasis upon the relationship between Berta and her mother.

The king and queen of Hungary, Berta's parents, are themselves the subject of a very beautiful medieval poem.

In reading this text the English-speaking person feels very close to that superb poet who above all others has taught us to be at home in a medieval setting, he who may also have read before us the *Berta* poem— Geoffrey Chaucer.

BERTA OF HUNGARY

Toward the end of April, on the kind of day which is soft and warm, when the green grass has sprung up all over the meadows and every little tree is longing to be crowned with flowers, I thought one Friday morning I would take a trip to Paris. I wanted to say prayers of thanksgiving in the Church of Saint Denis.

It was there that I became acquainted with a monk named Savary who, as we got talking, invited me to his library. He very kindly showed me a storybook which he allowed me to read. I was so fascinated that I stayed there reading a certain tale until the following Tuesday; and here that story is—not misunderstood as some apprentice minstrel or unskilled writer would tell it, but so rhymed and so truly recounted that the uninitiate will be amazed and the sophisticated reader delighted.

At that time when my story begins, there was in France a royal king named Charles Martel who had accomplished many deeds worthy of renown, such as: enemies overthrown, hauberks slit, peace assured. The king had two sons. Both were with him in Paris about Saint John's Day when roses are in bloom. The older, named Carlemans, had already been dubbed knight for about four years; he later took holy vows and retired to an abbey. The second son was named Pepin.

Pepin was little, only five feet six inches tall, but daring! One time the king his father and the court were dining in the garden when a fierce lion belonging to a Norman gentleman escaped from his cage, killed two attendant nobles, and forced King Charles and the queen to retire. Pepin rushed inside for a sword. In a twinkling he had faced the beast—not only faced him, actually killed him!

"Beautiful boy and very sweet son," his mother said to Pepin, "how could you even think of approaching such a hideous creature?"

"Lady," he answered, "when one is destined for kingship, one must not doubt one's powers to avert danger!"

Now Pepin was only twenty years old at the time! I'm sorry. I didn't mean to digress. I know you haven't all day to sit about and listen. . . . Well, Charles Martel passed away, so did his fair-faced queen, and

Pepin was crowned as the legitimate heir of France. He fought many wars, tumbled many a castle, and married a noble lady. However, he could not get an heir from her no matter how often they slept together. Finally she passed away. God rest her soul.

Then Pepin assembled his barons. The question was: Where should he find a wife? One of his nobles began to talk about a certain girl. "Sire, I know of a maiden who is supposed to be the most exquisite female creature from here to beyond the seas! She is the Princess of Hungary. I hear that she is named Berta the Debonaire."

"Sir," assented Pepin. "She is the very one for me! I'll take her as my wife and my queen."

The very next day Pepin sent a large party of knights into Hungary to make a formal request for the hand of the Princess Berta. They arrived on a Tuesday in time for dinner. Queen Blancheflor of Hungary summoned her daughter. When the French knights, who were all connoisseurs of feminine charms, saw this maiden they were stunned! She was so pink and white, so mantled in long, blond curls, so winsome, so slender and so dimpled, that they could hardly wait to snatch her away for King Pepin. It was agreed, the princess consenting, that they might take her back to France to make her a wife and a queen.

Berta's farewells were tearful. "Daughter," counseled her father, "try to resemble your mother. Be sweet and gentle to the poor. She who does good about her will be amply recompensed. Be kind. If you show them in France that you are debonaire, you then will be truly beautiful. My dear daughter, I recommend you to God's keeping."

In those days it was the custom for every lord and baron to keep French tutors in his domains, so that Berta had learned this language of culture as a child. In any case, her mother and father, King Floire and Queen Blancheflor, had learned French in Paris. They had been born and raised in this suburb of Saint Denis. They decided to send with the princess three of their own servants—an old woman named Margiste, her daughter Aliste, and their cousin Tibert. "Take care of these servants," counseled Blancheflor, "because I ransomed them from slavery out of my own pocket. Therefore I know that they will serve you faithfully. Moreover, the serving girl Aliste looks so exactly like you that her beauty will second yours."

"Lady," promised Berta, "they shall never lack. More than that, I shall arrange for Aliste to be well married in France."

When Princess Berta was seated on her bay palfrey, her weeping mother asked her daughter for the little ring she wore on her finger. When Berta had given her mother the ring, Blancheflor said, "Daughter, may God take good care of you for me! Try to ingratiate yourself with the scholars and intellectuals, for they are very troublesome in France."

"Mother, I promise. Oh, how can I leave you both? I feel as if someone were piercing my belly with a knife!"

"Daughter," comforted Blancheflor, "be smiling and merry. What is this talk about knives! Remember, you are going to be married, and traveling into France on this lovely, sunny day. My heart is really at peace for you. There are no gentler, finer people in all the world than the French!"

The pretty maiden wept so pitifully at leaving her mother and father that she drooped in the saddle and almost fainted away. However, the party finally finished their farewells and set out on their journey. They passed through Germany, crossed the Rhine at Saint Herbert near Cologne, and rode safely through the great forest of Ardennes. At the crossing of the Meuse they were entertained by the fabled hero, the

Duke Naimes, in whose honor the city of Namur was named. They rode into Paris early on a Sunday morning.

Pepin, escorted by seventeen hundred gaily bedecked cavaliers, jogged up to meet the Princess of Hungary. Church bells tolled merrily. There was not a street in all Paris that was not adorned with banners and spread with carpets. Bands of young girls in holiday finery strolled singing carols and strewing flowers. Pepin bowed low to his bride and she to him. Dashing young knights spurred their horses to get a closer look at the princess. "Oh, ho!" cried the French nobles. "Have we a springtime mistress!" and "Look at young youthfulness in person!"

Pepin married Berta on a day in mid-August. It was such a magnificent ceremony, without a raindrop or a breath of wind! The king was garbed in Eastern silk with a crown on his head worth at least 100,000 marks, maybe more. Berta was as pretty as a pink flower on a grafted fruit tree. A master tent was set in the palace garden for a hundred and thirty guests. Minstrels played violas, lutes, and harps. Many young ladies were presented to the queen. Everyone fought to be noticed by Berta. She had already charmed the younger knights who envied Pepin's possession of her. Berta was radiant—but soon she will be sent down a path that will cause her rosy cheeks to be furrowed with tears, all because of that rotten old bitch of a Margiste. May the Lord God confound her!

When the king rose—for he did not wish to delay the consummation of his marriage any longer—dukes, counts, and princes escorted the new queen to her bedchamber so that she could be disrobed. After Berta was arrayed for bed, her maid Margiste kneeling began to whisper to her, "When the King Pepin comes to you this night to do what a man in all firmness does to his wife, I have heard from a friend of mine that he intends to kill you. He has a knife. I have trembled so to tell this to you!"

As the innocent Berta heard these words, she began to shake and to cry. The old hag consoled her, however. "Lady, there's no use weeping. After the abbots and bishops have come in to bless your bridal bed, I'll put Aliste in it instead of you. If one of you is to be murdered, let it be she! I've already told her how she must perform. God knows, as I swear, that I'd much rather have her die than you. You know what your parents did for me." Then Berta was as relieved as if someone had given her all the gold of Montpellier!

Margiste trotted to her daughter's room. "Aliste," she said, "please God and Saint Peter, you shall be Queen of France! All we have to do now is to dispose of Berta. That won't be too difficult!"

"May God hear your prayer," chirped Aliste. "Go fetch our cousin Tibert, and we'll finish her off!" Fast as a greyhound the old woman ran to find the ruffian Tibert.

That night the unsuspecting Pepin covered the serving girl in bed so thoroughly that before morning she had conceived. All this time Margiste kept Berta in her room and laughed. Berta read a book while her husband did all his will and kingly duty to Aliste in the next room. In the morning, following Margiste's directions explicitly, Berta entered the bridal chamber and stabbed Aliste in the *thigh* with a little dagger Margiste had shown her how to use. Aliste screamed so sharp she awoke Pepin. Then Margiste cried, "Oh, look, Sire, my daughter has tried to murder your bride!"

Pepin sat up in bed and began to curse. "Have her destroyed, Sire," begged Margiste, "for I disown her utterly!" She cuffed Berta hard and shoved her out into the hall where Tibert swathed her in a cloak and pulled her away into Margiste's room. He forced a gag into her mouth, as one would a bit on a horse, tied her hands behind her back, and threw her on the bed with a sheet over her.

Soon after breakfast three sergeants were dispatched by the king secretly—for this attempted assassination was a nasty business—to escort Tibert out into the forest where Berta could be quietly beheaded. When they stopped at an inn for the night, they laid Berta on a bed. Tibert stood by her with drawn sword threatening to chop off her head if she made the slightest sound. After she had drunk some water, he replaced the gag and retied her wrists.

For five days they traveled in this fashion, Berta wrapped in a dark cloak and bundled on a pack animal, until they came to the lonely dark forest of Mans. There they halted under an olive tree. Tibert pulled Berta to the grass and unwrapped the thick cloak. The three sergeants gasped to see that the criminal they were hauling to execution was a fragile, winsome, blond princess. Berta stood trembling before them, her long golden hair falling almost to the ground. She wore a white silk tunic and a white cape. She gazed at the four men so imploringly that they pitied the poor girl, especially the King's sergeant Morans. Then when Berta saw Tibert's sword drawn to behead her, she fell to her knees and began to pray. The gag kept her from wailing. She could only moan.

"By God, Tibert," cried Morans, the first sergeant, "your heart is as hard as a rock. I'd sooner kill you right here and now and never return to France, than let you touch a hair of this maiden." The three sergeants grabbed Tibert and forced him to his knees. Then Morans untied Berta's hands and the gag. "Fly, Beauty, and may God help you," he said.

After Tibert saw that Berta had escaped through the trees, even in that extremity he thought of a way to save himself. He and the three sergeants killed a pig, cut out its heart, and carried it back to Margiste. She and Aliste rejoiced at the sight of what they thought was the heart of Berta.

Sobbing from fear, Queen Berta stumbled through the great forest. Night had fallen. All around her owls hooted from the treetops, and wolves howled in the distance. Streaks of lightning flared through the black tree trunks before the thunder shook the earth under her feet. Rain fell along with hail whipped by an icy wind.

"Sir God," wept Berta, "surely you will show me the way as you did to Gaspar, Melchior, and Balthazar when they sought the Virgin's son." On and on through the rainy woods she fled, tripping over slippery stones, switched by low-hanging branches. The wolves howled after her. "Alas, how could you have been so cruel to me, old woman?"

This was the Queen of France who stumbled through a black forest without a roof over her head or the rudest couch to lie upon, her dress torn and ragged and her pretty white hands scratched and bleeding. In the beating rain and darkness she came once to a river; but when she knelt to drink, the water was as cloudy as ale. Then she sped wearily on bumping into trees and fighting her way through thorns that pulled at her cloak, darting down one path to the right and another to the left as the lightning showed her an opening in the dense woods, not knowing which was the *right* road to take. When a huge gnarled branch clutched at her breast, she screamed for her mother. If Queen Blancheflor could have seen her darling child, her precious Berta whose cheeks were as red as the rose and whose skin was as white as the lily, how she would have wept too!

"Somebody, help me! Answer me! I'm afraid!" screamed Berta in terror as she turned about in the forest maze. "I am lost! Find me, somebody! . . . Oh, I thought I was mounting a throne when they sent me to Paris. Now I see the truth. I have only gone from bad to worse since I arrived in this land. Saint Denis! Help me! The wolves will surely eat me alive! Saint Catherine! Open the door of Paradise to me!"

The royal Berta finally made herself a bed of leaves in a hollow spot. No body has ever slept on the cold ground so pitifully all the way from Wales to Thessaly! She broke fronds from the ferns beside her. These were her blanket. Her pillow was a stone. There it was she finally fell asleep, lost and forlorn, this maiden so tender. Berta was at this time not more than sixteen years old. She slept soundly, however, because the harder was her lot, the more she trusted in God, laying her sorrow at His feet. Toward morning the rain ceased. Then it grew clear and bitter cold under the thick trees.

Berta woke up shivering. In the cold morning light she saw how dense the woods were and how forsaken. "Please God," she prayed, "to show me where to go, and I promise that I will henceforth be humble. *I will never tell who I am*, either that I am the daughter of Hungary or the wife of France. Only God grant me that I keep my maidenhood, . . . and I hope that Tibert dies for the injuries he has done me."

During the early daylight hours Berta wandered along the forest paths. Her body was blue with cold, for her silk chemise and cloak were wet and thin. She came to a spring of clear water. After she had drunk enough to quench her thirst, she grew even chillier. Then following a beaten path for some distance, she came to a hermit's cell. She beat upon his door with the wooden knocker that hung from a cord. The hermit slid open his wicket and peered at her.

"May I come in and warm myself, holy hermit?"

"Oh, by God," he replied, "I could never allow the enemy to gain such power over me! What is such a Beauty as you doing in these leafy woods? You must be the Devil come to tempt me! But God has promised me sanctity, and I shall never let you enter—you or any female creature!" Then he quickly made the sign of the cross.

"Oh, don't misunderstand me. I also have vowed my heart to God."

"Who are you then, and who are your parents?"

"I am only a poor girl. Please may I come in? I am so cold."

"Beauty," insisted the hermit, "I can let no fiend in, neither in summer *nor* in winter!"

Berta stood shaking with cold in front of his door. She was so frightened and so hungry that she began to wail again. In pity the hermit passed her a piece of black bread through the wicket. It was soggy and full of chaff. Berta thanked him, but her sobs wracked her so that she could not even taste it. She just stood and cried. It had begun to rain again.

"Beauty," called the hermit, "I know what you could do. You could go to the house of Simon and Constance. They would give you shelter."

"But I don't know the way if no one is here to show me."

"Don't be frightened, Beauty. Just keep straight down this path. It is not far."

"But I don't know what path you mean. As true as God sees me here, I am dead and gone forever if I have to sleep another night in these woods. Even if the Virgin Mary were to give me twenty lives, I would wear them all out before tomorrow morning."

At these words the hermit grudgingly consented to unbar the door and set her on the *right* path. Berta almost died of panic a little way down the trail when she saw a huge bear coming toward her. Her faith in the Virgin was upheld, however, for the bear lumbered off the road and disappeared into the trees. Finally Berta met the Sheriff Simon himself. He dismounted, amazed to see a shivering maiden trudging along the lonely road. It was Simon's duty to patrol the roads in this area of the forest.

"Beauty, who are you?" he inquired.

"Sir," Berta replied, "I am only the humble daughter of a vavasor from Alsace. I ran away from a stepmother who beats me. I have been wandering a long time in these woods. I am so cold and so hungry."

The warmhearted Simon took Berta to his manor house, where she was made welcome by his wife Constance and his two daughters, Ysabel and Aiglente. Within a few days the slender princess had become one of the family. Her new sisters marveled at Berta's beauty. They loved to comb her long curls, which were longer than Elaine's. They knew her name was Berta, but they all believed her story of how she had escaped through the forest. Berta and her foster sisters loved each other dearly. They spent long hours together working with silken and golden threads, which Berta taught them how to do. It occurred to none of them to wonder why the strange maiden was so often pensive and generally silent about herself.

Ysabel and Aiglente often told their mother that if Berta ever ran away from their house, they would accompany her. "Berta is sweeter than the wild rose in May," the girls never tired of saying. Berta lived in Simon's house as his niece for nine and a half years. Everyone agreed she was the most virtuous maiden, the most stainless young girl in all that lonely forest.

Pepin was living meanwhile with Aliste as man and wife. They had two sons, Rainfrois and Heudris, who were treacherous boys. The Hungarian queen, whom everyone believed was Berta, was loathed by her subjects because of the taxes and tolls she levied upon rich and poor regardless, even upon priories and abbeys. She and her mother Margiste collected taxes upon the sale of pepper, cumin, spices, and wax as well as upon wheat and wine. Both bent every effort to amass treasures by the power they had wheedled from Pepin. Aliste often sat playing with her treasures, counting them, and laughing; if she had been wiser, she would rather have cried to see them pile up about her!

In the meantime both Berta's brother and sister had died so that King Floire and Queen Blancheflor were faced with the lack of an heir to the throne of Hungary. They sent a messenger to Pepin to request that he dispatch his younger son to them so that Berta's child could be trained for kingship also. Although King Pepin was disposed to accept this honor, Aliste returned word that she could not and would not be deprived of one of her sons. Floire could hardly believe his ears when the messenger returned this answer.

That same night Queen Blancheflor, sleeping beside her husband, had a terrible dream. She dreamed that a wild bear was eating her ribs, her right arm, and her buttocks, that its claws were ripping her cheeks. She awoke from this nightmare weeping. As the king tried vainly to comfort her, Blancheflor told him that she felt her dream announced danger to Berta. She pleaded to be allowed to journey into France at holiday time. She had not seen her daughter for eight and a half years.

"How could we who love each other so dearly live so long apart?" asked the king; but Blancheflor replied that her mother's heart knew there was something amiss with Berta. He finally consented to her departure since he hoped she would bring back with her one of Berta's sons. The king ordered one hundred knights to accompany Blancheflor. "I want you to be splendidly escorted. You know how haughty the French are and how they judge by appearances."

Blancheflor had not penetrated very far into French soil before she began to hear the unpleasant reports about her daughter. "How could my Berta be so hated?" wondered the mother. "She never saw either rapacity or greed as a child. I know my own daughter's heart as every mother does who has trained her child's character. If this story is true, I shall certainly take her to task and make her return at once all the monies and treasures she has extorted."

Once Blancheflor met a poor peasant. "Lady, I complain to you about your wicked daughter," said he, grasping her mount's bridle. "I too once owned a horse that carried thatch and faggots into town. This Queen Berta we have in France confiscated my animal, our sole means of livelihood. Now my wife and little ones are starving. By the Lord who made Adam and Eve, I shall curse her from evening to daybreak and call upon God to avenge me." The queen gave him her purse.

Blancheflor and her retinue arrived into Paris on a Monday. Pepin was overjoyed to hear of it—not so Margiste, nor Aliste, nor Tibert! Those three sat on their cushions and wondered what to do. Margiste proposed that Aliste should pretend to have fallen ill suddenly, that she should go to bed, and be drawn out of it under no pretext whatsoever. Margiste also knew how to brew a poison that could be fed to Blancheflor in a pear or some cherries. Aliste preferred flight.

"I'm afraid," said Aliste, "because of my feet. You know my feet and heels are not half so wide as Berta's were. Let us load our wealth on mules and have Tibert lead us out of the country—into Sicily, perhaps. There we could get rich even faster through usury." They decided, however, to adopt Margiste's plan. They stopped up the windows with tapestries. After the room had been darkened, Aliste climbed into bed, pulling the covers up even over her chin, her nose, and her eyes.

Shortly the news of the queen's illness spread through the city; it caused a general rejoicing. Pepin started out from the palace, accompanied by his two sons, to meet Queen Blancheflor in Montmartre where she was hearing mass. Pepin bowed to his mother-in-law and embraced her. Blancheflor's first words were, "Tell me in the name of Jesus, how is my daughter?"

"Why, she was so overjoyed to hear of your arrival that she became ill. As soon as she sees you, however, I know that she will recover."

Blancheflor fell silent. Although Pepin tried to cheer her, she would not smile. When he presented his two sons to her, Blancheflor only nodded coldly to them. She looked each boy up and down without seeing in either face any family trait. She could not understand why Berta had not sent a personal message. With a white, stern face she looked down the hill of Montmartre at the fair city of Paris spread out in the valley below her. It would have charmed her eyes, had her heart been less heavy. She saw the high, square towers of Montlhéry castle, the broad Seine meandering between the vineyards, the cities of Pontoise, Poissy, Meulan along the highroad, Marly, Conflans, and Montmorency among their meadows, and many another large city that I will not even name. The queen sighed to see such a lovely countryside and wondered again how her daughter could have earned in this fair land such a black name.

Pepin escorted his mother-in-law across the marble courtyard of his palace. Then Margiste rushed up to her former mistress. She was as wild-eyed as a devil and had self-inflicted scratches on her cheeks.

"Margiste," commanded Blancheflor after she had raised the servant and embraced her, "where is my daughter? Have her shown to me at once."

"Lady," answered Margiste, "she was so overjoyed at your arrival that she fell into a dire illness. Let her sleep until vespers."

The queen was so rebuffed and so disappointed that she grew pale and silent again. To Pepin's attempts at consolation she replied, "The King Floire loves our child Berta more than anything in the world. I had thought also to take home her younger son to adopt him as our heir."

"Lady," said Pepin, "do it forthwith. I grant the request." Four hundred knights sat down to dinner in honor of Hungary's queen. At the end of the evening Margiste again asked Blancheflor to delay awakening "Berta."

"Willingly," answered the mother. "But by the will of the Almighty God, however, I shall sit myself right here—and hear you that I speak truly—nor leave this spot until I have seen with my own eyes the pretty body of my child and kissed her pretty lips." There Blancheflor, sad and worried, sat from early morning under an espalier tree in the courtyard. Once again she summoned Margiste. "Tell me why my daughter suddenly became so covetous of gold. Both young and old complain about her. It is not only unseemly conduct in her, but it is a trait of her nature that I as her mother do not recognize."

"They have only told you lies, and cursed be their hides," affirmed Margiste. "No kinder lady ever wore a golden ring!"

"Tell me," persisted the queen. "Where is your daughter Aliste?"

"Lady, I will tell you. She died suddenly one day as she was sitting on her stool. I don't know what disease she had on her cheek. I guess that in the end it was leprosy. Know that my heart under my breast was sore, for she was frank and vivacious. I had her buried in an old chapel, secretly, so the word would not spread."

For two whole days Blancheflor sat before that chamber door so vigilantly and so faithfully that the old hag could neither come nor go. Tibert and the bitch figured out pretexts to keep Blancheflor from Aliste's chamber. Then just before supper one evening, as dusk was falling, Queen Blancheflor lost her temper. She refused to endure one instant longer of not seeing her child. She called a young servant girl to fetch a candle, and despite Tibert's objection she forced her way into the bedroom.

All was dark inside. Like a cat Margiste struck the servant so hard that the poor girl fell in a pool of blood to the floor. The candle went out. Then Queen Blancheflor's suspicions about Margiste were confirmed. She walked straight to the bed and began to run her fingers over the coverlet.

"Mother," said the false Berta in a very plaintive voice, "how nice that you could come. How is my father whom God blesses?"

"Daughter, he was well when I had to leave him."

"May God be praised. . . . I regret not to be able to entertain you with festivities. It makes me so miserable that I think I shall die. I should like to divert you . . ." Aliste was so frightened and trembled so under the covers that she had lost all her taste for laughter. She twisted her head away from the queen and squirmed out of reach of her fingers.

"Daughter," said Blancheflor, "my heart breaks to see you so ill, as you say."

"Mother," whispered the servant Aliste, "I am suffering such martyrdom that I fear my white skin will become as yellow as wax. The physician tells me that light makes me worse, and talking too. Nothing is more aggravating to my condition. Therefore I cannot have visitors. Believe me, I am very annoyed, for my heart longs for gossip about father. I don't know what to do. I am so discomfited. Let me rest; and may Jesus thank you for it, because . . ."

When Blancheflor heard those mewing words, her heart sank to her toes. "Help me, dear God," she said, "who never lied; for this is not my daughter whom I have found in this bed! Why, if my daughter were half dead, even then she would have kissed me and shown me her love!" Blancheflor opened wide the door to the corridor and summoned the household. "Come here at once, all of you! Come running in the name of God! I have not found my daughter in this room, and I shall prove it to you promptly. Then she ordered the servants to strip the cloth-of-gold hangings from the windows. With her own hands she pulled down tapestries and draperies from the vaulted ceilings.

"Lady," shrieked Margiste, "for the love of God, do you want to kill your daughter? She hasn't slept for three days!"

"Shut up, old woman," snapped the queen. Neither Margiste nor Tibert could think of a further trick to thwart her anger.

Clear light from the setting sun flooded into the chamber. Aliste had pulled the covers up over her head. When the household had collected, Queen Blancheflor stepped up to the bed. With both hands she grasped the coverlet and pulled it entirely off the bed. Her eyes fell accusingly on the serving girl's feet. They were little, only half the size of Berta's. The queen cried in anguish and grew deathly pale. Quickly the agile Aliste pulled a sheet over herself and leaped for the door. Blancheflor caught her by her braids and threw her to the carpet.

"Halloo! Come here! Help! Help! This is no child of mine! Alas, and woe is me! This wench is the child of Margiste, whom I fed from babyhood. They have murdered my sweet Berta whom I loved more than my life!"

When Pepin heard that news, he also ran into the chamber. "French King," accused Blancheflor, "what have you done with my daughter? Where is my child, so blond, so sweet, so courteous, so well educated? Where is Berta the Debonaire? If I don't have word of her at once, you will feel the weight of my rage!"

Pepin was so astounded that he grew red with fury. He beckoned four sergeants to seize the old hag and hold her up before him. "Hag, you will burn for this, by the body of Jesus Christ!" Then Pepin retired to his throne room, followed by his barons. As the old hag was dragged before him, it began to storm and thunder. Pepin shuddered at the loathsome old woman who had forced her daughter upon him for so long. "She is the Antichrist!" he said. They put her to the torture, twisted her thumbs with screws until she was ready to confess to all her crimes, including the poison. She was condemned unanimously to the stake.

Then the rough Tibert talked fast. "Sir King, as far as I know, Berta is dead; for we left her in the forest where bears, lions, and wild boars roam. If it had not been for Morans, I would have cut off her head." More than seventeen hundred courtiers began to weep.

A great fire was kindled with thorns. Some piled on brush while others fanned it until the flames were white-hot. Then the rotten old bitch was thrown into it, and well had she deserved it! When her daughter Aliste saw this, she groveled on the floor before Pepin. Then Tibert was tied to horses and dragged outside the walls of Paris to the hangman's field at Montfaucon, where he was left dangling in the wind. And that was good for him!

The peers advised Pepin, "Do not take the serving girl's life if you wish to follow our counsel. Let her live it out since she has borne you children. However, from this day forth, she must never approach you again nor maintain contact with any noble of France."

Pepin sighed when he heard their verdict. "Sirs, she deserves to be stoned and destroyed; but I shall not countermand your decision."

Aliste pleaded with the king. "Sire, allow me to withdraw from the world to a nunnery in Montmartre. I know how to read and sing. Let me also take my wealth as a dowry. As for my sons, keep them with you, have them knighted, and find them rich wives. Remember our nights in bed together!" Pepin disdained a refusal, so disgusted was he!

It took eight days to transport all of Aliste's belongings to Montmartre, so much gold and silver was there, and that's not counting all her other divers and sundry riches which I won't trouble to list. Let me go on with the story.

Pepin was disconsolate. There never ruled in France a king with such a soft heart. He did his best as a gentle man to console Blancheflor; neither one of them could smile. Pepin ordered two of his most treasured palfreys brought. He helped Blancheflor into a litter that had been attached to the horses, for Berta's mother was too despondent to ride a horse. Followed by throngs of Parisians, some weeping for their lost queen, and others cursing Aliste and grumbling because she had not been executed and her wealth given to the poor, Pepin escorted Blancheflor all the way to Senlis.

"How shall I tell her father that his sweet child is dead?" moaned the queen. "Just imagine how he will tear his beard! There will not be such grief from Friesland to the sea. How is it that my heart under my breast does not break? I wish that I were dead and gone." There was general mourning in every Hungarian town. Then was hair pulled and palms beaten against each other! In every street people wept for Berta the Well-born.

Pepin summoned Morans to his presence. "Hear my thought," said the king. "I know that without you my wife would have been murdered. I think she was probably eaten alive by wild beasts; otherwise she would have returned. I want you to search the Forest of Mans. Ask every inhabitant throughout that region. See if you cannot find at least a piece of her dress. Know that I shall love her as long as I live. Know that I would kiss her evening and morning too." For fifteen days Morans and his men beat the countryside. They found no trace of Berta—nothing.

Sheriff Simon heard what had happened in Paris. He and his wife Constance were thoughtful. After some discussion they called Berta, told her the startling news, and asked, "Berta, are you the lady King Pepin is seeking?"

Although Berta grew pale with fright, she would not break her vow. "It is not I. Believe me, I deny it." When her foster parents replied not a word, Berta argued, "Do you think that I prefer a manor house in these woods to the king of France's palace?"

"Sire," reported Morans to Pepin, "we sought Madame with all our hearts. We questioned every knight, every bourgeois, every peasant, every serf. We asked every plowman, every coal miner, every belabored varlet. We stopped at each church and each chapel by the road. We even asked those sick-a-bed for news of the queen. We know no more today than nine years ago." Morans was so depressed, so sorrowful for his past deed that he made a pilgrimage *outremer* to do penance for his failure to save the queen of France. His two companions accompanied him, but only Morans lived to see France again. Only he returned from the Holy Land.

Pepin did not recover from his sorrow even when young Duke Naimes rode in from his lord, the Duke of Bavaria. Young Naimes and twelve nobles had been sent to request Pepin to ordain them as knights. Naimes gave Pepin very good advice. It was decided that the court would remove to the city of Mans, where at Pentecost the German knights were ceremoniously dubbed. During this celebration Duke Naimes asked Pepin why he did not take a new bride.

"Sirs," replied the king, "that shall I not do. . . . I loved the Princess Berta whom I only saw for a few precious hours. Then I was tricked and disgraced by a serving girl. When I think of my wedding day in Paris and of the gentle princess who was stolen right under my eyes, I feel like taking my own life. I dream only of caressing her fair body from evening until daybreak." The virgin knights were bewildered, for they did not know love.

On a Thursday morning the king rode into the forest to hunt deer; because he was melancholy he preferred to ride alone, apart from the hunting party. For hours he let his horse bear him wherever it willed, up one path and down another, until he came to that chapel where Simon and his family performed their daily devotions. Berta had remained in the holy place after the departure of the others. She had prayed very long that morning, asking God to give her special strength so that she could resist revealing her true identity and thus breaking her vow. She had just left the chapel, carrying her psalter and Book of Hours in her hand, when Pepin rode up the path toward her.

"Beauty, don't be alarmed," smiled Pepin. "I am a knight and vassal of that king to whom this whole sweet France belongs. In truth, I have lost my way, which pains me not a little. Is there a manor or fief in this vicinity where I could get redirected?"

"Sir," replied Berta, "Sheriff Simon, I believe, could do so."

"Why, thank you, Beauty." The more Pepin looked at her, the more he observed how crimson and white were her cheeks and how blond the little curls under her hood. Only then did he realize that quite by accident he had stumbled upon a very young and very desirable damsel. Without another word he dismounted. Before she could even gasp, he had pressed her close against him. When he felt to his surprise that she was struggling in his arms and twisting away from his lips, he urged her to answer his desires. "Look," Pepin whispered in her ear, "love me, Beauty. Make love to me . . . You shall come back into France. Will you love me? Why don't you give in? . . . You won't? Look, I will buy you any jewel that your little heart desires. I don't care how much it costs. . . . Won't you? Very well. I will settle a rich estate upon you." Pepin still held her close against him. He pushed back her hood. "Not a person will do you harm. . . ." The more he urged her, the harder she struggled. Berta didn't care a mint leaf for all his bribes. Pepin saw that this girl was actually terrified of his caresses and the strength of his arm.

"Oh, please," begged Berta. "Please let me go. My Uncle Simon will come looking for me. You must let me go. My Uncle Simon has to journey up to Mans today to carry victuals to the king."

"Beauty, tell me what you were doing alone in this wood."

"I was praying in the chapel, but a little angel came down to hear my pleas. I overstayed the mass."

Pepin scanned her face narrowly as she talked. It seemed to him that if he could not take her by force, he would be obliged to win her through love. Have her, he must. In his eyes she became more lovely every second. With her cape askew, he saw her lovely breasts and that her golden hair flowed in curls to the ground. "Beauty," pleaded Pepin, "I must make love to you. . . . I will honor you afterward. I promise I will take you back to France. I will give you so much wealth that no desire you have shall go unfulfilled. I am going to make you do my will anyway, whatever it may cost; you may as well yield right now."

"Sir, I forbid you to touch me!" replied Berta with great distinctness. Tears came to her eyes and slowly rolled down her cheeks. "I order you to step back, Sir Knight. You have offended me greatly. I am no ordinary damsel. I am the wife of Pepin, king of France. I am the daughter of the king and queen of Hungary. . . . Do not venture a step further in my direction. Know that I am the queen of France!"

Pepin was so amazed that he grew pale. He could not, indeed, take a step. He could not even speak. For several minutes he just stood and stared at her. Then he gulped and swallowed, for there was a lump in his throat. "Beauty," he said then softly, "if what you say is true, I wouldn't harm your person for one thousand marks in gold."

Berta walked along the forest path toward Simon's house while Pepin, leading his horse, followed her. Hard as he questioned her about herself, the maiden would not reply or volunteer any corroboration of her story. Simon greeted the strange knight and wondered at Berta's flushed face. He and Constance saw there had been an attempt at rape, but they could tell it had not succeeded. Pepin introduced himself as the king of Paris. He was very gallant toward Constance and her two daughters. The family saw that their strange guest was a nobleman.

As soon as an apt occasion presented itself, Pepin drew Simon aside to inquire about Berta's chastity. At once Simon called his wife. That lady scolded Pepin roundly, "Sir, our niece has been complaining about your conduct. It seems you tried to take her virginity. Our dear child is frightened. This was very unknightly of you."

Then Pepin decided to take them into his confidence. "Your Berta has just told me something that, if it is the truth, will bring down upon your heads the blessings of France. She told me she was the queen of France! Say what you know about this maiden, and beware of my ire if you lie to me."

"Sir," answered Simon, "all we know is that I found her wandering in the forest. She was blue with exposure and half dead from fright and hunger. We can both bear witness to her purity and honor. As far as we know, she came from Alsace. . . . In all this country she is the most pleasing and most gentle maiden. To this I can and will swear before you and before God."

"Simon," replied the king, "let us go all three of us and talk to her."

"Sir," answered Simon, "do you know what I suggest? If I were you, I would hide behind this curtain and listen to what she tells my wife and me. She will be frank and open with us."

Simon took Berta by the hand and led her into the hall where Pepin was concealed. "Berta," he told her kindly, "this noble knight has revealed your words, what you told him in the forest. They are very wonderful and joyous. Why did you hide your rank from us?"

"I beg you, dear Berta, to tell us the truth," urged Constance.

"I had to tell the knight that I was Berta the queen," she replied. Berta was so embarrassed that she could not meet their eyes. "It was the only way to save myself from being raped in the woods."

Constance led the slender Berta from the hall. Then she told the strange knight, "I do not know what to think now. Our niece would be delirious to hide such a fact from us who love her. She cannot be the queen of France!"

Pepin, with somber thoughts and wrinkled brow, took leave of his host and hostess. He had chased enough for that day. As soon as he arrived in Mans, however, he dispatched a messenger to bring Simon to him. "Simon," said Pepin, "you did not recognize me. I am Pepin the king."

"Oh, Sire," replied Simon, bowing low to show his awed respect, "had I known it was you, I should have made you many times more welcome in my home."

"Your reception was sufficient," sighed Pepin. "I am distraught because of my dear wife Berta who was stolen from me so many years ago. I cannot sleep nights because of my desire to hold her in my arms." After some deliberation between the two men, Pepin concluded, "Do you know what to do? You will return home and mention this occurrence to no one at all. My heart will not be denied. My heart tells me that the maiden in your house *is* my lost bride although the fact that she continues to deny it grieves me deeply."

"I can never believe either," mused Simon, "that this girl is not your wife whom you love so deeply. My idea is that when she found herself so chilled and so famished in the deep forest she made some vow which she now fears to break. Such a virtuous girl as she is would not endanger her salvation for all your gold and all your fair domains, not even for the kingdom of France."

"Simon," concurred Pepin, "I really think you have solved this mystery; on the other hand, you know how I was deceived by a scheming woman. You will understand my desire for proof. Therefore, since I must put my mind at rest, I shall send word to Hungary to ask her mother Blancheflor." Pepin called a chaplain to whom he dictated a letter.

Great was the rejoicing in Hungary when King Floire and Queen Blancheflor broke the seal of the king's missive and read his words. Early next morning they set out for France, traveling so hard that within a few days they had arrived in Paris. Pepin urged them not to delay but to set out at once for Mans. He was so eager to see Berta again that their whole party arrived in the city of Mans one day for dinner. However, Queen Blancheflor could neither eat nor drink, so anxious was she to clasp her beloved daughter in her arms.

Simon, summoned to the royal presence, asked, "Has Queen Blancheflor come?"

"Yes," replied Pepin, "only she is so upset that she can neither eat nor sleep."

"I am more and more certain our niece is your queen," said Simon. "Every time I mention your name, she hangs her head, blushes, and grows silent. Have no fear for her nature. She is the most honorable maiden in the land."

King Pepin and his royal guests were secretly escorted by Simon out of the city, through the forest, and into his home. "Where is Berta?" asked Pepin breathlessly.

"She is in my chamber repairing an altar cloth that was torn," answered Constance.

The whole party, excited and eager, burst through the chamber door and saw Berta sitting before her embroidery frame. As soon as her eyes fell upon Blancheflor, the maiden Berta rose to her feet. She ran across the room and sank down on her knees, burying her face in her mother's skirts. All could see that she had swooned.

"May God be praised," cried King Floire. "We have found our priceless daughter!" King Floire raised his child gently, drew his Berta into his arms, enfolded his slim daughter, stroked her hair, and kissed her face.

"Oh, God," cried Pepin, "who made heaven and earth, be praised for this our destiny. You have rewarded me so today, O God, You have so changed my sorrow into joy that any happiness I ever felt before is a hundred times doubled. May this day be honored long, the day when I again found my Lady!"

The news sped swiftly to Mans. All the church bells began to toll paeans of joy. Their peals carried through the trees into the room where Berta was being kissed and caressed by her parents. Then Pepin went up to her, bowed low, and said, "Sweet friend, for God's sake, say something to *me!* I am King Pepin, and I here crave your forgiveness for all the pain and the frights I have caused you."

Berta marveled deeply to hear his gentle words. Like a highborn princess she answered becomingly, "Sire, since it is really you, I thank the Holy Virgin who gave birth at Bethlehem."

Pepin called for his sergeant Henri, his marshal Gautier, and his chamberlain Tierri. "Ride into Mans and bring us tents and pavilions. Provide for our comfort here; here it was that I found all my joy, and here it is our pleasure to remain. Ask Duke Naimes and the new knights to join our company." So the court convened there in the forest, and that was on a Monday.

That night in the royal pavilion Pepin at long last slept with his wife and there also the three following nights. He caressed her from evening to morning. In the morning he dubbed Simon a knight at Berta's request. It was the Duke Naimes who buckled on the spurs, and Pepin who extended the sword, struck Simon on the shoulders, and ordained him knight. Simon kissed the king's foot and leg. Then Pepin raised Simon and kissed him on the cheeks. Afterwards Pepin bestowed on his new knight a thousand pounds of income per year in lands. He also gave five hundred pounds a year to each of his daughters. He ordered their coat of arms to be field-blue struck with white and a golden fleur-de-lys. Their heirs still bear this device today.

"Constance," said Berta, "you and your daughters shall accompany me into France. It is not right that I should have such honors and you such humility." Constance replied that they would all do her will gladly.

The royalty and their train of nobles made a solemn entry into the city of Mans on a Tuesday morning. Berta rode between the king and Duke of Naimes. They were met by the clergy, lay and ecclesiastical, who bore in their hands caskets containing holy relics, silver and gold censers, cloth of gold and silken fabrics. Ladies and nobles of the area thronged to be presented to the queen about whose distress they had long heard. The festivities lasted for eight days.

Then Pepin ordered their return to Paris. Near Berta rode Ysabel and Aiglente. The three young ladies were gay and merry all the way. The sun shone down over the beautiful fields of France. Through every hamlet and burg people crowded close to the queen. Many had journeyed long distances on foot and on horseback to glimpse her loveliness. They saw that she was *noble and humble*, and they blessed her mother for having brought her up so well. Minstrels accompanied them with lute and merry song all the way to Paris.

v. 3329.   *Grant joie orent en France li joene et li chenu.*
Encontre Pepin vinrent si ami et si dru,
Et encontre lor dame dont grant joie ont eü;
De ce qu'est retrouvée gracient moult Jhesu.
Tant vont que de Paris ont maint clochier veü;
Paris ert acesmée c'onques mais si ne fu,
Car moult furent la gent de grant joie esmeü
Pour le bien que il voient que Diex leur a rendu.
Ne remest en la vile ne chauf ne chevelu,
Ne moine ne abé, ordené ne rendu,
Qui à pourcession ne soient tuit venu.
Sachiez cel jour i ot maint grant destrier coru
Et i ot lainte lance brisie sor escu;
Berte la debonaire ot cel jour maint salu.

Great joy was had in France by young heads and hoary
Who greeted Pepin so friendly and so merry,
Then met his sweet lady whom they hailed joyfully;
People thanked Jesus she'd been found in safety.
They filed through Paris under tower and belfry—
Paris never was adorned so beautifully.
So moved were the people they turned prayerfully

To thank God above they should so honored be.
There remained in the town not a bald nor a curly,
No monk nor abbot, no ordained nor renegee;
But joined the procession and the ceremony.
Be sure great chargers spurred before the canopy.
Long lances and bright shields were shivered gallantly
For the debonaire Berta their homage and her fee.

The king and queen of Hungary were happy and comforted to watch this reception given to Berta by the Parisians. After eight more days of celebration during which Pepin outdid all previous records for grace, entertainment, and hospitality, Floire and Blancheflor returned to Hungary. They founded and endowed an abbey for sixty nuns in honor of their daughter's fortunate return to her rightful place upon the throne. This was not the only joy they carried back into Hungary with them. Within a few months Queen Blancheflor gave birth to a baby girl who was named Constance in honor of the fine lady who had rescued Berta. This is the Constance who in good time became the queen of Hungary.

Pepin and Berta ruled happily in France. When the unfortunate Sergeant Morans returned from outremer, Berta asked her husband to receive him. She pardoned him herself and thanked him; for, as she told him publicly, he had really saved her life. She further requested Pepin to confer knighthood upon Morans, and it was so done.

The first child born to Berta and Pepin was a lovely daughter who was gentle, teachable, and mild. This girl grew up to become the wife of Sir Milon d'Aiglent. Her son was the great hero Rollanz, he who never knew cowardice, he who was daring and bold, he who was the finest flower of chivalry.

The second child of Berta and Pepin was a boy. He it was who led great wars against the pagans, who upheld and enforced the laws of God, who drove the infidels out of many a fertile field, who pierced many a helmet, crumpled many a buckler, broke many a hauberk, cut off many an enemy's head, and fought his whole life long with all his mighty heart for his lands of France so valiantly, indeed, that the wide world mourns his passing even to this day. The second child of Berta and Pepin was named Carles.

He was great Charlemagne.

TWELVE
AUSTRIA
SIFRIT

The following chapter summarizes the first sixteen adventures from the *Nibelungenlied*, an Austrian poem of unknown authorship, composed about 1200. This work centers about the life of Sifrit, the Siegfried of the Wagnerian operas, who became the best-known hero of German and Scandinavian literature.

The *Nibelungenlied* is an amalgam of stories from three principal sources: actual history of the invasions of the fifth century, Scandinavian mythology—which in turn comes largely from Icelandic manuscripts—and Oriental legends partially remembered from Asia, the original home of the Indo-Europeans. As an historical document this poem corroborates the importance of certain kings and queens such as the Hun Attila who had 500,000 men under his command at one battle, men collected from Kiev to what is now Vienna.

In 430 Attila defeated and killed a Burgundian king named Gundicarius, the Gunther of our story. Attila himself, according to unproved suspicions of the time, was murdered in 453 by his Burgundian wife, Ildico, perhaps the Chriemhilde (*Chriem* = grim-grief; *hilde* = bearing) of our story. Our poet treats one of his characters, the knight Dietrich, with great respect; historians have seen in him Theodoric the Great, king of the Ostrogoths, who in actual fact reigned some fifty years after Attila.

The first half of this poem takes place at the court of Burgundy. The Burgundians were Germanic tribes who added to their domains until in the fifteenth century their alliance with Henry V of England prolonged the Hundred Years' War. When their empire was dismembered at the close of that century, its western half fell to France while its eastern half went to the husband of the Duchess Marie of Burgundy, a hitherto unimportant prince named Hohenzollern. Sifrit is said at first in our poem to have come from the Low Country at the mouth of the Rhine, a territory held by the Franks and called Austrasie. The Franks considered themselves descendants of the Trojans of Asia Minor. One character in the story, Hagen, comes from Tronje (New Troy) in Alsace. Sifrit comes from Santen (Troia Francorum).

Sifrit himself, however, seems rather to resemble Achilles. Both were young and courageous, both were invulnerable except in one spot, both fought a warrior maiden, and both were murdered. The tradition of the warrior maiden—in our present story she is Brunhilde (Brun = brunie-byrnie)—derives also from antiquity. Not only was there Penthesilea and Camilla, but also that Persian maiden named Gurdafrid, whom we met for a brief moment in the *Shah Nameh*. Brunhilde's original name in Scandinavian mythology was Sigrdífa. In those stories Sifrit was a descendant of the god Odin, or Woden (for whom Wednesday is named), recognized by the Romans as Mercury. (Wednesday is called *Mercredi* in French, and in Italian, *Mercoledi*.) Odin, like Sifrit, was closely associated with a galloping horse of gigantic size just as Suhrab and Rustam were in Persian legend.

The poet of the *Nibelungenlied* presupposes a certain acquaintance with Scandinavian legend, which tells of the Valkyrie Brunhilde lying in a magic sleep surrounded by fire; she is rescued and awakened by Sifrit. The poet gives no details of the Nibelungen treasure. Apparently the Nibelungenland was somewhere in the North, and a Nibelung was he who possessed this fatal hoard. The idea of gold bringing death we have seen in *Beowulf*.

The following adaptation follows closely a two-volume translation of the *Lied* into French, made in Russia in 1837 by a French schoolteacher, Mme. Charlotte Moreau de la Meltière. Her work has been checked against an original German text and also against two subsequent French translations of 1866 and 1909.

Mme. de la Meltière dedicated her book to Catharine the Great of Russia.

Sifrit and Chriemhilde

In the most ancient legends are recorded the names of the lovers Sifrit and Chriemhilde. In song and poem are commemorated their story— tales of his valor, of their undying love, of the festivals their presence graced, the pageantry of her tears and the wrongs they suffered, side by side with the prodigious exploits of bloodthirsty warriors.

There grew up in the pleasant land of Burgundy, protected and cherished by three mighty chiefs who were her brothers, this tender maiden whom we know by the name of Chriemhilde. Her beauty was so exquisite, so fragile that its fame and the prestige of this princess were celebrated by wandering bards throughout lands even beyond the Rhine. Chriemhilde, they said, declined to requite the love proposals of any suitor; they told how her reluctance was due to a dream.

She had once dreamed that two eagles, swooping down from the skies, devoured a sleek falcon which she had raised, loved and trained diligently. What a sorrow to the gentle girl was this presage! The maiden's mother, Queen Uta, explained to her child that this dream meant only that her pet bird was that great lord who would become her husband, he who would be torn apart by eagles if he were not carefully safeguarded.

"No," cried Chriemhilde. "I shall never marry. I see how great the sorrow of married women is."

"Make no hasty decisions," answered the queen. "Only the love of a man can transport you above all other joys. You are very beautiful. We shall hope for that great knight who surpasses all others for your husband." While she awaited her knight in shining armor, Chriemhilde lived in peace, hidden safely from rough warriors in her brothers' palace of Worms-on-the-Rhine.

On the lower reaches of this river, in the realms of the Franks, ruled a fabled king named Sigmund and his queen, Siglinde. Their son was already a hero. He was Sifrit. Although this youth had only been dubbed at the summer solstice, he had already worked fabulous deeds. He had fought a dragon, had bathed in its blood so that his skin had become as tough as horn, had stolen the magic cape which made its wearer invisible, and had seized the golden hoard of the Nibelungen. The young Sifrit, whose laughter and sunny beauty had already made him the object of amorous glances, had not felt love until he heard of the beauty of the hidden Princess Chriemhilde. Her inaccessibility seemed a challenge sufficient to his strength, particularly since her oldest brother Gunther ruled as many vassals and owned as much wealth as did Sifrit's own father in the Niderland. Therefore, overruling his parents' protests and refusing the aid of a host, Sifrit, accompanied by eleven knights, set out from Santen magnificently attired in golden armor and squirrel-skin robes to win all by himself the hand of the Princess Chriemhilde. Within seven days he had arrived at Worms.

King Gunther of Burgundy looked out his palace window to see the twelve strange knights in his courtyard. Their golden helmets flashed in the sun. He saw that their battle swords reached to their spurs. They were magnificently appareled. Gunther called for his uncle Hagen, for Hagen was bold and experienced. In the course of his adventures this dark knight had visited many lands and known many foreign kings.

Hagen leaned out the window and recognized the strangers. "I believe it is Sifrit of the Niderland," he said, "although I never saw him before. He won the treasure of the Nibelungen that was hidden under a mountain. He conquered the dwarf Alberich and made him a slave. From this hoard he took his mighty sword Balmung, and from Alberich the magic cape. He also killed the dragon that lived under the linden tree, bathed in its blood so that his skin became as hard as horn. No weapon can harm him. Let us receive this fair hero so kindly that we turn him into an ally, certainly not into an enemy."

Gunther, his brothers Gernot and Giselhers, and their uncle Hagen welcomed Sifrit into their hall and inquired about his voyage. "I am a warrior destined one day to wear a crown," boasted Sifrit. "I have heard that you Burgundians are valorous. Whether you like it or not, I have come to deprive you of your possessions and also to subdue your towns and villages."

"Why should I be stripped dishonorably of those lands which my fathers so long ruled honorably?" asked Gunther.

"I am sorry to see that you have come here for a quarrel," said Hagen.

"Sifrit, welcome to our lands," cried Giselhers, the youngest brother. "Let wine be brought to this hero!"

At his words and the subsequent welcome of Gunther, Sifrit became friendly. "All that we have is yours, royal guest," said Gunther. "We shall share our wealth with you. Only ask any favor of us, and it shall be granted."

The Burgundian lords entertained Sifrit at feastings and at tourneys where with lance, sword, and javelin Sifrit was every time first. The royal Princess Chriemhilde watched him secretly from her windows. She gasped at his beauty and skill. She knew he was the hero of the Franks and felt in her secret heart that he would be her one and only love. Sifrit did not know that the princess had seen him, or even that she had heard all about him. Inexperienced at intrigue, he could think of no way to meet her or to acknowledge his passion.

Their dalliance and their tourneys were interrupted by messengers from the two northern kings of the Saxons and the Danes. "Within twelve weeks our kings will pay you a visit, Gunther of Burgundy. They will come at the head of their hosts. Their purpose is conquest. Prepare to do battle!"

In Gunther's council it was Hagen who suggested that their guest Sifrit be notified of this threat. The young prince of the Niderland volunteered his aid at once. "Calm your fears," said Sifrit. "Even if the Saxons and Danes attack with thirty thousand men, I will meet them with only a thousand!"

Gunther's forces were assembled. They set out from Worms with the minstrel-knight Folker bearing the silken banner and Hagen in command of the columns. They passed through Hesse, burning villages and pillaging until they came to the frontiers of Saxony. There Hagen remained with the army while Sifrit, followed by chosen companions, led the attack into the enemy. After a bloody contest Sifrit took the Danish king prisoner and sent him back to Gunther at Worms. Three times Sifrit cut a path through the Saxon ranks until his arms ran in enemy blood from wielding his magic sword Balmung. When the Saxon king learned that his brother had been taken prisoner, and when he saw the design of the crown on the strange knight's buckler, he knew that his foe was the hero Sifrit. At once he ordered his banner to be lowered in sign of surrender. He too was ordered to Worms as a hostage. Stretchers transported the wounded into Burgundy along with five hundred captives. Runners carrying the news of this victory were dispatched to the Rhine.

Chriemhilde the Beautiful asked a messenger for news. "If you say good words to me, I will give you so much gold that you will be rich. Speak the truth, if you crave my favor. How did our Burgundians pursue the war? Which knight did the greatest exploits! That is what you are to tell me!"

"Since I must tell you, gracious Queen," replied the messenger, "it was in verity the arm of Sifrit alone that accomplished prodigies. The deeds of Hagen were nothing but the wind in comparison to those of Sigmund's great son. He has caused such grief among the Saxon women that they have now only to mourn and lament their whole lives long. Wherever he struck, the blood bubbled crimson and hot. Learn also that he overcame two battle-wise kings singlehanded, and that he is sending them as hostages to your brother Gunther. Great was the fury of the young Sifrit!"

As Chriemhilde listened, her glowing cheeks became as red as the rose. "You shall have ten marks and new livery," she replied. (One recites messages willingly to such rich ladies.) The damsels of Gunther's court hid behind their windows and watched the roads that led into the palace. Gunther greeted his victorious vassals and first the band of warriors who bore many a sword, many a captured shield, many a trophy. Then came the wounded and prisoners; only sixty Burgundians had been lost in that war. Gunther lodged his men in the town without forgetting to provide for the captives so that his magnanimity in victory would be remembered.

Gunther then began to plan a festival as a reward to his loyal subjects. Queen Uta opened chests and wardrobes so that the young ladies of her court could be splendidly attired. She heard that many noble warriors would be presented to her. Day after day knights arrived to do honor to the Burgundian royalty. Each was given rich robes and red gold for his love. Tiers of benches were built along the Rhine and places assigned according to each visitor's rank.

By Pentecost thirty-two princes and five thousand knights had jogged into Worms, each more nobly outfitted than the other. The Burgundians took Gunther aside and advised, "If you really wish this festival to be the most memorable ever attended, allow your noble guests to glimpse your sister Chriemhilde. What else warms the heart of a warrior? What greater compliment, what more suitable reward could you offer them than to let the knights parade before our hidden beauty whom no man has ever seen, but about whom all have heard? The poets sing her praises!"

Then did an excited princess and her damsels open the cases where the treasures of the kingdom were laid safely. More rich fabrics were ordered from the merchants. Wide ribbons were unrolled; jeweled clips, bracelets, pendants, and buckles were unwrapped and polished. Many warriors considered that the sight of this princess was, indeed, a boon far to be preferred to wealth and domains.

Gunther commanded one hundred knights with drawn swords to form an escort for his sister. The great hall, packed with thousands of knights, waited in silence as the procession of royal ladies ascended the stairs. First came Queen Uta followed by one hundred noble dames clad in satins and gleaming with jewels; then came Chriemhilde surrounded by a bevy of smiling young girls.

Chriemhilde walked into the hall, that gracious and shy young beauty, as pink as a morning sunbeam on drops of dew. Her cheeks were even brighter than the precious stones sewn over the skirt of her gown. She gleamed more luminously over the damsels in her train than does the moon over its surrounding stars. Sifrit, seeing for the first time her whom he loved, felt pride swell in his heart. Chamberlains ordered the cheering knights to step back so that no one approached the princess too closely.

"Brother," said Gernot to Gunther, "now is an opportunity to pay homage to Sifrit and thus bind this hero to us forever. Let the Princess Chriemhilde greet him! All present know that she has never greeted a knight in her life before. Let Sifrit approach, and bid her acknowledge him." Gunther so instructed his sister.

Others told Sifrit, "Approach. King Gunther is about to do you an unparalleled honor before all his court."

Sifrit, growing pale and red at the same time, advanced to the princess and bowed before her. To the delight of the court the princess— she who had up until this day lived a virginal life far from the sight of men—spoke to Sifrit. "Dear lord," she said, "good and noble knight, welcome." Sifrit bowed low before the maiden, but when he raised his head, their eyes locked. . . . Perhaps he disobeyed protocol and took her white hand. That would not be surprising, for joy ran fast through the heart of Sifrit those days in May.

Certain is it that Sifrit, escorting her from the church door one morning, whispered in her ear, "I shall serve you forever. I shall never rest until I have won your good graces. If I live, my life shall be consecrated entirely to you."

On the twelfth day of the festival Gunther consulted Sifrit about his two royal prisoners who were recovering from their wounds. "What do you think, Sifrit?" asked the king. "They will swear never to bring war parties into my lands again. They offer me all the gold that five hundred horses can carry in exchange for their freedom."

"To accept their gold would be acting dishonorably," replied Sifrit. "Ask them only to give you their hands on it that they will refrain from war. Take no gold from them, nothing. Give them their freedom, outside of Burgundy."

The Danish king took his leave, for the festival had drawn to a close. The Saxon king also took leave of Gunther and of his noble captors. Knights and vassals retired happily to their lands. Sifrit would have returned home to the Niderland, but he remained at Worms-on-the-Rhine because he had won the love of the Princess Chriemhilde.

Sifrit had won that love which meant death . . . the love of the Princess Chriemhilde. Through her undying love Sifrit was to find his death. In this love King Gunther of Burgundy also found death and also Chriemhilde's two brothers Gernot and Giselhers. Yes, even Giselhers, who was only a boy at the May festival given in honor of that war, also found death. Because of this love the minstrel-knight Folker, he who loved Hagen, also found death. Because of the love of Sifrit and Chriemhilde the terrible, black knight Hagen himself found death, far from home, in the burning palace of the awesome Attila, king of the Huns.

Such was the fate of them all because of the sleepless, passionate love the Princess Chriemhilde of Burgundy bore Sifrit.

Sifrit and Brunhilde

Meanwhile Gunther, king of Burgundy, had no bride for himself. He and the members of his royal court often heard tales of the extraordinary beauty possessed by princesses in exotic, distant lands, so much so that Gunther resolved to court one of those faraway beauties himself. Both his heroes and his warriors approved his decision especially when Gunther's thoughts turned to that princess who was by all reports the most hazardous to win, and the most glamorous.

Far across the sea, according to Gunther's informants, there reigned a foreign princess named Brunhilde. No lady had ever been like her, for she vanquished her suitors by feats of arms.

> *Den stein warf si verre,*   *dar nâch si wîten spranc.*
> *swer ir minne gerte,*   *der muose âne wanc*
> *driu spil an gewinnen*   *der vrowen wol geborn:*
> *gebrast im an eime*   *er het daz houbet verlorn.*

> A stone she heaved far   and reached it with one bound.
> He who sought her love   had dauntless to confound
> In three knightly tests   that maiden so well bred;
> If he failed one trial   then forfeit was his head.

All the suitors of Brunhilde had thus far, indeed, lost their heads. Gunther, however, would not be dissuaded. The more dangers his informers painted for him, the more eager was Gunther to pit his strength against such a fierce and heartless maiden.

"No matter what may befall," concluded Gunther, "I shall cross the western sea. I shall make my way to Brunhilde. I shall risk my life to win her love; even if I die in the attempt, I want her united to me in wedlock."

"I am opposed to such an enterprise," said Sifrit. "This queen has such barbarous customs that he who desires to serve her must pay dear for such an honor. You shall not find in me any encouragement for this sea voyage of yours."

"Hear now my opinion," said Hagen. "You must solicit from Sifrit himself help and counsel in such an immense voyage. I advise you this, for Sifrit *knows many things* about this Queen Brunhilde!"

"Sifrit, beloved friend," pleaded Gunther, "will you assist me to seek out this fabled Queen of Beauty? . . . If you accept, as I beseech you to do, and if Brunhilde ever falls into my possession, I shall place at your feet both my honor and my life."

Then Sifrit, son of Sigmund, replied, "Let it be as you desire. If you will give me your sister, the lovely Chriemhilde, I shall ask for no other guerdon."

"Here is my hand and oath on it," shouted Gunther. "Let once Brunhilde set foot in Burgundy, and Chriemhilde is yours. How joyously will you live with such a gentle beauty as my sister!" Sifrit laughed in anticipation of that moment while in the back of his mind he was remembering that he would need the magic cape which rendered him invisible and gave him the strength of twelve men if ever he was to surpass Brunhilde in agility and supernatural strength.

"Tell us then, Sifrit, how we shall arrange to appear before this barbarous queen in all our royal pomp and splendor. How many warriors shall we need? Will thirty thousand be sufficient, do you think?"

"No matter what your numbers, how valiant their hearts, or how strong the temper of their swords, they would all die in her fierce land," mused Sifrit. "That is not the way to capture her. Rather let us float down the Rhine in a small band. . . . Allow me in accordance with the laws of chivalry to name those valiant few who shall accompany you. I shall be one; you shall be second, Gunther; Hagen shall be third; and his brother Dankwart the fourth. Full thousands will not withstand our virtue and cunning."

"Tell me also, Sifrit, how I am to observe etiquette in her court, so that during our passage I shall be able to prepare my words and gestures."

"Believe me, Gunther, the most splendid attires that the minds of men could invent have already been paraded before her. However, let us be richly dressed so that the women of her court will not shame us when they gossip at their windows."

"Since that is the case, I shall ask my mother, Queen Uta, to choose for us that raiment which will do us the most credit and earn for us the greatest glory," replied Gunther.

Then Hagen interrupted brusquely, "Why go to your mother, Gunther? It seems to me you would do better to ask for the Princess Chriemhilde's opinion. She would know best what would delight a maiden."

Chriemhilde was notified in sufficient time of their desire for audience so that she and her court were attired radiantly. She led Gunther and Sifrit by the hand to seats of state beside her. While she had displayed before them cuts of richly painted silks heavy with gold thread, she and Sifrit exchanged looks of love secretly.

"I should be pained before all ladies," assured Chriemhilde, "if ever you were to appear at a disadvantage before another queen. Moreover, do not plead for my assistance; order me to advise you, for I shall always hasten to fulfill your commands joyously. Ask your servants only to bring me precious stones laid on a shield so that my women may set them in these silks which, as you see, are plentiful in my court. Who are these warriors I am to attire?" she inquired.

"There will be four of us," answered the king. "We shall each require three sets of garments, each one more ornate than the preceding." After he and Sifrit had bowed from her presence, Chriemhilde summoned thirty skilled women to work the jewels into the silk fabrics. She cut the heavy cloth herself, choosing Arabian silk as white and thick as snow, and green silk as bright and glossy as green clover leaves. She used sealskins and beaver for the hems and cuffs. For seven weeks Chriemhilde and her court worked on these magnificent garments, choosing other gold brocades from Libya and Morocco, which they edged with ermine. By the time that the ship which would bear the royalty over the ocean was launched on the Rhine, the women were sick from overwork.

"Brother," wept Chriemhilde, "you can still remain here. You will find just as beautiful a wife here in Burgundy." Her tears fell upon the gold of her dress and tarnished it in long streaks. "Sifrit," she sobbed, "I entrust my brother to your protection and recommend him to your vigilance. Let no shadow blacker than death creep over him in the barbarous land of this Brunhilde."

"While I live, Chriemhilde," he replied, "you need never fear. I shall bring him back home to you. Be sure of that."

As the young beauties of Burgundy watched from their windows, a breeze caught the sail of the king's ship and bore it swiftly downstream. "Who will be our pilot?" asked Gunther.

"I," replied Sifrit gaily, "for *I know the sea paths!*" Sifrit took the rudder then while Gunther leaned to an oar. Their horses were well stowed in the hold of the ship. Their food—many dainties too, and their Rhine wine were well battened down. The cables strained. The canvas bellied out to catch the wind. Before nightfall they had journeyed twenty miles, and at the end of the twelfth day they had come within sight of the dreadful Isenstein Castle in the kingdom of Brunhilde, a *country known only to Sifrit.*

"One word of caution before we arrive," warned Sifrit. "We must all tell the same story and never gainsay it, any one of us. Otherwise, there will befall awful disasters to each one of us. We must tell Brunhilde that Gunther is the king, and that I am only his vassal. If we make her believe this, and keep to our story, I have no doubt that we can take her alive. You must all give me your words now not to fail me in this." When they had pledged their solemn oaths as knights, Sifrit reminded them that he had undertaken this peril not for the sake of Gunther but only because he wanted to win the hand of Chriemhilde.

Their vessel floated so close under the many exterior ramparts of Isenstein Castle that the warriors could look up into the faces of the maidens who crowded its black walls and who gazed down upon them. Gunther exclaimed over and over at their exotic beauty.

"Quick," he urged Sifrit. "They are all so lovely! Tell me, I urge you, which one is Brunhilde."

Sifrit threw back his head and laughed. "Look them all over carefully, Gunther," he teased. "Pick out the one you would have as your wife in bed with you, and I will then say if she is Brunhilde."

After a careful scrutiny Gunther pointed upward and excitedly showed Sifrit the direction of his gaze. "Do you see that tall one, the maiden dressed in the long, white robe, as white as the driving snow, as majestic as a queen? That is the one I would choose. Is she the Queen Brunhilde?"

"Your eyes have not deceived you," laughed Sifrit. "That beautiful maiden is, well enough, the noble Brunhilde, the very woman your heart, your courage, and your virility have set out to master!"

When Brunhilde saw that the strange mariners were pointing at her, she withdrew haughtily from the walls and commanded her attendants to do likewise. At once her ladies rushed to deck themselves in finery. (Women are all vain, and that is their custom. When they meet heroes, they wish to be admired.) Some ladies disobeyed Brunhilde and continued to peek through the narrow windows.

As soon as the ship touched land, Sifrit led out two of the fine war horses they had brought, holding the head of one so that Gunther could mount. No one of the maidens missed a part of the proceedings! That was probably the first time that a king's son like Sifrit had ever held the stirrup for anyone! Then Sifrit mounted. Both knights wore the snow-white costumes. Both their horses were also pure white and mettlesome after their long sea crossing. And still the women watched from their windows. Both knights cantered up to the palace, the little golden bells on their saddles tinkling merrily. They had come to Brunhilde's throne just as they had intended.

Brunhilde covertly watched them approach. She marked their splendid attire, their newly sharpened lance points, their battle swords that hung to their spurs. Hagen and Dankwart advanced behind Gunther and Sifrit. Their costumes were as black and glistening as a raven's plumage. Their shields were brand-new, very wide, very polished, very solidly smithied. Upon their vestments gleamed precious gems from India. Brunhilde knew that they had moored their vessel casually upon her shores, with no one to guard it. Carelessly also had they penetrated her massive fortress, black rock piled tier on tier beneath eighty-six towers, three palace courts, a throne room constructed of marble as green as grass.

Courtiers and servants threw open the great hall of Iceland as the four from Burgundy clanked down the fortress corridors. When valets came to take their arms, Hagen refused angrily until Sifrit persuaded him by explaining that this was the Icelandic custom.

Brunhilde sent them the following greeting: "I wish to be informed without delay who these unknown warriors are who tramp through my palace so proudly, why these knights-at-arms have sailed to my shores."

One of her counselors advised, "None of them has been recognized, save one who resembles Sifrit. Let us make that one welcome with zeal and prudence. Another one is praiseworthy, I should say. He could be some great king who possesses vast domains. That is probably the case, for his bearing is haughty. The third is extremely tall but sinister of aspect. I can tell by the somber lights of his eyes that he is fierce and arrogant. The youngest of the four appears to be courtly. As a matter of fact, I admire the way he carries himself, modestly and gracefully as one who has just finished his apprenticeship as page and squire."

"Bring my reception attire," said Brunhilde. "If the mighty Sifrit has come to this land for love of me, he shall not escape with his life. I am not afraid of him, even so much as to think he may force me to become his wife."

Then escorted by five hundred Icelandic barons, each one with drawn sword in hand, Queen Brunhilde crossed the marble floor to the strangers. "Welcome in this land, Sir Sifrit. What is the purpose of your voyage?"

"Many thanks, sovereign Queen, most noble daughter of a king," he replied, "for greeting me first; but I must yield precedence to my liege lord here present, of whom I am only the vassal. He is the king of Rhineland. What more can I say but that he has crossed the sea desiring your love so ardently that he will never renounce it. His name is Gunther, this wealthy and dreaded sovereign. After he has vanquished you, no wish of his remains to be fulfilled. No wish on earth! He demanded my presence on this voyage, which I would rather of my own free will have declined."

"Are you, Sifrit, this king's vassal?" queried Brunhilde. "Is he your liege lord? Have you sworn fealty to this King Gunther? Does your lord know of the three trials he must undergo?"

Then Hagen cried rudely, "Woman, what are these so onerous trials? My king will bend every ounce of his great strength before he lets a woman defeat him!"

"First he must tilt with me. Then he is to throw a boulder, and then leap to it. Do not be so rash; for if he loses, so you will all lose your heads!" Brunhilde spoke eye to eye with Hagen. She was superb in her arrogance.

Sifrit whispered to Gunther to accept the challenge forthwith. "I am ready to contest you, magnificent Queen," said the king, "and either win you or die."

While judges of the bout were drawing a circle for the meet and taking their places and while seven hundred or more Icelandic knights were preparing to witness it duly, Sifrit slipped down to the ship, put on his magic cloak, and returned to Gunther's side, invisible. Brunhilde meanwhile had been attired in coat of mail, red-gold helmet, and shield upon which green stones had been set, stones greener than grass. (On my word, he was a daring man who thought to oppose her!) When Hagen saw the Icelandic queen easily lift her shield, cunningly fashioned of three thicknesses of gold and metal plate, even Hagen was daunted. He tried to discourage Gunther.

"What do you say, Sir Gunther?" cried Hagen, more and more intimidated. "This woman is the devil's bride, no other!"

Gunther himself fell back when he saw three servants staggering under the weight of Brunhilde's lance, so thick and broad, so powerful and pointed, so long and heavy and filed to a needle point was it! "If only I were home in Burgundy now," thought Hagen, "this barbarian could rule forever safe from my pursuit!"

Hagen's younger brother Dankwart thought to himself, "Has it come to this, that we must all perish because of a woman?" Despite himself Dankwart looked backward toward the palace, trying to think of a plan whereby he could retrieve his own weapons and those of the swarthy Hagen.

There was nothing bashful about Hagen; he spoke his defiance aloud. "If only I had a sword, we should see whether this proud woman should not find her temper softened!" Brunhilde smiled when she heard him. At her command courtiers returned their weapons to both Hagen and Dankwart. The younger brother blushed until he grew purple at this contemptuous gesture, but Hagen respected her for it.

As Gunther set his feet to receive Brunhilde's spear, he felt a hand on his arm. At first he could not imagine who had touched him, but hearing Sifrit's voice he grew reassured. Sifrit slipped his left arm into Gunther's shield strap and grasped Gunther's lance with his right hand. Even so, even the strength of both warriors together could not stop the force of her lance. With a clap like thunder it rang on the metal shield. Red sparks burst like blinding sunlight at the point of impact. The lance pierced the shield through and through, and clanged on Gunther's helmet. Its force threw both Gunther and Sifrit over backward to the earth!

Sifrit scrambled to his feet. Now it was Gunther's turn to throw the lance, and Brunhilde must fall also or they were lost. Sifrit drew back the lance until his hand was well behind his right shoulder. Then, leaping forward, he hurled it—he who had the strength of twelve men—so unerringly and so powerfully that Brunhilde in her turn spun around and fell to the earth. Opposite her Sifrit vomited pools of blood from his effort, and yet the onlookers saw only Gunther.

Trembling violently, Brunhilde, on her feet again, called across the lists, "Many thanks to you, Gunther, for such a fine blow!" It did not occur to her that Gunther had not aimed that lance, or even that he was far from capable of such a feat. Red with anger at her first defeat, the noble maiden strode with big steps up to the round boulder that no man alone could lift. Inspecting her arm bands to see that they were tight, she bent down, grasped the stone, set her feet, and then to the Icelanders' delight lifted it gracefully and hurled it a good distance from her. Then, feet close together, she leaped well beyond it, landing with a great ringing of armor.

In utter silence Gunther and Sifrit raised the boulder in their turn. The latter heaved it over seventy-two feet, and leaped well beyond it so easily that he was able to carry Gunther along with him.

When she recognized by these deeds that she had been fairly beaten, Brunhilde said to her subject in low tones, "Approach, relatives, friends, warriors. You have just become the subjects of this Burgundian king." Then all present laid down their arms and knelt before Gunther. All believed he had vanquished their queen justly by virtue of his superior strength.

Brunhilde took Gunther's hand and acknowledged before her courtiers that all her lands and wealth had also become his property. Of those present Hagen's face was the most triumphant. He grew even more pleased when he observed that the Icelandic queen received Gunther in her palace with every sign of honor and respect that she could make to his chivalry. Hagen's hatred of Brunhilde vanished. He admired her with all his heart.

After the agile Sifrit had run toward the ship and hidden his cloak, he entered the hall and asked the king respectfully, "When will the trials begin? Whom are you awaiting, O King? Let us find out the result!" So did the guileful Sifrit behave as if he knew nothing of what had transpired.

"How does it happen, Sir Sifrit," asked Brunhilde, "that you did not witness those games and did not see your liege triumph?"

Quickly Hagen answered, "Noble Queen, when you so impressed us with your overwhelming strength and superb skill, our Sifrit was at the ship."

"I am very happy to learn that my liege has won. That is good news, indeed," cried Sifrit. "Now is your pride humbled, Brunhilde. Now do you recognize your lord and master! Now, noble maiden, must you accompany us to Burgundy!"

Brunhilde dispatched messengers throughout her domains. When her friends and relatives had all assembled, she turned over her kingdom to an uncle. Then amid the tears and wails of her subjects she chose two thousand warriors, eighty-six matrons, and a hundred maidens to accompany her. It was decided that her wedding would be celebrated at Worms-on-the-Rhine. The voyage to the mouth of that river was long and perilous. Queen Brunhilde never saw her native Iceland again.

The double wedding took place at the palace of Gunther, where at the banquet Brunhilde wore the crown of her new kingdom. She wondered sadly why Gunther should have bestowed his sister upon a mere vassal like Sifrit, but promising that he would one day explain why he had conferred such an unparalleled honor upon the Niderland hero, Gunther refused at the moment to reveal his secret. During the wedding supper Brunhilde watched Sifrit and Chriemhilde sitting together wrapt

in their love. Despite her efforts to resign herself, the Icelandic queen's face grew dark; once tears came to her eyes.

That night Sifrit made to Chriemhilde the supreme offering of his love. They became one in flesh.

In the nuptial chamber of Gunther, however, there was another story! Once the servants and knightly escorts had withdrawn, Gunther hastened to close the door. Then he blew out the lights just as Brunhilde in her fine white linen nightgown walked toward the bed and lay down. "Now," thought Gunther, "I shall obtain what I have desired for so many endless days!"

Although not so beautiful as the Princess Chriemhilde, Queen Brunhilde was still splendid in her virginal loveliness. Gunther lay on the bed beside her and clasped her body close to him. His joy was great. He had already begun to open her robe and to caress her naked body when to his astonishment Brunhilde addressed him in tones of hatred and loathing!

"Noble knight, you must immediately renounce what you intend this night with me! I forbid you to touch me! Know once for all that I have decided to remain a virgin until I learn the secret you and your vassal Sifrit have between you. It concerns me too deeply, and I see that it also concerns your sister Chriemhilde who has greeted me so affectionately and so regally here in your land. Why have you married your sister to a vassal? It humiliates me even to think of it!"

Gunther, thinking that he could quell her by sheer force, now that she was undressed and weaponless, knowing also that once she yielded to him and lost her virginity she would also have lost her unnatural power both as a warrior maiden and as an individual reigning sovereign, gave no thought to her words. Instead he opened her gown and continued his caresses. Brunhilde, however, had not yet lost her power. Indignantly she wrenched off the braided silk rope she wore about her waist and despite Gunther's attempts to catch her hands, Brunhilde tied the sash tightly about both his feet and his hands. Then she carried him, bent double and trussed up firmly, to the wall, where she suspended him from a hook. Once she had disposed of King Gunther of Burgundy, Brunhilde straightened her robe and climbed back into bed.

"You can stop speaking love words to me, Gunther," she called across the dark room to him, "and stop disturbing my rest also!"

King Gunther was so tied, his head hanging down almost to the floor, that he could only gasp in mortification and pain, "Untie me, O Queen, I beg of you! Let me go. I swear that I shall never again try to vanquish you and that I shall only rarely approach your couch."

Brunhilde then walked over, untied him and stood him up on his feet. She allowed him to stretch out on the side of the bed so long as he did not touch her. She never would have endured his wrinkling and disarranging her white linen nightgown.

A radiant, merry Sifrit met only sour looks from Gunther the next morning. At Sifrit's request for information about his wedding joys, Gunther replied that Brunhilde had left him hanging from a hook all night long, right in his own palace!

"Oh, well, I'll take care of her once for all," laughed Sifrit. "I shall see that tonight you sleep so close against her that she never again dares to refuse your love. I shall use the magic cape. What you do is this: be sure to send away the chambermaids and the bedroom pages for the night so that we shall have neither witnesses nor any of her people about to whom she could call for help."

"In truth," said Gunther, "assist me in subduing her, for I have led a raging fiend into my bed."

"When you see the candle flames blown out tonight," continued Sifrit, "you will know that I am in the room. I shall quell her proud spirit so that she will lie patiently under your caresses from this night onward!"

"If you would do that, Sifrit," smiled Gunther, "then perhaps I could recover from my humiliation. Only don't go too far! Don't deflower her yourself! Whatever you invent to do, whatever way you choose to whip her will please me—only let me be the one to break open her body."

"On my honor, I don't want to make love to your Icelandic queen," laughed Šifrit. "You need not worry about that! Your lovely sister satisfies me completely, above all females!"

That day seemed as long to Gunther as thirty days. He could hardly sit still during the long banquet and actually dismissed the noble guests early. Sifrit was sitting holding hands with Chriemhilde when all at once he disappeared. "Where did King Sifrit go?" Chriemhilde asked her attendants. "He was here beside me just a few minutes ago. I didn't even feel his hands slip out of mine!" The Lady Chriemhilde, however, was wise enough to keep silent and to retire to her chambers. Sifrit joined her later.

In the royal chamber, as soon as the tapers were extinguished, Gunther hurried to double-bolt the heavy door. Then what screams and what cries came from the bed where Sifrit tried to hold down Brunhilde! Gunther's heart rose joyously and then sank when through the darkness he could tell that the maiden had thrown Sifrit off her!

"Go away from me. Go far away from me!" Brunhilde screamed. "Gunther! You shall be terribly chastised for this!"

Sifrit disguised his voice and in Gunther's tones ordered her to submit. From all the thrashing and gasping on the bed, Gunther could be sure that Sifrit was not consummating the marriage. Once Brunhilde threw Sifrit off the bed so violently that he cracked his head on a bench. After a deep breath Sifrit leaped on her again, pinning down her hands at her sides. Another time she escaped and stood up beside the bed.

"It is unseemly that a royal lady, a queen and the daughter of a king, should have her white shift torn from her body! You shall suffer for this outrage you do me, unfortunate wretch! You shall pay for this before you die!"

Then the struggle began afresh with even greater violence. When Brunhilde tried to tie Sifrit and hang him from the wall, she found that she could not hold him as she had so easily been able to do the preceding night. She squeezed his wrists so hard that the skin cracked and the bright blood ran down his fingers. In trying to untangle her belt so that she could tie at least his hands, she caught her own wrists. Then Sifrit held her on the bed. Then what vengeance did he take while Brunhilde screamed. . . She trembled from head to foot, and then grew quiet while Gunther consummated the marriage.

Once her strength was gone, Brunhilde knelt on the floor beside the bed and begged that her life be spared. She promised to be yielding and gentle henceforth and never to refuse her love. "You have shown me that you are my master," she confessed to Gunther.

Sifrit then released her and stole from the room carrying her braided sash and her golden *ring* that he had taken by force. With a merry laugh he gave both the ring and the belt as gifts to his beloved Chriemhilde.

After fourteen days the wedding celebrations drew to a close. Sifrit and Chriemhilde prepared to choose retainers and retire to their own Niderland kingdom. They could have required the attendance of Hagen, but that dour lord replied, "Do you not know the tradition of the heads of my house? My place shall always be, as it has been for my ancestors, close to the queen of Burgundy. I am henceforth a vassal of our Queen Brunhilde."

No princess was ever so joyously welcomed as was Queen Chriemhilde by Sifrit's parents in the Niderland. There they lived happily for many years.

Sifrit

Brunhilde maintained an outward calm in her new life, but her thoughts were troubled, for Gunther had never revealed his secret. Nor could Brunhilde understand why Sifrit, who she still believed was their vassal, never fulfilled his duties toward them, but on the contrary lived in far-distant Norway. Tortured by doubt, Brunhilde finally persuaded Gunther to invite them all to a tournament. To her delight Sifrit and Chriemhilde, as well as Sigmund and Siglinde, accepted the urgent and loving invitation.

During the course of this magnificent tournament, it happened one day that the two ladies Chriemhilde and Brunhilde were seated side by side at the table.

"All the lands of the earth should really belong to my handsome husband," sighed Chriemhilde. "Just see how gallant he is."

"That, of course, could never occur while King Gunther lives," replied Brunhilde in astonishment.

"See how my Sifrit shines like the moon among lesser lights!" boasted Chriemhilde.

"Shine as he may," answered Brunhilde curtly, "he cannot surpass my lord. I have heard your Sifrit swear with his own lips that he was the vassal of Gunther."

Chriemhilde answered furiously, "I shall have to ask you to cease such lies! Do you for a moment think that my brothers would have married *me* to a vassal? Moreover, you must well have observed that we never pay you any homage of fealty!"

"We shall see how high you have risen, my fine lady!" hissed Brunhilde, "and whether or not you are prompt in acquitting yourselves of those duties!"

"Indeed," taunted Chriemhilde, "I shall show you today which one of us takes precedence over the other at the church door! I tell you, I am above all queens who ever wore crown in this world!"

Each lady imperiously summoned her attendants and ordered them to outdo themselves in the splendor of their attire. Each lady walked confidently between the ranks of waiting knights who were amazed to see them arrive separately for the first time up to the portals of the church. Each queen wore her jewels and her most sumptuous gown. Chriemhilde was the more dazzling, however, because of the Nibelungen treasure her lord Sifrit had wrested from the dragon under the linden tree.

Raising her hand majestically, Brunhilde commanded, "Back, *vassal*, and stay far behind me! A mere vassal does not precede a queen into the minster!"

Then Chriemhilde cried in such a loud voice that the knights and courtiers all heard her clearly, "You would do better to curb your tongue, *concubine!* How can one man's concubine be the wife of an honorable king?"

"Whom are you calling a concubine?" gasped Brunhilde.

"You!" shouted Chriemhilde. "Sifrit, my beloved husband, possessed your body first. You were not a virgin when Gunther possessed you! Oh, no! It was not my brother Gunther who took your virginity!"

"On my honor," said Brunhilde, "I shall ask Gunther himself about that!"

"Do so," hissed Chriemhilde. "You have been blinded by your own ignorance. Your calling me a *vassal* has so kindled my anger that you have lost my friendship forever. Now go into the church and do penance for all your sins!"

While Brunhilde stood weeping at the church door, Chriemhilde swept past her with her train of attendants. When the service was ended, Brunhilde still stood at the minster door waiting for Chriemhilde to emerge. Brunhilde stopped her and said, "Do you still call me a concubine? If that fatal word is true, prove my crime to me now!"

"You would have done better to let me pass," replied Chriemhilde, "because I have the proofs right on my person. Here they are. This golden ring, which I am wearing on my finger, was a gift from my beloved Sifrit on the second day of my marriage."

"That royal ring was stolen from me," cried Brunhilde. "Now do I recognize the traitor who took it! It was you!"

"I did not steal your ring," affirmed Chriemhilde. "My husband Sifrit wrestled it from your hand and this braided sash also as proof that he was in your bed. Yes! My beloved Sifrit slept with you first!"

Chriemhilde swept haughtily away to her court. Brunhilde remained still weeping at the church door until Gunther could be notified. When the king, distressed and appalled at his wife's dishonor announced so publicly, inquired of her what reparation she demanded, Brunhilde assured him that if he did not avenge her, she would not receive him in her arms again.

Gunther assembled his court and required the presence of both queens and of Sifrit. Before his nobles he accused Sifrit of having vaunted the possession of Brunhilde. Before the black faces of the Burgundian nobles Sifrit swore that he had never done any such thing. The courtiers stared ominously at him. Gunther, however, believed Sifrit and pardoned him publicly. Sifrit then swore to silence his wife, and he suggested that Gunther do likewise. Both queens withdrew from the presence chamber, but Brunhilde hung her head in grief and shame. She now understood Gunther's secret. On her way out, she met the dark knight Hagen.

"Who has made my noble Queen weep?" questioned Hagen angrily. Sobbing, Brunhilde admitted her shame to him. Hagen's answer was solemn. Bending his knee before her, Hagen swore, "Chriemhilde's lord will bear the penalty for your dishonor, or I shall turn my back on the joys of this earth."

Several of the Burgundian knights during their next council thought also that Sifrit should be punished for Brunhilde's disgrace. Gunther did not consent, however; for, as he pointed out, Sifrit was too powerful an adversary for them to encounter. Like a refrain Hagen kept whispering to Gunther, "Just think, King, how many lands you would encompass, however, if he *were dead*." Gernot, one brother of the king, voted openly for Sifrit's death. Giselhers, the youngest brother, thought on the contrary that no woman's quarrel was worth the price of a man's life.

"My honor also is involved," argued Hagen. "What tarnishes the queen of Burgundy's name also defames me. Think, King Gunther, of Sifrit's Nibelungen treasure. It could all be ours. Think of the gold!" Because of Hagen's reasons it was agreed that he should kill Sifrit, lure him to his death by treachery even, if necessary.

The conspirators subsequently either withdrew or lost interest in the plot, all except Hagen. He arranged to have false messengers come from the Saxon and Danish kings to declare their sovereigns' intentions of making war on Burgundy. As Hagen had foreseen, Sifrit volunteered to serve Gunther as he had done previously. Then the implacable Hagen called upon Chriemhilde.

"How can I serve you best in this coming war, Lady?" he inquired.

"First you must not blame Sifrit for Brunhilde's anger," she replied. "Only protect my lord, for the fault was not his. It was mine, and he has chastised my body severely enough as my punishment."

"Tell me how I must protect your lord," Hagen urged. It was common knowledge that Sifrit's horny flesh was invulnerable. "I am your relative," Hagen reminded her, "and as such I only wish your lord all goodness."

"I should not worry at all," confessed Chriemhilde, "if someone during the battle were to curb his thirst for combat."

"Do you worry that some person could wound Sifrit?" persisted Hagen. "If so, you should tell me how I can safeguard him."

"My lord is daring, as you know, and he is wonderfully powerful. When years ago he vanquished the dragon on that mountain, brought that foul worm to his death under the linden tree, Sifrit then bathed

in the dragon's blood. What a great hero he is! Ever since that day my lord has been invulnerable. No arm, no weapon can pierce him. All the same, I worry when he rides impetuously through the crush of battle. Then do I tremble in fear that I shall lose his dear life. What anguish grips me then! (Chriemhilde should have said no more!)

"Hagen, I shall confide in you because you are my uncle. I enjoin you to keep faith with me, for I shall now reveal to you alone that one place on his body where Sifrit could be pierced, even to his death! That day when the red blood gushed from the dragon's dying carcass, as my Sifrit gloriously bathed in its crimson floods, a leaf from the linden tree dropped to his shoulders and adhered. Only in that one place can his body be wounded!"

The faithless Hagen then replied to Chriemhilde, "Embroider then, O Queen, a cross on the back of his robe so that I can see plainly, even through the clouds of dust, the place I must watch as I ride close behind him."

"That is exactly what I shall do," exclaimed Chriemhilde in relief. "I shall choose strands of silk and trace a mystic cross. May your protecting arm keep my lord safe for me!"

"Never fear, Lady," promised Hagen. "I shall not forget."

The next morning the Burgundian knights led by Gunther, Sifrit, and Hagen, attaching red streamers to their lances as was their custom in time of war, rode gallantly out of the city to battle. They had not gone far, however, when they were met by messengers who announced that the Saxon and Danish kings had revoked their warlike decisions. Despite their relief, the Burgundian knights were crestfallen. Rather than remain idle in their court, Gunther suggested that they prepare for a hunting trip into the Odenwald Forest. Gunther knew that Hagen was waiting for an opportunity to murder Sifrit.

The young Niderland king welcomed the suggestion of a royal hunt and listened to Hagen's clever description of bears and wild boars that roamed the deep woods in great numbers. They returned to the court to notify gamekeepers, masters of the hunt, and to loose the packs of dogs. Brunhilde prepared baskets of food which she sent ahead of them to a spring deep in the forest.

Chriemhilde wept bitterly, however, and pleaded with Sifrit to remain with her at the palace. "Last night I had such a lamentable dream. It was as if two fierce boars had pursued you over the heather. Then I saw the little flowers stained red with—! Ah, I have good reasons for my tears. I have a premonition—every now and then a shudder runs through me—that some implacable enemy is hovering over us with a hatred that no deed of mine can mollify."

"My beloved," comforted Sifrit, "no one hates us here. I have earned the ire of no man! These good warriors are our friends."

"No. It's not true, Sifrit. No, last night my dreams were black and funereal. It seems I dreamed two huge mountains toppled down upon your dear body. If I were never to look upon your face again, do you know what torture would burn into the depths of my being?" Sifrit held her in his arms and then left her chamber rapidly without another word.

When the royal huntsmen had come into the forest, Hagen suggested that he, Sifrit, and Gunther hunt separately so that he who brought down the largest game could be adjudged the winner. "Let us divide the valets and the dogs," proposed Hagen. "He who proves the most skillful forester shall receive our compliments."

"Oh," laughed Sifrit, "that's an excellent idea. Just give me one bloodhound, one which can scent the spoor of a bear through these dark trees, and I'll track down your Burgundian game for you!"

Then Sifrit spurred his fleet horse along the paths, over fallen tree trunks, urged him over streams so dexterously that no game raised by the hound was lost. He speared a fierce wolf-dog, and soon after felled a lion with one of his well-aimed arrows. The beast leaped thrice and rolled over dead. Then he killed a wild bull, a bison, and a buffalo. He also bagged several stags and does. Still his agile horse bore him swiftly through the tangled undergrowth. At last he killed, swinging his war sword with both hands, a monstrous boar as it rushed him with tusks lowered.

The master of the hunt recalled the hounds and ended the chase. The Burgundians laughed as Sifrit rode up to them. "Let a few of our animals live," they teased. "You have denuded our forest of game to-day." Sifrit laughed merrily with them. They rode together toward the sound of the horn that announced Gunther's camping area. On the way they spotted a huge bear.

"Loose my hound again," said Sifrit. "We'll have some fun with this old fellow." Then Sifrit dismounted and approached the bear which was trapped by the hunters on all sides of it. Easily Sifrit tied the bear's claws and slipped a noose on it, forcing the animal to trail after him like a dog on a leash. Thus Sifrit rode into Gunther's camp, leading a bear by the neck!

Sifrit's hunting costume was so splendid that there probably never was seen one so sumptuous in all Burgundy. His robe was of a thick, rich black. His toque was of sable as costly, surely, as the fur straps of his quiver. Wild panther skins decorated the quiver. Over his robes he wore a collar of white lynx scalloped with gold. He bore his fabled sword Balmung in his hand. From his quiver protruded arrows with shafts of gold.

As he rode into the circle where the king and his nobles reclined on golden chairs, while under the trees the cooks and kitchen boys roasted game over spits and spread delicious food on embroidered cloths, Sifrit released the bear that he had hauled behind him. Then he roared with laughter to see the fierce beast lumber between the campfires. The cooks fled clutching their utensils! The nobles holloed for the dogs to be untied, or called for their swords. Kettles and chairs went flying! Dogs barked and servants yelled. Then, still laughing, Sifrit killed the bear with one stroke of Balmung. Everyone agreed that he should be praised for his impromptu diversion. They complimented him on the blow that had slain the bear.

The nobles took places at the magnificently appointed tables where they were served the rich food that Brunhilde had ordered for their enjoyment. However, the wine stewards still had not arrived! Otherwise, no one could do anything but compliment Gunther upon his feast.

"Your cooks keep serving me one delicious roast after another," called Sifrit, "but where are your wine stewards? Either treat hunters better than this, or I shall leave off the chase altogether! Haven't I deserved a better reward than this?"

"Indeed, we shall repair such an oversight," called Gunther to Sifrit. "Besides, it is not I but Hagen who is responsible for this misdeed!"

"Truly, honored lords," apologized Hagen, "I thought we were going to hunt in another direction today. I sent our wines to that rendezvous. Therefore if we are all so thirsty already, I hope they will find us before long!"

"And I hope your body is torturing you with thirst also," replied Sifrit. "What we need here is seven draft horses heavily laden with mead and wine. Otherwise we should have camped closer to the Rhine."

This was what Hagen had carefully planned.

"There is a pure, crystal-clear spring not far from here, if you are so thirsty, Sifrit." Then as the Niderland king prepared to ride to the spring, Hagen continued, "Your noble Chriemhilde is always boasting of how fleet of foot you are, Sifrit. I for one should certainly like to race you."

"And I too," added Gunther.

"Very well," agreed Sifrit. "I'll race you both. And it shall be recounted afterward how you stripped down while I outpaced you both loaded with my heavy hunting suit, my sword Balmung, and my quiver full of arrows." As he spoke Hagen and Gunther were disrobing until they stood ready in their white shirt sleeves.

At a signal all three set off through the woods toward the linden-tree fountain. Sifrit won easily. He arrived long before them. Even so he would not commit the discourtesy of drinking before Gunther. To while away the time Sifrit unbucked his sword, stripped off his quiver and shield, and tossed them on a bed of moss. He laid his lance against the trunk of the linden tree; its point disappeared among the green leaves.

As soon as the others had arrived, Gunther threw himself face down beside the clear, limpid spring and drank. Then after him Sifrit did likewise. Behind him Hagen, marking well the cross, drove his lance at it and through Sifrit's body so carefully that the blood shot up from Sifrit's heart and wet Hagen—all over his white shirt. The lance stayed bolt-upright in the wound. That was the first time Hagen ever fled,— and the last time.

Shielding his eyes from the horrible sight, Hagen rushed away from Sifrit. . . . Sifrit raised himself to his knees, then to his feet. The iron tip of the lance protruded from his chest. His eyes sought his sword Balmung, but he could not reach it in time. All he could reach was his shield. This he heaved across the clearing at Hagen. Hagen fell to the ground, stunned by the impact. The precious gems from the shield rolled into the green moss. The clang re-echoed through the forest.

His blood poured from Sifrit. He tottered on his feet. Clots of red blood from his opened heart flowed upon the forest flowers at his feet, staining them all scarlet. Sifrit's knees buckled. He slipped to the ground.

"Misfortune upon both your heads, cowardly and faithless warriors. How have my exploits, accomplished at your request, served me? I kept faith with you, for which I now receive your payment. You have today betrayed also my wife, who is your relative. All your children will be held accursed for this your deed today. Your names shall be scratched from the roll of the valiant and honorable."

Little by little the other knights came by twos and threes to look upon the dying Sifrit. At their lamentations Gunther also began to weep. Sifrit taunted him then, "Let the author of this deed weep; that shall not efface his guilt. He could have renounced this plot."

"Ah," cried Hagen in disgust, "what are you all sniveling about? Our cares are over! Glory be to me who ended his domination!"

Desperately Sifrit struggled against death. "The day will come when you will regret my murder," he told them. "You can believe the dying words of him you have slain."

Carefully the warriors raised the corpse of Sifrit and laid it on his shield. They prepared to bear him through the trees. They debated what story of accident to invent for Chriemhilde and how to protect Hagen from her wrath.

"Bah!" snorted Hagen, picking up Balmung and buckling it to his own belt. "I myself shall carry Sifrit. I myself shall set his body outside his wife's chamber door. Let her find him at dawn when she starts for matins in the church. Let her weep! What do I care for the tears of a woman who brought shame to Queen Brunhilde of Burgundy?" [1]

Chriemhilde mourned Sifrit all the days of her life. Sigmund and Siglinde returned to the Niderland without her. She asked them for the Nibelungen treasure. When she had received her fabulous dowry, she thought to use it to buy knights who would avenge Sifrit; but Hagen stole the key to it. When Attila, king of the Huns, asked for her hand in

[1] The section that follows is a summary of Adventure 17 to 39 of the *Nibelungenlied*.

marriage, Gunther consented, glad to have her malevolence far in eastern lands, far away from him and his court. Although Hagen thought it was a mistake to let her assume such new riches and honors, Gunther allowed Chriemhilde to marry Attila.

Years later when Chriemhilde sent messengers to Worms-on-the-Rhine assuring them all of her pardon and undying affection and inviting them to a tournament at Attila's court, Hagen opposed their acceptance. Gunther, Gernot, and the youngest brother Giselhers, who had always adored Chriemhilde, accompanied by Hagen, Folker, and their most valiant knights, traveled royally down the Danube. There Chriemhilde sat in royal state awaiting them.

Her Huns murdered the Burgundians for her sake, all but Gunther and Hagen. Chriemhilde incited the Huns to chop down the Burgundians right in her mead hall; and when she saw that some were still alive, she set fire to the hall, trying to burn them alive. They became so parched with thirst that to survive they had to drink blood from the corpses. Finally, only Gunther and Hagen remained. The great warrior Dietrich brought them tied to Chriemhilde on condition that she spare their lives.

Chriemhilde broke her word to Dietrich. First she had Gunther beheaded. She carried his bleeding head to Hagen. "Now tell me where my Nibelungen treasure is," she ordered, "you loathsome devil!"

"Only I know, Lady, so be sure you will never find out for all your cruelty and treachery." Hagen had thrown the Nibelungen gold to the bottom of the Rhine. Wielding Balmung in both her hands, Chriemhilde beheaded Hagen herself. The Huns were so horrified from all the days and nights of carnage this fierce queen had caused in their land that one of them stepped forward and slew her where she stood.

Attila of the Huns watched her die. What happened after that I cannot say . . .

. . . But if you wish to see the linden-tree spring, walk through the forest of Odenwald near the village of Ottenheim. This fountain still flows limpid and pure, just as I tell you. Do not doubt me. You will find it.

THIRTEEN
RUSSIA
PRINCE IGOR

In the fifth century B.C. Herodotus in Book IV of his *History* speaks of the Scythians who inhabited northern Europe and Asia. He tells even then of their "gold-guarding griffins," and that they drank the blood of the first enemy that they conquered in battle, that they did not bathe in water, that they used the bark of the linden tree for prophecies, that they drank from the skulls of their conquered enemies, that they hung the scalps of those they killed on their bridle reins, and that they worshiped a sword fixed in the ground and watered with blood. We have already seen from the myths of the western invaders of Europe some survivals of these traits, particularly among the Goths and Huns as recollected in the *Nibelungenlied*.

Moving eastward from the Danube realm of Attila, we come to the area north of the Black Sea where the Slavs, another Indo-European people, appear in the pages of history with their own variations of culture and language and their own epic story or poem older by some fifteen years than the *Nibelungenlied*. It is the *Slovo o polku Igoreve*, or *The Lay of the Host of Igor*, which belongs to one particular group of Slavic peoples—the Russians.

In the ninth century, according to their first historian, a monk named Nestor who lived some 300 years later, they occupied a limited area around the Dnieper and Dniester rivers. They were surrounded by enemies—the Lithuanians on the west, the Finns on the north, and the Turks on the east and south. Their subsequent story is one of colonization and expansion.

In the ninth century Scandinavian conquerors called the Varangians crossed the Baltic and descended through Europe to Constantinople (Tsargrad). From their kings and heroes dates the history of the Russian people. Within a hundred years one of their rulers Olga had been converted to eastern Christianity, which brought the Greek alphabet to Russia; and around 1000 Vladimir, who like Olga became a saint, had tumbled into the Dnieper at Kiev the statue of the ancient Russian thunder god. Under Vladimir's son Jaroslav (1018?–1054) Russia was united around its splendid capital at Kiev which possessed like Tsargrad its cathedral of Saint Sophia and its Golden Door.

After the death of Jaroslav occurred a long period of civil wars in which warring princes struggled for supremacy. *Prince Igor* deals with this period. Our unknown author laments the dissension which has laid his land open to invasions from the Polovcians or Qumans (Kumans) who spoke a Turkic language. As a result of these wars and invasions Kiev ceased to be the center of Russia; its focus moved northward toward Novgorod and Moscow.

Our story tells of a particular invasion into Quman territory by a Russian prince named Igor Sviatoslavov from his home city of Novgorod-Severski in 1185. His Turkic-speaking enemies are nomads whose names, Qumans and Polovcians, mean "blond," or "fair-skinned." They may be the same Caucasian peoples whom the Persians in the *Shah Nameh* call the "white demons"; certain terms applied to them in the Russian epic recall similar appellations applied to the central Asiatic khan Afrasiab.

The story of Prince Igor's raid is historical. However, under these actual occurrences lies an invaluable and unique testimony to the pagan beliefs of the Slavic peoples. Here is the prime document which speaks of Horus, the Egyptian sun god; Voloss, guardian of herds and patron of poetry; Stribog, the wind god whose grandsons are the Russians; the thunder god Peroun who did not disappear even though Saint Vladimir destroyed his statue; and the swan-maiden of death. This last symbol was very widespread; it is found from the time of Aeschylus down to Lohengrin via *Beowulf* and Brunhilde.

One observes also in the *Igor* story an element of mythology that, passing through the folklore of Slavic, Turkish, Scandinavian, Germanic, Icelandic, and French cultures has left a superstition visible even in America today. Our author stops his narration to tell of a Russian prince named Vseslav who at night changed into a wolf. This is the werewolf myth (Anglo-Saxon *wer* = man) or the *loup-garou* of France. Popular belief through the ages was that a baby born with a caul about its head became bloodthirsty, crafty, lucky, swift of foot, wizardlike—a wolf at night. They thought his skin was as hard as horn and invulnerable, owing to the second skin or caul. After death he became a vampire, thus *Dracula* and *Dr. Jekyll and Mr. Hyde*. According to French tradition the lycanthrope or werewolf could only be killed by that person who wore or carried a four-leaf clover! It would seem as if this widespread superstition had colored the myth of Alexander the Great whose story was written and rewritten so many times during the Middle Ages, and also that of Sifrit.

The following adaptation of the *Slovo o polku Igoreve* is taken from the book *La Russie Epique* by the French scholar and Academician Alfred Rambaud (1842–1905), although historical elucidation comes from Professor Rambaud's *Historie de la Russie* (1878).

There was only one copy of this work, discovered in a Russian monastery in 1795 and subsequently burned during the Moscow fire of 1812. Professor Rambaud thinks it was written partly in poetry and partly in prose. It has been suggested that the work was composed by a friend of Prince Igor, perhaps by a warrior in his *droujina*, and that it may have been sung at the wedding of Igor's son Prince Vladimir. Many volumes were written in the nineteenth century to dispute its authenticity, which seems today unquestionable. Since Professor Rambaud does not give the whole text, some liberties have been taken with the narrative.

Among the many histories of Russia that appeared in the nineteenth century after Napoleon's invasion, is one written by Count Lamartine who is not only beloved as a romantic poet of France but respected as a scholar and statesman. In the introductory paragraph to this book he talks about the difficulty of tracing or establishing the history of those peoples whose mythology is the subject of this present book. He says:

An almost impenetrable mystery floats over the cradles of peoples, as there floats over the sources of those rivers which descend from their glaciers to flood a continent . . . a cloud. Whatever may be the struggles or the systems of scholars to retrace after the events, race by race and step by step, those immense and inexplicable migrations of men who according to the learned scholars seeped out of the high plateaus of Tartary, the mind becomes troubled at the hypothetical accounts of these *historians of mystery;* one can only glimpse flashes, one can only discern a confusion, one cannot explain one enigma by another enigma, and if one is then sincere and lucid, of a mind not satisfied with words alone, but wanting to walk toward the true light upon solid ground, one ends by abandoning those poets of darkness who are called erudite, and by uttering humbly the words of the profane, . . . which are also the words of the philosophers: "I do not know!"

Alphonse de Lamartine

THE HOST OF PRINCE IGOR

How shall we begin this story, brothers? In new words or in old? In what fashion shall we sing of the deeds of Prince Igor? Shall we mimic the verses of Boyan, the olden bard?

Boyan was a poet who knew how to stir the heart! When he consented to celebrate the deeds of a hero, his words ran as swift and as footless as a field mouse to the top of fancy's tree. Or like a lean, gray wolf he could slink, belly to the ground, across the deep ravines of poetry! Then in our listening ears he transformed himself into the blue and lonely eagle that soars over our heads until it has merged into the blue-gray thunderheads of autumn that drive northward from the sea. Such was the wizardry of that poet!

Do you not remember the spells of Boyan? As he sat meditating the works of the hero, some great *bogatyr*, Boyan would swiftly release ten falcons upon a flight of white swans that arched the southern blue. The first white wounded swan pierced by the swift avenger, had first to sing her plaintive melody faint as the dying words of the hero. Sad and thin were the words of Boyan as he charmed our ears: tales of Jaroslav the Elder, of Mstislav the Brave as he killed Rededya there before the Cherkess horde, and a pleasant lay about the fair warrior Roman, son of Sviatoslav.

Do we not know, my brothers, that the ten fierce hawks swift to cut the summer winds with their winged flight, were the ten slender fingers of Boyan which plucked the living strings of music? Those were the chords of memory his magician's fingers played upon. They sang the glory of our princes. . . .

We could have begun our lay with the life and works of Vladimir the Old. Let us not do so, brothers. Let our thoughts and our song drift down the winds of memory until they halt at the deeds of Prince Igor. He in our lifetimes has lived nobly. Prince Igor has dipped his soul into the well of truth and whetted his nerve like a steel blade. Let us likewise discard the rhapsodies of Boyan and tell only those true deeds of Igor; they will more than delight our souls.

Prince Igor set out from Novgorod with his train of warriors and rode due east. Warlike and valiant, the Russians under Igor spurred their swift chargers far from home, away from their peaceful fields and tame forest paths, eastward over the black earth of the steppes. Out of their warm, wind-sheltered homeland they rode gallantly toward the open prairies that stretch their rolling backs in grassy undulations far eastward toward the hordes of invading Qumans.

Then in a twinkling the sun hid its face. The whole earth grew black. Prince Igor sought in vain the bright sun's glare, sought in vain in the swift darkness the faces of his host. His men had reined in their horses and dismounted.

"Brothers and companions," said Igor, "mount up and ride. Is it not preferable to be hacked into pieces by the Qumans than to be captured here in this day that has turned to black night upon our shoulders? As for me, I have set out to strike my lance against the Quman breast plates! Ride forward, brothers! Let me leave my head upon these endless prairies, or let me pierce to where the Don rolls blue into the sea! I have sworn to drink his waters from my helmet!"

Boyan, you great poet of the bygone days, Boyan, nightingale from our distant past! You, and only you, Boyan, great poet, should have sung the host of Igor! For only you like the nightingale could hop upon the high tree of thought and fly in fancy through the fluffy clouds of summer. Only you could have chained these circumstances to the olden legends of Russia. Only you could have sprinted after Igor and caught him where he stood brave and unafraid on the grassy sea of the steppes.

Above the head of Prince Igor fierce hawks streak across the stormy sky! Above the wide plains, high over the wilderness of grass, masses of jackdaws flee in thick clusters toward the great Don.

Back in the homeland the call to arms thundered through Kiev! From Novgorod to the marches the shrill trumpet blared the alarm! Knights mounted their war horses. Banners were unfurled. The host fell into ranks behind Igor and set their faces eastward. Prince Igor waited for Vsevolod, his dear brother.

"Igor, my only brother," Vsevolod had told him, "saddle your war horse. Raise your battle flag. Are we not brothers? Are we not both sons of Sviatoslavov? . . . My warriors await you in Kursk. They are all tried men battle-proven and brave. They were born to the call of the trumpet, trained from childhood under their war helms, fed from a lance point! They know the roads to the Polovcian lands. They know every gulch and dry stream bed. Their bows are strung, their quivers are opened, their sabers are filed to a razor edge. They lope through the steppes like gray wolves in packs thirsty for glory for themselves and for us, the princes! Mount up, dear Igor, and ride!"

Then Igor set his foot in the golden stirrups and rode swiftly out into the black earth of the plains. Before him the sun dropped a curtain of darkness. Night blanketed the land. Igor listened to the voices of darkness. There was a moaning in the air so threatening it awakened the birds from their sleep. Around the host wild beasts roamed through the high grass and screamed their wild scream as they hunted. The little soft creatures huddled in fear, their eyes like pinpoints in the gloom. They flattened their bodies against the earth mother and listened. From a swaying treetop the fierce Diva shrieked the alarm to the foreign land upon which Igor had set his feet. "Awaken," cried the Diva, "awaken!" Thus she alerted the Volga, and also the Great Don, and the shores of the Black Sea.

By uncharted tracks the Quman hordes began to stream toward the Great Don. In the dark night the heavy wheels of their carts squeaked and squealed on the wooden axles like the terrified screams of wild swans overhead. Through the darkness they shuddered and wailed their piercing news, "Igor is leading the warriors toward the Don!" Then the earth creatures roamed smelling the smell of hot blood that will slake their thirst. In deep ravines the wolves howled to the moon. The eagles answered, summoning the toothed animals to the carrion piles. The foxes barked and snarled at the red shields of Igor.

Earth of Russia, where are you? Where are you, land of home? You are far behind the funeral mounds, far distant now for Igor who has crossed the soil of the steppes! Igor and his host stand alone on enemy earth in the trackless plains that stretch a long way to the Don.

Black night has changed to gray mists swirling their heavy webs over the host. White shrouds have lifted at dawn. Day has come to the prairie. The nightingales have hushed their cries as the daws croak and quarrel in the swaying grasses.

In a golden line the warriors of Igor have barred the roads to the west. In the white light of day they meet the Quman warriors and trample them into the earth. Like swift arrows the host of Igor pierces the heavy line of the foe and drives them about in panic. Pile after pile of rich fabric, silks and velvets, are torn from the Quman carts and trampled under foot. The foe are so loaded with cloaks, with fur robes, with brocades, with pavilions, that these stuffs under the horses' feet make a bridge through the marshy soil. The Russian horses tread on a causeway of furs and samite. The beautiful girls of the Qumans fall also as the spoils of war. The brave sons of Sviatoslavov take as their booty a red battle standard, a white banner, and a red yak tail on a golden staff.

That night in the lonely fields slept Igor and Vsevolod with the little princes, their sons. Lost, far in the trackless waste, slept the sons of Sviatoslavov. After their victory they had pushed on behind the scattered Qumans and camped for the night. Little did they know that the Khan Gza was on the march, swift and silent as the gray wolf of darkness. Little did they dream that the Khan Koncak of the Polovcians was streaking across the plains behind them to cut off their retreat.

You were not born, Prince Igor, to endure their insults nor those of the falcon, nor those of the hawk, nor yours either, black crow of a Quman, pagan Polovcian!

At daybreak a red sun, blood-red and fiery, flooded the plain where the Russians slept. The day dawned red under black thunderheads that drifted closer and closer from the sea, that descended slower and slower toward the orange earth. The rain clouds dropped their swaddling mists over the four sons, the four princes of Russia. From their black maw blue streaks of lightning hunted among the host of Igor. Thunder shook the earth and rattled the sabers. The horses rolled apprehensive eyes and pressed closer together for comfort.

Like stinging arrows the rain struck the host full in the faces. Like the sharp clang of steel-tipped arrows the rain, slanting sharply from the east, hammered at the Russian breast plates. From the Don came the driving shower of arrows. Lances shivered. Sabers blunted on conical helms. By the shores of the River Kayali the princes of Russia were surrounded by fierce Quman warriors. The battle thundered not far from the waters of the Great Don!

O land of home, where are you now? Where are you, earth of Russia? Igor and Vsevolod and the two little princes have left you far behind them. They have crossed the last mounds and plunged into the trackless prairies that lie between the Dnieper and the Great Don.

Fierce winds from the seacoast, those ungovernable sons of Stribog, are whipping Polovcian arrows against you! Full in your faces they rain the steely lances of battle. Under your feet the strange earth moans and disowns you. Beside you the strange river flows uneasily, hesitates turgidly, roiled with unknown blood from heroes it cannot welcome. Damp clouds of storm roll over your desperate arms. Back and forth the battle standards call to each other; they rally their friends in that tumult. The Polovcians pour on the battlefield from all directions, from the Don and from the Black Sea coast. Step by step the Russians retreat; their shields behind their backs, they form a circle facing inward.

And you, brave Vsevolod, impetuous bull, standing fierce at the rear guard, how you rake them with your arrows. How you beat upon their casques with your battle sword of hardned steel! This way and that you leap and plunge like a savage buffalo. Over here and then there your golden helm shines and glints. Under your hooves the earth is strewn with pagan heads. The Caucasian helmets crumple beneath your flashing blows. The nomads lie tangled upon their soil.

See his fury! Like a mad bull Vsevolod has struck from his mind all thoughts of home. In a flash he has forgotten the splendor of his princely life, his home city, the golden throne of his father, and the soft arms of his wife, that gracious daughter of Gleb. Vsevolod has forgotten a lifetime of happiness. What are wounds to him?

Did you hear that clang of metal? We have seen wars before and battles at Troy. All, all is past like the days of Jaroslav and the days of Oleg. He was a prince who brought disorder to our land so that harmony was broken. Prince fought prince and brother fought brother. In all these wars the grandsons of Dazbog laid down their lives over the fields of Russia where the carrion crows quarreled over their corpses while jackdaws grew fat from feasting. Those indeed were great battles, bloody and cruel; but none was so awful as that second day when Igor and Vsevolod fought the Quman hordes.

The black earth of the plains was churned by the furious horses. The very grass had been trampled so that it was stamped into the earth. No grass color showed any more. Bones and dying warriors, wounded and bleeding heroes lay in heaps across the prairie. What a crop of tears was planted in that rich earth!

What are those clinking sounds I hear? Ah, it is Igor's men riding again into the fray! Their armor clashes! Their swords ring against helmet in the heart of the Polovcian land. Igor could not let his brother think that he had been abandoned there at the rear guard! They had both fought hard all the first day. Then the battle had begun afresh in the rain of the second day's dawn. This was Sunday, the third day.

Not until noon of the third day did the torn banner of Igor tremble and fall! After that the brother princes were separated by the banks of the swift-flowing Kayali River.

The bloody red wine has all been spilled. The princes have risen from the feast and departed. The Polovcians are thirsty no more, for they have drunk their fill of blood. The Russians have lain down to die in the Quman fields. They have laid down their lives for their motherland. In sighing waves the long grasses of the plains have bowed their heads in sorrow. A tree, stricken with grief, has bent its head until its trembling fingers trail on the ground.

Then the goddess of Discord flew over the sleeping warriors. Lo! my brothers, sad is the hour when she glides down the wind! The wasteland has eaten our beloved friends and companions. The turf has sucked their blood. They have all been chewed and swallowed in that expanse of grass. All the "children of the glorious Sun" sleep now in darkness. Now over their dreamless bones flies the swan-winged goddess. See her glide through the blue skies! She has come from the Don to spread death among our peoples. All one will find in her path are mounds of bleaching bones!

Oh! how the swan goddess has brought in days of misfortune! How in Kiev the women wail! How the women of Novgorod weep and lament! Prince Igor's banner has fallen on the black soil of the prairies! How shall we sleep with the nomads at our doors? When shall we see our loved one riding up to the door? When shall we hear the sharp whinny of his horse? What black night shall we hear in our slumber the clang of his spurs on the threshold? When shall we feel his strong arms enfold our trembling shoulders?

What calamities did the warring princes bring upon us! How they have thrown our gold to the four corners of the Quman land! Why were they not all with Igor when he and Vsevolod affronted the hordes alone on the murmuring, foreign soil? What shall we answer, and where shall we hide when the fierce conquerors ride through our villages and call for a pelt at every door? We have made them rich, the fierce nomads of Quman. Their carts groan from the gold that overflows! Their rivers overflow from the golden swords, the gleaming helms, the gallants' shields that lie under their currents.

Prince Igor has just exchanged his golden saddle and his harness for a nomad's pony and a length of coarse rope!

In his palace at Kiev the crown prince of Russia dreamed that night, he who is suzerain lord to all the princes of Russia, he who is "uncle" of Igor. In his prime this Prince Sviatoslavov sent for swords from the Burgundian Franks. He used these weapons well. With his Frankish metal he cleaved a path that Quman chieftains remembered from father to son. Now in his palace the crown prince dreams.

"Hear my dream," cries Prince Sviatoslavov. "I thought that early last evening here on the hills near Kiev, they swathed me in a black shroud as I lay on my high-carved bed. They poured me wine that was cloudy and mixed with gall. Over my chest they emptied their quivers. The quivers of the heathen nomads were full of pearls! Huge, misty pearls rolled over my body. And lo! in my gold-domed palace the roof tree was missing; the mainstay of my house was gone! All through last night the black crows perched under the eaves of my house and croaked, cawed and croaked in my ears!"

The *boyars* replied to their prince, "Sorrow has stolen into your heart, and we understand your affliction. Your two young falcons have slipped their leashes and flown away from their father's throne. They have left your golden palace and galloped across the land toward the seacoast. They longed to drink the waters of the Don in their helmets. You have cause for grief, O Prince. Your dream was not false. The heathen Polovcians have snared your swift hawks in their nets. They have clipped their wings and chained them with iron fetters.

"On the third day of battle two princes radiant like dawns of royal

purple hue were hid by storm clouds and pelting flurries of arrows. Two boy princes, their sons, as slender and graceful as two crescent moons, were shrouded in cloud as they sank into the sea.

"All these disasters have brought abounding joy to the khans of the

Qumans who lope over our fields now like a band of hungry leopards. Black shame has, indeed, shrouded our former glory. Like the thunderbolts that fell upon Prince Igor have bondage and slavery fallen now upon all our people.

"The Diva, terrible goddess, croaks from our own treetops. Now that our warriors lie moldering, their bones bleaching beside prairie rivers, will not our defenseless homes invite the plunder of the hordes?

"Now the pretty handmaidens of the Goths, those allies and slaves of the Qumans, sing songs of our defeat all along the seacoast. They jingle our gold in their slender palms and hail the khans. For gold they sing songs of the long-dead chiefs of the Polovcians. For us, for you, Prince Sviatoslavov, there is no more joy!"

Then the crown prince in this golden palace at Kiev let fall his golden thoughts drenched in his tears, "Oh, my nephews, my children, Igor and Vsevolod! Too early, much too early, you rode forth into the rolling prairies of our enemies, thinking to cover yourselves with glory. You have not distinguished yourselves, young Princes! You have only let the blood of your faithful followers seep into the pagan soil. I know your hearts were valiant. I know your heads were high and your swords tempered in baths of courage. But look at the grief you have brought down upon my white head!

"See the sorrow I now must endure in my old age! Now I no longer see my valiant brother Jaroslav come riding at the head of his armed host, he so powerful and so rich, he whose warriors hastened to his banner from all the neighboring peoples. How would he have defeated the Qumans, my young fledglings?

"The host of Jaroslav in the old days had no swords like yours of tempered Frankish steel. With only a cutlass stuck in their boots, they spurred into the nomad hordes screaming their resounding war cries, raising the honor and renown of our cities! Jaroslav was the terror of the hordes!"

The old prince's head fell upon his chest. Of whom could he seek aid? One after another he passed in review the warring princes, those who had thundered across the plain, those whose sleds had sped swiftly down the frozen rivers in winter, whose oars in summer had raised showers of water drops from the Dnieper, from the Don, and from the Volga with their blades. It was up to the princes now that Igor had fallen. Only they together could stop the Quman invasion. If only Igor had not been so impetuous, they might have destroyed the enemies' winter homes while they were still in their northern pastures.

It was that Prince Vseslav who first years ago craftily brought the Qumans as mercenaries into Russian fields. He was not human, that Vseslav! At night like a wizard he slipped out of Kiev. He was no longer a man. At night he was the bloodthirsty werewolf. Through the forests he trotted from Kiev to Belgorod, all covered in a blue-gray fog. Then by morning he was thundering his battering rams against the oak gates of Novgorod. With his extra measure of good luck, Vseslav crushed the fame of Jaroslav.

Under cover of darkness Vseslav could leap all the way to the Nemiga in Lithuania where he drank much blood. During the day he sat in judgment over whole nations, handing over cities and villages to his followers. Every night he changed himself into a wolf and trotted through the moonlit forests from Kiev to the heathen idol at Tmutarakan before cockcrow. Thus in the form of a wolf he nightly followed the route of the sun god Horus. . . . If the princes do not rally to save Kiev, then we are lost!

What is that sound I hear? One would think at first the voice of the cuckoo. Do you hear its soft notes? It is not the weak cry of a bird. It is the lament of Jaroslavna, daughter of Jaroslav. Why does she weep? She weeps for the love of her beloved husband who is far away on the lonely prairies of the east. Jaroslavna weeps, ever so softly, poor lady, because her beloved husband Prince Igor is far from her arms. In the cuckoo's soft voice at dawn Jaroslavna weeps on the walls of Putivl' castle.

Leaning over the walls of her castle, straining her eyes toward the east, Jaroslavna weeps for her beloved.

"I shall fly like a cuckoo all the length of the Don. I shall fly to the Kalayi and dip my arms in its water . . . even up to the beaver cuffs of my sleeves. With my own hands I shall carry water and gently wash the wounds of my Prince Igor, all the bloody wounds there are on his powerful body."

Leaning over the walls of her castle, straining her eyes toward the east, Jaroslavna weeps for her beloved.

"O Wind, terrible Wind! Why, Sir Wind, do you blow so hard? Why do your light winds bear the arrows of the khan against my husband's warriors? Is it not satisfying enough to you to blow up high among the clouds? to rock the vessels on the blue sea? Why, Sir Wind, must you overthrow all my joy on the grass of the steppes?"

Leaning over the walls of her castle, straining her eyes toward the east, Jaroslavna weeps for her beloved.

"O glorious Dnieper! You whose swift current cut a bed through the stone mountains of the Polovcian land! O Dnieper, you willingly rocked the warships of Sviatoslavov when he carried his war into the land of the Khan Kobyak! Please, Sir River, carry my lord home to me. Then I shall no more have to send him my tears which drop now on your waters."

Leaning over the walls of her castle, straining her eyes toward the east, Jaroslavna weeps for her beloved.

"O, brilliant sun, you thrice brilliant sun! You warm us all with your yellow rays. You shine for us all. Why, Sir Sun, must you shoot your burning rays upon my husband's warriors? Why do you dry up their bows in their hands in that hot waste without water? Why do you make their quivers so heavy that they cut into the warriors' shoulders? Why, as they ride through that thirsty land?"

Toward midnight great swells mount in the sea. Huge funnels of fog rise from the deep and prowl inland over the coast. Their trailing veils cover the marshlands. They swirl their mysterious mists through the prairie grasses and engulf the camp of the Polovcians where Igor and the princes lie prisoner. God opens a path through fog, a clear path opening out to the west, a plain corridor of light down which a prince could walk between thick, gray blankets of cloud. If Prince Igor were to step boldly into that hallway, were to ride bravely down that unknown, midnight path, it would lead him surely to the golden throne of his fathers!

The evening dawn has finished her work. She has welcomed the horse of the Sun and prepared him for the second half of his daily journey over the heavens. She has lifted her purple robes and sunk to rest down the evening sky. Mist and darkness play at hide-and-seek on the prairie.

In the Polovcian camp the warriors sprawl in sleep, drunk with the sweet wine of victory. Does Prince Igor sleep? Can Prince Igor sleep when he knows what tidings of grief have already been carried back to the anxious cities of Kiev and Novgorod?

No, Prince Igor lies wakeful and watching among the prisoners. His eyes seek the path through the trailing, wet fog. In thought he measures the distance from the Great Don to the little Donets River. He rehearses the lie of the land, its folds and ravines, and counts off the tens of miles on his fingers. The most dangerous part of the journey would be the first day. As soon as the sun rose and dried up the fog, he would be clearly visible to his pursuers. For miles they would see him, one black speck, horse and rider, standing out clearly against the pale grass of the prairie. At night they could only guess the general direction of his flight from the distant, faint thunder of hoofbeats, if they laid their ears to the resonant earth, their earth of the steppes, friendly to them and hostile to Igor.

Just at the hour of midnight Prince Igor hears a low whistle. Cautiously he raises himself on his elbow and listens again. There it comes, a soft, low whistle from the reeds on the opposite bank of the Kayali. That was the signal he had arranged with the Polovcian Ovlor who had agreed to saddle a horse and lie waiting for Igor on the opposite shore of the river.

"You have a chance to escape. Fly back to Russia," his fellow prisoners had urged Igor.

"No man could do it," another argued. "No man alone with one horse, or even with two, could ride all those days alone over the prairie."

"No," replied Igor. "I was captured fairly. The Qumans rely on my word. For that they have allowed me to talk with my fellow prisoners."

"Fly, Prince Igor. Fly like a bird to the homeland," urged his attendants.

"No," replied Prince Igor, "and leave my comrades prisoner in the Quman camp? Perhaps if I were to escape, I might save my own life. Perhaps I might even arrive unscathed in our motherland again. No. We set out together to make this raid. It was on our own initiative, without the knowledge, the wise plans, or even the consent of Crown Prince Sviatoslavov. We rode together, and we shall die together as one man."

"Your thoughts run low like foxes, from burrow to burrow. Your thoughts are sad because your body is weary from wounds, from battle, and from the heavy shame of defeat. Be not a fox in your plans, Prince Igor. Let your hopes soar with the eagle who sees the two dawn goddesses at once. He flies so high that he looks from his flight of today backward into yesterday and forward into tomorrow.

"Fly, Prince Igor," urged the members of his *droujina*. "Remember that there is above us all a greater cause, that of our country. Kiev needs you now and Novgorod on the marches. The Qumans have defeated our armies. Their horses have trampled the sons of the Sun into the sod of the prairies. Let us not lose our leader also! Is it not terrible enough to have seen our warriors perish?

"Run the gauntlet of your pursuers, Prince Igor! Ride, leaning double over your horse's neck. Make a dash for freedom! Escape, Prince Igor, and may God go with you!"

Now in the midnight fog when the campfires are blackened ash and the creeping fog mantles the land, Igor has heard the whistle of Ovlor. "Do not stay here. Prince Igor! Come! Leave the Quman horde! Fly," it seems to say.

Cautiously Prince Igor rises to his feet and steps carefully over the legs of his sleeping companions. Silent and swift he makes his way through the fog to the outskirts of the camp, past the last blanketed forms, past the last tents and heavy carts, past the tethered horses of the enemy. The earth stirs and complains at his measured footfall. The treacherous grasses of that hostile land catch at his boots, swish against his spurs, murmur noisily at his passage. Like giant trees in the

gloom two Polovcian sentinels walk toward each other on his right hand. They have left the path clear in front!

Swift as an ermine Prince Igor darts into the reeds that cluster higher than his head along the Kayali shores. His feet sink into the wet soil which sucks loudly at his boots and tries to betray his passage. Like a teal, so swift in its flight, so rapid to fold its wings and dive headfirst into water, Prince Igor plunges under the Kayali current. With strong strokes he swims like a teal under the surface while over his legs the fog has covered the widening circles on the water. The river does not struggle against the swimmer. Prince Igor passes its water and wades ashore on the opposite bank.

There Ovlor awaits him, holding the bridles of their strong horses. Prince Igor vaults into the saddle and the horse awakens under him. Like the light-footed wolf used to running through fog and through darkness mile after mile, the mount of Prince Igor leaps over the grasslands. The only other sound is the pounding hoofs of Ovlor behind him. They cut a deep path in their flight, leave the grasses darker where they have passed because of the silver dewdrops that brush off on their horses' legs and on their flanks. Like a fierce hawk Prince Igor feels the wind on his head and senses which way is due west. They ride without stopping for breath, without once slackening speed, until both their horses heave and founder under them.

Then Prince Igor and Ovlor walk mile after mile through the rolling land on the eastern bank of the Donets. With their arrows they bring down wild swans and honking geese for their breakfasts, for noonday and for supper. As soon as they have eaten and stamped out their fires, they start out again under the blinding sun of day or wrapped in thick fog at night. Oftentimes they travel through grasses that are taller than their heads, where only the eagle could see their tracks, or the gray rabbit could hear their tread, until they come finally to the shores of the Donets.

Then that river, rolling its majestic way toward the Don, speaks clear words to Prince Igor. "Prince Igor," says the Donets, "as great glory as your escape will bring about your person, so will it bring equally great derision upon the Quman khans Gza and Koncak. You may be sure there will be great rejoicing throughout your native land."

"O Donets," answered the prince, "nor is there little glory for thee who has rocked so many princes gently upon blue waves. Was it not thee who through all time spread a carpet of thick grass so green and pleasant along thy silvery shores? Was it not thee who set the white ducks bobbing along the currents as sleepless sentinels? Was it not thee also, O Donets, who encouraged the sea gulls to patrol the estuary and the swift teal to span the course? The sluggish Stugna was never such a river as thou art! Scant and grudging are her treacherous waters that watched defeats by the Polovcians, encouraged them even by clawing at our friendly crafts and then ripping out their bottoms on hidden tree stumps!

"No praises shall I sing for the muddy Stugna's waters. What treachery did that river use! Surely thou rememberest, wise Donets! She caught our Prince Rostislav as he fought for his life in her bosom. She held his dear head down . . . down . . . thrice down under her waves until he rose no more to the sunlight! Now his mother wails and weeps, wakes and weeps for her son. All along the thin Stugna wild flowers bend their heads pensively as they see their faces in her mirror and are reminded of Prince Rostislav. Even the trees droop and mourn along her shores!"

Did you hear that? One would say a horde of magpies squabbling over seeds! Over there, beyond the grass! Do you hear it? One would say two magpies hurling insults at each other, coming in our direction! Hark! All of a sudden the crows have stopped circling and calling! Look! Look in the air above us! It is suddenly empty! Where are the jackdaws who swoop and wheel in the sun? The air is too silent! The earth is too still!

It was no horde of magpies whose chattering had drifted across the breeze to Prince Igor. That was the furious oaths of the Quman khans Gza and Koncak who fan out across the steppes and halloo up and down their lines as they hunt through the grasses for Igor! The crows caw no more. The magpies have ceased their chatter. Only the woodpeckers climbing nimbly over the gnarled willow trunks announce by their sharp little cries the line of the river.

Far in the distance the nightingale heralds a new day!

Riding hard, Khan Gza calls to Khan Koncak, "Since the Russian hawk has fled toward its golden nest, let us pierce his young fledgling prince with our golden arrows!"

Then Khan Koncak replies, "Since the proud Russian hawk has fled toward its golden nest, let us entangle his young fledgling in the meshes of a pretty, young Quman girl!"

Khan Gza replied, "If we let that fledgling get enmeshed in the charms of a pretty, young girl, we shall be able to keep neither him nor his lady love! You can see what would happen after that: in a few years time their young would fly vengefully at us and again lay waste the Polovcian fields!"

We must always return to the wise words of Boyan. You remember what Boyan said: "It is painful for a head to be without shoulders; and a misfortune for shoulders to be without a head is it also."

So would it have been for the Russian land a calamity to have been without Prince Igor and his son, Prince Vladimir!

No. Darkness did not fall upon us! Misfortune did not altogether lament and spread her wings over our land!

A new sun rose with a new dawn!

Prince Igor made his way back into the motherland. Maidens sang with joy all along the distant Danube. Their cries were wafted by the wind all the way from Kiev to the waters of the sea!

Prince Igor rode up the steep ravine of Baritchef, which led from the shores of the Dnieper to the high hill where gleamed the golden domes of Kiev! He knelt in prayer at the Church of the Virgin of the Tower. The motherland rejoiced. Bells rang in domed churches. Songs were sung in honor of the older princes, and new songs were composed at once for Prince Igor.

Poets sing of the glorious exploits of Igor, son of Sviatoslavov. They sing gladly of the impetuous buffalo, Vsevolod, of young Prince Vladimir, the fledgling and son of Prince Igor.

Long life and health to such princes and to their retinue who fight so nobly for the Chrstian people of Russia, against their pagan foes!

All hail to the Prince, and to his attendants.

AMEN

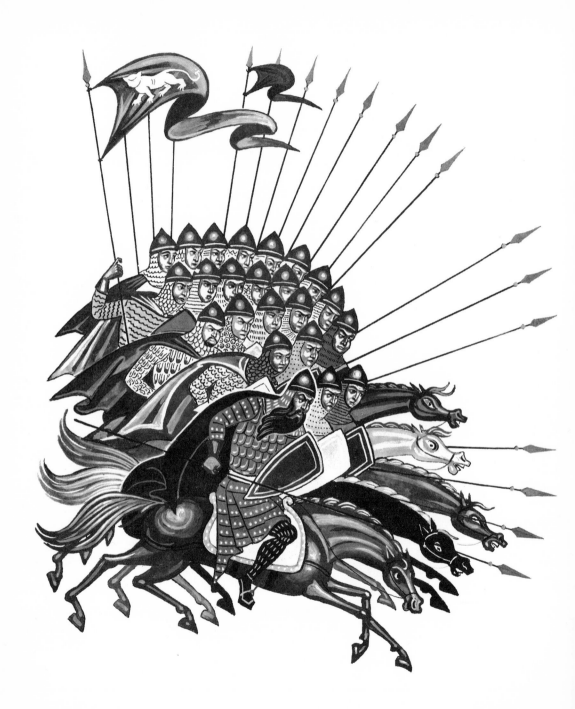

FOURTEEN
SPAIN
THE CID

How long poets in Spain had been celebrating the deeds of their medieval hero, Rodrigo Díaz of Vivar, before the Abbot Peter copied it
in the manuscript form that will be used here, is very difficult to say.
Rodrigo Díaz was born about 1043 (?). He actually did besiege and
conquer the beautiful city of Valencia on the eastern coast of Spain; he
ruled it for some five years with a clemency and skill that caused him to
be remembered and adored as their own hero by the simple people of
Spain; he did only leave Valencia in 1099 at the time of his death, leaving the reins of government in the hands of his wife, Doña Ximena; and
he was interred at the monastery of San Pedro de Cardeña near Vivar
and Burgos, where he was born. It is also true that great nobles, even
kings, are supposed to have descended from him. The family of our early
Floridian, Ponce de Leon, was one of them.

Rodrigo Díaz was called the Cid not by his fellow Castilians, but
strangely enough by his enemies, the Moors he defeated in Valencia and
elsewhere. The word Cid (sidi) means "champion" or "hero." Our
author calls Rodrigo Díaz endearingly Mío Cid—My Hero; he even
has Rodrigo call *himself* Mío Cid! In a medieval Latin chronicle this
champion is referred to as "*Ipse . . . Mío Cid semper vocatus,*" or "He
was always called Mío Cid." The reader will note in the following
abridged translation who among the characters in the story do not
refer to him by that affectionate nickname.

Our poet may have thought that he was composing in Latin, but
he was actually writing Spanish; this poem of the Cid coincides with
the birth of the Spanish language. It probably dates from the early
twelfth century (1140?) because it is much closer to Latin and to Old
French, much cruder in versification and elegance of expression than
the language of such poets as Don Gonzalez de Berceo who we know

wrote in the thirteenth century. Señor Juan Cabal in his book *Los Héroes Universales de la Literatura Española*, published in Barcelona in 1942, says that the *Poem of Mío Cid* would be more or less unintelligible to the average reader of Spanish. However that may be, it is true that a large part of our poet's vocabulary does not occur in a modern Spanish dictionary, but does occur in medieval French.

Some scholars in Spain hesitate to admit connections between this poem and French medieval epics, and yet it seems no reflection on the *Mío Cid* poet to remark that aside from the unexpected closeness of words and expressions, it does have traits that tie it to the *Song of Roland*, which is older, and to the *Berta* story, which is much more recent.

As the reader will see, Charlemagne did not have a monopoly on Saint Gabriel, nor on the possession of a magnificent beard. Prince Igor's father, who also dealt with the Franks, had a beard, and so does the Cid. The latter also has a pet lion in a cage as did the father of King Pepin. This king, by the way, had sent 25,000 men into Spain to fight the Moors in 735. . . . These traits, it may be argued, do not of necessity have to have been borrowed. Perhaps they only show the similarities between the European cultures. The reader, thinking back to the bleeding lance of the *Peredur* myth, will find its signification fully explained by Mío Cid's wife, Doña Ximena.

The land of Spain was settled and in touch with the other parts of the ancient world by at least 1500 B.C. It was colonized by Phoenicians, by Greeks, by Carthaginians, by Romans, and then early in the Middle Ages by the Goths and the Mohammedan Moors. It remained under Roman rule from about 218 B.C. for six hundred years during which time the Latin language became that of Spain. The Moors or Arabs invaded Spain around A.D. 711 and occupied its southern half for long centuries—the Dominion of the Almohads—until they were finally expelled in 1492.

By the thirteenth century, however, there was such a thing, despite all these mixtures of cultures, alphabets, and languages, as the Spanish tongue. There were great, *very* great "Spanish" authors living long before the days of our unknown poet who composed *The Poem of Mío Cid;* but they wrote in Latin, and their names are Seneca, Lucan, Quintilian, and Martial. In classical times Spain was known as Hesperia, a beautiful land somewhere in the west. The Romans knew its oranges, the "golden apples of the Hesperides," and its "dancing girls from Cadiz." Hannibal had come from Spain when he crossed the Alps into the Po Valley.

Spain and France were very close during the Middle Ages, as both the *Roland* and the *Cid* show us. In the thirteenth century the regent of France was the Spanish princess Blanche of Castile, one of the most pious and most remarkable women of the Middle Ages. Not only was she the mother of Louis IX of France, he who died in Africa during the last Crusade and was canonized in 1297 as Saint Louis, but she also helped establish the cult of the Virgin and the traditions of courtly love. One already notices in the *Cid* the emphasis upon women that became so strong during the Crusades when they assumed unwonted responsibilities of government and administration during their husbands' absences in the Holy Land.

Just as we have seen in the *Roland*, one good yarn deserves another. Poets therefore gave Charlemagne a childhood, and Roland also. Then they moved backward to give them ancestors whose lives made attractive subjects. The same is true of Rodrigo Díaz. The original poem passed through many hands into songs, poems, romances, and the glamorized accounts of early historians. From Guillén de Castro, a noted Spanish dramatist, it passed to France where it became the *Le Cid* (1636) of Pierre Corneille as French schoolchildren and students of French know. This masterpiece is to the lover of French classical literature what *Hamlet* or *Macbeth* would be to us. Rodrigo Díaz, no matter how humble his origins, has had a brilliant career in European culture!

The *Cid* is in a way the story of a self-made man. Although the actual life of Rodrigo Díaz was probably one of wandering and incessant quarreling with King Alfonso VI of Castile, our poet has, with almost the novelist's gift for characterization, presented us with the story of a real man's love and devotion to his family, his struggles to rise in the world and to become accepted by his social superiors. One knows the Cid better than one knows any other national hero of the Middle Ages. His words ring true; it is therefore no wonder that he is synonymous with Spanish! That very word "Spain" may convey instantly to the mind Don Quixote and Sancho Panza, or Don Juan, but most probably the first thought one has is Rodrigo, My Cid.

THE CID

. . . . then weeping and distressed Mio Cid said, "Father in heaven, you see what my wicked enemies have done to me!"

Mio Cid and his dear friend Alvar Fañez rode forth from Vivar. There was a black crow on their right; as they entered Burgos, there was a black crow on their left. Even so, Mio Cid shrugged his shoulders and held his head high. "Alvar Fañez," he sighed, "*we have been exiled from Castile!*"

Sixty of his knights, all bearing pennants, fell quietly in behind Mio Cid as he rode through the streets of Burgos up to his own palace. The city dwellers watched them from their balconies; no one dared greet Mio Cid on pain of the king's displeasure. Mio Cid dismounted before his own door. He knocked loudly on its panels. He knocked loudly and again. There was no answer from his people within the walls. Mio Cid turned away from his own door. Even that was barred against him.

That night Mio Cid camped outside the city on the banks of the Arlanzon just as if he were campaigning in the mountains. There Martin Antolinez of Burgos joined him and supplied food for the company in defiance of the king's injunction. Mio Cid was able to borrow six hundred marks from Señors Rachel and Vidas. At cockcrow he and his companions, those who had freely chosen an exile's wandering life with him, rode to the monastery of San Pero de Cardeña where their ladies had taken refuge.

"From this moment," said Mio Cid to those who still followed him, "since the king of Castile has seen fit to banish me, I am about to depart from this kingdom. I do not know whether I shall ever in my life enter my home again. Queen of glory, sustain me!"

He and his loyal knights arrived in the courtyard of the monastery just before daybreak. Doña Ximena, the wife of Mio Cid, and her two daughters, Doña Elvira and Doña Sol, were kneeling at matins when the word came of the knights' arrival. Joyously they ran into the dark courtyard where by the flare of candles and torches they recognized Mio Cid. Doña Ximena fell on her knees before her husband. She kissed his hands.

"I see that you are leaving us," she wept, "and that you and I must part even in our lifetimes."

Weeping also Mio Cid put his arms about his two young daughters. He pressed them close to him. "Yes, most accomplished Lady whom I love as I love my soul, I see that we must, indeed, part in our lifetimes. I must leave you here, Lady. May God grant me a few more days of life and happiness in this world. May He grant me to earn dowries for our young daughters. May He grant me life so that I may do you service and homage, most honored Lady, my wife."

During that day heralds rode about the countryside announcing the present departure of Mio Cid from the lands of King Alfonso of Castile, and inviting all men who so desired to rally to his banner. Within six days, 115 men-at-arms had joined Mio Cid. They knew he had no money, for he had left his cash at the monastery for the care of his wife and daughters. Whatever he still possessed, they knew he would share gladly down to the last coin. Since only three days remained before Mio Cid would be arrested by the king, his whole party prepared to ride at daybreak toward the frontiers of Castile.

Doña Ximena prayed, "Glorious Father, who art in heaven. Thou who appeared in Bethlehem, Thou whom Melchior, Gaspar and Balthazar came to adore, Thou who spent thirty-two years upon this earth, Thou who upon the cross did a wonderful deed! Longinos, who had been blind from birth, pricked Thee with the point of his lance so that Thy blood streamed down the lance's point and dripped on his hands. When Longinos lifted his hands to his eyes, they were *healed* and he saw! I adore Thee and believe in Thee with all my heart. I pray Saint Peter to keep Mio Cid from harm and to make us united again in this lifetime."

After Doña Ximena and her husband had heard mass together, they rose and left the chapel. Mio Cid kissed his wife tenderly, for she was weeping so hard she did not know what to do. He entrusted her and his daughters to the abbot, promising to reward the monastery for their trouble and expense. Then he tore himself from his family painfully, like a fingernail from the finger, and rode away over the eastern mountains at the head of his knights.

One night as Mio Cid lay sleeping alone and exiled near the Duero River, the Angel Gabriel appeared to him in a dream. "Ride forward, Cid, good Campeador! Never did baron ride into the eastern lands with such a promise as I now make you: as long as you live, Cid, your life will turn out well for you!"

By the time that Mio Cid had reached the Sierras, he could count three hundred lances behind him. How could he feed such a host? . . . He took the town of Casteion, captured its fortress, and received three thousand marks as a tribute. All this money, herds also, fell to Mio Cid who cared nothing for wealth. To each of his knights he gave one hundred silver marks and to each footsoldier fifty marks. Then he restored their freedom to the Moors he had vanquished, and to their women also, so that people would never speak badly of Mio Cid. He then set out again, for King Alfonso of Castile was still close behind him. Mío Cid would never have raised his lance against his liege lord.

Before the walls of Alcocer Mio Cid camped for fifteen weeks. He finally took that city also, by artifice. He left one tent pitched before the town, folded his other baggage, and set off down the riverbanks. The people of Alcocer, thinking that he had run out of bread for his men and barley for his animals, spurred after him. When he had drawn them far enough away from the gates, Mio Cid wheeled about, cut a path through his pursuers, and entered the city ahead of them. The banner of Mio Cid was raised over the citadel. He allowed the Moors to re-enter as his subjects.

When the neighboring cities of Teca, Teruel, and Calatayud heard of this victory, they sent a messenger to King Tanin at Valencia asking for aid before they too were seized. Two Moorish kings set out with three thousand well-armed Moors. They recruited supporters and came to besiege Mio Cid in Alcocer. They cut off the water supply to the city and waited. After three weeks Mio Cid and Alvar Fañez put all the Moors out of the city one night. Then they armed themselves for battle. They were six hundred. The honor of carrying their banner was accorded to Pero Bermuez. At daybreak they threw open their gate and plunged without warning into the Moors' encampment. . . . You should have seen the Moors scurry about to arm themselves! At the roll of their drums you would have thought the earth wanted to split!

The men of Mio Cid clutched their shields against their chests. They lowered their lances from which bright pennants streamed. They did this as one man. They bent their faces over their horses' necks. In stirring tones Mio Cid called to them, "Strike them, Knights, for the love of charity! I am Ruy Díaz, the Cid Campeador of Vivar!"

(V. 731)　*Trescientas lanzas son, todas tienen pendones.*
Sennos Moros mataron, todos de sennos colpes.
A la tornada que facen otros tantos son.
Veriedes tantas lanzas premer è alzar,
Tanta adarga aforadar é pasar,
Tanta loriga falsa desmanchar,
Tantos pendones blancos salir bermeios en sangre,
Tantos buenos cavallos sin sos dueños andar.
Los Moros laman Mafomat: los Christianos Sanctiague.

They are three hundred lances, all bearing pennants.
Each man killed a Moor, each one at one carom.
At the turning, as they wheel, they are still as many.
You should have seen those lances, lowered and raised,
So many bucklers pierced, so many perforated,
So many coats of mail broken and unlaced,
So many white pennants with red blood defaced,
So many fine horses without their riders stray.
The Moors call on Mohammed: the Christians on Saint James.

That day there were the following brave men with Mio Cid: Alvar Fañez, Martin Antolinez, Muño Gustioz, Martin Muñoz, Alvar Salvadoros, Galin Garcia, and Felez Muñoz, who was the Cid's nephew. They fought so valiantly that the Moorish kings fled the field of battle and rode for dear life into Teruel and Calatayud to nurse their wounds. Mio Cid pursued them right to the gates of Calatayud. Then he returned to the battlefield where the Moors lay dead and dying. Sword in hand he waited for his Castilians to rally around him. "Grace be to God that we have won this pitched battle," said Mio Cid. So much wealth lay in the Moorish camp that it seemed one could not count it.

Mio Cid allowed the Moorish people to return to their city. He also ordered that they should each be given something. Mio Cid's part of the spoils was one-fifth. In his share were one hundred war horses. He said to Alvar Fañez, "Ride back to Castile. Announce to my lord and king the news of this battle. Take him thirty caparisoned horses, each with a fine sword hanging from the pommel. Ask him to receive this gift from me. Take also this purse of gold and pay for the thousand masses I promised at Saint Mary of Burgos. Give what is left to my lady wife and to my daughters. Say to them that if I live, they shall all three become wealthy ladies."

382

In all Mio Cid's party now there was not a needy man. However, the Campeador could not stay in Alcocer, for the country was too bare and the land too poor to sustain him and his growing forces. When he prepared to ride forth, the Moors and their women sent their prayers along with him. They wept to see Mio Cid go. The Castilians camped on the high hill of Mont Real and sent requests for tribute to Teruel.

Meanwhile Alvar Fañez had arrived in Castile. Kneeling before the king, he begged him to accept Mio Cid's gift. "It is too early," said the king, "to pardon a vassal who has incurred my displeasure. However, I accept his offering, and I am happy for his success. I reinstate you, Alvar Fañez, in your fiefs. As for the Campeador, I have nothing to say except that I hereby declare that any knight who wishes to join him is free to do so. I also ordain that the hill of Mont Real where Mio Cid is encamped be duly and legally called from this day forth the Hill of Mio Cid." Alvar Fañez took two hundred more knights to his lord who had moved north to Saragossa and put it to ransom. Saragossa paid willingly; it congratulated itself to be acquitted so easily.

The news of Mio Cid's incursions in the north reached the Count of Barcelona, Raymond Bérenger. This Frankish nobleman was highly insulted and deeply offended. "Mio Cid de Vivar," said Count Raymond, who was a rash sort of fellow, "is dashing through lands which are under my protection. I never sent him a challenge. I never acted as the aggressor. Since he has dared to provoke me, I think I shall have to go ask him why."

Large forces of Christians and Moors flocked to the banner of this Frankish count. They caught up with Mio Cid as he was winding his way, heavily loaded with spoils, down a sierra into a valley. To the count's angry message Mio Cid sent this answer: "Tell the Count not to take it so badly. I am carrying away nothing that belongs to him. Tell him to let me go in peace."

Count Raymond replied haughtily. "He shall have to pay me now. This exile must learn that he has dishonored a count!"

Then Mio Cid ordered that the baggage be unloaded. He saw that Count Raymond would not let him escape without a battle. When Mio Cid observed the silken hose and cushioned saddles of the Franks, and compared them to his sturdy wooden saddles and coats of armor, he did not doubt but that three Franks would fall before each Castilian lance. In the ensuing short encounter Mio Cid easily won 1,000 silver marks, and took Count Raymond prisoner. The Frank was escorted to his captor's tent and served a delicious dinner.

As each dish was presented to him, Count Raymond turned up his nose in disdain. "I would not touch a mouthful of your food for all there is in Spain," he said scornfully. "I prefer to leave here both body and soul rather than to confess I was defeated by such a motley band of . . . leggings!"

Then Mio Cid told him, "Eat some of this bread, Count, and drink some wine. If you do what I advise, you will escape from your captivity. If not, then you will never see your Christian land again."

Count Raymond answered, "You eat, Don Rodrigo, and enjoy yourself. I prefer to die, for I refuse your food and your drink." For three days, while the Castilians were apportioning the booty, the Frankish count sulked and fasted.

Mio Cid watched him all this time. Again he said, "Eat something, Count, for if you do not eat you will never see Christians again. If you do eat enough to satisfy my honor, I will liberate you and two of your gentlemen as well. You shall be freed."

When he heard that, Count Raymond exulted. "If you really do it, Cid, I shall be marvelously pleased with you as long as I live."

"Then eat, Count, for when you have done so, I shall set you free with two others. However, know that of all the spoils I have taken from you, I shall not return a red cent. The men who follow me would be poverty-stricken if I did not provide. Therefore I need this plunder for myself and for them. We have to live by taking what we can find. Not only that! We have to lead this kind of life as long as it shall please our Holy Father, since I am a man who has incurred his sovereign's displeasure, for which I was banished."

Mio Cid was seated in his tent, higher than the count. "If you do not eat enough of my food to satisfy my honor, Sir, you and I shall never be free the one of the other."

"I accept with all my heart," said Count Raymond, "your gracious hospitality." Mio Cid was pleased when he saw the Frank call for water, wash his hands, and then plunge his flashing white fingers into the meats that were set before him. When both had dined, Count Raymond courteously thanked Mio Cid. "Since the day I was dubbed, I don't recall such a delicious meal," he said. "The pleasure it has afforded me will not soon be forgotten."

Three palfreys with beautiful saddles were brought, and heavy cloaks and furs. His Castilian host escorted the three Franks to the edge of the camp. "Are you leaving me so soon?" inquired Mio Cid. "And in such a Frankish manner? Let me thank you again for all the rich gifts you have left behind you. If it ever occurs to you to wish for revenge, and if you come looking for me, I am sure that you will find me. If you do not, on the other hand, send after me, but leave me alone, I shall see that you receive something from my wealth or from that of yours which I have."

"Give not a thought to it, Mio Cid," laughed Count Raymond. "You have nothing to fear from me. I have paid you enough tribute for one year. And as for seeking you out, I doubt if it will ever cross your mind."

Then the Frankish count dug both spurs into his palfrey's sides and looked over his shoulder, expecting that Mio Cid would repent and chase after him. His Highness (el Caboso) would never have committed such a disloyalty for anything in the world! Mio Cid returned to his

camp where he spent many more days distributing the plunder from this battle. He and his men were so rich now that they couldn't tell how much they had.

(V. 1094)   *Aquí s conpieza la gesta de Mio Cid el de Bibar.*

Here begins the story of Mio Cid of Vivar.

The Siege of Valencia

Mio Cid, leaving Saragossa and its lands far behind him, turned toward the sea, towards the east from which rises the sun. The more towns he seized on his passage, the more he came to understand that God was with him. His triumphs weighed heavily upon those in the princely city of Valencia; you may as well know it. Those of Valencia therefore took the initiative. They left their rich city and advanced to besiege the Castilians in Murviedro. Mio Cid was delighted. "Here we are," he said, "in their land, drinking their wine and eating their bread. They have every right to question our presence. If we wish to remain here, we must chastise them thoroughly. Let this night pass. On the morrow we shall advance and then see who among my followers is worth his pay."

Now listen to what Alvar Fañez replied. "Campeador, let us do what pleases you. Give me a hundred knights—I ask for no more. Attack them full in the face, and I know you will not flinch. I will circle round and strike them from the rear." His spirit always pleased Mio Cid.

At the very break of dawn Mio Cid aroused his men. Each one knew where to go and what to do. "Hit them hard," cried Mio Cid. "In the name of our Maker and the Apostle James, strike them, knights, will all your will and heart. For I am Ruy Díaz, Mio Cid of Vivar!"

There you would have seen the Castilians spur between the Moors' tents, slash the ropes, and topple the pegs! As the Moors tried to search for their leaders through that confusion of falling pavilions, Alvar Fañez struck them from behind. They had a choice then—to surrender or to run! Two Moorish kings were killed. Mio Cid pursued those who escaped all the way to Valencia; those who made it to that haven had only the fleetness of their horses to thank. Great was the joy of the Castilians, for they were rich beyond all their hopes. Nor did they stop there. Sleeping during the day and marching at night, Mio Cid spent three years taking one Moorish city after another. He gave them a good lesson in Valencia.

The news of his victories traveled across the sea to Morocco. The people of Valencia complained bitterly as they saw Mio Cid tightening the circle he had drawn around them. They no longer knew what to do, for all the roads were cut. No bread came into the city any more.

Father no longer fed son, nor son father. Friend no longer helped friend. They found no crumb of consolation. It is a disastrous state of affairs, sirs, not to have bread and to watch your women and children starve before your eyes. The king of Morocco knew this, and yet he sent them no aid.

When Mio Cid saw no reinforcements disembark, his heart was gladdened. He dispatched heralds throughout Aragon, Navarre, and Castile to proclaim far and wide: "He who wishes to lose all care and arrive at great riches, let him rally to Mio Cid, who desires to take a daring ride! Mio Cid intends to besiege lordly Valencia itself! He wants it to be in Christian hands. He will wait three days by the Canal of Celfa. Let each man who joins him do it of his own free will, and not under duress!"

After knights and footsoldiers had swollen his ranks, Mio Cid led his army to the very ramparts of Valencia. He besieged that great city honorably, without trickery, simply allowing no one to leave and no one to enter. He established and announced the delay he would grant the city: nine months and no more. He thought that their reinforcements, if any, would have ample time to succor the besieged if that was their intent. At the beginning of the tenth month lordly Valencia fell to Mio Cid. As he rode through its streets, those of his followers who had joined his ranks as simple footsoldiers were mounted and equipped as gallantly as knights. Who could begin to tell you the quantities of gold and silver each had earned? How happy was he as he watched his banner being raised to the top of the Alcazar!

Within a short time thereafter the king of Seville rode forth to challenge Mio Cid's possession of Valencia. Although this king had thirty thousand warriors under his banner, Mio Cid vanquished him. His share from Valencia, which was thirty thousand minted marks, plus this second landfall, surpassed his dreams. Each Castilian took from this battle one hundred silver marks, so you can imagine what Mio Cid's fifth was!

Then Mio Cid vowed that he would never pull a hair from his ample beard or cut it in any way. This would show his long trials, his great love for his lord Alfonso of Castile, and would be a subject of marvel for Moors and Christians alike. Next he decreed that any man who deserted Valencia without permission, and without having first kissed his hand, should be hanged and his wealth donated to the public coffers. He also appointed Alvar Fañez to have a census made of his followers, their lands and estates, and the amount of wealth they had earned. He found that his forces totaled 3,600. Smiling and satisfied at how his position had improved, he then asked Alvar Fañez to take one hundred horses as a gift to King Alfonso of Castile.

"Beg my king to spare me my lady and my daughters, so that I may now enjoy their gracious presence here in Valencia. Now that I am lord of this proud city, I can begin to do them honor. Therefore urge my suit before the king. . . . I can entrust my family's safety to you, dear Alvar Fañez, during the journey where they must be honorably escorted. Let no indignity fall upon them." Mio Cid dispatched one hundred men with Alvar Fañez and a gift of one thousand marks to the monastery which had provided shelter and care to his family.

While these deliberations were being taken, there arrived in Valencia from the Holy Land a distinguished priest and scholar named Don Jerome. Mio Cid was struck by this priest's learning and prudence; he observed also how Jerome sat a horse as skillfully as a knight, and how well he bore himself in all situations requiring learning and diplomacy. This erudite Jerome explained to Mio Cid that he was a militant priest who wished to share their fortunes and their rude trials. He said he expressly forbade any Christian to weep for him if ever he fell under a Moorish sword. Mio Cid studied this Frankish priest, his speech and his actions, and judged him to be honorable and holy. He therefore decided to elevate Jerome to the rank of bishop and to create a diocese for him in the city of Valencia. This decision was also to be announced to King Alfonso of Castile. There was great happiness in the city when the people learned that they now had within their walls their own Lord Bishop.

Alvar Fañez found the king of Castile in the estates of Carrion. He fell on his knees and presented Mio Cid's gift in full view of the populace one day as the king came out from mass. King Alfonso smiled as he heard from Alvar Fañez' lips the list of Mio Cid's conquests—Xerica, Onda, Almenar, Murviedro, Cebola, Casteion, Peña Cadiella, and Valencia—when he learned of the five pitched battles he had won, and of the wealth he had acquired for himself and his men. With his right hand King Alfonso made the sign of the cross at such good news. "My heart is glad," said the king. "I am pleased at the prowess of the Campeador. He brings me glory. I accept his gift."

Then Garci Ordoñez, long a bitter enemy of Mio Cid, added his acid comment, "It seems to me, Sire, that the Cid Campeador has not left us a single man alive in the land of the Moors."

"Stop such talk," commanded the king. "He serves me better than you do."

"Mio Cid craves your mercy," continued Alvar Fañez, "if such a request does not displease you. He asks that you permit his lady and daughters to leave their monastery and to journey to Valencia."

"I accede to his request," answered King Alfonso. "I wish also to provide for these noble ladies while they remain within my lands. See that neither insult, nor evil, nor dishonor fall upon them. Let your Mio Cid look to their safety at the frontier of Castile. Think of it, and make your plans accordingly.

"Now hear you all," continued the king, "I wish Mio Cid to be deprived of nothing. I hereby reinstate his vassals in all their lands and privileges and exempt them from my jurisdiction in cases of capital punishment. I do this so that they may be free to serve their feudal lord."

The two young princes, or Infantes, of Carrion were present at this interview. They spoke to each other secretly. "The fortunes of the Cid Campeador are increasing steadily. Perhaps we should marry his daughters. . . . However, how should we, Infantes of Carrion, propose such a thing to this adventurer, this Mio Cid, who is only from Vivar?"

"Tell your lord," said the crafty Infantes to Alvar Fañez, "that we greet him, that we are at his service as much as princes are able, and that he should think kindly of us. He could not lose thereby."

"I shall transmit your words," replied Alvar Fañez. "There is no trouble in that."

After he had humbled himself before Doña Ximena, and told her of her coming travels, Alvar Fañez sent three knights toward Valencia to tell Mio Cid that his family would be leaving Castile and that within five days he should have an escort waiting for them at the frontier. Then he spent five hundred marks in Burgos on palfreys for the ladies and their attendants, upon the saddles and accouterments so that they would suffer no indignity from their appearance.

Mio Cid, you may be sure, sent his most courageous and most trusted vassals to escort his precious ladies. He dispatched Muño Gustioz, Pero Bermuez, and Martin Antolinez with one hundred knights armed to the teeth, and he also asked Bishop Jerome to join their party. He instructed them to pass through Molina, which was ruled by the Moor Abengalvon, long a personal friend of Mio Cid. The Moor would surely add another hundred knights to the escort. "Tell my old companion Abengalvon that I count on him to do full honors to my family. I shall remain in Valencia because it is now my hereditary fief," declared Mio Cid. "I spent years to win this realm and will not lose it now."

The Moor Abengalvon, understanding the weight of his responsibility, set out to meet the ladies himself. Not satisfied with one hundred knights, he took two hundred with him. Nor would he accept any money for their maintenance. He ordered stores, lodgings, horses, servants for the entire company plus that of Alvar Fañez, all at his own expense. In this way were the ladies of Mio Cid honored. Their attendants rode the finest horses. Their palfreys were draped with satins and damasks. Silver bells hung from their saddles. Every knight's equipment was elaborate. Each lance bore a silken pannet. Every knight wore his shield hung about his neck. Their polish reflected the sunlight proudly. Alvar Fañez rode up and down the columns. He left nothing to chance. Abengalvon was equally vigilant and openhanded. He would not let Mio Cid's party pay for even a horseshoe!

When Mio Cid heard that the party was approaching the gates of Valencia, that his family were all well and not too tired from their travels over the Sierras, that they had been greeted everywhere with the greatest ceremony and show of respect, it was the happiest moment in his life!

Immediately he dispatched two hundred knights to ride forth from the gates. Mio Cid still remained in the Citadel, watching and standing guard. Then when he was notified that the party was almost at the gate, he chose men to stand guard in his stead. He deputed armed sentinels for every tower of the Alcazar, for every entrance and every exit, where they could within instants spread the alarm.

Then Mio Cid called for his horse, a new one named Babieca, which he had acquired recently. He did not know whether or not the horse was swift, whether or not it would stand for him. Mio Cid wanted to remain at attention just outside the city's main gate, where with his back to the wall he would be safe enough. Don Jerome arrived first and hastened to the chapel to put on his vestments and take the silver cross so that he could welcome the ladies.

Mio Cid put Babieca through his paces, guided him through intricate figures, and stopped him short at the gate. The new horse performed beautifully before all eyes. Then Mio Cid dismounted and advanced on foot towards the party. Babieca stood as still as stone. From that day forth the honor and reputation of this war horse traveled throughout Spain. What man did not dream of seeing the bearded Mio Cid astride Babieca!

Doña Ximena and her daughters wept so hard they could hardly see Mio Cid. "Thank you, Campeador," cried Doña Ximena, kneeling at her husband's feet. "You were, indeed, born at a marvelous hour! You have rescued me and my daughters from ugly humiliations! Here are your daughters. With God's aid and yours, they are well trained and good."

"Dear and esteemed Lady," said Mio Cid, "and daughters who are my heart and soul, I salute you. Do me the honor of allowing me to escort you into your new heritage, which I won only for you."

The lady and her daughters kissed Mio Cid's hand. They rode into the city, receiving the respect and honors due them. Mio Cid conducted them first to the highest tower of the Alcazar from which they could look down on Valencia's white streets spread out below them, and also eastward toward the blue Mediterranean. When they saw the beauty of their new home, how surrounded they were with thick groves of perfumed lemon and orange trees, the ladies lifted their hands to God in prayer. Mio Cid and his knights felt their hearts swell with pride. The winter sped by happily, and we come to the month of March.

Now I want to tell you about Morocco across the sea, and about its King Yucef, who lost his royal temper because of Mio Cid, Don Rodrigo. "He has entered my domains by violence," cried King Yucef. "And he only honors Jesus Christ!" The king of Morocco embarked with fifty thousand warriors to seek Valencia. He pitched his tents on the beach beside the city. Mio Cid saw him and was not afraid.

"All I have in this world is right before my eyes," mused Mio Cid. "I conquered Valencia fairly. I shall not abandon it except when I die. This city is my inheritance. I shall fight these Moors with my wife and daughters watching me. They will then see how an outcast gets a home in a strange land, and with their own eyes learn how an exile earns his bread."

He sent for Doña Ximena and her daughters to come to the tower of the Alcazar. Then he pointed downward where the Moorish tents blanketed the earth as far as one could see. "God save you!" they cried. "What is it, Mio Cid?"

"Why, that, honored wife, is no cause for alarm. That is more wealth about to drop into our coffers. Since you are newly arrived, the Moors are bringing you a gift. Since you have daughters to marry, they are bringing them African dowries. Watch the battle, if you like, here from the Alcazar. Have no fear on my account, Lady. I shall win it."

By the end of the second day the Moors were defeated and their treasure carted within the walls of Valencia. Mio Cid rode back from the battle, sword in hand. His face was dark and tired. He reined in Babieca before the ladies and dismounted. They knelt before him. "While you ladies kept Valencia for me," smiled Mio Cid, "I fought out in the orchards. Look at this bloody sword and sweating horse! With such a steed as Babieca, the Moors defeat themselves! Pray to God that Babieca lives for several more years. You may then be sure that many will humbly kneel to kiss your fingers!"

After they had entered their palace, Mio Cid, seated on his expensive bench, which had a backrest to it, announced welcome news. "I should like all in Castile to know that those ladies who escorted my señora and her daughters in days of misfortune have been amply rewarded. I hereby bestow a dowry of one hundred marks on each one of them. As for your daughters, Lady, that will come later."

Mio Cid was so enriched by this victory that no proper count of his wealth could be taken. The Moors who dwelled near Valencia were also bettered, particularly as Mio Cid let them keep the stray horses. Mio Cid decided to send King Yucef's pavilion—so large it was upheld by two posts inlaid in gold—to King Alfonso of Castile. From his fifth part Mio Cid granted one-tenth to the church. Don Jerome was delighted, he who had fought side by side with the Campeador, he who had killed uncounted enemies. The next morning Alvar Fañez set out for Castile, taking the tent and this time two hundred horses as a gift. He found the king in Valladolid.

Don Alfonso was overjoyed at the presents and wondered how he could reward the Mio Cid. Don Garcia, who hated the Campeador, regretted his successes. The young princes of Carrion again took counsel with each other. "The fortune of this Cid is still better," said they. "Sire, consent to ask for the hands of the Cid's daughters. We consent to marry them. It will be an honor for them and an advantage for us."

After an hour's reflection King Alfonso replied, "I exiled this good Campeador. I have done him only harm; he has returned only good for evil. I do not know whether he desires these marriages. Let us broach the subject." Then to Alvar Fañez and Pero Bermuez he said, "I pardon Mio Cid. Let him come to see me. Diego and Ferrando Gonzalez, the Infantes of Carrion, desire to wed his daughters. Tell your lord this union would do him great honor. Tell your lord to meet me at the frontier."

When Mio Cid heard the king's proposal, he thought for an hour. "These princes are haughty and have wide influence at court. I should not have desired these marriages. However, since he who is above us all has counseled it, we will with God's inspiration discuss the matter with him." Then Mio Cid sent a letter saying that he would meet the king at the Tagus River.

In three weeks' time both parties, magnificently attired, met at the river. The Infantes of Carrion rode beside the king in high spirits. They paid for this and that, right and left, on credit, knowing that they would soon have gold enough to last them all their lives. What sturdy mules there were in the two retinues! What prancing palfreys! What handsome coats of mail! What galloping horses! What gorgeous cloaks and satin cloaks and fur cloaks! Young and old, tall and short, wore robes of dazzling colors! Mio Cid rode gaily too, for he had left Valencia well defended with strict orders that not a person was to enter or leave the city until his return.

When he had come before the king, Mio Cid dismounted with fifteen of his chosen knights. He advanced on foot. He threw himself face down before his lord. He fastened his teeth on a clump of grass and wept bitterly, so happy was he! In this way, thudding his knees and his hands flat on the earth, he made his gesture of submission to Don Alfonso.

The king was pained. "Stand on your feet, Cid Campeador. Kiss my hands. As for my feet, no! Obey me, or you shall not receive my love."

Mio Cid did not rise. "I crave your mercy, my lawful lord. With me prostrate before you, give me back once more your love, so all present may hear you."

"Gladly," said the king, raising his voice. "I hereby pardon you, Mio Cid, and accord you my love. From this day forth receive access to all my domains."

"Thanks, great lord," cried Mio Cid, "I accept. Now surely God will protect me day and night." Rising, he kissed the king's hand. "Be my guest, Don Alfonso, my liege lord."

"That would not be fitting," replied the king. "We have been here since yesterday while you arrived only now. Tomorrow we shall do as you please. Today you are my guest."

Then the Infantes of Carrion humbled themselves before Mio Cid. "You were born in a good hour, Cid. As far as we are able, we shall walk toward your welfare."

"God willing," replied Mio Cid.

After two days of entertaining, during which the king feasted his eyes admiringly on the magnificent beard of Mio Cid and could not praise it enough, they heard mass celebrated by Don Jerome and then settled down to the weighty business at hand.

"Give us your daughters in marriage," said the king. "These princes ask it and I order it."

"I have no daughters to wed," replied Mio Cid. "I engendered them, but they are not mine. They are also of a tender age. These Infantes of Carrion could look for a much more honorable match, owing to their high birth. We are all of us at your mercy, Sire, Doña Elvira and Doña Sol as much as I am. Therefore here are the hands of your daughters, Don Alfonso. Bestow them as *you* please, and I shall be content."

"With these words then," ordained the king, "I bestow Doña Elvira and Doña Sol upon the Infantes of Carrion. Their troths are plighted. Take these sons-in-law to Valencia with you."

"I thank you, Sire," replied Mio Cid. "It is you who give my daughters in marriage, and not I." There was a celebration then for all present. Mio Cid bestowed gifts on every man who asked. Then leaping on Babieca, Mio Cid cried, "Let all who desire rich presents attended these weddings in Valencia!" It had been decided that Alvar Fañez would act in proxy for Don Alfonso, since Mio Cid repeated that he would not give away his daughters at the altar. As he rode back to Valencia, his party greatly increased and the king's diminished by those who accepted the cordial wedding invitation. Mio Cid asked Pero Bermuez and Muño Gustioz to watch the Infantes carefully, to report their personal habits to him, even after they were lodged in the palace he assigned to them in Valencia.

The wedding celebration was lavish and festive. Mio Cid outdid himself in generosity. For fifteen days he entertained his guests at tournaments and feasts. Everyone was pleased with the Infantes of Carrion. They remained in Valencia for two years.

(V. 2286)   *Las coplas deste cantar aqui s van acabando*.

The couplets of this song are just ending now.

May the Creator and all his Saints save you and keep you.

Dishonor and Revenge

(V. 2288)   Mio Cid was in Valencia with his vassals, and also with his sons-in-law, the two princes of Carrion.

One afternoon as Mio Cid lay sleeping on his high-backed bench, a frightful event occurred. A lion burst from its cage, broke its chain, and started roaming through the palace. Those brave men of the Campeador threw their capes over their right arms and retreated cautiously until they had formed a barrier between the huge cat and their master.

The Infante Ferrando saw no place to hide, no tower stairway unbolted, no chamber door open. In terror he crawled under the settee where the Campeador lay resting. The second Infante Diego darted out a door and squeezed himself between a beam and the wall, moaning, "Now I shall never see Carrion again!"

At this moment he-who-was-born-in-that-good-hour awoke. He saw his barons encircling his couch. "What is it, friends?" asked Mio Cid. "What do you want?"

"It is only, honored Sir, that a lion has escaped."

Mio Cid had his wide cloak about his shoulders. Rising to his feet, he walked deliberately toward the lion. The beast, seeing that man approach so confidently, was cowed. It drooped its head and looked toward the floor. Then Mio Cid grasped it by the mane and succeeded in turning it and forcing it back into the cage. All present were amazed. When they had recovered from their excitement, Mio Cid asked where his sons were. No one knew. Up and down the palace people called them. Neither one nor the other answered. Finally they were discovered hiding. Don Diego had soiled his shirt and his cloak. Both Infantes were as pale as sheets. You never saw such amusement as the looks of them caused at the court. Mio Cid had to forbid conversation on that subject! He saw that the Infantes were sensitive.

Before these jokes had ceased being remembered, a new force of fifty thousand Moors under King Bucar of Morocco—I suppose you have heard of him—came to besiege Valencia. From the Alcazar, Mio Cid saw their tents spread through his orchards, and their sight delighted him. He thanked his Maker that more booty was about to fall into his hands. The Infantes, on the contrary, were panic-stricken! "We'll be expected to leave our palace and advance to battle! What will happen to us then? These Moors could not have come at a better time! Now we shall certainly never see Carrion again!"

Muño Gustioz reported their conversation to his lord. "Your sons-in-law are so brave that they are frightened," he told Mio Cid. "They are so homesick that they can't go to battle! You should go and console them now, and may the Creator help you! Let them sit home and receive no share of the spoils. We will win this engagement also, if our Maker wishes!"

With a pleasant face Mio Cid strode to the Infantes. "Good day, my sons-in-law, Princes of Carrion. Why do you not today hold my daughters, they who are as bright as sunlight, in your arms while I go out to meet the Moors. You know I am for the war, and you are for Carrion. Amuse yourselves today here in Valencia. Do whatever you like for your pleasure. Leave the Moors to me. I am an old hand at this sort of nastiness. I assure you, the Moors shall be vanquished."

[Here the manuscript is torn; at least one page is missing, but the story of this day is told later by Pero Bermuez.]

The Infantes armed themselves for battle. Mio Cid asked his nephew Pero Bermuez to watch over the princes. Alvar Fañez stood ready to ride when Bishop Jerome rode through the press to Mio Cid.

"Today I said mass for you at Holy Trinity. Now you understand that I left France to fight the Moors. I came here to Valencia for that express purpose because here I could best serve my order. I demand the right to strike the first blow on this field. You see that I have raised my own pennant. You see that my arms are of the finest. If you refuse me this right to try my worth against our foes, I shall never serve you again!"

"I am pleased with your words," replied Mio Cid. "There the Moors are, right in front of you, Lord Bishop. By all means, go and test them. We shall watch from here how an abbot wages war."

Then all alone Bishop Jerome spurred into the enemy. He killed two at the first lance thrust and five more with his sword. Blows fell upon him from all sides; his armor was proof against them. He struck about him with heavy, ringing swings of his sword arm. Mio Cid waited until he saw that the bishop was heavily surrounded. Then, followed by his knights, Mio Cid spurred Babieca into the foe. What a battle was that! Heads and helmets fell to the ground and rolled in the grass! Riderless horses, maddened with wounds, plunged through the falling tents.

Mio Cid marked the African King Bucar. He gave chase, calling, "Wait for me, Bucar! You have traveled so far to meet me! Come greet the Cid of the long beard! We should salute each other like true knights! Who knows? We might strike up a friendship!"

"God damn such a friendship!" cried Bucar. "I know what you want to strike! If my mount neither falters nor stumbles, you will find me in the sea!"

"That's a lie, Bucar. I'll overtake you first!" cried Mio Cid. He spurred Babieca to great, thundering strides. Little by little he overtook the Moorish king, caught up with him about three lengths from the water. With one stroke of his sword Mio Cid dashed the jewels in the golden helm of Bucar over the sand, split the helm and all that was under it down to the waist. That blow ended the battle quickly, for the Moors hastened to lay down their arms. Mio Cid rode back through the tents. His forehead was wrinkled. Then he met the two Infantes in full armor there on the field. The sight of them delighted his heart.

"Come," smiled Mio Cid. "You are both of you now my real sons. Good news and high praise shall travel to Castile. All men shall know that you conquered Bucar, the king of Morocco. We shall all come out of this victory with pleasure and honor." Every good word Mío Cid said the two princes twisted into evil. When they had received their share of the booty, however, they saw that they would never need any more wealth as long as they lived.

"I thank God humbly," said Mio Cid. "I see laid out before me everything I have wished for all my life. My sons fought beside me on the field of honor. Once I was poor, and now I am a rich man. My dear daughters are wedded to princes. I win battles one after another thanks to my Creator. Over there in Morocco where the mosques are, men fear that some dark night I may take it into my head to cross the sea and besiege their cities. They have no basis for their suspicions. I never think of it. I shall never go to seek them. I shall live in Valencia and allow them to send me tribute instead."

Then the two princes—truly they were brothers—withdrew and whispered to each other. "Let us return to Carrion. We have stayed here long enough. We could never spend all this gold our whole lives long. Let us ask the Cid for our wives. We could tell him that we want to take them to Carrion. We have stayed here long enough. We could tell him we wish to show his daughters our lands and castles. Yes, say we want them to see their inheritance. Only let us escape his vigilance! Once on the road we'll go where we like and do as we please. Let us go before someone mentions that incident of the lion again. We were born princes of Carrion.

"We will transport out of Valencia all the wealth that we now have. Then let us humiliate these daughters of the Campeador. Let us revile them! We are rich enough at present. Let us think of marrying only the heiresses of kings and emperors. We are princely by birth and by taste. Let us abase his daughters before anyone mentions the incident of the lion again!"

At once they put their request, very courteously framed and delivered, to Mio Cid and to his favorites. The Campeador made no difficulty at all about granting their suit. He had no suspicions about their real intentions. "Yes, I shall give you my daughters, and something of mine also," he said proudly. "Let people up and down Castile see how richly my sons are wed. I am pleased that you have settled estates and revenues upon Doña Elvira and Doña Sol, who are the very coverings of my heart. I grant you 3,000 silver marks as an additional dowry. I present you with two fabled swords, which I wrested hardly from my foes. Here they are, Colada and Tizon. Serve my daughters well, for they are yours in holy wedlock. Honor them, and I shall reward you for it."

When Doña Elvira and Doña Sol were ready to take their leave, they knelt before their parents and said, "We beg your favor, father who engendered us, and mother who bore us. Señor and Señora, you are sending us now to the lands of Carrion. We are honored to do your bidding."

"Go, daughters," replied Doña Ximena, "and may the Lord preserve you. You have our favor, mine and your father's. Go now to Carrion where lie your inheritances. I think we have married you nobly."

Mio Cid and his knights escorted the girls out of the sunny city and through its surrounding orange groves with all the panoply of chivalry. Although their father rode joyfully before his knights, his mind was not entirely at ease because he had seen from omens that these marriages would not be without sorrow. However, he could not retract the contracts; both girls had been duly wedded. Because of his deep concern, however, he asked Felez Muñoz to accompany the girls to Carrion and then to bring him back word how they were received and how honored.

It was hard for Mio Cid to break away from his daughters, very painful for him to be obliged to turn his back on them, and return to Valencia. He wept, and so did his two girls. "We commit you to God's care, Doña Elvira and Doña Sol," he said. "Bear yourselves in such a way that we here in Valencia shall be happy."

The princes replied, "God willing."

Still Mio Cid could not depart. The separation was as painful to him as if a nail were being torn from his finger. "Listen, my nephew," he instructed Felez Muñoz, "pass through Molina. Tell my friend, the Moor Abengalvon, that my daughters are entering their estates at Carrion. Ask him to receive them, and to furnish them with anything whatsoever that they may require or desire. Tell him I wish his Moors to escort my children to the frontier. He will do this for love of me. He knows that I repay my debts. He knows what my word is worth."

The Infantes of Carrion, once Mio Cid had turned his back, thought only of covering ground as fast as possible. They soon arrived at Molina where Abengalvon met them with every sign of joy. God! How he served this company! Early next morning he awaited their departure and accompanied them with two hundred knights, for they had to cross high and lonely mountains in order to reach Castile. Abengalvon spared no expense. Every rich sword and jeweled helm in his kingdom was paraded in order to honor Doña Elvira and Doña Sol. He escorted them as if they had been born of princely rank, like their husbands.

"Look," whispered the brothers to each other, "since we have decided to leave the Campeador's daughters, we could kill this Moor Abengalvon; all his wealth would then accrue to us. As sure as we stand here, if the sum were added to what we now have, not even the Cid could bring us to a reckoning."

While they were plotting, a certain Moor who was a good Latinist overheard their conversation. Instead of keeping this secret to himself, he naturally hastened to Abengalvon. "Master," he warned, "be on your guard, as you are my liege. I heard the Infantes conspiring your death."

Abengalvon was a man of no uncertain courage. He did not stand on ceremony, even with princes. With his knights in close ranks behind him, and with his own sword drawn, he rode up to the princes, face to face. "Now tell me, Infantes of Carrion, what I have done to incur your wrath. I have gone to some inconvenience to do you service, without guile or malice. And you are planning to murder me! If I were not bound to refrain because of Mio Cid of Vivar, I would whip you now so soundly that the reports would re-echo about the world! I would then escort his daughters back to Mio Cid. And as for you, you wouldn't get to Carrion at all!

"I take leave of you here and now, for I see your rascality and your treachery! By your leave, Doña Elvira and Doña Sol, I shall retire from your company. I care little for the reports that may come from Carrion. May God ordain that Mio Cid have joy from these alliances." Leaving the Infantes highly outraged, Abengalvon like a sensible man returned home to Molina.

After the Moor had disappeared down the road, the Infantes ordered their party forward on the double. Not content with their previous rate of speed, they pushed on day and night until they were high in the Sierras de Miedes. Through these high, white peaks they hastened, forcing their horses and setting a hard pace. They passed gigantic caverns and precipices that dropped off into the dark forests below them until they came one evening to the deep woods where the trees were of a tremendous height. Their branches seemed to reach to the clouds. In a clearing they came upon a grove and a spring of clear water. Wild animals hunted for food even up to the edge of this encampment.

The Infantes selected a spot for their tent and allowed their weary wives to dismount. The whole company settled down for the night. The brothers from Carrion caressed their wives in their arms that night and gave them evidences of their love. . . . They will prove it to the poor Doña Elvira and to the poor Doña Sol when day breaks!

Early in the morning the horses and pack animals were saddled, the baggage was reloaded, the tents were folded and packed, and the party set off through the woods. The princes ordered everyone to leave. They said that not a man or a woman should remain at the campsite except themselves and their wives. They wanted to be quite alone with their ladies. According to their wishes, everyone rode ahead down the forest trail, leaving the four under the trees. . . . What do you think the Infantes of Carrion had been hatching?

"You may believe us when we tell you, Doña Sol and Doña Elvira, that you are now going to be disgraced," said the princes. "Here in these forbidding mountains you are both about to be debased. We shall continue on our journey; first of all, we have an account to settle before we abandon you here. This is as much portion of the princely domains of Carrion as you shall ever inherit. We want the news of your fate to reach the Cid Campeador. We intend to take our revenge here for that adventure of the lion."

Then before the horrified eyes of the two young ladies, the Infantes of Carrion took off their fur cloaks, and then their jackets. That was not all! They next proceeded to strip the ladies of their rich mantles. They ripped off their cloaks, their dresses, and left them naked in their thin shirts and tunics. They buckled on their spurs and unhooked the leather girths from their horses!

When Doña Sol saw them approaching herself and her sister with these straps in their hands, she spoke. Doña Sol said, "In the name of Heaven, Don Diego and Don Ferrando, do not use straps on us! Hear my plea! You both have swords that are strong and trenchant. I should know because I have often seen these blades in my father's hands. They are called Colada and Tizon. . . . Then use them on us! Cut off our heads, and give us martyrdom! Moors and Christians alike will declare that we have earned it. Even though we do not deserve to die, even though you will not treat us according to our actions, do not, I pray you, make upon our persons such a bad example. If you beat us here in the forest, you will only abase yourselves, not us! . . . You will be called to account for it too, either man to man or at the court of Castile!"

Doña Sol's prayer did not help either herself or her sister. Suddenly the Infantes raised the leather straps and began to rain stinging blows upon their naked shoulders. Leaving the girths unknotted and at their full length, they whipped the girls so unmercifully that both fainted. After both had fallen to the ground, the princes tore their shirts from their backs with their spurs and bruised the girls' hips and thighs. The bright, red blood flowed over their rags of tunics. The weeping girls felt each blow all the way to their hearts. What a blessing it would have been, had the Creator so willed, if the Cid Campeador had suddenly appeared riding through the trees!

The princes beat those ladies until they lay totally unconscious on the ground, their shirts and their tunics drenched with blood. They struck them until their arms were tired, for each one tried to get in the hardest strokes. For a long time neither Doña Sol nor Doña Elvira had made a sound. Then the Infantes picked up the girls' robes and cloaks, picked up their ermine shawls, mounted the palfreys, and rode away leaving their wives for dead where they lay. They abandoned their bloody remains to the birds of the mountain peaks and to the beasts of prey. They left them for dead, hear, and not for alive! What a blessing it would have been if the Cid Campeador had suddenly appeared before them, riding through the trees! Oh!

The Infantes of Carrion left the poor girls under the trees. Neither girl could even crawl to help her sister any more. Down the trails and out into patches of sunlight the brothers rode laughing and congratulating each other. "Now we have exacted our revenge for such marriages! We shouldn't have even welcomed such girls as these for concubines, unless, of course, their father begged us to do so on bended knee! They were not our equals. And to think we actually had to hold them in our arms! Another score too! We have also avenged ourselves for the lion.' So they rode down the mountainside, joking and thumping each other on the back.

Now I am going to tell you about Felez Muñoz, who was the nephew of Mio Cid the Campeador. He had been ordered that morning to ride ahead with the others, and he did so, but not of his own accord. As he followed the path, his heart ached and pained him so that he gradually slipped away from the others, down side paths. Then he stole backward along the trail, keeping to the thick underbrush, and making no noise. After a while he not only saw the Infantes riding down the trail; he also was able to overhear snatches of their banter. They neither saw Felez Muñoz nor suspected his presence. You may be sure that if they had, he would not have escaped with his life!

Felez Muñoz waited just long enough to let them get a good distance away. Then he dug his spurs into his horse's flanks and galloped frantically back up the trail. There he saw the pitifully wounded girls lying on the earth.

"Cousins! Cousins!" he cried, leaping from his horse and tying its bridle to a tree. "Cousins! My dear Cousins! Doña Elvira! Doña Sol! Oh, what evil have these princes done! I pray to God and to the holy Saint Mary that they receive as bad a punishment!" As gently as he could, Felez Muñoz turned each girl over on her back. Their eyes were closed. They did not breathe. Not a sound, not even a whimper came from either one. It would have broken your heart. "Cousins, live! Wake up! Awaken while it is daylight, while the forest creatures are in their lairs asleep. Wake up before the wild beasts eat us all!"

Then Felez Muñoz saw that the girls were coming to consciousness. Little by little their eyelids began to quiver. Then they opened their eyes and recognized their cousin leaning over them. "Take courage, Cousins, in the name of the Creator!" he urged them. "As soon as the Infantes of Carrion notice that I am no longer with them, they will send after me. If God does not provide for us, we shall all die here."

Then painfully Doña Sol said, "If our father the Campeador has ever merited your love, Cousin, bring us a little water . . . and may God bless you."

With his sombrero, which was a new and clean one he had recently

bought in Valencia, Felez Muñoz fetched water and poured it over the deep cuts on the two girls' bodies. He then helped them to sit up. He kept talking to them and encouraging them. He comforted them as best he could, for their bodies were bruised and torn. He pleaded and exhorted them to be brave. The girls with his help finally managed to limp to his horse, where he gently lifted each one to the saddle. Then wrapping them in his wide cloak, telling them all the time how proud he was of their courage, he left the campsite. Leading his horse by the bridle, he plunged under the trees and away from that bloody soil as fast as he could walk. At the hour between daylight and dusk they came down out of the mountain, up to the banks of the Duero River. He found shelter for the girls, for everyone knew their father, at the first castle on the river. Then he spurred hotly down the dusty road and into the nearest town to seek strong friends.

While Doña Elvira and Doña Sol were recovering from their wounds, surrounded by sympathetic and distressed friends, the news of their humiliation traveled westward to the king and eastward to Mio Cid the Campeador. When their father heard all the details of this premeditated outrage, he raised his hand, enjoining silence upon his court. For an hour he sat, stern and alone, digesting the awful news. Then, gripping his beard, he spoke. "Thanks be to Christ, Lord of the world, that the Infantes of Carrion have done me this signal honor. I shall see that their joy is short-lived. As for my daughters, I vow that they shall never again wed counts, only kings!" Then he dispatched two hundred knights under Alvar Fañez' command to bring home his beloved children.

Tears came to Alvar Fañez' eyes when he next looked upon the ladies Doña Sol and Doña Elvira. They said to him, "We are as happy to see you as if we were looking on the face of our Creator! Give thanks to Him that we are even alive! Please take us home. We will tell you all that happened when we are safely home again."

"Dry your tears, dear Ladies. It is enough for all of us that you are alive and well. Your father and mother send you their love. The day shall come very soon when we in Valencia shall have our revenge!"

There was a holiday in Valencia the day the daughters of Mio Cid rode into their home city again. Mio Cid smiled contentedly to see his dear girls safe in his palace again. Then he drew up a message to King Alfonso of Castile. "Tell the king that I sympathize with his affliction," dictated Mio Cid. "Say that I lament his dishonor, for it was he who gave my daughters in marriage. Ask Don Alfonso to summon these Infantes of Carrion to a tournament or to a plenary session of his court, for I am about to seek retribution for their insults, to say nothing of the wealth they took from me under false pretenses. Rancor lodges deep in the heart of a man like me."

When Don Alfonso heard Mio Cid's messengers, he deliberated and then announced that he would convene his court at Toledo. The king acted promptly. He sent his cards into all of his vast realms—throughout Castile, Leon, Saint-James, Portugal, and Galicia—summoning his vassals to Toledo in seven weeks' time. He who failed to appear would lose at least his titles and lands.

The Infantes of Carrion, having taken counsel with their family, asked to be excused from attending. They feared having to face Mio Cid. However, King Alfonso replied, "Absolutely not! You will attend my court or else leave my kingdom. You must give satisfaction to Mio Cid, who has complained to me about you." Don Garcia collected his friends, summoned all the great nobles who made up his faction to support the Infantes. Don Garcia, who had always hated Mio Cid, saw in this assembly an opportunity to insult Mio Cid himself.

The assembled court had to wait for five days until Alvar Fañez came to announce Mio Cid's arrival. Don Alfonso rode out of Toledo to meet him. Mio Cid came, escorted by all his chosen companions, all fully dressed in armor, all ready to defend their Campeador with every ounce of the strength and skill they possessed. As soon as he had come in plain sight of the king, Mio Cid dismounted and fell to his knees.

"By Saint Isidore," cried the king, "I will not allow you to humble yourself to me today. Mount up, or you will incur my displeasure. Let us greet each other in all sincerity of heart and soul. Know that my own heart is heavy with the weight that hangs upon you. May God grant that your presence may grace my court, Mio Cid."

"Amen," replied Mio Cid the Campeador. "I prostrate myself before you, Sire, and before these great nobles who accompany you. My wife, Doña Ximena, who is a lady of property, kisses your hand. My two daughters greet you humbly. May what has happened to us weigh heavily upon you."

."I shall attend to your plea," answered Don Alfonso, "and may God oversee us all."

King Alfonso of Castile returned to the city of Toledo, but Mio Cid remained that night by the banks of the Tagus River. He explained that he needed to await his men before crossing the river and entering the city. He also desired to spend the night in vigil in a holy place. "I shall present myself at court before dinner at noon," he promised.

"I consent willingly," answered the king.

All that night Mio Cid remained kneeling and praying in a holy place. He lighted taper after taper, taking counsel with his Lord as to how he should proceed on the following day. He knew that he had the faction of Don Garcia to outwit and intimidate. He realized what powerful friends and allies the Infantes of Carrion claimed among the great nobles. At daybreak Alvar Fañez found Mio Cid still at his devotions. He and his men then worshiped together. The mass was ended at sunrise. Mio Cid then made a handsome donation to the chapel and addressed his followers. He named his dearest, oldest companions as his escort and asked them to bring their number up to one hundred by designating others.

"Wear undergarments that will keep your full armor from chafing," said Mio Cid. "Dress yourselves as for battle in complete suits of armor and coats of mail underneath. Let your breastplates be as radiant as the sun. Then put over all this your ermine and your fur cloaks. Fasten them carefully at throat and waist so that the armor does not show. Under your cloaks be sure that your swords are sharp and ready. Wear them loose today. Thus garbed shall we fare to the court where I may say my say and demand justice; in the case that our princes of Carrion seek a quarrel, I shall have no fear with one hundred warriors like you. We know each other's worth, I think."

They answered to a man, "We shall do it, Señor."

While his knights were dressing, Mio Cid attired himself to go before the court. He drew on tights of fine wool, and a shirt of white linen as dazzling as sunlight. Its tucks were edged with gold and silver. Over his armor he wore a gold-brocaded tunic, bordered with so much gold that you would have said he gleamed like the sun itself. Then over his shoulders he draped a red fur scalloped with gold. On his head he fitted a cap of scarlet linen worked with gold and so cut that it covered all his hair that had not been trimmed. To protect his beard in like fashion he tied it with a scarlet ribbon and tucked it inside his tunic. Over this he fastened a sweeping cloak that fell from his shoulders to the ground in such ample folds that it hid his sword perfectly. He leaped to Babieca's back and rode into the city of Toledo at a sharp clip.

Mio Cid dismounted at the palace door. Surrounded on all sides by his hundred magnificently attired knights, he entered the audience hall. Courteously the king arose, and so did most of his nobles. Not so Don Garcia and the Infantes of Carrion.

"Come sit beside me," invited the King Don Alfonso. "You shall take this seat of honor, here upon this bench which has a backrest. It is the one you so thoughtfully presented me. Certain people here may be afflicted because of the honor I do you, but sit down. You will be more comfortable than all of us."

"Pray keep your seat," answered Mio Cid humbly. "Sit on your high-backed bench as a king and great liege lord should do. I shall sit here with my men around me." When Mio Cid had taken his place, all eyes in the room were free to inspect his splendid attire. Such elegance had never before been paraded, except by the king. They noticed how full his beard was and how he had tied it with a satin cord. They were impressed by his manner, that of a great baron accustomed to rule. The Infantes alone could not meet his gaze. When they felt Mio Cid direct his glance in their direction, they bowed their heads. They were ashamed to meet his eyes.

"Hear ye, gentlemen of my house, if you wish the Creator to hear you," began King Alfonso of Castile. "Since my coronation I have held only two plenary sessions of all my vassals, one at Burgos and one at Carrion. I have seen fit to convoke this third at Toledo out of love for Mio Cid, who was born in a good hour, in order that he may receive his right from the Infantes of Carrion. They did him a great wrong; we know this. Let Count Don Anrrich and Count Don Remond of Burgundy be our judges; they are unaffiliated with either faction. You will all hear this case, inasmuch as you are thoughtful and experienced, so that justice may be done; I shall sanction no injustice. Let the one side be for this day at peace with the other. I swear by Saint Isidore that whoever causes commotion in my court today shall be exiled from my realm. I shall side with the right. Let us hear the demands of Mio Cid first and then the replies of the Infantes of Carrion."

Mio Cid rose and kissed the king's hand. "I give you thanks for having convened this assembly out of love for me. Here is what I demand: in the case of my daughters that these princes have left me, I feel no dishonor; for you married them, Sire, and you know what to do about them today. However, when these princes led my daughters out of lordly Valencia, because I loved them in my heart and in my soul, I gave them two swords, Colada and Tizon. I had won these blades like a baron with the intention of using them for your glory and vassalage, Sire. Now since these princes have abandoned my daughters in the woods, it is clear that they no longer cared about me. In consequence they have lost my love. I ask that they return the swords to me since they are no longer my sons-in-law."

The judges decreed, "All is reasonable."

Then the Count Don Garcia spoke for his faction. "We must deliberate this point." After he, the Infantes, and their friends had spoken together, and had agreed, Don Garcia counseled them secretly, "This Cid Campeador still shows us his love, since he does not call for a reckoning today concerning his daughters. We shall give Don Alfonso satisfaction on that score. Let us give up the swords since this Cid limits himself to that penalty. After he receives them, the court will be adjourned. The Cid Campeador will have lost his opportunity; he never will extort satisfaction from us then!"

The party of Don Garcia and the Infantes replied in open court, "Thanks, King Don Alfonso. We do not deny that he gave us the swords. Since he calls for them and desires them, we wish to deliver them to him in your presence." They unsheathed the swords and laid them on the king's hands. A murmur of admiration moved the courtiers. The pommels of these blades were so bright that they lighted up the room. When Mio Cid took them, he smiled at their beauty, perhaps at the pleasant memories of his victories.

The swords sparkled in the hands of Mio Cid, who smiled broadly and thought to himself, "By this beard which no man has ever dared pluck, we shall see how Doña Elvira and Doña Sol shall be avenged!" Mio Cid called his nephew by name. Holding out Tizon to him, he said, "Felez Muñoz, take this beauty. You are worthier of her." He then stretched out Colada. "Martin Antolinez, vassal of renown, Colada is for you. I earned her from a gentleman, Count Raymond the Frank of Barcelona. I entrust her to you. Care for her well. If you have occasion to wield her, she will earn you fame and high esteem." Martin Antolinez took Colada reverently, bent low, and kissed Mio Cid's hand.

Mio Cid then rose to his feet again. "Thanks be to God, and to you also, King, that I have been put at rest concerning Colada and Tizon! When they led my daughters out of Valencia, I gave them 3,000 silver marks. While I was thinking of gifts for them, they were planning to execute another project. Let them return my money since they are no longer my sons-in-law." You should have heard the complaints of the Infantes then!

Count Don Remond instructed them, "Answer yes or no."

Then the Infantes replied, "We returned his swords to the Cid Campeador so that he would not ask for anything else. That was all he demanded. May it please the King; that is our answer."

The king intervened, "To this demand of the Cid, you must also give satisfaction. I decree it."

Alvar Fañez then said hotly, "Insist, O Mio Cid, Campeador. Part of that money was mine. I also demand restitution."

The Infantes took counsel together. It was a staggering sum of silver, which they had already spent. They pleaded with the court, "He is pressing us sorely, this Cid who conquered Valencia. Now he covets our wealth! We shall have to pay him later, out of our lands at Carrion."

"You must pay him here and now, before this court," advised the judges.

"Mio Cid is right," said the king, "and he must be paid. The Infantes of Carrion gave me two hundred marks, which I now return. Since they are to transmit this money, I don't want it."

The Infantes' faction complained, "We don't have the money."

The judges answered, "You mean you have spent it. Then pay its equivalent in kind." When the Infantes understood that there was no other alternative, they began to round up whatever they could. You should have seen their finest charges, mules, palfreys, swords, equipment, furs! Mio Cid accepted it all at the court's evaluation, except for the two hundred marks of King Alfonso. The Infantes paid him the whole sum finally, even though they were obliged to strip themselves and borrow right and left in order to adjust the amount. You may as well know; they came off badly jolted.

"Ah, thanks, Sire, for your love and kindness to me!" said Mio Cid, again rising to his feet. "However, I still cannot forget my wrongs. Let me speak to you now about my greatest source of grievance. Hear me, nobles, and then assess my injury. . . . Without a challenge I cannot dismiss these Infantes of Carrion who have so basely dishonored me. Infantes, tell me how I offended you! Did I do it in banter? Did I do it maliciously? In what way did I do you wrong? Where was my crime? I want to hear it *now!*

"When you led my daughters out of Valencia, why did you tear in such a way the very coverings of my heart? I gave you my daughters. I gave you my wealth without stinting; openhanded I poured my riches and my love upon you! If you no longer wanted my daughters, treacherous dogs, why did you take them out of their fief at Valencia? Why did you strike my daughters with leather straps and with your spurs? Why did you abandon them in the deep woods where they were to fall prey to ravening beasts and flesh-eating birds? All this you did to *my daughters*, which has by so much diminished your manhoods! Let this court now sentence you for this crime, and give me satisfaction."

Don Garcia replied to Mio Cid's demands. "Greatest King of Spain, here is before you this Cid, who has had his entrance proclaimed by heralds, who has let his beard grow so long that it frightens some and amazes others! Our Infantes of Carrion are such that they could not accept his daughters even as concubines! Who would have given them such women as their wives? In deserting them, these princes were within their rights. We take no account whatsoever of the Cid's accusations."

Mio Cid leaped to his feet and stood stroking his beard. "What insolence is this for you of all people to criticize my beard? My beard has never been plucked by any man of woman born, by neither Moor nor Christian! Can you say as much? Is it not the plain truth that I once pulled your beard, Don Garcia, the day I stormed your castle?"

Ferrando Gonzalez of Carrion rose to his feet. In a loud voice he interrupted, "Enough talk, Cid. You have been paid. There is no more quarrel between us. We were born Infantes; that is our princely nature. We should rather have been married to the daughters of kings and emperors. Daughters from your station were not highly born enough for us. In so deserting them we were within our rights. We have grown in self-esteem because of this action, not sunk!"

"Very well," replied Mio Cid. "We have been polite long enough. Pero Bermuez the Mute, you may now speak, if you wish."

"You are a liar, Ferrando of Carrion," cried Pero Bermuez, "a liar in every word you utter! Had you remained with the Campeador, and only then, your true natures would have been concealed! Now let me remind you what sort of man you are! Think back to the battle we fought at Valencia. You asked the Campeador to let you fight, and he instructed me to watch over you. Suddenly, brave Infante, you spied a Moor. You started toward him! Then what? Then you wheeled about and ran! That's what! I took your place. I slew the Moor. I gave you his horse, which you promptly showed Mio Cid, saying that you had done this brave deed. I kept your secret. Right until this day I never broke faith, never spread abroad the tale of your cowardice. I let you brag how brave you were! People believed you out of love for Mio Cid. You may be handsome, but you are surely not manly! You are all tongue, with no hands to act! Say, Ferrando, do I speak the truth about you?

"Let's also gossip about the lion, Ferrando. Where were you hiding when the lion threatened Mio Cid? Ferrando, I challenge you to a single combat because you are a liar and a traitor. I shall fight you here before Don Alfonso of Castile to test my statements. As for the daughters of Mio Cid, you lie! The both of you have sunk, not risen, because of that action. They are only women, and you are supposed to be men! Whichever way you look at it, they are worth more than you! The day we meet in combat, I shall force you to admit all this publicly."

Diego of Carrion then addressed the court. "We are by birth the purest of counts. If only it had not pleased God to saddle us with such alliances! Imagine, having this Cid, Don Rodrigo, for a father-in-law! That we deserted his daughters, we have today no compunction. As long as they live, let them sigh after us! They should be reproached to have thought of touching us! I am ready to fight the most valiant man there is to prove that we were right!"

Martin Antolinez jumped up and cried, "Shut your mouth, you liar, you mouth-without-truth! Don't forget the incident of the lion, Diego Gonzalez! You squeezed yourself in between the pillar and the wall! You never again could wear the clothes you had on that day! I shall fight you for it! I want to know from you why you deserted the daughters of Mio Cid. Know in any case, they are worth more than you are! When you leave the field of combat, I shall hear you admit it too, plus the fact that you are a traitor, and that you have lied today in every word that you have uttered!"

At that moment appeared in the courtroom Asur Gonzalez. He strolled into the room, dragging his cloak on the floor behind him. His face was scarlet, for he had just finished eating. In any event, he had no reputation for intelligence. "Well! Well! Barons!" scoffed Asur Gonzalez. "Did you ever see such a fuss about nobody? Somebody tell me about this Cid of Vivar. Where is he, out filling up feedbags with grain? Out at his mill? That's the way he lives, you know. Whoever put it into his head to aspire to alliances with Carrion?"

"Shut up, you traitor! Liar! Scoundrel!" shouted Muño Gustioz. "You've been out stuffing yourself instead of praying, as you should have been doing. Every time you get close enough to a man to open your mouth, you disgust him! You speak the truth neither to friend nor to lord. You are false to all, even to your Creator. I wish to have no share of your friendship. I propose to make you own up to what you are."

"Let all talk stop here," decreed King Alfonso. "Those who have challenged will fight. Otherwise, may God help them!"

He had hardly uttered these words when two handsome young knights entered the courtroom. All eyes turned in their direction, watched them approach the king. It was the two royal Infantes, one named Oiarra and the other Yenego Simenez. One was the heir apparent to the kingdom of Navarre and the other the heir of the kingdom of Aragon. Bending low to kiss the hand of Don Alfonso, the two crown princes asked that he bestow upon them the hands of Doña Elvira and Doña Sol in marriage. The king so ordained. Mio Cid, you may be sure, submitted joyously to the king's will.

Then Alvar Fañez asked permission to say what was on his mind. "My resentment against the Infantes of Carrion," began Alvar Fañez, "is great. It was I who at the request of King Alfonso gave these ladies at the altar. I am glad that they shall now become queens of Spain. Now you Infantes of Carrion will have to kiss their hands and call them Señora. No matter what spite you feel, you will now have to attend upon them. So have we seen, from day to day, the honor of Mio Cid increase. As for you, Infantes, you are none the less liars and traitors! Will no one stand up and fight me for my words?"

"Enough," said the king. "Not another word. Let the three challengers appear at dawn tomorrow. The issue will be settled on the field of combat."

"Please, Sire," then pleaded the Infantes, "give us a delay. Those of the Cid are armed and ready, but we must return to Carrion first!"

"Will you name the place and the time?" King Alfonso asked Mio Cid.

He replied with a smile, "Why, yes. Let them come to Valencia."

"Be reassured," answered the king. "Entrust your knights to me. I will guarantee their safety. I hereby decree that the combats will take place in my presence three weeks from today at Carrion. He who does not present himself accordingly shall forfeit the privilege and be branded a traitor."

Mio Cid then thanked the judges, gave rich gifts to those who loved him, and prepared to take his leave. The king told Mio Cid that he was the finest baron in all his realm. As Mio Cid bade farewell, he made one last gesture to show his love for Don Alfonso. "You ordered me, Sire, to ride Babieca into your enemies, Moors and Christians alike. This horse has not his like in all the world. I give him to you now, Sire. Have him led away to your stables."

"I have no such desire," replied the king. "Such a splendid horse and such a splendid rider belong together. I am not the man to mount your Babieca! If any person else were to ride him, God would surely not come to his aid! It is because of you, Mio Cid, and because of your horse that our realm has been so favored."

Mio Cid then took leave of his vassals, the three challengers. "Stand firm on that field," he told them. "Fight like barons. Let the news that reaches me in Valencia be good."

"Why do you say that, Señor?" asked Martin Antolinez. "We made this contract ourselves, and we shall fulfill it. You may learn that we were killed, but you will never learn that we were defeated!" Mio Cid was pleased at those words. Light at heart, he set out for his fief at Valencia.

In three weeks' time the king and his challengers waited at the field of combat. The Infantes were two days late. Finally they came, escorted by their relatives and friends. If they could have murdered Mio Cid's men, they would have done so. Fortunately, they did not attempt it, so great was their fear of King Alfonso of León. That night was spent in vigil.

By morning a large crowd of knights thronged the field to see these trials and to hear Don Alfonso's verdict as to which party could claim the right on its side. On one end of the field Mio Cid's men were armed. The Infantes prepared themselves on the opposite side. As they were being dressed, Count Garci Ordoñez briefed them. Then the Infantes sent word to Don Alfonso entreating him to debar Colada and Tizon, the two trenchant swords, from the combat. They regretted having returned these wonderfully cutting blades to Mio Cid.

"I did not see you draw these swords when you wore them to my court," the king replied shortly. "If you possess other good swords, they will give you their aid. The same will be true for the Campeador's men. Therefore stand up, Infantes of Carrion, and enter the lists. You are now obliged to combat. Therefore acquit yourselves like noblemen. If you ride victorious from this field, great honor will accrue to you. Be sure that your opponents have overlooked nothing, and that they intend to win. If you are vanquished, don't complain to me about it; for everyone here knows that you brought it all upon yourselves."

When the Infantes heard the reply of King Alfonso, they sorely repented their past deeds. They would not have committed them again, had they to relive that past year, for all their estates at Carrion.

Meanwhile the king in like measure had instructed Mio Cid's knights. They replied, "We kiss your hand, since you are our king and lord. Be our judge today. Protect us with your might and justice against any unfair play. The Infantes are on their home ground, surrounded by their vassals. We don't know whether or not they are plotting against us. Mio Cid entrusted us to you, Señor. Uphold the right in the name of the Creator."

"With heart and soul," pledged the king.

The three knights mounted. They adjusted their shields and checked their stirrups. They raised their lances so that the pennants blew in the breeze. Then, making the sign of the cross over their saddles, they rode, all three side by side, up to the barrier. There they waited silently until the Gonzalez brothers rode to the barrier opposite, and halted while the king appointed judges so that there could be no recourse. The king then harangued the combatants carefully and clearly.

"Listen to what I say, Infantes of Carrion," began Don Alfonso. "You were to have competed this trial at Toledo, but you would hear of no such thing. Remember that I am the sponsor of these three vassals of Mio Cid, and that I conducted them to your estates. Seek only your due. If you overstep the bounds of justice, I shall mishandle you badly from one end of my realm to another."

Then the judges measured off the lists as the crowd stepped back away from the barriers. They called out the rules, saying that any knight who left the lists was adjudged to have forfeited the contest. They ascertained that the spectators were maintaining a safe distance of six lance lengths on all sides. Lots were drawn for positions so that those who were lucky had the sun at their backs instead of in their faces. Then the judges retired from the center of the arena.

The three of Mio Cid faced the three from Carrion. Each man glared fixedly at his adversary. Each man clutched his shield against his chest, lowered his lance until the pennants hung straight down, bent forward with his body over the pommel of his saddle, dug his spurs into his horse's sides, and shot forward. . . . The spurt was so great the ground thundered underfoot. Each man aimed at his foe. They joined in a shock of metal. . . . The watchers were sure that all six were dead.

Pero Bermuez, who first had challenged his man, met Ferrando Gonzalez face to face. Each one struck the other's shield, with no decisive result. On the second exchange Ferrando Gonzalez pierced the shield of Pero Bermuez, but his lance came out into air instead of into flesh. In two places he broke the wood of his lance. Pero Bermuez sat firm in the saddle. He was not even jolted. Since he had taken a blow, he gave one in return. His stroke broke the shield strap from Ferrando Gonzalez' neck. The shield fell to one side. Then Pero Bermuez pierced him, for his cover was gone. Then he pierced his chest, for the cover was gone. Ferrando wore three thicknesses of mail, which stood him in good stead. Two were shattered, but the third held well. The lance, however, had driven his shirt and the padded doublet he wore under his armor into his chest, to about the depth of a man's hand. Blood spurted from Ferrando Gonzalez' mouth. His stirrup straps broke; neither one held firm. Pero Bermuez threw him to earth over his horse's haunches. The spectators thought he was wounded to death. Pero Bermuez dropped his lance and grasped his sword. Then Ferrando Gonzalez, looking up at him, recognized Tizon! Instead of awaiting its blow, he cried, "I am vanquished." The judges acknowledged his submission and called Pero Bermuez from the lists.

Meanwhile Martin Antolinez and Diego Gonzalez were dealing each other heavy blows—so hard, in fact, that both their lances were shivered. When Martin Antolinez then unsheathed Colada, the light from this blade flashing in the sunlight flooded the field of combat, so clear and white was it! At the first swift stroke he severed the straps of Diego Gonzalez' helmet. Then he knocked it from his head. Next he lifted off his mail hood. He then snipped off the top of his cloth hat. With a swishing sound that was almost a whistle, he lopped off his hair and cut to the scalp. Pieces of flesh fell to the ground. When Diego Gonzalez saw with what precision Colada could be wielded, he realized that he would not escape her alive. He yanked the reins of his horse away from the blows. Then Martin Antolinez whacked him with the flat of the blade, not with the point! Although Diego Gonzalez had his own sword in hand, he made no effort to use it. "Help me, glorious God! . . . Señor, save me from that blade!" Turning his horse's head about in a desperate effort, he bounded out of the lists!

"Come, Pero Bermuez, beside me," called the king. "You have won decisively." The judges concurred. Two knights from Valencia had triumphed, and I shall now tell you of the third.

Muño Gustioz was matched against Asur Gonzalez, who was agile, strong, and courageous. Both knights dealt telling blows upon each other's shields. Asur Gonzalez broke the shield of Muño Gustioz and also broke his armor. When the lance pierced the broken shield, however, it passed into empty air on the other side. Then Muño Gustioz at the next exchange cracked Asur Gonzalez' shield in the middle. Aiming carefully, he drove his lance as he rushed forward right through the shield with such a momentum that it passed through his opponent's body and came out, pennants and all, on the other side. It came out about two arms' length on the back of Asur Gonzalez' body. Then Muño Gustioz toppled him from the saddle and let him slip the length of the lance to the ground. The lance came out red with blood, tip, wood, pennants! Muño Gustioz sat over his opponent, his lance pointed downward until the judges shouted, "In the name of God, do not strike him! You have won the trial." Everyone thought Asur Gonzalez was dead.

The good King Alfonso ordered the field to be cleared and the weapons lost there to be confiscated for himself. The champions of Mio Cid left the lists amid warm congratulations. The sorrow in Carrion was great.

That very night the king dispatched Mio Cid's three knights to Valencia so that they might risk no reprisal nor any fear of such. Like devoted vassals they rode day and night to make their report. They had proven the Infantes of Carrion to be evil men, and they had accomplished the duty required of them by their lord.

Mio Cid the Campeador was satisfied. Then was he satisfied. Great, indeed, was the shame that had fallen publicly upon the Infantes of Carrion. May a similar punishment, or a worse one, fall upon any man who so jeers at a fine lady and then deserts her!

Now let us leave to themselves the Infantes of Carrion and concern ourselves rather with him who was born in such a favorable hour . . . The beautiful city of Valencia laughed and rejoiced because of the honor their champions had brought upon every one. Mio Cid stroked his beard contentedly and said, "Thanks to the King of Heaven, my daughters have been avenged. I shall be able without shame to marry them to men of great rank or not, as I wish."

Meanwhile the Princes of Navarre and Aragon pursued their courtships of Doña Elvira and Doña Sol. They had a new interview with King Don Alfonso. They made before him new marriage vows, more solemn than the first. You see how the reputation and honor of Mio Cid had increased!

Now, the daughters of Mio Cid became the queens of Navarre and Aragon! The king of Spain today is one of their descendants. Everything he touched turned to glory for Mio Cid, who was born at such a good hour.

Mio Cid departed from this world at a Pentecost. May Christ have mercy on his soul. May He have mercy on us all, the righteous as well as the sinners.

This is the story of Mio Cid, the Campeador. Here ends the tale.

May God be pleased to grant Paradise also to him who wrote this book. Amen.

The Abbot Per wrote it in the month of May in the year of our Lord MCCXLV.

APPENDIX TO
MEDIEVAL MYTHS

The seven medieval hero stories come originally from handwritten, parchment manuscripts which are among the treasures of the western world. Many of these manuscripts are close to the oldest documents we possess in the following modern languages: Welsh, English, French, Spanish, German, and Russian. With one exception these stories date from the early Middle Ages.

The term "Middle Ages," as opposed to "Ancient World," and the word "modern" (*modus* = manner; *hodiernus* = of today) dates, according to Professors Kukenheim and Roussel, from 1469 (*media tempestas* = middle of the storm), 1518 (*media aetas* = middle age), and 1604 (*medium aevum* = middle period).

The sources were as follows:

EIGHT
BEOWULF

Only one manuscript exists. It was discovered in England in the seventeenth century by Sir Robert Cotton among nine other parchments which together form the Codex Vitellius in the British Museum. Sir Robert Cotton had spent many years acquiring manuscripts that had been dispersed throughout England after the seizure and destruction of the monasteries. After his collection was sold in 1700, the manuscripts were lodged in Ashburnham House. In 1731 the *Beowulf* manuscript was damaged by fire as the charred corners one sees in photographs of it attest. In 1753 it was placed in the British Museum.

The first two copies were made in 1786 by the Danish scholar G. J. Thorkelin, one by Thorkelin himself and one by a copyist. These two handwritten copies are in a Copenhagen museum today. Aside from early printings referred to in the introduction to Chapter 8, one could list many others and many translators of this work into poetry and into prose. These are four unabridged translations to which the interested reader should refer, since each one of them is in itself a masterpiece: Francis B. Gummere (Harvard), Charles W. Kennedy (Princeton), Edwin Morgan (Glasgow University), and William Ellery Leonard (Wisconsin). The *Beowulf* of this book is an original version, made without reference to the preceding, and done despite their superb scholarship in order to establish the literary themes which are the subject of this half of the book.

NINE
PEREDUR, SON OF YORK

The manuscripts of the *Mabinogion* are in Peniarth Castle in Wales. They were published and translated for the first time by Lady Charlotte Guest from 1838 to 1849, and subsequently in Paris by H. de Villemarqué (1842) and J. Loth (1899, 1913). The diplomatic text was established for *The Red Book of Hergest* by the Welsh scholars J. Rhys and John Gwenogvryn Evans in 1887 and for *The White Book of Rhydderch* by John Gwenogvryn Evans in 1907. Both of these definitive texts include the Peredur story. The abridged translation presented in this volume is taken principally from a text of the manuscript called Peniarth 4, which forms a part of the White Book *Mabinogion*. Scholars have believed that it was written before, or contained parts of earlier material than that in the *Red Book of Hergest*, which appears from the character of its script to date from *c.* 1375 to 1425. Both Padraic Colum and Sidney Lanier have written about Peredur. There is a modern translation (1948), by Gwyn and Thomas Jones, entitled *Mabinogion*.

TEN
THE STORY OF ROLAND

This present translation follows the manuscript called Digby 23, from the Library of Oxford University, the handwriting of which is believed to be that of an Anglo-Norman scribe. The only other principal manuscript, dating from the fourteenth century, is in Venice. An early Latin adaptation is called *Carmen de prodicione Guenonis*. The Roland story was translated during the Middle Ages into Welsh, German, English, and Dutch. With so many "Franks," as the Crusaders were called, around Constantinople, Syria, Palestine, and Egypt during the Crusades, one could easily believe that the *Roland* served as a prototype for all medieval epics.

The Oxford manuscript was printed in France by Francisque Michel (1837, 1869), by Clédat (1870, 1887), by Léon Gautier (1872). Mrs. A. C. Marsh made an English translation in 1854. The best-known edition and translation is that of Professor Joseph Bédier. Variants of 484 verses from five manuscripts (another from Venice, Paris, and Châteauroux) are given in the *Chrestomathie* of Karl Bartsch, Edition XII (New York, 1958). There is a modern translation by Merriam Sherwood (New York, 1938).

One approaches this poem with a very real reverence, for it is, in its way, as beautiful and as unique a work of art as the *Beowulf*.

ELEVEN
BERTA OF HUNGARY

The story which the present author calls *Berta of Hungary* exists, in the version written by the Belgian minstrel Adenes li Rois, in six manuscripts. There is also another version of the same story, *Berta de li gran pie*, in manuscript form: MS. fr. XIII, Library of Saint Mark, Venice. Four of the manuscripts of Adenes are in the National Library of Paris (MSS. 778, 1447, 12467, 22404), and another is in Rouen (Belles Lettres 175). The story was first published in Paris in 1832 by Paulin Paris, the father of the brilliant medievalist Gaston Paris.

The text followed in this book is the manuscript called Belles Lettres 175, in the Library of the Arsénal, Paris. It was collated and printed in Brussels in 1874 by August Scheler. The reader will note that all the other material in this book dates from the early Middle Ages, the period Professor Gustave Cohen called the "Age of Genesis." Only the *Berta* story falls into the so-called Classical or Great Century of the Middle Ages, the thirteenth. This might explain why there are so many manuscripts, aside from the fact that our author served Guy de Dampierre, Count of Flanders, as well as Marie de Brabant, Queen of France. He was also a protégé of the Princess Blanche, daughter of Saint Louis.

The *Berta* story was written in modern French by Louis Brandin (Paris, 1924); in his version, according to information given in the preface, the Adenes manuscript was supplemented by other incidents from the Venice manuscript. Dean Arthur Sideleau in his excellent book *Chansons de Geste* (Montreal, 1945) has translated into modern French a part of the *Berta* story. I know of no translation into English.

TWELVE
SIFRIT

There are altogether twenty-eight manuscripts of *The Nibelungenlied*, but three are considered the best: the Munich manuscript, the parchment manuscript in the monastery of St. Gall, and the third in the "ducal library of Donaueschingen." The scholar Karl Lachmann announced its first publication at the University of Berlin in 1816, and it has been printed many times, especially the three best manuscripts. This volume follows a text of the St. Gall manuscript and is particularly indebted to its earliest translation into French, as the introduction to Chapter 12 explains. This earliest French translator spent ten years on her work, basing it upon the St. Gall text, comparing it with editions published by Hagen, Lachmann, Karl Simrock, M. Schoenhüth, and then referring it painstakingly to the St. Gall manuscript itself. The English reader may remember William Morris' *Sigurd the Volsung*. There are many translations, among them one by Professor

Daniel B. Shumway (1909), one in rhyming couplets by Dr. Arthur S. Way (1911), and ones by S. H. Hamer and Gertrude Henderson.

THIRTEEN
PRINCE IGOR

In a manuscript entitled *Sbornik*, Count Pushkin discovered the Prince Igor story-poem, which he printed for the first time in Russia in 1800. He had bought the manuscript from a monk. Since the original burned during Napoleon's invasion of Moscow (1812), the *Igor* was reprinted in 1864 by Pokarsky from a copy found in the archives of Catherine the Great. A polyglot edition, Russian, Polish, and Czech, was printed in Lwow, Poland, in 1886 by Soltykov-Romanski. It was also published in Berlin by Boltz and by Eichoff in Paris (1839)—neither of which revision the present author has found. The Rambaud partial translation used in this volume is from 1876. Subsequent scholarly studies have been made by two modern authorities, Professors Henri Grégoire and Roman Jakobson.

FOURTEEN
CID

There is only one manuscript of the *Poem of Mio Cid*. The noted Spanish scholar Ramón Menéndez Pidal says that this precious document was preserved in the Convent of Franciscan Nuns at Vivar, the town where El Cid was supposedly born. I believe that the manuscript has been privately owned since 1775. It was first published in 1779 by C. Tomas Antonio Sánchez in Volume I of his anthology, *Coleccion de poesías castellanas anteriores al siglo XV*. The second publication was in Paris in 1858, and the third was in Spain in 1864. The first English version may have been that of Robert Southey, *Chronicle of the Cid*, London, 1808. This epic was the subject of Victor Hugo's magnificent poem *Le Cid Exilé* and also of the Massenet opera *Le Cid*.

In his dedication to his edition and translation published in 1942 by the Hispanic Society of America, Mr. Archer M. Huntington tells us that the manuscript was privately owned at that time by Don A. Pidal y Mon of Madrid. Mr. Huntington was fortunate to have made his edition and his verse translation from the manuscript itself. This present abridged translation follows the original Sánchez text. The reader should be alerted to the fact that there had apparently been some tampering with the manuscript through the ages, and that the date given in its last lines should not be taken too seriously, as it appears to have the number *C* (100) missing from it, owing to erasure.